Communications
in Computer and Information Science 1797

Rationale

The CCIS series is devoted to the publication of proceedings of computer science conferences. Its aim is to efficiently disseminate original research results in informatics in printed and electronic form. While the focus is on publication of peer-reviewed full papers presenting mature work, inclusion of reviewed short papers reporting on work in progress is welcome, too. Besides globally relevant meetings with internationally representative program committees guaranteeing a strict peer-reviewing and paper selection process, conferences run by societies or of high regional or national relevance are also considered for publication.

Topics

The topical scope of CCIS spans the entire spectrum of informatics ranging from foundational topics in the theory of computing to information and communications science and technology and a broad variety of interdisciplinary application fields.

Information for Volume Editors and Authors

Publication in CCIS is free of charge. No royalties are paid, however, we offer registered conference participants temporary free access to the online version of the conference proceedings on SpringerLink (http://link.springer.com) by means of an http referrer from the conference website and/or a number of complimentary printed copies, as specified in the official acceptance email of the event.

CCIS proceedings can be published in time for distribution at conferences or as postproceedings, and delivered in the form of printed books and/or electronically as USBs and/or e-content licenses for accessing proceedings at SpringerLink. Furthermore, CCIS proceedings are included in the CCIS electronic book series hosted in the SpringerLink digital library at http://link.springer.com/bookseries/7899. Conferences publishing in CCIS are allowed to use Online Conference Service (OCS) for managing the whole proceedings lifecycle (from submission and reviewing to preparing for publication) free of charge.

Publication process

The language of publication is exclusively English. Authors publishing in CCIS have to sign the Springer CCIS copyright transfer form, however, they are free to use their material published in CCIS for substantially changed, more elaborate subsequent publications elsewhere. For the preparation of the camera-ready papers/files, authors have to strictly adhere to the Springer CCIS Authors' Instructions and are strongly encouraged to use the CCIS LaTeX style files or templates.

Abstracting/Indexing

CCIS is abstracted/indexed in DBLP, Google Scholar, EI-Compendex, Mathematical Reviews, SCImago, Scopus. CCIS volumes are also submitted for the inclusion in ISI Proceedings.

How to start

To start the evaluation of your proposal for inclusion in the CCIS series, please send an e-mail to ccis@springer.com.

Isaac Woungang · Sanjay Kumar Dhurandher ·
Kiran Kumar Pattanaik · Anshul Verma ·
Pradeepika Verma
Editors

Advanced Network Technologies and Intelligent Computing

Second International Conference, ANTIC 2022
Varanasi, India, December 22–24, 2022
Proceedings, Part I

Springer

Editors
Isaac Woungang
Ryerson University
Toronto, ON, Canada

Sanjay Kumar Dhurandher
Netaji Subhas University of Technology
New Delhi, India

Kiran Kumar Pattanaik
ABV-Indian Institute of Information
Technology and Management
Gwalior, India

Anshul Verma
Banaras Hindu University
Varanasi, India

Pradeepika Verma
Indian Institute of Technology
Patna, India

ISSN 1865-0929   ISSN 1865-0937 (electronic)
Communications in Computer and Information Science
ISBN 978-3-031-28179-2   ISBN 978-3-031-28180-8 (eBook)
https://doi.org/10.1007/978-3-031-28180-8

Preface

The 2nd International Conference on Advanced Network Technologies and Intelligent Computing (ANTIC-2022) was organized by Department of Computer Science, Institute of Science, Banaras Hindu University, Varanasi, India in hybrid mode from 22nd to 24th December 2022. ANTIC-2022 aimed to bring together leading academicians, scientists, research scholars, and UG/PG students across the globe to exchange and share their research outcomes. It provided a state-of-the-art platform to discuss all aspects (current and future) of Advanced Network Technologies and Intelligent Computing. This enabled the participating researchers to exchange ideas about applying existing methods in these areas to solve real-world problems.

ANTIC-2022 solicited two types of submissions: full research papers (equal to or more than 12 pages) and short research papers (between 8 and 11 pages). These papers identify and justify a principled advance to the theoretical and practical foundations for the construction and analysis of systems, where applicable supported by experimental validation. A total 443 research papers were received through the EquinOCS portal of Springer and 79 papers (17.83%) were accepted after the rigorous review process. Out of 79 accepted papers, 68 papers (86.07%) are full papers and 11 papers (13.92%) are short papers. All 79 accepted papers have been selected for publication in the Communications in Computer and Information Science (CCIS) series of Springer. These are grouped into two thematic categories: Advanced Network Technologies and Intelligent Computing.

We would like to thank everyone who helped to make ANTIC-2022 successful. In particular, we would like to thank the authors for submitting their papers to ANTIC-2022. We are thankful to our excellent team of reviewers from all over the globe who deserve full credit for the hard work put in to review the high-quality submissions with rich technical content. We would also like to thank the members of the Advisory Committee and the Program Committee for their guidance and suggestions in making ANTIC-2022 a success. We would also like to thank all the Track Chairs, Organizing Committee and Technical Program Committee members for their support and co-operation.

December 2022

Isaac Woungang
Sanjay Kumar Dhurandher
Kiran Kumar Pattanaik
Anshul Verma
Pradeepika Verma

Organization

Chief Patron

Sudhir K. Jain (Vice-chancellor)   Banaras Hindu University, India

Patron

V. K. Shukla (Rector)   Banaras Hindu University, India

Co-patrons

A. K. Tripathi (Director)   Institute of Science, Banaras Hindu University, India
Madhoolika Agrawal (Dean)   Institute of Science, Banaras Hindu University, India

Advisory Board

Anil Kumar Tripathi   Indian Institute of Technology (BHU), Varanasi, India
Jagannathan Sarangpani   Missouri University of Science and Technology, USA
Jawar Singh   Indian Institute of Technology, Patna, India
Manish Gaur   Institute of Engineering & Technology, Lucknow, India
Pradip Kr. Das   Indian Institute of Technology, Guwahati, India
Rajeev Srivastava   Indian Institute of Technology (BHU), Varanasi, India
Rajkumar Buyya   University of Melbourne, Australia
Sanjay Kumar Madria   Missouri University of Science & Technology, USA
Sundaraja Sitharama Iyengar   Florida International University, USA

General Chairs

Isaac Woungang   Toronto Metropolitan University, Canada
Sanjay Kumar Dhurandher   Netaji Subhas University of Technology, India
K. K. Pattanaik   ABV-Indian Institute of Information Technology
                               and Management, Gwalior, India

Conference Chair

Vivek Kumar Singh   Banaras Hindu University, India

Program Chairs

S. Karthikeyan   Banaras Hindu University, India
Pramod Kumar Mishra   Banaras Hindu University, India
Anshul Verma   Banaras Hindu University, India

Convener

Anshul Verma   Banaras Hindu University, India

Organizing Secretaries

Gaurav Baranwal   Banaras Hindu University, India
Ankita Vaish   Banaras Hindu University, India
S. Suresh   Banaras Hindu University, India
Pradeepika Verma   Indian Institute of Technology Patna, India

Track Chairs

Himanshu   Punjabi University, Patiala, India
Karm Veer Arya   ABV-Indian Institute of Information Technology
                               and Management, Gwalior, India
P. K. Singh   ABV-Indian Institute of Information Technology
                               and Management, Gwalior, India
Rajiv Ranjan Tewari (Retd.)   University of Allahabad, India
Sanjay Kumar   Pt. Ravishankar Shukla University, Raipur, India

Udai Shanker	Madan Mohan Malaviya University of Technology, Gorakhpur, India
Alireza Izaddoost	California State University, Dominguez Hills, USA
Binod Kumar Singh	National Institute of Technology, Jamshedpur, India
Divakar Singh Yadav	National Institute of Technology, Hamirpur, India
Huy Trung Nguyễn	People's Security Academy, Vietnam Ministry of Public Security, Vietnam
Joshua D. Reichard	Omega Graduate School, American Centre for Religion/Society Studies, USA
Lalit Garg	University of Malta, Malta
Pradeepika Verma	Indian Institute of Technology Patna, India
Shensheng Tang	St. Cloud State University, USA
Yousef Farhaoui	Moulay Ismail University, Morocco
Jatinderkumar R. Saini	Symbiosis Institute of Computer Studies and Research, India
Priyanka Sharma	Rashtriya Raksha University, India

Organizing Committee

Achintya Singhal	Banaras Hindu University, India
Manoj Kumar Singh	Banaras Hindu University, India
Rakhi Garg	Banaras Hindu University, India
Manjari Gupta	Banaras Hindu University, India
Vandana Kushwaha	Banaras Hindu University, India
Awadhesh Kumar	Banaras Hindu University, India
Manoj Mishra	Banaras Hindu University, India
S. N. Chaurasia	Banaras Hindu University, India
Sarvesh Pandey	Banaras Hindu University, India
Vibhor Kant	Banaras Hindu University, India
Jyoti Singh Kirar	Banaras Hindu University, India

Publication Committee

Sanjeev Sharma	Indian Institute of Information Technology, Pune, India
Vibhav Prakash Singh	Motilal Nehru National Institute of Technology, Allahabad, India
Dharmendra Prasad Mahato	National Institute of Technology, Hamirpur, India

Vijay Bhaskar Semwal	Maulana Azad National Institute of Technology, Bhopal, India
Bhawana Rudra	National Institute of Technology, Karnataka, India

Publicity Committee

Prashant Singh Rana	Thapar Institute of Engineering & Technology, India
Harish Sharma	Rajasthan Technical University, India
Puneet Misra	University of Lucknow, India
Sachi Nandan Mohanty	College of Engineering, Pune, India
Koushlendra Kumar Singh	National Institute of Technology, Jamshedpur, India

Finance Committee

Praveen Kumar Singh	Banaras Hindu University, India
Kishna Murari	Banaras Hindu University, India
Sunil Kumar	Banaras Hindu University, India
Shashi Shukla	Banaras Hindu University, India
Santosh Kumar	Banaras Hindu University, India
Saurabh Srivastava	Banaras Hindu University, India

Technical Program Committee

A. Senthil Thilak	National Institute of Technology, Surathkal, India
Abdus Samad	Aligarh Muslim University, India
Abhay Kumar Rai	Banasthali Vidyapith, India
Abhilasha Sharma	Delhi Technological University, India
Ade Romadhony	Telkom University, Indonesia
Afifa Ghenai	Constantine 2 University, Algeria
Ajay	Shree Guru Gobind Singh Tricentenary University, India
Ajay Kumar	Chandigarh University, India
Ajay Kumar	Central University of Himanchal Pradesh, India
Ajay Kumar Gupta	Madan Mohan Malaviya University of Technology, Gorakhpur, India
Ajay Kumar Yadav	Banasthali Vidyapith, India

Ajay Pratap	Indian Institute of Technology (BHU), Varanasi, India
Akande Noah Oluwatobi	Landmark University, Nigeria
Akash Kumar Bhoi	KIET Group of Institutions & Sikkim Manipal University, India
Alberto Rossi	University of Florence, Italy
Aleena Swetapadma	Kalinga Institute of Industrial Technology, India
Ali El Alami	Moulay Ismail University, Morocco
Amit Kumar	BMS Institute of Technology and Management, India
Amit Kumar	Jaypee University of Engineering and Technology, Guna, India
Amit Rathee	Government College Barota, India
Angel D.	Sathyabama Institute of Science and Technology, India
Anil Kumar	London Metropolitan University, UK
Anirban Sengupta	Jadavpur University, India
Anita Chaware	SNDT Women's University, India
Anjali Shrikant Yeole	VES Institute of Technology, Mumbai, India
Anjula Mehto	Thapar Institute of Engineering and Technology, India
Ankur Jain	IGDTUW, India
Ansuman Mahapatra	National Institute of Technology, Puducherry, India
Antriksh Goswami	Indian Institute of Information Technology, Vadodara, India
Anupam Biswas	National Institute of Technology, Silchar, India
Anuradha Yarlagadda	Gayatri Vidhya Parishad College of Engineering, India
Anurag Sewak	Rajkiya Engineering College, Sonbhadra, India
Arun Kumar	ABV-Indian Institute of Information Technology and Management, Gwalior, India
Arun Pandian J.	Vel Tech Rangarajan Dr. Sagunthala R&D Institute of Science and Technology, India
Ashish Kumar Mishra	Rajkiya Engineering College, Ambedkar Nagar, India
Ashutosh Kumar Singh	United College of Engineering and Research, India
Aymen Jaber Salman	Al-Nahrain University, Iraq
B. Surendiran	National Institute of Technology, Puducherry, India
B. Arthi	SRM Institute of Science and Technology, India
B. S. Charulatha	Rajalakshmi Engineering College, India

Balbir Singh Awana	Vanderbilt University, USA
Baranidharan B.	SRM Institute of Science and Technology, India
Benyamin Ahmadnia	Harvard University, USA
Bharat Garg	Thapar Institute of Engineering & Technology, India
Bharti	University of Delhi, India
Bhaskar Mondal	National Institute of Technology, Patna, India
Binod Prasad	ABV-Indian Institute of Information Technology and Management, Gwalior, India
Boddepalli Santhi Bhushan	Indian Institute of Information Technology, Allahabad, India
Brijendra Singh	VIT Vellore, India
Chanda Thapliyal Nautiyal	DU Govt. Degree College, Narendra Nagar, India
Chandrashekhar Azad	National Institute of Technology, Jamshedpur, India
Chetan Vyas	United University, Prayagraj, India
Chittaranjan Pradhan	Kalinga Institute of Industrial Technology, India
D. Senthilkumar	Anna University, India
Dahmouni Abdellatif	Chouaib Doukkali University, Faculty of Sciences of El Jadida, Morocco
Darpan Anand	Chandigarh University, India
Deepak Kumar	Banasthali Vidyapith, India
Dharmveer Kumar Yadav	Katihar Engineering College, India
Dhirendra Kumar	Delhi Technological University, India
Dinesh Kumar	Motilal Nehru National Institute of Technology Allahabad, India
Divya Saxena	The Hong Kong Polytechnic University, China
Ezil Sam Leni A.	KCG College of Technology, India
Gargi Srivastava	Rajiv Gandhi Institute of Petroleum Technology, India
Gaurav Gupta	Shoolini University, India
Gyanendra K. Verma	National Institute of Technology, Kurukshetra, India
Hardeo Kumar Thakur	Manav Rachna University, India
Hasmat Malik	Netaji Subhas University of Technology, India
Inder Chaudhary	Delhi Technological University, India
Itu Snigdh	Birla Institute of Technology, Mesra, India
J. K. Rai	Defence Research and Development Organisation, India
J. Jerald Inico	Loyola College, India
Jagadeeswara Rao Annam	Gudlavalleru Engineering College, India
Jagannath Singh	Kalinga Institute of Industrial Technology, India

Jagdeep Singh	Sant Longowal Institute of Engineering and Technology, India
Jainath Yadav	Central University of South Bihar, India
Jay Prakash	National Institute of Technology, Calicut, India
Jaya Gera	Shyama Prasad Mukherji College for Women, India
Jeevaraj S.	ABV- Indian Institute of Information Technology & Management, Gwalior, India
Jolly Parikh	Bharati Vidyapeeth's College of Engineering, New Delhi, India
Jyoti Singh	Banaras Hindu University, India
K. T. V. Reddy	Pravara Rural Education Society, India
Kanu Goel	Amity University, Punjab, India
Koushlendra Kumar Singh	National Institute of Technology, Jamshedpur, India
Kunwar Pal	National Institute of Technology, Jalandhar, India
Lakshmi Priya G.	VIT University, India
Lalatendu Behera	National Institute of Technology, Jalandhar, India
Lokesh Chauhan	National Institute of Technology, Hamirpur, India
M. Joseph	Michael Research Foundation, Thanjavur, India
M. Nazma B. J. Naskar	Kalinga Institute of Industrial Technology, India
M. Deva Priya	Sri Krishna College of Technology, India
Mahendra Shukla	The LNM Institute of Information Technology, India
Mainejar Yadav	Rajkiya Engineering College, Sonbhadra, India
Manish Gupta	Amity University, Gwalior, India
Manish K. Pandey	Birla Institute of Technology, Mesra, India
Manish Kumar	M S Ramaiah Institute of Technology, India
Manpreet Kaur	Manav Rachna University, India
Mariya Ouaissa	Moulay Ismail University, Morocco
Mariyam Ouaissa	Moulay Ismail University, Morocco
Meriem Houmer	Ibn Zohr University, Morocco
Minakhi Rout	Kalinga Institute of Industrial Technology, India
Mohd Yaseen Mir	National Central University, Taiwan
Mohit Kumar	National Institute of Technology, Jalandhar, India
Monica Chauhan Bhadoriya	Madhav Institute of Technology & Science, India
Muhammad Abulaish	South Asian University, India
Mukesh Mishra	Indian Institute of Information Technology, Dharwad, India
Mukesh Rawat	Meerut Institute of Engineering and Technology, India
Mukta Sharma	Michigan State University, USA

Nagarajan G.	Sathyabama Institute of Science and Technology, India
Nagendra Pratap Singh	National Institute of Technology, Hamirpur, India
Nandakishor Yadav	Fraunhofer Institute for Photonic Microsystems, Germany
Narendran Rajagopalan	National Institute of Technology, Puducherry, India
Neetesh Kumar	IIT Roorkee, India
Nisha Chaurasia	National Institute of Technology, Jalandhar, India
Nisheeth Joshi	Banasthali Vidyapith, India
Nitesh K. Bharadwaj	OP Jindal University, India
Om Jee Pandey	SRM University, Andhra Pradesh, India
P. Manikandaprabhu	Sri Ramakrishna College of Arts and Science, India
Partha Pratim Sarangi	KIIT Deemed to be University, India
Pavithra G.	Dayananda Sagar College of Engg., India
Pinar Kirci	Bursa Uludag University, Turkey
Piyush Kumar Singh	Central University of South Bihar, Gaya, India
Pooja	University of Allahabad, India
Prabhat Ranjan	Central University of South Bihar, Gaya, India
Pradeeba Sridar	Sydney Medical School, Australia
Pradeep Kumar	University of KwaZulu-Natal, South Africa
Prakash Kumar Singh	Rajkiya Engineering College, Mainpuri, India
Prakash Srivastava	KIET Group of Institutions, India
Prasenjit Chanak	Indian Institute of Technology (BHU), Varanasi, India
Prateek Agrawal	Lovely Professional University, India
Praveen Pawar	Indian Institute of Information Technology, Bhopal, India
Preeth R.	Indian Institute of Information Technology, Design and Manufacturing, Kurnool, India
Preeti Sharma	Chitkara University Institute of Engineering and Technology, Punjab, India
Priya Gupta	ABVSME, Jawaharlal Nehru University, India
Priyanka Verma	University of Galway, Ireland
Pushpalatha S. Nikkam	SDM College of Engineering and Technology, Dharwad, India
R. Rathi	VIT, India
Raenu Kolandaisamy	UCSI University, Malaysia
Rahul Kumar Verma	Indian Institute of Information Technology, Lucknow, India
Rahul Kumar Vijay	Banasthali Vidyapith, India

Ramesh Chand Pandey	Rajkiya Engineering College, Ambedkar Nagar, India
Rashmi Chaudhry	Netaji Subhas University of Technology, India
Rashmi Gupta	Atal Bihari Vajpayee University, India
Ravilla Dilli	Manipal Institute of Technology, India
Revathy G.	Sastra University, India
Richa Mishra	University of Allahabad, India
Rohit Kumar Tiwari	Madan Mohan Malaviya University of Technology, Gorakhpur, India
Rohit Singh	International Management Institute, Kolkata, India
S. Gandhiya Vendhan	Bharathiar University, India
Sadhana Mishra	ITM University, India
Sanjeev Patel	NIT Rourkela, India
Santosh Kumar Satapathy	Pandit Deendayal Energy University, India
Saumya Bhadauria	ABV-Indian Institute of Information Technology and Management, Gwalior, India
Saurabh Bilgaiyan	Kalinga Institute of Industrial Technology, India
Saurabh Kumar	The LNM Institute of Information Technology, India
Seera Dileep Raju	Dr. Reddy's Laboratories, India
Shailesh Kumar	Jaypee Institute of Information Technology, Noida, India
Shantanu Agnihotri	Bennett University, India
Shiv Prakash	University of Allahabad, India
Shivam Sakshi	Indian Institute of Management, Bangalore, India
Shivani Sharma	Thapar Institute of Engineering & Technology, India
Shubhra Jain	Thapar Institute of Engineering & Technology, India
Shyam Singh Rajput	National Institute of Technology, Patna, India
Siva Shankar Ramasamy	International College of Digital Innovation - Chiang Mai University, Thailand
Sonali Gupta	J.C. Bose University of Science and Technology, YMCA, India
Sonu Lamba	Thapar Institute of Engineering & Technology, India
Sri Vallabha Deevi	Tiger Analytics, India
Srinidhi N. N.	Sri Krishna Institute of Technology, India
Sudhakar Singh	University of Allahabad, India
Sudhanshu Kumar Jha	University of Allahabad, India
Suneel Yadav	Indian Institute of Information Technology, Allahabad, India

Sunil	Jamia Millia Islamia, New Delhi, India
Sunil Kumar Chawla	Chandigarh University, India
Suparna Biswas	Maulana Abul Kalam Azad University of Technology, India
Suresh Raikwar	Thapar Institute of Engineering & Technology, India
Sushopti Gawade	Pillai College of Engineering, India
Syed Mutahar Aaqib	Government Degree College, Baramulla, India
U. Anitha	Sathyabama Institute of Science and Technology, India
V. D. Ambeth Kumar	Panimalar Engineering College, Anna University, India
Venkanna U.	National Institute of Technology, Trichy, India
Vijay Kumar Dwivedi	United College of Engineering and Research, India
Vikas Mohar	Madhav Institute of Technology & Science, India
Vinay Kumar Jain	SSTC-SSGI, India
Vinay Singh	ABV-Indian Institute of Information Technology and Management, Gwalior, India
Vinita Jindal	Keshav Mahavidyalaya, University of Delhi, India
Vinod Kumar	University of Allahabad, India
Vishal Pradhan	KIIT University, India
Vishal Shrivastava	Arya College of Engineering and IT, India
Vivek Kumar	PSIT Kanpur, India
Yadunath Pathak	Visvesvaraya National Institute of Technology, Nagpur, India
Yogish H. K.	M. S. Ramaiah Institute of Technology, India
Vijay Kumar Sharma	Shri Mata Vaishno Devi University, India
Muhammad Sajjadur Rahim	University of Rajshahi, Bangladesh
Anjana Jain	Shri G. S. Institute of Tech. and Sc., India
K. Ramachandra Rao	Shri Vishnu Engineering College for Women, India
Mamta Dahiya	SGT University, India
Satyadhyan Chickerur	KLE Technological University, India

Contents – Part I

Contents – Part II

Advanced Network Technologies

Vehicle Routing Problem with Value Iteration Network

Ashok Kumar Khatta, Jagdeep Singh$^{(\boxtimes)}$, and Gurjinder Kaur

Department of Computer Science and Engineering, Sant Longowal Institute of
Engineering and Technology, Longowal, Punjab, India
`jagdeep@sliet.ac.in`

Abstract. Multi Vehicle routing to service consumers in dynamic and
unpredictable surrounding such as congested urban areas is a difficult
operation that needs robust and flexible planning. Value iteration networks hold promise for planning in vehicle routing problem. Conventional approaches aren't usually constructed for real-life settings, and
they are too slow to be useful in real-time. In comparison, Vehicle Routing Problem with Value Iteration Network (VRP-VIN) offers a neural
network model based on graphs that can execute multi-agent routing in
a highly dispersed but connected graph with constantly fluctuating traffic conditions using learned value iteration. Furthermore, the model's
communication module allows vehicles to work better in a cooperative
manner online and can easily adapt to changes. A virtual environment is
constructed to simulate real-world mapping by self-driving vehicles with
uncertain traffic circumstances and minimal edge coverage. This method
beats standard solutions based on overall cost and run-time. Experiments
show that the model achieves a total cost difference of 3% when compared with a state-of-art solver having global information. Also, after
being trained with only 2 agents on networks with 25 nodes, can easily
generalize to a scenario having additional agents (or nodes).

Keywords: Reinforcement learning · Vehicle Routing Problem · Value
iteration networks · Graph attention layer · Multi-agent communication

1 Introduction

As vehicles grow increasingly widespread, one of the most basic issues is understanding how to navigate a fleet of vehicles to perform a specified job. Also,
the huge population densities in our cities today put all existing infrastructure,
especially urban transportation networks, under strain. With the progression of
services like e-commerce and vehicle sharing, these congested cities transportation demands have also gotten more complicated. So, it is very important to
route vehicles in way so as to reduce overall cost, time and congestion. Different
methods have been proposed to route vehicles. One of the classic methods in
which a single agent is entrusted with determining the shortest path between
a set of sites and destinations is known as Travelling Salesperson Problem [1].

© The Author(s), under exclusive license to Springer Nature Switzerland AG 2023
I. Woungang et al. (Eds.): ANTIC 2022, CCIS 1797, pp. 3–15, 2023.
https://doi.org/10.1007/978-3-031-28180-8_1

The multi-agent approach to this problem is called the Vehicle Routing Problem (VRP) [1]. In VRP, multiple agents try to find an optimal route by visiting a set of locations exactly once. Even after having a huge number of solvers, they are primarily built to perform planning offline and cannot modify solutions when used online. Also, agents can't communicate online when using these types of solvers.

Deep Learning approaches like Vinyals [2], Khalil [3], Kool [4], Deudon [5] show great results with faster runtime. They are, however, often evaluated on simple planar network benchmarks with limited exploration in multi-agent environments. Furthermore, none of these solutions were created for dynamic contexts where online communication may be quite advantageous.

We have given a fleet of cars in a multi-agent environment. We have to determine the minimum total cost for mapping a given graph under traffic conditions, such that all routes are traversed not less than a defined number, and this number is not known prior.

The Vehicle Routing Problem value iteration network is a distributed neural network designed for managing multiple vehicles intended to complete a specific task. Each agent has a value iteration module to carry out its own planning with the help of communication between agents via an attention mechanism. In the attention mechanism [6], only a subset of the input characteristics (value function) is meaningful for a specific label prediction (action). It is also well known that attention improves learning performance by reducing the number of network parameters that are actually used in course of learning. The dense adjacency matrix is used for encoding paired edge information to accelerate information sharing and allow for more complex encoding since our focus is on sparse road graphs. Using actual traffic flow simulation, we illustrate the usefulness of VRP-VIN on actual road maps derived from eighteen different cities around the world. A random sub-graph of those cities was used to produce training and evaluation examples comprising real-world mapping difficulties, and then a random number is selected, which determines how many times each node in each graph is covered. The fleet will be unaware of this knowledge until they reach this number. We use the total time taken for traversal as our major evaluation criterion, demonstrating that this technique outperforms both conventional VRP solvers and recently suggested deep learning models. Moreover, VRP-VIN adapted effectively to the graph size and agent count.

The rest of the paper is organized as follows: Sect. 2 takes on the previous work related to our work. The system model is described in Sect. 3. Section 4 illustrates the working, structure, and parameters of VRP-VIN. Section 5 shows a numerical experiment for comparing models with deep learning solvers. Section 6 concludes the investigation and future work.

2   Related Work

In [7], Tamar et al. proposed a planning module-equipped neural network. They are able to prepare and foresee the results of planning, like reinforcement learning. They have excellent planning capability and can generalize better in diverse set of tasks. They are based on a differential estimation of the value-iteration algorithm using CNN. Value iteration is a technique based on the Markov decision process. The MDP's purpose is to discover a policy that in turn optimizes our expected return. Vn (state value function at iteration n) converges to V* (ideal state value function) using the value iteration technique as n approaches infinity. The VI module in the VIN takes advantage of the fact that each iteration of VI can be visualized as a previous Vn and the reward function passes through a convolutional and max pooling layer. The Q function for every channel in the convolution layer refers to a specific action. As a result, K iterations of VI are equivalent to K times of applying a convolutional layer. The value function peak at the goal, so the high-value function means destination.

In [8], Lu et al. suggested a distributed cooperative routing method (DCR) based on evolutionary game theory to coordinate vehicles. This solution combines edge computing and intelligence to run on roadside units. Nash equilibrium is achieved under DCR. No vehicle can find a path more suitable than the one currently under Nash equilibrium. In [9], Tang et al. proposed a reinforcement learning model with multi-agents for centralized vehicle routing in order to improve spatial-temporal coverage. Two reinforcement learning: proximal policy optimization and deep q-learning have been used to create routing policies. A centralized routing method is proposed for vehicular mobile crowd-sensing systems (VMCS) to expand their range of sensing based on MARL. The author initiates by customizing an environment for reinforcement learning in order to get the maximum feasible spatial-temporal coverage based on user preferences for various regions. They designed two MARL algorithms based on the Deep Q network and Proximal Policy Optimization (PPO). Then, they do comparisons and sensitivity analyses to figure out how well the two methods work for VMCS problems.

Niu et al. proposed multi-agent graph-attention communication (MAGIC) in [10]. It is a novel multi-agent reinforcement learning algorithm with a graph-attention communication protocol having: 1) a Scheduler to aid the challenge of when and to whom messages should be sent, 2) a Message Processor employs Graph Attention Networks (GATs) [11] comprising dynamic graphs for handling communication signals. A combination of a graph attention encoder and a differentiable attention mechanism is used to develop the scheduler that provides dynamic, differentiable graphs to the Message Processor, allowing the Scheduler and Message Processor to be trained at the same time.

3   System Model

The Routing Path can be represented as a strongly connected graph (G) with edges (E) and vertices (V), where we want to generate a routing path for D agents R(i)D, and each vertex in the graph is traversed D_v time across all agents. Until a specific number is reached, D_v is unknown to the agents, and local traffic information is the only thing that can be observed. Each agent collects surrounding environment observation and information gathered from other agents and then outputs the next step's route (Tables 1, 2 and 3).

Table 1. Notations

Symbol	Representation
t	Current timestamp
G	Graph of road map
L	No of Agents
n	No of graph nodes
f	Policy of Routing and Communication
π	Routing Policy
F	Time Cost given a route R
o	Agent i's observation at time t
s	Agent i state at time t
a	Agent i action at time t
m	Message vector sent by agent i at time t
D_v	No of times node v needs to be visited
Z_i	At the kth value iteration, Agent i's node feature
Y_i	Agent i's input communication feature

A route is defined as a sequence of action $R(i) = [s_0^i, ..., s_N]$, where s_0^i represents routing steps taken by agent i in time t, suggesting node to be traversed next, and each step represents an intermediary destination. The strategy of a single agent can be described as a function of

1) graph of the road network;
2) surrounding environment observation bi;
3) the communication messages sent by other agents y j;
4) current status of an agent ji.

$$s_t^i, y_t^i = f(G, b_t^i, \{y_{t-1}^j\}_{j=1}^M; j_t^i), \qquad (1)$$

Considering a traffic model D determines how long it takes to travel a route, we want our system to accomplish the following goal:

$$min_R(i) \sum_{X=1...L} D(R^i), \qquad (2)$$

subject to

$$\sum_i T(R^i, v) \geq T_v, v \qquad (3)$$

where T(R, v) tells how many times a node v should be visited in path R.

It's worth noting that the model is resilient and failure-proof as the model runs locally on all the agents, which allows it to scale better with the number of agents. VRP-VIN has two main components:

1) Asynchronous communication module saves messages sent by agents in a temporary unit and retrieves information via the agent-level attention method. This information is received by the value iteration network for path planning in the future.
2) Value iteration network operates locally on each node repeatedly to calculate the value of traveling to each node for its next route.

After that, LSTM [12] planning unit with attention mechanism repeatedly refines the node features and produces a value function associated with each node. The next destination will be selected on the basis of the value function, so the node with the highest value function will become the next destination.

3.1 Value Iteration Module

The road network is represented by a tightly linked graph G(V, E). Each graph node represents a street segment, and each agent's goal is to choose a node. That node will become the next destination of the agent. Node's initial features are refined by passing them through a graph neural network [13] for specific iterations. Then, these features are turned into a value function, and the next destination is the node with the highest value. Let $Z = (z_1, z_2, ..., z_n)$ represents a vector with initial node features, where n denotes number of nodes, and $Y = y_1, y_2, ..., y_n$ denote the node features of the input communication. A linear layer encodes node input features to produce an initial feature for the value iteration module:

$$Z^0 = (Z||Y)W_{enc} + b_{enc} \qquad (4)$$

We conduct the following iterative update across neighboring nodes at each planning iteration z using an attention LSTM:

$$Z^{(k+1)} = Z^{(k)} + LSTM(Att(Z^{(k)}, A); H^{(k)}) \qquad (5)$$

where K denotes the number of value iteration steps, hidden states $H^{(t)}$ in LSTM, and adjacency matrix A. Floyd Warshall method is employed to compute dense distance matrix, which is then used as an input to this model, rather than using the adjacency matrix as an input to the network. This ensures that our model uses more useful information. The Floyd-Warshall algorithm generates a matrix, $D_{i,j} = d(v_i, v_j)$, which represents the shortest path between any two nodes in terms of pairwise distance. This matrix is then normalized to create a dense adjacency matrix. $A = (D - \mu)/\sigma$ where μ is the mean of the elements of D and σ is the standard deviation of the elements.

3.2 Graph Attention Layer

The graph attention layer(GAL) is responsible for the exchange of information within a graph. The attention module used in VRP-VIN is a transformer layer [14] that receives adjacency matrix and node features, then outputs modified features. First, the values of the key, query, and value function for each node are calculated.

$$Q^{(k)} = Z^{(k)}W_q + b_q \qquad (6)$$

$$K^{(k)} = Z^{(k)}W_k + b_k \qquad (7)$$

$$V^{(k)} = Z^{(k)}W_v + b_v \qquad (8)$$

The node feature vector is multiplied by the weight vector to calculate the key, query, and value. Then we form an attention matrix by computing attention between the node and each other nodes.

$$A_{att} = Q^{(k)}.K^{(k)T} \qquad (9)$$

To express edge features, we mix adjacency matrix A and attention matrix in a multi-layer neural network g as shown below.

$$A(k) = softmax(g(A_{att}^{(k)}, A)) \qquad (10)$$

The values of new nodes are calculated by merging the values generated by the other nodes in the merged attention matrix according to the attention. The output of GALs is sent into the LSTM module.

$$Z^{(k)} = Z^{(k)} + LSTM((A^{(k)}, V^{(k)}; H^{(k)}) \qquad (11)$$

Before decoding, the entire procedure is performed for a fixed no. of iterations, $k = 1. \ldots .K$.

Each node feature is translated into a scalar value function on the graph after iterating the attention LSTM module for K iterations. Then SoftMax function is applied across the rest of the nodes to derive action probabilities, masking off the value of any node that is not required to be visited anymore because they're fully traversed.

$$\pi(s_i; j_i) = softmax(Z^k W_{dec} + b_{dec}) \qquad (12)$$

Lastly, the node with the highest probability value is chosen as the next destination. With the help of the shortest path algorithm, a full path is constructed by linking the latest node with the node chosen as the next destination. The graph weight is calculated by dividing the length of a road segment by the average speed of the car driving it. It shows how long it is expected to take to drive from one road segment to the next.

3.3 Communication Module

As our problem is dynamic in nature, it is best for agents to communicate their desired path, thus encouraging more collaborative behavior. In order to do this, VRP-VIN includes a communication module based on the attention mechanism, in which attention is now focused on the agents as opposed to the street segment earlier in VI module. Whenever an agent acts, it outputs some communication vector: $y^{(i)}$. It is subsequently transmitted to each agent using $Z^{(K)}$, the value iteration module's final encoding. The communication vector is expressed as a set of node attributes in order to obtain the topology of the street graph. At the receiver end, each sender's current communication vector is stored temporarily. Every agent has an attention layer that compiles data from the receiver's inbox, whenever an agent wants to take a new action. Let $M^{in} = m^1, ..., m^L$ represent concatenated messages received by an agent from others, where L represents the number of agents. The agent creates a query and a value vector by transforming the communication vectors.

$$Q_{com} = M_{in}W_{q,com} + b_{q,com} \qquad (13)$$

$$V_{com} = M_{in}W_{v,com} + b_{v,com} \qquad (14)$$

The key vector is generated by the agent's last outputted communication vector.

$$k_{i,com} = M_{in}W_{k,com} + b_{k,com} \qquad (15)$$

We then perform the dot product of this key vector with each agent's query vector to generate a learned linear combination of all other agent's communication vectors. Then combined communication is computed as U_i.

$$Y_i = \sum_j \alpha_{i,j}V_j \qquad (16)$$

$$\alpha_i = softmax(Q_{com}k_{i,com}) \qquad (17)$$

For the next stage, node feature Y_i will be put to use as inputs to the autonomous mapping benchmark module. VRP-VIN can be trained using reinforcement learning. We presume there is a teacher(oracle) that can answer these planning difficulties for imitation learning. But this approach requires a completely observable environment. The teacher solver frequently slows down the training process because each roll-out generates a training graph, but always provides an optimum result. Reinforcement learning, on the other hand, uses a trial and error process, where the correct move is rewarded and the erroneous move is punished. Reinforcement learning is quite challenging to train but improves the eventual goal. LKH3 solver [15] is provided with knowledge regarding each problem to be resolved as a completely observable environment to build the ground-truth a* that we wish to replicate. Each agent attempts to forecast the upcoming move "a" based on the ground-truth historical trajectory. Cross-entropy loss is minimized for each action and summed over roll-out, "teacher-forcing" is used to train the agent. Agents are pushed to perform the same actions equivalent to ground truth, and if their actions do not resemble those of their "teacher" they are penalized.

$$L = -E\sum_{(t,i)} log\pi(s_t^{(i)*}; y_t^{(i)}) \qquad (18)$$

where $\pi(s; y)$ is the likelihood of performing action s provided a state y The expert demonstration is beneficial for imitation learning, but it may not always be available in actual situations. We can instead employ reinforcement learning. The network is trained through episodic reinforcement learning using REIN-FORCE [16]. The reward function will be set as the negative of the total cost required to complete the traversal, which is normalized over a set of mini-batches.

$$r = \sum_i F(p^{(i)}), \tilde{r} = (r - \mu_r)/\sigma_r, \tag{19}$$

$$L = -E_\pi \tilde{r}, \nabla L = E_\pi[\tilde{r} \sum_{(t,i)} \nabla log\pi(s_t^{(i)}; (y_t^{(i)})] \tag{20}$$

4 Evaluation

A 3-layer MLP with 16 dimensions each, with ReLU activation is utilized to combine the dot-product attention with the distance matrix. The encoding vectors have a 16-dimensional size. Adam optimizer is used to set the model's learning rate during training to be 1e−3. The decay rate is set as 0.1 per 2000 epochs. The model is trained for 5000 epochs. Each of the 50 graphs in our batch size has a maximum of 25 nodes. We just use two agents to train our network and one to nine agents to analyze it.

There are 22,814 directed road graphs in the collection, which were collected from 18 cities on six continents. For testing, we pick a different location, and for validation, we utilize 10% of the training set. We also include actual traffic situations and mapping issues in this benchmark. Extra problems fall into three groups: random revisits, realistic traffic, and asynchronous execution.

In the real world, the environment is dynamic, and mapping a road could fail due to failure in sensors or harsh weather. As a result, we have to traverse a road an indeterminate amount of times until the graph network is completely traversed. Every node in the graph is assigned a random number ranging from one to three during training, which specifies the number of times it must be traversed before the graph is completely covered. When testing, this value is sampled evenly from 1 to 3 at random, except when explicitly tested for alternate distribution.

Unknown traffic congestion is also simulated for each road. We employ the flow equations presented by Tampere et al. [17] for estimating the node's equilibrium congestion. This method models traffic as a flow issue in which the goal is to maximize overall vehicle movement while sticking to a set of junction limitations. The congestion is begun at random using a uniform distribution from 0 to 1, and the flow constraints are produced by multiplying the no. of arriving and departing lanes by the speed limit of those lanes. After that using Sewall et al. [18], velocity at each road v is defined as: $v = v_{max}(1 - \rho^\gamma)$, where v_{max} is the road's speed limit, and ρ is the road's traffic congestion, and γ denotes hyper-parameter (fixed at 3) helps in reducing the impact of traffic. Therefore, anytime an agent visits a certain node, the traversal cost of that node goes up by $1/(1 - \rho^\gamma)g$. To make sure that the traveling cost to nodes with the most congestion does not reach infinity, we set this factor to a maximum of 4. Depending on the equilibrium congestion, the edge traversal cost can range from one to four times its initial value. It's worth remembering that until an agent visits a node, the congestion value is unknown. Each agent works in a synchronous manner during the training phase, where each agent performs some action serially until every node in the graph has been traversed. However, this ignores the amount of time needed for each action. Instead, we simulate the time it takes to execute each activity during the evaluation phase. As a result, agents act in a non-synchronous manner depending on the length of time it takes to execute each action.

Table 2. Total cost (Runtime in Hrs)

	No of vehicles			
No of nodes	1	2	3	4
20	1.1	1.1	1.4	1.9
30	1.2	1.4	1.8	2.2
40	1.4	1.6	2	2.6
50	2	2.2	2.6	3.2
60	2.1	2.3	2.7	3.3
70	2.2	2.4	2.8	3.5
80	2.6	2.9	3.2	4
90	2.9	3	3.6	4.2
100	3.5	3.8	4.3	5.1

4.1   LKH3

LKH3 is the best-performing iterative solver with available data. First, the solver chooses the best route for precisely covering all nodes exactly once. After that, the solver determines a new optimal route across each of the nodes that still need to be traversed. Until every node has been completely mapped, this is repeated. Basically, the solver does VRP traversals until the required number of nodes has been visited.

4.2   Oracle

If an agent had been given global knowledge of every hidden state, this is the best possible performance that could have been obtained. By giving the LKH3 solver information about every hidden variable and doing an optimal plan search, the solution is discovered. By duplicating the nodes and raising the node's edge weights affected by traffic congestion, we alter the adjacency matrix.

Table 3. Average traversal cost on real graphs; Time cost (hrs); Runtime (ms)

	25 Nodes, 1 Vehicles		
Method	Cost	Gap	Runtime
Oracle	1.16	0.00%	71.3
LKH3	1.26	8.84%	71.2
GAT	1.53	32.50%	43
VRP-VIN (IL)	1.37	18.00%	62.8
VRP-VIN (RL)	1.25	8.17%	62.8
	25 Nodes, 2 Vehicles		
Method	Cost	Gap	Runtime
Oracle	1.28	0.00%	438
LKH3	1.8	40.50%	438
GAT	1.56	21.60%	29.1
VRP-VIN (IL)	1.42	11.30%	66.6
VRP-VIN (RL)	1.32	2.87%	56.6
	50 Nodes, 2 Vehicles		
Method	Cost	Gap	Runtime
Oracle	1.85	0.00%	902
LKH3	2.54	37.30%	902
GAT	2.58	39.70%	38
VRP-VIN (IL)	2.21	19.00%	71.5
VRP-VIN (RL)	2.12	14.50%	71.4
	100 Nodes, 5 Vehicles		
Method	Cost	Gap	Runtime
Oracle	3.19	0.00%	2430
LKH3	6.14	92.50%	2430
GAT	5.43	70.20%	38.2
VRP-VIN (IL)	4.36	36.70%	72.8
VRP-VIN (RL)	4.62	44.90%	72.8

4.3   Graph Attention Network

GATs exchange complex information between the nodes based on the attention mechanism. Normally, GAT architectures, on the other hand, presume that all edges have equal weight rather than encoding the information about the distance matrix, which restricts their potential. Although GATs aren't always made to address TSP or VRP issues, they are still among the most cutting-edge options for graph and network encoding (Figs. 1, 2 and 3).

The performance of VRP-VIN is the best over a range of agent counts and graph sizes. Notably, this technique with 25 nodes and two agents using rein-

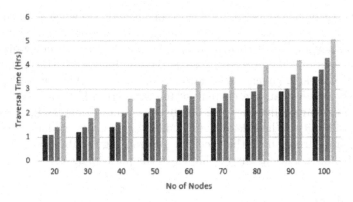

Fig. 1. Total cost graph

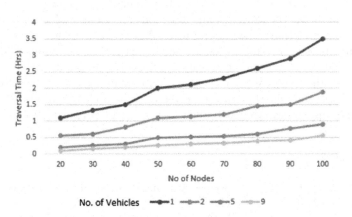

Fig. 2. Cost per agent (Runtime in Hrs)

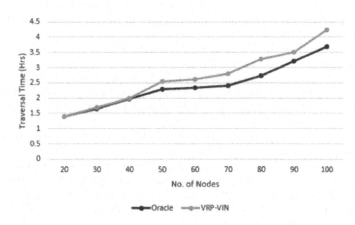

Fig. 3. Oracle vs VRP-VIN (Runtime in Hrs)

forcement learning achieves a total cost of around 3% when compared with oracle. We discovered that the model that included imitation and reinforcement learning outperformed all rival models. The model's overall generalization to multiple agents and larger graph sizes is outstanding. Each traversal's cost is distributed across the agents in a fairly equal manner. The method performs significantly better than the current state-of-the-art, LKH solver. The overall cost increases marginally when the number of agents is increased, demonstrating high scalability. When dealing with more agents, the models trained with reinforcement learning have the excellent generalizing capability. Increasing the number of value iterations further increases the performance.

5   Conclusion

VRP-VIN can easily route multiple vehicles online in a real-world environment with dynamic obstacles. This model beats all current approaches on real road graphs by leveraging the learned value iteration transitions and a communication protocol based on the attention mechanism. Also, it can be scaled up or down to different numbers of agents and nodes without requiring retraining. Communication is a key component in multi-agent systems learning coordinated behavior. So, Future studies will involve a more in-depth examination of the information stored in the communication and its semantic value. There will also be further research into approaches that will allow this system to operate on huge graphs.

References

1. Toth, P., Vigo, D. (eds.): The Vehicle Routing Problem. Society for Industrial and Applied Mathematics, Philadelphia (2002)
2. Vinyals, O., Fortunato, M., Jaitly, N.: Pointer networks. In: Advances in Neural Information Processing Systems, vol. 28 (2015)
3. Khalil, E., Dai, H., Zhang, Y., Dilkina, B., Song, L.: Learning combinatorial optimization algorithms over graphs. In: Advances in Neural Information Processing Systems, vol. 30 (2017)
4. Kool, W., Van Hoof, H., Welling, M.: Attention, learn to solve routing problems!. arXiv preprint arXiv:1803.08475 (2018)
5. Deudon, M., Cournut, P., Lacoste, A., Adulyasak, Y., Rousseau, L.-M.: Learning heuristics for the TSP by policy gradient. In: van Hoeve, W.-J. (ed.) CPAIOR 2018. LNCS, vol. 10848, pp. 170–181. Springer, Cham (2018). https://doi.org/10.1007/978-3-319-93031-2_12
6. Vaswani, A., et al.: Attention is all you need. In: Advances in Neural Information Processing Systems, vol. 30 (2017)
7. Tamar, A., Wu, Y., Thomas, G., Levine, S., Abbeel, P.: Value iteration networks. In: Advances in Neural Information Processing Systems, vol. 29 (2016)
8. Lu, J., Li, J., Yuan, Q., Chen, B.: A multi-vehicle cooperative routing method based on evolutionary game theory. In: 2019 IEEE Intelligent Transportation Systems Conference (ITSC), pp. 987–994. IEEE, October 2019

9. Tang, B., Li, Z., Han, K.: Multi-agent reinforcement learning for mobile crowd-sensing systems with dedicated vehicles on road networks. In: 2021 IEEE International Intelligent Transportation Systems Conference (ITSC), pp. 3584–3589. IEEE, September 2021

10. Niu, Y., Paleja, R.R., Gombolay, M.C.: Multi-agent graph-attention communication and teaming. In: AAMAS, pp. 964–973, May 2021

11. Veličković, P., Cucurull, G., Casanova, A., Romero, A., Lio, P., Bengio, Y.: Graph attention networks. arXiv preprint arXiv:1710.10903 (2017)

12. Hochreiter, S., Schmidhuber, J.: Long short-term memory. Neural Comput. 9(8), 1735–1780 (1997)

13. Wu, Z., Pan, S., Chen, F., Long, G., Zhang, C., Philip, S.Y.: A comprehensive survey on graph neural networks. IEEE Trans. Neural Netw. Learn. Syst. 32(1), 4–24 (2020)

14. Yun, S., Jeong, M., Kim, R., Kang, J., Kim, H.J.: Graph transformer networks. In: Advances in Neural Information Processing Systems, vol. 32 (2019)

15. Helsgaun, K.: An Extension of the Lin-Kernighan-Helsgaun TSP Solver for Constrained Traveling Salesman and Vehicle Routing Problems, pp. 24–50. Roskilde University, Roskilde (2017)

16. Williams, R.J.: Simple statistical gradient-following algorithms for connectionist reinforcement learning. Mach. Learn. 8(3), 229–256 (1992)

17. Tampère, C.M., Corthout, R., Cattrysse, D., Immers, L.H.: A generic class of first order node models for dynamic macroscopic simulation of traffic flows. Transp. Res. Part B Methodol. 45(1), 289–309 (2011)

18. Sewall, J., Wilkie, D., Merrell, P., Lin, M.C.: Continuum traffic simulation. In: Computer Graphics Forum, vol. 29, no. 2, pp. 439–448. Blackwell Publishing Ltd., Oxford, UK, May 2010

Design of an Energy Aware Cluster-Based Routing Scheme to Minimize Energy Consumption in Wireless Sensor Networks

Shashank Barthwal[1] , Sumit Pundir[1]([⊠]) , Mohammad Wazid[1] , D. P. Singh[1] ,
and Sakshi Pundir[2]

[1] Department of Computer Science and Engineering, Graphic Era Deemed to be University,
Dehradun 248 002, India
sumitpundir1983@gmail.com
[2] Department of Management, Graphic Era Hill University, Dehradun 248 002, India

Abstract. Efficient usage of sensor nodes has fascinated researchers and scientists so that energy depletion of network can be decreased. Heterogeneous protocols are considered of paramount significance for fulfilling this purpose. Typically, energy of two or three levels of nodes are considered in heterogeneous protocols. But in real life, due to manufacturing variations, diversity in morphological factors and uneven physical terrain of sensor nodes, a broad range of energy levels exist. We propose an improved energy aware cluster-based routing mechanism to minimize energy consumption in wireless sensor networks (in short IEACRP). Through proposed mechanism, the lifetime, stability and throughput of network can be enhanced. Here, WSN contains sensor nodes with four energy levels, and some of the sensor nodes are kept into sleep mode if they have energy less than threshold. Sleep awake mechanism works as energy hole removing mechanism. Simulation results show that proposed mechanism attains longer stability, lifetime and throughput in comparison of EEAHP, TEEN, MODLEACH, DEEC, LEACH, E-MODLEACH and SEP.

Keywords: Wireless sensor network (WSN) · Clustering · Cluster head (CH) selection · Energy efficiency

1 Introduction

A wireless sensor network comprised of numerous nodes, which emphasize data gathering from inaccessible regions and then forwarding it to the base station. Sensor nodes play a momentous role in monitoring numerous environmental factors like humidity, sound, lightning, temperature, pressure etc. [3]. It is well understood to get the primary consideration of foot building and deploying buy less sensor networks of safety, dependability, and energy efficiency [19]. As a result of unattainable characteristics and the difficulty to recharge the node WSNs are hot subject of study [2]. The sensor nodes in WSN have restricted energy (e.g., 1.2 V, 0.5 AH batteries) and they work in unreachable regions, hence, recharging or replacing their batteries is impossible. If a sensor

© The Author(s), under exclusive license to Springer Nature Switzerland AG 2023
I. Woungang et al. (Eds.): ANTIC 2022, CCIS 1797, pp. 16–28, 2023.
https://doi.org/10.1007/978-3-031-28180-8_2

node drains its energy, then it is considered dead and if all nodes exhaust their energy, then the entire network becomes lifeless [18]. Hence, the energy of nodes should be utilized efficiently so that entire energy expansion of sensor nodes can be minimized [5, 20]. Amongst various routing methods, cluster-based routing is of utmost significance, it distributes the load among nodes in such a manner that the energy depletion is balanced amid sensor nodes [1, 7]. Clustering is a method of dividing a sensor field into teams referred to as clusters and selecting a team lead referred to as cluster head for all respective clusters [17]. The main responsibility of CHs is to gather the data and then forward it to the sink. CHs suffer from additional workload due to their member nodes. For distributing this workload, the position of CH is revolve along nodes. CHs spends more energy as compared to sensor nodes because of their additional functionalities. By performing the role of an intermediator between nodes and sink, clustering avoids multi-hop communication and reduces communication cost. Clustering based WSN are categorized into two categories i.e., homogeneous WSN and heterogeneous WSN [24]. In homogeneous networks entire nodes have equivalent energy, coverage, connectivity, and computational abilities. However, homogeneity doesn't exist in an ideal world [23]. On the other side, in heterogeneous networks, nodes have different energies, coverage, connectivity, and computational abilities [8]. Nodes with extra energy help in achieving network longevity [4].

Now by the radio energy dissipation model in Fig. 1 [10], for transfer of L-bit data over a distance d, the expanded energy is:

$$E_{TX}(L, d) = \begin{cases} LE_{elec} + Ld^2 \, E_{fs} & \text{if } d < d_0 \quad (1) \\ LE_{elec} + Ld^4 \, E_{mp} & \text{if } d \geq d_0 \quad (2) \end{cases}$$

Here, the receiver/transmitter circuit consume E_{elec} energy per bit and if distance (d) is greater or equals to threshold (d_0) then multi path energy model works (E_{mp}) or else, the free space (E_{fs}). The threshold distance (d0) is:

$$d_0 = \sqrt{\frac{E_{fs}}{E_{mp}}} \tag{3}$$

The Energy required to receive K-bit data (ERX) is:

$$E_{RX}(L) = L * E_{elec} \tag{4}$$

During data fusion, the following amount of energy is expended:

$$E_{dx}(L) = p \cdot L \cdot E_{da} \tag{5}$$

Here, p is the number of data packets and Eda is the energy expended in data fusion of 1-bit data.

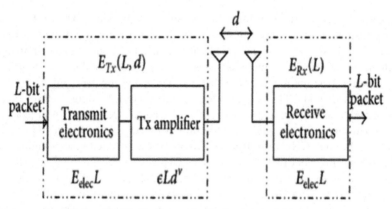

Fig. 1. Radio energy dissipation model

2 Literature Review

WSN protocols are considered of paramount significance for fulfilling the purpose of improving the network lifetime [9]. Heinzelman et al. discussed LEACH. In WSN, LEACH is considered as the earliest reactive and hierarchical routing protocol [21]. Firstly, it forms clusters and then selects a CH for respective clusters. For selection of CH, all sensor nodes generate a random number in the network and then calculate a threshold value for all nodes [11]. LEACH has flaws such as clusters of varying sizes, a low energy node as the cluster leader, a highly fluctuating CH count, and a non-uniform distribution of CHs [10]. MODLEACH is the extension of LEACH [22]. It considers efficient CH replacement methods with dual transmitting power levels of nodes for reducing energy consumption of nodes. Here CH remains the same for the successive round if threshold energy is less than residual energy. TEEN uses stratified grouping, in which cluster is formed between closer nodes, and this procedure is imitated until the BS (sink) is reached [15]. SEP is the first heterogeneous protocol having two levels of sensor nodes [12]. In this, some are advanced nodes, and the rest are normal nodes. The heterogeneity of sensor nodes assures the reliability of sensor network. It works on weighted election probability [14]. DEEC examines two node energy levels, and CH is chosen based on the network's residual and average energy ratio [13]. High energy nodes have a better likelihood of becoming CHs than low energy nodes. E-MODLEACH uses an approach based on remaining energy of the node for cluster head selection [25]. In EEAHP, CH selection is based on recasting the CH election threshold [16]. Thereby increasing lifetime and stability period of sensor network. Sink mobility possess a challenge while designing WSN [6, 26]. So to achieve better results all sensor nodes are aware of the position of sink [27].

3 Proposed Mechanism

In proposed IEACRP four levels of heterogeneous nodes are used. Total n sensor nodes are deployed out of which some are ultra-nodes, hyper nodes, advance nodes and normal nodes. Let normal nodes have E_0 energy.

c_0 -> Fraction of ultra-nodes and have φ times more energy than normal nodes. So, energy of ultra-nodes can be calculated as follows:

$$E_u = nc_0E_0(1 + \varphi) \tag{6}$$

c_1 -> fraction of hyper nodes and they have Ψ times more energy than normal nodes. So, energy of hyper nodes can be calculated as follows:

$$E_h = nc_1E_0(1 + \Psi) \tag{7}$$

c_2 -> fraction of advance nodes and they have $¥$ times more energy than normal nodes. So, the energy of mega nodes can be calculated as follows:

$$E_a = nc_2E_0(1 + ¥) \tag{8}$$

Remaining nodes are normal nodes which have E_0 energy. So, normal node's energy can be calculated as follows

$$E_n = nE_0(1 - c_0 - c_1 - c_2) \tag{9}$$

The overall energy of the system is calculated as:

$$\begin{aligned} E_{Total} &= E_u + E_h + E_a + E_n \\ &= nE_0(1 + c_0\varphi + c_1\Psi + c_2¥) \end{aligned} \tag{10}$$

Energy dissipation of cluster per round is:

$$E_{cluster} = E_{CH} + \frac{n}{k}E_{nonCH} \tag{11}$$

The CH energy dissipation in a round is given by:

$$E_{CH} = LE_{elec}\left(\frac{n}{k} - 1\right) + LE_{DA}\frac{n}{k} + LE_{elec} + LE_{fs}d_{toBS}^2 \tag{12}$$

Here k -> number of clusters
E_{da} -> processing cost of a bit per signal
d_{toBS} -> Proximity between CH and BS.

The CM's energy consumption is equal to:

$$E_{nonCH} = LE_{elec} + LE_{fs}d_{toCH}^2 \tag{13}$$

where d_{toCH} is the separation between a CM and its CH. It can be calculated as follow:

$$d_{toCH}^2 = \int\int \left(x^2 + y^2\right)p(x, y)dxdy = \frac{M^2}{2\pi k}$$

$$d_{toCH} = \frac{M}{\sqrt{2\pi k}} \tag{14}$$

$\rho(x, y)$ -> node distribution.

The total energy consumption of the network:

$$E_t = L\left(2nE_{elec} + nE_{da} + kE_{fs}d_{toBS}^2 + nE_{fs}d_{toCH}^2\right) \tag{15}$$

The average d_{toBS} is given by

$$d_{toBS} = \int_A^{\sqrt{}} x^2 + y^2 \frac{1}{A} dA = 0.765\frac{M}{2} \tag{16}$$

Now, to find optimal no. of constructed clusters we must differentiate E_t w.r.t. k by equating it to 0.

$$K_{opt} = \sqrt{\frac{n}{2\pi} \frac{M}{d_{toBS}}} = \sqrt{\frac{n}{2\pi} \frac{2}{0.765}} \tag{17}$$

At any round R, the average energy:

$$E(R) = \frac{1}{n}E_{Total}\left(1 - \frac{R}{R_T}\right) \tag{18}$$

Here, R-current round
E_{Total}-total energy of the system
R_T- total rounds.

The total rounds (R_T) can be calculated as follows

$$R_T = \frac{E_{Total}}{E_t} \tag{19}$$

The threshold energy of nodes is calculated as:

$$E_{TH} = ((E_{TX} + E_{DA}) * D) + \left(E_{mp} * D * d_{ex}^4\right) \tag{20}$$

D-Length of data packet
d_{ex}-Separation between farthest node and BS.

The node will only communicate if residual energy is greater than threshold energy otherwise the node moves towards sleep.

Here the probability of each node is essential for CH election. The probabilities are calculated as:

$$P_u = \frac{P_0(1 + \varphi)}{1 + b_0\varphi + b_1\Psi + b_2\yen + b_3\eta + b_4\delta} \tag{21}$$

$$P_h = \frac{P_0(1 + \Psi)}{1 + b_0\varphi + b_1\Psi + b_2\yen + b_3\eta + b_4\delta} \tag{22}$$

$$P_a = \frac{P_0(1 + \delta)}{1 + b_0\varphi + b_1\Psi + b_2\yen + b_3\eta + b_4\delta} \tag{23}$$

$$P_n = \frac{P_0}{1 + b_0\varphi + b_1\Psi + b_2\yen + b_3\eta + b_4\delta} \tag{24}$$

If random number < threshold value, then node will be CH.
Else, the node will be CM.
The threshold can be calculated as follows:

$$Th_u = \begin{cases} \frac{P_u}{1-P_u\left(r,mod\,\frac{1}{P_u}\right)} \frac{E_{Res}}{E_{AVG}*d_{toBS}*K_{opt}} & if\ N_u \in A' \\ 0 & otherwise \end{cases} \tag{25}$$

$$Th_h = \begin{cases} \frac{P_h}{1-P_h\left(r\,mod\,\frac{1}{P_h}\right)} \frac{E_{Res}}{E_{AVG}*d_{toBS}*K_{opt}} & if\ N_h \in A'' \\ 0 & otherwise \end{cases} \tag{26}$$

$$Th_a = \begin{cases} \frac{P_a}{1-P_a\left(r\,mod\,\frac{1}{P_a}\right)} \frac{E_{Res}}{E_{AVG}*d_{toBS}*K_{opt}} & if\ N_a \in A''' \\ 0 & otherwise \end{cases} \tag{27}$$

$$Th_n = \begin{cases} \frac{P_n}{1-P_n\left(r\,mod\,\frac{1}{P_n}\right)} \frac{E_{Res}}{E_{AVG}*d_{toBS}*K_{opt}} & if\ N_n \in A'''' \\ 0 & otherwise \end{cases} \tag{28}$$

A', A'', A''', A'''', are the set of ultra, hyper, advance, and normal nodes that are not CH in the last $1/P_u$, $1/P_h$, $1/P_a$ and $1/P_n$ rounds, respectively.
The E_{AVG} can be calculated as

$$E_{AVG} = \frac{1}{n}E_{Total} \tag{29}$$

Flow chart of the proposed mechanism is given in Fig. 2.

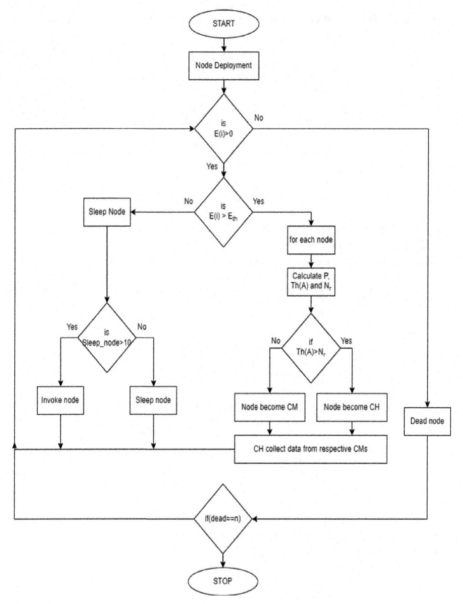

Fig. 2. Flowchart of proposed mechanism

4   Results and Future Work

For simplicity, we have taken immobile nodes. The mechanisms, which are compared with proposed IEACRP include EEAHP, MODLEACH, LEACH, E-MODLEACH, TEEN, SEP and DEEC. Here $c0 = 0.1$, $c1 = 0.2$ and $c3 = 0.3$. The details of nodes are given in Table 1

Table 1. Details of different nodes

Type of node	Number of nodes
Normal nodes	40
Advanced nodes	30
Hyper nodes	20
Ultra- nodes	10

Radio parameters are kept same for the proposed mechanism. The details are given in Table 2.

Table 2. Details of simulation parameters

Parameters	Description	Value
x_m, y_m	Dimension of field	200×200 m^2
n	Number of sensor nodes	100
E_0	Energy dissipated in transmitting data	1 J
E_{TX}	Energy dissipated in receiving data	50×10^{-9} J/bit
E_{RX}	Amplification energy when d is less than d_0	50×10^{-9} J/bit
E_{fs}	Amplification energy when d is less than d_0	10×10^{-12} J/bit/m^2
E_{mp}	Amplification energy when d is more than d_0	1.3×10^{-15} J/bit/m^2
E_{DA}	Data aggregation energy	10×10^{-9} J

4.1   Number of Alive Nodes Against Rounds

As shown in Fig. 5, IEACRP-WSN covers a greater number of rounds in comparison to EEAHP, TEEN, MODLEACH, DEEC, LEACH, E-MODLEACH and SEP. The improvement in alive nodes is because of the CH selection based on residual energy and optimum number of clusters.

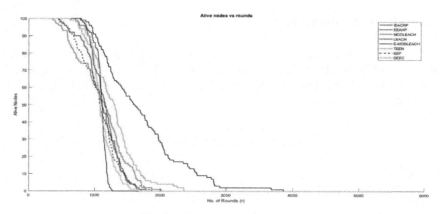

Fig. 3. Alive nodes versus rounds

4.2 Throughput

As shown in Fig. 4, IEACRP transmits 85166 packets whereas EEAHP, MODLEACH, LEACH, E-MODLEACH, TEEN, SEP and DEEC transmits 58247, 83268, 55429, 29250, 43713, 55491 and 44065 packets, respectively. IEACRP enhanced throughput in comparison to other protocols.

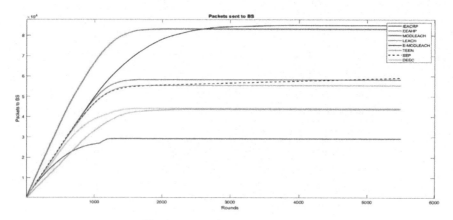

Fig. 4. Packets to BS versus rounds

4.3 Number of Dead Nodes Against Rounds

As illustrated in Fig. 3, the stability period of IEACRP is greater than the rest of the protocols. The first node dies at 782 round.

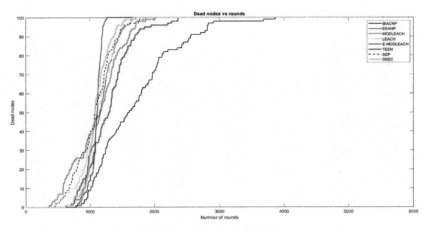

Fig. 5. Dead nodes vs rounds

4.4 Instability Period

As illustrated in Fig. 6, instability period of IEACRP is greater than the rest of the protocols. The instability period is 3082 round.

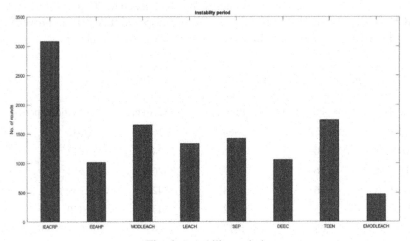

Fig. 6. Instability period

4.5 Stability Period

As illustrated in Fig. 7, stability period of IEACRP is greater than the most of the protocols. The stability period is 782 round.

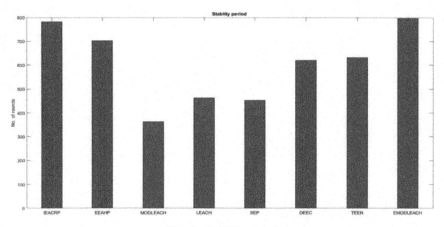

Fig. 7. Stability period

5   Conclusion

Proposed mechanism (IEACRP), an energy conservation clustering protocol is good for heterogeneous WSNs, with four variety of nodes. Residual and average energy are affecting CH selection. Thus, high energy nodes have more probability of getting nominated as a CH, in contrast of nodes with low energy. When matched to EEAHP, MODLEACH, LEACH, E-MODLEACH, TEEN, SEP and DEEC, proposed IEACRP has proven better protocol in terms of throughput, lifespan, and stability period (Table 3).

Table 3. Performance comparison

Protocols	First death	Lifetime	Throughput	Instability period
IEACRP	782	3864	85166	3082
EEAHP	703	1716	58247	1013
MODLEACH	363	2017	83268	1654
LEACH	463	1794	55429	1331
SEP	452	1872	55491	1420
DEEC	620	1677	44065	1057
TEEN	633	2370	43713	1737
EMODLEACH	796	1267	29250	471

Future Work
Although ample of research work has been done in the field of WSN but still there is a huge scope of improvement. The proposed mechanism can be improved further

by inscribing Machine Learning. WSN, IOT and ML combined can make a huge breakthrough in the Wireless Sensor networks.

Limitation

Although proposed mechanism is proved to be better than other protocols, but it is assumed that the environment conditions are standard, there can be no disruptions in the network, the nodes or the system has no manufacturing defects, and all conditions are standard and stable. Some limitations are:

- Node heterogeneity is limited to 4.
- Nodes cannot die unless their energy is exhausted.
- No external interference is there.
- Sink is not mobile.

References

1. Salam, T., Hossen, M.S.: Performance analysis on homogeneous and heterogeneous routing protocols in wireless sensor networks (2021). https://doi.org/10.1109/ACMI53878.2021.9528242
2. Verma, R.K., Pattanaik, K.K., Bharti, S.: An adaptive mechanism for improving resiliency in wireless sensor networks. In: 2015 IEEE 10th International Conference on Industrial and Information Systems (ICIIS), pp. 525–530 (2015). https://doi.org/10.1109/ICIINFS.2015.7399067
3. Lanzolla, A., Spadavecchia, M.: Wireless sensor networks for environmental monitoring. Sensors (2021). https://doi.org/10.3390/s2104117
4. Mehto, A., Verma, R.K., Jain, S.: Efficient trajectory planning and route adjustment strategy for mobile sink in WSN-assisted IoT. In: 2022 IEEE Region 10 Symposium (TENSYMP), pp. 1–6 (2022). https://doi.org/10.1109/TENSYMP54529.2022.9864434
5. Roundy, S., Steingart, D., Frechette, L., Wright, P., Rabaey, J.: Power sources for wireless sensor networks. In: Karl, H., Wolisz, A., Willig, A. (eds.) EWSN 2004. LNCS, vol. 2920, pp. 1–17. Springer, Heidelberg (2004). https://doi.org/10.1007/978-3-540-24606-0_1
6. Verma, R.K., Jain, S.: Energy and delay efficient data acquisition in wireless sensor networks by selecting optimal visiting points for mobile sink. J. Ambient Intell. Hum. Comput. (2022). https://doi.org/10.1007/s12652-022-03729-9
7. Rozas, A., Araujo, A.: An application-aware clustering protocol for wireless sensor networks to provide QoS management. J. Sens. (2019)
8. Jain, S.K., Venkatadari, M., Shrivastava, N., Jain, S., Verma, R.K.: NHCDRA: a non-uniform hierarchical clustering with dynamic route adjustment for mobile sink based heterogeneous wireless sensor networks. Wirel. Netw. **27**(4), 2451–2467 (2021). https://doi.org/10.1007/s11276-021-02585-3
9. Bazzi, H.S., Haidar, A.M., Bilal, A.: Classification of routing protocols in wireless sensor network. In: International Conference on Computer Vision and Image Analysis Applications, pp. 1–5. IEEE, January 2015
10. Ketshabetswe, L.K., Zungeru, A.M., Mangwala, M., Chuma, J.M., Sigweni, B.: Communication protocols for wireless sensor networks: a survey and comparison. Heliyon **5**(5), e01591 (2019)

11. Heinzelman, W.R., Chandrakasan, A., Balakrishnan, H.: Energy-efficient communication protocol for wireless microsensor networks. In: Proceedings of the 33rd Annual Hawaii International Conference on System Sciences, pp. 10-pp. IEEE, January 2000
12. Wang, J., Zhang, Z., Shen, J., Xia, F., Lee, S.: An improved stable election based routing protocol with mobile sink for wireless sensor networks. In: 2013 IEEE International Conference on Green Computing and Communications and IEEE Internet of Things and IEEE Cyber, Physical and Social Computing, pp. 945–950 (2013). https://doi.org/10.1109/GreenCom-iThings-CPSCom.2013.163
13. Qing, L., Zhu, Q., Wang, M.: Design of a distributed energy-efficient clustering algorithm for heterogeneous wireless sensor networks. Comput. Commun. **29**(12), 2230–2237 (2006)
14. Khan, A.A., Javaid, N., Qasim, U., Lu, Z., Khan, Z.A.: HSEP: heterogeneity-aware hierarchical stable election protocol for WSNs. In: 2012 Seventh International Conference on Broadband, Wireless Computing, Communication and Applications, pp. 373–378. IEEE, November 2012
15. Manjeshwar, A., Agrawal, D.P.: TEEN: a routing protocol for enhanced efficiency in wireless sensor networks. In: ipdps, vol. 1, p. 189, April 2001
16. Kashaf, A., Javaid, N., Khan, Z.A., Khan, I.A.: TSEP: threshold-sensitive stable election protocol for WSNs. In: 2012 10th International Conference on Frontiers of Information Technology, pp. 164–168. IEEE, December 2012
17. Shemim, K.F., Witkowski, U.: Energy efficient clustering protocols in WSNs: performance analysis and comparison of EEAHP protocol with LEACH and EAMMH using MATLAB. In: 2020 Advances in Science and Engineering Technology International Conferences (ASET), pp. 1–5. IEEE
18. Pundir, S., Wazid, M., Bakshi, A., Singh, D.P.: Optimized low-energy adaptive clustering hierarchy in wireless sensor network. Next Gener. Inf. Process. Syst. (2021)
19. Gupta, N., Wazid, M., Sharma, S., Singh, D.P., Goudar, R.H.: Coverage lifetime improvement in wireless sensor networks by novel deployment technique. In: IEEE International Conference on Emerging Trends in Computing, Communication and Nanotechnology (ICECCN) (2013)
20. Mohd, N., Singh, A., Bhadauria, H.S.: A novel SVM based IDS for distributed denial of sleep strike in wireless sensor networks. Wirel. Pers. Commun. (2020)
21. Shukla, K.: Research on energy efficient routing protocol LEACH For wireless sensor networks. IJERT (2013)
22. Mahmood, D., Javaid, N., Mahmood, S., Qureshi, S., Memon, A.M., Zaman, T.: MOD-LEACH: a variant of LEACH for WSNs. In: 2013 Eighth International Conference on Broadband and Wireless Computing, Communication and Applications (2013)
23. Barthwal, S., Pundir, S., Wazid, M., Singh, D.P.: An improved energy conservation routing mechanism in heterogeneous wireless sensor networks. In: Choudrie, J., Mahalle, P., Perumal, T., Joshi, A. (eds.) IOT with Smart Systems. Smart Innovation, Systems and Technologies, vol. 312, pp. 37–48. Springer, Singapore (2023). https://doi.org/10.1007/978-981-19-3575-6_5
24. Barthwal, S., Barthwal, N.: An introduction to wireless sensor networks, its challenges and security. Int. Res. J. Eng. Technol. (IRJET) **06**(09) (2019)
25. Hossain, Md.A., Reza, Md.M.: E-MODLEACH: an extended MODLEACH protocol for wireless sensor network. J. Netw. Secur. Comput. Netw. **6**(1), 26–30 (2020)
26. Jain, S., Verma, R.K., Pattanaik, K.K., et al.: A survey on event-driven and query-driven hierarchical routing protocols for mobile sink-based wireless sensor networks. J. Supercomput. **78**, 11492–11538 (2022). https://doi.org/10.1007/s11227-022-04327-4
27. Jain, S., Pattanaik, K.K., Verma, R.K., et al.: EDVWDD: event-driven virtual wheel-based data dissemination for mobile sink-enabled wireless sensor networks. J. Supercomput. **77**, 11432–11457 (2021). https://doi.org/10.1007/s11227-021-03714-7

Email Spam Detection Using Multi-head CNN-BiGRU Network

Ayush Gupta[✉], Jitendra Patil, Somesh Soni, and Alpana Rajan

Computer Division, Raja Ramanna Centre for Advanced Technology, Indore, India
{ayushgupta,jpatil,somesh,alpana}@rrcat.gov.in

Abstract. Spam emails refer to unsolicited email messages, usually sent in bulk to a large list of recipients with the purpose of marketing, or luring individuals to download malware or click on phishing links. Although much research has been done on this topic, our study reveals that less attention is given to combatting the tactics used by spammers, like purposely forging spellings and the usage of smart sentence structuring. This work attempts to fill this void by using sub-wording and context-based methods. The sub-wording method is used to combat the usage of forged spellings while the context-based method is used to counter smart sentence structuring tactics used by spammers. Also, most of the prevalent methods have been evaluated only for one class weight. As the models' performance can vary over class weights, we have used two class weights i.e., balanced and unbalanced for evaluation. The proposed model is designed by using a multi-head approach integrated with the Convolutional Neural Network and Bidirectional Gated Recurrent Unit network. The proposed model has been evaluated on the Lingspam and Spamtext datasets. Another issue neglected in prevalent methods is catastrophic forgetting, to consider it we have used a combination of the two datasets. The evaluation is done in terms of f1_score, accuracy, and receiver operator characteristic curve. The proposed model performs well, giving 99.75% accuracy for the Spamtext dataset and 99.79% accuracy for the Lingspam dataset. Obtained results are compared with state of art models available in the previous literature works.

Keywords: Spam · GRU · CNN · Lingspam · fastText · Inception · Catastrophic forgetting

1 Introduction

Email is one of the preferred methods for interpersonal communication over the Internet. According to statistics, in 2022, 4.258 billion people use email worldwide, this number is about 0.7 billion more than active social media users. This statistic emphasizes the outreach of email communication systems.

Email is also preferred for communication because it is one of the most systematic methods of communication to maintain records of information, documents, and media. But just like the two sides of coins, email's accessibility, and popularity make it an award-winning method for malicious activity and marketing. Statistics say that about 298 billion emails are sent every day among them more than 50% are spam. These

I. Woungang et al. (Eds.): ANTIC 2022, CCIS 1797, pp. 29–46, 2023.
https://doi.org/10.1007/978-3-031-28180-8_3

spam emails are expected to cost organizations nearly $200 billion annually [1]. Spam emails are also known as Unsolicited Bulk Emails (UBE). They can be sent for multiple purposes. One of the purposes is for identity and financial information theft by luring users using lucrative context to download malicious software or click a malicious link. Another usage of spam email is for marketing purposes. In this work, both types are collectively termed spam and legitimate emails are termed ham.

Automated spam detection can be done conventionally in many ways. For example, using blacklisting/whitelisting/greylisting methods, hashing-based methods, authentication-based methods, or any other customized denial method. But these methods are not able to cope with advancements in spam generation techniques thus giving large false positives or low accuracy. A lot of research has been done on improving spam-detecting methods. But in our study, we have found that less work has been done to handle situations when spammers employed techniques like purposefully using wrong spellings or smart sentence structuring. The core idea behind such a tactic is to leave the words and sentences understandable to the target individual (who can easily identify the intended term for such misspellings and can summarize the context of text) but make them unrecognizable by spam defensive systems.

Also, our study reveals that most of the methods in literature performed adequately only on a particular textual statistic and class weight. Above mentioned issues are addressed in our proposed model. To overcome the drawbacks of conventional methods, we have used a Deep Learning (DL) based model. The advantage of DL-based systems is that they can self-learn the behaviors of spam and ham without extensive human intervention.

Our proposed model uses DL and Natural Language Processing (NLP) for spam identification. We have used two publicly available email datasets i.e., Spamtext and Lingspam for evaluating our proposed model. In the proposed model, the datasets are first preprocessed using NLP methods. And then this preprocessed data is passed to the DL-based method in two phases, first for training and then for testing. This research is aimed to build a DL-based method using, an integrated approach of fastText word embedding, Bi-directional Gated Recurrent Unit (Bi-GRU), and an Inception-based multi-head network. FastText is an open-source lightweight library developed by the Facebook AI research team (FAIR). A pre-trained model of fastText word embedding is used to convert textual information into computer-interpretable float format. FastText is a character-level embedding, so unlike other word-level embeddings, it can deal with forged spellings. Bi-GRU is used for the extraction of context in text, based on both words' occurrence as well as their relative position in the text. And being bidirectional gives Bi-GRU an extra advantage for longer texts. Usage of the Inception-based network for classification increases the number of network parameters without depreciating the gradient of network parameters. The multi-head nature of the model allows it to learn the behavior of text from different perspectives, thus enhancing its range of suitability.

To validate the model for suitability over a wide range of text statistics and class weights evaluation is done on both balanced as well as the unbalanced version of datasets and the selected datasets are statistically different. Also, the combination of the datasets is used to verify the model's stability with respect to catastrophic forgetting [2]. Catastrophic forgetting is the tendency to forget previously learned information when learning new information. Improvements brought by the proposed model are validated quantitatively. Obtained results are compared with state of art models available in the literature. The results show that the proposed model performed adequately well and validates our claims.

The rest of the paper is structured in the following manner: Sect. 2 discusses related work. Section 3 explains the methodology and architecture of the proposed model. Experimental results are discussed in Sect. 4. Section 5 concludes our work and gives future direction.

2 Literature Survey

Various approaches for detecting spam emails have been developed. Some of the existing methodologies and strategies utilized by researchers for email spam detection are discussed in this section.

Kaya and Ertuğrul (2016) proposed an approach based on the usage of the statistics of characters with similar UTF-8 values. It used one-dimensional local binary pattern (shifted-1D-LBP) for feature generation [3]. For classification Fisher linear discriminant analysis (FLDA), Functional Tree (FT), Random Forest (RF), and BayesNet (BN) were used. Three benchmark email corpora were used for analysis.

Wijaya and Bisri (2016) proposed a hybrid combination of Logistic Regression (LR) and Decision Tree (DT) [4]. LR is used for threshold manipulation, while DT performs actual classification. An already preprocessed spam base dataset is used, this dataset has predefined rule-based features.

Gashti (2017) proposed an algorithm which is hybrid of the Harmony Search Algorithm (HSA) and ID3 DT for selecting the best features and classification [5]. 57 rule-based features were used for the purpose. Comparison with Support Vector Machine (SVM), Gaussian Naïve Bayes (NB), Radial Basis Function (RBF), LR, and Multi-Layer Perceptron (MLP) models with suggested method was also done.

Trivedi and Panigrahi (2018) performed a comparative study between various decision tree classifiers (such as AD tree, decision stump, and REP tree) with/without different boosting algorithms (bagging, boosting with re-sample, and AdaBoost) [6]. Feature generation is done using the Bag of Words (BoW) method. For comparison, Lingspam and Spamassassin datasets were used. In their results REP tree combined with AdaBoost algorithm outperformed other mentioned 5 algorithms.

Hassan and Mtetwa (2018) compared the effectiveness of term frequency-inverse document frequency (TF-IDF) and BoW feature generation methods [7]. Two different supervised machine learning classifiers namely SVM and NB were compared for spam email detection. SVM combined with TF-IDF was found to perform better.

Jawale et al. (2018) proposed a hybrid of SVM and NB algorithms [8]. Feature generation was done using BoW. Analysis was done on the Lingspam dataset. It was found that their approach gives more accuracy than separately implemented NB and SVM algorithms.

Gibson et al. (2020) compared four algorithms for hyperparameter optimization of five classifiers with different train-test split ratios [9]. Out of these two algorithms namely, Particle Swarm Optimization (PSO) and Genetic Algorithm (GA) were bio-inspired, and the other two algorithms were Grid Search CV (GSCV) and Random Search CV (RSCV). Feature generation was done using TF-IDF.

Roy et al. (2020) compared two deep learning methods namely Convolutional Neural Network (CNN) and Long-short term memory cell (LSTM) with state of art ML methods like NB, and SVM [10]. Also, hyperparameter optimization was used. Early stopping with accuracy threshold was used to control iterations' number.

Zagabathuni (2021) used a pre-trained word2vec model for generating vectors which are then fed to a LSTM network consisting of LSTM and dense layer and the classification result is then compared with the state of art DT algorithms [11].

Douzi S, AlShahwan FA, Lemoudden M, and Ouahidi B. (2020) proposed an ensemble feature generation method using DOC2vec and TF-IDF features [12]. They used DT as classifiers. Better results than conventional BoW methods were shown using the Enron dataset. The LSTM-based classifier was shown to perform better on the Spamtext dataset. Preprocessing is performed by text normalization and stop word removal. Further in this work authors have used different feature generation methods: Term Document Matrix (TDM), TF-IDF, TDM with Singular Value Decomposition (SVD), TDM with Negative Matrix Factorization (NMF), TF-IDF with SVD, TF-IDF with NMF, Keras embedding, Neural Bag-of-Words (NBOW), and Word2Vec word embeddings. Generated features are then applied to different classifiers: Dense Neural Network, CNN, Recurrent Neural Network (RNN), LSTM, CNN-LSTM, LR, NB, K-nearest neighbor, Decision Tree, AdaBoost, Random Forest, and Support Vector Machine. Their comparative study show that the deep learning architectures performed better when compared to the standard machine learning classifiers.

Natarajan et al. (2021) proposed a hyperparameter optimization algorithm for better performance of the classification algorithm [13]. Authors have used the big bang algorithm for the exploration part of the population, while the big crunch algorithm takes care of the convergence of the population. To solve the problem of exploration within a small sub-domain ant miner plus algorithm is used. This algorithm is further used for the classification process. Their result shows that the suggested algorithm performs better than ant miner, ant miner2, ant miner3, and ant miner plus algorithms.

Tida V.S. and Hsu S. (2022) proposed a technique that uses Bidirectional Encoder Representations Transformers (BERT) for feature generation [14]. Authors have used dense layers, with dropout as the classifier, for spam email identification.

The study on related works reveals that most of the authors have used BoW and frequency-based methods for feature generation as in [6–9]. A disadvantage with these methods is that if a spammer can know which of his emails were blocked then he can reverse engineer statistics of training data, and subsequently pass spam emails through the filter by forging spellings or grammar. Some authors have also used transformer-based classifiers and feature extractors as in [14, 37], for using transformers they have assumed a maximum length of the email. This limitation can also be abused by a spammer. In some other research works, Decision Trees and SVM are used for classification. In these methods, features have to be hand-coded or frequency based. If spammers can reverse engineer the rules used, they can restructure spam emails to pass through the filter. Also, these rules are static and may be specifically good for some particular text statistics. The features generated using frequency-based methods are of high dimensionality and are highly sparse, this not only introduces noise but also reduces resource utilization efficiency. Some authors have also used word-level embeddings for feature generation as in [11]. This method conventionally suffers from out-of-vocabulary (OoV) words. To handle OoV in some works stacked embeddings are used as in [12]. Although this method gives a good correlation between related words, it cannot handle forged spellings efficiently. Many works have also been conducted in the utilization of DL-based methods like CNN and LSTM for email spam detection but most of them use algorithms for hyperparameter and epoch optimization for each dataset, thus the developed models are overfitted to specific datasets. This can reduce the reproducibility of results on different datasets.

This paper aims at countering some of the above-mentioned shortcomings and filling the research gap. This paper also tries to contribute to the relatively less touched-upon topic of the simultaneous use of sub-wording and contextual information extraction for spam email identification. The usage of information from different perspectives using multi-head architecture is also introduced and explored in this work. Further usage of GRU cells, instead of LSTM cells which are generally used in related literature is validated.

3 Methodology

In this section, the approach used in the proposed method of spam email detection is described. Parts of the methodology employed are described briefly in Fig. 1.

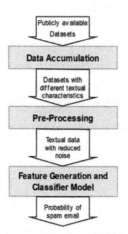

Fig. 1. Sequence of methodology

Python language is used for implementation in this work. Parts of the methodology employed are explained further in the order they were used.

3.1 Data Accumulation

Two publicly available datasets are used in this work. Both datasets consist of only the text in the body part of the email and the class label showing if the email is spam or ham. The first data set used is the open-source data set from Kaggle [15], it consists of 5,572 samples out of which 86% of the messages are legitimate. The second dataset used is not preprocessed folder in the Lingspam dataset derived from [16]; it consists of 2,893 samples out of which 84% are legitimate. Two datasets of different lengths and different textual statistics were chosen to validate the reliability of the proposed model over real-life data with wider statistics.

By exploring the numbers of class labels, it can be observed that both datasets are unbalanced, where the spams are much less than the hams. New datasets with a balanced number of mails are constructed by merging spam samples that are randomly selected from respective datasets such that the total number of spam classes becomes equal to that of the ham class. These new datasets consisted of 9696 samples and 4860 samples respectively. Thus, a total of 6 cases are used for evaluation as shown in Fig. 2. Total data is then divided into two parts in the ratio of 1:1 for training and testing purposes respectively.

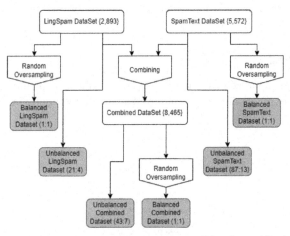

Fig. 2. Organisation of datasets Spam:Ham is shown in small brackets while the total size of the respective dataset is shown in curly brackets.

3.2 Preprocessing

After the collection of data, it is preprocessed using NLP methods to remove noise. Steps used for preprocessing are stop-word removal (SWR), text case normalization, lemmatization, tokenization, and punctuation removal. These steps are applied sequentially and, in the order, mentioned. For preprocessing spacy library is used.

Table 1 shows the change in mean word counts per email, concerning preprocessing steps. As punctuation removal and case normalization steps do not affect word counts, they are not included in Table 1. Also, note that the Spam class is more affected by the process of lemmatization than the Ham class. It can be observed that both datasets defer massively in mean word count and dataset length. These datasets also react differently to preprocessing methods, for example, while the Lingspam dataset is more affected by stopword removal, the Spamtext data set is more affected by the lemmatization step. Thus, they can be said to be statistically different.

Table 1. Mean number of words in emails after different preprocessing steps

Datasets	Class	Preprocessing steps			
		No preprocessing	Lemmatization	Stopword removal (SWR)	SWR & lemmatization
Lingspam	HAM	3165	3105	2507	2069
	SPAM	3808	3732	2649	1907
Spamtext	HAM	16	12	15	10
	SPAM	4	2	3	2

3.3 Feature Generation and Classification

After preprocessing text is fed to feature generation and classification block. As DL-based methodology is used feature generation step is integrated with the classifier.

Feature Generation. Feature generation here refers to the process of converting tokenized words to vectors of decimal numbers. The vectors are so assigned as to increase the correlation of vectors assigned to similar words and decrease the correlation with vectors assigned to the dissimilar word. This map between a word and its corresponding vector is stored in a matrix known as the embedding matrix present in the embedding layer. For feature generation, fastText word embedding is used.

FAIR provides many pretrained fastText models. We have used the fastText model, which has been pretrained on sub-words (with n-grams = 2), skip-gram & negative sampling techniques.

FastText is chosen as it performs better for OoV words and misspelled words by using character-level embedding on sub-words. Used fastText word embedding is pretrained on common crawl data [17]. The formula used for the loss function used for the generation of the feature is shown in Eq. (1).

$$L(t, c) = -\log[\sigma(c, t)] + \sum_{n \in N} \log[\sigma(-n, t)] \tag{1}$$

Note that in Eq. (1), 't' is the targeted word, 'c' is the context word, N is the group of negative words for 't', 'n' is a sample of 'N', and 'σ' stands for softmax function. The output of fastText is a vector of k elements, where k is the dimensionality of fastText. Each element of the vector represents a property of the word. Thus, each of these elements can be termed a feature of the word.

Classifier Model. After features have been generated from the textual information, the classifier model is then trained based on the generated features. This section describes the classifier model used in the proposed model.

Cells. This sub-section describes the cells and their need in the proposed classifier model. The description of cells used along with the reason for their usage is briefed below:

- CNN cells (CONV1D) are used to emphasize the effect of relationships between different features of a word in the classification process [18]. These features are the output of the embedding layer. This layer also helps in feature extraction using existing features. And multiple filters in CNN, combined with multi-head nature, enhance perspective toward text. Thus, improving the range of suitability.
- Bi-GRU cells are used to extract and use context information by using previous, future, and current feature vectors [19]. Bi-GRU can achieve similar performance as Bi-LSTM, for language processing of large sentences. Also, Bi-GRU gives better computational efficiency than Bi-LSTM [20].
- The Average Pooling cell computes the average of the values present in the window region of the filter. The average pooling cell is used to reduce translational invariance and reduce the ill effect of high dimensions (curse of dimensionality) on the classification process [21].
- Dense cells receive the input from the previous layers. It tries to find how output probability can be related to the output of the previous layers by learning a series of nonlinear combinations of the same [22].

Architecture of the Proposed Feature Generation and Classifier Model. This section describes the structure of the proposed model. Model architecture is inspired by the inception model which is used in image classification as described in [23]. The thought process behind the choice was that as deeper models tend to overfit, they will tend to show unstable performance in the case of multiple class weights and combined datasets. Also in the proposed model, each path tends to provide a new perspective of the same information [24]. The binary cross-entropy function is used as the loss function. The embedding layer uses an embedding matrix obtained using the fastText model whose dimensions are chosen to be 256. Cells are arranged as shown in Fig. 3.

The hyperbolic tangent function is used as the activation function for GRU cells while the sigmoid function is used as recurrent activation in GRU. For all other cells except the last two, the 'si' function, is used as the activation function. The last layer uses the sigmoid function as the activation function.

$$\tanh(z) = \frac{\left(e^z - e^{-z}\right)}{\left(e^z + e^{-z}\right)} \tag{2}$$

$$\text{sigmoid}(z) = \frac{1}{\left(1 + e^{-z}\right)} \tag{3}$$

$$\text{si} = \sin(z)^2 \tag{4}$$

where: z is the output of matrix multiplication of weights and input to layer

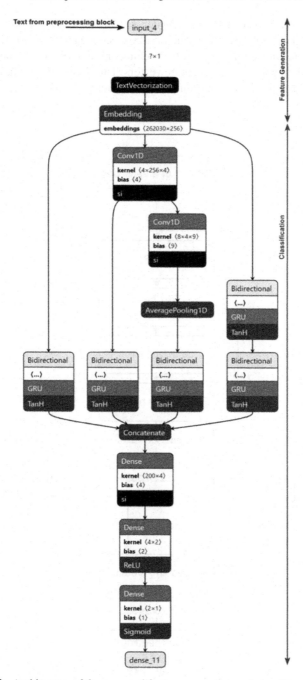

Fig. 3. Architecture of the proposed feature generation and classifier model.

The text vectorization layer divides the denoised text into a list of subsequences separated by space. Each sub-sequence contains a consecutive group of words and is known as an ngram. The embedding layer in the architecture described contains a dictionary of ngrams and their corresponding feature vectors. This dictionary is obtained using the fastText model. The flow of data and output type of each part of the algorithm is depicted in Fig. 4.

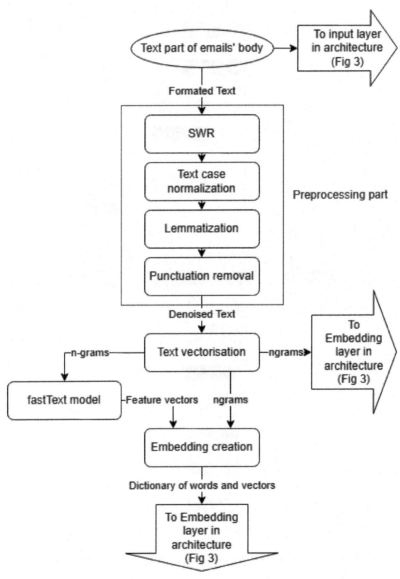

Fig. 4. Flow of data in architecture depicted in Fig. 3

4 Experimental Results

This section describes the performance metrics used and then discusses the result obtained by using the proposed model.

4.1 Performance Metrics

To assess the performance of the proposed model, we employ six popular assessment metrics: recall, accuracy, precision, f1_score, and Area Under Curve (AUC) of the Receiver Operator Characteristic (ROC) curve. These performance metrics can be calculated using the confusion matrix parameters as shown in Table 2.

Table 2. Confusion matrix showing representations used

	Predicted SPAM	Predicted HAM
Actual SPAM	True positive (TP)	False negative (FN)
Actual HAM	False positive (FP)	True negative (TN)

Precision. The precision metric shows how many of the predicted spams detected were actually spams. It can be calculated using Eq. (5).

$$\text{Precision} = \frac{TP}{TP + FP} \tag{5}$$

Recall. The recall is the likelihood of properly categorizing spam emails. Higher recall suggests that the filter does not tend to produce FN but may produce FP. It can be calculated using Eq. (6). It can be seen from equations that there exists a trade-off between precision and recall, one can alter a model to boost precision at the expense of lower recall or, conversely, to boost recall at the expense of lower precision.

$$\text{Recall} = \frac{TP}{TP + FN} \tag{6}$$

F1_Score. The f1_score metric is the harmonic mean of precision and recall, and it shows how much balanced is the tradeoff between precision and recall. It can be calculated using Eq. (7). Due to the tradeoff between precision and recall their harmonic mean will be high if both are nearly the same. Thus, a high f1_score indicates fewer chances of overfitting to any one class. This metric gives better interpretation than accuracy if data is unbalanced [25].

$$f1\_\text{score} = \frac{2}{2 + \frac{FP}{TP} + \frac{FN}{TP}} \tag{7}$$

ROC Curve. ROC curve is the plot between the true positive rate (TPR) against the false positive rate (FPR) for different thresholds. Formulas for TPR and FPR are mentioned in Eq. (8) and Eq. (9) respectively. A random classifier is expected to give points lying along the FPR = TPR line. In our case, high AUC implies that the model's output probabilities are near extrema (0 and 1). This means lower dependence of the classifier on the prediction probability's threshold for decision. The optimum threshold tends to change when slight noise or structural changes are introduced. Thus, a high AUC also means that the model can be used to reliably classify data that have slight structural changes compared to the training data [25, 26].

$$TPR = \text{Sensitivity} = \frac{TP}{TP + FN} \tag{8}$$

$$FPR = 1 - \text{Specificity} = \frac{FP}{TN + FP} \tag{9}$$

Accuracy. The accuracy metric shows the capability of the method to correctly classify legitimate emails and spam emails. It can be calculated using Eq. (10).

$$\text{Accuracy} = \frac{TP + TN}{TP + FP + TN + FP} \tag{10}$$

4.2 Results and Discussion

This section describes the performance of the proposed model over all 6 cases of datasets. The model was trained for 100 iterations. The confusion matrices for the evaluation of the proposed model for all 6 cases are shown in Fig. 5, Fig. 6, and Fig. 7 for Spamtext, Lingspam, and the combined dataset respectively.

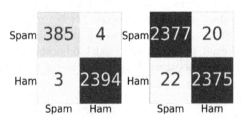

Fig. 5. Confusion matrix for Spamtext dataset left one shows the unbalanced version while the right one shows the balanced version. The labeling convention is the same as shown in Table 2

Performance metrics of the proposed model for all the datasets are presented in Table 3 and results for the balanced versions of the same are mentioned in Table 4.

Some inferences which can be drawn are:

- The proposed model performs well for both balanced and unbalanced datasets. Balancing of the datasets only slightly affects the performance of the proposed model. This observation implies that the proposed method can perform stably over a wide range of class weights.

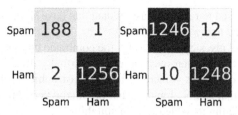

Fig. 6. Confusion matrix for Lingspam dataset left one shows the unbalanced version while the right one shows the balanced version. The labeling convention is the same as shown in Table 2

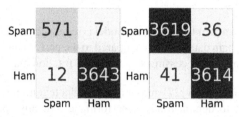

Fig. 7. Confusion matrix for combined dataset left one shows unbalanced version while the right one shows the balanced version. The labeling convention is the same as shown in Table 2

Table 3. Result of the proposed model for the unbalanced version of datasets

Datasets	Precision	Recall	f1_score	Accuracy	ROC-AUC
Spamtext	99.22%	98.97%	99.10%	99.75%	0.991
Lingspam	98.94%	99.47%	99.21%	99.79%	0.992
Combined	97.94%	98.79%	98.37%	99.56%	0.989

Table 4. Result of the proposed model for the balanced version of datasets

Datasets	Precision	Recall	f1_score	Accuracy	ROC-AUC
Spamtext	99.08%	99.17%	99.12%	99.12%	0.995
Lingspam	99.20%	99.05%	99.12%	99.13%	0.989
Combined	98.88%	99.01%	98.95%	98.95%	0.989

- It can be observed that the precision and recall metrics do not defer much indicating both true positives and true negatives contributing nearly equally toward accuracy despite the presence of class imbalance.
- F1_score for all cases is high indicating the model's low tendency to overfit to features of the majority class.
- The proposed model gives adequate ROC-AUC for all cases. This implies that model prediction is less ambiguous. Also as discussed in Sect. 4 it can be deduced that the

model can also be used to reliably classify data that have slight structural changes or is noisy as compared to the training data.

- The proposed model gives good scores for the combined dataset. It indicated that the model could detect spam even over larger and textually diverse datasets. This also implies that the model is less vulnerable to the catastrophic forgetting effect.
- Another inference that can be drawn is that the model performs adequately well for all cases, thus validating its wide range of suitability.

4.3 Comparison of Performance of the Proposed Model with Existing Techniques in Related Works

In this section performance of the proposed model is reviewed on the unbalanced version of Spamtext and Lingspam datasets and compared to the performance of relevant models on the same datasets but preprocessing steps and test fraction may vary.

For the Spamtext Dataset. In [27] authors proposed a text mining approach and used the spam text dataset to demonstrate its performance. In this approach, verbs were removed in preprocessing and tags tokens were maintained for spam and ham. It showed 91.41% accuracy. In [28] authors proposed another algorithm that is based on the word cloud. It gave an FPR of 86.3% and an accuracy of 97.64%. Tida et al. proposed an algorithm based on BERT and fixed-length sequence for the classification of Spamtext this algorithm gave an accuracy of 98%, f1_score of 93.96%, precision of 95%, and recall of 93%. In [29] authors proposed a method that uses linear regression between tagged words for the classification of text, this technique gave 0.9885 AUC and 98.85% accuracy. In [11] suggested algorithm's performance shown in terms of accuracy, precision, recall, and f1_score is 98%, 96%, 92%, and 94% respectively. In [30] authors have done a comparative analysis of 9 commonly used classifiers. The result of their work shows that the SVC classifier is the best among the 9 classifiers, it gives 99%, 98%, 91%, 99%, and 0.99; accuracy, precision, recall, f1_score, and AUC respectively. In [31] authors were able to demonstrate an AUC of 0.94. In [32] authors investigated the usage of the clustering method for spam email identification. Their model gave 91.96 as the best f1_score for the Spamtext dataset. In [10] authors obtained an AUC of 0.968. Our proposed model achieved 99.56% accuracy, 98.97% recall, 99.22% precision, 99.10% f1_score, and 0.991 AUC on the same dataset. The results are briefed in Table 5.

For the Lingspam Dataset. In [33] authors proposed an algorithm that used the Naïve Bayes algorithm along with Particle Swarm Optimization for spam email detection, algorithm gave accuracy, precision, recall, and f1_score value as 95.5%, 96.4%, 94.5%, and 95.4% respectively. The algorithm proposed by Tida et al. gave values of accuracy, f1_score, precision, and recall as 98%, 94%, 90%, and 98% respectively. Samira. Douzi et al. proposed a method for spam identification that used ensemble features obtained using PV-DM and TF-IDF techniques, their method gave accuracy, precision, and f1_score of 98.27%, 97.97%, and 98.97% respectively. In [34] authors have proposed email summarization and keywording-based feature generation method, for the choice of classifiers comparison was done among multiple state of art classifiers like logistic regression, SVM, etc. Their method was able to give 98.85%, 96.1%, 78.3%, and

Table 5. Results of the proposed model and techniques given in relevant previous works for the Spamtext dataset

References for work	Year	Accuracy %	Precision %	Recall %	f1_score %
[27]	2017	91.41	88.73	98.43	93.32
[28]	2021	97.64	99	92	95.37
[14]	2022	98.00	95	93	93.96
[36]	2021	98	–	–	–
[11]	2021	98.00	96	92	94
[31]	2022	98.07	–	–	–
[29]	2019	98.85	–	–	–
[32]	2020	–	–	–	91.96
[30]	2022	99	98	91	99
[10]	2020	99.44	–	–	–
Proposed model	2022	99.75	99.22	98.97	99.10

86.2% accuracy, precision, recall, and f1_score values. In [35] authors have compared the combination of different classifiers and hyperparameter optimization algorithms. SGD classifier optimized by the genetic algorithm was found to be the best, it gave 98.77, 100.00, 94.21, 97.02 as accuracy, precision, recall, and f1_score values respectively. In [36] authors have proposed a simple RNN-based algorithm for SPAM identification. In this work proposed algorithm was compared with other commonly used algorithms and found to give a better result, it gave an accuracy of 99%. In [37] authors have used the pretrained BERT model for SPAM identification. Their model gave 99.13, 96.41, 98.79, and 97.58 as accuracy, precision, recall, and f1_score values. Natrajan et al. proposed a self-adaptive hybrid algorithm of big bang-big crunch with the ant colony optimization for email spam detection, algorithm demonstrated 99.1% accuracy and recall of 94.79%. Our proposed model achieved 99.79% accuracy, 99.47% recall, 98.94% precision, 99.21% f1_score, and 0.992 AUC on the same dataset. The results are as in Table 6.

Discussion. The comparison with related works for both datasets brings out some notable inferences, which are stated below:

- There was a large difference between precision and recall values for studied literature works, indicating high chances of their model overfitting to the majority class. This further indicated that the models may not reproduce similar performance in case the dataset becomes balanced. The proposed model seems to give the most analogous results for precision and recall among the literature works reviewed.
- The proposed model gave good accuracy and f1_score compared to reviewed works. Also, it gave a good AUC score pointing to stability in performance.

Table 6. Results of the proposed model and techniques given in relevant previous works for the Lingspam dataset

References for work	Year	Accuracy %	Precision %	Recall %	f1_score %
[3]	2016	92.56	92.50	92.40	92.00
[33]	2018	95.50	96.42	94.5	95.45
[8]	2018	97.56	–	–	–
[6]	2018	98.2	–	–	98.2
[14]	2020	98.27	90	98	86.29
[12]	2020	98.27	97.97	100.00	98.97
[35]	2020	98.77	100.00	94.21	97.02
[13]	2021	98.85	96.1	78.3	86.2
[3]	2021	99	–	–	–
[37]	2022	99.13	96.41	98.79	97.58
[32]	2020	–	–	–	93.24
[9]	2020	99.48	–	–	–
Proposed model	2022	99.78	98.94	99.47	99.21

5 Conclusion and Future Scope

As spam detection techniques are getting evolved, spammers are also developing new ways to circumvent spam detection systems, such as obfuscating message contents. A spam detection system should be able to perform well for a wide range of class weights. It should also be able to handle datasets with different characteristics efficiently. This research attempts to address these issues by building a multi-headed model that can work efficiently over a large range of class weights as well as can handle emails with different textual characteristics.

The proposed model is expected to perform well even for emails with misspelled words. Incorrect grammar, and smartly structured sentences. We have used character-level embedding rather than word-level embedding to meet this expectation. This claim has been validated by comparing the obtained results with existing methods in the previous literature works.

To validate our claim of a wide range of suitability, the model was tested on two statistically different datasets and with different class weights. Both the datasets used have large statistical differences. The proposed algorithm performed well for both; thus, it can handle data with different textual characteristics.

Also, most previous research models have demonstrated their performance on individual datasets. If these models were to replicate on different datasets, their performance may vary due to the catastrophic forgetting effect. In this manuscript, this issue is addressed by evaluating the proposed model over the combined dataset as well.

The performance of the proposed model is shown in Sect. 4. The model gives 99.75% accuracy and 0.991 AUC for the Spamtext dataset. And for the Lingspam dataset, gives 99.79% accuracy and 0.992 AUC.

For upcoming endeavors, a more exhaustive study can be done on preprocessing methods and their correlation study. Hyperparameter and threshold tuning for the email spam detection algorithm can be further studied. The scope of metrics used for performance evaluation can be further increased to include parameters like memory consumption, training time, prediction time, etc. Different methods can be studied which can speed up training and prediction time. Our study considers the body's text content for detecting spam. The study may be extended to include attachments, links, images, and header information embedded in the email. The proposed model can be refined in the future using active and reinforced learning for unlabeled data.

References

1. Email usage statistics 2022: How many people use email? https://wpdevshed.com/email-usage-statistics/. Accessed 01 May 2022
2. Catastrophic interference. https://en.wikipedia.org/wiki/Catastrophic_interference. Accessed 10 Aug 2022
3. Kaya, Y., Ertuğrul, F.: A novel approach for spam email detection based on shifted binary patterns. Secur. Commun. Netw. **9**(10), 1216–1225 (2016)
4. Wijaya, A., Bisri, A.: Hybrid decision tree and logistic regression classifier for email spam detection. In: 8th International Conference on Information Technology and Electrical Engineering (ICITEE) (2016)
5. Gashti, M.Z.: Detection of spam email by combining harmony search algorithm and decision tree. Eng. Technol. Appl. Sci. Res. **7**, 1713–1718 (2017)
6. Trivedi, S.K., Panigrahi, P.K.: Spam classification: a comparative analysis of different boosted decision tree approaches. J. Syst. Inf. Technol. **20**, 298–105 (2018)
7. Hassan, M.A., Mtetwa, N.: Feature extraction and classification of spam emails. In: 5th International Conference on Soft Computing & Machine Intelligence (ISCMI) (2018)
8. Jawale, D.S., Mahajan, A.G., Shinkar, K.R., and Katdare, V.V.: Hybrid spam detection using machine learning. Int. J. Adv. Res. Ideas Innov. Technol. **4**(2), 2828–2832 (2018)
9. Gibson, S., Issac, B., Zhang, L., Jacob, S.M.: Detecting spam email with machine learning optimized with bio-inspired metaheuristic algorithms. IEEE Access **8**, 187914–187932 (2020)
10. Roy, P.K., Singh, J.P., Banerjee, S.: Deep learning to filter SMS SPAM. Future Gener. Comput. Syst. **102**, 524–533 (2020)
11. Zagabathuni, Y.: Spam text classification using LSTM recurrent neural network. Int. J. Emerg. Trends Eng. Res. **9**, 1271–1275 (2021)
12. Douzi, S., AlShahwan, F.A., Lemoudden, M., Ouahidi, B.E.: Hybrid email spam detection model using artificial intelligence. Int. J. Mach. Learn. Comput. **10**, 316–322 (2020)
13. Natarajan, R., Mehbodniya, A., Ganapathy, M., et al: Hybrid big bang–big crunch with ant colony optimization for email spam detection. Int. J. Mod. Phys. C (2021)
14. Tida, V.S., Hsu, S.H.: Universal spam detection using transfer learning of BERT model. In: Proceedings of the Annual Hawaii International Conference on System Sciences (2022)
15. Spam detection using tensorflow. https://www.kaggle.com/code/akanksha496/spam-detection-using-tensorflow. Accessed 18 May 2022
16. Sakkis, G., Androutsopoulos, I., Paliouras, G., et al.: A memory-based approach to anti-spam filtering for mailing lists. Inf. Retr. **6**(1), 49–73 (2003)

17. FastText. https://fasttext.cc/. Accessed 02 May 2022
18. O'Shea, K., Nash, R.: An introduction to convolutional neural networks. arXiv preprint arXiv: 1511.08458 (2015)
19. A guide to bidirectional RNNS with keras. https://blog.paperspace.com/bidirectional-rnn-keras/. Accessed 04 May 2022
20. Nosouhian, S., Nosouhian, F., Kazemi, K.A.: A review of recurrent neural network architecture for Sequence learning: comparison between LSTM and GRU (2021). https://doi.org/10.20944/preprints202107.0252.v1
21. A gentle introduction to pooling layers for Convolutional Neural Networks. https://machinelearningmastery.com/pooling-layers-for-convolutional-neural-networks/. Accessed 04 May 2022
22. Huang, G., Liu, Z., Van Der Maaten, L., Weinberger, K.Q.: Densely connected convolutional networks. In: Proceedings of the IEEE Conference on Computer Vision and Pattern Recognition, pp. 4700–4708 (2017)
23. Szegedy, C., Vanhoucke, V., Ioffe, S., Shlens, J., Wojna, Z.: Rethinking the inception architecture for computer vision. In: 2016 IEEE Conference on Computer Vision and Pattern Recognition (CVPR) (2016)
24. Qin, R., Liu, Q., Gao, G., et al.: MRDet: a multihead network for accurate rotated object detection in aerial images. IEEE Trans. Geosci. Remote Sens. **60**, 1–12 (2022)
25. Ferri, C., Hernández-Orallo, J., Modroiu, R.: An experimental comparison of performance measures for classification. Pattern Recognit. Lett. **30**(01), 27–38 (2009)
26. PR vs ROC Curves. https://cosmiccoding.com.au/tutorials/pr_vs_roc_curves. Accessed 12 May 2022
27. Ratniasih, N.L., Sudarma, M., Gunantara, N.: Penerapan text mining dalam spam filtering untuk aplikasi chat. Majalah Ilmiah Teknologi Elektro **16**(03), 13–18 (2017)
28. Kulkarni, A., Shivananda, A.: Deep learning for NLP. In: Natural Language Processing Recipes, pp. 213–262. Apress, Berkeley (2021)
29. Chatterjee, R., Acharya, V., Prakasha, K., Arjunan, R.V.: Text based machine learning using discriminative classifiers. J. Adv. Res. Dyn. Control Syst. **11**(07), 32–41 (2019)
30. Aliza, H.Y., Nagary, K.A., Ahmed, E., et al.: A comparative analysis of SMS SPAM detection employing machine learning methods. In: 6th International Conference on Computing Methodologies and Communication, pp. 916–922 (2022)
31. Oswald, C., Simon, S.E., Bhattacharya, A.: SpotSpam: intention analysis driven SMS spam detection using BERT embeddings. ACM Trans. Web **16**(14), 1–27 (2022)
32. Sahin, D.O., Demirci, S.: Spam filtering with KNN: investigation of the effect of K value on classification performance. In: 28th Signal Processing and Communications Applications Conference, pp. 1–4 (2020)
33. Agarwal, K., Kumar, T.: Email spam detection using integrated approach of naïve Bayes and particle swarm optimization. In: Second International Conference on Intelligent Computing and Control Systems, pp. 685–690 (2018)
34. Islam, A.M., Mahbub, S., Kaushal, C.: Spam-detection with comparative analysis and spamming words extractions. In: 9th International Conference on Reliability, Infocom Technologies and Optimization (Trends and Future Directions), pp. 1–9 (2021)
35. Alanazi, H.K., Alruwaili, R.H.: Exploring the role of machine learning in email filtering. In: International Conference on Business Analytics for Technology and Security, pp. 1–7 (2022)
36. Nisar, N., Chhabra, M., Rakesh, N.: Spam filtering using deep neural network. In: SPAST Abs, vol. 1, no. 01 (2021)
37. Sahmoud, T., Mohammad, M.: Spam detection using BERT, 7 June. arXiv.org, http://arxiv.org/abs/2206.02443 (2022)

Validation of Nonlinear PID Controllers on a Lab-Scale Batch Reactor

Prajwal Shettigar J[1], Ankitha Pai[2], Yuvanshu Joshi[1,2],
Thirunavukkarasu Indiran[1,2(✉)], and Shreesha Chokkadi[1,2]

[1] Department of Mechatronics Engineering, Manipal Institute of Technology MAHE,
Manipal, India
[2] Department of Instrumentation and Control Engineering,
Manipal Institute of Technology, MAHE, Manipal, India
it.arasu@learner.manipal.edu

Abstract. With wide acceptance of batch processes for polymer production, this study aims to model the temperature dynamics of a batch polymerization reactor using Hammerstein and neural network approaches. And to design nonlinear PID controllers in combination to the models to control the temperature of exothermic reactions happening inside the reactor. A temperature trajectory is used as reference signal which is designed based on reactor safety constraints for the reaction of choice Acrylamide Polymerization. The Hammerstein Model based nonlinear PID (HNPID) makes use of polynomial structures to approximated the inverse of the model, so that a higher order model can be used that provides better accuracy. On the other hand, the neural network based PID (NNPID) uses an optimization approach to tune the PID gains. With Batch Reactor as system of interest, both the controllers are validated in simulation to account for energy consumption by each of them. It is noted HNPID consumes less power than NNPID with better tracking hence a perfect candidate for polymer production in realtime.

Keywords: Hammerstein model · Neural networks · HNPID ·
NNPID · Batch reactor · Acrylamide polymerization

1 Introduction

Polymer production is the prominent application of batch reactors, by nature these reactions are exothermic which makes the process nonlinear. The closed system characteristics along with uneven heat addition forms an unsteady condition, which makes modelling and control of the polymerization batch reactors difficult and challenging. The extensive developments in the field of artificial intelligence have presented various data driven methods of modelling a system, hence capture internal dynamics that may go unnoticed in traditional mathematical modelling.

Among them neural networks have proven to be the most effective and have been used to model batch process [1,2]. "The neural network with sufficient number of nodes in hidden layer can approximate any continuous accurately", [5].

© The Author(s), under exclusive license to Springer Nature Switzerland AG 2023
I. Woungang et al. (Eds.): ANTIC 2022, CCIS 1797, pp. 47–59, 2023.
https://doi.org/10.1007/978-3-031-28180-8_4

The neural networks gives the freedom of selection of its structure to the user, also with a simple three layered model complex dynamics can be easily captured. [6] demonstrated the efficacy of neural network trained using back propagation in modelling and control of chemical process of pH balance in CSTR. The extended capability of neural networks to model multi-variable system was shown by [7]. Neural network with Internal model control for conical tank process can be found in the works of [8]. Other examples to the popular modelling structures include the Hammerstein and Wiener models [3,4], which captures the linear and non-linear parts of the system separately, thus providing the user an option to invert the model. Various algorithms have been presented in literature for identification of Hammerstein model, [9] proposed a neural network approach of identifying Hammerstein model, where the nonlinear static part and linear dynamic part are trained/identified separately. [10] the multivariable identification of Hammerstein model using Narendra-Gallman algorithm. An analytical approach to identifying the Hammerstein model using special test signal is proposed by [11]. [12] have compared the effectiveness of parameter identification algorithms iterative least square and recursive least square in offline and online scenarios and were found to be effective for Hammerstein identification.

Batch reactor control is an important aspect of the control domain as it helps regulate process outcomes, thereby eliminating redundant reactions from taking place. Since the chemical process being non-linear it requires a nonlinear controller to achieve desired outcomes. PID control being popular in industries worldwide, cannot be directly used in batch control, in this regard several research have been conducted to add nonlinear capabilities to PID. Nonlinear PID with linearized neural networks can be found in [18]. An online identification and internal model control based PID tuning is given in the study by [16]. Nonlinear PID with two tracking differentiators for noise cancellation and sector bound gain cascade with conventional PID controller [17]. PI and PID in combination with Fuzzy Logic is presented by [14] and [13]. A neural network based nonlinear PID the uses Levenberg-Marquardt algorithm to update the gains at every time instant is proposed by [15].

Addressing the issue that literature lacks more experimental studies related to batch reactor with chemical feed, to decide on controllers with satisfactory tracking in real time scenario, this study presents an extension of Hammerstein based nonlinear PID with polynomial structures [3] to bath control which presents a inverse model strategy with PID and comparing it with neural network PID [1] which utilizes adaptive PID approach. Thus deciding the best controller through simulation and validating it on a lab-scale batch reactor undergoing exothermic polymerization reaction. The paper is further explains the batch reactor system and reaction in Sect. 2, the modelling and control methodology in Sect. 3, the simulation and real-time results are presented in Sect. 4 and conclusion remarks in final section.

2 Reaction and System Description

The study utilized a lab-scale batch reactor facility of 1 liter capacity shown in Fig. 1. The system consist of main vessel where the reaction takes place, ceramic band heater that supplies the energy through radiation required to activate the chemicals. To regulate the temperature coolant is supplied through the flow control station consisting of rota-meter with electro-pneumatic valve that controls the flow rate of coolant to the reactor through cooling coil. The temperature developed inside the reactor is measured using a resistance temperature detector (RTD). The system and computer is interfaced through wireless data acquisition card (DAC), that provides real-time sensor readings to the algorithm and supplies the control signal from algorithm to the flow control valve. The various components of the reactor system is given in the schematic Fig. 2. The physical dimensions and technical specifications of the batch reactor used in this paper can be found in [19].

Fig. 1. Lab-scale pilot plant batch reactor

The study makes use of Acrylamide polymerization reaction, where the acrylamide monomer with ammonium per-sulphate initiator undergoes reaction to form poly acrylamide, the quantity of chemicals used, reaction kinetics with first principles model and the details about reference trajectory is given in [20].

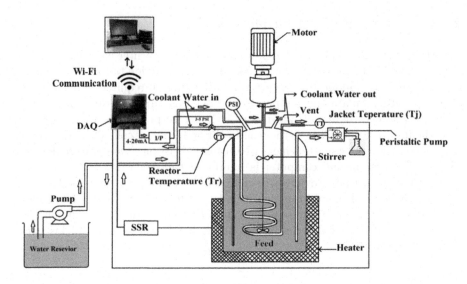

Fig. 2. Schematic representation of pilot plant batch reactor

Throughout this study batch reactor is treated as SISO system with coolant flow rate as input and reactor temperature as output.

3 Methodology

The details of error based control strategy in combination with model strategy implemented for batch reactor is presented in this section. Firstly, the Hammerstein and neural network model identification procedure is conveyed, later subsections deals with the development of nonlinear PID strategies.

3.1 Hammerstein and Neural Network Model Identification

The input-output data is obtained from batch reactor i.e. the percentage current supplied to the coolant valve and the corresponding reactor temperature of 160 samples is collected for PRBS input. The data collected is given in Fig. 3.

Hammerstein Model
The Hammerstein model is described as association of a nonlinear block with a linear block as show in Fig. 4, and is represented using following equations,

$$y_k = \frac{B(q^{-1})}{A(q^{-1})} v_k \tag{1}$$

$$v_k = f(u_k) \tag{2}$$

where,

$$A(q^{-1}) = 1 + a_1 q^{-1} + \ldots + a_{n_A} q^{-n_A}$$
$$B(q^{-1}) = b_1 q^{-1} + \ldots + b_{n_B} q^{-n_B}$$
$$v_k = d_1 u_k + d_2 u_k^2 + \ldots + d_N u_k^N$$

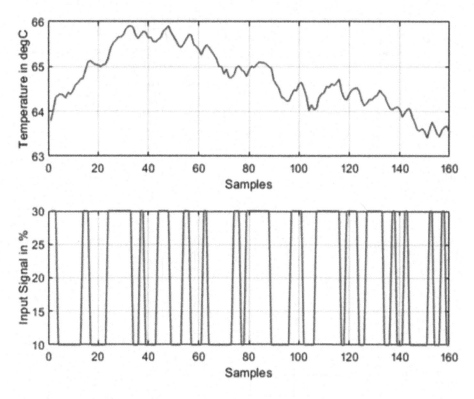

Fig. 3. Input output data collected from batch reactor

With u_k as input to the model, output of nonlinear block $f(.)$ is v_k which serves as input to linear block $\frac{B(q^{-1})}{A(q^{-1})}$ and y_k is the output from Hammerstein model. The powers n_A, n_B represents the lag terms and N the order of input, a_i, b_i and d_i are parameters to be identified. Considering $d_1 = 1$, Eq. (1) can be expanded as,

$$y_k = -\sum_{i=1}^{n_A} a_i y_{k-i} + \sum_{i=1}^{n_B} b_i \left(u_{k-i} + \sum_{p=2}^{N} d_p u_{k-i}^p \right) \qquad (3)$$

which can be written in linear in parameters form as,

$$y_k = \varPhi_k^T \theta_k \qquad (4)$$

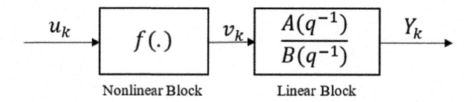

Fig. 4. Hammerstein model

with,

$$\Phi_k = \begin{bmatrix} Y_k \\ U_k \end{bmatrix}, \; \theta_k = \begin{bmatrix} a_k \\ b_k \\ c_k \end{bmatrix},$$

$$Y_k = \begin{bmatrix} -y_{k-1} \\ -y_{k-2} \\ \vdots \\ -y_{k-n_A} \end{bmatrix}, \; U_k = \begin{bmatrix} U_{1k} \\ U_{2k} \\ \vdots \\ U_{Nk} \end{bmatrix},$$

$$U_{jk} = \begin{bmatrix} u^j_{k-1} \\ u^j_{k-2} \\ \vdots \\ u^j_{k-n_B} \end{bmatrix}, \; \forall j = 1, 2, \dots, N$$

$$a_k = \begin{bmatrix} a_{1k} \\ a_{2k} \\ \vdots \\ a_{n_A k} \end{bmatrix}, \; b_k = \begin{bmatrix} b_{1k} \\ b_{2k} \\ \vdots \\ b_{n_B k} \end{bmatrix}, \; c_k = \begin{bmatrix} d_{2k} b_k \\ d_{3k} b_k \\ \vdots \\ d_{Nk} b_k \end{bmatrix}$$

Neural Networks Model

The Auto-regression with Exogenous inputs neural network (ARXNN) is comparable to Hammerstein model in the sense that it takes in previous outputs and inputs of the system to calculate the current output. The neural network model represents the system as a single nonlinear entity divided into input, hidden and output layers. The input vector to ARXNN at time t is given by,

$$\phi(t) = \begin{bmatrix} y(t-1), \dots, y(t-n_y), \\ u(t), u(t-1), \dots, u(t-n_u) \end{bmatrix}^T \tag{5}$$

The intermediate calculations in a single neuron of hidden layer involve the product of inputs to their corresponding weights plus the neuron bias this is given by Eq. (6). The intermediate output $m_c(t)$ is passed through the hidden layer activation function f_H to get hidden layer output.

$$m_c(t) = \sum_{i=1,j=i}^{n_y} w_{c,j}^h y(t-i)$$ (6)

$$+ \sum_{i=0,k=i+n_y+1}^{n_u} w_{c,k}^h u(t-i) + w_{b,c}^h$$

The activated outputs from hidden layer is multiplied with their corresponding weights in output layer, the sum of these outputs and bias gives the neural network output represented in Eq. (7).

$$\hat{y}_{NN}(t) = \sum_{c=1}^{n_H} w_c^o f_H[m_c(t)] + w_b^o$$ (7)

This network makes use of hyperbolic tangent and linear activation functions at hidden and output layers respectively. The weights and biases are estimated using gradient descent algorithm.

The identification and validation fit for both the models to actual data is given in Fig. 5, the hyper-parameters of the model are reported in Table 1. The modelling accuracy's are reported in Table 2.

Table 1. Model hyper-parameters

Hammerstein model	Neural network model
$n_A = 3$	$n_y = 3$
$n_B = 2$	$n_u = 2$
$N = 4$	$n_H = 10$

Table 2. Modelling accuracy (Mean Squared Error)

Model	Identification	Validation
Hammerstein	0.008225	0.014907
Neural network	0.005600	0.010712

3.2 Hammerstein Based Nonlinear PID Using Polynomial Structures

To approximate the inverse of higher order model the output of nonlinear block is represented in terms of polynomial structure as follows,

$$v_k = \tilde{w}_{1,k}^1 U_k + \tilde{w}_{2,k}^1 \tilde{U}_k^{[2]} + \tilde{w}_{3,k}^1 \tilde{U}_k^{[3]} + O\left(U_k^{[4]}\right)$$ (8)

where $U_k = [u_k \ u_{k-1}]^T$, $\tilde{w}_{1,k}^1 = [1 \ 1]$, $\tilde{w}_{2,k}^1 = [\alpha_{1,k} \ \alpha_{2,k} \ \alpha_{3,k}]$, and $\tilde{w}_{3,k}^1 = [\alpha_{4,k} \ \alpha_{5,k} \ \alpha_{6,k} \ \alpha_{7,k}]$. The $U_k^{[i]}$ represents the Kronecker power of U_k.

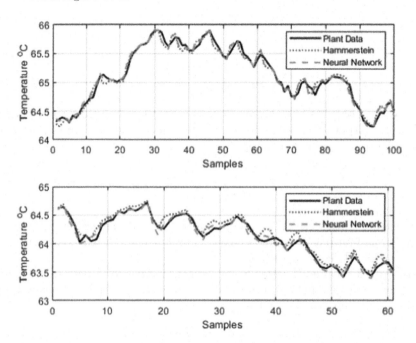

Fig. 5. Hammerstein and neural network model identification (Top) and validation (Bottom)

Considering following structure for linear part of Hammerstein model,

$$y_k = -a_{1,k}y_{k-1} - a_{2,k}y_{k-2} + b_{1,k}v_{k-1} + b_{2,k}v_{k-2} \tag{9}$$

Combining Eqs. (8) and (9) the entire model in terms of nonlinear polynomial structures can be written as,

$$y_k = -a_{1,k}y_{k-1} - a_{2,k}y_{k-2} + \tilde{w}_{1,k}^2 U_k + \tag{10}$$
$$\tilde{w}_{2,k}^2 \tilde{U}_k^{[2]} + \tilde{w}_{3,k}^2 \tilde{U}_k^{[3]} + O\left(U_k^{[4]}\right)$$

where,

$$\tilde{w}_{1,k}^2 = [b_{1,k}, \ b_{1,k} + b_{2,k}]^T,$$
$$\tilde{w}_{2,k}^2 = [b_{1,k}\alpha_{1,k}, \ b_{1,k}\alpha_{2,k}, \ b_{1,k}\alpha_{3,k} + b_{2,k}\alpha_{1,k}]^T,$$
$$\tilde{w}_{3,k}^2 = [b_{1,k}\alpha_{4,k}, \ b_{1,k}\alpha_{5,k}, \ b_{1,k}\alpha_{6,k}, \ b_{1,k}\alpha_{7,k} + b_{2,k}\alpha_{4,k}]^T$$

The parameters of above model is identified using RLS algorithm.

The Hammerstein based nonlinear PID is the combination of general PID and inverse function of nonlinear polynomial structure, that can be viewed as a linear block (general PID) followed by nonlinear block (inverse polynomial structure).

$$PID_{non-linear} = PID f_{approx}^{-1}(.) \tag{11}$$

Here the general PID provides the intermediate output of Hammerstein represented as $\tilde{v}_k$, which serves as input to the approximate inverse function to calculate the current input signal u_k,

$$u_k = f_{approx}^{-1}(\tilde{v}_k) \tag{12}$$
$$= \tilde{w}_{1,k}^3 \tilde{V}_k + \tilde{w}_{2,k}^3 \tilde{V}_k^{[2]} + \tilde{w}_{3,k}^3 \tilde{V}_k^{[3]} + O\left(\tilde{V}_k^{[4]}\right)$$

where,

$$\tilde{V}_k = [\tilde{v}_k,\ \tilde{v}_{k-1}]^T, \tilde{w}_{1,k}^3 = [\beta_{1,k}, \beta_{2,5}],$$
$$\tilde{w}_{2,k}^3 = [\beta_{3,k}, \beta_{4,k}, \beta_{5,k}], \tilde{w}_{3,k}^3 = [\beta_{6,k}, \beta_{7,k}, \beta_{8,k}, \beta_{9,k}]$$

From the identified coefficients of Eq. (8), the coefficients of (12) are given as,

$$\beta_{1,k} = 1, \beta_{2,k} = -1, \beta_{3,k} = -\alpha_{1,k},$$
$$\beta_{4,k} = 2\alpha_{1,k} - \alpha_{2,k}, \beta_{5,k} = \alpha_{2,k} - \alpha_{3,k},$$
$$\beta_{6,k} = 2\alpha_{1,k}^2 - \alpha_{4,k}$$
$$\beta_{7,k} = 3\alpha_{1,k}\alpha_{3,k} - 6\alpha_{1,k}^2 + 3\alpha_{4,k} - \alpha_{5,k},$$
$$\beta_{8,k} = -3\alpha_{1,k}\alpha_{2,k} + 5\alpha_{1,k}^2 - 3\alpha_{4,k} - 2\alpha_{5,k}$$
$$-\alpha_{6,k},$$
$$\beta_{9,k} = \alpha_{4,k} + 3\alpha_{1,k}^2 + \alpha_{1,k}\alpha_{2,k} + \alpha_{2,k}\alpha_{3,k}$$
$$+3\alpha_{5,k} + \alpha_{6,k}$$

3.3 Neural Network Based Nonlinear PID

The NNPID works by adaptively tuning the PID parameters such that it minimizes the predicted tracking error, the general form of PID represented in Eq. (13) becomes computationally expensive due to integration, therefore the control update is written in terms of velocity form of PID,

$$u(t) = k_c \left[e(t) + \frac{1}{\tau_i} \int e(t)dt + \tau_d \frac{de(t)}{dt} \right] \tag{13}$$

With error as difference between desired and actual output, $e(t) = y_{des}(t) - y(t)$. The PID parameters k_c, τ_i and τ_d are proportional gain, integral and derivative time constants respectively. The velocity form of PID by trapezoidal approximation with Δt as sample time is given by,

$$\Delta u(t) = u(t) - u(t-1) \tag{14}$$
$$= k_c \left\{ [e(t) - e(t-1)] + \frac{\Delta t}{2\tau_i} [e(t) + e(t-1)] \right.$$
$$\left. + \frac{\tau_d}{\Delta t} [e(t) - 2e(t-1) + e(t-2)] \right\}$$

By rearranging and simplifying Eq. (14),

$$\Delta u(t) = k_0 e(t) + k_1 e(t-1) + k_2 e(t-2) \tag{15}$$
$$= E(t)K(t)$$

With $K(t) = [k_0, k_1, k_2]^T$ and $E(t) = [e(t), e(t-1), e(t-2)]$, where $k_0 = k_c \left(1 + \frac{\Delta t}{2\tau_i} + \frac{\tau_d}{\Delta t}\right), k_1 = -k_c \left(1 - \frac{\Delta t}{2\tau_i} + \frac{2\tau_d}{\Delta t}\right), k_2 = \frac{k_c \tau_d}{\Delta t}$.

The controller aims at determining the optimal $K(t)$ such that it minimizes the following objective function,

$$J = \frac{1}{2}\left[\hat{e}^2(t+1) + \mu \Delta u^2(t)\right] \tag{16}$$

where,

$$\hat{e}(t+1) = y_{ref}(t+1) - \hat{y}_{NN}(t+1) \tag{17}$$

The neural network part of the Eq. (17) in optimization will add excessive computational load in control loop, to speed up this process without much loss in accuracy linearized neural network is used which is given by,

$$\hat{y}_{NNl} = bias - \sum_{i=2}^{n_y} a_i y(t-i) - \sum_{i=1}^{n_u} b_i u(t-i) \tag{18}$$

The network coefficients a_i and b_i are obtained as first partial derivatives of neural network with respect to output and input respectively evaluated at $\phi(t) = \phi(\tau)$ as shown below,

$$a_i = \frac{\partial \hat{y}_{NN}(t)}{\partial y(t-i)} = \sum_{c=1}^{n_H} w_c^o \frac{\partial f_H(t)}{\partial m_c(t)} w_{c,i}^h, \forall i = 1, 2, \ldots, n_y \tag{19}$$

$$b_i = \frac{\partial \hat{y}_{NN}(t)}{\partial u(t-i)} = \sum_{c=1}^{n_H} w_c^o \frac{\partial f_H(t)}{\partial m_c(t)} w_{c,(i+n_y)}^h, \forall i = 1, 2, \ldots, n_u \tag{20}$$

The linear neural network output is used in place of $\hat{y}_{NN}$ term of Eq. (17), for faster optimization. To achieve further computational efficiency the PID parameters are updated through optimization only when the moving average of previous n errors is less than a specified threshold ε.

4   Results and Discussion

The effectiveness of the above algorithms for controlling a nonlinear batch reactor performing acrylamide polymerization is described in this section, prior to real time studies the simulation is performed to estimate the amount of energy consumed (control cost) for each of the controller thus select best candidate for experimental validation. The process batch time is taken to be 30 min, aiming to track a given nonlinear reference trajectory. The manipulated variable refers to the percentage opening of the coolant flow control valve.

Both algorithms are initialized at same PID gains i.e. $K_p = 0.9, K_i = 0.01$ and $K_d = 0.003$. The simulation result showing tracking is given in Fig. 6, it can be noted that HNPID provides good tracking throughout the batch time, while NNPID takes some time to stabilize the output thus has high oscillations in the

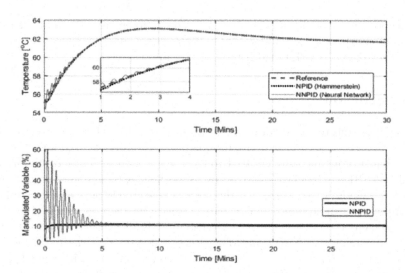

Fig. 6. Closed loop control of batch reactor comparison of Hammerstein and Neural Network based nonlinear PID (Simulation)

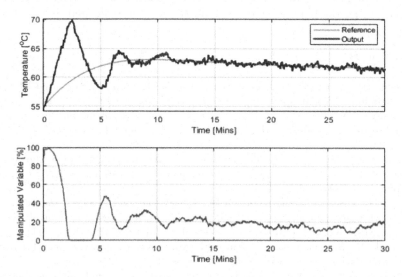

Fig. 7. Closed loop control of batch reactor with Hammerstein based nonlinear PID (Real-time)

manipulated variable leading to greater energy consumption, hence inefficient in a real experimental scenario. Form this observation the real time application of HNPID is performed on a lab scale batch reactor with acrylamide polymerization, the so obtained tracking result is give in Fig. 7.

Although there is initial overshoot in reactor temperature, the controller was successful in bringing the temperature to desired value in short span, thus proves the efficacy of the HNPID algorithm.

5   Conclusion

In this paper, authors have addressed the modeling of the lab scale batch reactor using data driven method, here the Hammerstein modeling is used for obtaining the nonlinear modeling. Further to it to track the nonlinear temperature profile, a nonlinear PID controller is designed by using the inverse of higher order model through polynomial structures. In this paper, neural networks based nonlinear PID approach using dynamic NPID gains at every instead of error is simulated and implemented on a pilot plant batch reactor. It is also observed that this approach of modeling and NPID controller design helps to track desired trajectory with minimum error as well as with minimum control efforts. The control signal plot is also presented in the paper. There is initial oscillations in the process variable, but it gradually decreased and settled finally to track trajectory. The experimental study carried out reveal that HNPID is able to overcome the heat released during the reaction and maintain the reactor at desired temperature.

References

1. Chen, J., Huang, T.-C.: Applying neural networks to on-line updated PID controllers for nonlinear process control. J. Process Control **14**(2), 211–230 (2004)
2. Billings, S.A., Jamaluddin, H.B., Chen, S.: Properties of neural networks with applications to modelling non-linear dynamical systems. Int. J. Control **55**, 193–224 (1992)
3. Rayouf, Z., Ghorbel, C., Benhadj Braiek, N.: Identification and nonlinear PID control of Hammerstein model using polynomial structures. (IJACSA) Int. J. Adv. Comput. Sci. Appl. **8**(4) (2017)
4. Peng, J., Dubay, R., Hernandez, J.M., Abu-Ayyad, M., et al.: A Wiener neural network-based identification and adaptive generalized predictive control for nonlinear SISO systems. Industr. Eng. Chem. Res. **50**(12), 7388–7397 (2011)
5. Hornik, K., Stinchcombe, M., White, H.: Multilayer feedforward neural networks are universal approximators. Neural Networks **2**, 359 (1989)
6. Bhat, N., McAvoy, T.J.: Use of neural nets for dynamic modeling and control of chemical process systems. Comput. Chem. Eng. **14**, 573 (1990)
7. Narendra, K.S., Parthasarathy, K.: Identification and control of dynamic systems using neural networks. IEEE Transient Neural Networks **1**, 4–27 (1990)
8. Srivignesh, N., Sowmya, P., Ramkumar, K., Balasubramanian, G.: Design of neural based PID controller for nonlinear process. Procedia Eng. **38**, 3283–3291 (2012)
9. Su, H.T., Mcavoy, T.J., Luyben, W.L.: Integration of multilayer perceptron networks and linear dynamic models: a Hammerstein modeling approach. Ind. Eng. Chem. Res. **26**, 1927–1936 (1993)
10. Lakshminarayanan, S., Shah, S.L., Nandakumar, K.: Identification of Hammerstein models using multivariate statistical tools. Chem. Eng. Sci. **50**, 3599–3613 (1995)

11. Sung, S.W.: System identification method for Hammerstein processes. Ind. Eng. Chem. Res. **41**, 4295–4302 (2002)
12. Ding, F., Chen, T.: Identification of Hammerstein nonlinear ARMAX system. IEEE Trans. Autom. Control **41**, 1479–1489 (2005)
13. Chabni, F., Taleb, R., Benbouali, A., Bouthiba, M.A.: The application of fuzzy control in water tank level using Arduino. Int. J. Adv. Comput. Sci. Appl. **7**, 261–265 (2016)
14. Chainho, J., Pereira, P., Rafael, S., Pires, A.J.: A simple PID controller with adaptive parameter in a dsPIC; case of study. In: Proceedings of the 9th Spanish-Portuguese Congress on Electrical Engineering (2005)
15. Hong, X., Iplikci, S., Chen, S., Warwick, K.: A model-based PID controller for Hammerstein systems using B-spline neural networks. Int. J. Adapt. Control Signal Process. **28**, 412–428 (2014)
16. Zhu, Y.: Robust PID tuning using closed-loop identification. In: Preprints of the International Symposium on Advanced Control of Chemical Processes ADCHEM, vol. 1, pp. 165–170 (2004)
17. Su, Y.X., Sun, D., Duan, B.Y.: Design of an enhanced nonlinear PID controller. Mechatronics **15**, 1005–1024 (2005)
18. Tan, Y., Dang, X., van Cauwenberghe, A.: Generalised nonlinear PID controller based on neural networks. In: 1999 Information, Decision and Control. Data and Information Fusion Symposium, Signal Processing and Communications Symposium and Decision and Control Symposium. Proceedings (Cat. No. 99EX251), pp. 519–524 (1999)
19. Yadav, E.S., Shettigar J, P., Poojary, S., Chokkadi, S., Jeppu, G., Indiran, T.: Data-driven modeling of a pilot plant batch reactor and validation of a nonlinear model predictive controller for dynamic temperature profile tracking. ACS Omega **6**(26), 16714–16721 (2021)
20. Shettigar J, P., Lochan, K., Jeppu, G., Palanki, S., Indiran, T.: Development and validation of advanced nonlinear predictive control algorithms for trajectory tracking in batch polymerization. ACS Omega **6**(35), 22857–22865 (2021)

Automation with Blockchain: Creating a Marketplace for IoT Based Irrigation System

Usha Divakarla[1][✉] and K. Chandrasekaran[2]

[1] NMAM Institute of Technology, Nitte, Karkala, Karnataka, India
ushachavali@gmail.com
[2] National Institute of Technology Karnataka, Surathkal, Mangaluru, India
kch@nitk.edu.in

Abstract. The next revolutionary technology to emerge since the creation of bitcoin in 2008 is blockchain technology. The Internet of Things (IoT), security, and other industries have all adopted blockchain technology. The article discusses the use of smart contracts, an Ethereum blockchain feature, to automate transactions in the Ethereum blockchain-based marketplace platform for Internet of Things devices. The following is demonstrated as a proof of concept by building a prototype of the suggested platform utilising Ethereum, Ganache, Web3, and Metamask. This exemplifies how transactions can be automated using smart contracts on the blockchain. When the land's moisture content is less than some critical value, the prototype concentrates on automating the watering of the land. Real-time monitoring of the moisture level of the consumer's land is possible. On the basis of the centralised paradigm, attempts are being made to construct such a system. The goal is to automate every activity. In the blockchain, the smart contract functions like a living thing. Because of this, automating is made possible. The blockchain also gives each gadget a unique account, considering them as participants in the transaction rather than just the sold goods, increasing the potential for automation.

Keywords: Ethereum · Blockchain · IoT · Automation

1 Introduction

The Internet of Things (IoT) has significantly altered our way of life. From smart wearables to smart refrigerators that adapt to our demands, it has permeated every aspect of our life. Additionally, automobiles use them (self-driving). Today's fuel is data. It is currently utilised throughout all sectors of society.

The three technologies that are closely related to data are blockchain, machine learning, and the internet of things. The creation of data and services is made possible by the Internet of Things devices, which also give computers a way to communicate with the real world. Blockchains offer a mechanism to record data and transactions in an unchangeable form. Machine learning is used to make sense of the data obtained and use those insights to achieve a larger goal.

IoT devices and data will be sold as commodities in the market, just like cloud services and physical goods, as a result of the IoT ecosystem's rapid expansion. A significant

I. Woungang et al. (Eds.): ANTIC 2022, CCIS 1797, pp. 60–72, 2023.
https://doi.org/10.1007/978-3-031-28180-8_5

IoT service exchange is creating a trade platform. Attempts have been made to create a system where IoT services are traded like commodities. However, the primary issues here are data security and privacy [4]. For the reasons outlined in the following sections, a centralised system where one must blindly trust a third party is no longer a viable option in the current world. A decentralised system built on the blockchain is required because it eliminates the requirement for a reliable third party by enabling users to independently verify data and ensure its immutability [5]. IoT devices can use blockchain to register themselves and organize store, share streams of data effectively and reliably.

Blockchains like Ethereum provide a notion of smart contracts. On the blockchain, smart contracts are stored as code or scripts.

They are set off by specific circumstances. The ability to automate processes on the blockchain is provided by smart contracts to developers. Like entities that live on the blockchain, smart contracts. On the blockchain, they are connected to their own address and account. The project's goal is to use smart contracts to automate exchanges of goods, services, and data between two entities on the blockchain with little to no human involvement. Every gadget whose data or service is available for trade or exchange can be given an account using blockchain technology. Therefore, by giving the devices access to their blockchain, the blockchains deal with the devices as participants in the exchange, which prevents fraud in transactions.

A basic trading platform for irrigation services between farmers and the service providers who have placed IoT devices all over the place is constructed as a proof of concept. This platform can be very helpful in a nation like India where agriculture is significant. The farmers sign up for the site and are given a blockchain-connected account that they may use to conduct transactions. They might request that the soil moisture be monitored and that it be irrigated when it falls below a certain threshold. These kinds of attempts are made utilising the conventional centralised client-server approach, which has a lot of issues [3]. With the exception of the farmer's first request, all of these tasks are entirely automated. The fact that the blockchain has cryptocurrency associated with it, which can be used for payments, is another benefit of it. The moisture level of the soil in the farmers' fields can be updated in real time. When irrigation is required, automatic transactions between the accounts linked to the device and the farmer take place. The smart contract is written in Solidity, and the prototype is built on the Ethereum blockchain.

Section 2 gives the brief overview of the works previously done in the field. Section 3 contains information about the Approaches and Mechanisms used to build the prototype. Section 4 contains information about the results obtained, i.e the working of the prototype. Section 5 contains discussion regarding the advantages and disadvantages of using blockchain as a basis for such a platform and also how the present model can be extended.

2 Literature Review

The project's objective is to provide a platform where farmers can easily and safely access irrigation services from a variety of vendors. This entails offering farmers IoT device-based services for tracking the soil's moisture content and also implementing irrigation when the moisture content is low. Farmers ought to be able to monitor the soil's moisture level in real time. Additionally, as much as practicable, the actions conducted are to be automated.

In order to develop such an Internet of Things (IoT) based system for tracking the moisture level of the fields, Rao et al. [3] discuss the numerous tools and equipment required. In this article, the authors primarily concentrate on the actual tools required to monitor and irrigate the field. The authors also provide the fundamental circuitry needed to construct such an infrastructure.

Hub et al.'s [6] discussion of the framework needed to combine the physical IoT infrastructure with the blockchain-based platform for managing and monitoring IoT device performance. The mechanism is automated through the use of smart contracts and the Ethereum [2] blockchain. Additionally, it advises using asymmetric key cryptography to give the system the necessary security.

The best practises for combining blockchain technology with IoT devices are discussed by Fernandez et al. [4] and Christidis et al. [7], S. Huh et al. [11]. According to Dogan et al. [5], creating the data marketplace utilising blockchains for data produced by IoT devices is discussed. Additionally, by developing a prototype for the same on the Ethereum network, this gives a clear proof of concept.

3   Approaches and Mechanisms

3.1   Comparison of the Two Model - Cloud Based and Decentralized

As was already noted, the project's objective is to provide a platform where farmers can easily and safely access irrigation services from a variety of providers. In order to do this, IoT device-based services are offered to farmers, who can use them to monitor the soil's moisture level and apply irrigation when it is low. Farmers ought to be able to monitor the soil's moisture level in real time. Additionally, the steps conducted must be as automatic as possible.

In order to build a system or platform where the IoT devices are exchanged or are allowed to be used in exchange for money, two approaches can be used [3, 4].

- Centralized Cloud model: The first system is a centralised one that uses cloud computing resources. When IoT device services or transactions take place through the platform, the cloud serves as the platform's trusted third party. As a result, attacks like Denial of Service are possible given this centralised approach (DoS). A single point of failure exists in the centralised system as well. Additionally, a significant number of IoT devices are being used in our daily lives, and more are predicted to be added rapidly in the near future. We utilise gadgets like wearable smart devices, smart air conditioners, and smart refrigerators every day. Therefore, there are too many devices for a single centralised system to manage. IoT devices are also available whose services are needed in real-time by customers. However, in a centralised system, every data travelling must contend with other internet traffic in order to reach its destination, stopping at the cloud for any additional processing. This is a slightly inappropriate way to establish the market for IoT device services on top of it due to all of these problems.

Various stakeholders are interested in such a platform, which is centred on exchanging or selling IoT services. Five essential primitives (roles), according to the National Institute of Standards and Technology, are utilised in actual Internet of Things applications [8].

- IoT sensors are devices that produce data.
- Data aggregation infrastructure includes edge, fog, and mist.
- Communication channels: services offered by communication service providers for wired or wireless communication.
- eUtility: Cloud-based SaaS, PaaS, and IaaS services.
- Processes for enacting decisions, such as pipelines for data analysis.

Each of these services is frequently offered by a distinct provider who is unaware of the identity of the other supplier. So the only option is to put your trust in a single party. The party which gives the sensor data has no idea how the data will be used by the party consuming it. Additionally, the entity consuming the data is unaware of the accuracy of the data it has received. Thus, we require a different strategy.

So we need a different approach.

- Blockchain-based decentralised model: Establishing trust amongst the numerous parties participating in such a system is one of the main challenges. Users of the cloud-based approach are compelled to believe the centralised cloud without question. They lack any other option. But it shouldn't be like this. The blockchain is a novel data sharing mechanism that resolves this problem by doing away with the requirement for a reliable third party. It brings in the needed trust by maintaining the immutable database or ledger, which cannot be easily tampered with. All the participants hold a copy of this, and the system tries to maintain consensus among the participants, by using several distributed consensus algorithms. As a result, the following benefits [8] can be attained by employing the blockchain to oversee the trade of IoT device services:

  - IoT devices may share data through the blockchain without relying on a third party.
  - The blockchain entries, which keep track of all the transactions, can be used to track the data produced by various sources.
  - Better service providers gain significantly more than less effective service providers.
  - The supplied data's integrity is safeguarded.

Therefore, rather than building it on the cloud, it is preferable to develop the aforementioned platform (marketplace for IoT device-based services) on blockchain technology.

3.2 What is Block Chain?

A Blockchain is a distributed data structure, whose copies are stored in the nodes of the network. These copies, ideally, are exactly the same as each other. The concept of

Blockchainwas introduced as part of the Bitcoin [1], a cryptocurrency aimed at solving the double spending problem. The blockchain is nothing but a linked list that is supposed to be immutable. Blockchain consists of a series of blocks that are time-stamped and identified by their unique cryptographic hash. Every block references the hash of its previous block. This is one of the main reasons for the immutability property of the blockchain. This forms a link between the block and its previous one, leading to the formation of a chain of blocks, called blockchain.

Every node on the blockchain network holds a copy of this blockchain. A node can act as an entry point for many users (of blockchain) into the network. These nodes form a peer-to-peer network. In this network [7]:

- The users hold private-public key pairs. The private key [10] is used by the user to sign his transaction. Therefore the private key acts as the digital signature of the user in the blockchain network. The public key, which is accessible to other users in the network, is used to verify the signed transactions. The use of asymmetric cryptography brings authentication and integrity into the blockchain network.

  Such signed transactions are broadcasted by a users node to its neighbours (one-hop peers).
- The neighbouring peers check the validity of the transaction before relaying it to its neighbours. Invalid transactions are dropped. Eventually, the transaction is broadcasted to the entire network.
- The above valid transactions are collected and packaged into a time stamped candidate block. This process is called mining. The mining node issues this block back to the network.
- The nodes check the broadcasted block for its validity and add it to their blockchain if valid.

As said before, there is no trusted third party in a blockchain network. So a way has to be found to help the network reach **consensus**, mainly regarding the validity of the blocks.

So a blockchain network needs a set of rules to which all its nodes should oblige. These rules are programmed into the nodes, which are used when creating a transaction or while receiving one. When each node in the network follows the set rules, it is possible to bring consensus without having to blindly believe a third party. Here belief is on the mathematics of cryptography used and not on a third party. So a blockchain operates in a **trustless environment**.

Using a blockchain provides a convenient billing layer for using the services and gives way to the creation of a marketplace of services between devices [7]. Using this technology, we can allocate an account to every IoT device, treating them as participants of the transactions and not just objects that are traded. This further helps in the main goal of automating all these transactions.

3.3 How to Apply the Above-Mentioned Concept to the Problem of Creating a Market Place for Sharing Irrigation Service and also Automating It?

A blockchain for the platform has to be created. The service providers should register every one of their devices they intend to use. This creates an account for every device. The consumer should also register and create an account in the blockchain. Therefore this blockchain is a permissioned one that is not open to everyone but should register with the platform before being able to use the blockchain.

There can be two types of blockchains.

- Permissionless blockchain: This is an open network that allows anyone to join or quit the network. The incentives are provided for being a part of the network and mining the blocks. The consensus mechanisms used are mostly Proof-of-Work or Proof-of-Stake.
- Permissioned blockchain: Only the registered participants are allowed to participate in the blockchain network. Privacy is preserved as the public is not allowed to participate. Consensus mechanisms like Byzantine Fault tolerance used. Incentives for participation rarely seen.

Once the account is created, the service providers create a smart [11] contract on the blockchain for every device, which controls the way the device has to behave and the way the money (or cryptocurrency) is transferred between the account of the device and that of the consumer, who in this case is the farmer requesting the services. All the transactions occur according to the rules set by the smart contract. As the smart contract is visible to everyone on the network to see, no fraud can be done. The block chain will be based on Ethereum, which also provides the needed smart contracts. The smart contracts will be run on the EVM (Ethereum virtual machine) on the nodes of the Ethereum network

3.4 Ethereum

Ethereum [2], proposed by Vatalik Buterin in 2013, is a public blockchain-based distributed computing platform. Unlike, bitcoin, the original blockchain network, it can work as a computer. But the performance is lower compared to normal cloud-based computing. The code that is stored on Ethereum is called smart contract and is written in languages like Solidity. The code is compiled to bytecode and stored on the Ethereum blockchain. Ethereum nodes comprise of three components.

- The blockchain
- The peer-to-peer communication layer.
- The Ethereum virtual machine

The Ethereum virtual machine is what runs the byte code of the smart contract. Ethereum combines the computing system with blockchain. Storing the code on the blockchain saves it from malicious tampering. Processing code on Ethereum costs gas, which acts as the economic incentive to the nodes performing the computation

3.5 Smart Contracts

A computerised transaction system called a "smart contract" [2] performs a contract's terms. Smart contracts are scripts that are kept on the blockchain in the context of the technology. They have a specific blockchain address. They could be seen as autonomous actors, or entities that live on the blockchain. As a result, the idea of decentralised autonomous organisations is born. The smart contract is activated under specific circumstances, which causes the programming it contains to run. Smart contracts enable general-purpose computations to take place across the chain. A smart contract is a piece of deterministic code that, when executed under identical circumstances, produces the same outcome. In essence, a smart contract connects several entities to create a system that performs specific activities. We can run general-purpose code on the blockchain, more precisely the Ethereum Virtual Machine (EVM) of the network's nodes, thanks to the Turing-complete characteristic of smart contracts in Ethereum.

3.6 How to Use the Proposed Marketplace Platform?

The consumer (farmer) interacts with the blockchain and obtains the services offered by the registered devices using the web-based interface. He chooses the necessary instrument and instructs it to begin monitoring the amount of moisture in the soil in his field. These tools are deployed in the farmers' fields by the provider and are the providers' property, not the farmers'. If the device detects during tracking that the moisture level is below the critical level, it begins irrigating the land with the available water supply while deducting the appropriate amount from the customer's account. Everything is carried out automatically. The procedure is therefore automated. The moisture level of the farmer's land is constantly visible. As all the transactions are saved in the blockchain with the timestamp, it is almost impossible to perform any fraudulent activities.

3.7 A Prototype of the Idea as Proof of Concept

A prototype of the model as the proof of concept to the above idea has been created. The created model simplifies the problem statement by providing provision for a single consumer and a single device from the given provider. This model can be extended to allow multiple users and multiple parallel transactions. The code for the model can be seen at https://github.com/govardhangdg/seproject

Ganache is used to produce the in-memory Ethereum test blockchain needed for the model, which can be accessed and interacted with via the JSON-RPC protocol as advised by Ethereum to create dApps (decentralized applications). The service's necessary files are provided to the customer's browser via the prototype, a NodeJS programme that runs an HTTP server. The Solidity programming language is used to create the smart contract for the code. Web3.js is used to programmatically connect with the blockchain from the NodeJS app.

An add-on called Metamask, which internally uses the same web3.js as mentioned above, is used to transform a standard browser into one that can communicate with the blockchain. The official solc compiler is used to translate the solidity code into bytecode that the Ethereum Virtual Machine (EVM) can understand. Then, as the first block following the genesis block, the byte code is introduced to the blockchain. Every subsequent transaction uses the smart contract's address, which is kept.

To provide a web-based interface for the software, a simple HTML page is created. A process that delivers simulated moisture levels at regular intervals is created in order to imitate the sensor readings. When the moisture condition is lower than the critical moisture condition, the main app responds in response to this. Every time the moisture content falls below the threshold, an event is set off, a new blockchain transaction is made, and the moisture content is raised by simulated watering (which is just a message from the main process to the process simulating sensor readings). Once the time of tracking asked by the consumer is passed, the tracking is stopped.

4   Results

A prototype is made as a proof-of-concept to demonstrate how the suggested model for automating transactions between the device and the consumer for the irrigation service will operate. The Ethereum blockchain is used to build the prototype, and smart contracts are used to automate the transactions. The smart contract keeps track of the two parties' transaction's current state and is programmed to start various actions when certain conditions are satisfied, such as when moisture content falls below a threshold. The prototype's smart contract is depicted in the diagram below. Its user interface is web-based. The smart contract for the prototype is given in the Fig. 1. The web interface shows the address where the necessary contract is set up as well as the accounts linked to the customer and the service-providing device. The user must specify how long he wants the device to keep an eye on his field. When the duration has passed, a smart contract event is triggered, ending the tracking.

The contract is initially deployed to the blockchain when the app is launched using the code contained in the deploy.js and compile.js files. When this occurs, a little amount of ether is taken out of the device's account to cover the cost of deploying the contract. Following the contract's deployment, the customer specifies the number of hours he wants to use the service; this generates a transaction that modifies the smart contract's state and adds a new block to the blockchain. The sequence diagram for the proposed model as shown in Fig. 2.

The expense of the tracking is transferred to the account of the device. The prototype also offers the opportunity to view the field's moisture content. The result is as shown in Fig. 3.

The link opens up a graph that shows the moisture in real time. Every time the moisture goes below critical level an event is triggered and transfer of funds from the consumer to device occurs and the service (irrigation) is provided.

```solidity
pragma solidity 0.4.25;

contract Service {

    address public provider;
    bool public working;
    bool public tracking;
    uint256 public endTrackingTime;

    event trackingEvent (
        bool active,
        uint256 endTrackingTime
    );

    event workingEvent (
        bool active
    );

    constructor() payable public {
        provider = msg.sender;
        tracking = false;
        working = false;
        endTrackingTime = 0;
    }

    function startTracking(uint8 _time) public
        payable
    {
        require(tracking == false && working ==
            false,"conditions for startTracking not
            met");
        require(msg.value == 5 * _time * 1e18,"
            proper ether value not sent");
        provider.transfer(msg.value);
        tracking = true;
        endTrackingTime = block.timestamp + _time *
            3600;
        emit trackingEvent(tracking,endTrackingTime)
            ;
    }

    function startWorking() public payable {
        require(working == false && tracking == true
            ,"conditions for startWorking not met");
        require(block.timestamp < endTrackingTime,"
            endTrackingTime already passed");
        require(msg.value == 4 * 1e18,"proper ether
            value not sent");
        provider.transfer(msg.value);
        working = true;
        emit workingEvent(working);
    }

    function stopWorking() public {
        require(working == true && tracking == true,
            "conditions for stopWorking not met");
        working = false;
        emit workingEvent(working);
    }

    function stopTracking() public {
        require(tracking == true,"conditions for
            stopTracking not met");
        working = false;
        tracking = false;
        endTrackingTime = 0;
        emit trackingEvent(tracking,endTrackingTime)
            ;
    }
}
```

Fig. 1. Smart contract prototype

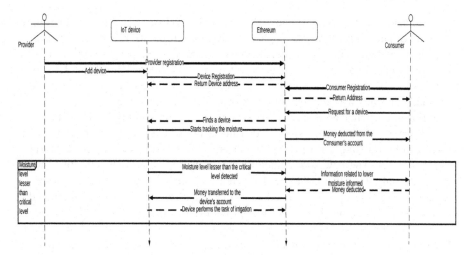

Fig. 2. Sequence diagram of the model

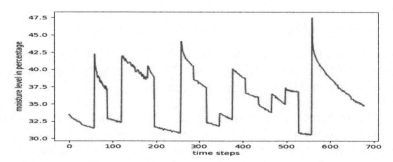

Fig. 3. The graph depicting the performance of the model when provided with the soil moisture data from the data hosted

5 Discussion

The presented simulates the actual functioning of a similar platform in real life. Attempts are made in creating a similar system, based on the Cloud-based model. The major disadvantages of using a cloud-based model have been discussed in the above sections.

The project can be extended in directions as mentioned below:

- IPFS: A distributed storage system that is compatible with the Ethereum blockchain is IPFS. https://ipfs.io/. It can be used to give the data generated during the tracking period a storage facility. Scientists and data analysts can use the generated data to gain profound insights into specific issues. The same methodology can be utilised to construct a data marketplace where this data is sold as a commodity. The real-time data that is gathered can be saved on IPFS as a file (csv). The consumer with the proper private key can access the data stored in the IPFS and encrypt it using asymmetric key cryptography techniques [5].

- The inclusion of multiple providers, devices and consumers: To simplify the implementation, The simple case of a single provider, a single device and a single consumer is considered here. This can be extended to include multiple parties interacting with each other in a suitable manner. A system to search providers, who fall under certain conditions, can also be implemented. A chat system can also be created between two interacting parties with the help of whisper protocol of Ethereum.
- Addition of the actual hardware: To make the implementation simpler, Here, moisture values from the sensor are simulated using a method. Instead, the model can be improved by utilising a Raspberry Pi and the appropriate sensors to read the soil's moisture level. The new sensor module should merge seamlessly with the current code. The only thing that has to be changed is the source of the incoming data stream from the readings simulator procedure to the actual sensor data [3]. Including edge nodes for computation: Instead of just providing raw data to the consumers, edge nodes (fog computing concept) can be added to the platform at the edges (next to IoT sensors) to process the data before providing it to the consumers. A RaspberryPi may be used to process the data obtained from the sensors before providing it to the consumers, in the extension mentioned above [9].

5.1 Concerns Regarding Using Blockchain for Such a Platform

Even though using Blockchain as the basis for the proposed platform brings a lot of advantages, it is not the silver bullet that solves all the problems. Instead, it brings along its own set of concerns [4].

- Passing ownership of the devices: Suitable steps should be taken when the ownership of the device is transferred. This is very important because the trust of the consumers on the new provider and hence the device in question can be affected. The data possessed by the device can be used by the new owner in a way that is not recommended.
- Bringing about the privacy of transactions: This is really a tough problem to solve as even though public keys are used to identify a device or a consumer on the blockchain, these devices or consumers can be identified in the real world based on the coincidences in the activities on the chain and in the real world. So a balance in the privacy and openness in the transaction history is to be achieved, which is a delicate matter.
- Throughput and latency: Blockchains deliberately restrict the number of transactions that can be made in a given time. This affects the performance of the system when a lot of IoT based transactions have to be made simultaneously. Hardcore real-time applications suffer from this. Even though the problem cant be completely solved, steps must be taken in eradicating the problem.
- Energy efficiency: Mining nodes with consensus mechanisms like Proof-of-Work is computationally expensive. As computing is inevitable, something useful is to be com puted. Like the primes etc.
- Adoption Rate: The blockchain enables pseudonymity. Thus people can misuse this privacy given to them. This is not a problem in the permissioned blockchains but may turn out to be one if public blockchains are to be used for the purpose.
- Usability: Creating applications over blockchain is not as easy as creating one over the traditional and conventional, centralized server-client model. As a result, there aren't

many people who are interested in taking up such ambitious projects. The problem is expected to be mitigated with the formation and development of a community worldwide who are interested in creating decentralized applications or dApps.

- Dealing with forks: As blockchain is a distributed system, disagreements regarding the state of the blockchain can occur, mainly in the form of the forks. It is very important to deal with the forks in a way that doesn't cause problems to the consumers or providers using the platform.
- Lack of legal governance: Rules regarding the usage of blockchain technology are not strict or not even formed in many countries. Lack of such rules severely hinders the widespread adoption of the technology

6 Conclusion

As discussed in the previous sections, there can be two important approaches to building a marketplace for the IoT device based services. One is the traditional centralized system and the other is the blockchain based decentralized system. As mentioned above, the centralized system requires too much of trust to be placed on the third party, which can be dangerous and is also subjected to problems like single point of failure etc. On the other hand, the blockchain based solution solves most of the problems faced by the centralized system. But this comes with its own set of problems, which can be solved with proper legal support. In the end, the blockchain based solution provides the required security and protection for the proposed system.

References

1. Nakamoto, S., et al.: Bitcoin: a peer-to-peer electronic cash system (2008)
2. Wood, G., et al.: Ethereum: a secure decentralised generalised transaction ledger. Ethereum Proj. Yellow Pap. **151**, 1–32 (2014)
3. Rao, R.N., Sridhar, B.: IoT based smart crop-field monitoring and automation irrigation system. In: 2018 2nd International Conference on Inventive Systems and Control (ICISC), pp. 478–483. IEEE (2018)
4. Fernández-Caramés, T.M., Fraga-Lamas, P.: A review on the use of blockchain for the Internet of Things. IEEE Access **6**, 32979–33001 (2018)
5. Özyilmaz, K.R., Doğan, M., Yurdakul, A.: IDMoB: IoT data marketplace on blockchain. In: 2018 Crypto Valley Conference on Blockchain Technology (CVCBT), pp. 11–19. IEEE (2018)
6. Huh, S., Cho, S., Kim, S.: Managing IoT devices using blockchain platform. In: 201719th International Conference on Advanced Communication Technology (ICACT), pp. 464–467. IEEE (2017)
7. Christidis, K., Devetsikiotis, M.: Blockchains and smart contracts for the Internet of Things. IEEE Access **4**, 2292–2303 (2016)
8. Yu, B., Wright, J., Nepal, S., Zhu, L., Liu, J., Ranjan, R.: Trustchain: establishing trust in the IoT-based applications ecosystem using blockchain. IEEE Cloud Comput. **5**(4), 12–23 (2018)
9. Tuli, S., Mahmud, R., Tuli, S., Buyya, R.: FogBus: a blockchainbased lightweight framework for edge and fog computing. arXiv preprint arXiv:1811.11978 (2018)

10. Huh, S., Cho, S., Kim, S.: Managing IoT devices using blockchain platform. In: 2017 19th International Conference on Advanced Communication Technology (ICACT), pp. 464–467 (2017). https://doi.org/10.23919/ICACT.2017.7890132
11. Pranto, T.H., Noman, A.A., Mahmud, A., Haque, A.B.: Blockchain and smart contract for IoT enabled smart agriculture. PeerJ Comput. Sci. 7, e407 (2021). https://doi.org/10.7717/peerj-cs.407

An Intelligent Behavior-Based System to Recognize and Detect the Malware Variants Based on Their Characteristics Using Machine Learning Techniques

Vasudeva Pai⬤, Abhishek S. Rao$^{(\boxtimes)}$ ⬤, Devidas⬤, and B. Prapthi

Department of Information Science and Engineering, NITTE (Deemed to be University),
NMAM Institute of Technology (NMAMIT), Nitte 574110, Karnataka, India
abhishekrao@nitte.edu.in

Abstract. An Intrusion Detection System's (IDS) primary goal is to safeguard the user and their equipment against malicious malware. IDS offers more security than more established techniques like firewalls. Malware software affects the integrity, confidentiality, and availability of data by launching cyberattacks from a computer-based system. There has been a lot of advancement in computer crime, and IDS has grown tremendously to keep up with it. Researchers have been trying to advance in this field and increase the chances of detecting an attack while also maintaining the working system and network. In this research, we provide a novel approach to identifying and detecting malware programs based on their attributes and behavior, using machine learning techniques. The paper also suggests several techniques for analyzing malware behavior, including filtering useful system operations, defining the type of action, generating behavior, and assessing risk score and frequency. The proposed method achieved higher accuracy of 94% using the Random Forest machine learning classifier when compared to other classifiers.

Keywords: Intrusion detection system · Cyber security · Malware detection · Risk score calculation · Machine learning

1 Introduction

The frequency and variety of cybercrime attacks have significantly increased in recent years. Almost everyone uses the internet in some aspect of their everyday lives. The internet and related technology have significantly influenced our way of life. We utilize the internet for marketing, social media, online banking, and business-related activities. More crimes are perpetrated online than in real life due to the prevalence of the internet and its significance in daily life. After identifying the victim computers, malicious malware launches its payloads on them, and this malicious program is used by criminals to start their online crimes. Different virus types frequently cause cyber-attacks.

I. Woungang et al. (Eds.): ANTIC 2022, CCIS 1797, pp. 73–88, 2023.
https://doi.org/10.1007/978-3-031-28180-8_6

Any software that uses security holes in computer and network systems to commit crimes and make money is considered malware [1]. Some examples of malware include ransomware, Trojans, rootkits, worms, viruses, and backdoors. They are designed in such a way that one of them can "launch distributed denial of service (DDoS) assaults and enable remote code execution," while another can steal confidential information [2]. Multiple malware variants are used in sophisticated and clever attacks. The malware was initially very basic and was only applied to simple tasks. This type of threat is referred to as traditional malware. Modern malware is far more sophisticated and may operate in kernel mode, making it riskier and more evasive to detection. Earlier malware just used one process. They do not use any tricks to hide their identities. But the most recent virus makes use of complex and sophisticated tactics to conceal itself and spread unchecked within the targeted system. Next-generation malware, in contrast to older malware, has greater detrimental impacts. Due to consumers' increased network workloads, there is a rise in the production of malware. The emergence of malware is aided by the creation of numerous new applications and the addition of more hardware, including the Internet of Things. It is difficult to keep track of viruses today because of the massive volume of data being produced. Sometimes the virus cannot be discovered using conventional techniques because the malware variants use complex hiding mechanisms to evade detection systems. Attacks with malware are extremely harmful and have significantly impacted the economy. Researchers claim that cyberattacks have a trillion-dollar negative impact on the global economy. Attack strategies have changed quickly, and the quantity of damage that was done has increased significantly. Malicious emails, phishing scams, and exploiting user trust are a few instances of the attack spread strategy in action. By the end of 2019, the ransomware virus will cost the world over $11.5 billion, according to cybersecurity ventures [3]. This is due to a significant increase in the amount of fraudulent mobile applications, banking Trojans, and backdoors. Additionally, there is an increase in social media attacks, data theft from the healthcare business, privacy concerns, cryptocurrency fraud, and many more. Malware detection is a tedious process where we determine whether the erroneous program is harmful or benign. Despite having several limitations, the signature-based detection method is frequently used to detect malware. This method has significant critical flaws, one of which is that it cannot recognize and categorize brand-new, or unnamed malware. Different methods for detecting malware offer varying degrees of detection precision. Researchers have proposed a variety of cutting-edge methods, including deep learning detection, IoT detection, mobile device detection, cloud detection, and others to detect different types of malwares [4]. Malware detection methods such as heuristic-based detection, model checking-based detection, and behavioral-based detection frequently use machine learning and data mining techniques [3, 5, 6]. These methods have demonstrated effectiveness in identifying unknown malware [7]. Against unknown and complex malware, model checking-based, behavior-based, or cloud-based techniques perform better. Results have been positive for identifying both known and undiscovered malware when using new technologies like deep learning, IoT-based technologies, and others [8]. The superiority of one detecting method over another is not supported by any hard data. Every detection technique will result in different results under different circumstances. There is a very low possibility that all the sophisticated and emerging malware can be found using a single method. This highlights the intricacy of the current problem and highlights the need for developing identification methods that are even more potent. The drawback of using signature-based detection is that it is unable to recognize and detect unidentified malware with numerous signatures. With numerous variants of the same virus, the method of signature-based detection performs remarkably well. The vast majority of zero-day malware can be successfully identified using behavior-based, heuristic-based, and model-checking-based techniques [9]. Malware, however, might be hard to find if it uses sophisticated packaging techniques. Using deep learning-based or mobile device-based detection approaches, we have seen an improvement in the detection rate (DR). However, it can be challenging to identify those that behave differently from malware that has been found. Additionally, various servers can use a range of detecting techniques. Using different algorithms increases the effectiveness of malware detection while reducing false positive (FPR) or negative rates. Hence, our study suggests an intelligent behavior-based malware detection system to recognize and detect the various malware variants based on their characteristics and behavior.

2 Methodology

This section offers a comprehensive explanation of the proposed framework, including model design, dataset, characteristics, and recognition methods. The file is run and executed by numerous virtual machines (VMs). The execution's outcome is gathered and put together utilizing the appropriate tools. The behavior is produced once the developed follows are gathered by the detection system. To generate features, the defined rules join instances of related behavior. The components are created via the Subtractive Center Behavior Model (SCBM). The proposed method then chooses the most discriminative attributes, and the features are subsequently transmitted to the detection system in a learning-based way. Selected highlights in a learning-based model are produced using an ML calculation such as a logistic model tree (LMT), simple logistic regression (SLR), j48, random forest (RF), and sequential minimum optimization (SMO). Each instance is then categorized as either benign or malware and saved in the data collection. The database stores the values of data, whether they are malicious or benign.

2.1 Proposed System Architecture

The process diagram for the malware detection model is shown in Fig. 1.

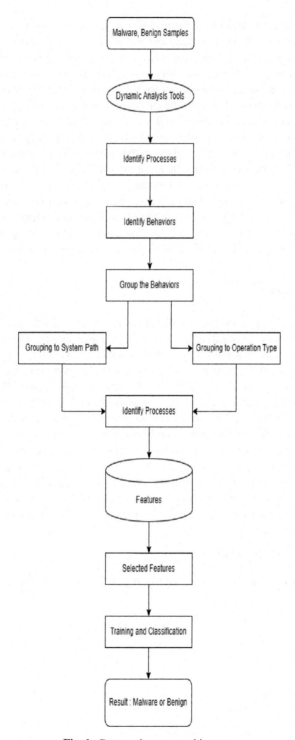

Fig. 1. Proposed system architecture

2.2   Behavior Formation, Extraction of Features, and Feature Selection

Active real-time document inspection tools like API Monitor, Process Monitor, Process Explorer, Autoruns, or Debuggers are used to examine each suspicious record's components while they are being created [10]. The subsequent phase involved gathering every execution and transmitting them to the detecting system. The system's behaviors and features were developed using the SCBM model. The malignant characteristics are those that are detected in suspicious codes but not typically in non-revengeful testing [11]. To distinguish between harmful attributes, we employ system call pathways, system calls, and document types. During this phase, the prime goal is to compile and identify all the key qualities of the suspicious codes. It is essential to create links between various system calls to construct behaviors. One of the several system calls must be capable of managing large amounts of movement and producing behavior. Algorithm 1 lists the activities (F1), and the system calls to be used as input, and in response filters them and returns them as F2. The path scores are displayed along with a subfolder structure for each technique and attributes along with behaviors are produced using these techniques. The model list of system movement paths is shown in Table 1, and the path score estimations for behaviors are depicted in Algorithm 2.

Algorithm 1: System Operation Filtering

Input: List of activities/system calls (F1)
Output: List of activities/system calls (F2)

---

1. for each system call F1i do
2.   if F1[i][oper]! = F1[i+1] [oper] then
3.   if F1[i][oper] is not a process closing operation then
4.   write F1[i] into F2
5.   end if
6.   end if
7.   if F1[i][oper] == F1[i+1] [oper] then
8.   if F1[i][path]! = F1[i+1] [path] then
9.   if F1[i][oper] is not a process closing operation then
10.   write F1[i] into F2
11.   end if
12.   end if
13.   end if
14. end for

Table 1. Malware trace execution path

Action System Path
' c:\windows', system folder
' hklm\system ', system folder
' c:\windows\system32', system folder
'c:\program files', third party folder
'c:\program files (x86)', third party folder
'\....\suspicious file', self-folder
' c:\users\...\startmenu\...\startup', auto start location
' hklm\software \microsoft\active setup\installed components', auto start location
'hkcu\software\Microsoft\windows\currentversion\runonce\setup', auto start location
'hklm\software\microsoft\windows\currentversion\run', auto start location
'c:\documents and settings\ user name\local settings\temp', temporary folder
'c:\ users\user name \appdata\local\temp', temporary folder

Algorithm 2. Action Type naming

Input: List of activities/system calls (F2)
Output: List of activities/system calls with action types (F3)

---

1. for each system call F2i do
2.   at=' '
3.   if F2[i][path] == 'System' or 'HKLM' or 'Windows' then
4.   at = 'SY'
5.   elif F2[i][path] == 'Program Files' then
6.   at = 'TP'
7.   elif F2[i][path] == 'Start Menu' or 'Run' then
8.   at = 'AS'
9.   elif F2[i][path] == 'Temp' then
10.   at = 'TE'
11.   elif F2[i][path] == 'App Data' then
12.   at = 'SF'
13.   end if
14.   write F2[i] into F3
15.   write it into F3
16. end for

As shown in Algorithm 2, when a system call is made in the system folder, the following rules are taken into account.

1. If a disassembled program test connects effectively to the operating framework documents and registers, it is graded as typical. System administrators, background programs, and DLLs for the operating system frequently provide these interactions. Because these transactions are seen as routine, the risk associated with these links will either be minimal or significant depending on the other circumstances.
2. Code insertion is possible in the DLLs and exes of the framework. This cooperation is most feasible considering how negatively such behavior is seen by others [7]. The following rules must be followed when a system call is placed in a third-party envelope.

    i. The degree of risk associated with these connections will change based on the other variables, such as whether a defective program test necessitates the successful completion of other projects.
    ii. However, such activities are regarded as harmful and the risk level of these communications will be high if it is thought that actions are being done on third-party data and catalogues that are unrelated to the test that was performed.

Algorithm 3 depicts the risk score calculation to produce the list of activities with action types and path scores.

Algorithm 3: Risk Score Calculation,

Input: List of activities/system calls with action types (F3)

Output: List of activities/system calls with action types and path score (F4)

---

1. for each system call F3i do
2.   rs=' '
3.   if F3[i][atype] == 'SF' then
4.   if process_name in F3[i][path] then
5.   rs = 0
6.   elif '.exe' and 'system' in F3[i][path] then
7.   rs = 2
8.   else
9.   rs = 1
10.   end if
11.   elif F3[i][atype] == 'SY' then
12.   if process_name in F3[i][path] then
13.   rs = 0
14.   elif '.exe' and 'system' in F3[i][path] then
15.   rs = 3
16.   elif 'microsoft' and 'currentversion' in F3[i][path] then
17.   rs = 2
18.   elif '.dll' or '.exe' in F3[i][path] then
19.   rs = 1
20.   else
21.   rs = 0
22.   end if
23.   elif F3[i][atype] == 'AS' then
24.   if '.dll' or '.exe' in F3[i][path] then
25.   rs = 3
26.   else
27.   rs = 2
28.   end if
29.   elif F3[i][atype] == 'TP' then
30.   rs = 1
31.   else
32.   rs = 3
33.   end if
34.   write F3[i] into F4
35.   write into F4
36. end for

The following principles are taken into account while processing the system call in its organizer:

1. Even though a piece of malfunctioning software needs a small bit of data from its database or record, the steps it takes to operate are legitimate and cannot be labeled malicious.
2. However, the risk level of these collaborations will be considered if a deconstructed program test executes library- and organization-related operations inside specific records or transfers the contents of its document to other documents.

It is important to explore several strategies, including the use of temporary folders and auto-start locations. This is because most malware uses brief organizers while performing malicious activities and makes use of document library regions with auto-start capabilities to remain persistent in the system. There is a significant risk involved with these connections because of a failing software test using a temporary folder or auto-start regions. As a result of this information, risk scores are assigned to each system call and used in further feature extraction. Algorithm 3 completes this task by using the file types described in the previous algorithms. Algorithm 4 introduces feature extraction. When features are constructed from behaviors, twenty continuous behaviors are considered. This stage involves calculating the scores for the routes, features, and feature activity categories.

Algorithm 4. Behavior Creation

Input: List of activities/system calls with action types and path score (F4)
Output: List of behaviors (F5)

---

1. for each system call, F4i do
2.   namei = F4[i][oper]
3.   for j = i+1 to i+20 do
4.   namej = F4[j][oper]
5.   if namei == 'Read File' and namej == 'Write File' and F4[i][path] != F4[j][path] then
6.   write namei+namej into F5
7.   write 3 into F5
8.   elif F4[i][atype] == F4[j][atype] and namei != namej then
9.   if F4[i][path] == F4[j][path]
10.   write namei+namej+F4[i][atype]
11.   write F4[i][rs] into F5
12. end for

Algorithm 5 introduces frequency calculation. First, each property's frequency of occurrence is established. We make every effort to use fewer different features during the element recurrence estimation.

Algorithm 5. Frequency Calculation

Input: List of behaviours (F5)
Output: List of behaviours with frequency (F6)

---

1. for each system call F5i do
2.   calculate FeatureFrequecny()
3.   write (F5[i][oper], F5[i][rs], frequency)
4. end for

Following recurrence computation, features are selected considering path scores and activity states. The related attribute is chosen if the score for the route is moderate, high, or extremely high.

2.3 Learning-Based Detection

After the selection of the attributes, a row vector is used to address each program test. Recurring esteem is established for each quality. The risk score is multiplied by x to determine how frequently a property will be rehashed; if not, the frequency value is set to 0. WEKA is used to perform classification after the dataset has been assembled using feature vectors. A learning-based model prepares the chosen features using machine learning algorithms including J48, LMT, RF, SLR, and SMO.

3 Implementation

The data set creation model is implemented using the Python programming language. WEKA and numerous Python modules are utilized to create an accurate model-based detection. The construction and presentation of the data, the operation of the model, and the evaluation are clearly explained in the following sections.

3.1 Data Gathering and Characterization

The Malware DB, Das Malwerk, Tekdefense, Malware Bazaar, Malware Benchmark, VirusShare, and ViruSign were some of the sources used to collect malware tests [1, 9]. A substantial dataset was gathered from numerous groups, including gaming data, company documents, system tools, and mediator software. All the acquired samples, 15 benign and 10 malicious, were examined on a variety of virtual machines and conventional systems. The "Virustotal" utility was used to label the malware samples that were collected. The collected malware tests were run in several VMs, and the execution routes were sent to the identification expert. The execution was made to follow using Process Monitor, Process Explorer, and Autoruns. Figure 2 depicts the collection, analysis, and representation of information. Every activity was run for 5 to 15 s, depending on the number of viruses generated. Using our suggested approach, execution pathways were broken down to produce the behaviors as shown in Fig. 3 and 4, respectively. The recommended computations were performed using the Python programming language. The features that were chosen for risk ratings are shown in Fig. 5. Each sample is treated as a line feature vector for learning-based identification, as depicted in Fig. 6. The component's occurrence for a linked case triggers the recording of the redundancy's recurrence. If the element is not reused for a related instance, the value '0' is written. Since "0" is composed of unique qualities, the list of capabilities rapidly elongates.

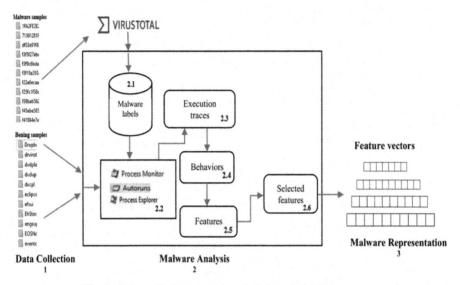

Fig. 2. Data gathering, assessing, and characterization process.

12:19.4	1.exe	5488	RegOpenKey	HKLM\Syste	NAME NOT	Desired Access: Query Value
12:19.4	1.exe	5488	RegOpenKey	HKLM\SYSTE	REPARSE	Desired Access: Query Value, Enumerate Sub Keys
12:19.4	1.exe	5488	RegOpenKey	HKLM\Syste	SUCCESS	Desired Access: Query Value, Enumerate Sub Keys
12:19.4	1.exe	5488	RegSetInfoKey	HKLM\Syste	SUCCESS	KeySetInformationClass: KeySetHandleTagsInformation, Length: 0
12:19.4	1.exe	5488	RegQueryValue	HKLM\Syste	NAME NOT	Length: 24
12:19.4	1.exe	5488	RegCloseKey	HKLM\Syste	SUCCESS	
12:19.4	1.exe	5488	CreateFile	C:\Users\id	SUCCESS	Desired Access: Execute/Traverse, Synchronize, Disposition: Open,
12:19.4	1.exe	5488	Load Image	C:\Windows	SUCCESS	Image Base: 0x75f50000, Image Size: 0xf0000
12:19.4	1.exe	5488	Load Image	C:\Windows	SUCCESS	Image Base: 0x76940000, Image Size: 0x215000
12:19.4	1.exe	5488	RegQueryValue	HKLM\Syste	NAME NOT	Length: 528
12:19.4	1.exe	5488	QueryNameInforma	C:\Windows	SUCCESS	Name: \Windows\SysWOW64\KernelBase.dll
12:19.4	1.exe	5488	RegQueryValue	HKLM\Syste	NAME NOT	Length: 528
12:19.4	1.exe	5488	QueryNameInforma	C:\Windows	SUCCESS	Name: \Windows\SysWOW64\KernelBase.dll
12:19.4	1.exe	5488	RegOpenKey	HKLM\Syste	REPARSE	Desired Access: Read
12:19.4	1.exe	5488	RegOpenKey	HKLM\Syste	SUCCESS	Desired Access: Read
12:19.4	1.exe	5488	RegSetInfoKey	HKLM\Syste	SUCCESS	KeySetInformationClass: KeySetHandleTagsInformation, Length: 0
12:19.4	1.exe	5488	RegQueryValue	HKLM\Syste	NAME NOT	Length: 548
12:19.4	1.exe	5488	RegQueryValue	HKLM\Syste	SUCCESS	Type: REG_DWORD, Length: 4, Data: 0
12:19.4	1.exe	5488	RegCloseKey	HKLM\Syste	SUCCESS	

Fig. 3. Collected behaviors

Name	Risk Score
Load ImageSY	1
CreateFileSY	0
RegOpenKeyRegSetInfoKeySY	0
RegOpenKeySY	0
RegQueryValueSY	0
RegOpenKeySY	0
RegOpenKeySY	0
RegOpenKeySY	0
RegOpenKeyRegSetInfoKeySY	0
RegOpenKeyRegSetInfoKeySY	0
RegOpenKeySY	0
RegQueryValueSY	0
CreateFileQueryNameInformationFileSY	0
CreateFileSY	0
RegOpenKeySY	0
RegQueryValueSY	0
Load ImageSY	1
Load ImageSY	1
CreateFileSY	1

Fig. 4. Feature generation feature generation

CreateFileMappingLoad ImageSY	1
CreateFileMappingCreateFileSY	1
CreateFileMappingQuerySecurityF	1
CreateFileMappingSY	1
QueryStandardInformationFileCre	1
QueryStandardInformationFileLoa	1
QueryStandardInformationFileCre	1
QueryStandardInformationFileQue	1
QueryStandardInformationFileSY	1
CreateFileMappingLoad ImageSY	1
CreateFileMappingCreateFileSY	1
CreateFileMappingQuerySecurityF	1
CreateFileMappingSY	1

Fig. 5. Selected features

3.2 Model Performance and Evaluation

After the feature identification procedure is completed, learning-based recognition techniques start assessing how well the suggested model works. To verify the effectiveness of the model, the following performance metrics such as accuracy, false-positive rate, f-measure, and detection rate were used. The metric True Positive (TP) measures how accurately malware is categorized. False Positive (FP) refers to the number of instances where harmless instances are incorrectly classified as malware, while True Negative

FileName	Load Imag	CreateFile	RegOpen	RegOpen	RegQuery	CreateFile	CreateFile
CodeBlocks.csvtest.c	135	0	0	0	0	0	416
4malware.csvtest.cs	1133	0	0	0	0	0	5264
854137.exe_malwar	50	0	0	0	0	0	85
Eclipse.csvtest.csv	118	0	0	0	0	0	200
Python.csvtest.csv	1907	0	0	0	0	0	2406
Skype.csvtest.csv	0	0	0	0	0	0	0
spyder.csvtest.csv	26	0	0	0	0	0	2
5malware.csvtest.cs	316	0	0	0	0	0	16876
6malware.csvtest.cs	211	0	0	0	0	0	18003
7malware.csvtest.cs	1660	0	0	0	0	0	8953

Fig. 6. Feature vectors

(TN) refers to the number of instances where harmless situations are correctly classified as benign, and False Negative (FN) refers to the number of instances where malware tests are incorrectly classified as benign.

4 Results

The results section summarizes the key findings of the experiment and discusses the use of the suggested framework. Various algorithms are utilized for learning purposes at the point when execution is evaluated. The best results are obtained when designing and analyzing machine learning models using cross-validation with k = 10. The statistics that are used to evaluate test results include Detection Rate (DR), False Positive Rate (FPR), F-score, and Accuracy. The model was designed and verified with three major classifiers of machine learning such as J48, Random Forest (RF), and Logistic Model Tree (LMT) to estimate the best-suited classifier for the study [12]. After the experimentation, the model achieved the results shown in Fig. 7.

Classifier	DR (%)	FPR	F-score (%)	Accuracy (%)
J48	88.8	37.5	80	76.4
RF	100	12.5	94.7	94.11
LMT	88.8	25	84.2	82.35
SLR	88.8	25	84.2	82.3
SMO	88.8	25	84.2	82.3

Fig. 7. Classification results

Fig. 8. Model results (a) Operation filtering (b) Action type naming (c) Risk score (d) Frequency and features

(d)

Fig. 8. (*continued*)

It is clear from Fig. 7 that the model achieved better accuracy for the Random Forest classifier. Figure 8 displays each algorithm's model results.

5 Conclusion and Future Work

To gather execution routes across many Virtual Machines and transmit them to the behavior-detection system, the study started the process by thoroughly analyzing the file samples using key tools. The behavior detection system was used to refine the data. This identification technique generates behaviors and features using the suggested SCBM. This includes different file types, system types, system call paths, and system calls. Corresponding to this, malicious feature routes are distinguished from harmful ones. The final output following frequency computation is recorded in a CSV file after going through all refinement steps. The learning-based system will then get this file and train on it. Finally, these models were utilized to determine whether the samples were harmful. Our evaluation results show that the suggested computations combined with AI (ML) classifiers result in a detection rate of 90.4%, a false-positive rate of 2.3%, and an accuracy of 83.5%. Our findings imply that by combining the recommended feature extraction and selection phases with a suitable learning-based detection method, the outcomes may be enhanced. We found that the Random Forest Classifier performed better than the other classification models. We have currently investigated malware on several Windows Operating System versions. The proposed framework may be expanded in a subsequent effort to accommodate Linux and macOS OS frameworks.

References

1. Havanje, N.S., Kumar, K.R., Shenoy, S.N., Rao, A.S., Thimmappayya, R.K.: Secure and reliable data access control mechanism in multi-cloud environment with inter-server communication security. Suranaree J. Sci. Technol. **29**(3) (2022)

2. Liao, H.J., Lin, C.H., Lin, Y.C., Tung, K.Y.: Intrusion detection system: a comprehensive review. J. Netw. Comput. Appl. **36**(1), 16–24 (2013)
3. Aslan, Ö.A., Samet, R.: A comprehensive review on malware detection approaches. IEEE Access **8**, 6249–6271 (2020)
4. Gibert, D., Mateu, C., Planes, J.: The rise of machine learning for detection and classification of malware: research developments, trends and challenges. J. Netw. Comput. Appl. **153**, 102526 (2020)
5. Calix, R.A., Singh, S.B., Chen, T., Zhang, D., Tu, M.: Cyber security tool kit (CyberSecTK): a Python library for machine learning and cyber security. Information **11**(2), 100 (2020)
6. Rao, A.S., Aruna Kumar, S.V., Jogi, P., Chinthan Bhat, K., Kuladeep Kumar, B., Gouda, P.: Student placement prediction model: a data mining perspective for outcome-based education system. Int. J. Recent Technol. Eng. (IJRTE) **8**, 2497–2507 (2019)
7. Nagesh Shenoy, H., Kumar, K.A., Shenoy, S.N., Rao, A.S., Rajgopal, K.T.: Exploring deep learning techniques in cloud computing to detect malicious network traffic: a sustainable computing approach. Int. J. Wirel. Microw. Technol. (IJWMT) **11**(5), 9–17 (2021)
8. Shhadat, I., Hayajneh, A., Al-Sharif, Z.A.: The use of machine learning techniques to advance the detection and classification of unknown malware. Procedia Comput. Sci. **170**, 917–922 (2020)
9. Singh, J., Singh, J.: Detection of malicious software by analyzing the behavioral artifacts using machine learning algorithms. Inf. Softw. Technol. **121**, 106273 (2020)
10. Aslan, Ö., Ozkan-Okay, M., Gupta, D.: Intelligent behavior-based malware detection system on cloud computing environment. IEEE Access **9**, 83252–83271 (2021)
11. Chemmakha, M., Habibi, O., Lazaar, M.: Improving machine learning models for malware detection using embedded feature selection method. IFAC-PapersOnLine **55**(12), 771–776 (2022)
12. Rao, A.S., Sandhya, S., Anusha, K., Arpitha, C.N., Meghana, S.N.: Exploring deep learning techniques for kannada handwritten character recognition: a boon for digitization. Int. J. Adv. Sci. Technol. **29**(5), 11078–11093 (2020)

Constraint Based Clustering Technique for Web Services

Sumathi Pawar[(⊠)], Manjula Gururaj, Roopa, Nirajan N. Chiplunkar,
and RajaLaxmi Samaga

Nitte (Deemed to be University), NMAMIT, Karkala, Karnataka, India
pawarsumathi@gmail.com

Abstract. Web services are loosely coupled methods which need to be located and used according to the requirement. Loose coupling nature of Web services made the system to integrate or combine constituent Web services of a standalone business. A Web service application that can compose the Web service from different organizations will have transactions that span the multiple services. It is difficult for an application to create a software component and use it if it is unlikely to be reused. Therefore, this system provides reusability feature that allowed composing the Web services and these composable services are integrated into an application. Service composing is an ability to combine Web Services into complex applications to get the coarser grained behavior. The Web services may contain more than one operation. These operations are required to be clustered according to the required constraints. This paper is focused on constraint-based clustering to group the Web services according to user request for faster access. Constraint based clustering is a technique to integrate Web services according to required constraints. The system performance is checked with real time available Web Services during dynamic composition. This is a novel approach of clustering due to dynamic technique of collecting data during run-time.

Keywords: Constraint based clustering · Web services · WSDL · Composite services

1 Introduction

Constraint based clustering is a process of grouping the service operations according to assumed conditions. Integration of operations is the process of connecting the operations according to the input requirements [16, 17]. To get large information through a flow, it is required to compose Web services. Service designers create services for independent reuse using bottom-up design. So single web service may not be sufficient to satisfy user requests. Therefore, integration or composition of these modular Web services/operations is necessary to develop an application for user requirement. For example "invoice processing" service is a complex service which uses a "bank service", a "customer service", and description of an item ordered. These services can be used separately or together as complex service. The interaction among these services should take care about service parameters like pre-condition, post-condition, type of web service composition.

The core of the service composition is sequencing and correlation. If the system has to understand the step by step operations of the business, the user must provide these steps of operations and system must provide a technique to maintain information across operations invoked, which is called as correlation. To fully automate the creation of a composed Web Service application, the user need additional information such as service availability, response time and service quality information. It is difficult to get these information without service execution (no UDDI). In early days QoS information of the Web services was stored by UDDI. Because of the absence of UDDI it is possible to get QoS information such as availability, response time and security information only after execution of the services.

The existing systems used to pass the transaction context from service to service are Business Transaction Protocol (BTP) from OASIS, WS-Transaction from IBM and Microsoft and Activity Service from OMG that provide reliable outcomes. JTS and JTA transaction managers are used to manage and coordinate distributed, ACID transactions.

1.1 Web Service Composition

In this research, Web service composition is also referred as integration. Composition models are organized into three dimensions-orchestration, choreography and coordination. Composition language like WS-BPEL (Web Service Business Process Extraction Language) can be relatively translated onto classes of formalism like automata, Petri net, process alzebra and other formalisms.

But the proposed research is not using UDDI registry as the third party because of unavailability of public UDDI registries. [16, 17] Instead, this research is using Bingo search engine technique. The user of the proposed system gives the required functional word as a query to the search engine in the form "functional_word?wsdl" during run-time. Then the search engine returns various links of WSDL to related services. The input parameters of the operations of these WSDL are compared with user queried parameters and those having non-zero support value are considered.

1.2 Web Service Description Language

The WSDL describes the service which belongs to service description layer.

This layer describes the three aspects of the web services.

- Operations of a Web Service
- Messages of the service that accepts
- Binding protocols to access the service

Web services are described by the Web Service Description Language (WSDL) by which the service consumer is able to discover a set of useful operations. In this research, WSDL's abstract descriptions and concrete descriptions are processed to get service information for satisfying the user request or for integration of the service.

1.3 Location Transparency

According to the Web service concept, service environment achieves location transparency because the location of Web service is stored in a registry. But service registry UDDI is not public as specified in the literature review. In this research UDDI is not used. But location transparency is achieved by the Bingo search engine which finds the service even though the service is moved from one location to another. Bingo searches the WSDL of the service and even though service is moved from one plat-form to another, no changes to the client application is necessary.

1.4 Scalability and Availability

This system is scalable because at the client side, client only knows interface of the service and not its implementation. At the server side any number of services can be added without overhead at the client application. In this system, availability of the service is high because even though one service fails, other similar service's information are stored in the cluster and used for satisfying the user request.

1.5 Dynamic Web Service Discovery

The constraint based clustering is helpful in discovering Web services dynamically. Exiting researches were discovering Web services using UDDI. According to the survey conducted, it is practically checked that UDDI is absent since the year 2006. This motivated our research to use search engines. The search engine used in this system is Bingo. The search result retrieved from the Bingo gives discovered information of the Web services from all the servers in World Wide Web in the form of WSDL. The search query that can be given to the search engine is prepared according to the user given request during run time, which makes the system dynamic.

1.6 Dynamic Web Service Invocation

Clusters which stores the operations are helpful in dynamic service invocation which is done at run time by filling the required parameters for invocation of the Web service dynamically. The parameters need to be filled are according to the user requested function and matched parameters are extracted from suitable WSDL of the Web services and populated in the place of the unknown parameters. The entire process is automatically executed and input parameters are asked from the user if user knows it. In the proposed research, human interaction is required only to enter the input parameter's value if input is known to the user. Or else, this system automatically searches the unknown input by using available Web services. These values are searched automatically in the online World Wide Web to satisfy the user requests. This reduces the burden of the user filling the unknown parameters of the required Web services.

1.7 Automatic and Dynamic Web Service Composition or Integration

The proposed constraint algorithm is also helpful in integration of the Web services that involves the task of service search, service selection and the connecting required operations of the Web services. The connecting of different operations is done only when it is required to resolve the values of unknown parameters which are resulted into the Web service composition. Many existing researches did service composition using different techniques, which need some prior information about the selection of services. But in the proposed research, without any knowledge-base, Web services are composed or integrated according to the requirement of the user which makes the system fully dynamic. In the proposed system, to overcome dynamic nature of the Web services, search of composable service is performed automatically by using search engines to get the available online Web service operations through clusters.

1.8 Automatic Web Service Execution Monitoring

The proposed provides clusters with input parameters and operation names of Web services. In the existing researches, the automatic service execution is not resolved by filling the parameters dynamically. The monitoring of the service execution is necessary to get information about the availability of services and the response time. Now a day due to absence of UDDI, no source like UDDI gives information about the QoS of the services. This information are noted during execution of Web services and stored in the repository, so that these information are used in the future during the composition of the Web services. The failing of the service execution is also recorded, so that in future the same service is not used and instead other similar services may be used. The composition plan generated in this system is tested for availability and response time and gives QoS to future requests.

1.9 Scope of the System

The proposed system is implemented as client for using existing online Web services. This research is implemented for information retrievable online Web services and not for transactional Web services. Because transactional operations cannot be implemented without co-ordination between executions of operations and there are no such free transactional Web services.

There are very limited WSDL described Web services available in the online nowadays and most of these services are information retrievable Web services. Therefore scope of the system is information retrievable Web services and the present system is beneficial only when there are composable Web services available in the online. By considering the atomicity of the operations, Web services are maintaining fine grained level of information. Hence scope of this system is, also to get coarse grained information by dynamically composing the operations.

2   Literature Survey

[1] Authors proposed Ontology based context models for context aware applications. They provided a discovery algorithm which matches the requested word with service

Ontology and which gives best matched service to the user. Authors considered location, time, person or agent as key contexts and included service Ontology in Context broker architecture.

[2] Each incoming request randomly chooses the one k dominating services to respond to the request. The Web services selected by top-k dominating services reduce the computation space instead of selecting the best solution. When concurrent requests are given to the same service, response time of that service may reduce due to many reasons. But in this system as k increases, the time of retrieving top-k dominating service also increases. Hence the response time of this system also increases. Authors provided an algorithm for selection of top k dominating Web services by calculation of the scores. But the cost of calculating the score of the Web services depends upon the efficiency of the algorithm and in order to quickly obtain the top k dominating services, they aggregate R-tree (aRtree). But in the proposed research, selection of Web services depend on user opinion, and hence user interaction is very important in the selection of Web services.

[3] The quality of Service is a factor to enhance the efficiency of Web Services. Technical quality and managerial quality are 2 kinds of qualities of Web services. The operational aspects of Web services are called technical quality. Technical quality deals with performance, response time, reliability, latency, execution time, throughput, dependability, availability, reliability, failure semantics, failure masking, operation semantics, exception handling, compensation, robustness/ flexibility, capacity, scalability, security, continuous availability, compliance, reputation/positive feedback and network related QoS. The managerial qualities deal with management information such as ownership, contact, payment etc.

But no such QoS parameters are available nowadays for real-time Web services because of a permanent shutdown of UDDIs. Therefore the proposed system could not use QoS parameters, instead it gives user satisfaction as feedback to rank the Web services.

[4] Depending on the nearest location of the service, service invocation is done to minimize data transmission time and cost. They did it by first selecting the k number of abstract services' service library, and then from each group selecting the one candidate service. But they assumed that service is gathered as a set of services within one area and not randomly distributed. By considering the returning time of service result, they calculated the distance of the service from the consumer.

[5] Maintenance of RESTful Web service is easier than the maintenance of SOAP-WSDL Web services. RESTful web services communicate using XML files and HTTP-GET and SOAP-WSDL Web services communicate using HTTP-POST. Authors proved that maintenance of RESTful web services at server side is easier than SOAP-WSDL Web services because they are light weight.

[6] TESSI, a tool based on TASSA, is a solution for WSDL-based testing of both single and composite web services. Test cases are defined in the XML form and each test case has two parameters, test case name and test case template. TASSA carries out the tasks such as identification of service operations, the creation of SOAP request messages, the definition of assertions at BPEL variable level, execution of test cases with sending and receiving of SOAP messages and collection of test outputs for result analysis.

TASSA framework tests the Web services for not only functional correctness but also for performance. Black box testing for BPEL is also followed which checks end-point orchestrations. Execution of test cases provides details about the behavior of the service.

Isolation tool, Data Dependency Analysis tool, Value Generation Tool, Injection tool and Test Case Generation tool are different tools available in TASSA framework. But the tool is applied only during design time testing of service Oriented Applications.

[7] The network usage is better than WS-Management, because the size of SOAP request and response messages is larger in WS-Management than in SNMP. But in Web Service-based management middle-ware models they managed single service at a time and not considered complex composite services. In the proposed research, the network load will be reduced because of usage of MOLAP to handle big size of WSDL of single Web services.

BPMN [8] modelor and tactic models are created to specify different steps of the composition and each tactic is implemented by service operations. Discovering the requirements are affected by unknown context is handled by creation of rule. Observation of context and collection of context information is done by Evelution planners.

But creation of composition models is static in nature which does not handle the dynamic requirements without the knowledge of context. The proposed research handles dynamic requirement by dynamic searching of Web services and by generating dynamic composition plans.

[9] In a sensor network performance of REST is better compared to SOAP, and it is recommended by equipment vendors to use RESTful Webservices for applications consuming embedded resources. But the proposed system works on only information retrievable services which are able to provide secured data transfer for future works. Therefore this system is not using RESTful Web services.

[10] The combinatorial optimization problem is composed by many services to build Service Networks that satisfy many requirements based on cost-effectiveness. Execution Time, reliability and price of services are used as QoS parameters. The performance is measured based on single requirement and also based on multiple requirement. This system uses Service Network as a tool which gives number of connections between services and the QSC approaches, which provides global QoS performance. Performance of the system is measured with total benefit and execution time. But in the proposed research, service execution performance is increased using MOLAP data model.

Due to removal of some Web services and change of information such as change of transaction fees, the authors created the concept of [11] change management of long term composition [12]. The failure in distribution of reputation values is that, the component Web service is never be penalized for poor performance of other peer component Web services. This is done by reputation propagation by changing the behavior of the individual services and thus increasing the reputation of the composite Web services. They divided the service composition into horizontal composition, vertical composition and hybrid composition. Web service composition is done by an agency which distributes the reputation values fairly. Here reputation is consumers perception about Quality of Service such as performance, reliability and availability, about the service they invokes. But when the consumer invokes composite Web service, their perception will be about composite Web services and these perceptions will not be about component Web services. Therefore average of reputation value is computed and distributed to component Web services. Reduction of reputation values are handled by composition orchestrator and perform the decision in finding the malicious Web services. It is a very important role of orchestrator to make decision.

[13] Another important issue of QoS is Trust based management of Web service which is divided into different types-Policy-based trust, Reputation-based trust etc. Trust Metrics given for the Web services are Execution Time, Response Time, Latency, Availability, Reliability and Remedies. As given in the survey WS-POLICY is the policy document that provides the policy-information and reputation is based on user perception reputation of the Web services [14]. In existing system, term pairs are entered in the Google search engine and snippet retrieved from Google search engine is used to get association of words such as "apple computer", "hardware software" etc. They categorized those terms into particular contexts and then generated the context vectors by computing the TDF/IDF values. This context is used to calculate the service similarity.

In proposed system, after extracting the WSDL elements of Web services, the elements such as service name, operation name, input and output features are compared to the service elements of the cluster of the Web services. Precision, recall and F-Measure are the factors used to measure the performance of the system. In the proposed research, every component Web services' availability and performance time is recorded and do not depend on one centralized system. In the proposed system, QoS factors are recorded during each Web service composition and current values are considered for next transaction.

3 Clustering Web Services with Constraint-Based Clustering

In this algorithm the WSDL links of each requested functional words are given as input to the procedure named constraint Based Clustering. The operations of each service are compared with each other for exact, partial and synonym matching factors and stored in the appropriate clusters as given in the pseudo-code below.

Procedure constraintBasedClustering(RetrievedWSDL_Links)
Step 1: Initialize I to 0
Step 2: For each WSDL_Links of RetrievedWSDL_Links extract i^{th} service name
Step 3: Extract operation names for i^{th} service
Step 4: Keep the operations in the ith cluster : i=i+1
Endfor
Step 5: initialize j to 0
Step 6: For each jth operation of cluster
Step 7 : Apply Decomposition Rules on j^{th} operation and store functional part of operation name in sourceOp:
* k=0*
Step 8: for each kth operation of the cluster
Step 9 : Apply Decomposition Rules on k^{th} operation and store functional part of operation name in destOp
Step 10 : If sourceOp and destOp exactly matches then
Step 11 : store destOp in ExactMatchingCluster(j) : j=j+1
Else
Step 12: if sourceOp and destOp matches partially then
Step 13: store destOp in partialMatchingClusters(i) : j=j+1
else
Step 14: Retrieve words similar to destOp from Wordnet and store it in SynonymWords
Step 15: For each synonym of SynonymWords
Step 16: Compare sourceOp to synonym
Step 17: If matches then store destOp in synonymMatchingClusters(j) :j=j+1
Step 18 : Break :Endif: Endfor: Endif : Endif : k=k+1: Endfor: Endfor : End Procedure

---

Fig. 1. Constraint based clustering

The constraint-based clustering is algorithm shown in the Fig. 1. The flow of this clustering process is shown in the Fig. 2. In this clustering, the operation names of retrieved WSDL links of requested functional word are stored in the cluster C1 initially. After applying decomposing process to operation names of each operation, the clusters are formed as shown in the pseudo code of the Fig. 2.

As an example input to the proposed system, consider the user requested function is "Weather". The different WSDL links retrieved for this request are given in the Table 1 of Sect. 5. Among the operations of the "GlobalWeather" service, the operations "GetWeather" and "GetCitiesByCountry" are to be tokenized using decomposition rule. The sets generated are S1 = {Get, Weather} and S2 = {Get, Cities}. In the operation "GetCitiesByCountry" the token after the stop word "By" is "Country". This token is considered as input token and stored in the input set of this operation.

The requested function "Weather" is compared with the tokens of first set S1. If it matches exactly to any token, then the <operation> name belong to this set is stored in the exact matching cluster of this service. Otherwise if it matches partially, then the <operation> name belong to this set is stored in the partially matched clusters of this service.

If in both situations if the requested token does not match, then words similar to the <operation> name element is retrieved from the *Wordnet* dictionary and compared against the user requested functional word. If any of the synonym word matches to the user requested function exactly, then this <operation> element is stored in the synonym matching clusters of this service. Finally all the exact matching clusters are merged together. Similarly the partially matching and synonym matching clusters also merged.

In the "getWeather" operation, the "Weather" token of the set S1 is matched with the requested functional word "Weather" exactly. Since "GetWeather" operation is stored in the exact matching clusters. There are no matching tokens in the set S2 for the requested functional word.

Each operation name is *Decomposed* first. Care is taken when stop words are removed because the operation name "GetWeatherByZipcode" and "ZipcodeToCityState" are not similar operations even though it contain "zipcode" as common word. Therefore when tokenizing the operation names, the words like "By", "To" are interpreted properly. The operation names which have tokens before "By" are interpreted as operation name and tokens which come after "By" are interpreted as input names. The names of the operations which come before the "To" are treated as input parameter name and parameters which come after the "To" are operation names. Therefore these two operations belong to different clusters.

The operations of other semantically matched service for "Weather" request are operations of "WeatherForecast" service i.e. "GetWeatherByZipCode" and "GetWeatherByPlaceName". Here token sets of these operations are S1 = {"Get", "Weather"} and S2 = {"Get", "Weather"} respectively. These tokens exactly match with the requested functional word and stored in the exact matched clusters. Tokens after the stop word "By" are "ZipCode" and "PlaceName" are considered as sets of inputs of respective operations.

The flow of forming the cluster of operations of retrieved WSDL links are shown in the pseudo code of Fig. 2.

C1 = Cluster of Retrieved WSDL links of requested functional word.

CO(k) = k^{th} Cluster of operations of services of kth WSDL link where k ranges from 1 to n and n is an element of finite set of natural number.

CEM(k) = k^{th} Cluster of exactly matching operations to the functional word.

CPM(k) = k^{th} Cluster of partially matching operations to the functional word.

CSM(k) = k^{th} Cluster of synonym matching of operations of this service to requested functional word.

Here exact matching (CEM(k)), partial matching (CPM(k)) and synonym (CSM(k)) matching clusters are three constraint based clusters formed through this process.

The clustering process with score is shown in the Fig. 3.

At first each of the WSDL link is considered to extract operation names. Each operation name is decomposed and requested functional word is compared with decomposed tokens. The cluster of exactly matching services CEM(k) stores the operations which exactly matches to the requested functional word. The weight given to the tokens/operations matches exactly is 0.5. The partially matching operations to the functional word are given by weight 0.3 and stored in the cluster CPM(k). The synonym matched operations to requested functional words are stored in the cluster CSM(k) and weight given to synonym match is 0.2.

Initially all the operations of the service$_1$ to service$_n$ of retrieved WSDL links are stored in the cluster called C_1 to C_n Where n is the element of finite set of natural numbers.

Then requested functional word is compared with the decomposed operation names of C_k and if requested functional word matches exactly then that operation name will be stored in the CEM(k).

If Requested functional word does not match exactly to any operation of C_k then CPM(k) and CSM(k) are formed for partial matching and synonym matching where k is the element of finite set of natural numbers.

All exactly matching operations are merged into exact matching clusters. This CEM cluster gives all exactly matching operations to the requested functional word. All synonym matching operations are merged into synonym matching clusters and all partial matching clusters are merged into partial matching clusters. If exactly matching clusters are empty for a functional word then partial matching clusters are considered. If partial matching clusters are also empty then synonym matching clusters are considered. If all the clusters are empty then it is concluded that requested functional words does not exist as Web services in the online.

During selection of matched operations, if no operation is matched exactly then the partial matching operations are retrieved from already framed partial matching clusters. If partial matching clusters are empty then operations from synonym matching clusters are retrieved.

3.1 Clustering for Integration of Web Services

Some of the operations of a service can form a cluster because these operations are linked to each other and are integrated according to the user requirement. Different types of clusters formed are given in the following sections.

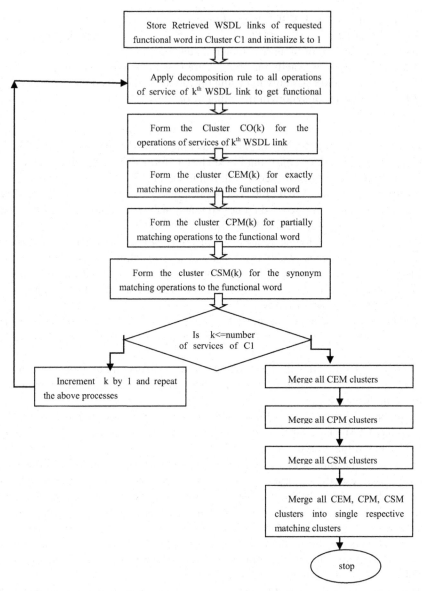

Fig. 2. Flow of process of clustering of operations which matches functional word through constraint-based clustering.

3.1.1 Self link Clusters

One of the constraint used in this research is, all operations of a service which are supplement to each other are belong to the same cluster. This is shown in Table 2 where all operations of a particular Web service are given together. For example in

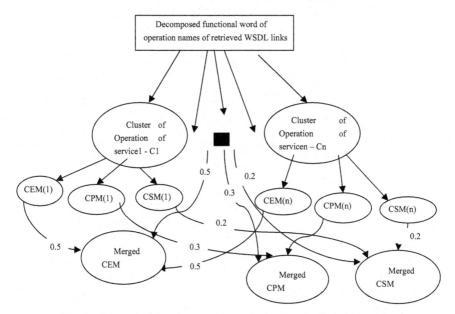

Fig. 3. Exact, partial and synonym matched constraint based Clustering

"GlobalWeather" service the operation "GetWeather" and "GetCitiesByCountry" are related because for GetWeather operation inputs are "CityName" and "CountryName".

To get information about names of cities of different countries it is required to invoke the operation "GetCitiesByCountry". Therefore both "GetWeather" and "GetCitiesByCountry" will be belonging to one link-based cluster. This is justified by comparing input elements of "GetWeather" with <operation>/<output> elements of "GetCitiesByCountry".

Each input element of the all the operations of the required service are compared with <operation>/<output> elements of all the remaining operations of the same service. Clusters will be framed for operations which are supplement to each other within the same service for getting the value of input of operations. This type of clustering is called *self-link clustering*. In the self link clustering the input of particular operation is satisfied by output of other operations of same services (Fig. 4).

3.1.2 Output-to-Input Linked Clustering

The output-input linked clusters contain operations which are linked together. The services which require to get the input from the output of operations of other services are gathered into a cluster called output-input linked clusters. Comparing the input elements to the <operation>/<output> elements is done by exact matching function.

In the Fig. 5 the following abbreviations used.

CS – Composit Service.
CS1 – "Input1 of the Composit Service".
CS2 – "Input2 of the Composit Service".

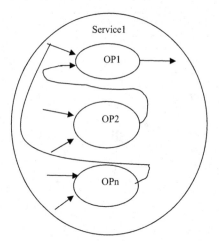

Fig. 4. Self-link clusters

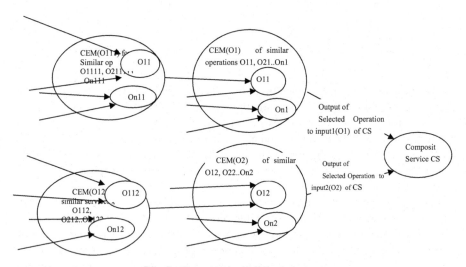

Fig. 5. Output to input linked clusters

CEM(O1) – "Cluster of exact matching operations which has matching output to the input1 of composit service".

CEM(O2) – "Cluster of exact matching operations which has matching output to the input2 of composit service".

CEM(O111) – "Cluster of similar operations which matches input1 of operation O11".

O1 – "Operation1 which matches input1 of CS".

O2 – "Operation2 which matches input2 of CS".

O1111 – "Operation1 which matches input1 of the operation11".

On111 – "Operation which matches input1 of the operation11".

O1122 – "Operation1 which matches input2 of the operation12".

On122 – "Operation which matches input2 of the operation12".

The above Fig. 5 shows the output-input link based clusters which have similar services of different community. Consider the composite service CS which has unknown input value for both input1 and input2. When there is a search for input1 it is called as composit search1 (CS1) for input1 and when there is a search for input2, then it is called as composit search2 (CS2) for input2.

In the Fig. 5 which shows output-input link based clustering, the similar operations which match the input1 of CS (complex service), form the cluster CEM (O1). From this cluster, suitable operation is selected by using weight matrix of WSDL. The cluster CEM (O1) gives similar operations O11, O21…On1 which matches the input1 of complex service CS. The value of another input of complex service (CS2) is also unknown. The cluster CEM (O2) includes similar operations O12, O22..On2 (n operations) which have matching output to the input2 of complex service(CS). The cluster of similar operations CEM (O111) gives matching operations which have the output that matches to the name of input1 of the operation O11.

4   Implementation

This research is implemented by using existing Web services in the online. The Web services can also be created in the local server. To create the Web services in the local server the Tomcat server is used in the proposed system. In one Tomcat instance, one service is started. Number of Web services is kept in the run mode in different instances of Tomcat Web server. Each Web service is running in the one instance of the Tomcat. But because of bottleneck of the capacity of the server, thousands of Web services cannot be kept in the run-mode simultaneously. For this purpose number of servers are required. Therefore it is recommended to use available online Web services. But available online Web services consume enough bandwidth to retrieve WSDL and more storage space to process and store the WSDL elements.

This research is implemented in Java Eclipse framework with 8 GB Ram and i5 processor. Code is written and executed for real time Web services. To store the operation elements of WSDL in the, it is required to extract operation elements from the WSDL. The <operation> element is extracted from the WSDL using.

WSDLHelper.GetOperations(portTypes) statement.

The portTypes is the element of WSDL which contains set of operation elements. The portTypes is extracted by using the statement.

portTypes = WSDLHelper.getPortTypes(WSDLdefinition).

Each operation is to be iterated and stored in the cluster using operation_keylevel2[cnt][count] = Searchops.get(count).getName() statement.

The input parameters are stored using the statement.

inputlevel3[cnt][count][j]   =   WSDLHelper.getInMessageParts(Searchops.get (count)).

The above statement stores the input parameters of the searched operations. If the input parameters store correct parameter names, then it is helpful to the user to enter the value of input parameters. If the input parameter names are given as "parameters" in WSDL, then the real input parameters' names are obtained by mining same operation name's binding information. It is already observed from the WSDL data set that, unknown input parameters can be mined by different binding information of the same operation.

Code snippet to interpret the input parameter names from the <operation> element

```
String s = Searchops.get(count).getName().toString(); //To get searched operation
    String[] r = s.split("(?=\\p{Upper})"); // To split according to Camel Case
    for(int i=0;i<r.length;i++)
    {
    if(r[i].equalsIgnoreCase("By"))
    {String[] r2 = s.split("By");
            inpString=r2[1];
            break;}
    else
            if(r[i].equalsIgnoreCase("To"))
            {String[] r2 = s.split("To");
            inpString=r2[0];
            break;}
            else
            inpString="parameters"; }}
            else
            inpString=Require_Input_List.get(j).getName();
```

Fig. 6. Code snippet to extract input parameters from operation names of the Web servic

This code snippet of Fig. 6 splits the operation name according to the camel case. For example if the operation name is "GetWeatherByZipcode" then it is splitted as Get Weather By Zipcode. If the operation name is "CityStateToZipcode" then it is splitted as City State To Zipcode. Here the word after "By" and word before the "To" are input parameter. This word is stored in the place of unknown parameter name.

As a search result, Web services with "UsZip" and "AddressLookup" services are received as results. In this "UsZip" service is matched partially to the "zipcode". Therefore the operations of this service "GetInfoByAreaCode", "GetInfoByZIP", "GetInfoByCity" and "GetInfoByState" are listed and shown to the user. Among these operations if the user selects "GetInfoByZIP" then the input parameter "UsZip" is unknown to the user. Therefore, this operation cannot give required output and the user has to select "GetInfoByCity" where the output parameter is "Zipcode" and input parameter is "City". This operation matches with the unknown element because the search technique found the unknown input in the output of this operation element.

When the operation selected by the user is "GetInfoByCity", then the input parameter of this service "UsCity" is shown to the user and user is allowed to enter the city name. If the city name is entered by the user then the system invokes "GetInfoByCity" operation of the "USZip" service and returns the result. The returned results are very large and are in the XML form which has more than 300 rows of zipcodes of different areas. But there will be a deserialization problem in getting these results because some of the XML data types of these results cannot be deserialized by the java data types. Therefore invocation of "UsZip" service results in the exception and fails in returning results. Hence the query for the same service with populated operation name and input parameters are given as URL in the browser in the following form.

URL = http://www.webservicex.net/uszip.asmx/GetInfoByCity?UsCity=Washington

At first the above query is stored in the URL object and given through the J2EE API as

BufferedReader in = new BufferedReader(new InputStreamReader (URL.openStream()));

The above method creates the buffer to store the results and XML results will be processed to extract suitable data.

5 Results

The below Table 1 shows the links retrieved for the request and returned results' operation names are clustered using constraint-based clustering technique. Support and confidence of search precision is calculated.

Table 1. Links of retrieved WSDL links for request Weather?wsdl

Requested word	Service name	Retrieved WSDL links
Weather	GlobalWeather	http://www.webservicex.com/globalweather.asmx?WSDL
	TemperatureConversions	http://webservices.daehosting.com/services/TemperatureConversions.wso?WSDL
	WeatherForecast	http://www.webservicex.net/WeatherForecast.asmx?WSDL
	CurrencyConvertor	http://www.webservicex.net/CurrencyConvertor.asmx?WSDL
	Service	http://www.ejse.com/WeatherService/Service.asmx?WSDL
	Service1	http://www.tempe.gov/wx/Default.asmx?WSDL

Figure 7 shows the graph of support(S) value of integrated/composed web services to give result of complex web services. Here request given by user is weather of a country of unknown input parameter value. Then this unknown input parameter will be resolved by the system with the help of constraint-based clustering. The result gives 40%, 60% and 40% support values with the real time web services for different composition plans. Support and confidence value of composition is increased if there is a greater number of similar services available during runtime.

Table 2. Cluster of Operations and input parameters of retrieved WSDL links for request Weather?wsdl

Service key	Operation name	Input parameters
Weather	Get_Weather	Parameters
	Get_Cities_By_Country	Parameters
	Get_Weather	CountryName CityName
	Get_Cities_By_Country	Country
	Get_Weather	CountryName CityName
	Get_Cities_By_Country	Country
WeatherForecast	GetWeatherbyPlaceName	Parameters PlaceName
	GetWeatherbyPlaceName	PlaceName
	GetWeatherbyPlaceName	Parameters
	GetWeatherbyZipcode	Zipcode
	GetWeatherbyZipcode	Zipcode
	GetWeatherbyZipcode	

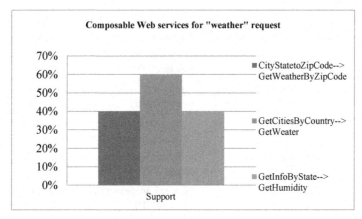

Fig. 7. Support of multiple composition plans using constraint based clustering

Precision, recall and f-measure are calculated using Eqs. 4, 5 and 6. As shown in the graph of Fig. 8, performance is calculated in percentage values. Precision is 58%, recall is 59% and F-measure is 52% for a particular request. This performance varies for different requested Web services according to user requirement.

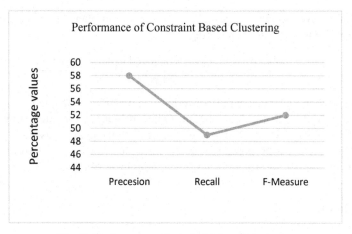

Fig. 8. Performance of constraint based clustering

6 Analysis

In this research using constraint-based clustering, service composition is achieved with following performance factors.

6.1 Support and Confidence of Search Precision

To measure the precision of WSDL retrieval, support and confidence factors are used. The precision is given with the following equation

$$\text{Precision} = \frac{Retrieved \cap relevant}{retrieved} \tag{1}$$

The search precision of retrieved matched WSDL from the Bingo search engine is calculated as dividing the count of relevant WSDL by count of retrieved WSDL.

In the same way support and confidence of matched operation in the retrieved Web services are calculated in Eq. 2 and Eq. 3 as

$$\text{Support} = \frac{count\ of\ matched\ term\ in\ any\ element\ of\ WSDL}{count\ of\ retrieved\ WSDL} \tag{2}$$

$$\text{Confidence} = \frac{Count\ of\ requested\ functionality\ in\ operation\ element}{total\ number\ of\ operations} \tag{3}$$

$$\text{Recall} = \frac{Retrieved \cap relevant}{relevant} \tag{4}$$

$$\text{F-Measure} = \frac{2*Precision * Recall}{(Precision + Recall)} \tag{5}$$

Performance of this system varies according to real time available services because this is dynamic real time Web service clustering system.

Equation 6 gives support(S) of multiple composition plans [1] of real time Web services using constraint based clustering

$$S = \frac{\text{Number of Web services invloved in the composition}}{\text{Total retrieved WSDL links}} \quad (6)$$

It is found that constraint-based clustering is a novel approach and constraint can be changed according to the requirement. Other techniques for integrating the web services includes WS-BPEL which requires separate tool and also it is static version of the composition. But our proposed research is dynamic version of composition method which produces output according to run-time requirement of user.

7 Conclusions

Existing systems are focused on clustering of Web services using machine learning which produces models of context from the terms retrieved from the Web. The training of SVM is done separately for each domain. This system uses the result snippet of the search engines manually such as Wikipedia and Google to get retrieved results. But the proposed system processes the search results of search engine automatically and uses search precision and response time for measure the performance of the system.

The usage of constraint-based clustering in the proposed system not only increases the performance in terms of speed but also saves the storage space. WSDL is big in size which has several elements. Storing all the retrieved WSDL elements consumes more storage space. Retrieving WSDL every time through the internet increases the bandwidth consumption. Hence the proposed system saves the usage of internet in retrieving the remote WSDL and made the system more efficient compared to other systems. Invocation of Web services requires service name element, operation element, input element, target namespace and WSDL link of the suitable Web services. The usage of this technique to store these elements makes the system more efficient because this occupies very less space. It is known that service has different operations and the operation has different input elements which are stored in the cluster. Retrieval of elements of cluster is fast because no need to process the entire WSDL to extract the required elements.

References

1. Sumathi, Pandith, K., Chiplunkar, N., Shetty, S.: Dynamic search and integration of Web services. In: Choudrie, J., Mahalle, P., Perumal, T., Joshi, A. (eds.) IOT with Smart Systems. Smart Innovation, Systems and Technologies, vol. 312, pp. 613–625. Springer, Singapore (2023). https://doi.org/10.1007/978-981-19-3575-6_60
2. Zhang, J., Zhong, F., Yang, Z.: Efficient approach to top-k dominating queries on service selection. In: Proceedings of the 6th IEEE Joint IFIP Wireless and Mobile Networking Conference (WMNC), Dubai, pp. 1–8(2013)
3. R-tree an Article About Data Structure. https://en.wikipedia.org/wiki/R-tree. Accessed 25 Oct 2013
4. Li, Y., Luo, Z., Yin, J.: A location-aware service selection model. Int. J. Serv. Comput. 1(1), 52–66 (2013). IEEE

5. de Oliveira, R.R., Sanchez, R.V.V.: Comparative evaluation of the maintainability of RESTful and SOAP-WSDL web services. In: Proceedings of 7th IEEE International Symposium on the Maintenance and Evolution of Service-Oriented and Cloud-Based Systems (MESOCA), Eindhoven, Netherlands, pp 40–49 (2013)
6. Ilieva, S., Pavlov, V., Manova, I., Manova, D.: A framework for design-time testing of service-based applications at Bpel level. Serdica J. Comput. **5**, 367–384 (2011)
7. Lu, Z., Jie, W., Patrick, H.: Web services standard-based system resource management middleware model, scheme and test. Int. J. Serv. Comput. (IJSC) **2**(1), 25–44 (2015). ISSN 2330-4472
8. BPMN2 Modeler. https://www.eclipse.org/bpmn2-modeler/. The Eclipse Foundation Copyright© 2016. Accessed 12 Mar 2013
9. Lee, S., Jo, J.-Y., Kim, Y.: Environmental sensor monitoring with secure restful web service. Int. J. Serv. Comput. **2**(3), 30–43 (2014). ISSN 2330-4472
10. Wang, Z., Jing, N., Xu, F., Xu, X.: Cost-effective service network planning for mass customization of services. Int. J. Serv. Comput. **2**(4), 15–27 (2014). ISSN 2330-4472
11. Liu, X., Bouguettaya, A., Yu, Q., Malik, Z.: Efficient change management in long-term composed services. Int. J. Serv. Orientat. Comput. Appl. (SOCA) **5**(2), 87–103 (2010). Springer
12. Nepal, S., Malik, Z., Bouguettaya, A.: Reputation management for composite services in service-oriented systems. Int. J. Web Serv. Res. **8**(2), 1–26 (2011)
13. Joseph Manoj, R., Chandrasekar, A.: A literature review on trust management in web services access control. Int. J. Web Serv. Comput. (IJWSC) **4**(3), 1–18 (2013)
14. Kumara, B.T.G.S., Paik, I., Koswatte, K.R.C., Chen, W.: Improving web service clustering through post filtering to bootstrap the service discovery. Int. J. Serv. Comput. **2**(3), 1–13 (2014). ISSN 2330-4472
15. Sumathi, Chiplunkar, N.N., Ashok Kumar, A.: Dynamic discovery of web services. IJITCS **6**(10), 56–62 (2014). ISSN: 2074-9015. https://doi.org/10.5815/ijitcs.2014.10.08
16. Sumathi, Chiplunkar, N.N.: Necessity of dynamic composition plan for web services. In: Proceedings of 2015 International Conference on Applied and Theoretical Computing and Communication Technology (iCATccT), Davangere, pp. 737–742 (2015)
17. Sumathi, Chiplunkar, N.N.: Populating parameters of web services by automatic composition using search precision and WSDL weight matrix. IJCSE (2018, in press). ISSN:1742-7193

Modified K-Neighbor Outperforms Logistic Regression and Random Forest in Identifying Host Malware Across Limited Data Sets

Manish Kumar Rai[✉], K. Haripriya, and Priyanka Sharma

Rashtriya Raksha University, Gandhinagar, India
{manishkumar.rai,priyanka.sharma}@rru.ac.in

Abstract. Using probabilistic risk assessment and decision-making methodology, this study analyzes and manages risks to Supervisory Control and Data Acquisition (SCADA) systems that are made on purpose. Seemingly, the attacker can launch attacks anywhere in the world from a single place. Viruses and other dangerous executables tend to stay in the system for a while and then spread their copy to other systems on the network. One of the greatest issues for security experts is detecting cyber-attacks and starting immediate recovery from them when they have spread across the entire system at a triggered time and are doing significant harm. Any SCADA system that has been compromised can have an effect on the functioning of functional blocks and measured parameters, changes in the operating circumstances of the installations, and abnormal beginnings, stops, and modifications to the installed units as instructed by the attackers. Samples are represented as a separate byte file in this study after the raw dataset has been preprocessed. The byte file is used for both testing and training prediction models using statistical processes, which can then be utilized to detect malware in critical infrastructure systems. Finding malicious executables based on both nature and signature is the focus of this study. Each model's conclusion is found on limited malware data samples; however, these samples produce convincing results for previously unidentified malware. The results of the experiments reveal that, when there are few training samples available for a given harmful file, modified K-neighbor outperforms Logistic Regression and Random Forest.

Keywords: SCADA · Wastewater treatment · Stuxnet · Log loss · Confusion matrix · Precision matrix · Recall matrix · Modified K-neighbor · Logistic regression · Random Forest

1 Introduction

The world will never go for permanent peace. Wars occur constantly, either between nations, states, or even individuals. It is just the mode and approach that will shift. Way back when, two kings had fought to the death over territory and resources. Swords, knives, and other cutting implements of the time were used in the attacks (Singh 1989). Swords and knives were phased out in the late 1990s in preference of firearms, tanks, missiles,

I. Woungang et al. (Eds.): ANTIC 2022, CCIS 1797, pp. 108–124, 2023.
https://doi.org/10.1007/978-3-031-28180-8_8

and other high-tech armament. It appears that the world is once again shifting from using physical weapons to using digital ones. In recent years, the world has witnessed the rise of digital warfare, in which harmful data are sent from one country (Geers et al. 2014) or a group of people to another country in an effort to compromise its key infrastructure (Mwiki et al. 2019). Because this type of infrastructure is essential for the functioning of any nation and the daily lives of its citizens. An attack was discovered on 5 February 2021 at the water treatment facility in Oldsmar, Florida, where the NaOH concentration had been raised from 100 ppm to 11,100 ppm (Cervini et al. 2022). The current conflict between Russia and Ukraine is the latest instance of a hybrid Cyber/conventional war (Mohee 2022; Brantly et al. 2022).

A Wastewater Treatment Plant is an example of Critical Infrastructure where a large mass of raw material processing is done for wastewater treatment procedures (WWTP) and is one of the largest industries in the world (Mathur and Tippenhauer 2016). SCADA (Stouffer and Falco 2006) is frequently used in water and wastewater treatment plants applications (Tuptuk et al. 2021) to connect distant and/or native sensing devices to a central monitoring point, from which coordinated reactions to monitoring data may be launched. WWTPs (Adepu and Mathur 2018) are complex, vibrant systems that are challenging to run and need durable knowledge and continuous observation to operate efficiently. In a WWTP, the number of steps involved in the process are: The mechanical treatment step consists of the following components—The installation of a rare-hole automated sieve; pumping station for raw water; power-driven cleaning gratings, unsanding, and bubbling fat extractor in a compact module; Imhoff type primary deck settler (Mathur and Tippenhauer 2016).

The biological cleansing stage entails—Basins for de-nitrification; basin of nitrification; external activated sludge pumping station; domestic activated sludge recirculation pumping station; an additional settler; wastewater treatment plant control and service module; purified water measurement parameters (Mathur and Tippenhauer 2016).

The sludge treatment stage consists of—Excess sludge from automatic pump stations; sludge thickening, stabilization basins, and main and overflow sludge; sludge drying beds that have been stabilized; creating mud puddle; sludge dewatering on the go.

SCADA is used to monitor and control all the aforementioned operations. A Supervisory Control and Data Acquisition (SCADA) system (Stouffer and Falco 2006) is used to manage a wide variety of processes, such as those described by Karnouskos (2011): the command segment and computerization would allow the observation and control of technical processes, while also assisting the operator by simplifying mass balances, such as those of solids in suspension. The installation of RTU to the SCADA system, which will be installed in the building for directorial dispensation and registration, computerization, and protection of the building, will ensure the regulation, operation, and safety of a wide variety of equipment (including pumps of any type and blowers, air compressors, and power-driven motors in general) (Karnouskos and Colombo 2011).

The native electrical panels will have a human/automated interface with buttons and switches for manual override. The engine will start and stop at certain intervals, and the time it was on will be logged. When the thrusts (and instruments in general) are positioned in accordance with backup equipment, the technique enables automated cyclic permutation of the unit. All pumps will be protected from dry running by means of strategic pressure level placement or a level measurement structure; pumps whose operation is determined by the water level in water retention structures (pools) are referred to as level sensors or level monitors (Adepu and Mathur 2018). The entrance to the combined treatment plant, the mechanical displacer in the pipeline that clusters the water supply pump, and the electromagnetic flow meters are all places where the flow rate must be continuously monitored and recorded. PH, temperature, and quality metrics such as diffused oxygen and suspended particles in aeration tanks, NO2, NOs, NH4, and turbidity, are displayed at the station's entrance, as are the numbers for these variables. All data was collected by SCADA and entered into a historical database (Fernandez and Fernandez 2005). The data collected was used to direct the actions of the mechanical device.

2   Details Experimental

2.1   Background Review

Smart water treatment operations accommodate numerous overlapping duties by communicating and interacting amongst themselves (Yaacoub et al. 2020). Customer Information Schemes, Demand Response Arrangements, Meter Data Management Systems, and Distribution Management Systems are all examples of systems that interact through the economic network (Mahmoud et al. 2015). It is important to put in a lot more consideration when discussing vulnerabilities in industrial networks (Mathur and Tippenhauer 2016) because they are more sensitive than the traditional network. Protecting an industrial network requires an in-depth knowledge of the various entry points a potential attacker can use (Amin et al. 2012). An attacker can assess a company's security by looking at its first footprints (such as its network areas, IP universe, Extranets, and other vital information). The problem is that industrial networks (Gungor et al. 2011) are niche and hard to access.. Unfortunately, it is just as easy to find details about other networks, with tools like Shodan (Bodenheim et al. 2014), a search engine like google, but more powerful because it has the ability to search for the devices that are connected to the internet. Also it enables searches of internet-connected systems by port and protocol, country, and other parameters.

Ping sweeps are frequently used as the first step in network scanning, both for locating devices and hosts and for using ICMP's advanced features to glean additional information such as netmask and port. As Windows is widely used in manufacturing environments, it is essential that Windows user accounts be enumerated according to industry standards and are completely compliant with all necessary processes. Receiving host authentication allows full access over the Open Platform Communications (OPC) environment, which is notably important for Windows-based Object Linking and Embedding (OLE) and Distributed Component Object Model (DCOM)-based Open Platform Communications (OPC) Classic systems (Kang and Robles 2009). In contrast, scanning an industrial network can be used to disrupt and penetrate business networks. This is because many commercial protocols are fragile, and the introduction of a huge amount of unexpected traffic might cause the protocol to fail. If infiltration rather than disruption is the goal, a technique similar to Stuxnet (Karnouskos 2011) could be utilized as an example. In order to infect Windows, Stuxnet (Chen and Abu-Nimeh 2011) employs a zero-day exploit technique (Zhu et al. 2011), attempting to bypass behavior blocking, infecting typically by injecting the entire DLL into another process, checking for windows version Antivirus installed, spreading laterally through (infected network, USB, step 7 project file), injecting code blocks into the target Programmable Logic Controller (PLC) that interrupt processes, and using one possible approach would able to conduct a threat analysis to determine where and how an attacker might get access to an industrial network and whether they were successful in their attempt.

There are a variety of vulnerabilities (Fernandez and Fernandez 2005), but one of the most important challenges is to identify such vulnerabilities in a timely manner, in order to minimize the impact. The goal of this research is to create an intelligent model that monitors the entire system's activity. It will continually learn the system's behavior and will have no effect on the system's performance. It will forecast and sustain a small change system based on past information. It will examine the system's vulnerabilities and suggest ways to improve performance. This technique will make it possible for these models to make judgments such as isolating the infected network or restoring prior conditions. When dealing with unpredictable or uncertain events, there are two basic approaches—computer science and computational intelligence techniques (Mills and Legg 2020).

Although all approaches appear to be similar at first look, AI (Gupta et al. 2020) and computational intelligence methodologies differ in how they address complicated issues. Computing approaches use a goal-oriented approach, in the sense, issues are based on detailed descriptions of the world, and links are made between the problem to be addressed and the activities that would assist in obtaining the desired state. However, in instances where stochastic processes are involved, this solution for complicated issues is not very suitable. Computational intelligence techniques, which include well-known concepts like evolutionary computation, mathematical logic and AI, are the best way to handle the openness of those circumstances. The unifying feature of these techniques is that, rather than being offered as a result of prior information defining activities associated with objectives, they rely on stochastic processes, including repetitive creation and assessment cycles. For a complex network, a traditional industrial network security approach is not sufficient to handle. On the other hand, Computational intelligence functions (like Machine learning and Artificial Intelligence) are performing well in those situations.

The value of computational intelligence in the smart grid context is thus based on its capacity to enable intelligent conduct in the face of uncertainty. As a result, this part is devoted to analyzing the most effective strategies as well as the prospective issues (Zhioua 2013) that those techniques will be able to handle. Computational intelligence approaches have made the largest contributions to the smart grid industry (Stouffer and Falco 2006). The potential of such strategies to anticipate significant information that aids in the decision-making process is their most intriguing aspect. Furthermore, these technologies make it possible to control the grid in a dependable and timely way. The greatest distinguishing aspect of neural networks (Jha et al. 2020; Alabadi and Celik 2020) is that, rather than being programmed to do certain tasks, they are taught to recognize specific data patterns.

3 Dataset

The majority of the currently available datasets do not appear to be available for research, and the majority of the time, the datasets that are obtained are not in the correct format for data processing and machine learning techniques. There are not a huge number of data samples available for new kinds of malware (Kumar et al. 2019). This study focuses on a specific set of files that have been identified as malicious software (Wangen 2015) and comes from nine different families. The dataset of the 52 malware samples from 9 different hazardous families are collected from different sources, such as Virus Share, Microsoft Malware Repository and so on. Each threat file includes an identification number, a hash value of 20 characters that uniquely identifies it, and a group, which is an integer that represents one of the nine dangerous family names. These three pieces of information are all kept in a single location. The different types of malwares, together with their respective parent groups, are presented in Table 1.

Table 1. Malware dataset of nine different malware families (Source: Virus Share, Microsoft Malware Repository, etc.)

Class	Family name	Type	First seen
1	Stuxnet	Worm	2010
2	Snake	Ransomware	2020
3	DoppelPaymer	Ransomware	2017
4	Havex	Backdoor	2013
5	Black Energy	Trojan	2007
6	Crashoverride	Backdoor	2016
7	Lollipop	Adware	2013
8	Tracur	Trojan Downloader	2011
9	Obfuscator.Acy	Obfuscated Malware	2012

In the dataset, each piece of information was displayed without the Portable Executable (PE) header, and the hexadecimal representation was included in the binary content of the raw data for each individual file. This was done to guarantee the data's purity. A metadata manifest is also provided, which is a log that contains various metadata information obtained from the binary, such as function calls, strings, and so on. This information may be found in the metadata manifest. The Interactive Disassembler (IDA) is a program that can take machine executable code and create the associated assembly code for it. Our goal is to come up with the most efficient approach to classify files according to whether they belong to the train set or the test set based on their respective family relationships.

4 Methodology

Training a prediction model using data that has already been labeled is required in supervised learning in order to achieve the goal of properly predicting the label of incoming data points. The two most common approaches of supervised learning are known as classification and regression. Classifier models are utilized while attempting to make a prediction regarding a discrete class. Regression models are used to make predictions about continuous variables. Because supervised learning relies on labeled data, the data that are provided need to have accurate labels attached to them.

In logistic regression, a correlation is established between a dependent variable and one or more independent variables by employing a straight line. This is accomplished by multiplying all the inputs by constants and adding the resulting values. The coefficients of the model can be calibrated using a variety of approaches, the most common among them is called the method of least squares. Notable benefits associated with linear models are how simple they are to implement and how easily they can be interpreted.

The many stages of the experiment are broken down and discussed in Fig. 1. These stages range from the processing of the raw sample to the training and testing of the various models. The first phase demonstrates the extraction of features from a byte file (Singh et al. 2019). It is essential to investigate recently discovered malware before training the model in order to have an understanding of the associated threats and goals.

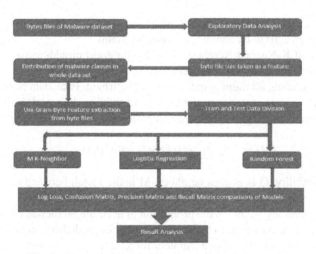

Fig. 1. Steps of malware identification through byte file

The dataset has several features that can be accessed by looking into the byte of the malicious program. An exploratory data analysis is conducted by taking few features into consideration and representing them in pictorial format, also feeding them to few machine learning algorithms. These features include the unique identifier of each sample as well as the class that is associated with it. Additionally, the size of each byte file is taken into consideration as a feature file. Another feature considered is the number of unigrams and bigrams in each sample and are represented in a tabular form (Fig. 7). The next step in the process involves dividing the dataset into two distinct parts or subgroups. The initial subset, that is utilized in the modeling process, is referred to as the training dataset. The model is not trained using the second subset; rather, it is provided as the input element of the dataset. After that, its predictions are created and compared to the predicted values of the problem. The test dataset serves as a second dataset that is used for evaluating the accuracy of the models.

In our tests, the following metrics are utilized to quantify the performance of malware detection algorithms.

The K-Nearest Neighbor algorithm (Giria et al. 2022) can categorize new data by analyzing how closely it resembles previously trained data. This particular class of test data was compiled using the vast majority of classes in the K data set. K represents the number of data points that are located at the closest distance to the test data; it is also often referred to as the test data's nearest neighbor. The K-Nearest Neighbor technique provides access to a variety of distance computations, one of which is a Euclidean distance calculation. The goal of the computation is to determine how far apart the two points are, namely the point in the training data (t) and the point in the testing data (t1). Equations may be used to determine the Euclidean distance between two points.

$$S((t_i, t_{1i})) = \sqrt{\sum_{i=0}^{N} (t_i - t_{1i})^2} \dots \dots \tag{1}$$

S is the space between two points, t is training data, t_1 is testing data, i represents the range between zero to N, and N is the number count.

The Modified K-Nearest Neighbor (MK-NN) algorithm adds class name and file size computations to the K-NN approach.

Before proceeding, all training data must be confirmed. Each data point relies on its neighbors. The validation step is performed on all training data, and the validity result is utilized to calculate weights afterwards. Equation calculates predictability:

$$p(t) = 1/Q \sum M (class(t), class(t_i)) \dots \dots \tag{2}$$

p is predictability, Q is nearest neighbor, M is the match between t and i^{th} nearest neighbor. M can be defined as 1 if t and t_i are the same otherwise 0.

The term "accuracy" refers to the proportion of accurate predictions made across all classes that is expressed as a ratio to the total number of predictions made. The stronger capacity of the detection model to accurately forecast the ground truth is shown by the fact that it has a greater accuracy.

$$Accuracy = \frac{TP + TN}{TP + TN + FP + FN} \dots \dots \tag{3}$$

TP = True Positive, TN = True Negative, FP = False Positive, FN = False Negative.

The number of cases that were wrongly labeled is just the misclassification rate of the classifier, which can be found as

$$Misclassified = \frac{FP + FN}{TP + TN + FP + FN} \dots \dots \tag{4}$$

The term "precision" refers to the proportion of harmful files that were accurately identified relative to the total number of files that were identified as malicious.

$$Precision = \frac{TP}{TP + FP} \cdots \cdots \tag{5}$$

The term "recall" refers to the percentage of harmful apps that were accurately predicted to the total number of malicious applications present in the dataset.

$$Recall = \frac{TP}{TP + FN} \cdots \cdots \tag{6}$$

5 Results and Discussion

Within this section, the results of each stage, which are outlined in the methodology section, have been broken down and discussed. The raw data were preprocessed so that they could be converted into the format that was wanted, which was byte format. The first phase discusses the files of the bytes dataset that contain malware: It was decided to upload the data sets to Google Drive to segregate the byte files from the larger dataset. In order to carry out the execution, the Google Colaboratory (Colab) platform was utilized. In the beginning, Drive is connected to Colab so that users can gain access to the data set that is displayed in Fig. 2. For the purpose of data analysis, byte files were segmented off into their own distinct folder (referred to as byte File) within the overall data collection, which contained a variety of data formats. 52 different datasets were used in this experiment to carry it out. 39 data files were utilized for training, 11 data files were used for testing, and 9 data files were used for cross-validation. The 52 samples were divided into test, train, and cross-validation sets so that the model output can be verified. In the course of this experiment, a deliberately limited dataset was collected in order to evaluate how well the model performed in relation to the newly discovered form of malware. Figure 3 depicts the distribution of each different family of malware throughout the dataset.

```
{

from google.colab import drive
drive.mount('/content/mdrive')

root_path = '/content/mdrive/MyDrive/train/'

}
```

Fig. 2. Code to mount Google Drive with Google Colab

To ensure that the 52 data samples selected are representative of the full malware data set, we randomly selected them from the entire collection. Malware families were examined for their representation in the sample pool. The dataset is heavily skewed toward class 3, while class 5 is underrepresented.

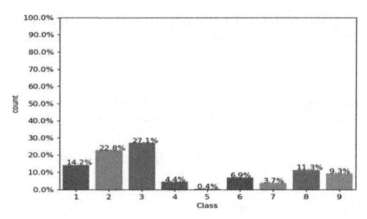

Fig. 3. Class distribution of malware in the dataset

The percentages of each class found in the sample are as follows: 14.2%, 22.8%, 27.1%, 4.4%, 0.4%, 6.9%, 3.7%, 11.3%, and 9.3% for classes 1, 2, 3, 4, 5, 6, 7, 8, and 9. In order to reduce the amount of inherent bias in the dataset, each class was assigned a certain probability throughout the selection process which is based on the availability of the samples for the dataset.

After the data set has been preprocessed, the size of each byte file is considered a significant element. The output of the program is depicted below in Fig. 4. This output includes information on the malware, such as its ID as a unique hash id, its size, and the class that is associated with each malware.

The dataset should be segmented into a train set, a test set, and a cross validation set, with the proportions of samples in each class being kept exactly the same as they were in the initial dataset. The most important customizable aspect of the approach is the size of the sets that are used for testing and cross validation.

In this experiment, the training set size is 0.61 (i.e. 61%), which indicates that the remaining percentage (i.e. 0.21 (21%)) is allocated to the test set, and the rest of the data sample (i.e. 18%) was utilized for cross validation.

Figure 5 and Fig. 6 shows the class distribution in train and test data set in graph format. In Fig. 5, Train data set has 9,6,5,5,3,2 and 2 files from class 3,2,6,7,1, 4 and 5 respectively. Similarly, in Fig. 6, the Test data set has 3,2,2,2,1 and 1, files belonging to classes 3,2,5,6,1 and 4, respectively.

Extraction of the Uni-Gram Byte Feature from Byte Files is the next feature that needs to be dealt with now as this one has been completed. Extraction of features using unigrams and bigrams has been attempted to achieve better results. The results of the programme are displayed in Fig. 7, and they include the number of unigrams and bigrams (Li et al. 2020) that are found in each byte file that was used for the sample. The number of unigrams and the bigrams present in the byte file will help to classify the malware samples with respect to their family to some extent.

	ID	size	Class			ID	size	Class
0	0cfIE39ihRNo2rkZOy5H	6.703125	3	30	0BKcmNv4iGY2hsVSaXJ6	8.941406	3
1	0czUXKSCiGY2j5mxLdWa	0.574219	9	31	0dnTixlMYzDUpsvEVrGc	6.902344	2
2	0cTu2bkefOAJqIhYUWFK	0.925781	8	32	0ACDbR5M3ZhBJajygTuf	4.523438	7
3	0bN6ODYWW2xeCQ8n3tEg	7.160156	2	33	0DNVFKwY1cjO7bTfJ5p1	0.691406	1
4	0aVxkvmflEizUBG2rHT4	0.363281	8	34	0DTs2PhZfCwEv7q8349K	6.703125	3
5	0CPaAXtyswrBq83D6VEg	4.441406	9	35	0Cq4wfhLrKBJiut11YAZ	2.378906	6
6	0D9IedmC1viTPuglRWX6	6.714844	3	36	0co46B8IkPt2UN3HSaw7	0.433594	9
7	0CzL6rfwaTqGOu9eghBt	6.703125	3	37	0cdnSIvN489sFUwY1rMQ	8.941406	3
8	0Dk7Wd8MERu3b5rmQzCK	6.714844	3	38	0dkuzUXLTEFwW71vP5b5	6.714844	3
9	0BIdbVDEgmPwjYF4xzir	4.183594	7	39	0C4aVbN5801nAigFJt9z	0.585938	8
10	0AnoOZDNbPXIr2MRBSCJ	0.468750	1	40	0DTpS9Av1RLifoKlUdm7	3.449673	2
11	0BZQIJak6Pu2tyAXfrzR	0.562500	6	41	0A32eTdBKayjCWhZqDOQ	3.438000	2
12	0b5LqcWix3J4fGIEhXQu	3.562500	7	42	0daTri9PSkeEsVHu5Dhw	6.703125	3
13	0DM3hS6Gg2QVKb1fZydv	6.082031	2	43	0AV6MP1rTWG4fVI7NBtQ	3.796875	9
14	0EAdHtLDypMcwjTFJziC	6.585938	2	44	0BFIPv1rO83whtpMYyAs	0.363281	8
15	0aSTGBVRXeJhx5OcpsgC	6.703125	3	45	0BEsCP7NAUy8XmkenHWG	5.425781	2
16	0DqUX5rkg3IbMY6BLGCE	0.539062	1	46	0akIH1MRxLmv34QGhEJP	0.996094	8
17	0AguvpOCcaf2myVDYFGb	0.972656	8	47	0csgzpwdL3FbZEJu6DjO	6.703125	3
18	0B2RwKm6dq9fjUWDNIOa	3.820312	9	48	0DbLeKSoxu47wjqVHsi9	0.867188	2
19	0aU7XWsr8RtN94jvo3lG	6.703125	9	49	0BLbmzJRkjNynCgQIdtV	6.703125	3
20	0bjN3Kgw5OATSreRmEdi	3.820312	9	50	0aVNj3qFgEZI6Akf4Kuv	0.351562	8
21	0cGWK6VvCkm7O2AxDjtw	6.703125	3	51	0BY2iPso3bEmudlUzpfq	1.218750	8
22	0dauMIK4ATfybzqUgNLc	0.667969	9				
23	0ASH2csN7k8jZyoRaqtn	6.070312	2				
24	0cfGJLYgE6ROaZH7KT1h	6.925781	3				
25	0dhL83vcswa7U1qHiDS5	0.644531	9				
26	0AWWs42SUQ19mI7eDcTC	0.597656	1				
27	0df4cbsTBCn1VGW81QRv	0.773438	6				
28	0cH8YeO15ZywEhPrJvmj	0.421875	1				
29	0akIgwhWHYm1dzsNqBFx	4.984062	2				

Fig. 4. Dataset distribution over different classes with the file size

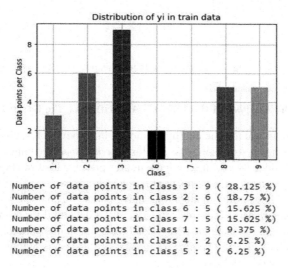

Distribution of yi in train data

```
Number of data points in class 3 : 9 ( 28.125 %)
Number of data points in class 2 : 6 ( 18.75 %)
Number of data points in class 6 : 5 ( 15.625 %)
Number of data points in class 7 : 5 ( 15.625 %)
Number of data points in class 1 : 3 ( 9.375 %)
Number of data points in class 4 : 2 ( 6.25 %)
Number of data points in class 5 : 2 ( 6.25 %)
```

Fig. 5. Distribution of data in the train dataset

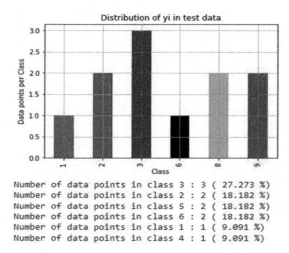

Number of data points in class 3 : 3 (27.273 %)
Number of data points in class 2 : 2 (18.182 %)
Number of data points in class 5 : 2 (18.182 %)
Number of data points in class 6 : 2 (18.182 %)
Number of data points in class 1 : 1 (9.091 %)
Number of data points in class 4 : 1 (9.091 %)

Fig. 6. Distribution of data in the test dataset

ID	0	1	2	3	4	5	6	7	8	9	0a	0b	0c	0d	0e	0f	10	11	12
0	0cRE39iiRNo2iKZOw5H	10042	5481	3273	3266	3368	3320	3203	3282	3192	3209	3187	3314	3204	3241	3234	3279	3300	3147	3156
1	0czU0XSClGY2j5nxLdiVa	82010	786	470	562	608	775	407	356	717	407	399	439	575	748	376	856	662	568	331
2	0cTu2bkefOAJqbhYUWFK	50359	266	163	248	249	141	139	73	166	97	303	53	141	56	68	216	153	76	78
3	00N6ODYWw2xeCOBn3IBp	63417	23412	19933	20481	24362	20307	19275	20620	23246	13523	13324	24318	24379	9113	5054	18513	21302	13047	13054
4	0aVkkvmfEizU8G2dM74	19811	717	295	489	552	407	245	225	393	239	221	226	423	693	216	285	455	279	220
5	0CPaAXtysvrBq83D6VEp	649008	4080	3392	3697	3979	4161	3471	2999	3096	3377	3809	3045	3108	5135	3821	3156	4184	3057	2915
6	009edmC1viTPugLRiXX6	11267	5830	3127	3250	3331	3199	3256	3289	3162	3320	3209	3358	3286	3145	3203	3263	3321	3181	3250
7	0CzL6rfvaTqGOu9eghBi	8510	4238	3117	3177	3044	3131	3086	3093	3190	3072	3071	3049	3104	3179	3120	3049	3090	3069	3063
8	0DX7Wd8MERs0b5mQzCK	10541	5492	3227	3243	3249	3245	3213	3271	3153	3286	3172	3265	3286	3293	3209	3205	3329	3257	3103
9	08Id0tVOEgmPwjYF4xdr	6453	66	30	22	27	20	9	10	16	5	4	5	21	7	3	9	23	11	4
10	0AnoOZDNbPXiz2MRB5CJ	25791	1202	569	750	948	456	405	517	754	494	388	323	628	419	315	857	1391	327	287
11	08ZQUJI8k5Pk2yAXfzR	5147	726	689	641	653	722	617	602	693	664	704	654	684	637	628	645	867	674	661
12	0b5LqSWaXJ4fGiEbXQu	4936	102	55	74	44	34	19	14	65	10	14	9	32	20	36	14	89	7	8
13	0DM3hS6GgGQVKb1f2ydv	702234	14914	9142	7806	22000	11673	14100	10992	9315	284	247	10761	9671	313	245	15483	11821	171	483

Fig. 7. Unigram and bigram feature output

5.1   Result of the Analysis of the MK-NN Algorithm on the Given Data Set

In order to both train and test the intelligent model, the modified K–neighbor (MK-NN) technique was utilized. Analyzing the log loss for the specified input using multiple values of k can be done by anyone using the figures presented below (Fig. 8 and Fig. 9). This model demonstrates the best result at point 3 along the x-axis in the graph that is associated with it. In a similar manner, one may conduct an analysis of the same thing using the confusion matrix. The truly little amount of data used for training meant that the model was unable to locate the categorized location. In this particular instance, the number of incorrectly classified points was 27.28, and its results will be compared with those of the other two models.

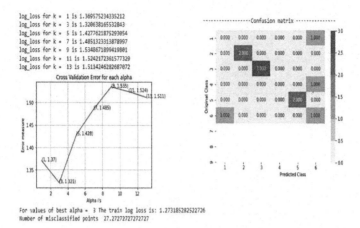

For values of best alpha = 3 The train log loss is: 1.273185282522726
Number of misclassified points 27.27272727272727

Fig. 8. Log loss and confusion matrix through modified K neighbor model

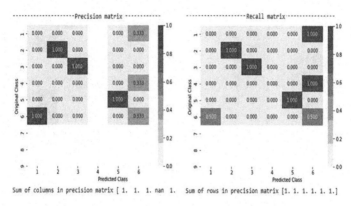

Sum of columns in precision matrix [1. 1. 1. nan 1.   Sum of rows in precision matrix [1. 1. 1. 1. 1. 1.]

Fig. 9. Precision and Recall matrix for MK-NN model

5.2 Result of the Analysis of the Logistic Regression Model on the Given Data Set

The intelligent model was trained and tested with the help of an algorithm called Logistic Regression. An examination of the log loss for the supplied input was carried out, and the results are depicted in Figs. 10 and 11, where the values of C ranged from 0.0001 to 1000. This model produces the best outcome at the beginning point, which is located over the x-axis in the graph. However, the number of points that were incorrectly classified in this model was 45.45, which is an increase of more than 18 when compared to the K-neighbor model. Similarly, the analysis of the same thing may be done from the Confusion Matrix, the True Positive, False Positive, True Negative, and False Negative were used to examine the Confusion Matrix, Precision Matrix, and Recall matrix, respectively. Within the Precision matrix, there is discussion on the total positive in relation to the true positive and the false positive. After doing a study of the Precision Matrix, it was discovered that the majority of the points cannot be recognized since the training data set contains a small amount of not a number (nan) output.

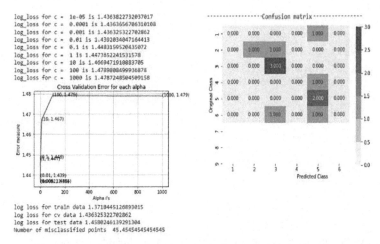

Fig. 10. Log loss and confusion matrix for each class in the data set

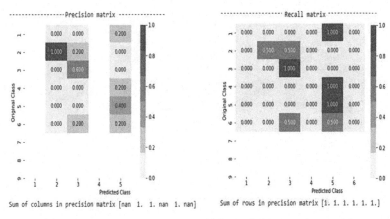

Fig. 11. Precision and Recall matrix for logistic regression model

5.3 Result of the Analysis of the Random Forest Model Algorithm on the Given Data Set

Training and testing the smart model were accomplished with the help of the Random Forest algorithm. Figures 12 and 13 show the results of a log loss analysis performed on the provided input for a range of C values (10–3000). The optimal outcome for this model lies at the highest x-coordinate in the graph. The model could not locate the categorized points because of the limited size of the training and testing datasets. There were 36.36 points that were incorrectly categorized. However, when comparing this model to the logistic regression model, it shows the best outcome and the modified K-neighbor model, with respect to the number of misclassified points, gives the best outcome. In a similar vein, the Confusion Matrix can perform an investigation of the same phenomenon.

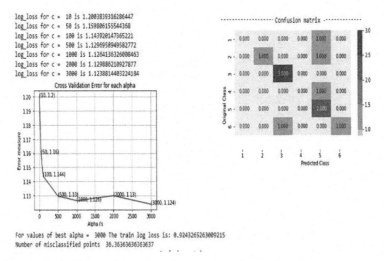

Fig. 12. Log loss and confusion matrix through the random forest model

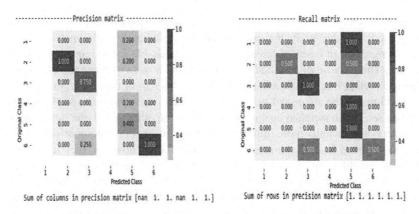

Fig. 13. Precision and Recall matrix for the random forest model

In Fig. 14, The number of misclassified points yielded by the three AI algorithms, Modified K neighbor, Logistic Regression and Random Forest Algorithm is plotted in the graph. The Modified K neighbor displayed the lowest number of misclassified points which is 27.28 makes it the best algorithm among all for the limited dataset. Logistic Regression gave the output of 45.45 as the number of misclassified points, which depicts the same as the worst algorithm for small dataset. The Random Forest algorithm has given an output for the number of misclassified points as 36.36 which is average in nature.

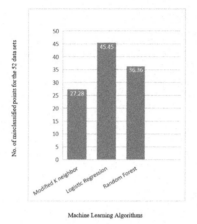

Fig. 14. Performance comparison of three models

6   Conclusions

Malware that is most recent both in its nature and its signature is able to circumvent the security model. In this study, the question of "how efficiently such types of malwares can be recognized, in cases of having fewer data available for training the model," is addressed. The purpose of this study is to determine how to increase the likelihood of detecting a certain form of malicious software. In this part of the article, the researcher trained and tested the AI model using the debate that took place across the relatively small data set. When weighed against the results of the other model, the outcome of the first model is significantly more important. The conclusion draws comparisons between the results obtained from the various models depending on how well they function. The modified K-neighbor model provides a better response than the other two models in terms of the misclassified point on the limited dataset, however the logistic regression model displays the lowest performance in this particular scenario. As a result of this experiment, by analyzing the output, the modified K-neighbor model was able to detect the virus, which is novel in nature and has very less information accessible from the systems in comparison to the Random Forest and Logistic Regression models. In the future, there should be more study done in this direction to detect unidentifiable malware from an exceedingly small quantity of information, which will help to secure the critical infrastructure systems from the various attackers.

References

Adepu, S., Mathur, A.: Distributed attack detection in a water treatment plant: method and case study. IEEE Trans. Depend. Sec. Comput. **18**(1), 86–99 (2018)

Alabadi, M., Celik, Y.: Anomaly detection for cyber-security based on convolution neural network: a survey. In: 2020 International Congress on Human-Computer Interaction, Optimization and Robotic Applications (HORA), pp. 1–14. IEEE (2020)

Amin, S., Litrico, X., Sastry, S., Bayen, A.M.: Cyber security of water SCADA systems—Part I: analysis and experimentation of stealthy deception attacks. IEEE Trans. Control Syst. Technol. **21**(5), 1963–1970 (2012)

Brantly, A.F., Kostyuk, N., Lindsay, J.R., Maschmeyer, L., Pakharenko, G.: The cyber dimension of the crisis in Ukraine: an expert panel discussion (2022)

Chen, T.M., Abu-Nimeh, S.: Lessons from Stuxnet. Computer **44**(4), 91–93 (2011)

Fernandez, J.D., Fernandez, A.E.: SCADA systems: vulnerabilities and remediation. J. Comput. Sci. Coll. **20**(4), 160–168 (2005)

Geers, K., Kindlund, D., Moran, N., Rachwald, R.: World War C: understanding nation-state motives behind today's advanced cyber-attacks. Technical report, FireEye, Milpitas, CA, USA, September 2014 (2014)

Gupta, M., Mittal, S., Abdelsalam, M.: AI assisted malware analysis: a course for next generation cybersecurity workforce. arXiv preprint arXiv:2009.11101 (2020)

Gungor, V.C., et al.: Smart grid technologies: communication technologies and standards. IEEE Trans. Ind. Inf. **7**(4), 529–539 (2011)

Jha, Sudan, Deepak Prashar, Hoang Viet Long, and David Taniar(2020). "Recurrent neural network for detecting malware." Computers & Security 99: 102037

Kumar, N., Mukhopadhyay, S., Gupta, M., Handa, A., Shukla, S.K.: Malware classification using early stage behavioral analysis. In: 2019 14th Asia Joint Conference on Information Security (AsiaJCIS), pp. 16–23. IEEE (2019)

Kang, D.J., Robles, R.J.: Compartmentalization of protocols in SCADA communication. Int. J. Adv. Sci. Technol. **8**, 27–36 (2009)

Karnouskos, S.: Stuxnet worm impact on industrial cyber-physical system security. In: IECON 2011 - 37th Annual Conference of the IEEE Industrial Electronics Society, pp. 4490–4494. IEEE, November 2011

Karnouskos, S., Colombo, A.W.: Architecting the next generation of service-based SCADA/DCS system of systems. In: IECON 2011-37th Annual Conference of the IEEE Industrial Electronics Society, pp. 359–364. IEEE, November 2011

Li, X., Qiu, K., Qian, C., Zhao, G.: An adversarial machine learning method based on OpCode N. IEEE (2020)

Mills, A., Legg, P.: Investigating anti-evasion malware triggers using automated sandbox reconfiguration techniques. J. Cybersecur. Priv. **1**(1), 19–39 (2020)

Mohee, A.: Cyber war: the hidden side of the Russian-Ukrainian crisis (2022)

Mwiki, H., Dargahi, T., Dehghantanha, A., Choo, K.-K.: Analysis and triage of advanced hacking groups targeting western countries critical national infrastructure: APT28, RED October, and Regin. In: Gritzalis, D., Theocharidou, M., Stergiopoulos, G. (eds.) Critical infrastructure security and resilience. ASTSA, pp. 221–244. Springer, Cham (2019). https://doi.org/10.1007/978-3-030-00024-0_12

Nicholson, A., Webber, S., Dyer, S., Patel, T., Janicke, H.: SCADA security in the light of Cyber-Warfare. Comput. Secur. **31**(4), 418–436 (2012)

Singh, A., Handa, A., Kumar, N., Shukla, S.K.: Malware classification using image representation. In: Dolev, S., Hendler, D., Lodha, S., Yung, M. (eds.) CSCML 2019. LNCS, vol. 11527, pp. 75–92. Springer, Cham (2019). https://doi.org/10.1007/978-3-030-20951-3_6

Stouffer, K., Falco, J.: Guide to supervisory control and data acquisition (SCADA) and industrial control systems security. National Institute of Standards and Technology (2006)

Tuptuk, N., Hazell, P., Watson, J., Hailes, S.: A systematic review of the state of cyber-security in water systems. Water **13**, 81 (2021)

Mathur, A.P., Tippenhauer, N.O.: SWAT: a water treatment testbed for research and training on ICS security. In: 2016 International Workshop on Cyber-Physical Systems for Smart Water Networks (CySWater), pp. 31–36. IEEE (2016)

Mahmoud, R., Yousuf, T., Aloul, F., Zualkernan, I.: Internet of Things (IoT) security: current status, challenges and prospective measures. In: 2015 10th International Conference for Internet Technology and Secured Transactions (ICITST), pp. 336–341, December 2015

Wen, Q., Dong, X., Zhang, R.: Application of dynamic variable cipher security certificate in internet of things. In: 2012 IEEE 2nd International Conference on Cloud Computing and Intelligence Systems, vol. 3, pp. 1062–1066. IEEE, October 2012

Wangen, G.: The role of malware in reported cyber espionage: a review of the impact and mechanism. Information 6(2), 183–211 (2015)

Yaacoub, J.P.A., Salman, O., Noura, H.N., Kaaniche, N., Chehab, A., Malli, M.: Cyber-physical systems security: limitations, issues and future trends. Microprocess. Microsyst. 77, 103201 (2020)

Zhioua, S.: The middle east under malware attack dissecting cyber weapons. In 2013 IEEE 33rd International Conference on Distributed Computing Systems Workshops, pp. 11–16. IEEE (2013)

Zhu, B., Joseph, A., Sastry, S.: A taxonomy of cyber attacks on SCADA systems. In: 2011 International Conference on Internet of Things and 4th International Conference on Cyber, Physical and Social Computing, pp. 380–388. IEEE, October 2011

Singh, S.D.: Ancient Indian Warfare: With Special Reference to the Vedic Period. Motilal Banarsidass Publ., Delhi (1989)

Cervini, J., Rubin, A., Watkins, L.: Don't drink the cyber: extrapolating the possibilities of oldsmar's water treatment cyberattack. In: International Conference on Cyber Warfare and Security, vol. 17, no. 1, pp. 19–25, March 2022

Giria, I.N.Y.T., Putria, L.A.A.R., Giria, G.A.V.M., Putraa, I.G.N.A.C., Widiarthaa, I.M., Suprianaa, I.W.: Music genre classification using modified k-nearest neighbor (MK-NN). Jurnal Elektronik Ilmu Komputer Udayana (2022). p-ISSN 2301-5373

Bodenheim, R., Butts, J., Dunlap, S., Mullins, B.: Evaluation of the ability of the Shodan search engine to identify Internet-facing industrial control devices. Int. J. Crit. Infrastruct. Prot. 7(2), 114–123 (2014)

Performance Analysis of a Hybrid Algorithm for Lost Target Recovery in Wireless Sensor Network

Alpesh Sankaliya[1,2](✉) 🆔 and Maulin Joshi[2] 🆔

[1] Gujarat Technological University, Gujarat, India
alpeshrs@gmail.com
[2] Sarvajanik College of Engineering and Technology, Surat, India

Abstract. Constructing a successful framework for recovering a lost target is a well-researched problem in wireless sensor networks. Better target prediction algorithms can reduce the overall energy consumption of the network. These can be accomplished by carefully choosing the best nodes for continuous target monitoring situations. Traditional prediction algorithms, on the other hand, were limited to constant motion models and typically failed in fast target movements. Designing prediction algorithms for resource-constrained micro sensor nodes is typically a difficult issue, but neural networks' capacity to understand all nonlinearity between input and output can be used. Recovery of the target after it has been lost in the network is one of the main problems with tracking applications. An efficient recovery method for applications involving linear and nonlinear target tracking is presented in this paper. The suggested method learns the temporal correlation between subsequent samples of a target trajectory using Kalman and time delay neural network (TDNN) models. Hybrid method that further improvements in terms of energy efficiency are realized taking into consideration geometrical shapes (circle, contour) and velocity of target while executing recovery algorithms. A hybridization of the present framework is suggested using a direct broadcast-based technique for targets that have been lost for longer periods of time.

Keywords: Wireless sensor network (WSN) · Hybrid recovery algorithm · Target tracking · Efficient target recovery · Loss target

1 Introduction

A surveillance area may have network irregularities due to rugged terrains, it requires proper communication mechanism. WSN sensor nodes can be used to track enemy vehicle (target) as soon as it enters inside coverage area of any sensor node in give network. Target is sensed by sensor node and then sensor node generally transmits information that can be useful for tracking systems to be able to compute current and possible future locations of target vehicle. Such systems can also be used in disaster relief operations, earthquake operations to track lost person [1, 2].

© The Author(s), under exclusive license to Springer Nature Switzerland AG 2023
I. Woungang et al. (Eds.): ANTIC 2022, CCIS 1797, pp. 125–140, 2023.
https://doi.org/10.1007/978-3-031-28180-8_9

Target tracking is done by sensor nodes which are located inside clusters and controlled by respective cluster heads. The use of energy is crucial since the power available to the sensor node is constrained. Single sensor node will only be able to monitor limited region so multiple nodes are used to locate the target [3, 4]. The main goal is to discover the target under various circumstances while using energy wisely. In comparison to previous methods, time domain neural network (TDNN) techniques are suggested as a better solution for target tracking [1].

Target may get lost where sensor nodes are not able to detect target location [5]. Sensors may not able to detect target locations due to various reasons. Holes in network are major causes for target lost. Holes can be classified in three categories mainly coverage holes, routing holes and jammer holes. Coverage hole defines area which is not covered by sensor nodes. Routing holes where sensor node cannot track target due to energy exhaustion. Jammer holes defines area where sensor nodes can track the target but may not able to communicate with them due to network jamming [6, 7].

Due to network abnormalities and variations in target velocity, tracking methods may occasionally fail to follow the target; in these circumstances, recovery techniques are utilised to find the lost target [15]. As far as target movement is concerned there are two possibilities that either target is moving at constant velocity or there can be a change in target velocity. If target is moving at constant velocity, recovery method should use optimum coverage area which uses optimum number of sensor nodes to locate the target. When target is moving at constant velocity, velocity-based methods can be used for recovery but it may not work when there is drastic change in velocity of target because lost target might not have remained in nearby region. The target may not be tracked if it is not in a local region if the target is lost because of a sharp change in velocity, prompting the currently employed recovery algorithms to cover a larger coverage area [8].

The hybrid technique solves the energy consumption issue with earlier methods while retrieving the specified target from a lost state. The method being proposed is a mix of a broadcast-based algorithm and a velocity-based algorithm. The suggested approach attempts to locate the target by first using a velocity-based strategy. If the target cannot be found at the initial level, the range is extended and additional tries are made. If the target still cannot be located, the broadcast algorithm is activated, which uses the best possible area with the best possible number of sensor nodes to find the target.

The remainder of the paper is arranged as follows. The discussion of the studied literary works is found in Sect. 2. Different strategies for target recovery are presented in Sect. 3. The simulation setups and their results are presented in Sect. 4, where various tracks are examined using various target recovery algorithms and comparisons of various recovery techniques in terms of recovery energy are made. Finally, Sect. 5 has drawn to a conclusion.

2   Literature Survey

The Kalman-based strategy essentially involves two steps of tracking, the first of which involves predicting the target's future position and the second of which involves correcting that prediction using observations. When the target's velocity changes suddenly, Kalman-based algorithms may not function at their optimum [9, 10].

Predicted position (a_{n+1}) and correction variance (C_{n+1}) can be defined as follows:

$$a_{n+1} = F * a_n \tag{1}$$

$$C_{n+1} = F * P_n * F^T + \tau Q \tau^T \tag{2}$$

Corrections are made in kalman filter using measurement Noise R. First kalman filter gain is calculated using Eq. 3.

$$Q_{n+1} = C_{n+1} * H^T * (H * C_{n+1} H^T + R)^{-1} \tag{3}$$

Correction variance (C_{n+1}) can be calculated from its previous value and filter gain as follows:

$$C_{n+1} = (1 - K_{n+1} * H) * C_n \tag{4}$$

Finally, next predicted state (a_{n+1}) can be calculated using

$$a_{n+1} = (1 - Q_{n+1} * H * a_n) \tag{5}$$

Figure 1 displays time delay neural networks (TDNN). Where each of them is coupled to a neuron layer, data from delayed input time series is utilized. To predict the target's subsequent state, a neural network employs delayed inputs and the current state [11].

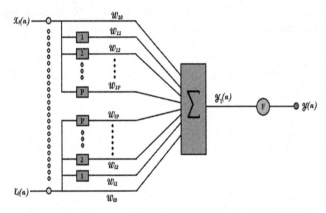

Fig. 1. Architecture of Time delay neural networks (TDNN)

Suppose, p is time delay and x(n) to x(n − p) are inputs. W_{ij} is weighted matrix, then output y_i (n) can be determined using

$$y_1(n) = \sum_{i=0}^{n} \sum_{j=0}^{p} w_{ij} x_i(n - j) \tag{6}$$

Sigmoidal function is used as activation function as follows:

$$f = \frac{1}{1 + e^{-\gamma [y_1(n)]}} \tag{7}$$

Finally, output can be derived using

$$y(n) = F(y_1(n)) \tag{8}$$

When monitoring a target, a fixed area and a fixed number of nodes are taken into account. Targets can occasionally become lost due to holes in networks or other circumstances, such as a lack of adjacent nodes in a certain area [12–14]. Target recovery method is employed in these circumstances.

3 Different Methods for Recovery of Loss Target

In this part, various target recovery models in circular and contoured geometrical shapes are shown. Later, we also describe our hybrid approach for finding a lost target.

3.1 Circle_fixed Method for Recovery of Loss Target

The conceptual diagram of the Fixed circle approach for target recovery is shown in Fig. 2. Apparent problem with this approach is that in each iteration, wider and wider area been covered, network activates large number of nodes and hence this approach seems more energy consuming. If target is in nearby regions, still this approach will use large area and large number of nodes. Advantage may be seen when there is abrupt change in velocity of target and if target has moved little far away or has suddenly changes direction from its previous correctly detected location then Fixed circle approach may be useful as it expands in all directions and covers large area [15].

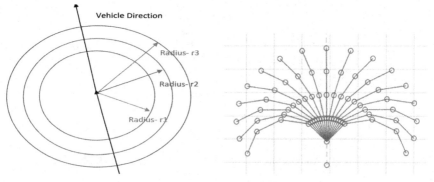

Fig. 2. Diagram of *Circle_fixed* (fixed circle) approach for target recovery

Fig. 3. Diagram of *Contour_fixed* (fixed contour) approach for target recovery

3.2 Contour_fixed Method for Recovery of Loss Target

Figure 3 illustrates a contour-based technique that takes the target's movement into account. In this approach, contours are made by identifying 80 lines at −40 to +40 angles. First slope of line is calculated using coordinates where (x_1, y_1) and (x_2, y_2) are previous coordinates of target.

$$slope = \frac{y_2 - y_1}{x_2 - x_1} \tag{9}$$

New coordinates are calculated for all lines for different angles. Coordinates are calculated for (2 * Recovery level) points using forward kinematics equations:

$$x_{present} = x_{previous} + \cos(angle) * V \tag{10}$$

$$y_{present} = y_{previous} + \sin(angle) * V \tag{11}$$

Above Eqs. (10) and (11) are similarly used to update coordinates for all lines.

3.3 Circle$_{velocity}$ Method for Recovery of Loss Target

This method computes a circular zone for the search of the lost target based on the velocity of the target once the target has been calculated and saved. As search area is a changeable function of current target velocity, this strategy promises to offer a better result than a fixed approach. If the target's velocity right before it became lost was lower, the search area will also be smaller, requiring fewer nodes to be activated and requiring less energy to retrieve the target.

3.4 Contour$_{velocity}$ Method for Recovery of Loss Target

This method is comparable to the *Contour$_{fixed}$* concept, except the contour's shape is determined by the target's velocity. When compared to earlier techniques, the search area needed for target loss is less, and if the prediction algorithm is strong enough, it can offer an energy-efficient solution.

3.5 Hybrid Method for Recovery of Loss Target

Target moving with constant or reasonable change in velocity decides to change its velocity all of sudden. In such cases incremental velocity based approaches may not be useful. Initial higher fixed radius approaches may work but still it may not be able to provide energy efficient solutions as they tend to cover lot of area so more energy will be used. Figure 4 is a screenshot of a search utilizing a hybrid method for target recovery, while Fig. 5 illustrates the conceptual flow of the hybrid method. In this work, we offer a method where the velocity contour approach is applied up to the first few levels in the beginning part. If the target is not located in the initial trial, several additional trials are carried out by creating a huge area in contour directions and repeating the search. If the target is still unfound, the broadcast technique is utilized in place of the contour velocity method, inviting all neighbouring clusters to participate in the search. All neighbouring cluster heads receive a "loss of target" notification from the cluster head where the target was lost. Each cluster head in the area will then ask its nodes if the target is still available.

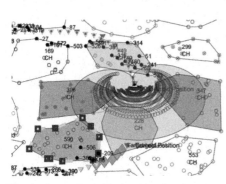

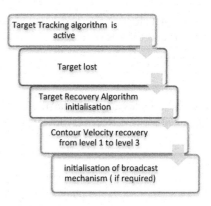

Fig. 4. Screenshot showing search using hybrid method for target recovery

Fig. 5. Flowchart of hybrid method

Relocation of target used in WSN is explained as algorithm:

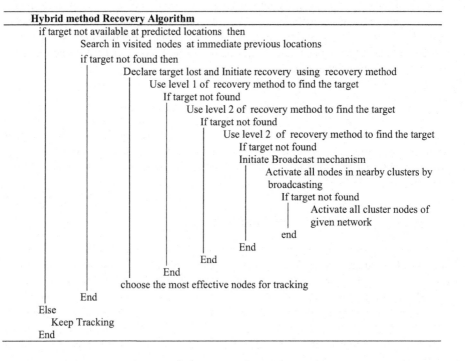

4 Experimental Results and Discussions

A 100×100 m^2 region with 14 clusters and 600 nodes is taken into consideration. The selection of cluster heads takes into account static clustering. Multiple tracks are used to examine the performances of various target recovery models, as mentioned in Sect. 3. The parameters for the target tracking and recovery algorithms are listed in Table 1 according to [11]. For target tracking and recovery, cluster heads in each cluster region communicate with sensor nodes.

Table 1. Parameters used for simulation

Parameter	Value
Initial node energy	2 J
Energy while sensing	9.6×10^{-3} J/Second
Energy while transmission	5.76×10^{-3} J/Byte
Energy while receiving	0.88×10^{-3} J/Byte
Energy while processing	4.0×10^{-9} J/Instruction
Energy while in sleep mode	0.33×10^{-3} J/Second
Size of message	64 Byte

4.1 Case A: Target Moving with Constant Velocity

Figure 6 depicts a typical tracking scenario with a target travelling at a constant speed. Additionally, it has a network hole region where a target may get lost if it goes through. As previously described, simulations are run for target moving using either TDNN-based tracking or Kalman-based tracking techniques. Figure 7(a) for $Circle_{fixed}$, Fig. 7(b) for $Circle_{velocity}$, Fig. 7(c) for $Contour_{fixed}$ and Fig. 7(d) for $Contour_{velocity}$ correspondingly demonstrate simulation results for target movements and executions of recovery algorithms with Kalman based tracking methods. In this simulation, the blue dot represents the original track. Target's real location is shown by the green triangle, its anticipated location is shown by the red triangle, and the network's active nodes are shown by the black dot. After three levels recovery has been conducted, the target may be observed to have been recovered using all models. The energy analysis in Table 2 includes the overall recovery energy used as well as the relative energy savings in various target recovery methodologies. In comparison to the $Contour_{velocity}$ model, $Circle_{fixed}$, $Contour_{fixed}$ and $Circle_{velocity}$ are seen to consume higher energy values during target recovery. $Circle_{fixed}$ and $Circle_{velocity}$ models require more sensor nodes since they need a larger coverage area, which increases the energy required to find a lost target. $Contour_{fixed}$ appears to use more energy because it is based on the contour region but still has a fixed radius. As it just awakens nodes in the contour zone and is velocity based, $Contour_{velocity}$ uses less energy. It should be noted that the hybrid method in this situation operates similarly to the $Contour_{velocity}$ model up to three levels because the target is recovered within that degree of recovery. According to the last column in Table 2, compared to the fixed circle approach, ***Contour***$_{velocity}$ and hybrid recovery models can save up to 66% of the energy needed for recovery.

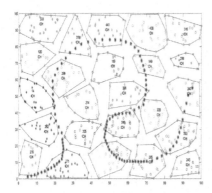

Fig. 6. Track 1 scenario illustrating the movement of the target with constant velocity

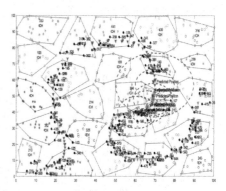

Fig. 7(a). ***Circle***$_{fixed}$ method performance in track 1 following Kalman based tracking (Color figure online)

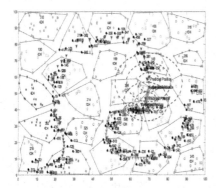

Fig. 7(b). ***Circle***$_{velocity}$ method performance in track 1 following Kalman based tracking (Color figure online)

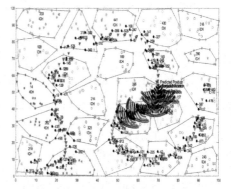

Fig. 7(c). ***Contour***$_{fixed}$ method performance in track 1 following Kalman based tracking (Color figure online)

Figure 8(a) shows target recovery performance of fixed circle (***Circle***$_{fixed}$) model in track I. It is having TDNN based approach as tracking of the target. It can be seen that target that is lost at hole region, cannot be tracked by ***Circle***$_{fixed}$ approach in level 1 recovery. Level 1 recovery covers area around circle with 10 m radius. Then with each increment level, radius of circle is increased by 10 m. Finally it gets tracked in level 2 of recovery. However, it can be seen that it covers more of area, requiring many nodes and hence much more energy is being utilized in recovery.

Figure 8(b) demonstrates results for target recovery performance of velocity based circle (***Circle***$_{velocity}$) model. In this approach level 1 recovery covers area around circle with radius equal to target velocity. Then with each increment of level, radius of circle is calculated by multiplying level with target velocity. It can be observed that target has

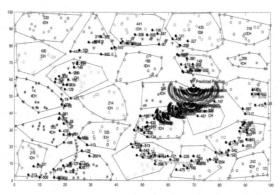

Fig. 7(d). *Contour$_{velocity}$* method performance in track 1 following Kalman based tracking (Color figure online)

Table 2. Energy analysis and energy saving with different approaches for track 1

Tracking algorithm	Recovery algorithm	Recovery energy (Joules)	% energy saved (compared to Circle$_{fixed}$)
Kalman	Circle$_{fixed}$	57.259	0
	Circle$_{velocity}$	45.6415	20.28
	Contour$_{fixed}$	51.8134	9.51
	Circle$_{velocity}$	19.2165	66.43
	Hybrid method (Contour velocity plus broadcast)	19.2165	66.43
TDNN	Circle$_{fixed}$	34.6196	0
	Circle$_{velocity}$	29.5322	14.69
	Contour$_{fixed}$	13.1501	62.01
	Circle$_{velocity}$	5.675	83.60
	Hybrid method (Contour velocity plus broadcast)	5.675	83.60

been able to be recovered at level 3 recovery. However, it is interesting to note that as this model covers less area as compared to fixed circle approach, it requires 14.69% less energy to recover as compared to fixed circle approach, as shown in Table 2.

Similarly, Fig. 8(c) highlights target recovery performance of contour based fixed (*Contour$_{fixed}$*) in track 1. It can be seen that here again lesser area and lesser nodes are used for recovery approximate 62% energy being saved to recover the target as compared to *Circle$_{fixed}$*. Figure 8(d) shows target recovery performance of Velocity based contour

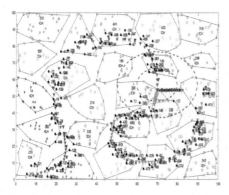

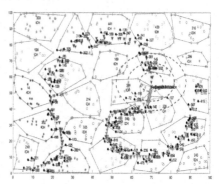

Fig. 8(a). *Circle$_{fixed}$* method performance in track 1 following TDNN based tracking

Fig. 8(b). *Circle$_{velocity}$* method performance in track 1 following TDNN based tracking

(*Contour$_{velocity}$*) in track 1. This approach proves even better and saves up to 83% energy compared to *Circle$_{fixed}$* approach. Hybrid model in this work will have similar performance as *Contour$_{velocity}$* approach as target is in nearby region and it is able to recover lost target within 3 initial levels of *Contour$_{velocity}$*.

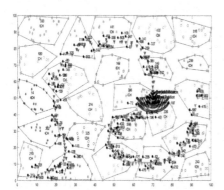

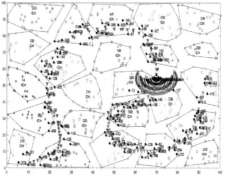

Fig. 8(c). *Contour$_{fixed}$* method performance in track 1 following TDNN based tracking

Fig. 8(d). *Contour$_{velocity}$* method performance in track 1 following TDNN based tracking

4.2   Case B: Target Moving with Sudden Change in Target Velocity

Figure 9 depicts a typical tracking scenario of a target travelling with an abrupt change in velocity. Additionally, it has a network hole region where a target may get lost if it goes through. As previously described, simulations are run for target moving using either TDNN-based tracking or Kalman-based tracking techniques. Figure 10(a) for *Circle$_{fixed}$*, Fig. 10(b) for *Circle$_{velocity}$*, Fig. 10(c) for *Contour$_{fixed}$*, Fig. 10(d) for *Contour$_{velocity}$*, and Fig. 10(e) for the hybrid approach show the simulation results for target movements and executions of recovery algorithms with Kalman based tracking algorithms, respectively.

Figure 10(a) shows target recovery performance of fixed circle (***Circle**_{fixed}*) model in track 2. It is having Kalman based approach as tracking of the target. It can be seen that target that is lost at hole region, cannot be tracked by ***Circle**_{fixed}* approach in first level recovery. Finally it gets tracked by increasing the area of circle. It requires 48.11% less energy to recover as compared to velocity based circle (***Circle**_{velocity}*) approach, as shown in Table 3.

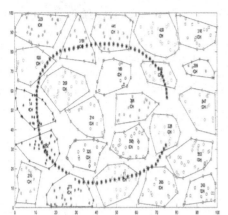
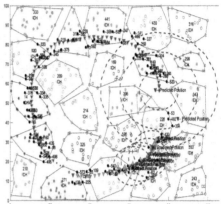

Fig. 9. Track2 scenario illustrating the movement of the target with sudden change in velocity

Fig. 10(a). *Circle*$_{fixed}$ method performance in track2 following Kalman based tracking

Figure 10(b) demonstrates results for target recovery performance of velocity based circle (***Circle**_{velocity}*) model following Kalman based approach. Target is recovered at level 8 recovery. It requires 256.571 J energy to recover the target, as shown in Table 3. It can be seen that it covers more of area, requiring many nodes and hence much more energy is being utilized in recovery. Figure 10(c) target recovery performance of fixed contour based (***Contour**_{fixed}*) approach in track 2. It can be seen that lesser area and lesser nodes are used for recovery approximate 66.58% energy being saved to recover the target as compared to ***Circle**_{velocity}* approach. Figure 10(d) shows target recovery performance of Velocity based contour (***Contour**_{velocity}*) in track 2. Here target is tracked in level 7 recovery. This approach saves up to 40.13% energy, as shown in Table 3. Figure 10(e) shows target recovery performance of hybrid based approach in track 2. This approach proves better and saves up to 84.76% energy compared to ***Circle**_{velocity}* approach. Here as per table 3 energy analysis, Hybrid method provide better results as compared to other methods.

Simulation results for target movements and executions of recovery algorithms with TDNN based tracking algorithms are shown in Fig. 11(a) for Circlefixed, in Fig. 11(b) for Circlevelocity, in Fig. 11(c) for Contourfixed, Fig. 11(d) for Contourvelocity, and Fig. 11(e) for hybrid approach respectively.

Figure 11(a) shows target recovery performance of fixed circle (***Circle**_{fixed}*) model in track 2. It is having TDNN based approach as tracking of the target. It requires 59.12% less energy to recover as compared to velocity based circle (***Circle**_{velocity}*) approach, as

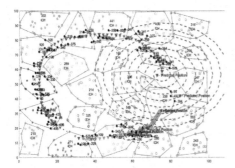

Fig. 10(b). *Circle_velocity* method performance in track2 following Kalman based tracking

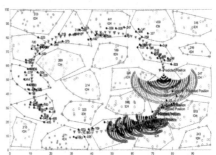

Fig. 10(c). *Contour_fixed* method performance in track2 following Kalman based tracking

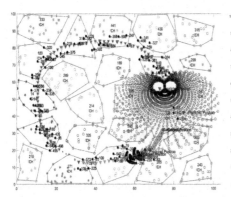

Fig. 10(d). *Contour_velocity* method performance in track2 following Kalman based tracking

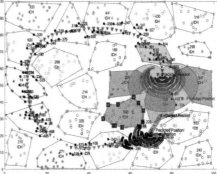

Fig. 10(e). Hybrid method performance in track2 following Kalman based tracking

shown in Table 3. Figure 11(b) demonstrates results for target recovery performance of velocity based circle (*Circle_velocity*) model for track 2. It requires 244.368 J energy to recover the target, as shown in Table 3 which is highest among all recovery methods. Figure 11(c) shows target recovery performance of fixed contour based (*Contour_fixed*) approach in track 2. It can be seen that here lesser area and lesser nodes are used for recovery 87.36% energy being saved to recover the target as compared to *Circle_velocity* approach. Figure 11(d) shows target recovery performance of Velocity based contour (Contour_velocity) in track 2. This approach saves up to 39.5% energy compared to *Circle_velocity* approach. Figure 11(e) shows target recovery performance of hybrid based approach in track 2. This approach proves most better and saves up to 89.91% energy compared to *Circle_velocity* approach. Here also Hybrid method provides better results as compared to other methods. As it can be seen in Table 3 *Circle_velocity* method uses maximum energy to recover lost target. Hybrid method with TDNN tracking provides 89% energy saving as compared to *Circle_velocity* approach.

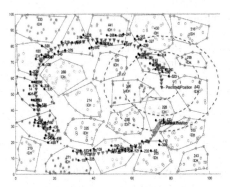 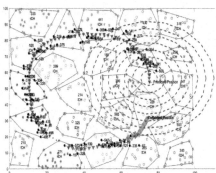

Fig. 11(a). *Circle_fixed* method performance in track2 following TDNN based tracking

Fig. 11(b). *Circle_velocity* method performance in track2 following TDNN based tracking

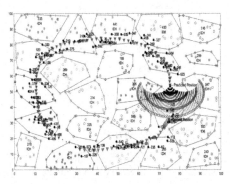 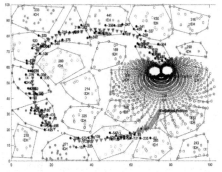

Fig. 11(c). *Contour_fixed* method performance in track2 following TDNN based tracking

Fig. 11(d). *Contour_velocity* method performance in track2 following TDNN based tracking

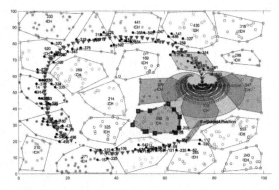

Fig. 11(e). Hybrid method performance in track2 following TDNN based tracking

Table 3. Energy analysis and energy saving with different approaches for track2

Tracking algorithm	Recovery algorithm (Joules)	Recovery energy (Joules)	Percentage of energy saved compared to $Circle_{velocity}$
Kalman	$Circle_{velocity}$	256.57	0
	$Contour_{velocity}$	153.58	40.13
	$Circle_{fixed}$	133.134	48.11
	$Contour_{fixed}$	85.7293	66.58
	Hybrid method (Contour velocity plus broadcast)	39.0922	84.76
TDNN	$Circle_{velocity}$	244.368	0
	$Contour_{velocity}$	147.729	39.5
	$Circle_{fixed}$	99.8794	59.12
	$Contour_{fixed}$	30.8664	87.36
	Hybrid method (Contour velocity plus broadcast)	24.6338	89.91

Table 4. Recovery energy (Joules) comparison with different tracks.

Track details	Tracking method	Recovery Models	Chart showing Recovery energy (Joules)
Track 1	Kalman / TDNN	$Circle_{fixed}$	
		$Circle_{velocity}$	
		$Contour_{fixed}$	
		$Contour_{velocity}$	
		Hybrid method	
Track2	Kalman / TDNN	$Circle_{velocity}$	
		$Contour_{velocity}$	
		$Circle_{fixed}$	
		$Contour_{fixed}$	
		Hybrid method	

It can be seen in Table 4, Hybrid method uses less energy in recovery of lost target for both tracks as compared to other methods. Table 4 shows overall comparison with different tracks.

5   Conclusions

In order to address the problem of energy efficiency in wireless sensor networks, a hybrid solution for target recovery is suggested. The hybrid model addresses the problem of lost target recovery by addressing drawbacks of previous approaches and utilizing advantages of broadcast based algorithm in addition to contour based recovery method. For various tracks under various velocity scenarios, various techniques, including $Circle_{fixed}$, $Circle_{velocity}$, $Contour_{fixed}$, $Contour_{velocity}$, and the suggested hybrid algorithm, have been analyzed. Results show that, in comparison to existing methods, the suggested hybrid algorithm offers an energy-efficient option for recovering lost targets.

References

1. Sankaliya, A., Joshi, M.: Performance evaluation of prediction algorithm-based tracking methods in a recovery of a lost target using wireless sensor network. In: Thakkar, F., Saha, G., Shahnaz, C., Hu, Y.-C. (eds.) Proceedings of the International e-Conference on Intelligent Systems and Signal Processing. AISC, vol. 1370, pp. 103–118. Springer, Singapore (2022). https://doi.org/10.1007/978-981-16-2123-9_8
2. Feng, W., Wang, F., Xu, D., Yao, Y., Xu, X., Jiang, X.: Joint energy-saving scheduling and secure routing for critical event reporting in wireless sensor networks. IEEE Access **8**, 53281–53292 (2020)
3. Delavernhe, F., Lersteau, C., Rossi, A., Sevaux, M.: Robust scheduling for target tracking using wireless sensor networks. Comput. Oper. Res. **116**, 104873 (2020)
4. Ahmad, T., Abbas, A.M.: EEAC: An energy efficient adaptive cluster based target tracking in wireless sensor networks. J. Interdiscip. Math. **23**(2: Sustainable Computing), 379–392 (2020)
5. Demigha, O., Hidouci, W.K., Ahmed, T.: On energy efficiency in collaborative target tracking in wireless sensor network: a review. IEEE Commun. Surv. Tutor. **15**(3), 1210–1222 (2013)
6. Jiang, B., Han, K., Ravindran, B., Cho, H.: Energy efficient sleep scheduling based on moving directions in target tracking sensor network. In: Proceedings of the 22nd IEEE International Parallel and Distributed Processing Symposium, Program and CD-ROM (2008)
7. Anvaripour, M., Saif, M., Ahmadi, M.: A novel approach to reliable sensor selection and target tracking in sensor networks. IEEE Trans. Ind. Inf. **16**(1), 171–182 (2020)
8. Tamtalini, M.A., Alaoui, A.E.B.E., Fergougui, A.E.: ESLC-WSN: a novel energy efficient security aware localization and clustering in wireless sensor networks. In: 1st International Conference on Innovative Research in Applied Science, Engineering and Technology. IEEE Explorer (2020)
9. Wang, X., Zhang, H., Han, L., Tang, P.: Sensor selection based on the fisher information of the Kalman filter for target tracking in WSNs. In: Proceedings of the 33rd Chinese Control Conference, pp. 383–388. IEEE (2014)
10. Wu, J., Li, G.: Drift calibration using constrained extreme learning machine and Kalman filter in clustered wireless sensor networks. IEEE Access **8**, 13078–13085 (2019)

11. Munjani, J., Joshi, M.: A nonconventional lightweight Auto Regressive Neural Network for accurate and energy efficient target tracking in Wireless Sensor Network. ISA Trans. **115**, 12–31 (2021)
12. Zhuang, Y., Wu, C., Zhang, Y.: Coverage hole recovery algorithm for wireless sensor networks based on cuckoo search. In: The 7th Annual IEEE International Conference on Cyber Technology in Automation, Control and Intelligent Systems (2017)
13. Jondhale, S.R., Deshpande, R.S.: Kalman filtering framework based real time target tracking in wireless sensor networks using generalized regression neural networks. IEEE Sens. J. **19**(1), 224–233 (2019)
14. Khare, A., Sivalingam, K.M.: On recovery of lost targets in a cluster-based wireless sensor network. In: IEEE International Conference on Pervasive Computing and Communications Workshops, pp. 208–213 (2011)
15. Patil, S., Gupta, A., Zaveri, M.: Recovery of lost target using target tracking in event driven clustered wireless sensor network. J. Comput. Netw. Commun., Tab8 (2014)
16. Asmaa, E.Z., Said, R., Lahoucine, K.: Review of recovery techniques to recapture lost targets in wireless sensor networks. In: International Conference on Electrical and Information Technologies (ICEIT) (2016)

Power Aware Non-Orthogonal Multiple Access for IEEE 802.11ah Based IoT Networks

Badarla Sri Pavan[1]([✉]) and V. P. Harigovindan[2]

[1] E.C.E Department, Nitte Meenakshi Institute of Technology,
Bangalore 560064, India
sripavan.rvce@gmail.com
[2] E.C.E Department, National Institute of Technology Puducherry,
Karaikal 609609, India
hari@nitpy.ac.in

Abstract. IEEE 802.11ah is a Wi-Fi standard promoted for Internet of things (IoT) applications. We propose a power aware non-orthogonal multiple access (NOMA) method for improving the performance of IEEE 802.11ah network. The restricted access window (RAW) mechanism in this standard reduces contention in dense IoT networks. Initially, with the power-domain NOMA (PD-NOMA), the data rates of devices are computed. Further, the user-clusters are formed with devices from each region using the proposed method. This further reduces contention and the user-cluster devices concurrent transmissions is possible using PD-NOMA. Using analytical model, the throughput of network is computed. From results, the proposed power aware NOMA method provides substantial improvement in performance compared to conventional IEEE 802.11ah network. The results are validated with simulations.

Keywords: Internet of things · IEEE 802.11ah · power-domain NOMA

1 Introduction

The information technology have witnessed rapid changes and IoT plays major role in this aspect. The connectivity among the devices at any time is very essential for sharing information. Nowadays, the devices are exponentially increasing especially those are connecting to the Internet. Different IoT applications such as smart city, smart health, industrial IoT, etc. are facing daunting challenges towards connectivity issue [1]. The IEEE 802.11ah is an upcoming Wi-Fi standard promoted for IoT applications [2]. It specifies physical and medium access control (MAC) layer features. The RAW mechanism is an innovative feature in IEEE 802.11ah which minimizes the contention. The RAW period (δ_R) is divided into RAW slots, devices into R groups. Every group is alloted with one RAW slot [3].

© The Author(s), under exclusive license to Springer Nature Switzerland AG 2023
I. Woungang et al. (Eds.): ANTIC 2022, CCIS 1797, pp. 141–148, 2023.
https://doi.org/10.1007/978-3-031-28180-8_10

For wireless communication, the spectrum resources are very congested and limited. Due to the limited resources in wireless spectrum, the proper multiple access technique can utilize the resources efficiently in dense IoT networks. Thus, the IEEE 802.11ah standard with a suitable multiple access technique can provide an excellent improvement in network performance in dense networking scenarios for next-generation IoT applications [2,4]. Recently, NOMA got attention of researchers because of their advantages over OMA techniques. Also, multiples transmissions in a resource block can be possible using NOMA non-orthogonally [5]. In PD-NOMA, the devices use different power levels for transmission of data [6]. In this paper, a power aware NOMA method is proposed to enhance the performance of IEEE 802.11ah network. The connectivity is very important for upcoming IoT applications.

2   Related Work

From literature, very limited works were endowed for NOMA in WLANs [7–10]. Authors of [7] targeted a mechanism for data transmission using uplink NOMA in Wi-Fi networks. From [8], a NOMA technique was included in WLAN that allowed to transmit simultaneously. In [9], an uplink NOMA was introduced in CSMA/CA networks. Authors of [10] used PD-NOMA in IEEE 802.11ah that provides improved network performance.

3   Network Architecture

The IEEE 802.11ah based network architecture with N devices as showed in Fig. 1 are deployed over access point (AP). The transmission range of AP is

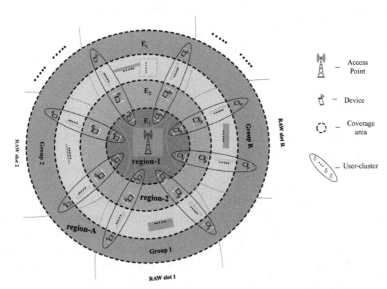

Fig. 1. Network architecture

Table 1. Data rates

Regions	1	2	3	4
$M_i^{(E_i)}$ (m)	0.16A	0.38A	0.63A	0.88A
E_i (Mbps)	8.85	2.59	0.60	0.16

classified into A regions with $a_i | i \in [1, A]$ is the radius of region-i. The data rates supported are $E_i | i \in [1, A]$. We consider the channel gain with near region has high gain and region at the fringes has low gain $\{\phi_1 \geq \phi_2 \geq \cdots \geq \phi_i\}$. From AP, the average distance of devices in region-i is,

$$M_i^{(E_i)} = \int_{a_{i-1}}^{a_i} a f_A(a) \, da \qquad (1)$$

The power levels are computed using the path loss expression $L(M_i^{(E_i)}) = 8 + 37.6 \log_{10}(M_i^{(E_i)}) + (F)_{dB}$ with the constrained nonlinear minimization using MATLAB R2021b and F is fade margin. The signal to interference noise ratio (SINR) with region-i devices is expressed as [10],

$$S_i = \frac{\mathbb{P}_{ti} \phi_i}{\mathbb{T} + \mathbb{U} + \mathbb{W}}, \qquad (2)$$

where $\mathbb{W}$ is AWGN, $\mathbb{P}_{ti}$ is transmit power and the channel gain is given by,

$$\phi_i = \frac{\mathbb{G}_{ti} \mathbb{G}_{ri}}{L(M_i^{(E_i)})}$$

The residual terms that exists during successive interference cancellation (SIC) process are represented in the denominator of Eq. (2), which are,

$$\mathbb{T} = \sum_{k=i+1}^{A} \mathbb{P}_{tk} \phi_k$$

$$\mathbb{U} = \eta \sum_{j=1}^{i-1} \mathbb{P}_{t(i-j)} \phi_{i-j}.$$

where η is SIC parameter. Further, the data rate of devices are provided in Table 1 using following relation [10],

$$E_i = \omega \log_2(1 + S_i), \qquad (3)$$

where ω is bandwidth.

The power aware NOMA based user-clustering algorithm for IEEE 802.11ah based IoT network is explained in Algorithm 1 [4,10]. Here, the data rates of devices are computed based on the assigned power levels. Further, these data rates are share with the AP through PLCP header. Now, the user-clusters are created

---

Algorithm 1. Power aware NOMA based user-clustering algorithm

1: Initialize δ_R, N, regions;

2: With PD-NOMA, compute the data rate of devices using the assigned power levels;

3: Share these data rates with the AP;

4: The user-clusters are created with one device from every region;

5: These user-clusters are uniformly divided into groups. Every group allot with a RAW slot as given in Fig. 1;

6: The devices in a particular group can contend in a RAW slot;

---

with one device from every region. These user-clusters are uniformly divided into groups and allot a group for every RAW slot. The devices in a particular group can contend in RAW slot. Once, the devices in near region got the channel access, it sends request to send (RTS) frame and AP reply with clear to send (CTS) with address of device won the contention. Now, the user-cluster devices transmit simultaneously in a RAW slot and the decoding is possible with the SIC technique.

For the analysis, the network does not have hidden devices and saturated conditions. The channel has mini-slots (δ_m) in a RAW slot. The rth group devices starts contention process with distributed coordination function (DCF). The transmission probability of rth group device is determined using mean value analysis in a RAW slot, which is given by [3],

$$\tau_r^{(E_i)} = \frac{\mathcal{M}_r[Y]}{\mathcal{M}_r[B] + \mathcal{M}_r[Y]}, \tag{4}$$

here $\mathcal{M}_r[B] = \frac{1}{2} \sum_{x=1}^{m} 2^{x-1} W_0 \left(P_{c,r}^{(E_i)} \right)^{x-1}$ is mean count of back-off slots, retry limit $m = 7$, and $\mathcal{M}_r[Y] = \sum_{x=1}^{m} \left(P_{c,r}^{(E_i)} \right)^{x-1}$ gives retransmission attempts.

3.1   Power Aware NOMA for IEEE 802.11ah Based IoT Network

The data rates are computed based on the assigned power levels as provided in Sect. 3. Using the proposed method, near region devices in r^{th} group can only compete for channel contention in a RAW slot. The collision probability having rate E_1 in a RAW slot is given by [10],

$$P_{c,r}^{(E_1)} = 1 - (1 - \tau_r^{(C_1)})^{(g_r^{(E_1)} - 1)}. \tag{5}$$

The Eqs. (4) and (5) are solved using MATLAB R2021b. The success probability having rate E_1 in a RAW slot is given by,

$$P_{s,r}^{(E_1)} = \frac{g_r^{(E_1)} \tau_r^{(E_1)} (1 - \tau_r^{(E_1)})^{g_r^{(E_1)} - 1}}{P_{tr,r}^{(E_1)}}. \tag{6}$$

Here, $P_{tr,r}^{(E_1)}$ is expressed as,

$$P_{tr,r}^{(E_1)} = 1 - (1 - \tau_r^{(E_1)})^{g_r^{(E_1)}} \tag{7}$$

Further, the transmission duration is considered with lower rate devices, i.e., the highest rate devices can transmit within that time. Hence, the rth group device with rate $E_i | i \in [1, A]$ of user-cluster in a RAW slot is expressed as [10],

$$\Delta_{nh}^{(E_i)} = \sigma_R + \sigma_C + \sigma_h^{(E_i)} + \max \left(\sigma_{\mathbb{E}[P]}^{(E_1)}, \sigma_{\mathbb{E}[P]}^{(E_2)}, \cdots, \sigma_{\mathbb{E}[P]}^{(E_i)} \right) + 3\sigma_s + \sigma_a + 4\delta. \quad (8)$$

In Eq. (8), the terms sequentially denotes the duration of RTS, CTS, header, payload, SIFS, acknowledgement, and propagation delay. The probability of Δ_ζ having ζ transactions in a RAW slot with λ mini-slots used can be expressed as [2,3],

$$P_{\Delta_\zeta}(\lambda) = \binom{\lambda - \zeta\Delta'_{nh} - 1}{\lambda - \zeta\Delta'_{nh} - \zeta} (P_{tr,r}^{(E_i)})^\zeta (1 - P_{tr,r}^{(E_i)})^{\lambda - \zeta\Delta'_{nh} - \zeta}, \quad (9)$$

where $\Delta'_{nh} = \Delta_{nh}^{(E_i)} + \sigma_d$. The random variable $\mathcal{D}$ gives the transactions in effective slot duration $\delta_{R',r} = \delta_{R,r}$—holding period. Then, the following term gives the count of mini-slots used for ζ-transactions in a RAW slot.

$$P_{\mathcal{D},r}^{(E_i)}(\zeta) = \sum_{x=\zeta}^{\delta_{R',r} - (\zeta-1)\Delta'_{nh} - \sigma_d - \delta_m} P\left\{ \sum_{r=1}^{\zeta} \lambda_{b,r} = x \right\}, \quad (10)$$

Here, the mean value of $\mathcal{D}$ in a RAW slot is,

$$\mathbb{M}_r^{(E_i)}[\mathcal{D}] = \sum_{\zeta=1}^{\mathbb{N}_t(\delta_{R',r})} \zeta P_{\mathcal{D},r}^{(E_i)}(\zeta).$$

where $\mathbb{N}_t$ is the maximum transmissions,

$$\mathbb{N}_t = \lfloor \frac{\delta_{R',r}}{\Delta'_{nh} + \delta_m} \rfloor$$

The throughput of user-cluster devices in r^{th} group in a RAW slot is [3,10],

$$\mathbb{T}_{nr} = \sum_{i=1}^{A} \frac{R \, \mathbb{M}_r^{(E_i)}[\mathcal{D}] \, P_{s,r}^{(E_i)} \mathbb{E}[P]}{\delta_R}. \quad (11)$$

Finally, the aggregate throughput using proposed method is computed as,

$$\mathbb{T}_{tn} = \sum_{r=1}^{R} \mathbb{T}_{nr}. \quad (12)$$

4   Results and Discussion

We provide analytical results with MATLAB R2021b and simulations with ns-3 [11]. An IEEE 802.11ah network having 5000 devices considered around AP. The network is divided into 4 regions. The user-clusters are created using proposed

Table 2. System parameters

Parameter	Value
$\mathbb{E}[P]$	64 bytes
δ_m	52 μs
Physical header	156 bits
RTS	20 bytes
CTS	14 bytes
DIFS, σ_d	264 μs
SIFS, σ_s	160 μs
σ_a	14 bytes
W_0	32
δ_R	1000 ms
δ	1 μs
m	7

method and devices compete in respective RAW slot. The parameters are given in Table 2. For results, the data rates with respect to four regions considered as given in Table 1. The region-1 devices have 8.85 Mbps data rate and far devices have 0.16 Mbps [10].

The aggregate throughput analysis of power aware NOMA with IEEE 802.11ah network using RTS/CTS is provided in Fig. 2. With the assigned power

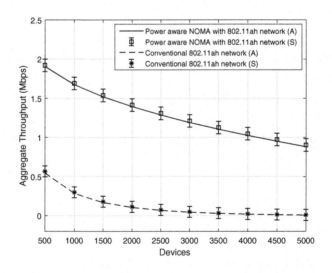

Fig. 2. Aggregate throughput

Table 3. Connectivity analysis

| N | Aggregate throughput (Mbps) | | | |
| | Power aware NOMA with 802.11ah network | | Conventional 802.11ah network | |
	Analytical	Simulation	Analytical	Simulation
500	1.9062	1.9196	0.5471	0.5675
1500	1.5191	1.5376	0.1684	0.1798
2500	1.2877	1.3085	0.0687	0.0750
3500	1.1033	1.1254	0.0301	0.0335
4500	0.9507	0.9731	0.0134	0.0152

levels using NOMA, the user-cluster devices can start concurrent transmissions. Also, the number of competing devices will be reduced, which results in decreased collisions. Hence, the power aware NOMA with IEEE 802.11ah network shows superior performance than the conventional IEEE 802.11ah.

Table 3 explores the connectivity point of view for network sizes $N \in \{500, 1500, 2500, 3500, 4500\}$. The proposed method with the devices of $N = 4500$ depicts improved aggregate throughput than conventional network for $N = 500$. The reason for this is because of proposed method using PD-NOMA. The above results clearly shows improved performance in power aware NOMA with IEEE 802.11ah network than the conventional network.

5   Conclusion

For the IEEE 802.11ah standard, a power aware NOMA method has been proposed for enhancing the performance of dense 802.11ah based IoT network. Here, the data rates are computed based on PD-NOMA and user-clusters are created using proposed method. Furthermore, analytical model has been presented for the IEEE 802.11ah using NOMA and computed the throughput. From results, it is evident that the IEEE 802.11ah network using power aware NOMA showed improved performance in terms of saturation throughput.

References

1. Fizza, K., et al.: QoE in IoT: a vision, survey and future directions. Discov. Internet Things **1**, 4 (2021). https://doi.org/10.1007/s43926-021-00006-7
2. Badarla, S.P., Harigovindan, V.P.: Restricted access window-based resource allocation scheme for performance enhancement of IEEE 802.11ah multi-rate IoT networks. IEEE Access **9**, 136507–136519 (2021)
3. Zheng, L., Ni, M., Cai, L., Pan, J., Ghosh, C., Doppler, K.: Performance analysis of group-synchronized DCF for dense IEEE 802.11 networks. IEEE Trans. Wireless Commun. **13**(11), 6180–6192 (2014)
4. Pavan, B.S., Harigovindan, V.P.: A novel channel access scheme for NOMA based IEEE 802.11 WLAN. Sādhanā **46**, (144) (2021). https://doi.org/10.1007/s12046-021-01669-2

5. Pei, X., Chen, Y., Wen, M., Yu, H., Panayirci, E., Poor, H.V.: Next-generation multiple access based on NOMA with power level modulation. IEEE J. Sel. Areas Commun. **40**(4), 1072–1083 (2022)
6. Liaqat, M., Noordin, K.A., Latef, T.A., Dimyati, K.: Power-domain non orthogonal multiple access (PD-NOMA) in cooperative networks: an overview. Wirel. Netw. **26**(1), 181–203 (2020)
7. Korolev, G., Kureev, A., Khorov, E., Lyakhov, A.: Enabling synchronous uplink NOMA in Wi-Fi networks. In: 2021 International Conference Engineering and Telecommunication, pp. 1–5 (2021)
8. Pavan, B.S., Harigovindan, V.P.: Improving the aggregate utility of IEEE 802.11 WLAN using NOMA. In: Woungang, I., Dhurandher, S.K., Pattanaik, K.K., Verma, A., Verma, P. (eds.) Advanced Network Technologies and Intelligent Computing. ANTIC 2021. Communications in Computer and Information Science, vol. 1534, pp. 168–176. Springer, Cham (2022). https://doi.org/10.1007/978-3-030-96040-7_13
9. Kwon, Y., Baek, H., Lim, J.: Uplink NOMA using power allocation for UAV-Aided CSMA/CA networks. IEEE Sys. J. **15**(2), 2378–2381 (2021)
10. Pavan, B.S., Harigovindan, V.: Power-optimized NOMA with TXOP tuning based channel access scheme for IEEE 802.11ah dense IoT Networks. IEEE Netw. Lett. **4**(4), 179–183 (2022)
11. Tian, L., Šljivo, A., Santi, S., De Poorter, E., Hoebeke, J., Famaey, J.: Extension of the IEEE 802.11ah ns-3 simulation module. In: Proceedings of the 10th Workshop on ns-3, pp. 53–60. WNS3 2018, ACM, New York, NY, USA (2018)

Effective Link Prediction in Complex Networks Using Differential Evolution Based Extreme Gradient Boosting Algorithm

Agash Uthayasuriyan[1], G. R. Ramya[2], and G. Jeyakumar[2(✉)]

[1] Department of Electrical and Electronics Engineering, Amrita School of Engineering, Amrita Vishwa Vidyapeetham, Coimbatore, India
cb.en.u4elc19005@cb.students.amrita.edu
[2] Department of Computer Science and Engineering, Amrita School of Computing, Amrita Vishwa Vidyapeetham, Coimbatore, India
{gr_ramya,g_jeyakumar}@cb.amrita.edu

Abstract. Link Prediction is the estimation of missing links or possible future links between any two nodes in a network. Based on the type of network, the use cases for these models may vary. Recommendation systems in eCommerce websites, relationship prediction in social media networks, and biological gene link assessment in the Human body are a few examples of the application of Link Prediction. The conversion of this problem into a supervised classification model is expected to yield reliable results. Ensemble learning models such as XG – Boost (XGB) combine multiple small decision trees to learn the input data and produce accurate results. But the results produced by the model vary highly based on the hyperparameters of the XGB. With the help of Differential Evolution (DE), these parameters can be optimized to perfectly fit the dataset. This paper attempts to solve the link prediction problem in complex networks using Differential Evolution-based XGB (DXGB). The working of DXGB is tested extensively on various real-world complex networks and is showcased. The experimental results reveal that the usage of DE with XGB produces a better prediction of links in complex networks. The implementation along with the results obtained is presented in this paper.

Keywords: Network analysis · Link prediction · Ensemble learning · Extreme Gradient Boost · Differential Evolution

1 Introduction

The recent innovations and advancements in the field of information technology have led to the formation of large - complex networks that consist of several nodes and links. A detailed understanding of these networks with the help of data mining techniques can be useful for solving analytical tasks on the network [1, 2, 20]. Links are the interconnections between nodes in the network and the prediction of it is expected to either anticipate future possible links in the network or find the missing link between any two nodes. Since

I. Woungang et al. (Eds.): ANTIC 2022, CCIS 1797, pp. 149–163, 2023.
https://doi.org/10.1007/978-3-031-28180-8_11

these complex networks are dynamic and evolve by the addition of new nodes or links, understanding the underlying mechanism of link formation between any two nodes in a network is a potential research problem. One of the many approaches to solving this problem is through supervised machine learning models.

Ensemble machine learning models like XG – Boost, combines the results from multiple decision trees through parallel and distributed computing and generally possess better learning of the data by producing appreciable results. However, these results largely depend on the values of the hyperparameter the XGB gets modeled with. Since there are many hyper-parameters involved in the design of XGB, and each parameter has a range of values to choose from, the selection of the best set of hyperparameter values is a crucial task and there is a need for optimization.

On the other hand, Differential Evolution, a subset of Evolutionary Algorithms, works based on the mechanisms drawn from nature to solve optimization problems by simulating principles of Darwin's survival theory. is one of the most powerful optimization algorithms and can optimize single or multiple objective functions.

This paper attempts to solve the Link Prediction problem in complex networks with a hybrid model (DXGB) consisting of XG- Boost and DE algorithm. The hyperparameter of the XGB will be optimized with the help of DE and make the hybrid model fit exactly for the network data provided. By this, a better link prediction can be achieved as the hybrid model leverages the benefits of both ML and EA algorithms.

The remainder part of the paper is organized as follows. Section 2 presents the work related to evolutionary algorithms, complex networks, and solving link prediction by using supervised learning. Section 3 explains the exact methodology carried out and followed in this paper. The results recorded and the inferences obtained are presented in Sect. 4, and finally, Sect. 5 concludes the paper.

2 Literature Review

There have been several notable research works in the field of complex networks and network link prediction. These works have been studied as a part of research to obtain a view of the present advancements relating to the field and are summarized in this section.

The improvements and future of social network analysis are presented in [7] where the author of the paper emphasizes the importance of the data mining techniques and argues that the analysis of a network should be approached with inter-disciplinary cooperation of various domains. An extensive survey presented by the researchers of [6] was studied to understand the various link prediction techniques, and their applications in real-world scenarios. The work also addresses the prediction tasks in all types of networks and concludes that there is a need for a model that works efficiently in large networks. The authors of [8] showcase the study conducted on various link pre-diction frameworks such as topic modeling and network topology in a bi-partite terrorist network.

Various methodologies followed in the anticipation of links have been reviewed such as [10] were, the temporal nature of networks is considered to solve the link prediction problem by the usage of common neighbors around two hops in the network. The degree updation based on these common neighbors was also considered as a part of the work employed. According to the research work [9], the authors explain that the global and local-based approaches of network understanding and a followed prediction task is ineffective in several cases and suggest a matrix-based mathematical model for fast and accurate link prediction. The experiment was validated in a few datasets with different characteristics to showcase the results of the matrix model. The long-term prediction problems in social networks are addressed using a long-short term deep learning model in [11] along with an encoding decoding technique for representation of data. The work takes account of the historical snapshot of the data and learns continuously to forecast links in the network.

The logistic Regression model was used in [5] to predict the links between friends in the Flickr network by following various hypotheses on the data and also prove that the application of these techniques leads to high prediction accuracy. A detailed feature extraction done in the network and assessment of link prediction in various network presented in [12] using supervised algorithms discusses the importance of these predictions and also present an experimental analysis that the individual similarity measure does not perform prediction of links well in a network. A few papers related to evolutionary algorithms were studied for a better understanding of the workings of the individual models.

In [15], The Biased Random-Key Genetic Algorithm (BRKGA) is applied to the traveling sales man problem and explains that BRKGA is an efficient methodology for solving problems involving combinatorial optimization, but it needs its parameters tuned to ensure that the algorithm's intensification and diversification are balanced. While examining the connection between the best possible mutation rate and problem complexity, the authors of [19] present that they are inversely proportional in the case of Genetic Programming [16], a part of the Evolutionary Algorithm. The base paper for XG - Boost algorithm presented in [13] has been re-visited in the view of learning the algorithm from the creator's point of view and understanding the working of it [14].

After analyzing these prior and related works, this paper aims to solve the link prediction problem in complex networks with a hybrid model of Differential Evolution and XG - Boost.

3   Proposed Method

Link Prediction in complex networks like social media networks, Transportation networks, Protein Interaction networks, etc., helps in identifying the relationship between nodes and suggests the prospective possible link or missing link in the network. Since real-life networks are complex in nature with thousands of nodes and links, predicting the links can be a challenging task. However, the task can be converted into a classification problem and solved using various algorithms like SVM, K – Nearest Neighbors, and Naïve Bayes Classifier.

Further, the learning and prediction of links in complex networks can be improved by using Ensemble learning algorithms like the Extreme Gradient Boosting algorithm (XGB) as a classification model. These ensemble algorithms integrate the results of many weaker and simpler models and predict the target class more accurately.

Although XGB assures better learning and prediction, the presence of several hyper-parameters makes it difficult to find the optimal set of them. Therefore, there is a need to optimize the XGB to be exactly suitable for the provided network as input. Evolutionary Algorithms like Differential Evolution, Genetic Algorithms can help fine-tune the parameters of the XGB and make the model a perfect fit for the provided dataset.

This paper attempts to predict the prospective links in networks using Extreme Gradient Boosting algorithm that is optimized with Differential Evolution by the following three steps:

1. Pre-processing of the network data given as input
2. Extraction of features using various measures and forming a dataset
3. Using the new dataset to predict links in the network with Differential Evolution based XG – Boost algorithm

3.1 Data Pre-processing

Most of the real-life network data only contain the already present links in the network and fail to accommodate the missing links. So, it is an important process to extract the missing links from the network data. In pre-processing, we generate the missing links and form a dataset through the class_generator algorithm. The working of the class_generator algorithm is depicted in Fig. 1. This process is also significant because, in modeling the link prediction task as a classification algorithm, the present/already available links will be mapped to one class and the missing links will be mapped to another. Since there is a high probability of the number of missing links in the network being larger than the present links, only missing links equal number to the number of present links is extracted from the network data.

```
Input: Raw Network Data with node pairs of present links
Output: Binary class dataset with present & missing links

Function class_generator (network data):
    1. Initialize network data
    2. nodes ← number of nodes
    3. links ← number of links between node pairs
    4. missing_links ← {}
    5. dataset ← []
    6. while length (missing_links) < links:
        6.1 a ← random number in range (0, nodes)
        6.2 b ← random number in range (0, nodes)
        6.3 if edge does not exist between (a, b) and
            Shortest path (a, b) > 2:
                6.3.1 add link in missing_links
    7. for each pair of datapoints in network:
        7.1 set class = 1
        7.2 add node pair with class in dataset
    8. for each pair of datapoints in missing_links:
        8.1 set class = 0
        8.2 add node pair with class in dataset
    9. return dataset
```

Fig. 1. Class_generator algorithm

By this, there is a balance achieved between the number of data points in each class and it also rules out the possibility of an imbalanced dataset. This generated dataset will be used to extract features.

3.2 Feature Extraction

Any machine learning algorithm's most significant stage is the extraction of the appropriate feature set. For link prediction, it is best to pick features that show some sort of relationship between the two vertices that will be useful for the machine learning model to classify data points based on these extracted feature attributes.

The feature vector preparation for each of the nodes in the network is implemented by using several similarity-based feature extraction techniques. For the calculation of a few parameters and to work with graphs, a python library named "networkx" is used. Networkx library hosts a variety of operations that can be performed on the network dataset. In the network that is given as input, each of the nodes is chosen individually or as a combination along with their source/destination node and is used to calculate the below-mentioned features.

Page Rank
Page rank, founded in 1996, by Larry Page and Sergey Brin was named after the founder. Using the Page rank technique, an importance score is assigned to the network nodes. The summation of all page rank values of nodes in the network will add up to 1, and this score will also be a non-negative real number. Page rank values for both the source node and destination nodes will be calculated and represented as individual feature vectors with the help of "networkx" library.

Katz Centrality
A node's Katz centrality in a network is a measure of the centrality of that node and is used to evaluate a node's relative level of influence within a network. Katz centrality counts all of the walks between any two nodes to determine influence and is implemented with the help of the "networkx" library that possesses a built-in function for the calculation of Katz centrality. Individual Katz Centrality feature vectors will be calculated and used to represent the source and destination nodes, respectively.

Shortest Path
The shortest path between two nodes is computed using the python library "networkx".

Similarity Measures
Similarity measures such as Jaccard's coefficient, cosine similarity, and Adamic Adar are calculated using the function "calculator". The steps followed in the algorithm are depicted in Fig. 2.

```
Input: Node pairs
Output: Various calculated values from the node pairs

Function calculator (node1, node2):
  1.  a ← node1
  2.  b ← node2
  3.  a_s ← set of successors for node 1 extracted using
      "networkx" library
  4.  b_s ← set of successors for node 2 extracted using
      "networkx" library
  5.  a_p ← set of predecessors for node 1 extracted
      using "networkx" library
  6.  b_p ← set of predecessors for node 2 extracted
      using "networkx" library
  7.  inter_s ← mathematical set intersection
operation
      of a_s & b_s
  8.  uni_s ← mathematical set union operation
      of a_s & b_s
  9.  inter_p ← mathematical set intersection operation
      of a_p & b_p
 10.  uni_p ← mathematical set union operation
      of a_p & b_p
 11.  jc_s ← length(inter_s) / length(uni_s)
 12.  jc_p ← length(inter_p) / length(uni_p)
 13.  c_s ← length(inter_s) / ( square root of
      (length(a_s)) * square root of (length (b_s)) )
 14.  c_p ← length(inter_p) /
      square root of (length(a_s) * length (b_s) )
 15.  adar ← 0
 16.  for each node in inter_s:
        16.1 p ← set of predecessors for node
        16.2 log_value ← log( length(p) )
        16.2 adar ← adar + (1/ log_value)
 17.  return jc_s, jc_p, c_s, c_p, adar
```

Fig. 2. Function calculator

A detailed description of the following similarity measures is as follows.

Jaccard's Coefficient. The Jaccard similarity coefficient, also known as the Jaccard similarity index, analyses the nodes in two sets to identify those that are shared and those that are unique. It serves as a comparison between the two sets of data in terms of similarity. For a set of node pairs, Jaccard Coefficient is calculated based on the provided nodes' successors as well as their predecessors as given in in (1) where n1, n2 are the nodes in the network and the numerator points to the number of successors or predecessors common in them while the denominator denotes the total number of number of successors or predecessors present in n1 and n2.

$$J(n1, n2) = |n1 \cap n2|/|n1 \cup n2| \tag{1}$$

Cosine Similarity. The cosine similarity between two nodes has a value that falls between 0 and 1. When the value is 1, it means that the neighbors of the two vertices are the same; when it is zero, there are no neighbors in common. Cosine Similarity is calculated based on the provided nodes' successors as well as their predecessors and is given by (2), where the n1, n2 are the nodes in the network and the numerator points to the number of successors or predecessors common in them while the denominator denotes the product of the square rooted value of the degree of successors/ predecessors for each node.

$$C(n1, n2) = |n1 \cap n2|/(\sqrt{\text{len}(n1)} * \sqrt{\text{len}(n2)}) \tag{2}$$

Adamic Adar. According to the number of shared links between two nodes, Lada Adamic and Eytan Adar developed the Adamic-Adar index in 2003 to anticipate links in a social network. It is described as presented in (3) where n1, n2 are the nodes in the network. For every common node in present in n1 and n2, the inverse logarithmic value of its length of predecessors is calculated and summated overall.

$$A(n1, n2) = \sum_{k \varepsilon N(n1) \cup N(n2)} 1/\log(N(k)) \tag{3}$$

Following feature extraction, each feature vector is rescaled and standardized with the help of the python library "sklearn". The values produced are centered on the mean and have a unit standard deviation. As a result, the DXGB algorithm finds it easier to process all the features as they are nearly the same size and are given equal importance.

3.3 Differential Evolution Based XG – Boost Algorithm

XG – Boost (XGB) uses ensemble learning with the help of gradient boosted decision trees. Ensemble learning techniques aggregates the result of various machine learning models in order to improve the overall accuracy rates and learning of given input data [21]. This technique when used as classification models [22], reduces the probability of a data point to be mapped to an incorrect class by having several weak classifiers to make a strong classifier. At each stage, the proceeding model tries to mitigate the errors of the previous model. This process is followed until the input data is learnt correctly.

In XGB, the decision trees are generated one after the other and each feature in the dataset provided is given a weight before them being subsequently fed into the trees that predict the outcomes. In the proceeding trees, the weight of the features of the wrong predictions are increased and then fed into the tree. These distinct classifier trees are then combined to produce a robust and accurate model. Since, XGB involves multiple models and methods, there are a number of hyper-parameters involved in the design of XGB. These hyper parameter values contribute largely to the prediction done by the XGB algorithm.

In the link prediction problem, the XGB will solve a binary classification problem. For a binary classification problem, as a part of the experiment, the parameters of XGB such as 'tree_method' is set to "hist", 'grow_policy' is set to 'lossguide', 'objective' is set to 'binary: logistic' and 'eval_metric' is set to 'auc'. Although these parameters are pre-set, there are a few parameters that have to be set based on the dataset provided to the XGB. These parameters, along with their short description and considered range of values in the experiment is presented in Table 1.

Table 1. Description on a few hyper parameters of XGB

Hyper parameter	Short description	Considered range of values
n_thread	Number of parallel threads to be run	(1, 10)
eta	Step size to prevent overfitting	(0.001, 1)
max_depth	Maximum depth of a tree	(0, 20)
max_leaves	Maximum number of nodes	(3, 1500)
min_child_weight	Sum of weights of all observations	(0.001, 1)
alpha	L1 regularization	(2, 8)
scale_pos_weight	To balance positive and negative weights	(1, 10)
sub_sample	Fraction of observations for sampling	(0, 1)
colsample_bytree	Subsample ratio of columns occurring for each tree	(0.001, 1)
colsample_bylevel	Subsample ratio of columns occurring for each depth level	(0.001, 1)
seed	Random number seed	(1, 10)

Since, finding the best set of hyper parameter values is a computationally challenging task, optimization algorithms such as Differential Evolution can help find the values of each parameter that makes the model learn better on the provided dataset.

Differential Evolution (DE) is a part of the Evolutionary Algorithm family. Evolutionary Algorithms (EAs) use natural mechanisms to solve optimization issues by mimicking the behaviors behind the survival of the fittest principle. The EAs are frequently utilized as a pre-made tool for a range of optimization challenges that arise in the real world, as well as for improving the accuracy of machine learning models by optimizing their hyper-parameters of them. DE is a simple, yet powerful stochastic global optimizer for a continuous search domain. It has been demonstrated to be a reliable global optimizer and has been used to solve numerous global optimization issues [3, 4, 18].

DE stands out of the EA family by employing a unique mutation operator in the creation of the offspring population. The DE approaches the optimization of hyper parameters of XGB by the methodology depicted in Fig. 3.

The DE model, starts with an initial population (N) that consisting "D" real parameters, the DE algorithm runs for several generations (G) and in each generation, the solution set gets updated. Considering the target vector $x_{i,G} = [x_{1,i,G}, x_{2,i,G}, \ldots x_{D,i,G}]$ where 'i' ranges from 1, 2, 3 … N. The population consists of a set of hyperparameter values which are chosen individually from their range. First, the mutation operation is applied. Mutation operation enables the DE to expand the search space for the solutions

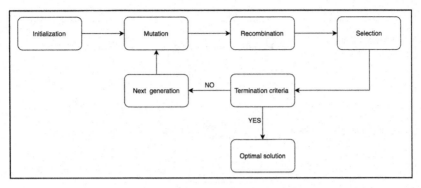

Fig. 3. A sample working of Differential Evolution algorithm

[19]. Although there are many variants of the mutation operation, the basic and most used DE/rand/1 operation is followed in this experiment as depicted in (4) where F is the mutation factor and is designed based on the data given as input.

$$v_{i,G+1} = x_{r1,G} + F(x_{r2,G} - x_{r3,G}) \tag{4}$$

For each of the vectors, three random solutions are chosen from the population set to form a new solution $v_{i,G+1}$ (donor vector) by adding the weighted difference of the two of the vectors to the third vector. After mutation, recombination is done which helps to incorporate the best solutions of the before generation. In recombination, a trial vector $u_{j,i,G+1}$ is formed from the target vector and donor vector where the elements of the donor vector enter the trial with a probability value (CR). The trial vector is decided based on Eq. (5).

$$u_{j,i,G+1} = \begin{cases} v_{j,i,G+1} & \text{if rand}_{j,i} \leq CR \text{ or } j = I_{rand} \\ x_{j,i,G} & \text{if rand}_{j,i} > CR \text{ and } j \neq I_{rand} \end{cases}$$
$$i = 1, 2, \ldots, N; \; j = 1, 2, \ldots, D \tag{5}$$

I_{rand} ranges from $1, 2, 3 \ldots D$ and ensure that the $v_{i,G+1}$ is not equal to $x_{i,G}$. The target vector is then compared with the trial vector and the one with the highest fitness value is considered for next generation. This process is continued for the given number of iterations (termination condition). By this process, the hyperparameters of the XGB can be optimized and the best solution set can be obtained. The overall proposed methodology in this experiment can be visualized as presented in Fig. 4.

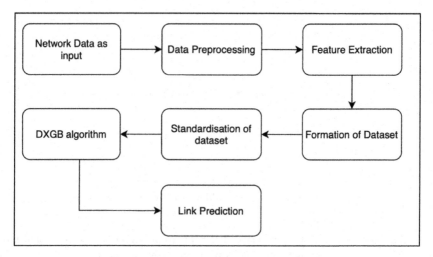

Fig. 4. Methodology followed in experiment

4 Experimental Results and Discussion

4.1 Data Set Considered

To test the robustness of the model, the experiment was conducted on 8 different real-world datasets which were obtained from the open-source platform KONECT Project [17]. Additionally, the dataset set "Twitch" is obtained from online website – Kaggle [23], for further testing of the model. These datasets were carefully selected from a variety of domains to generalize the link prediction among all types of networks. The considered networks are chosen to be directed in nature, uni-partite, and those which do not have self-loop. A detailed description of experimented datasets is presented in Table 2.

4.2 Experimental Setup and Results

For each of the networks, after completion of the pre-processing stage and feature extraction, the dataset obtained is then split into testing and training data. 60% of the data was used for training the model and the remaining 40% of the data was used to test and validate.

The Differential Evolution algorithm was run up to 230 iterations with a population size of 10. The values of mutation and recombination rates were designed as 0.1 and 0.3 respectively. Throughout the process, the loss (1 − accuracy) value is obtained along with the search space of all the hyperparameters ranging through all iterations and is visualized. The general notation used in this paper to represent hyper – parameters is presented in Table 3.

As a sample of obtained plots, the hyper – parameter search space along with the fitness values (loss) for the Wikipedia network is visualized in Fig. 5. For Wikipedia Network as shown in Fig. 5, the values for each hyper-parameter of the XGB is randomly searched initially and as the iterations increases, the search space gets limited to

Table 2. Dataset description

Name	Type of network	Number of nodes	Node meaning	Number of links	Link meaning
Twitter	Social media network	23,370	User	33,101	Follows
Google Plus	Social media network	23,628	User	39,242	Friendship
Epinions	Trust network	75,879	User	508,837	Trust
Cora	Citation network	23,166	Paper	91,500	Citation
Human protein	Protein interaction network	2,239	Protein	6,452	Interaction
Wikipedia	Wikipedia links network	2,929	Article	118,603	Wiki - link
Chicago road	Road transportation network	12,982	Node	39,018	Road
Dolphins	Community of bottle nose dolphins	62	Dolphin	159	Association
Twitch	Gamers who stream	7,126	Streamers	35,324	Friendship

Table 3. Hyper-parameter notation

Hyper – parameter in XGB	Notation used
eta	W1
max_leaves	W2
max_depth	W3
subsample	W4
colsample_bytree	W5
colsample_bylevel	W6
min_child_weight	W7
alpha	W8
scale_pos_weight	W9
nthread	W10
seed	W11

obtain the best possible value. This makes the loss of XGB reduce from 0.2 to around 0.02. Therefore, indirectly increasing the accuracy from around 80% to 97.81%. This improvement in XGB through continuously optimizing the parameters with help of the Evolutionary Algorithm, makes the link prediction more accurate and reliable.

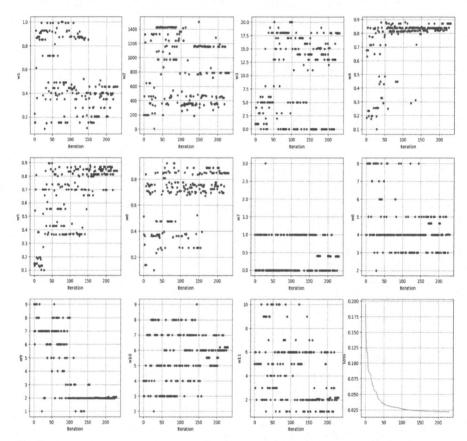

Fig. 5. Hyper parameter search space across iterations and fitness values for Wikipedia dataset

The best hyperparameter values obtained for each of the considered networks along with their accuracy, and the comparison with standard XGB is presented in Table 4, showcasing the improvement in accuracy of the prediction task by using DXGB.

In Fig. 6, the DE initially starts with random hyper-parameter values for the XGB, accounting for the low fitness (high loss). But across iterations, as the optimal settings for each of the hyper-parameter is found, the fitness value can be observed to increase. The same is visualized and is presented for each of the considered datasets.

The experiment carried out intending to reduce loss and increase the accuracy of the model was achieved with the help of optimizing the 11 hyperparameters of XGB by DE. Although the initial solutions provided by Differential Evolution do not possess high

Table 4. Best values obtained for considered datasets along with comparison to standard XGB

Name	W1	W2	W3	W4	W5	W6	W7	W8	W9	W10	W11	Acc. DXGB	Acc. XGB
Twitter	0.44	615.63	14.66	0.83	0.98	0.82	0.29	3.02	1.47	3.82	3.0	**96.4%**	**91.7%**
Google Plus	0.97	370.75	16.26	1.0	0.95	0.69	0.90	6.28	2.34	8.58	9.30	**99.3%**	**92.2%**
Epinions	0.95	995.5	15.56	0.91	0.83	0.94	0.86	4.38	4.68	8.91	3.82	**99.2%**	**96.6%**
Cora	0.86	344.97	15.05	0.73	0.78	1.0	0.55	2.60	1.01	1.16	1.93	**99.0%**	**95.2%**
Human protein	0.76	1139	13	0.99	0.42	1.0	1.0	6.0	1.0	8.0	6.0	**88.6%**	**80.2%**
Wikipedia	0.45	788.48	17.96	0.86	0.83	0.85	0.39	4.01	2.07	6.20	2.16	**97.8%**	**94.6%**
Chicago road	0.56	1205.91	6.81	0.57	0.51	0.88	0.19	3.94	1.31	8.70	7.51	**82.9%**	**82.3%**
Dolphins	0.88	1332.49	3.60	0.82	0.18	0.19	0.36	2.63	2.07	7.60	2.64	**74.3%**	**60.1%**
Twitch	0.56	798.74	8.58	0.82	0.73	0.57	0.75	2.38	1.0	8.20	1.08	**82.7%**	**76.5%**

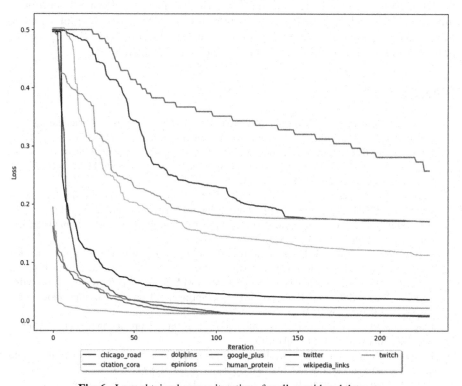

Fig. 6. Loss obtained across iterations for all considered datasets

accuracy, as the number of iteration increase, the DE manages in identifying the right and optimal set of hyperparameter values.

This makes the XGB model fit exactly to the dataset of the individual networks and learns to predict the links in the network more accurately and precisely. However, this set of optimal solutions comes at a cost of high computation and time complexity since the model is run several times continuously for a longer time.

5 Conclusions and Future Work

This work is an attempt to hybridize the Extreme Gradient Boosting algorithm and Differential Evolution algorithm to solve the Link prediction problem in complex networks. Extensive feature extraction from the networks is employed and the dataset is formed. The dataset is then used to test the working of the DXGB algorithm. Real-world network data such as social networks, citation networks, transportation networks, etc. is used to assess the performance and robustness of the model. The inferences of the results obtained revealed that the usage of DE with XGB provides a better link prediction in networks. However, the limitation observed is that to obtain the better optimal solution, the DE algorithm has to be run several times which comes as a downside concerning time complexity and computational costs. Further, to check the possibilities of obtaining a better and quick solution, the XGB algorithm can be hybridized with other algorithms of the EA family which will be carried out as a part of our future work.

References

1. Nair, M.R., Ramya, G.R., Bagavathi Sivakumar, P.: Usage and analysis of Twitter during 2015 Chennai flood towards disaster management. Procedia Comput. Sci. **115**, 350–358 (2017)
2. Ramya, G.R., Bagavathi Sivakumar, P.: An incremental learning temporal influence model for identifying topical influencers on Twitter dataset. Soc. Netw. Anal. Min. **11**(1), 1–16 (2021). https://doi.org/10.1007/s13278-021-00732-4
3. Rubini, N., Venkata Prashanthi, C., Subanidha, S., Jeyakumar, G.: An optimization framework for solving RFID reader placement problem using differential evolution algorithm. In: The Proceedings of International Conference on Communication and Signal Proceedings (ICCSP), Chennai, pp. 1290–1294. IEEE Xplore (2017)
4. Saketh, K.H., Sumanth, K.B.V.N.S., Kartik, P.V.S.M.S., Aneeswar, K.S.S., Jeyakumar, G.: Differential evolution with different crossover operators for solving unconstrained global optimization algorithms. In: Chen, J.-Z., Tavares, J.M.R.S., Shakya, S., Iliyasu, A.M. (eds.) ICIPCN 2020. AISC, vol. 1200, pp. 381–388. Springer, Cham (2021). https://doi.org/10. 1007/978-3-030-51859-2_35
5. Liaghat, Z., et al.: Application of data mining methods for link prediction in social networks. Soc. Net. Analy. Min. **3**, 143150 (2013)
6. Kumar, A., Singh, S.S., Singh, K., Biswas, B.: Link prediction techniques applications and performance: a survey. Phys. A Stat. Mech. Appl. **553**, 124289 (2020)
7. Scott, J.: Social network analysis: developments, advances, and prospects. Soc. Netw. Anal. Min. **1**(1), 21–26 (2011)
8. Anil, A., et al.: Link prediction using social network analysis over heterogeneous terrorist network. In: 2015 IEEE International Conference on Smart City/SocialCom/SustainCom (SmartCity), pp. 267–272 (2015)

9. Papadimitriou, A., Symeonidis, P., Manolopoulos, Y.: Fast and accurate link prediction in social networking systems. J. Syst. Softw. **85**(9), 2119–2132 (2012)
10. Yao, L., Wang, L., Pan, L., Yao, K.: Link prediction based on common-neighbors for dynamic social network. Procedia Comput. Sci. **83**, 82–89 (2016)
11. Chen, J., et al.: E-LSTM-D: a deep learning framework for dynamic network link prediction. IEEE Trans. Syst. Man Cybern. Syst. **51**(6), 3699–3712 (2021)
12. Kumari, A., Behera, R.K., Sahoo, K.S., Nayyar, A., Kumar Luhach, A., Prakash Sahoo, S.: Supervised link prediction using structured-based feature extraction in social network. Concurr. Comput. Pract. Exp. **34**, e5839 (2020)
13. Chen, T., Guestrin, C.: XGBoost: a scalable tree boosting system. In: Proceedings of 22nd ACM SIGKDD International Conference on Knowledge and Discovery Data Mining, pp. 785–794 (2016)
14. Chen, J., Zhao, F., Sun, Y., Yin, Y.: Improved XGBoost model based on genetic algorithm. Int. J. Comput. Appl. Technol. **62**(3), 240–245 (2020)
15. Srinivas Rao, T.: An ant colony TSP to evaluate the performance of supply chain network. Mater. Today Proc. **5**, 13177–13180 (2018)
16. Piszcz, A., Soule, T.: Genetic programming: analysis of optimal mutation rates in a problem with varying difficulty. In: The Proceedings of Artificial Intelligence Research Society Conference, vol.19, Flairs, FL, pp.451–456 (2006)
17. Kunegis, J.: KONECT—the Koblenz network collection. In: Proceedings of the 22nd International Conference on World Wide Web, pp. 1343–1350 (2013)
18. Jeyakumar, G., Shunmuga Velayutham, C.: Heterogeneous mixing of dynamic differential evolution variants in distributed frame work for global optimisation problems. Int. J. Adv. Intell. Paradig. **22**(3–4), 318–335 (2022)
19. Dhanalakshmy, D.M., Akhila, M.S., Vidhya, C.R., Jeyakumar, G.: Improving the search efficiency of differential evolution algorithm by population diversity analysis and adaptation of mutation step sizes. Int. J. Adv. Intell. Paradig. **15**(2), 119–145 (2020)
20. Anusha, K., Chokkalingam, S.P.: Detecting stress based social interactions in social networks. Test Eng. Manag. (TEM) **81**, 5465–5471 (2019)
21. Ramesh, T.K., Shashikanth, A.: A machine learning based ensemble approach for predictive analysis of healthcare data. In: 2020 2nd PhD Colloquium on Ethically Driven Innovation and Technology for Society (PhD EDITS), pp. 1–2 (2020)
22. Chandralekha, M., Shenbagavadivu, N.: An improved tree model based on ensemble feature selection for classification. Turk. J. Electr. Eng. Comput. Sci. **27**(2), 1290–1307 (2019)
23. https://www.kaggle.com/datasets/andreagarritano/twitch-social-networks

Hybrid Partitioning for Embedded and Distributed CNNs Inference on Edge Devices

Nihel Kaboubi[1,2]() , Loïc Letondeur[1] , Thierry Coupaye[1],
Fréderic Desprez[2], and Denis Trystram[2]

[1] Orange SA, Grenoble, France
{nihel.kaboubi,loic.letondeur,thierry.coupaye}@orange.com
[2] Univ. Grenoble Alpes, Inria, CNRS, Grenoble INP, LIG, Grenoble, France
{frederic.desprez,denis.trystram}@inria.fr

Abstract. Convolutional Neural Networks (CNNs) and Deep Neural Networks (DNNs) are ubiquitously utilized in many Internet of Things applications, especially for real-time image-based analysis. In order to cope with concerns such as resiliency, privacy and near real time analysis, these models must be deployed on edge devices. Particularly for large models, the large number of parameters becomes a bottleneck for the inference process because edge devices are resource constrained, subjects to failures and/or hardware faults. New solutions to cope with these issues are required. This paper proposes a hybrid partitioning strategy, architecture and implementation (called HyPS), which identifies the best positions in the model structure to split the network structure into small partitions that fit resources constraints of edge devices noticeably by decreasing instantaneous memory needs. The generated partitions consume less memory than the original network and each partition can be processed almost separately, resulting in new ways to process CNN's execution at the edge. Thanks to this partitioning strategy, large CNNs inference can be run without modifying the main model architecture. The proposed approach is assessed on the well-known neural network structure of VGG16 for image classification. The results of the experimental campaign show that the partitioning method allows for the successful inference of large models on devices with limited overhead and high accuracy.

Keywords: Distributed inference · Edge computing · Edge intelligence · Convolutional Neural Networks · Internet of Things

1 Introduction

Internet of Things (IoT) and Artificial Intelligence (AI) affect our daily lives in a revolutionary way. Billions of connected devices should be deployed in homes, buildings, vehicles, cities, and industries. Connected devices product data and

I. Woungang et al. (Eds.): ANTIC 2022, CCIS 1797, pp. 164–187, 2023.
https://doi.org/10.1007/978-3-031-28180-8_12

offer interactions used to enhance smart services in their surrounding environment. AI models can be used and are based on DNNs and noticeably on CNNs on various tasks such as image recognition, video analysis, or object detection.

CNNs are typically deployed on remote cloud servers, requiring the upload of data through all the communication infrastructure. This can be an issue regarding infrastructure solicitation and latency. Such uploads are also problematic concerning privacy [1,2] as data are shared with third-party and hackers might access this information along the way [3]. Performing inference in the cloud can be a problem for some critical applications for a big telecommunications operator, which nevertheless has an extensive infrastructure at the network periphery (e.g.: relay antennas, network point of presence (POPs), internet access boxes, etc.) [4].

A better alternative solution is to relocate CNN models at the edge of the network. This process is known as Edge intelligence, i.e., Edge computing applied to AI [5]. The edge intelligence paradigm moves computing resources from clouds and data centers as close as possible to the originating data source. Edge infrastructure is composed of one or more edge devices that will leverage deep learning models to implement accurate predictions, make decisions, and decode behavior behind sensors' data.

However, inferring pre-trained large CNNs consumes significant time, memory, and computational resources that can be higher than most edge devices' capabilities. Some existing works use model compression techniques [6,7] to adapt CNN models to run at the edge. Others use partitioning strategies to split CNN's structures into small partitions that fit edge devices [8,9]. Besides hardware capabilities, edge devices often suffer from failures that result in unpredictable service loss because edge devices are often located in unprotected areas (e.g., customers' homes). Another tremendous topic related to edge intelligence is the protection of secrets. This issue concerns data to process and the used AI models themselves. If various approaches intent to fill the gap between resources demands of CNNs models and edge devices capabilities for inference, they do not cover the subject as proposed in this paper, that is without impacting accuracy, without requiring to re-train a model and/or without complex computations before deployment. The proposed solution also brings preliminary answers concerning secrets protection and execution reliability. Other existing approaches only partially cover the described problems.

The main contributions of this work are listed below:

- **a strategy which couples different partitioning methods. It offers the opportunity to effectively partition a large CNN model by identifying the best partitioning points while minimizing the communication cost and inference response latency.** This strategy allows inference processing using large CNNs without modifying their main architecture and guarantees high accuracy. **Partitioned CNNs can be easily executed on one device or can be distributed across a cluster of multiple edge devices,**

- **an orchestration architecture** for hybrid distributed inference. This architecture also exhibits good properties in terms of reliability, resilience, and privacy,
- **a prototype** that demonstrates the functional behavior of the proposed concepts of HyPS assessed by **experimental results on an actual testbed**.

The paper is organized as follows. Section 2 presents the background, context and objectives of this work, and introduces illustrative use cases which will be used throughout the article. Section 3 presents the proposed solution and architecture overview. Section 4 discusses the evaluation of HyPS on a defined testbed and the analysis of experimental results. Section 5 briefly reviews the relevant existing researches related to the proposed work. Section 6 concludes and introduces some perspectives for future works.

2   Background, Context, and Objectives

2.1   Overview of CNNs

A CNN specializes in processing data with a grid-like topology, such as an image. CNN architecture is essentially composed of two parts: *feature extractor* and *classifier*. Feature extractor layers process the original input, and classifier layers then classify the resultant features. A CNN model mainly includes *Convolution layers (Conv)*, *Pooling layers (Pool)*, *Batch Normalization layers (BN)*, and *Fully Connected layers (FC)*. A CNN can be deployed monolithically on a single-edge device or partitioned into multiple partitions. CNNs have a chain topology as each layer only depends on the previous layer's output and not on the other layers. This characteristic will help us to distribute partitions on one or multiple devices and sequentially perform inference, which will be detailed later.

A well-known CNN example is VGG16 [10], used as an illustrative example in the rest of this article. Visual Geometry Group (VGG) is a popular and clear-in-structure CNN model that includes all mainstream layer types. VGG16 (cf. Fig. 1) is trained with 16 layers consisting of 13 convolution layers and three fully connected layers.

VGG architecture has been retained in this article because it has proven to be a reference in many complex tasks such as object detection, image recognition and image classification. Noticeably, VGG16 achieves 92.7% top-5 test accuracy in ImageNet [11], a dataset of over 14 million images belonging to 1000 classes. We chose VGG16 as a representative architecture of CNN models. VGG16 represents a great potential for applications in several real-world use cases such as smart factory [12] and autonomous vehicles [13]. Therefore, performing VGG16 inference at the edge can benefit to many IoT applications.

2.2   Context

The VGG16 model needs more than 520 MB in memory and requires 15.5G multiply-accumulate operations [14] to classify one image with a 224 * 224 resolution. The training of a VGG model can require 2–3 weeks [15] on advanced

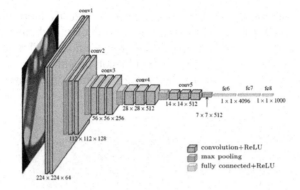

Fig. 1. VGG16 architecture. (Source: Researchgate.net)

GPUs. Because subsequent CO_2 emissions have an impact on the environment [16], the proposed approach aims at capitalizing on the AI models existing training without requiring any re-training phase. Even during inference, these pre-trained models often present a high computational cost, that prevents their execution on constrained devices. In this work, we will use a specific strategy that allows performing inference of partitioned VGG16 on edge infrastructure while minimizing induced overhead and solving resource constraints issue.

2.3   Objective: CNN Model Partitioning Strategies

CNN inference is usually computation-intensive, especially when CNN models are large. They require a lot of memory to run inference calculations but many edge devices do not have enough resources. To this, many previous works have proposed strategies for deploying CNNs models on resource-constrained devices. Besides following concepts and definitions, further details are given in the related works section.

Among existing kinds of strategies, *partitioning* refers to the splitting of an entire model on specific locations to obtain one or more partitions. A first partitioning strategy is *data partitioning*: dividing the input data given to every CNN layer into several small partitions. Weight partitioning is not considered, and each partition includes all layers of the CNN model. The input data to layer L_i of partition P_i may have to be shared with layers from other partitions. After the computation of all partitions, outputs may be fused to get the final inference output. This does not decrease memory requirements and implies a high complexity to synchronize all the inference.

A second partitioning strategy is *vertical model partitioning* which consists in building partitions made of one or several complete layers named V-partition. In Fig. 2, partitions are represented by rectangles colored in blue, and each of them includes one or a group of consecutive layers. Each layer keeps weights and parameters fixed during the training phase. Going deeper into the network, the complexity increases, and filters are applied to identify more prominent elements. Vertical partitioning strategy is easier to deploy and run as pre-trained models can be divided into multiple layer groups and distributed to different edge nodes. Nevertheless, this strategy could not be sufficient to decrease the memory footprints of partitions as they are a combination of entire layers.

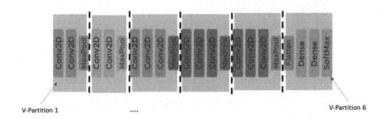

Fig. 2. Vertical partitioning.

A third partitioning strategy is *horizontal model partitioning* which partitions the weights across layers. A partition can include one or more units from different layers. The input data are sent to all partitions. All partitions must communicate and synchronize with each other because all the output data must be concatenated with the output data from the different partitions to get the final output. The horizontal strategy is efficient regarding memory footprint limitation for each partition, but at the cost of a high complexity concerning deployment and execution, as it requires more synchronizations than the vertical strategy.

This article proposes to combine advantages of existing partitioning strategies and more precisely to combine vertical and horizontal partitioning. Because only these two strategies can reduce memory requirements, a heuristic is also proposed: it mainly consists in using vertical partitioning as a bootstrap for distributed execution of CNNs and then horizontal partitioning but only when needed and on a single partition at a time. As shown further in this article, this approach permits to achieve good performances, enable reliable execution of a CNN on a typical edge infrastructure and open new use cases.

2.4   Illustrative Real Life Use Cases

The hybrid partitioning strategy proposed in this article is helpful in several real-life use cases. For example, consider an AI service company sells an image recognition system linked to surveillance cameras. This system can be integrated into any embedded device that composes a typical Telecommunication company.

For instance, an image recognition task can be performed on an internet gateway. Such a device can not run many CNNs by itself without optimizations. Our proposed strategy addresses resource constraints by distributing inference in time on a single device or multiple devices. Model partitioning reduces the size of the tasks assigned at a time to each device, reducing memory consumption and avoiding calculation problems.

Because internet gateways can also be abruptly unplugged, all the processed data can be lost, and the inference must then be restarted from scratch. In our solution, intermediate inference outputs after each partition are saved, avoiding restarting calculations from scratch. Interrupted calculations can thus be resumed making inference more reliable on edge devices.

A second use case is that of a smart factory, a digitized manufacturing facility that uses connected devices, machinery, and production systems to collect and share data continuously. Image recognition models are used to improve the productivity and detect defective pieces rapidly. This smart factory is composed of different production areas. Each area takes charge of a part in the manufacturing process. The available machines in the production are dedicated to do a specific production task and are very constrained in memory and computing capacity.

Generally, the manufacturer wants to avoid buying more powerful machines to classify images but instead takes advantage of their existing machines. These machines must give a real-time response. So, running the whole AI model on one machine can increase the computational load, cause memory saturation, and increase subsequent response latency. HyPS solves this problem by sequentially running a partitioned model on one or multiple machines. Indeed, the execution of one partition will be less expensive than the whole model in one block. The collected data are used locally and are not accessible by other production units. So, the proposed strategy helps the factory to improve the quality of construction pieces without slowing the production process nor causing damages to the machinery. It also permits to preserve data and model privacy since each machine only deals with specific partitions of the global model. The following sections present the proposed partitioning strategy and discuss the architecture details for HyPS implementation.

3 Proposed Approach: Vertical, Horizontal, and Hybrid Partitioning Strategies

The methods of partitioning a network have been already proposed in previous papers, but the novelty here is the strategy of mixing two ways of partitioning (vertical and horizontal). This technique aims at deploying trained CNN model on edge device(s) without any modification in the entire architecture or loss in accuracy while optimizing the computation time as much as possible.

The main objective of this contribution is to capitalize on the AI models previous training phase, use it actively on inference and avoid the re-training phase as much as possible. In Sect. 3.1, the vertical partitioning method is introduced and presented over different cases. In Sect. 3.2, a second existing way of partitioning, namely horizontal partitioning, is presented. Finally, Sect. 3.3 contains the new partitioning strategy and the benefits behind coupling two strategies of partitioning.

3.1   Vertical Partitioning Strategy

Vertical partitioning is a valuable strategy that splits a large pre-trained CNN structure so that each partition includes a set of consecutive layers. This strategy does not divide the calculated weights for each layer. Each V-partition is defined by a specific output layer and generates its feature map. Dimensions of feature maps produced by the output layer can vary considerably, resulting in a possible huge communication. Therefore, the choice of the output layer is essential. The output layer is the decisive point in the dimensionality of the generated feature map, which will be transmitted to the next partition. The feature map shape through the CNN layers is irregular, and it depends on the filter size applied in the layer, the input dimension or the feature map output of the prior layers, and the type of the layer.

As mentioned in Subsect. 2.1, all layers in CNNs are arranged following a specific pattern. The output feature map of a convolutional layer is a complex matrix with high dimensions. After each convolution block, there is a pooling layer. This layer performs the dimensionality reduction on the input by reducing the number of parameters. V-partitions can be deployed separately on devices with limited memory and low computation capacity. However, to get a final inference response, it is necessary to ensure feature map transmission between partitions. This process generates high communication costs if the transmitted data are extensive and may increase latency. Fortunately, the communication charge in a vertical partitioning strategy is less than the communication cost in a horizontal partitioning strategy, as explained in the following subsection.

3.2   Horizontal Partitioning Strategy

As mentioned in the previous section, the vertical partitioning splits the DNN model at the layer granularity while horizontal partitioning splits a DNN layer at the neurons granularity. Horizontal partitioning is the thinnest way of partitioning. Inside a model, layers have different number of parameters and for some layers this number of parameters can be very high. Those layers demand a powerful computing capacity to generate feature map. For limited resources devices, it could be impossible to perform calculations of complex layers in one operation. So, vertical partitioning alone is insufficient to perform CNN inference efficiently on edge devices.

For example, our experiments showed it was impossible to run the VGG16 model without horizontal partitioning on Raspberry Pi 3B+ with 1 GB of RAM. This specific layer has a number of parameters that exceeds one hundred two million $(102 * 10^6)$ parameters which is too high for a device as a Raspberry Pi. The horizontal partitioning strategy splits a given complex layer into small groups of neurons, whereas the input data layer is not partitioned.

In Fig. 3, the complex layer in the VGG16 structure is partitioned into four H-partitions which are represented by a green rectangle (four H-partitions are chosen to simplify the presentation in the figure). In this case, partitioning one layer into H-partitions reduces the number of parameters, storage needs,

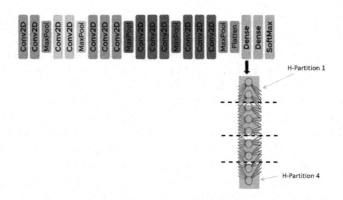

Fig. 3. Horizontal partitioning of the first fully connected layer in the VGG16 structure.

and the memory required to compute layer features. Therefore, the CNN layer that includes intensive computations is divided into many H-partitions. Each H-partition is only responsible for computing a part of the output of the current layer. At the same time, a specific algorithm collects and merges all the output's H-partitions to get the full feature map before executing the next layer.

Partial features maps collection and merging is a synchronization process that introduces a synchronization cost. This cost does not exist for vertical partitioning, so to preserve performance, horizontal partitioning must be used as few as possible. The following section describes how HyPS takes the highest benefits from both sorts of partitioning.

3.3   Hybrid Partitioning Strategy

Customers and industrial users need help choosing the best partitioning strategy that enables large CNN model inference on resource-constrained device(s). A preliminary decision support system that provides a guided partitioning strategy is proposed. HyPS takes input information about the global model structure to be partitioned and the characteristics of the target edge infrastructure. Afterward, the proposed approach helps to identify the strategic split points to get partitions and precise the type of partitioning to be applied.

Using either vertical or horizontal strategy could not solve entirely the problem of edge infrastructure incapacity to run a given model partition. For a large CNN model like VGG16, vertical partitioning generates V-partitions that are still computationally intensive and complex to be executed on a edge device(s). On the other hand, horizontal partitioning splits the CNN layers into thinner H-partitions. However, H-partitions must also be fused to obtain the final result of the partitioned layer: this fusion increases both the communication and the computing times.

In consequence, we argue that H-partitions must be restricted to avoid ineffective operations. The intended solution aims to minimize computational costs related to H-partitions synchronization and prevents any degradation in model accuracy. The hybrid partitioning strategy provides a solution to identify *mandatory partitioning points* and *optional partitioning points* on the CNN structure. HyPS prioritizes vertical partitioning and applies horizontal partitioning, if it is mandatory, to perform the CNN partition execution on the target edge infrastructure. The proposed algorithm starts by going through all the model layers one by one and checks if it is possible to run it on the edge device. The program runs this process until reaching a complex layer which results in three vertical partitions for one particular complex layer: one V-partition before the first added mandatory split point, a second after the second mandatory split point and a third constituted of the complex layer itself and alone. Then, the third V-partition containing the complex layer is itself partitioned into H-partitions as small as required to fit targeted execution infrastructure. HyPS operates H-partitioning when required and on a single layer at a time, to preserve original model performances. Algorithm 1 allows to identify the mandatory partition points for an input CNN model.

Algorithm 1. Get mandatory split points

Require:
1: *Model*: CNN model
2: *Threshold* : maximum number of parameters supported by the device
Ensure: *LM* : list of total mandatory split points
3: **for** each layer in *model* **do**
4:     **if** number of parameters > Threshold **then**
5:         *LM* ← Mandatory Split Points
6:     **else if** the last layer **then**
7:         **return** *LM*
8:     **end if**
9: **end for**

After a first step consisting in the identification of the possible mandatory split points, HyPS identifies optional split points in a second step. Optional split points are particular locations in the NN architecture where partitioning operation allows to obtain smaller V-partitions to cope with particular needs related to the use of the NN (e.g. privacy concerns). HyPS identifies all pooling layers as so called *Optional Split Points*. The benefits of using pooling layers include reducing the complexity, speeding up the calculations, and improving the efficiency of HyPS. Indeed, pooling layers are the most suitable output layer for the model partitions. This type of layers reduces the dimension of the output feature map resulting in a minimal data transfer between consecutive V-partitions. HyPS takes advantage of these layers to reduce the communication overhead of feature map transmission between V-partitions.

On a CNN structure, there are two main scenarios. First, it is possible to apply only vertical partitioning on the optional split point on the condition that the generated V-partitions are uncomplicated and can be executed on edge device(s). Otherwise, applying vertical and horizontal partitioning is indispensable enable the partitioned model inference.

The optional split points are helpful in several use cases, when the user needs to distribute the partitioned model inference on multiple devices, and/or wants to increase the number of V-partitions. According to the user objective, HyPS provides final output partitions ready to be deployed on the target edge device without any bottlenecks. HyPS can be used by a simple customer or can be integrated into a software program that provides an automated deploying solution of NN. Thanks to HyPS, the edge infrastructure can be covered more easily. The model structure, in addition to edge infrastructure, should be known before starting the partitioning process.

Identifying these optional split points leads to making several combinations. In the case of the VGG16 structure, there are five strategic split points (five pooling layers), so there are several possible V-partitions. The pooling layers throughout the VGG16 model have different output dimensions. The pooling layers' output dimensions decrease when going closer to the final output layer. For example, the VGG16 output feature map dimension passes from $112 * 112$ in the first pooling layer to $7 * 7$ in the last. Theoretically, splitting the model on the last strategic point, with the most miniature feature map, is more efficient in minimizing communication overhead.

In this work, HyPS was applied to the VGG16 model to perform the model inference on Raspberry PI 3 B+. The VGG16 model requires horizontal partitioning on the first fully connected layer (fc6), which is very complex and cannot be executed on the targeted infrastructure. Figure 4 shows the VGG16 structure with the positions of the mandatory partitioning locations represented by continuous red lines and optional partitioning locations represented by dashed green lines. Mandatory split points are located before and after the first fully connected layer. So, VGG16 must be partitioned vertically on this position, and the fc6 must be split horizontally. The optional split points bring the opportunity to get more than three V-partitions, while minimizing the communication overhead.

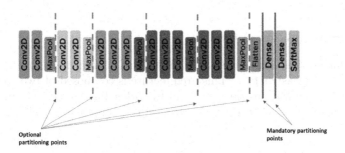

Fig. 4. Mandatory and optional split positions of VGG16 model structure.

The generated partitions can be deployed separately and distributed either over time, or spatially into multiple devices. The way how partitions are executed is known as scheduling. Figure 5 reveals only one distribution scenario among several, to illustrate the proposed contribution well. This figure reveals only one distribution scenario among several to illustrate the proposed contribution well. The cluster is composed of four edge devices. In this schema, T1, T2, T3, T4, and T5 are consecutive partitions' instantiation and execution times. In this case, the VGG16 is partitioned into four V-partitions represented by blue rectangles. The first fully connected layer (L19) is divided into four H-partitions: HP1, HP2, HP3, and HP4, represented by green rectangles. Four is the minimum number of H-partitions for which the number of parameters is sufficiently reduced to fit a specific edge device, as discussed further in the evaluation part of this article.

The inference of the partitioned VGG16 is launched following a sequential process. The V-partitions are executed one after the other. Only the H-partitions of the fc6 can be performed in parallel, as shown in Fig. 5. Besides this particular scenario, advanced scheduling possibilities exist and are led to further publications. The next subsection describes HyPS architecture entities responsible for partitioning and scheduling.

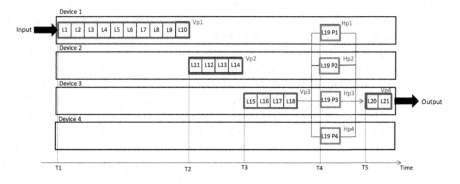

Fig. 5. Hybrid partitioning of VGG16 model deployed on a cluster of four edge devices.

3.4   Architecture Overview

A particular architecture is defined to distribute inference and run partitioned model on edge infrastructure. This architecture is composed of two tree topologies: one for computations purposes and the other for related communications. Each topology is formed through the instantiation of a hierarchical star pattern at each level.

Computations Topology. The computations topology comprises two types of entities: one *manager* and multiple *workers*. The manager is responsible for the

AI model partitioning and the partition distribution on device nodes. A manager can have workers that serve as sub-managers that manage a distinct group of workers. Every manager manages the execution of a given AI model through successive jobs, by scheduling the execution of partitions on different workers. The different entities constituting the computations topology can be seen in Fig. 6. Figure 6 shows an example of a distributed inference of a partitioned VGG16 that is used in an industrial use case inspired by [17]. The manager is denoted "M1" while the workers are denoted "W machine". The manager decides the number of partitions taken by every worker. To simplify, only one manager and three workers are represented in Fig. 6. Nonetheless, this number can be significantly higher in reality. A worker can receive and execute one or more partitions submitted by its direct manager. The dotted lines represent the communication links between the entities.

Communications Topology. The communications topology is an overlay of the computations topology. It manages data exchanges between entities. A communication hub (denoted "C1" in Fig. 6) transmits data between the manager and its workers.

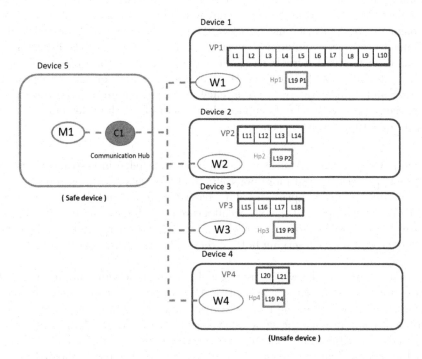

Fig. 6. Example of distributed inference architecture of VGG16 model.

The manager and the workers know how to contact the communication hub. This one separates their communications thanks to a specific addressing policy. The communication hub allows for a reactive approach for each worker, where each starts computing only when data are effectively present at a given address. For example, Worker W3 in Fig. 6 does computations of V-partition 3 (Vp3) only when the feature map coming from computations of V-partition 2 done by worker 2 (Vp2) is returned to the communication hub.

The proposed architecture presents different advantages concerning edge infrastructure specificities, in particular resilience, reliability issues and also secrets protection.

Resilience and Reliability. In addition to limited computing and memory resources, edge devices can suffer from many dysfunctions. Among them, energy cutoffs can occur, as is the case with customers who abruptly unplug their internet gateway to save energy. HyPS offers resilience to NN inference execution at the edge by enabling backups policies, such as those described and used for the IoT in [18].

HyPS permits the recovery of already done computations because the communication hub ensures the persistent storage of the intermediate data exchanged between workers. Such reliable storage is fundamental in case of a problem during the inference process. The stored data can then be used as backups to resume the inference, without restarting from scratch. Furthermore, thanks to distributed infrastructure, it is possible to run the same partition on several edge devices. This redundancy guarantees a high quality of service for the user and reduces the response latency in case of failure. Inference results of the same partitions can be done on multiple nodes for failure detection purpose [19], thanks to a voting consensus.

Secrets Protection. Another concern, regarding edge infrastructure, relates to secrets protection, and more precisely, to all possible information disclosures. Possible disclosures comprise the data passed in input and obtained from the output of a given NN, and the NN architecture itself. If data can unveil industrial or private secrets, NN models are assets in which investments were made for their design and training. Preserving both of them is an important concern that HyPS addresses.

Each worker only knows its manager, the communication hub, a part of the entire model, and the data it processes. Also, the manager knows all the architecture, all the workers, the communication hub, and the data processed. The communication hub has the same knowledge as the manager. As a consequence, two kinds of entities can be identified regarding secret protection. The manager and the communication hub must be protected. They must be hosted on safe devices that cope with strong security policy (represented in the green rounded corner rectangle in Fig. 6). The workers are considered "unsafe" (described in the red rounded cornered rectangles in Fig. 6). Regarding entities' knowledge about described secrets in the Fig. 6 example:

- Only M1 and C1 know the full AI model,
- Only M1 and C1 know the entire data,
- Other entities only know a part of the AI model,
- Other entities only know a part of the data.

Thanks to these different roles, *it is possible to manage not only the possible data divulgation but also, the NN model divulgation. To the best of our knowledge, the literature weakly covers this second aspect.* Workers outside the safe zone will receive only partial data already executed. HyPS uses the distributed inference process to guarantee data privacy even when workers run on unsafe machines. Indeed, only the manager and the communication hub have the actual image, while related workers (including sub-managers) only have intermediate feature maps. In the absolute, each manager is ensured neither to know the entire NN nor the actual data because it could be a sub-manager. Therefore, revealing the actual image after layers operations is difficult. It is demanding to interpret the partial data since having undergone several unknown transformations.

HyPS architecture and principles have been implemented in a prototype that permits a first round of experiments.

4   Implementation and Experimental Results

This section details the system setup, implementation of the proposed approach, and interpretation of experimental results that show the behavior of HyPS execution, with a real use case on a practical testbed.

4.1   System Setup

The methodology used consists in two steps. First, partitioning the model into sequential sub-networks which can then be sent to edge nodes. The partitioning function is implemented in Python, using TensorFlow and Keras libraries. Second, after the partitioning phase, the distributed inference process is executed on a realistic collaborative edge computing testbed that consists of four Raspberry Pi's: 1 Raspberry PI 3 model B (ARM Cortex-A53 Quad-Core processor - 1 GB RAM) and three Raspberry PI 3 model B+ (Broadcom BCM2837B0, Cortex-A53 64-bit SoC @ 1.4 GHz - 1 GB RAM). All devices are connected within the same network via a LAN cable. The capabilities of those nodes represent typical edge devices [17]. According to the official website of Keras, VGG16 is a large model (528 MB) and it comprises 138.4 M of parameters. Experiments are done using the VGG16 NN model that is specified by a chain topology, and trained with the ImageNet dataset. In the following experiments, images of fixed size of 224×224 are used.

4.2   Experimental Results

In this section, experimental results are presented. It was not possible to achieve direct comparison of performances between HyPS and other existing solutions, as it appears to be not relevant. As described further in this article, existing solutions either imply to offload computations in the cloud, or do modifications to the original NN resulting in accuracy loss. HyPS permits to process inference at the edge, without requiring offloading or NN modification. These characteristics cope with industry realistic use cases for which, strict performances must be guaranteed To evaluate the proposed strategy, a set of experiments was carried out to observe the effects of running inference of partitioned model on the inference time and the communication overhead. The following metrics are measured for each experiment:

- *Inference time:* the time necessary for the whole inference. It includes both the computation and communication time.
- *Computation time:* the duration for nodes to process an inference, excluding communications.
- *Communication time:* the transfer time of intermediate feature map from one partition to another.

Experiments are performed in two steps. The first step consists in the identification of both the mandatory and the best optional split points in this model structure. For this purpose, the vertical partitioning is applied in different locations on the VGG16 structure to compare the quality of partitioning for each case and the impact on communication overhead. After choosing the best positions to split the model, the horizontal partitioning is applied in the second step to enable the execution of each complex layer. This second step is discussed further, noticeably to measure the impact of the number of H-partitions on the inference performances.

The first experimentation objective is to evaluate the impact of vertical partitioning and layer types on communication overhead and inference time.

Impact of the Vertical Partitioning on the Communication Overhead
The VGG16 model is partitioned vertically to get the smallest possible V-partitions: one partition includes only one layer. 21 V-partitions are generated since the model contains 21 successive layers. Figure 7 shows the positions of the vertical partitioning.

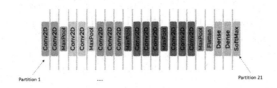

Fig. 7. VGG16 model partitioned vertically on 21 partitions.

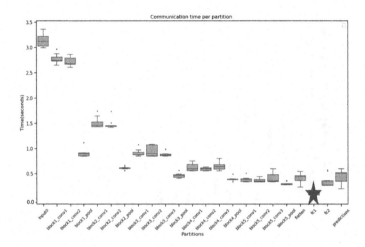

Fig. 8. Communication overhead of partitioned VGG16 model vertically on 21 partitions deployed on Raspberry Pi.

The next step is to distribute the partitioned model inference over time, and execute partitions on the testbed. The execution of the whole VGG16 is done on the Raspberry Pi with one exception: the V-partition that contains the first fully connected layer. Because this layer in too complex, it cannot be executed without a horizontal partitioning. This particular point is discussed further, but for the present experiment, the problematic V-partition is simply offloaded onto a PC. In this experimentation, the measures on the following figures related to the offloaded partition (represented by a blue star) are ignored. Only measures of the V-partitions executed on edge devices are under consideration. This experimentation allowed to precisely locate the layer that poses a problem when running VGG16.

Figure 8 presents the communication overhead for the 20 V-partitions runnable on a Raspberry Pi. The communication overhead decreases from one layer to another. This decrease is explained by the reduction of the dimension of the feature maps generated by the pooling layers. It appears that the communication overhead depends on the dimension of the feature map, the larger the feature map, the slower it is transmitted. The number of parameters does not impact the communication cost because the convolution layers with the lowest communication cost are the layers with a high number of parameters Fig. 9 presents the measured feature map size generated by each V-partition. The measured size of data transmitted between V-partitions appears to be directly correlated to the feature map dimensionality and by extension, to the communication overhead measured above. This chart shows local minima in the feature map size map generated by the pooling layers.

Orange color arrows indicate these local minima in Fig. 9 which correspond to pooling layers in the VGG16 structure. To minimize the communication overhead, it is efficient to split the model after the pooling layers. This positions

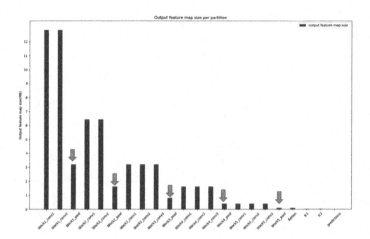

Fig. 9. Output feature map size per V-partition.

represented the optional strategic split points. Besides, all the pooling layers do not have the same impact on the communication overhead: the closer to the output the pooling layer, the less the communication overhead. Therefore, the optional split points that are close to the output layer should be favored.

Figure 10 shows a vertical partitioning on two different locations in the VGG16 structure: (a) presents the VGG16 model partitioned on nine partitions, the output layer of the first five partitions is a convolutional layer, (b) gives the VGG16 model partitioned on nine partitions, the output layer of the first five partitions is a pooling layer. The main goal of this experimentation is to measure the communication overhead in the two cases and compare the results. The difference between convolutional and pooling layers is that the convolutional layer serves to detect patterns, in multiple sub-regions, in the input feature map, using different filters. In contrast, the pooling layer progressively reduces the representation's spatial size, reducing the number of parameters and amount of computations in the CNN. In the two ways of partitioning, the transmitted feature map's size differs because the output layer in the nine partitions is not the same.

The box plots (a) and (b) in Fig. 11 show, respectively, the overall communication time when, the output layer in the partitions of the VGG16 are either convolutional layers or, pooling layers. The values measured for the fc6 are ignored because it is offloaded on a PC. For the first five partitions, the communication overhead, when the output layer is a pooling layer, is lower than the communication overhead when the output layer is a convolution layer. For the partition nř1 in graph (a), the communication time is two times higher than the communication time in a graph (b). The difference between the cases is the size of data transmitted between partitions because the pooling layers reduce

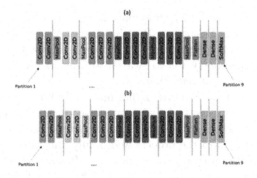

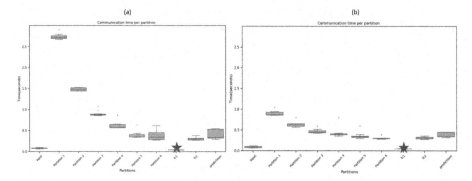

Fig. 10. (a) VGG16 model partitioned vertically on convolutional layers (b) VGG16 model partitioned vertically on pooling layers.

Fig. 11. (a) Communication time of partitioned VGG16 on convolutional layers (b) communication time of partitioned VGG16 on pooling layers.

the shape of the feature map generated by the convolution layer just before. To conclude, these experiments show that:

1. **the best optional positions, to split the model and reduce communication overhead, are the pooling layers,**
2. **applying only vertical partitioning is not enough to deliver VGG16 inference on the testbed,**
3. the V-partition that obstructs the inference process contains the first fully connected layer, and this is why two mandatory split points are required: after and before the fc6, to isolate this particular layer into a separated V-partition that will be then H-partitioned. **This demonstrates the relevance of the proposed hybrid partitioning.**

Next experiments aims determining the optimal number of H-partitions for the particular case of the VGG16 that allows fc6 inference on edge device.

Impact of the Hybrid Partitioning on the Inference Time and the Communication Overhead. VGG16 is partitioned first vertically, on the mandatory split points and then, horizontally on the fc6 split point. Partitions are executed on a single Raspberry Pi using a wide range of H-partitions numbers. During the inference executions, it appears that a too small number of H-partitions leads Raspberry Pis to swap, resulting in very poor performances due to Raspberry Pis resources exhaustion.

The swap activation adds more virtual memory, allowing the system to deal with more memory-intensive tasks without out-of-memory errors or, having to shut down other processes. However, the downside is that accessing the swap file significantly slows down the process and finally, increases the inference time. Swapping is not satisfactory regarding devices efficiency. That is why, for next experiments, we deactivate swap to ensure partitions are light enough.

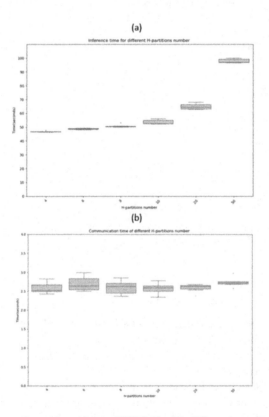

Fig. 12. (a) Inference time of partitioned VGG16 with different number of H-partitions. (b) Communication overhead of partitioned VGG16 with different number of H-partitions.

VGG16 is partitioned on the mandatory split points identified by HyPS. These points are shown in red lines in Fig. 4, then the complex layer fc6 is partitioned horizontally into H-partitions. According to the memory constraints, it is mandatory to split the fc6 at least into four H-partitions. With more than four H-partitions, a Raspberry Pi is able to support the inference of the entire VGG16. This number should not be too high to prevent from getting a huge communication overhead.

The next step is to try a different number of H-partitions and to observe if it impacts the inference time and the communication overhead. Figure 12 shows the results of testing VGG16 inference on a single device with different H-partitions numbers. The box plots in graph (a) show that inference time is relatively constant, until 8 H-partitions, and then, increases exponentially. For 50 H-partitions, the inference time is two times higher than partitioning the fc6 into 4 H-partitions. The graph (b) in Fig. 12 presents the communication overhead for different numbers of H-partitions. To minimize the communication overhead, four H-partitions is the optimal number.

These experimental and practical results, based on the implemented prototype, validate the proposed approach. Indeed, horizontal partitioning leads to high communication overhead. All H-partitions need to be fused to obtain the output feature map, which adds synchronization time to the computing time of each H-partitions apart. Therefore, **it is imperative to avoid non-mandatory horizontal partitioning and use hybrid partitioning strategy**.

5 Related Work

This section discusses a variety of related approaches which perform DNN inference on resource-constrained edge devices. Existing solutions are classified into two categories to address this issue. First, many works reduce the model size using specific model compression techniques that modify the model architecture, and make it lighter by reducing model parameters. There are four main categories of model compression techniques: quantization [20,21], pruning [22], Knowledge Distillation(KD) [23], and low-rank factorization [24]. Model Compression broadly reduces model size and latency overhead, and allows DNN inference at the edge. However, these techniques reduce accuracy for large and complex models, and require retraining to recover the model performance. The proposed solution avoids the retraining step, and provides an inference response with the original model accuracy.

Second, several approaches adopt different partitioning strategies to split DNN structure into small partitions that can be distributed and deployed separately on IoT devices. A lot of research consider DNN structure as a graph, and use graph partitioning techniques to split the NN [25–27]. Some researches focus on DNNs with chain topology, and apply partitioning strategy according to the characteristics of NN structure.

In [28], *Zhao et al.* proposed DeepThings, a locally distributed and adaptive CNN inference framework in resource-constrained IoT devices. DeepThings proposes a Fused Tile Partitioning (FTP) which consists in partitioning all convolutional layers horizontally into independent tasks. This approach allows to minimize the RAM memory footprint by reducing the sizes of input and output activations. However, its main drawback is the replication of the network's parameters on all the devices, thus increasing the memory footprint at system level. The CNN layers with huge number of parameters (e.g., fully connected layers) are not partitioned, and they are deployed on powerful gateway device. In contrast, our methodology focuses on partitioning large CNNs, and deploys all model partitions on resource-constrained devices.

In [29], *Mao et al.* partitions layers horizontally and the layers' input and output data, using the Biased One-Dimensional Partition (BODP) method. MoDNN treats each computing part of every single layer as an individual task, leading to high synchronization costs among devices. The mutual waiting would also greatly increase the inference latency. When the number of workers increases, the latency of MoDNN increases rather than decreases. Due to the frequent synchronization, MoDNN is sensitive to the network environment. In contrast, horizontal partitioning is restricted as much as possible to a single layer. Moreover, increasing the number of workers reduces the inference time, thus reducing latency.

Vertical partitioning has been used in many previous works. For example, *Tang et al.* in [30] proposes a vertical partitioning strategy to split the CNN model and perform inference at the edge. This work aims to reduce the memory requirement per edge device. The algorithm used to do vertical partitioning is not suitable for complex problems because it requires more significant amounts of computing power and extremely complex fitness models. Also, this algorithm is computationally expensive and time-consuming. On large CNNs, more than vertical partitioning is needed to obtain inference response on the edge device. The advantage of HyPS is the simplicity of the partitioning strategy, and the coupling of both vertical and horizontal partitioning.

In the same direction, *Kang et al.* in [31] propose to partition a DNN model vertically, and distribute partitions between cloud server and mobile device, according to the network situation. Neurosurgeon is one of the first works to investigate layer-wise partitioning. The split point is decided intelligently depending on the infrastructure network conditions and devices capacities.

In this work, partitioning at the layer granularity can provide significant latency and energy efficiency improvements. Partitioning between the last pooling layer (pool5), and the first fully connected layer (fc6 in Fig 1) of the Alex Net architecture, achieves the lowest latency. In our work, we split the DNN model systematically based on the layer's type, and we distribute partitions across only edge devices without any recourse to cloud servers. Authors in [32] proposed a CNN splitting algorithm that efficiently splits CNN vertically, in exactly two parts, between edge and cloud, and reduces bandwidth consumption. Various parameters are considered, such as CPU/RAM load at the edge, input image dimensions, and bandwidth constraints, to choose the best splitting layer.

F. Xue et al. in [33] proposed a locally distributed DNN inference framework based on layer-wise and fused-layer parallelization. EdgeLD can dynamically and flexibly partition a DNN model for parallel execution, to adapt to heterogeneous computing resources and different network conditions. However, our strategy enables sequential inference execution and aims to reduce communication costs.

6   Conclusion and Future Works

This article proposes a hybrid partitioning strategy that performs partitioning of large CNNs thanks to the identification of the best split points. Large CNNs can successfully be run on the resource-constrained device(s), while minimizing inference time and communication overhead.

The main contributions of this paper are: i) a hybrid partitioning strategy for running large CNN model inference on resource-constrained edge devices including a method for identifying mandatory and optional split positions in a CNN structure. ii) an architecture and a prototype (called HyPS) that implements the proposed approach, and iii) first experiments and evaluation of HyPS on a realistic testbed concerning a typical CNN.

Experimental results show that: i) the split point position impacts communication overhead, ii) the number of partitions from a horizontal partitioning influences the overall communication overhead, and iii) partitions can be scheduled sequentially on a single device or distributed on multiple devices. Experiments highlight that HyPS helps to choose the right partitioning, generates partitions ready to be deployed separately at the edge, and schedules subsequent tasks execution.

This work opens multiple perspectives. First, many other experiments have been left for the future. For instance, it would be interesting to analyze the experiment results of running a partitioned model on multiple devices. Another promising direction could investigate *batch inference*, which would generate predictions on a batch of observations on single and multiple devices.

Acknowledgement. This work was partially supported by the Multi-disciplinary Institute on Artificial Intelligence MIAI at Grenoble Alpes (ANR-19-P3IA-0003), and by the IOLab Inria-Orange joint laboratory.

References

1. Raza, M.R., Varol, A., Varol, N.: Cloud and fog computing: a survey to the concept and challenges. In: 2020 8th International Symposium on Digital Forensics and Security (ISDFS). IEEE (2020)
2. Abdalla, P.A., Varol, A.: Advantages to disadvantages of cloud computing for small-sized business. In: 2019 7th International Symposium on Digital Forensics and Security (ISDFS). IEEE (2019)
3. Krutz, R.L., Krutz, R.L., Russell Dean Vines, R.D.V.: Cloud Security a Comprehensive Guide to Secure Cloud Computing. Wiley, New York (2010)
4. Venugopal, S., et al.: Shadow puppets: cloud-level accurate AI inference at the speed and economy of edge. In: USENIX Workshop on Hot Topics in Edge Computing (HotEdge 2018) (2018)
5. Deng, S., et al.: Edge intelligence: the confluence of edge computing and artificial intelligence. IEEE Internet Things J. **7**(8), 7457–7469 (2020)
6. Ademola, O.A., Leier, M., Petlenkov, E.: Evaluation of deep neural network compression methods for edge devices using weighted score-based ranking scheme. Sensors **21**(22), 7529 (2021)

7. Berthelier, A., et al.: Deep model compression and architecture optimization for embedded systems: a survey. J. Sig. Process. Syst. **93**(8), 863–878 (2021)

8. Kang, Y., et al.: Neurosurgeon: collaborative intelligence between the cloud and mobile edge. ACM SIGARCH Comput. Archit. News **45**(1), 615–629 (2017)

9. Zhang, S., et al.: Deepslicing: collaborative and adaptive CNN inference with low latency. IEEE Trans. Parallel Distrib. Syst. **32**(9), 2175–2187 (2021)

10. Kim, J.H., Poulose, A., Han, D.S.: The customized visual geometry group deep learning architecture for facial emotion recognition. Available at SSRN 4087604

11. Russakovsky, O., et al.: ImageNet large scale visual recognition challenge. Int. J. Comput. Vision **115**(3), 211–252 (2015). https://doi.org/10.1007/s11263-015-0816-y

12. Althubiti, S.A., et al.: Circuit manufacturing defect detection using VGG16 convolutional neural networks. Wirel. Commun. Mob. Comput. **2022** (2022)

13. Khanum, A., Lee, C.-Y., Yang, C.-S.: Deep-learning-based network for lane following in autonomous vehicles. Electronics **11**(19), 3084 (2022)

14. Zhou, Z., Chen, X., Li, E., Zeng, L., Luo, K., Zhang, J.: Edge intelligence: paving the last mile of artificial intelligence with edge computing. Proc. IEEE **107**(8), 1738–1762 (2019)

15. Simonyan, K., Andrew, Z.: Very deep convolutional networks for large-scale image recognition. arXiv 1409.1556 (2014)

16. Strubell, E., Ganesh, A., Mccallum, A.:Energy and policy considerations for deep learning in NLP, 3645–3650 (2019). https://doi.org/10.18653/v1/P19-1355

17. Letondeur, L., Ottogalli, F.-G., Coupaye, T.: A demo of application lifecycle management for IoT collaborative neighborhood in the Fog: practical experiments and lessons learned around docker. In: IEEE Fog World Congress (FWC) 2017, pp. 1–6 (2017). https://doi.org/10.1109/FWC.2017.8368526

18. Ozeer, U., Letondeur, L., Salaün, G., Ottogalli, F.-G., Vincent, J.-M.: F3ARIoT: a framework for autonomic resilience of IoT applications in the Fog. Internet Things **12**, 100275 (2020). ISSN 2542-6605

19. Chaurasia, B., Verma, A.: A comprehensive study on failure detectors of distributed systems. J. Sci. Res. **64**(2) (2020)

20. Gholami, A., et al.: A survey of quantization methods for efficient neural network inference. arXiv preprint arXiv:2103.13630 (2021)

21. Garifulla, M., et al.: A case study of quantizing convolutional neural networks for fast disease iagnosis on portable medical devices. Sensors **22**(1), 219 (2021)

22. Lin, Shaohui, et al. "Towards optimal structured cnn pruning via generative adversarial learning." Proceedings of the IEEE/CVF Conference on Computer Vision and Pattern Recognition. 2019

23. Wang, G.-H., Ge, Y., Wu, J.: Distilling knowledge by mimicking features. IEEE Trans. Pattern Anal. Mach. Intell. (2021)

24. Noach, M.B., Goldberg, Y.: Compressing pre-trained language models by matrix decomposition. In: Proceedings of the 1st Conference of the Asia-Pacific Chapter of the Association for Computational Linguistics and the 10th International Joint Conference on Natural Language Processing (2020)

25. Zhang, B., et al.: Dynamic DNN decomposition for lossless synergistic inference. In: 2021 IEEE 41st International Conference on Distributed Computing Systems Workshops (ICDCSW). IEEE (2021)

26. Hu, C., Li, B.: Distributed inference with deep learning models across heterogeneous edge devices. In: IEEE INFOCOM 2022-IEEE Conference on Computer Communications. IEEE (2022)

27. Jeong, H.-J., et al.: IONN: incremental offloading of neural network computations from mobile devices to edge servers. In: Proceedings of the ACM Symposium on Cloud Computing (2018)
28. Zhao, Z., Barijough, K., Gerstlauer, A.: DeepThings: distributed adaptive deep learning inference on resource-constrained IoT edge clusters. IEEE Trans. Comput.-Aided Des. Integr. Circuits Syst. (2018)
29. Mao, J., Chen, X., Nixon, K.W., Krieger, C., Chen, Y.: MoDNN: local distributed mobile computing system for deep neural network. In: Design, Automation and Test in Europe Conference and Exhibition (DATE), pp. 1396–1401 (2017). https://doi.org/10.23919/DATE.2017.7927211
30. Tang, E., Stefanov, T.: Low-memory and high-performance CNN inference on distributed systems at the edge. In: Proceedings of the 14th IEEE/ACM International Conference on Utility and Cloud Computing Companion. Association for Computing Machinery, New York (2021). Article 26, 1–8. https://doi.org/10.1145/3492323.3495629
31. Kang, Y., et al.: Neurosurgeon: collaborative intelligence between the cloud and mobile edge. ACM SIGARCH Comput. Archit. News. **45**, 615–629 (2017). https://doi.org/10.1145/3093337.3037698
32. Mehta, R., Shorey, R.: Deepsplit: dynamic splitting of collaborative edge-cloud convolutional neural networks. In: 2020 International Conference on COMmunication Systems NETworkS (COMSNETS). IEEE (2020)
33. Xue, F., Fang, W., Xu, W., Wang, Q., Ma, X., Ding, Y.: EdgeLD: locally distributed deep learning inference on edge device clusters. In: Proceedings of IEEE 22nd International Conference on High Performance Computing and Communications; IEEE 18th International Conference on Smart City; IEEE 6th International Conference on Data Science and Systems (HPCC/SmartCity/DSS), December 2020, pp. 613–619 (2020). DSS50907.2020.00078. https://doi.org/10.1109/HPCC-SmartCity

Application of Abelian Mechanism on UFS-ACM for Risk Analysis

Padma Lochan Pradhan[✉]

Nalla Malla Reddy Engineering College, Hyderabad, India
pradhan.cse@nmrec.edu.in

Abstract. This proposed research paper focuses on and takes care of Abelian-Mudulo's application over a Unix Access Control Mechanism to resolve the unordered, unset-up, uncertainty of the UFS. The purpose of the Abelian mechanism is going to implement the UFS ACM at the right time in the right way by applying the attributes of a Unix File System (Read, Write, Execute). This Abelian (RWX) access control mechanism is the process of communicating and transforming every request of the customer to use any device, components, data, and applications over Edge Computing. This Abelian Mechanism resolves protection issues to determine the client's response as well as qualities of services (QoS) to be invested into the classification, normalization, and frequent pattern mechanisms deciding on the major components of Reading, Writing, and Execute to access the data and information on anywhere of the globe through the UNIX Server and Web Portal. The prevention is inversely proportional to a set of risks. The attributes about attributes (Meta Attributes) provide prediction of current, and future security, and the risks pattern. Finally, this research work covers a wide range of Standardization, Normalization, Optimization, and Fuzzy Laws for risk assessment.

Keywords: Unix File System (UFS) · Access Control Mechanism (ACM) · Read Write Execute (RWX) · Abilen mechanism · Risk assessment · Unix operating system

1 Introduction

This proposed research paper is the vital role and responsibility of the UNIX FILE SYSTEM, that is, creating, collecting, storing, reporting, and updating the valuable data and programs as per requirement all the time and every time. It is always required in the past, present, and future for carrying and storing a large amount of data from one location to another or from source to destination around the globe. The valuable data and, finally, the information is carried in the file system. The file system is creating, storing, and managing as a file, subdirectory, and directory. This file system organization is storing, organizes, managing, and working on various types of operating systems like DOS, Windows, and UNIX. We have to prevent, detect, and correct the file system with the help of the Access Control Mechanism [15]. The file contains data and the

© The Author(s), under exclusive license to Springer Nature Switzerland AG 2023
I. Woungang et al. (Eds.): ANTIC 2022, CCIS 1797, pp. 188–201, 2023.
https://doi.org/10.1007/978-3-031-28180-8_13

program, File is stored on Disk. The file system, Shell, and kernel make an operating system. The operating system manages the file system. The logical file system is responsible for interaction with the user and application. It provides the vital data and user program, and application (API) for file operations—OPEN, CLOSE, and READ, etc., and passes the requested operation to the layer below it for processing. The logical file system manages the open file table entries and per-process file descriptors. This layer provides "file access, directory operations, [and] security and protection. A file system is a process of managing how and where data is on a storage disk, which is also referred to as file management (UFS) [12–15]. It is a logical disk component that compresses files separated into groups, which are known as directories. It is abstract to a human user and related to a computer; hence, it manages a disk's internal operations. The files and additional directories and sub-directory can be depended on all the time. Although there are various file systems with Windows, FAT, NTFS UFS are the most common in modern times. It would be impossible for a file with the same name to exist and also impossible to remove installed programs and recover specific files without file management, as well as files would have no organization without a file structure [15]. The file system enables you to view a file in the current directory as files are often managed in a hierarchy. The role and responsibilities are creating, writing, reading, updating, transferring, collecting, and storing are major functions and operations on big data, data science, business analytics, and analysis in Morden computing and technology [27–29]. Therefore, protection, detection, and correction are the major security in multi-tire complex architecture. Now day-to-day security and risk management are great responsibilities for managing the day-to-day business in all aspects like connecting, Create, Manage, Deploy, Run, Monitor, Maintain, and Scale Business Logic as well as Analytics Apps at the Edge [38].

1.1 Architecture of UNIX File System (META FILE SYSTEM)

The file system is a process of managing how and where data is on a storage disk, which is also referred to as file management or UFS. It is a logical disk component that compresses files separated into groups, which are known as directories. It is abstract to a human user and related to a computer; hence, it manages a disk's internal operations. Files and additional directories can be in the directories [12–15]. Although there are various file systems with Windows, NTFS, and UFS are the most common in modern times. It would be impossible for a file with the same name to exist and also impossible to remove installed programs and recover specific files without file management, as well as files would have no organization without a file structure. The file system enables you to view a file in the current directory as files are often managed in a hierarchy [15].

2 Background

The objective of the access control mechanism is to provide accountabilities, authentication, and right to clients as well as users to be able to use the global service around the world. Therefore, the execution of policies, procedure, process, actions, and reactions that are defined by the security management and business owner. The access control

Table 1. Unix file system

UFS - Unix File System

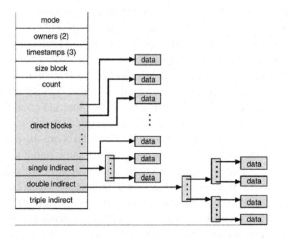

mechanism is required for any operating system designed to restrict user and client access to the file system according to predefined roles and responsibilities. The purpose of the access control mechanism is to minimize the security risk of unauthorized access to physical and logical systems [22–24].

The access control mechanism (RWX) is a fundamental component of the Unix file system that optimizes the risk detection of who is allowed to access and use organization information and resources. Although, accountability, authentication, and authorization, access control policies make sure that the users are who they are and that they have appropriate access to the Unix file system (UFS). The access control mechanism is a means of safeguarding the security by detecting and preventing unauthorized access and by permitting authorized access in an automated system. The Access control enables multiple users to access a single system, maintaining the privacy and security of each user's profile. It also protects the critical system files (UFS) from being altered or tampered with, optimizing the likelihood that the Unix operating system will malfunction and uninterrupted [15].

The attributes of the UNIX File System (RWX) may be classifying and reorganized as per organization policy and procedure. The files are stored on disk or other storage and do not disappear when the user logout and login. The Unix files have names and are associated with access permission that permits controlled sharing (RWX). These files are arranged or more complex structures to reflect the relationship between them (Ref to Table 1). The file has a name and data that are reflected in Table 1. Moreover, it also stores metadata information like file creation date and time, current size, last modified date, etc. All this information is called the attributes of the Unix file system [12–15].

File access is a process that determines the way that files are accessed and read into memory. Generally, a single access method is always supported by any operating systems. Although there are some operating system which also supports multiple access methods like Unix Operating system [38].

3   Data Collection and Analysis

Table 2. Allocation of UFS-ACM attributes

Octal	RWX	Attributes	Role & Right	USR	RISK
0	000	None/Blank (-)	Nil	No Body	Nil
1	001	execute only(x)	Any One	Any	L
2	010	write only(w)	Reserved	R	H
3	011	write and execute(w-x)	Reserved	R	H
4	100	read only(r)	Top Mgmt	UG	M
5	101	read and execute (r x)	Top Mgmt	UG	M
6	110	read and write (r w)	Developer	UG	H
7	111	read, write, and execute (full permissions) (r w x)	Developer	UGO	H

Table 3. Sample of UFS data (RISK-DSS)

ACM	Inode Subject Link U G Date Stamp UFS(Object)	Risk
777	134208 -rwxrwxrwx 1 plpl 727 2014-11-08 16:02 menu1.sh 141049 -rwxrwxrwx 1 plpl 461 2014-11-08 16:17 menu4.sh 141050 -rwxr-xr-x 1 plpl 547 2014-11-08 16:37 menu5.sh 140886 -rwxrwxrwx 1 plpl 505 2014-11-09 16:52 menu	H(RWX)
444	123412 -r--r--r-- 1 plpl 727 2014-11-08 16:02 menu1.sh 321456 -r--r--r-- 1 plpl 461 2014-11-08 16:17 menu4.sh 751231 -r--r--r-- 1 plpl 547 2014-11-08 16:37 menu5.sh 432123 -r--r--r-- 1 plpl 505 2014-11-09 16:52 menu.sh	M(R)
111	367231 ---x--x--x 1 plpl 727 2014-11-08 16:02 menu1.sh 213814 ---x--x--x 1 plpl 461 2014-11-08 16:17 menu4.sh 151232 ---x--x--x 1 plpl 547 2014-11-08 16:37 menu5.sh 451649 ---x--x--x 1 plpl 505 2014-11-09 16:52 menu.s	L(X)
000	753232 ---------- 1 plpl 727 2014-11-08 16:02 menu1.sh 651241 ---------- 1 plpl 461 2014-11-08 16:17 menu4.sh 251201 ---------- 1 plpl 547 2014-11-08 16:37 menu5.sh 751231 ---------- 1 plpl 505 2014-11-09 16:52 menu.sh	0 Access Deny

4   Problem Statements

There is a great issue regarding the resource allocation and distribution of Read, Write and Execute on various level of users. As per above data collection, the access control mechanism is not available on the recent Real Time Unix ACM and the corrective action and reaction on file system, application & resources is a big concern on this current security age like IOT, Cloud Computing, and Edge Computing. The multiple Relation,

Function, Operation and Services are happening over a multiple clients, business, application and resources on a complex heterogeneous IT infrastructure. Therefore, resource conflicts are the biggest issue over a complex network, platform and user application. Therefore, there is no balance ratio among the Risk, DSS, and Resource Management. There is a vital issue regarding the resource allocations of the combination of Read, Write, and Execute on the UFS at various level of resources management (Developer, Top, Medium & Lower mgmt.).

Machine Level Problem

- One User exist with one or many group.
- One User have one or many file system and Onefile system have one or many processes.
- One User have one or many attributes (R, W, X), that USR link to one or many more file system (UFS-ACM).
- We have to mapping the User, Group, Others to File system and then Processes through the attributes read, write and execute, due to risk mitigation over a Unix RTOS. Each UFS is associated with inode and that may be soft link or hard link.
- Shared lock [R-Read] & Exclusive locks [W-Write].

5 Proposed Research Methodology

This research paper contributes to the define, design, development of an optimization and normalization model that aims and objective to determine the optimal cost, time and maximize the Quality of Service to be implemented into the dynamic Abelian model & mechanisms deciding on the measure components of Read, Write, and Execute as follows.

We have to define, design, develop and deployment the large datasets, key parameter, pattern, mechanism, relation, function, operation & services to fix up dynamic, integration, structure, classification, frequent patten by applying Abelian Algebra based on RWX ACM concepts. Meanwhile, we can maintain the organizational DSS by applying automated method, model, mechanism (M^3) & tools on UFS to maximize the decision management to achieve the highest business objective.

We have to move forward to finding alternate solution and algorithm for Access Control Mechanism on Unix File System based on the Abelian Group. This reliable, transformation, and scalable complex Read (R), Write (W), and Execute (X) RWX definitely will be resolve our purpose on complex real time Access Control Mechanism for all the times. We have to design and develop these seven objects is a set of elements as follows: {X, W, WX, R, RW, RX, RWX}. This seven objects ordering (Relation & Function) apply to our designing methodology and as per top management decision and requirement of the current and future business.

Prove that the set {1, 2, 3, 4, 5, 6, 7} = {{X, W, WX, R, RW, RX, RWX}. is a finite Abelian (Addition Mudulo) combinatory order& unordered composition. Whereas, S = {X, W, WX, R, RW, RX, RWX} = {{X, W, WX, R, RW, RX, RWX}.

Let us take a relation R (X, W, WX, R, RW, RX, RWX); we have following dependencies for a relation R, and we have to consider each element for managing the ACM role and right. These parameters are applied to the Abelian Addition Modulo to achieve Risk Assessment.

Define the Abelian Addition Modulo:

- Prove that the set {1, 2, 3, 4, 5, 6, 7} is finite Abelian Group of order 7 under addition modulo 5 as composition.
- Solution. To test the nature of the system (G, +7) where G = {1, 2, 3, 4, 5, 6, 7}

Implementation of Abelian Group on RWX to achieve the RISK.-Refers to Table No.2

Table 4. Implementation of Abelian addition modulo.

+7	1	2	3	4	5	6	7
1	2	3	4	5	6	7	0
2	3	4	5	6	7	0	1
3	4	5	6	7	0	1	2
4	5	6	7	0	1	2	3
5	6	7	0	1	2	3	4
6	7	0	1	2	3	3	5
7	0	1	2	3	4	5	6

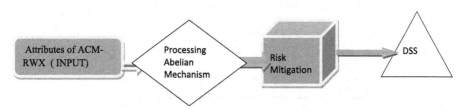

Fig. 1. Framework of Abelian mechanism

The inputs are attributes of the ACM (RWX) Mechanism applied to the Abelian Addition Modulo to achieve the best ACM Pattern & Process for the right decision. We have to prove that the Abelian Group resolving the various ACMs pattern based on UFS (RWX) mechanism. This proposed Abelian theorem resolving our Uncertain and unordered to get the right ACM pattern for our dynamic decision support system.

The proposed Abelian's Addition Modulo resolving the uncertain, unordered relationship and achieving the right ACM pattern for the risk mitigation process.

The above Abelian's Addition Modulo resolving the uncertain, unordered relationship and achieving the right ACM pattern for the risk mitigation process on IoT and

Table 5. Implementation of Abelian's addition modulo - RWX ACM model

+7	X	W	WX	R	RX	RW	RWX
X	W	WX	R	RX	RW	RWX	0
W	WX	R	RX	RW	RWX	0	X
WX	R	RX	RW	RWX	0	X	W
R	RX	RW	RWX	0	X	W	WX
RX	RW	RWX	0	X	W	WX	R
RW	RWX	0	X	W	WX	R	RX
RWX	0	X	W	WX	R	RX	RW

Note: Refers to Table 4.

Table 6. Design the RWX ACM based on abelian model-identified the best ACM pattern (mentioned by narrow mark)

+7	X	W	WX	R	RX	RW	RWX
X	W	WX	R	RX	RW	RWX	0
W	WX	R	RX	RW	RWX	0	X
WX	R	RX	RW	RWX	0	X	W
R	RX	RW	RWX	0	X	W	WX
RX	RW	RWX	0	X	W	WX	R
RW	RWX	0	X	W	WX	R	RX
RWX	0	X	W	WX	R	RX	RW

EDGE platform. Now it is on the cluster level, therefore, we have to normalize as per our best requirement and better risk assessment.

We have to find out the uncertainty, unordered, unreliable, and un setup ACM pattern of the dataset and remove it from the above table.

Now we have to take care and focus to find out the reliable and high availability (riskless) pattern to integrate and communicate with the EDGE Computing. The R, RX, X are the right pattern for reliable and high available data processing on EDGE Computing. Now we should be removed RW, WX & RWX patterns, because the Read, Write, and Execute is a very high risk for data processing. We have to resolve the uncertainty, unordered, unreliable, and un setup ACM Data sets for better data processing.

Table 7. ACM pattern (mentioned by narrow mark)

+7	X	W	WX	R	RX	RW	RWX
X				R	RX		0
						RWX	
W		R	RX		RWX	0	X
WX	R	RX		RWX	0	X	
R	RX		RWX	0	X		
RX		RWX	0	X			R
RW	RWX	0	X			R	RX
RWX	0	X			R	RX	

Note: Ref to Table No 2 & 3

Design the RWX ACM Based on Abelian Model- Redefined the reliable pattern. Now we have to focus and emphasize the RX & X ACM Pattern and remove RWX & RW.

Therefore, we have moved forward to identification, classification, normalization, frequent pattern as follows:

N1 - Normalization & Optimization RX (Read and Execute)

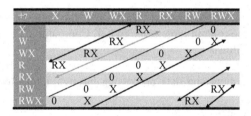

Now, we have to normalize further the RX & X ACM pattern on Abelian Model and filter the reliable RX, X ACM Pattern (Mentioned by Narrow Mark).

The above Read (R & Execute (X) pattern is highly available and reliable for data processing business purposes. Therefore, the first normalization (N1) is closely supported to the and EDGE Computing.

The End Users and business client and can be able to Connect, Create, Deploy, Run, Monitor, Maintain & Scale Business Logic & Analytics Apps at the Edge.

N2 - Normalization-Optimization (R - Read ACM Pattern Only)

+7	X	W	WX	R	RX	RW	RWX
X			R				0
W		R				0	X
WX	R				0	X	
R				0	X		
RX			0	X			R
RW		0	X			R	
RWX	0	X			R		

Note: Ref to Table No 2 & 3

The purpose of this RRR (Read) pattern is useful for Review the data, but cannot process the data. The XXX pattern execution of data, finally data can be processed at Edge based on RX concept. That is called data processing & analysis in IoT & EDGE Computing environment. Therefore RX is the right ACM pattern for all the time and every time. This RRR & XXX pattern is a great use for data analysis.

N3 - Normalization-Optimization (X-ACM Pattern Execute Only)

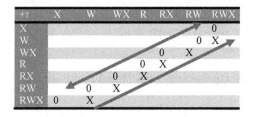

The purpose of the normalization (N3) is that the data processing and analysis can be available all the time in large-scale EDGE Computing. The benefit of the third normalization is as follows:

- Better data management and data processing through automated ACM patterns or scripts.
- better security practices

Reliable, high available, and uninterrupted connectivity for data processing. The data can be collected and analyzed in a faster reliable way, which will be a support to the risk mitigation as well as decision.

N4 - Normalization-Optimization (000-Pattern No One Access)

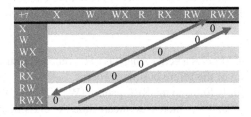

The above normalization/optimization is revered for top management for future reused purpose.

This Pattern (000) is required for Business Continuity Program for top management.

Finally, the Abelian's Model will be established the ACMs process and response as well as qualities of services (QoS) to be invested into the RWX frequent pattern mechanisms deciding on the major components of the set S = (X, W, WX, R, RW, RX, RWX) data security and risk assessment for IOT & EDGE Computing. The generating primary pattern (RWX), secondary pattern (RW0), WX0 are high risk & the third stage pattern (RX0), X0, R, X are required for EDGE Computing as well as risk assessment. Now identification, classifying, optimizing and frequent Pattern is a great benefits for Risk Assessment on EDGE Computing for faster data processing and better decision support system for top management.

6   Result Analysis

The purpose of the research paper improving the right access control mechanism for better preventive control (PC) and risk assessment. The preventive control (ACM) is inversely proportional to risk and DSS closely associate with our propose ACM data sets {1, 2, 3, 4, 5, 6, 7} = {{X, W, WX, R, RW, RX, RWX}. Now, the PC, ACM, DSS, and RISK datasets are interdependencies with each other for risk assessment. Finally, preventive control is inversely proportional to the risk and decision support system. When the preventive control increasing the risk assessment cost will be reduced. The maximum and stronger generation, classification, the frequent pattern of the attributes of RWX, and frequent pattern establishing the Anti-Fragile relationships for ACM process for top management. We can apply Fuzy's system in optimization (High, Medium & Low). Therefore, Abelian's finite group is applied to the UFS-RWX dataset to evaluate the relationship among the various risk assessment and decision processes. The optimization and normalization process will be a great contribution towards risk, cost, and DSS.

- Improve the meta data sets, order, identification, classification, and frequent patterns on UFS ACM.
- Improve the metadata (RWX) sets as well as the quality of Access Control Mechanism and services (QoS).

- Improve the high reliable and available operational & services for (DDSS) Dynamic Decision support system all the time and every time.
- Improved customer satisfaction due to better preventive control.
- Improve the ACM Pattern and Process for Risk Mitigation at the right time for EDGE Computing.

More accurate UFS ACM gives a better Analysis of current and future Security and Risk Assessment forecasting of the future business process.

Note: X Read Color belongs to the Risk pattern (W, WX, RW, RWX).

When a large ACM datasets increases, meanwhile the classification, identification, sequencing, ordering, and ACM & RISK pattern visualization are very much crystal clear for risk and DSS.

The metadata right ACM pattern (X, W, WX, R, RX, RW, RWX) is inversely proportional to the RISK% (Preventive control (RX) is inversely proportional to the Risk). At this point Read and Execute is the best preventive control for any business.

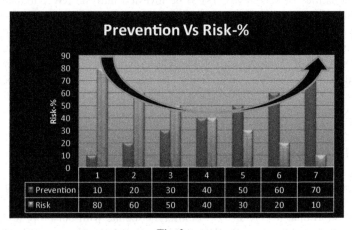

Fig. 2. .

7 Discussion (Practical and Managerial Activities)

The preventive control is inversely proportional to the risk and decision support system. When a large number of the frequent pattern increases, meanwhile the identification, classification, sequencing, ordering of ACM pattern generating and matching for the batter to butter ACM pattern and the Risk (HML) assessment will be easier and resource cost, DSS, and risk will be optimized. Meanwhile, improve the reliable operation & services on IoT and EDGE Computing will be improved all the time. The objects, subjects, input, output, and domain & range would be mapping orderly to integrating, communicating, transforming & synchronizing with (RWX) along with R, W, and X on UFS. The risk and decision are always two sides of the coin. Therefore, improve performance and safety, automate all core business data processing and ensure the high availability available of reliable data for better services. Edge Computing is important because it **creating new and improved ways for large enterprise-level businesses** to maximize reliable operational efficiency services all the time and every time.

8 Future Research

The major role of Abelian Group, functional dependency, relation, function, Set, Group, Partial order sets, Cartesian Product, Circular Queue, permutation, and combination are generating, classifying, ordering, identifying, and frequent pattern matching to achieve the desired ACM and Risk Pattern for risk assessment as well as dynamic decision support system. Based on these mathematical ideas new theory can be explored on the field of computer security, risk pattern and data science.

9 Conclusion

This proposed Abelian's Mechanism on UFS-ACM generating, classifying, and frequent pattern mechanism analysis provides a better and faster decision support system for risk mitigation over EDGE Computing. This mechanism is accomplished through Real-Time systems as well as Virtualization that regenerate the UFS ACM process for dynamic decision support for top management. These ACM patterns are high availability, reliability, scalability, integration, and integrity. They are part of UFS-ACM. This research paper is a more practical idea and less theoretical approach as well is available in both analytical as well as graphical methods. The attributes of UFS-ACM (metadata) patterns are providing a dynamic decision support system for Risk Assessment. The attributes of the ACM (UFS-RWX) that applied to the dynamic are unordered, unset up and uncertain. In this way, we can achieve the secure operational and service goal, and finally, maintain the better services to top management. This Abelian ACM frequent pattern is very helpful to present dependable technology (IoT, Cloud Computing, and EDGE COMPUTING)) to co-op with the Abelian Algebra, Circular queues, Cartesian Product, and Combination Algebra resolving to the unordered, uncertain environment as well as a dynamic and self-autonomy system for UFS-ACM for all the time and every time. This Abelian ACM mechanism resolves the DSS for top management to improve the business pattern and process, Quality of Service, scalability, reliability, and availability all the time.

References

1. Asthana, A., Pradhan, P.: Dynamic butterfly ACM for risk optimization on the real-time Unix operating system. Int. J. Softw. Innov. (IJSI) **10**(1) (2022). https://doi.org/10.4018/IJSI.297505
2. Asthana, A., Pradhan, P.: Proposed abelian ACM method optimizing: the risk on a real-time Unix operating system. Int. J. Secur. Priv. Pervasive Comput. (IJSPPC) **13**(4) (2022). https://doi.org/10.4018/IJSPPC.2021100103
3. Asthana, A., Pradhan, P.: Proposed L-shape pattern on UFS ACM for risk analysis. J. Digit. Forensics Secur. Law (2022). https://doi.org/10.15394/jdfsl.2022.1728

4. Andrew, Richard: UNIX Network Programming. Person Education India, New Delhi (2011)
5. Arnold, D.M., Rangaswamy, K.M. (eds.): Abelian Groups and Modules. Dekker, New York (1996)
6. Antonio, F.S., Ramos Jose, L.H., Moreno, M.V.: A decentralized approach for security and privacy challenges in the Internet of Things. In: Proceedings of the IEEE World Forum on Internet of Things; Seoul, Korea. 6–8 March 2014, pp. 67–72 (2014)
7. Tang, A.: A guide to penetration testing. Netw. Secur. **8–11**, 2014 (2014)
8. Devis, A.: What is critical to your infrastructure? Infosecurity **8**(5), 18–21 (2011)
9. Webb, A.: UNIX: who manages your system? Computer Audit Update. Elsevier Science Ltd., April 1994
10. Platts, A.: New technology - servant or master? Computer Audit Update. Elsevier Science Ltd., December 1997
11. Karabacak, B., Sogukpinar, I.: ISRAM: information security risk analysis method. Comput. Secur. **24**, 147–159 (2005)
12. Balagurusamy, E.B.: Programming in Java. Tata McGrawHill, New Delhi (2007)
13. Ritche, C.: Operating System in Unix & Window. BPB Publication, New Delhi (2006)
14. Charles, Shari, Deven: Security in Computing. Pearson Education India, New Delhi (2007)
15. Coriolis: CISSP Exam Cram. Coriolis Group Books. Dreamatech, New Delhi (2012)
16. Klaus, C.W.: Network security: anything but bulletproof. Inf. Secur. Tech. Rep. **2**(3), 28–32 (1997)
17. Hsu, C.-H.: Real-time embedded software for multi-core platforms. J. Syst. Archit. **60**, 245–246 (2014)
18. Sumitabh, D.: UNIX System V UNIX Concept & Application. Tata McGraw Hill, Delhi (2017)
19. Hussein, D., Bertin, E., Frey, V.: A community-driven access control approach in Distributed IoT environments. IEEE Commun. Mag. **55**(3), 146–153 (2017)
20. Deng, Y.: Linux network security technology. IEEE (2011). ISBN 978-1-4577-0860-2/11
21. Schofield, D.: Know the risk – learning from errors and accidents: safety and risk in today's technology. Risk Manag. **7**, 67–68 (2005). https://doi.org/10.1057/palgrave.rm.8240222
22. Kirda, E., Jovanovic, N., Kruegel, C., Vignac, G.: Client-side cross-site scripting protection. Comput. Secur. **28**, 592–604 (2009)
23. Heinlein, E.B.: Principles of information systems security. Comput. Secur. **14**, 197-198 (1995)
24. Baiardi, F., Coro, F., Tonelli, F., Sgandurra, D.: Automating the assessment of ICT risk. J. Inf. Secur. Appl. **19**, 182–193 (2014)
25. Donovan, F.: Compliance strategies-A.K.A. alphabet soup. Infosecurity **8**(6), 22–25 (2011)
26. Ren, H., Song, Y., Yang, S., Situ, F.: Secure smart home: a voiceprint and internet-based authentication system for remote accessing. In: Proceedings of the 11th International Conference on Computer Science and Education, ICCSE 2016, pp. 247–251, August 2016
27. Nosworthy, J.D.: A practical risk analysis approach: managing BCM risk. Comput. Secur. **19**(7), 596–614 (2000)
28. Saurabh, K.: Unix Programming. Wiley India, New Delhi (2014)
29. Liu, Y., Peng, Y., Wang, B., Bai, X., Yuan, X., Li, G.: The Internet of Things security architecture based IBE integration with the PKI/CA. In: Proceedings of the Advanced Science and Technology Letters; Harbin, China. 18–20 April 2013, pp. 243–246 (2013)
30. Bach, M.J.: The Design of Unix Operating System. Wiley, New Delhi India (2016)
31. Trnka, M., Cerny, T.: Authentication and authorization rules sharing for Internet of Things. Softw. Netw. **1**, 35–52 (2017)
32. Mohamed, A.F., Leandros, M., Sotiris, M., Helge, J.: Deep learning for cyber security intrusion detection: approaches, datasets, and comparative study. JISA **50**, 102419 (2020)
33. Pradhan, P., Patra, P.: Integrated dynamic model & mechanism optimizing the risk on RTOS. IJISP **8**(1), 38–61 (2014). ACM, INSPEC, SCOPUS, Thomson, Web Science

34. Pradhan, P., Patra, P.: Dynamic value engineering method optimizing the risk on real time operating system. IJEEI **2**(2), 101–110 (2014)
35. Pradhan, P.: Dynamic Semi-Group CIA Pattern Optimizing the risk on RTS. IJDFC **9**(1), 51–70 (2017). WOS, Scopus 1941-6210
36. Pradhan, P.: A literature Survey on Unix operation system for risk assessment. IJAPUC **11**(3) (2019)
37. Tasali, Q., Chowdhury, C., Vasserman, E.Y.: A flexible authorization architecture for systems of interoperable medical devices. In: Proceedings of the 22nd ACM Symposium on Access Control Models and Technologies, SACMAT 2017, USA, pp. 9–20, June 2017
38. Steinberger, R.: Vulnerability management in Unix environments. Inf. Secur. Tech. Rep. **7**(1), 26–36 (2002)
39. Kondakci, S.: A new assessment and improvement model of risk propagation in information security. Int. J. Inf. Comput. Secur. **1**(3), 341–366 (2007)
40. Kim, S.-J., Son, C.-W., Lee, C.-W.: Linux based unauthorized process control. IEEE (2011). ISBN 978-1-4244-9224-4/11
41. Lee, S., Choi, J., Kim, J., et al.: FACT: functionality-centric access control system for IoT programming frameworks. In: Proceedings of the 22nd ACM Symposium on Access Control Models and Technologies, SACMAT 2017, USA, pp. 43–54, June 2017
42. Tanenbaum: Operating System Design and Implementation. Person Education India, New Delhi (2010)
43. Thomas, T.: A mandatory access control mechanism for the Unix file system. Motorola Inc., Microcomputer Division, IEEE (1988)
44. Ron, W.: Information System Control & Audit. Person Education India, New Delhi (2002)

Support Systems and Technological Capabilities in Digital Transformation According to the Nature of the Company

Reynier Israel Ramirez Molina[1] ![ORCID], Ricardo Romario Antequera Amaris[1]([✉]) ![ORCID], Diego Alberto Baez Palencia[1] ![ORCID], Nelson David Lay Raby[2] ![ORCID], and Lydia López Barraza[3] ![ORCID]

[1] Universidad de la Costa, Barranquilla, Colombia
{rramirez13,ranteque2,dbaez}@cuc.edu.co
[2] Universidad Andres Bello, Viña del Mar, Chile
nelson.lay@unab.cl
[3] Universidad Autónoma de Occidente, Culiacán, Mexico
lydia.lopez@udo.mx

Abstract. The evolution of markets has encouraged the use of technologies in different areas; in business and industry, their use has increased since these tools and technologies allow efficient management of resources and generate better products and services; in this sense, the technological capacities allow a correct use of the different elements and technology resources to be able to carry out productive, commercial and management processes, as well as the use of tools such as the support system. This research evaluates the effect of technological capabilities in operations and information technology capabilities in business support systems on the company's digital transformation. Four categorical regression models are estimated, controlling for economic activity, for a sample of companies from different industries. The findings show an influence of capabilities on the propensity for digital transformation and a moderation effect due to economic activity. Information technology capabilities influence service companies, while the digital transformation of manufacturing organizations depends on the technological capabilities in operation with a more significant effect. It is concluded that the development of technological skills, both in operation and in support, serve as inducers of digital business models. However, their adoption will depend on the nature of the firm. Changes in the technological support capabilities further underpin the probability of more extraordinary digital transformation in service, opposite for those who operate the production of tangibles.

Keywords: Support systems · Technological capabilities · Digital transformation

1 Introduction

The constant evolution of the markets has led organizations to join forces in innovating to offer products and services with more novel characteristics, leading to the generation

I. Woungang et al. (Eds.): ANTIC 2022, CCIS 1797, pp. 202–214, 2023.
https://doi.org/10.1007/978-3-031-28180-8_14

of a competitive environment in the different segments and markets; this dynamism boosts economies. Moreover, strengthening the elements adds value according to new needs; within this, companies also need to renew their technological capabilities, which allow an adaptation to new tools and processes that involve the use of Information and Communication Technologies (from now on ICT) and new technologies. In the same way, it is essential to have tools such as support systems, which suggest better decisions in the different situations of the organization and its environment.

Technological capabilities are defined as the grouping of skills, competencies, and knowledge that become relevant for the excellent management of technological and scientific resources, resulting in an organization that is more willing to innovate [11]. In this sense, the objective is to have the necessary elements and knowledge to operate equipment, software, tools, and machines, allowing maximum use of resources, and promoting proactive attitudes and innovative strategies in the organization's different areas.

Assistance tools for decision-making are part of those elements under which it is required to know, such as technological capacity; the so-called support systems are responsible for processing data to provide decision suggestions in complex or uncertain situations, for [10], support systems allow making assessments and suggestions on decisions in situations of uncertainty, where management requires precise movements that minimize risks and losses, for which it is relevant to have the resources and technological capacities to be able to work with said systems.

The situation at the global level is unequal; on the one hand, there are developed territories that have policies and programs that promote science and technology in associations, schools, universities, and industries, resulting in a population with high levels of qualification, competitiveness, and economic capabilities, these nations prioritize the use of technology due to the consideration that it is directly related to economic growth and competitiveness. [4] agrees with the diagnosis of the current situation, these authors point out that there is a non-uniform distribution between regions and countries and that knowledge is mainly concentrated in countries with high levels of industrialization.

The panorama of highly industrialized countries predominates in European and North American nations. The technological countries of Asia, the economic conditions, and the historical disposition towards industrialization are positive and aligned with the economic objectives of each country; on the contrary, in Latin America, Africa, and Oceania, industrialization is different and has delays in its implementation. It, therefore, affects the economy and the opportunity for large-scale production, considering innovation, creativity, and the market situation.

Developing countries do not have sufficient financial and political muscle to implement successful policies that promote science and technology; in the case of Colombia, a positive evolution has been evidenced in line with the strategies carried out by developing countries, among them is the creation of the Ministry of Science, Technology, and Innovation, which has established policies, programs and incentives for the promotion of science and formation of human capital, resulting in a more educated society capable of to develop with the help of technology. However, years of continuous work are required to prioritize research, science, and technology as one of the pillars of the Colombian economy.

While the case of the city of Barranquilla is like the panorama of the country, there are significant advances in favor of promoting technologies and science. However, there is a lack of curricula and training by the entities in related areas. ICT, automation, systems, and big data, among others, so the population does not have full knowledge of these elements. Identifying as a problem the lack of knowledge and resources to develop a total technological capacity, therefore, the impossibility of using tools and support systems, which may be caused by the non-training of personnel, for economic reasons, of personnel, or because of the lack of interest in said topic. Therefore, there is little added value for the companies, so they are not sustainable over time, leading to not obtaining economic income that, in turn, generates the loss of jobs and the obsolescence of the work.

It is predicted that the situation of absence could worsen as a result of the emergence of new technologies and the non-adaptation and appropriation of the same by organizations; this would generate an economic decline given by the volatility of industries and companies, for which is suggested to control said forecasts, encouraging private and public capitals to promote and train their personnel continuously in the use and development of technologies that optimize operations and processes. Given the situation described, the following problem question arises: What is the effect of support systems and technological capabilities in the digital transformation of companies?

1.1 Support Systems and Technological Capabilities in Digital Transformation: Conceptual Aspects and Contributions

Digital transformation in organizations goes hand in hand with various requirements: to have the initiative for transformation and to financial, technological, and knowledge resources; for the latter, it is necessary to educate and train for the development of capacities. This transformation will allow the organization to improve its internal and external communication, market services and products through massive social media, and negotiate trade agreements. The technological capacity, according to [1], is the basis for starting to develop a lasting competitive advantage over time; at the same time, these capabilities allow for solving the multiple problems of the economic society in a more efficient and timely manner. On the other hand, [2] define technological capabilities as the ability to develop new businesses, products, and services channeled in the strategic plan based on innovation.

In the same way, [2] provide that the technological capabilities are directly related to the organization's performance, and the digital capabilities provide the technical support required for the generation of value. Likewise, [3] points out that technological capabilities refer to the skills for efficiently managing resources such as hardware and software; this allows executing processes to carry out any technological changes. For [16] it is important the integration of organizational, cognitive and technological skills, added to research and development management, technology management, digital and technological transformation to lead a successful strategic management that allows to take advantage of internal and external strengths to adapt optimally and achieve competitive advantages. In the same way [17, 18] relates the relevance of the organizational capacity to group and create exploitable knowledge for appropriation that generates value and drives dynamic capabilities that favor the companies, not leaving aside the environment and the other companies in the market.

Therefore, the authors point out that these capabilities are the accumulation of knowledge acquired from experiences and accumulated skills. While for those who investigate, technological capacities refer to the organizational and individual capacity for the development, management, and execution of the various processes that involve the use of technologies; this capacity implies knowing how to do, knowing how to operate, and knowing how to solve, for which fosters a favorable climate for competitiveness and efficiency, allowing us to be alert to changes in order to face them with the knowledge and technologies acquired.

On the other hand, support systems enter as tools for the timely management of the organization and its resources, [7] indicates that support systems have contributed to reducing uncertainty by formulating suggestions for decision-making. In addition, it is indicated that these systems have pillars such as (1) data management, (2) model management, and (3) interface, for which generic and specific knowledge is required in terms of technologies to carry out each of the management processes.

In agreement, [8] contemplate that the support system enables the analysis of situations from various perspectives through the unification, management, and analysis of data to provide relevant information. In this sense, for those who investigate, support systems are technological tools that aim to support organizations in times of crisis where decisions imply risks for it; in this system, data management is used through software that results in usable information that works as a guide for decisions.

1.2 Indicators for Digital Transformation

Technological capabilities and support systems make it possible to carry out a digital transformation that benefits organizations, thus ensuring the use of knowledge, tools and resources to adapt to new models, technologies and needs. Therefore, it is essential to identify what elements constitute and support them, defining relevant indicators for the full development of capabilities that favor the use of software and tools for management.

The indicators are: (1) technology and product development, which refers to the formulation and design of products and services that have innovative characteristics that generate added value through the use of technologies, (2) automation of the manufacturing/service process is the operationalization and standardization of processes through technology and regulations that allow a manual process to be operated by equipment and programs, generating cost reduction and minimization of errors, next is (3) technology development, which refers to the adaptation of technologies, methods, and tools that facilitate the performance of tasks following a standard of quality and efficiency.

As the fourth indicator is the (4) prediction of technological changes in the industry, which contemplates the qualification and skills of the collaborators and the organization itself to study the differences, threats, and opportunities of the environment, as the following indicator is (5) technological structure in production is related to the existence of resources and elements that allow productive development to be carried out, where they are counted as software, machines, norms, and standards, later there is the (6) technology in the control of the product/service. This indicator is linked to the resources and elements available to operate the various types of rules efficiently [12].

In seventh place is the (7) functional integration indicator, which is an approach that integrates components and systems to ensure that functionality is operative correctly, followed by (8) technological knowledge: specific knowledge that allows the design, management, and validation of technical elements such as computer programs, systems, machines, etc. Another indicator includes (9) knowledge of the market, which is the ability to interact with the context to identify customer needs, news, technologies, opportunities, skills, and others. Moreover, finally, there is the indicator of (10) Internal and external communication, which refers to the ability and capacity to communicate with collaborators and consumers, so there must be elements such as channel, sender, receiver, message and context to carry out a correct communication process [9].

2 Methodology

2.1 Measurement and Theoretical Model

By the preceding literature, the study performs an empirical validation of the digital transformation (From now on DT) of the company based on the technological capabilities (From now on TC) immersed in the productive operation or the provision of the service and the capabilities of information technologies (From now on IC) that provide support to the business from non-core activities. For technological capabilities, digital technology was considered from the conception of the product to its final control, as well as the adoption and transfer in the primary processes. It was evaluated through the manager's perception of i) technology in product development, ii) automation of the manufacturing/service process, iii) technology development, iv) prediction of technological changes in the industry, v) technological structure in production, vi) technology in product/service control.

Similarly, information technology capabilities evaluated the use of information systems that provide support to the main activity of the company from different angles, such as i) product development, ii) functional integration, iii) technological knowledge, iv) knowledge of the market, v) internal communication and towards the market. These variables influence the propensity for the digital transformation of the company. This aspect was evaluated by considering the strategic orientation of the company and its organizational structure, work culture, and performance control, elements that enable a digital model in the company.

Thus, the theoretical model evaluated is expressed in Fig. 1:

Considering that the difference between the economic activity of the companies analyzed can influence the calculated effects on digital transformation, this variable was included as a control of the model. The measurement was made through an instrument applied by direct collection in education, retail, and textile companies in Bogotá, Colombia. The sample reached was 236 organizations, the informant being a manager in the company.

The instrument to measure capabilities was applied and validated in [5], while the digital transformation variable used the tool validated in [6]. In addition, the scale's reliability was evaluated using Cronbach's Alpha, reaching an acceptable score for the three variables (TC = 0.71; CI = 0.68; SD = 0.61). An odd semantic differential scale was considered in the three constructs, ensuring equidistant intervals for modeling.

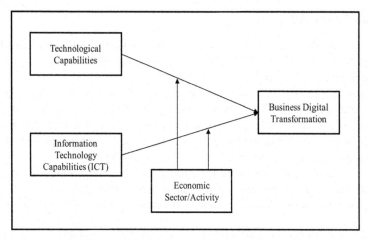

Fig. 1. Theoretical model. Source: Own elaboration (2022).

The measure of technological capacity and information technology was obtained from aggregation to the mean. While the extent of the propensity for digital business transformation was categorized by collection under a membership function:

$$M = \begin{cases} 0 \; si \; 1 \leq \sum_{i=1}^{3} x_i/3 < 4 \\ 1 \; si \; 4 \leq \sum_{i=1}^{3} x_i/3 < 7 \\ 2 \; si \; 7 \leq \sum_{i=1}^{3} x_i/3 \leq 9 \end{cases} \tag{1}$$

where M is the membership category obtained by the firm, x_i is the response value in indicator i in the digital transformation construct, the levels are M = 0: Low propensity, M = 1: Medium propensity, and M = 2: High propensity.

Therefore, the methodological steps used in this research as show in Fig. 2:

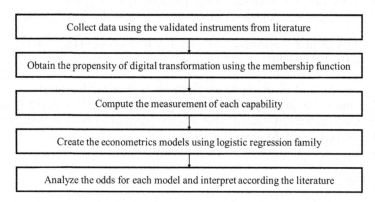

Fig. 2. Methodological model. Source: Own elaboration (2022).

2.2 Statistical Models

Regarding the methodology used to understand the influence that capabilities have on the digital transformation of the business, multinomial regression models were used. Four models were performed.

The first two models considered the digital transformation propensity depending on the technological capabilities and information technologies capabilities (ICT), also include the type of industry as a covariate which moderates the effect on digital transformation. Industry is a dummy being 1 is the firm is a service company, and 0 is the firm is a manufacturing business; zero was the reference level.

Thus, the model (2) contains the three variables and interaction terms as the control variable is included. While (3) is the parsimonious model that only considers the covariates as possible drivers of the dependent variable. The models are as follow:

$$
\begin{aligned}
\text{Logit(Digital Transformation)} &= \alpha_i + \beta_i \text{Technological Capabilities} \\
&+ \theta_i \text{ICT Capabilities} + \delta_i \text{Industry} + \gamma_{i1} \text{Industry} \times \text{Technological Capabilities} \\
&+ \gamma_{i2} \text{Industry} \times \text{ICT Capabilities}
\end{aligned} \tag{2}
$$

$$
\begin{aligned}
\text{Logit(Digital Transformation)} &= \alpha_i + \beta_i \text{Technological Capabilities} \\
&+ \theta_i \text{ICT Capabilities} + \delta_i \text{Industry}
\end{aligned} \tag{3}
$$

In addition, being companies of three different objects, the particular type of economic activity was included as a different control variable through two dummies as follows: Education being 1: education company, and 0: another case; and Retail being 1: retail company, and 0: another case; textile company is assumed when they are 0 in both dummies. Thus, those control variables and their interaction terms are included in the model (4). While (5) is the parsimonious model from (4). The models are as follows:

$$
\begin{aligned}
\text{Logit(Digital Transformation)} &= \alpha_i + \beta_i \text{Technological Capabilities} \\
&+ \theta_i \text{ICT Capabilities} + \vartheta_i \text{Education} + \varphi_i \text{Retail} + \lambda_{i1} \text{Education} \\
&\times \text{Technological Capabilities} + \lambda_{i2} \text{Education} \times \text{ICT Capabilities} \\
&+ \pi_{i1} \text{Retail} \times \text{Technological Capabilities} + \pi_{i2} \text{Retail} \times \text{ICT Capabilities}
\end{aligned} \tag{4}
$$

$$
\begin{aligned}
\text{Logit(Digital Transformation)} &= \alpha_i + \beta_i \text{Technological Capabilities} \\
&+ \theta_i \text{ICT Capabilities} + \vartheta_i \text{Education} + \varphi_i \text{Retail}
\end{aligned} \tag{5}
$$

Being $i = \{0, 1, 2\}$ according to the levels of the membership function in (1) and taking 0 as the reference category. For all the models, assumptions were validated, fit tests were made, and the likelihood value was compared to establish the significance of the moderation effects of the control variables.

3 Results

3.1 Measures of Capabilities

A measurement of the capabilities in the total sample of companies analyzed shows that there is a medium level in the perception of the managers both in the technological capacities of operation and in the information technologies for support; even with a close rating (Technological Capabilities = 5.73; ICT Capabilities = 5.13). However, it is interesting to know the measure differentiated by the type of economic sector and its economic activity. Table 1 shows the summary:

Table 1. Aggregated measures of capabilities by control variables

	IND		EDU	RET	Textile
	Services	Manufacturing	Education	Retail	
Technological capabilities	4.73	5.89	5.01	4.23	5.89
Information technology capabilities	6.13	4.97	6.67	5.18	4.97

Source: Own elaboration (2022)

Note the relationship trend between capacity and activity type. Those companies focused on manufacturing have a better level of technological capabilities, those that influence the company's production process. At the same time, service providers offer more significant emphasis on the capabilities of information systems to support their core business. If it is analyzed particularly by economic activity, retail companies value their capabilities to a lesser extent than the other companies in the sample. However, it must be considered that they are all small businesses, and their geographical scope of action is limited, so they do not tend to use technology on a large surface scale. Regarding education and textile companies, the trend found in aggregate by the type of economic sector is maintained.

3.2 Estimation Results

The estimation of models (2) to (5) presented statistical evidence for the significance of the independent variable, although some of them do not find this significance for the control variable. However, it must be considered that since it is a multinomial model (three categories), if significance is obtained in at least one of the models, the variables must be maintained in the rest. Under this precept, the results of the estimates are reflected in Table 2 for the models that control by economic sector and Table 3 for the control in company activity.

From model (3), information technology capabilities show the statistical effect on digital transformation. Although the other variables do not reflect it in the parsimonious model, when the moderation by the control variable is included (model 2), all the variables included are statistically significant in at least one estimate. However, the term the interaction of control with technological capabilities shows that the economic sector does not generate an intervening influence on the relationship between these capabilities and digital transformation.

Although significance is shown at least for the control by ICT, that is, digital transformation depends on information technology capabilities given the conditions of the economic sector. A hypothesis test was carried out to assess whether the effect occurs or

Table 2. Estimated models controlled by economic sector

Reference level	Model (2)			Model (3)		
0:Low propensity	Coef.	Std. err.	P-value	Coef.	Std. err.	P-value
Estimation TD = 1:Medium						
Constant	−12.161	3.460	0.000[a]	−3.576	0.995	0.000[a]
Technological Cap.	0.768	0.374	0.040[b]	0.244	0.164	0.137
ICT	1.414	0.449	0.002[a]	0.338	0.149	0.024[b]
Industry	9.447	3.605	0.009[a]	−0.365	0.451	0.419
Industry × Technological Cap.	−0.569	0.422	0.177			
Industry × ICT	−1.235	0.480	0.010[a]			
Estimation TD = 2: High						
Constant	−6.438	2.822	0.023[b]	−1.591	1.078	0.140
Technological Cap.	0.254	0.338	0.454	0.092	0.176	0.602
ICT	0.899	0.379	0.018[b]	0.099	0.164	0.542
Industry	5.094	3.058	0.096[c]	−0.751	0.487	0.123
Industry × Technological Cap.	−0.103	0.403	0.797			
Industry × ICT	−1.012	0.423	0.017[b]			
Goodness of fit by frequencies			0.262			0.184
Deviance			0.647			0.506

Significance level: [a]0.01, [b]0.05, [c]0.1
Source: Own elaboration (2022)

not, comparing the complete model (2) and the parsimonious one (3). The results showed in Table 4 allow rejecting the null hypothesis of equality to zero in the coefficients for control covariates. Therefore, there is a moderation effect of information technology capabilities and a non−moderation effect of technological capabilities on the propensity to digital transformation.

Regarding the inclusion of the dummy variables that identify the company's economic activity, all the individual covariates presented statistical significance in at least one estimate. However, only the interaction term of education and information technology capabilities allows us to assume a coefficient other than zero. This agrees with the parsimonious model, which only showed significance for the ICT variable. In addition, the companies of this economic activity presented a more excellent perception of this capacity than those operating in technology.

Note that this evidence does not allow rejecting the null hypothesis of the effect coefficient equal to zero (see Table 4). Thus, there is no moderating effect since the parsimonious model (5) equally captures the influence of technological capabilities. However, for information technology capabilities, it is convenient to read from the complete model (4). Next section discusses the interpretation of the effects.

Table 3. Estimated models controlled by primary activity of the company

Reference level	Model (4)			Model (5)		
0:Low propensity	Coef.	Std. err.	P-value	Coef.	Std. err.	P-value
Estimation TD = 1:Medium						
Constant	−12.161	3.460	0.000[a]	−3.966	1.086	0.000[a]
Technological Cap.	0.768	0.374	0.040[b]	0.255	0.165	0.123
ICT	1.414	0.449	0.002[a]	0.407	0.167	0.015[b]
Education	10.278	3.771	0.006[a]	−0.594	0.508	0.243
Retail	7.868	3.913	0.044[b]	−0.172	0.525	0.743
Education × Technological Cap.	−0.639	0.435	0.142			
Education × ICT	−1.307	0.501	0.009[a]			
Retail × Technological Cap.	−0.392	0.526	0.456			
Retail × ICT	−1.079	0.557	0.053[c]			
Estimation TD = 2: High						
Constant	−6.438	2.822	0.023[b]	−3.079	1.224	0.012[b]
Technological Cap.	0.254	0.338	0.454	0.143	0.188	0.447
ICT	0.899	0.379	0.018[b]	0.339	0.190	0.075[c]
Education	2.499	3.812	0.512	−1.724	0.620	0.005[a]
Retail	3.727	3.277	0.255	−0.027	0.540	0.960
Education × Technological Cap.	−0.077	0.509	0.880			
Education × ICT	−0.718	0.541	0.185			
Retail × Technological Cap.	0.013	0.467	0.977			
Retail × ICT	−0.736	0.489	0.132			
Goodness of fit by frequencies			0.997			0.913
Deviance			0.584			0.520

Significance level: [a]0.01, [b]0.05, [c]0.1
Source: Own elaboration (2022)

Table 4. Likelihood-ratio test for models (2) vs. (3) and models (4) vs. (5)

	Model (3) nested in (2)	Model (5) nested in (4)
Likelihood-ratio test	13.84 (0.0078)	12.43 (0.1332)

LR (p-value). Significance level: [a]0.01, [b]0.05, [c]0.1.
Source: Own elaboration (2022)

3.3 Effects of Technological and Information Technology Capabilities on Digital Transformation

Considering the previous results, it is possible to analyze the increases in the probability due to changes in some of the capacities. Considering that the complete models allow evaluation of the effects, and that the change of economic activity is not a viable process in the short term for the company, the odds for models (2) and (4) are analyzed. For model (2), statistical significance was found for the two capabilities in the estimation of medium-level propensity to digital transformation. In contrast, only the capacity of information technologies is significant in the model of high propensity to digital transformation (4).

Based on the above, an increase of one unit in technological capabilities increases more than doubles ($RRR_{1,0} = 2.15$) the probability of having a medium-level stance, concerning low-level propensity, towards the digital transformation of the business.

Regarding the information technology capabilities, this variable was significant in both complete models (2) and (4), for each estimated category. This shows the relevance for service companies of information systems as support for their primary and secondary operational processes. This finding is consistent with perspectives by [13], who point out that ICT is an innovative driver to move companies into digital transformation.

Further, the interaction terms to control the model were also significant in models (2) and (4), and they changed the significance of the covariates compared with models (3) and (5). This finding shows that the economic sector of the company and its economic activity are relevant in the digital transformation.

Then, when the model includes the economic sector as showed in (2), an increase in one unit in the ICT capabilities increases 19% the probability of having a medium-level in the propensity of digital transformation, regarding the low-level. In the case of moving into a high-level propensity, this is 11,96% more likely than a low-level propensity to digital transformation when ICT capabilities increase in one unit.

On the other hand, model (3) got statistical significance for both moderator variables in estimating category medium. Therefore, regarding the low-level propensity to digital transformation, an increase of one unit in ICT capabilities boosts the probability of having a medium-level propensity in 11,29% and 39,79%, for educational services and retail companies respectively, compared to textile firms.

These results show the importance of support systems, as a part of ICT capabilities, for the digital transformation of the company. This agrees with what [14] stated that as much progress is made in data analysis and its applicability and adoption in business, the digital transformation of firms is currently relevant for most companies regardless of their size and nature. In addition, it is a current factor of interest for the academic community [15].

4   Conclusions, Limitations, and Future Research

This study attempted to analyze the relationship between digital transformation and technological and ICT capabilities in multiple industries. The effect of each capability was evaluated in three levels of propensity to the digital transformation that the company has. The findings allow to conclude that digital transformation in business model of Colombian companies exists to the extent that firms develop better capabilities related to the technological factor, either for products and primary processes, or for information systems that support business decisions.

The technological capabilities involve into the production process promote digital transformation as long as the company develops industrial manufacturing activities. But this capability is not a driver of digital transformation for service companies. While ICT capabilities promote the transformation of the business model regardless of the economic activity of the company. This is relevant since Colombia has a GDP distribution of almost the same proportion between the manufacturing and extractive sectors and the services sectors.

Some limitations were found. First, the digital transformation in companies can be produced not only by the technological and ICT capabilities that the company possesses. This change can be influenced by internal factors such as competitive strategy or the flexibility of the structure. Also due to external aspects such as the competitive dynamics of the firm's strategic domain, or the encouragement and control actions carried out by the government. Therefore, the independent variables in the model should be considered when interpreting the results. Second, the findings are obtained from the analysis of three industries which group the important economic sectors, but findings should not be generalized to the reality of all Colombian industries.

Three future lines of research emerge from the results. First, an evaluation of the drivers of digital transformation in developed countries will serve as a point of comparison for changes in organizational capabilities that companies can carry out autonomously, as well as a point of reference for government policies.

Second, digital transformation is a complex construct that can have different scopes depending on the business area to be evaluated. Therefore, a split in the measurement of this variable leads to analyze the specific dynamic capabilities that the company can boost according to its strategy and the intended focus of change. Third, a measurement of digital transformation based on hard data rather than manager insight may provide a better benchmark for establishing capability effects.

Acknowledgement. Research supported by Red Sistemas Inteligentes y Expertos Modelos Computacionales Iberoamericanos (SIEMCI), project number 522RT0130 in Programa Iberoamericano de Ciencia y Tecnologia para el Desarrollo (CYTED).

References

1. Ahn, S., Kim, K., Lee, K.: Technological capabilities, entrepreneurship and innovation of technology-based start-ups: the resource-based view. J. Open Innov.: Technol. Mark. Complex. **8**(3), 156 (2022)
2. Heredia, J., Castillo-Vergara, M., Geldes, C., Carbajal Gamarra, F., Flores, A., Heredia, W.: How do digital capabilities affect firm performance? the mediating role of technological capabilities in the "new normal." J. Innov. Knowl. **7**(2), 100171 (2022)
3. Morrison, A., Pietrobelli, C., Rabellotti, R.: Global value chains and technological capabilities: a framework to study learning and innovation in developing countries. Oxf. Dev. Stud. **36**(1), 39–58 (2008)

4. Archibugi, D., Coco, A.: A new indicator of technological capabilities for developed and developing countries (Arco). World Dev. **32**(4), 629–654 (2004)
5. Baez Palencia, D., Mariño-Jiménez, J., Parra Moreno, C., López Barraza, L.: Capacidades estratégicas en instituciones de educación para el trabajo y desarrollo humano de Bogotá, Colombia. Revista Espacios **41**(50), 183–205 (2020)
6. García Samper, M., et al.: Digital transformation of business models: influence of operation and trade variables. Procedia Comput. Sci. **203**(1), 565–569 (2022)
7. Sánchez Céspedes, J., Rodríguez Miranda, J., Ramos Sandoval, O.: Decision support systems (DSS) applied to the formulation of agricultural public policies. Tecnura **24**(66), 95–108 (2020)
8. Mendoza Becerra, M., Camayo Otero, A., Martínez Molina, A., Martínez Flor, E., Cobos Lozada, C.: Sistema de soporte a la toma de decisiones para el análisis multifractal del genoma humano. ITECKNE **10**(1), 45–56 (2013)
9. Ramírez, R., Villalobos, J., Lay, N.D., Herrera, B.A.: Medios de comunicación para la apropiación del conocimiento en instituciones educativas. Información tecnológica **32**(1), 27–38 (2021)
10. Londoño Mora, P., Kurlat, M., Agüero, M.: Desarrollo de un Sistema de Soporte a la Toma de Decisiones y su Aplicación en la Empresa. Cienc. Tecn. **13**, 323–332 (2013)
11. García Velázquez, A., Pineda Domínguez, D., Andrade Vallejo, M.: Las capacidades tecnológicas para la innovación en empresas de manufactura. Universidad & Empresa **17**(29), 257–278 (2015)
12. Baez Palencia, D., Lopez-Barraza, L., Mariño-Jimenez, J.: Organizational capabilities and competitive strategies in a developing country: an empirical analysis. Procedia Comput. Sci. **210**(1), 358–362 (2022)
13. Eom, T., Woo, C., Chun, D.: Predicting an ICT business process innovation as a digital transformation with machine learning techniques. Technol. Anal. Strat. Manag. (1), 1–13 (2022)
14. Machado, A., Secinario, S., Calandra, D., Lanzalonga, F.: Knowledge management and digital transformation for industry 4.0: a structured literature review. Knowl. Manag. Res. Pract. **20**(2), 320–338 (2022)
15. Shi, L., Mai, Y., Wu, Y.: Digital transformation: a bibliometric analysis. J. Organ. End User Comput. **37**(7), 1–19 (2022)
16. Teece, D., Pisano, G., Shuen, A.: Dynamic capabilities and strategic management. Strateg. Manag. J. **18**(7), 509–553 (1997)
17. Ettlie, J., Pavlou, P.: Technology-Based New Product Development Partnerships. Decision Sciences (2006)
18. Sukier, H. B., Ramírez Molina, R.J., Ramírez M., R.I., Lay Raby, N.D.: Administración estratégica en el sector salud desde el enfoque organizacional. Revista Venezolana de Gerencia (RVG) **25**(04), 206–221 (2020)

An Improved Approach of Image Steganography Based on Least Significant Bit Technique for Secure Communication in Cloud

Md. Khorshed Alam(✉) ⓘ, Samia Nushrat, Md. Amir Hamza Patwary, Ahsan Ullah, and Kazi Hassan Robin

Department of Computer Science and Engineering, World University of Bangladesh, Dhaka 1230, Bangladesh
khorshedalam.kbd@gmail.com, {ahsan.ullah,robin1}@cse.wub.edu.bd

Abstract. Cloud computing allows for a simple, distributed pool of reconfigurable computers with widespread network connectivity. But maintaining data security and privacy is very difficult. In order to guarantee the privacy and security of data in cloud computing, this study developed an efficient and enhanced method that involves concealing data inside pictures. The authors have proposed Multi Level Encryption Algorithm (MLEA) and Two-Level Encryption Algorithm (TLEA) and also processed the image in various steps to achieve better security. The objective is to design and develop an image steganography method based on the Least Significant Bit (LSB) technique that can secure the data during sharing or storing. The authors used the LSB technique of image steganography and encrypted data using MLEA and TLEA. The authors compared different methods and proved their research provides better security than the existing ones. This research demonstrates that the proposed method has performance with an average of 19.7814% better than other existing schemes.

Keywords: Steganography · LSB · Cloud computing · TLEA · MLEA

1 Introduction

Users store their data on the cloud, and data of every type must be secure on the cloud. Cloud computing is made up of computer and network applications. Data sharing is a key activity in the cloud. Small, medium, and large businesses use the cloud to store their data for a low leasing fee. In recent years, cloud computing has proven its value in terms of application sharing, resource and network sharing, and data storage usefulness. As a result, the majority of clients prefer to use cloud features and services. So, security is a critical consideration for both customers and vendors. In terms of data service, privacy of data, and data management, there are various challenges that must be addressed. Among the most critical problems in cloud computing is the security of stored data and information. We can fix a lot of security issues by using good access control protection strategies. Accept that controlling the privacy and security of information on the internet is extremely difficult.

© The Author(s), under exclusive license to Springer Nature Switzerland AG 2023
I. Woungang et al. (Eds.): ANTIC 2022, CCIS 1797, pp. 215–233, 2023.
https://doi.org/10.1007/978-3-031-28180-8_15

By creating a cover channel, steganography is mostly utilized for confidential conversations. Steganography is the technique of encoding secret information such that only the intended receiver is aware it exists. Steganography is a well-liked method for concealing sensitive data in digital material, including text, images, videos, and audio files. Other methods, on the other hand, include confidential information in network protocols. Three key criteria capacity, robustness, and security are used to assess the research on steganographic systems. The total number of secret messages that are concealed in the cover medium is measured by capacity. Robustness refers to resistance to the concealed data's destruction or change (a steganogram). Security evaluates an eavesdropper's capacity to find concealed information. Security is often the quality that people value most, however. LSB is a well-known technique that is used in steganography. The least significant bit (LSB) is a process where the least significant bit of the image is converted into a data bit. By changing the LSB, the image doesn't change its visual representation, and it doesn't catch on the HVS (Human Visual System). So, an unauthorized person can't read or find the hidden image.

The paper is organized as follows, Sect. 1 contains the introduction of cloud computing, Image Steganography and LSB technique; Sect. 2 contains the related works; Sect. 3 contains proposed method and algorithm; Sect. 4 contains results and discussion; Sect. 5 explains the conclusion of this research.

2 Related Works

A unique steganography paradigm was suggested that is visible to any hacker and resistant to recognition and unsealing secret data. Two qualities help us achieve these goals: the data are not modified, and the secret is distributed on a multi-cloud storage server, which permits us to conceal the presence of the private channel between communication parties. In most cases, related works conceal data in covert media. The converted media serves as a guide to the content of this work. As a result, the file contains the information without being altered, and the key is the only method to access it. Experiments have revealed that when the value of the chosen base increases, the secret distribution in the clouds diminishes [9].

An effective method for ensuring data integrity. In this architecture, the data that has been sent to the server is sealed beyond the pictures. As a consequence, because the data is hidden, unauthorized access cannot view it. Although the suggested approach uses picture steganography to protect data integrity, which is an outstanding solution, data security during transmission is not addressed at all. As a result, while this is a novel technique, it might have been much better if data integrity and secrecy could be managed at the time of loading to a cloud server [11].

Encryption, information concealment, and hashing techniques are used to improve the security of cloud data. The author used hybrid encryption in the data encryption phase, combining the AES256 symmetric encryption technique with the RSA asymmetric encryption algorithm. Using the LSB method, the encrypted data was then buried in an image. The SHA hashing method was utilized in the data authentication phase [12].

To improve the strength of the proposed strategy, the digital content was initially exposed to DRT transformation. The embedding rate increased once it was changed to

Base B. The cover picture was then given an IWT. The Base B transform interactions of the altered digital material were inserted inside the altered cover picture using the diamond encoding technique. With the aim of creating the stego image, the created image—which was afterwards saved in cloud storage—was put through the inverse of IWT. These stego pictures were unloaded from the cloud as required, and the genuine mixed media data was acquired in a similar way. The testing outcomes demonstrate that the created stego picture had architectural similarities with the cover image [4].

Integrating three methods, they were able to guarantee data security in cloud computing. First, they used DSA for data verification and authentication. Then, to ensure optimum data security, use the technique to protect data and steganography to secure data inside the audio files. Because it is a one-by-one process, this model meets both authenticity and security [17].

Method for sharing and storing private information in the cloud that employs multiple steganography techniques, including the Hash-LSB technique and the AES algorithm, allowing users to upload the solitudes of hidden data stored in the cloud Simultaneously, all saved data is available from any location at any time [3].

A mutual authentication system that allows the user and cloud server to verify each other's identities. They use steganography and secret sharing to establish mutual authentication in this article. The protocol is split into four parts: registration, login, mutual authentication, and password change. In this convention, the user, AS, and CS are the main participants. Their protocol was created in such a way that steganography is used as an extra encryption mechanism. The system uses secret sharing to achieve authentication. When the AS provides the secret and obtains the user data from it, the user will be authorized [12].

Examine some of the steganography approaches proposed in numerous papers to improve cloud data security and resistance to cyber-attacks and spying. Steganography is widely regarded as one of the most fruitful techniques for safeguarding cloud communication. Steganography is the practice of composing concealed texts in such a way that the sender and receiver are able to secretly read and transmit the message through a communication medium. Despite the fact that they are completely different terms, steganography and cryptography are sometimes misunderstood. Cryptography is in charge of privacy, while steganography is in charge of secrecy [15].

Security issues in cloud computing and how they can be avoided; in this case, steganography and cryptography were used to secure data. RSA is a more secure algorithm than other algorithms. The RSA method was combined with other algorithms to provide additional data security. During the steganography, an encoded image is created that looks the same as the cover image to the naked eye. The discrepancies can be noticed by analyzing the image binary codes. Otherwise, it won't be able to tell which image is the original. The technique taken in this study will aid in the creation of a solid structure for data security in the cloud computing industry [18].

Steganography and cryptography were used to achieve cross-system communication and a comparative analysis of steganography and cryptography was performed. Several techniques for combining cryptography and steganography methods in a single system were examined. The K-Strange Clustered Algorithm was improved, and the LSB steganography approach was used to protect information within an image [10].

Strategy that uses the Rivest–Shamir–Adleman (RSA) algorithm as a digital signature and image steganography to increase cloud security. The RSA algorithm is used to generate public and private keys, which are used for authentication rather than repudiation, to offer a message digest to authenticate the user. Once the information has been validated, it is concealed using image steganography in order to execute a plane transfer without the intruders becoming aware of it. The researchers measured network bandwidth, memory storage, CPU processing time, and power [2].

The security of data stored in the cloud, which is a major concern because the data is kept in locations where specific machines can access it, Data security is extremely difficult to achieve. The authors created a data concealing technique to boost data security when transmitting and while living in the cloud. They improved data security by concealing it within the color image's margins. The major purpose of this study is to prevent adversaries from obtaining data. Substitution techniques were employed for steganography. The Robinson Mask with LSB technique is used to conceal hidden data inside the cover picture [6].

The HCIS algorithm (hybridized cryptographic-integrated steganography) includes additional data inputs for an IoT-enabled cloud environment with safe data sharing for the city transportation system. To protect communications within the IoT-based cloud server for the urban transportation system, cryptography uses a collection of techniques known as ciphers to encrypt and decode data. Key exchange, encryption, and authentication are all done using cipher suites. Steganography is a technique for hiding secret and non-secret information within private data that is extracted by the recipient. The advantages of steganography may be used with encoding as an additional means of safeguarding or hiding information. In cloud computing, the suggested HCIS approach accomplishes effective data transmission [5].

The AES 128 algorithm scrambles the communications using LSB steganography to disguise the scrambled messages. Using Steg-Spy, the data was evaluated. According to the findings of this investigation, the Platform as a Service (PaaS) cloud computing service produced ciphertext that was connected to JPG and JPEG images using the Least Significant Bit (LSB). In five (five) of the trials, the encryption result on JPG and JPEG files was larger than the original file. The size of JPG and JPEG files will grow in proportion to the number of characters in the inputted text [14].

Three image steganography algorithms are used in this technique. The primary idea behind the purpose of these methods is to include the weak point in the host medium without first encrypting the data that will be buried, and to do so in a way that is purely dependent on quantum walks. It also presents the possibility of combining quantum technology with data-concealing methods to improve security. The given technique employs grayscale or color images as a secret item to be protected within the carrier picture. The recommended algorithms offer good condition and great security, which depends on QWs and high encoding magnitude in compliance with security research and tentative results [1].

The concealing method is used to hide data behind images. The user uploads the data and encrypts it with a powerful algorithm like the AES in this algorithm. The data is subsequently synced to the server in encrypted form. When input from the user is received, a hiding method is used to select bits from images where data is to be kept at random [7].

3 Proposed Method and Algorithm

The proposed algorithm is to conceal information inside a cover medium, which is an image. In this algorithm, a Multi-Level Encryption Algorithm (MLEA) has been used to secure the secret message and a Two-Level Encryption Algorithm (TLEA) to secure the secret key. This secret message and secret key have been inserted inside the cover picture. The cover image turns into a stego image, which consists of an encrypted secret message.

3.1 Proposed Encryption and Decryption Method

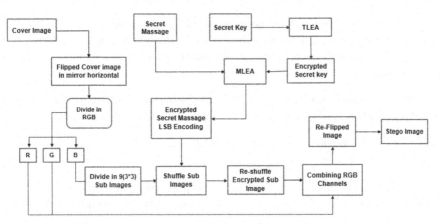

Fig. 1. Proposed encryption method

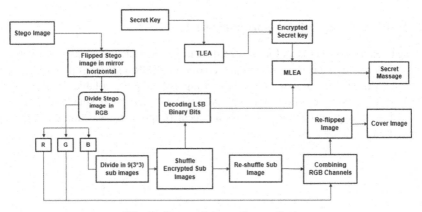

Fig. 2. Proposed decryption method

Description of Proposed Encryption & Decryption Method. For Fig. 1 and Fig. 2, the following terms are described below.

Cover Image. A cover image is the image chosen for hiding data in or within using the proposed method.

Cover Image in Horizontal Mirror. Flipping an image means changing the pixel position of the image. Mirror flip flips the image from left to right, and the horizontal is reversed.

Divide in RGB: Color Images have color channels: Red Channel, Green Channel, and Blue Channel. Divide in RGB means dividing the image into these three-color channels and selecting the Blue channel of the cover image.

Divide into 9 Sub-Images. Dividing the whole image into 9 parts by a 3*3 matrix, which means 3 rows and 3 columns. Each part is called a sub-image.

Shuffle Sub-Images. Changing the positions of sub-images using a secret shuffling pattern. The sub-image in position 1 can be replaced with the sub-image in positions 4 or 5 or any other position. Each sub-image will change position, and then we will get the shuffled image.

Reshuffle Encrypted Sub-Images. Returns all sub-image positions to their original positions. And here, every sub-image will contain the encrypted message.

Combining RGB Channels. Combining the Red, Green, and Blue channels together to have a colored image as before.

Re-flipped Image. Flipping the image back from upside down and from right to left. The image looks exactly like the cover image but contains a hidden secret message.

Stego Image. After hiding the secret message into the cover image using the proposed method, this image is called a stego image.

3.2 Two-Level Encryption Algorithm (TLEA)

Aiming to encrypt secret keys for increased security, the TLEA is a simple yet effective method. There are two primary components to it: bit-XOR and secret pattern-based bit shuffling. Although a number of encryption algorithms are available for these tasks, including Advance Encryption Standard (AES), Data Encryption Standard (DES), and Blow-fish, their appropriateness for real-time security applications is limited by the high computational cost of these methods.

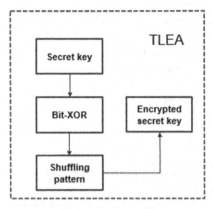

Fig. 3. TLEA block diagram

Algorithm:

Step 01: Select the secret key and convert into binary 8 bits.
Step 02: Taking the XOR of all bits by logical 1
Step 03: Using an 8-bit combination, the third bit is switched for the sixth bit, the second bit for the eighth bit, the seventh bit for the fifth bit, and the fourth bit for the first bit.
Step 04: Store all bits in an encrypted secret key (ESK)

3.3 Multi-level Encryption Algorithm (MLEA)

The real secret data is encrypted using the MLEA to make it challenging for an attacker to extract it from the stego picture. Its primary argument for selection is that it is reasonably lightweight when compared to complicated algorithms like AES, DES, and others. It is composed of four procedures: bit-XOR, secret bit block division, secret key-based shuffling, and encrypted secret key-based encryption [11].

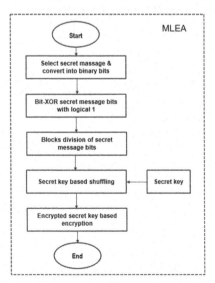

Fig. 4. MLEA block diagram

BSM = Bit-XOR Secret Message
MB = Message Block
BSMB = Bit-XOR Secret Message Block
SKBSM = Secret key based Secret Message
ESK = Encrypted secret key
ESM = Encrypted secret Message

Algorithm:

Step 01: Select a secret message & convert it to binary 8 bits
Step 02: XOR all bits using logical 1
Step 03: Take an 8-bit combination & divide it into 4 Massage Blocks (MB_1, MB_2, MB_3, MB_4) [16]. MB_1 is all the eighth and first bit; MB_2 is all the seventh and second bit; MB_3 is all the sixth and third bit; and MB_4 is all the fifth and fourth bit of each 8-bit combination.
Step 04: Take the ith digit from the secret key.
Step 05: Separate the secret bit in the ith digit position from BSMB.
Step 06: Concatenate the separated bit with SKBSM and increment the value of i
Step 07: Repeat step (4) to (6) until all bits of the BSMB are shuffled
Step 08: Initialize the loop counters j and k such that $j = 0$ and $k = 0$
Step 09: Select the jth secret bit from SKBSM
Step 10: Select the kth bit from the encrypted secret key ESK
Step 11: If the kth bit of the secret key ESK is 1
    i. Perform Temp = ($SKBSM_{(j)} \oplus$ logical 1)
    ii. Concatenate Temp with ESM
      Else
            Concatenate $SKBSM_{(j)}$ with ESM without bit-XOR operation
      End
Step 12: Increment j and k by 1
Step 13: Repeat step (9) to step (12) until all bits are encrypted.

3.4 Proposed Encryption and Decryption Algorithm

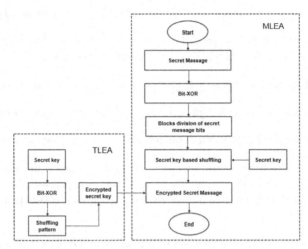

Fig. 5. Encryption algorithm block diagram

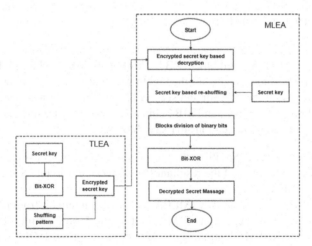

Fig. 6. Decryption algorithm block diagram

Description of Proposed Encryption & Decryption Algorithm. For Fig. 5 and Fig. 6, the following terms are described below.

TLEA. It composed of two procedures; bit-XOR and Secret Pattern based bit shuffling.

MLEA. It is composed of four procedures: bit-XOR, secret bit block division, secret key-based shuffling, and encrypted secret key-based encryption [11].

Secret key (TLEA). Select a Secret Key (SK) and convert the key into binary 8 bits.

Secret Key (MLEA). Select an 8-digit secret key and the secret key digit must be 1 to 8.

Bit-XOR. Applying the bit-XOR function to Secret Key binary bits with a logical 1.

Shuffling Pattern. After Bit-XOR, bits are shuffled according to this pattern, i.e., the fourth bit is swapped with the first bit; the second bit is swapped with the eighth bit; the third bit is swapped with the sixth bit; and then the seventh bit is swapped with the fifth bit.

Encrypted Secret Key. The combinations of the secret pattern base shuffled bits are the Encrypted Secret Key (ESK).

Secret Massage. Select a massage and convert the American Standard Code for Information Interchange (ASCII) to binary 8 bits.

Blocks Division of Secret Bits (Fig. 5). Secret Massage bits divided into four massage blocks first block MB1, Second block MB2, Third block MB3 and fourth block MB4.

Massage block MB1 contains all the eighth and first bit of each byte of the secret bits; MB2 contains all the seventh and second bit of each byte; MB3 contains all the sixth and third bit of each byte; and MB4 contains the fifth and fourth bit of each byte of message. Finally combine the four-massage blocks.

Secret Key-Based Shuffling. Shuffling the bits of Bit-XOR Secret Massage Bits (BSMB) on the secret key (MLEA) and the resultant bits stored in a variable Secret Key Based Secret Message (SKBSM).

If the first digit of the secret key (MLEA) is 8 so the eighth bit from BSMB will be stored in SKBSM. If the next digit of the secret key is 5, so the fifth bit of BSMB is concatenated with SKBSM. Continuing the same procedure for BSMB bits, the resultant bits are stored in SKBSM.

Encrypted Secret Massage. Select SKBSM and ESK resulting from TLEA. Storing the final resultant bits into an array Encrypted Secret Massage (ESM).

Select the ith secret bit from SKBSM and Select the jth bit from Encrypted Secret Key (ESK). If the jth bit of ESK is 1 then bit-XOR i^{th} with logical 1 and Store in ESM otherwise store i^{th} bit in ESM without bit-XOR operation.

Encrypted secret key-based decryption. Select ESM and ESK resulting from TLEA. Storing the final resultant bits into an array Secret Key Based Decrypted Secret Message (SKBDSM).

Select the ith secret bit from ESM and Select the jth bit from Encrypted Secret Key (ESK). If the jth bit of ESK(j) is 1 then bit-XOR i^{th} bit with logical 1 and Store in SKBDSM otherwise store i^{th} bit in SKBDSM without bit-XOR operation.

Secret Key-Based Re-shuffling. Re-shuffling the bits of SKBSM based on the secret key (MLEA) and the resultant bits stored in a variable BSMB.

If the first digit of the secret key (MLEA) is 8 so the eighth bit from SKBSM will be stored in BSMB. The next digit of the secret key is 5, so the fifth bit of SKBSM is concatenated with BSMB. Continuing the same procedure for SKBSM bits, the resultant bits are stored in BSMB.

Blocks Division of Secret Bits (Fig. 6). BSMB divided into four massage blocks first block MB1, Second block MB2, Third block MB3 and fourth block MB4.

Massage block MB_1 contains all the eighth and first bit of each byte of the BSMB; MB_2 contains all the seventh and second bit of each byte; MB_3 contains all the sixth and third bit of each byte; and MB_4 contains the fifth and fourth bit of each byte of message. Finally combine the four-massage blocks.

Decrypted Secret Massage. Convert the binary bits into ASCII codes and get the Decrypted secret massage.

3.5 Description of Embedding Algorithm

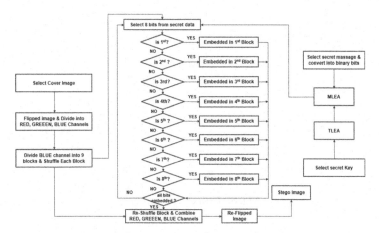

Fig. 7. Embedding algorithm

In Fig. 7, the RGB color space is used by the embedding algorithm. The cover image is first flipped in a mirror horizontal and after that divided into its three channels that is red, green, and blue channels. The blue channel is used to hide the secret data. Before embedding, the blue channel is divided into nine equal blocks, and then each of the block is shuffled with the Secret Shuffled Pattern [16]. On the other hand, the secret key is encrypted by a two-level encryption algorithm (TLEA), and the secret message (ASCII codes) was encrypted using a multi-level encryption algorithm (MLEA). Blue channel was choosed for embedding secret messages, which are divided into nine equal blocks. We select 8 bits of secret message, embed the first two bits in the 1st block of the blue channels, the second bit into the 2nd block, the third bit into the 3rd block, the fourth bit into the 4th block, the fifth bit into the 5th block, the sixth bit into the 6th block, the seventh bit into the 7th block, and the eighth bit into the 8th block of the blue channels, respectively. All bits are embedded in the image's blue channel, then the blocks are reshuffled and the RBG channels are combined [16]. The image was refilled. Finally getting the Stego image.

LSB Encoding. Select 8 bits of secret message and embed the first bit into the 1st block, the second bit into the 2nd block, the third bit into the 3rd block, the fourth bit into the 4th block, the fifth bit into the 5th block, the sixth bit into the 6th block, the seventh bit into the 7th block, and the eighth bit into the 8th block of the blue channels, respectively [16]. These details are used to generate the cover image. These values are inserted into the 1-bit LSB of the cover image's successive pixels.

3.6   Description of Extracting Algorithm

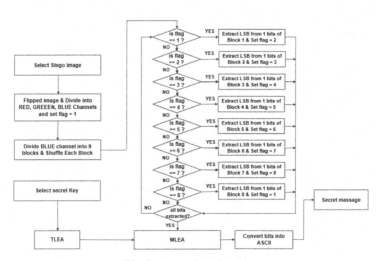

Fig. 8. Extracting algorithm

In Fig. 8, the extraction algorithm. The embedding algorithm has been accomplished but in reverse order. First, the stego-image is flipped back horizontally, mirrored, and divided into the red, green, and blue channels. The blue channel is then divided into nine equal blocks, and every block is shuffled using a Secret Shuffle pattern. The LSB of 1 pixel from each block is decrypted repetitively up to the end of the embedded data [16]. TLEA and MLEA are used to decode the extracted data. Then converting every eight-bit combination into an ASCII value. Finally getting the secret massage.

LSB Decoding. The 1-bit LSB of every pixel value from each block is extracted periodically from the end of the embedded data in the Stego image. The first bit will be extracted from the first block, the second from the second, the third from the third, the fourth from the fourth, the fifth from the fifth, the sixth from the sixth, the seventh from the seventh, and the eighth from the eighth block. For every 8-bit combination of Secret Message.

3.7 Proposed Encryption Method for Cloud

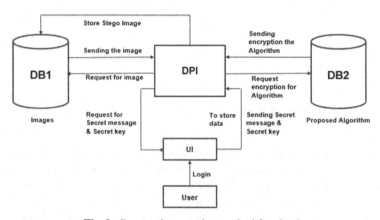

Fig. 9. Proposed encryption method for cloud

In Fig. 9, the model of the proposed encryption method in a cloud environment where data will be encrypted using the proposed Encryption algorithm. Whenever the user wishes to store their data in the cloud, the below operations will take place: The user enters their user ID and password to access the user interface (UI). The user requests to store data in the cloud database (DB). Data Processing Interface (DPI) re-quests an image from DB1. DB1 provides a valid image to DPI. DPI requests for the data-hiding encryption algorithm, which is reserved in DB2. DB2 provides the encryption algorithm to DPI. DPI requests Secret Message & Secret key from the user. The user provides their Secret Message & Secret key to DPI. In compliance with the encryption algorithm, the data is embedded in the pixel values of the image, which are taken from the DB1. Finally, the Stego Image will be stored in DB1 [11].

3.8 Proposed Decryption Method for Cloud

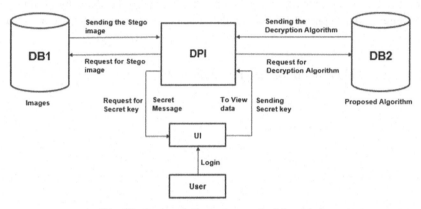

Fig. 10. Proposed decryption method for cloud

In Fig. 10, the model of the proposed decryption method in a cloud environment to extract data using the proposed decryption algorithm. The following mechanisms will be used whenever the user wishes to view or retrieve data: The user enters their user ID and password to access the user interface (UI). The user requests to view or retrieve data from the cloud database (DB). Data Processing Interface (DPI) requests Stego Images that are affiliated with the Secret Message that users want to view or retrieve. DB1 provides the associated Stego Image to DPI. DPI requests the data retrieval and decryption algorithm, which is stored in DB2. DPI receives the decryption algorithm from DB2. Then DPI requests a secret key from the user. DPI processes the decryption algorithm on the stego image which is provided by DB2 and stores the data after retrieval into a temporary file. This file is represented to the user, and after performing any action on this data. It will be de-allocated from the User Interface (UI). Before the user logs out of the User Interface, the temporary file will be impulsively deleted from the system [11].

4 Results and Discussion

The image, which will include the concealed information contained, is the cover image. The outcome is the Stego Image (which will, surely be the same size of the cover image). Peak Signal-to- Noise Ratio (PSNR) [19], a computation of stego picture quality, is computed. A statistical metric called PSNR is used to evaluate the quality of digital images and videos. The easiest way to determine PSNR is to use the Mean Squared Error (MSE) [19] for two M × N ferrotype pictures, f and g where one image is thought of as a noisy approximation of the other images.

4.1 Mean Squared Error (MSE)

$$MSE = \frac{1}{MN} \sum_{i=0}^{M-1} \sum_{i=0}^{N-1} \left[f(x, y) - g(x, y) \right]^2 \qquad (1)$$

Table 1. MSE value for different dimensions of the same images

MSE	128 × 128	256 × 256	512 × 512	1024 × 1024
Baboon Image	0.0031	0.00073242	0.00018819	0.000042915
Lena Image	0.0028	0.00071208	0.00018311	0.000045776
House Image 1	0.0030	0.00071208	0.00017166	0.000046730
House Image 2	0.0031	0.00069682	0.00018438	0.000045141

4.2 Peak Signal to Noise Ratio (PSNR)

The calculation of the quality between the cover image f and Stego Image g of sizes M × N is defined by PSNR as:

Where, $\mathbf{MSE} = \frac{1}{MN} \sum_{i=0}^{M-1} \sum_{i=0}^{N-1} \left[f(x, y) - g(x, y) \right]^2$

$$\mathbf{PSNR} = 10 \log_{10} \frac{255^2}{MSE} \qquad (2)$$

4.3   Representation of Baboon, Lena, House Image-1 and House Image 2 Images of Different Sizes and PSNR Value

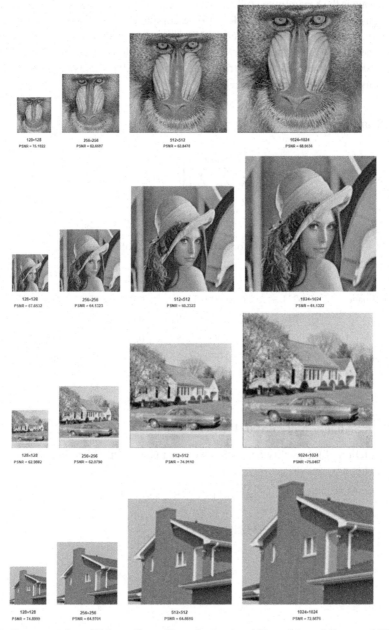

Fig. 11. Representation of Baboon, Lena, House Image-1 and House Image-2 images of different sizes and PSNR value

4.4 Calculation and Analysis Based on PSNR

Experimental Setup and Simulation Tools. The simulators used for the proposed method is PyCharm (Python Integrated Development Environment) and MATLAB. The PSNR and MSE parameters are used to compute the quality of the Cover Image and Stego Images of various sizes (128 × 128, 256 × 256, 512 × 512, 1024 × 1024).

PyCharm is used for Embedding the Secret Massage in the Cover Image and Extracting the Secret Massage from the Stego Image. MATLAB is used to calculate the MSE from the Eq. 1 and PSNR from the Eq. 2.

Table 2. Comparison of proposed method with other mentioned techniques, encrypting same size of Secret Message in selected standard images of different sizes based on PSNR

Image Name	Image dimensions (In pixels)	Classic LSB Method PSNR (dB)	PIT PSNR (dB)	Karim's Method PSNR (dB)	Muhammad et al. [Muhammad, Ahmad, Farman et al. (2015)] Method PSNR (dB)	Fahad et al. [Fahad, Fazal, Georgios et al. (2020)] Method PSNR (dB)	Proposed Method
Baboon Image	128 × 128	64.9939	48.6326	50.2716	65.6754	75.1022	73.1710
	256 × 256	55.8862	50.2321	49.6829	62.4044	62.6587	79.4832
	512 × 512	61.882	50.1906	50.0517	59.4242	62.8478	85.3847
	1024 × 1024	67.8306	50.2001	50.1669	65.5012	68.9636	91.8074
	Average	**62.6482**	**49.81385**	**50.0433**	**63.2513**	**65.9681**	**82.461575**
Lena Image	128 × 128	42.4947	45.3316	42.5020	58.3332	67.6532	73.7108
	256 × 256	49.1185	50.1136	52.4134	52.4134	64.1323	79.6055
	512 × 512	49.8277	50.0932	49.9546	57.0021	60.3323	85.5038
	1024 × 1024	50.0299	50.1004	50.0645	59.7532	61.1322	91.5244
	Average	**47.8677**	**48.9097**	**48.0198**	**56.8725**	**60.3125**	**82.586125**
House Image 1	128 × 128	43.5487	44.3455	47.5464	63.6754	62.9882	73.4325
	256 × 256	49.4532	49.2130	50.4567	62.4044	62.9790	79.6055
	512 × 512	48.8743	50.1110	51.5643	59.3032	74.9110	85.7841
	1024 × 1024	51.8974	50.4311	52.4531	65.3212	75.0467	91.4348
	Average	**48.4434**	**48.5251**	**50.5051**	**62.6760**	**75.0467**	**82.564225**

(*continued*)

Table 2. (*continued*)

Image Name	Image dimensions (In pixels)	Classic LSB Method PSNR (dB)	PIT PSNR (dB)	Karim's Method PSNR (dB)	Muhammad et al. [Muhammad, Ahmad, Farman et al. (2015)] Method PSNR (dB)	Fahad et al. [Fahad, Fazal, Georgios et al. (2020)] Method PSNR (dB)	Proposed Method
House Image 2	128 × 128	62.7293	67.5132	62.7137	69.3076	74.8999	73.2278
	256 × 256	56.6697	54.7702	53.3682	64.8565	64.9701	79.6996
	512 × 512	62.7405	54.754	54.3691	63.3443	64.6510	85.4737
	1024 × 1024	68.8288	54.7901	54.6877	72.4734	72.5676	91.5158
	Average	**62.7421**	**57.95688**	**56.2847**	**67.4932**	**69.2771**	**82.49225**

The proposed method and other mentioned methodologies are compared using PSNR in the table. The same-sized text (12 KB) is encapsulated in identical pictures that are varying sizes (128 × 128, 256 × 256, 512 × 512, and 1024 × 1024). (Lena, Baboon, House Image 1, House Image 2). The findings unequivocally show that the proposed method performs better than other existing methodologies, with an average score improvement of 19.7814%.

5 Conclusion

The authors propose the LSB substitution technique and multi-level encryption to create a security system that balances picture quality, computational complexity, and security as well. This paper describes the TLEA for encrypting the secret key and the MLEA for encrypting the secret data. They applied the LSB substitution technique for data encryption to establish extracting the data more difficult for adversaries. The proposed method strengthens steganography and improves the security of existing information-hiding technologies. Applying the RGB shading space, they exhibited a novel and improved method that is more powerful and secure than previous methods. Future work will be on audio and video file encryption.

References

1. El-Latif, A.A.A., Abd-El-Atty, B., Elseuofi, S., et al.: Secret images transfer in cloud system based on investigating quantum walks in steganography approaches. Physica A 2019 (2019)
2. Ismail Abdulkarim, A., Souley, B.: An enhanced cloud based security system using RSA as digital signature and image steganography. Int. J. Sci. Eng. Res. **8**(7) (2017)

3. Ranjan, A., Bhonsle, M.: Advanced system to protect and shared cloud storage data using multilayer steganography and cryptography. Int. J. Eng. Res. **5**(6), 434–438 (2016)
4. Sukumar, A., Vijayakumar, S., Ravi, L.: A secure multimedia steganography scheme using hybrid transform and support vector machine for cloud-based storage. Springer Science + Business Media, LLC, part of Springer Nature 2020 (2019)
5. Bi, D., Kadry, S., Kumar, P.M.: Internet of things assisted public security management platform for urban transportation using hybridised cryptographic-integrated steganography. IET Intell. Transp. Syst. **14**(11), 1497–1506 (2020)
6. Hadi Saleh, H.: Increasing security for cloud computing by steganography in image edges. Al-Mustansiriyah J. Sci. (ISSN: 1814–635X), **27**(4) (2016)
7. Karun, H.A., Uma, S.I.: Data security in cloud computing utilizing encryption and steganography. Worldwide J. Comput. Sci. Mobile Comput. **4**(5), 786–791 (2015)
8. Muhammad, K., Ahmad, J., Ur Rehman, N., Jan, Z., Sajjad, M.: CISSKA-LSB: color image steganography using stego key-directed adaptive LSB substitution method. Multimed Tools Appl. (2016)
9. Moyou Metcheka, L., Ndoundam, R.: Distributed data hiding in multi-cloud storage environment. J. Cloud Comput. **9**(1), 1–15 (2020). https://doi.org/10.1186/s13677-020-002 08-4
10. Khan, M.A., Hassan, T., Ullah, Z.: information security for cloud using image steganography. LGU Res. J. Comput. Sci. Inf. Technol. **5**(1) (2016)
11. Sarkar, M.K., Chatterjee, T.: enhancing data storage security in cloud computing through steganography. ACEEE Int. J. Netw. Secur. **5**(1) (2014)
12. Abbas, M.S., Mahdi, S.S., Hussien, S.A.: Security improvement of cloud data using hybrid cryptography and steganography. In: 2020 International Conference on Computer Science and Software Engineering (CSASE), Duhok, Kurdistan Region – Iraq (2020)
13. Nimmy, K., Sethumadhavan, M.: Novel mutual authentication protocol for cloud computing using secret sharing and steganography. J. Inf. Secur. Res. **5** (2014)
14. Astuti, N.R.D.P., Aribowo, E., Saputra, E.: Data security improvements on cloud computing using cryptography and steganography. IOP Conf. Ser. Mater. Sci. Eng. **821**(1), 012041 (2020)
15. Ahmed, O.M., Abduallah, W.M.: A review on recent steganography techniques in cloud computing. Acad. J. Nawroz Univ. (AJNU), **6**(3) (2017)
16. Rahman, S., et al.: A novel approach of image steganography for secure communication based on LSB substitution technique. Comput. Mater. Continua CMC, **64**(1), 31–61 (2020)
17. Adee, R., Mouratidis, H.: A dynamic four-step data security model for data in cloud computing based on cryptography and steganography. Sensors **22**, 1109 (2022). https://doi.org/10.3390/s22031109
18. Pant, V.K., Prakash, J., Asthana, A.: Three step data security model for cloud computing based on RSA and steganography techniques (2015)
19. MathWorks PSNR Documentation, https://www.mathworks.com/help/vision/ref/psnr.html. Accessed 13 June 2022

Enhanced Horse Optimization Algorithm Based Intelligent Query Optimization in Crowdsourcing Systems

M. Renukadevi[1]([⊠]), E. A. Mary Anita[2], and D. Mohana Geetha[1]

[1] Department of Electronics and Communication Engineering, Sri Krishna College of Engineering and Technology, Coimbatore, Tamil Nadu, India
renukadevimohanram@gmail.com
[2] Department of CSE, School of Engineering and Technology, CHRIST University, Bengaluru, India

Abstract. Crowdsourcing is a strategy of collecting information and knowledge from an abundant range of individuals over the Internet in order to solve cognitive or intelligence intensive challenges. Query optimization is the process of yielding an optimized query based upon the cost and latency for a given location based query. In this view, this article introduces an Enhanced Horse Optimization Algorithm based Intelligent Query Optimization in Crowdsourcing Systems (EHOA-IQOCSS) model. The presented EHOA-IQOCSS model mainly based on the enhanced version of HOA using chaotic concepts. The proposed model plans to accomplish a better trade-off between latency and cost in the query optimization process along with answer quality. The EHOA-IQOCSS is used to compute the Location-Based Services (LBS) namely K-Nearest Neighbor (KNN) and range queries, where the Space and Point of Interest (POI) can be obtained by the conviction level computation. The comparative study stated the betterment of the EHOA-IQOCSS model over recent methods.

Keywords: Query optimization · Crowdsourcing · EHOA-IQOCSS · Location-based services

1 Introduction

Crowdsourcing refers to a pattern of human-powered problem-solving, has gained popularity in the time of Internet of Things [1]. Abilities upon which crowdsourcing relies, namely textual document gathering and data source connection, were innate in framework of the World Wide Web (WWW). In the early stage, linguistic analysis can be utilized for answering open-domain questions in a conventional framework. Afterward, depending on questions, inputs having its queries were structured. The fundamental target of crowdsourcing system is to offer the right answer. Thus, search engine assessments need extra attempts and difficult linguistics analysis. Data streaming together with real-time processors can be utilized for separating analytic challenges. A very famous process on the internet was searching for the keyword. Depending on the interface, the

I. Woungang et al. (Eds.): ANTIC 2022, CCIS 1797, pp. 234–249, 2023.
https://doi.org/10.1007/978-3-031-28180-8_16

search engine renders outcomes in the form of links. Figure 1 showcases the overview of Crowdsourcing System.

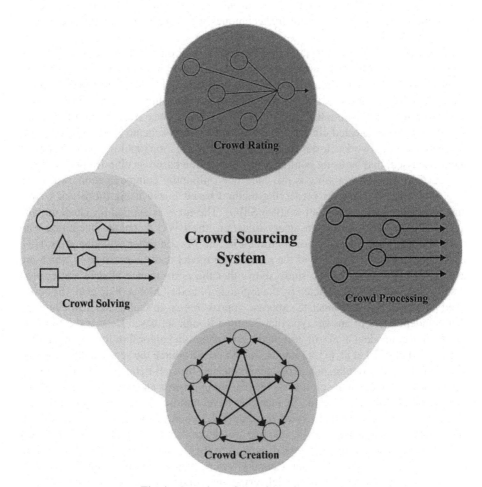

Fig. 1. Overview of crowdsourcing system

2 Related Work

In recent times, crowdsourcing patterns were grabbed more interest in real-life applications because of its effectiveness. The end-user submits or asks queries and gains the appropriate answer from the crowd and the optimal crowdsourcing were listed as Quora, Yahoo!, and Stack overflow. Crowdsourcing was a group collection of opinions, information, and work of people that were connected through the Internet. WWW was to present a collection of textual files and the connection of data resources. The requester and workers plays an vital role in crowdsourcing systems. Workers simply resolve a task by making use of crowdsourcing methods. Whenever adding people to crowdsourcing platform, several difficulties arise due to latency, human worker predictability, cost, and quality [2, 10]. The declarative crowdsourcing was enabled for solving challenging problems. Recently, evolutionary techniques were executed well for engineering perplexities.

Renukadevi et al. [3] introduce an Efficient Fuzzy Logic Cluster Formation Protocol (EFLCFP) for cluster formation and employ cluster cranium (CC) for reporting and aggregation of the data. The author, extended the feature of cluster cranium by improving the tendency to accomplish data aggregation and reporting by the requester without scarifying their confidentiality. Vinodha et al. [13] introduce a novel multifunctional multiparameter concealed cluster-based data aggregation scheme (NMFMP-CDA) for wireless sensor networks clusters in a hierarchy with a 'n' hop topology. Also the author have discussed, that by using homomorphic encryption based on elliptic curves, source and destination confidentiality is provided with minimum communication cost. Priya et al. [4] suggest a privacy preserving method based Fuzzy using the Black widow and Spider Monkey Optimization (BW–SMO). The fuzzy is applied for clustering the query solution. To improve the query selection, the BWO technique integrated with the SMO approach and they are controlled by the FL controller. Vinodha et al. [14], the author presented a review of the networking model and the procedures which are used to provide privacy. This study shows that the performance of data aggregation systems is significantly impacted by the topology of nodes. Moayedikia et al. [5] developed an unsupervised manner to expertise approximation in microtask crowdsourcing that is independent of answer type that is called Rough set based Expertise estimation (ROUX). Renukadevi et al. [6] designed a crowdsourcing algorithm for optimizing the latency and cost. Li et al. [7], examines how to crowd source the sense making method via a pipeline of modularized steps interconnected by well-defined input and output. The crowd intermediate result reveals the reasoning process and provides evidence that justifies the conclusion. Ye et al. [8], identifies novel multi-center-based task distribution problems in terms of Spatial Crowdsourcing (SC), whereby multiple allocation center exists. The first step is to use the adaptive weighted Voronoi diagram-based approach and the basic Voronoi diagram-based method to divide the research region according to the distribution center. A Graph Neural Network (GNN) with the attention model is used to learn the embedding of the delivery point worker and allocation centers before we apply a Reinforcement Learning model to complete the job distribution.

This article introduces an Enhanced Horse Optimization Algorithm based Intelligent Query Optimization in Crowdsourcing Systems (EHOA-IQOCSS) model. The proposed model plans to accomplish a better trade-off between latency and cost in the query optimization process along with security. Besides, homomorphic encryption technique is utilized for data encryption process. In addition, the EHOA-IQOCSS model optimizes the select and join queries having minimal latency and cost.

3   The Proposed Model

In this study, a new EHOA-IQOCSS technique was proposed for query optimization process. The presented EHOA-IQOCSS model mainly based on the enhanced version of HOA using chaotic concepts.

3.1 System Architecture

In a crowdsourcing system, the end user creates the group based on the Location-based Service (LBS) and invites their friends, relatives, and neighbours to join this group. The terms and conditions will determine how the group members participate. The location-based services (such KNN-query and Range query) are assessed depending on the end user's location. In order to deliver services, the LBS makes use of information from its specific geographic position. The group's formation makes it possible for the customer to get in touch with group members to evaluate queries. Each group member estimates the queries from the given database. Along with the query, the space data and point of interest will be returned. Since the group members do not want to share their information with a specific person in the group, they can feel free to exit the gang anytime. Either a sequential or parallel query assessment technique is utilized to balance the cost of transmission and processing time.

3.1.1 Parallel Processing

The KNN and Range query is used for handling with parallel processing. The user send the Location and the query to group members. Each group member estimates their individual native database queries, and return the space information and POI to the requester (i.e. the user who requested). Once after receiving the result from the group member the user performs the analysis and evaluate the conviction level of the query answers. Scalability is the primary benefit of the parallel method, and the query processing environment has several group members. Group members' computations can be done in parallel. Otherwise, parallel processing (shown in Fig. 2) will have an impact on numerous group members who utilize the same data space and POI, increasing the communication cost [9, 11].

Fig. 2. Parallel processing

3.1.2 Sequential Processing

In order to minimize the communication overhead sequential processing is used. In this Sequential processing (shown in Fig. 3) the query will be distributed to the selected member of the group. The member from the group is chosen along with the MID (member ID) and the same is posted to every member in the group of those who is having visited flag [9, 11].

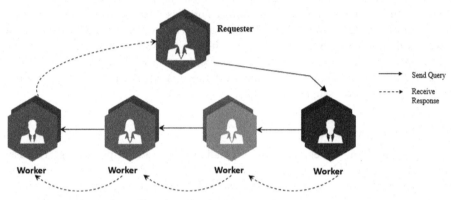

Fig. 3. Sequential processing

The visited flags are fixed as false initially. The member who is received the query will evaluate the query from the local database and add the POI and space information from the local database. Finally, the query requestor processes the queries for the chosen members and collects the results until they obtain accurate answers. Thus, the computational overhead is decreased by this query processing. However, the calculating time may grow, which would raise the computational cost.

3.1.3 Space Knowledge Index

A space-tree, sometimes known as a quad-tree, is a hierarchical data structure that is recursively divided into four quadrants, with the root node representing the whole space. When a quadrant is classified as known or unknown or when the space-maximum tree's depth is reached, the quadrant's decomposition comes to an end [9]. If the area represented by the node is part of the known region, the related tree node for the quadrant is tagged with a 1 and is considered to be known. If a quadrant does not cross the known region, it is considered unknown and its corresponding tree node is marked with a zero. If a region only partially covers a certain area, we label the node with a zero and divide the remaining space into four quadrants.

3.1.4 Conviction Level Computation

In this study, the distance and area-dependent trust stages [10] are used to measure the query-answer standard. It's important to note that the POI range query only looks at the trust stage area when determining the optimal response quality. In the case of a KNN question, the query answer that includes every POI and their trust level is also reviewed in comparison to the query answer that uses the average k trust stage. The jth-neighbor POI is represented by the response group Q in the form of q_j of p.

$$Nj = A(L_j)/A(C_j)$$

4 Conviction Level Computation – KNN Query Using EHOA-IQOCSS

Next, query processing with optimal or conviction level KNN query selection is carried out by Enhanced Horse Optimization Algorithm based Intelligent Query Optimization in Crowdsourcing Systems. This means a new bio-inspired method presented with its main resource of inspiring the features of horse herd [12]. The features assumed in original article are: (a) the group of horses in herd so every herds can be led by dominant stallions, (b) replacing dominant stallion of herd by superior rival stallions, (c) various gaits, (d) considering of running as the optimal defines system, (e) excellent long run memory of horses, (f) hierarchical association of the herds, that adjusts accessibility to several sources namely food, shelter, and water and (g) the rearrangement of horses has lesser fitness values (FV).

The HOA involves instruction flow and configuration parameters. Some configurable variables were particular to HOA, namely: the horse distribution rate (*HDR*), the dominant stallion percent (*DSP*), the single stallion percent (*SSP*), and the horse memory pool (*HMP*). At the same time, some configurable parameters of HOA were typical to other bioinspired approaches, namely: the reorganization frequency (M), the size of population (N), and the amount of iterations (I) and dimensions (D). Figure 4 depicts the steps involved in HOA. The major stages of the HOA are discussed below:

Step 1. N horses $\{h_1, \ldots, h_N\}$ were prepared at a random fashion in the D dimension searching spaces.

Step 2. The process calculates FV by means of objective functions and updates values of h_{gbest}.

Step 3. The value of iteration is set to 0.

When iteration is lesser than I, then there exist two conditions: when the iteration modulo M equivalents 0, then the process continues to Step 4, or else the process continues to Step 8. When the iteration is larger than or equivalent to I, then the process continues to Step 18.

Step 4. The $N \times DSP$ optimal horse based on the FV is the leader of the herd from set T of recently initialized herds so $|T| = |N \times DSP|$.

Step 5. The $N \times SSP$ best horse based on FV is single stallion and form set S.

Step 6. The residual horse is randomly assigned to herds from T.

Step 7. The worst $N \times HDR$ horse in terms of fitness values are randomly distributed in the D dimension searching space, the fitness value is re-calculated, and accordingly the value of h_{gbest} is upgraded.

Step 8. For every herd $\{h_1, \ldots, h_K\}$ of size K from T, rank is from $\{\frac{1}{K}, \frac{2}{K}, \ldots, 1\}$ so that the maximum rank value is allocated to the horse with best FV that is the maximal value in the event of maximization problem or minimal value in the event of minimization problem. When 2 horses with indices i, j from $\{1, \ldots, K\}$ have a similar FV, so that $i < j$, horse with j index contains a highest rank when compared to the horse with i index. The center of herd is calculated as a weighted arithmetical mean of the position of the horse so the weight is the rank.

The instruction from Steps 9 to 14 is implemented for every horses.

Step 9. The gait was upgraded to an arbitrary number from [1, 2].

When the horse was single then the velocity was upgraded in Step 10, or else velocity was upgraded in Step 11.

Step 10. The equation to update location for a single stallion was:

$$v^{iteration+1} = vteration + r \times h_{gait} \times (nherd_{center} - x^{iteration}), \tag{1}$$

so that $v^{iteration+1}$, $v^{iteration}$ are the value of velocity in $iteration + 1$ and iteration r refers to an arbitrary number within [0, 1], h_{gait} indicates the gait of horse h, $nherd_{center}$ represent the center of adjacent herd, that is Euclidean distance among the center of herd and the location of stallion is minimal, and $x^{iteration}$ represent the location of the stallion in the existing iteration.

Step 11. When the horses belong to a herd, the velocity is upgraded as follows:

$$v^{iteration+1} = vteration + h_{rank} \times h_{gait} \times (herd_{center} - x^{iteration}), \tag{2}$$

so that h_{rank} and $herd_{center}$ represent the rank of h and the centre of herd, respectively.

Step 12. The equation to update location is given as follows:

$$x^{iteration+1} = x^{iteration} + v^{iteration+1}, \tag{3}$$

In Eq. (3), $x^{iteration+1}$ and $x^{iteration}$ represents the position in iteration +1 and iteration, respectively. The *HMP*-dimension memory pool can be upgraded by:

$$M^{iteration+1} = \begin{bmatrix} m_{1,1}^{iter.aii.on+1} & \cdots & m_{1,D}^{iier.aii.on+1} \\ \cdots & \cdots & \cdots \\ m_{HMP,1}^{iteraiion+1} & \cdots & m_{HMP,D}^{iteraiion+1} \end{bmatrix} \tag{4}$$

For any $k \in \{1, \ldots, HMP\}$ the equation for the memory updating is represented as follows:

$$m_k^{iteraiion+1} = x^{iteraiion+1} \times N(0, 1), \tag{5}$$

So that $N(0, 1)$ refers to the standard distributed number with standard deviation1 and mean 0. Step 14. The novel FV was calculated as best value among FV of location $x^{iteration+1}$ and the fitness value of $M^{iteration+1}$ element. When $x^{iteraion+1}$ has a higher fitness value than h_{gbest}, then h_{gbest} is upgraded to $x^{iteration+1}$. When $M^{iteraiion+1}$ element contain a higher FV than $x^{iteraiion+1}$, then $x^{iteraiion+1}$ is upgraded to value of that elements.

Step 15. For every herd $\{h_1, \ldots, h_K\}$ of size K from T, rank is from $\{\frac{1}{K}, \frac{2}{K}, \ldots, 1\}$ so that the maximum rank value is allocated to the horse with best FV that is the maximal value in the event of maximization problem or minimal value in the event of minimization

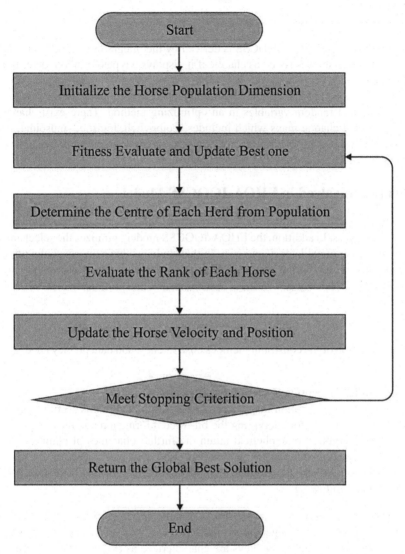

Fig. 4. Steps involved in EHOA-IQOCSS

problem. When 2 horses with indices i, j from $\{1, \ldots, K\}$ have a similar FV, so that $i < j$, horse with j index contains a highest rank when compared to the horse with i index. The center of herd is calculated as a weighted arithmetical mean of the position of the horse so the weight is the rank.

Step 16. For every stallion from S, the adjacent herd was defined. Once the stallion contains a higher FV than stallion of herd, then both stallions get switched: (1) single stallion becomes leader of herd, (2) herd becomes a single stallion, as well as (3) position of both stallions get swapped.

Step 17. The value of iteration was increased by 1.

Step 18. The process returns value of global best solution h_{gbest}.

In this study, the EHOA-IQOCSS is derived by the integration of HOA and chaotic theory. A mechanism was stated as chaotic if it displays a type of random deterministic conduct in bounded yet non-converging search spaces. Most of the stochastic optimizing issues were trapped in local optima. Essentially, chaotic optimizing means sine chaotic series rather than random variables in an optimizing method. There exist changes in one-dimensional chaotic maps which includes, Leibovitch, logistic, sinusoidal, circle, iterative, chebyshev, sin, intermittency, sawtooth, singer, tent, and piecewise. But this article takes logistic map for HOA randomization.

5   Process Involved in EHOA-IQOCSS Model

In the EHOA-IQOCSS technique, homomorphic encryption technique is utilized for data encryption process. In addition, the EHOA-IQOCSS model optimizes the select and join queries having minimal latency and cost. In this study, we have improved the objective function of latency and cost in query optimization. The fitness value of crowdsourcing can be assessed by the latency ($CRWD_{latency}$), data privacy, and minimized cost ($CRWD_{cost}$) as follows.

$$Fitness = CRWD_{latency} + CRWD_{cost} + CRWD_{data\_privocy}. \tag{6}$$

The derivation of the constraint includes cost, latency, and data privacy are discussed below.

Homomorphic Encryption System for Data Privacy
The homomorphic encryption for data privacy is formulated in this section. This technique is well-organized for encrypting the bit–wise information and the computational outcomes of decryption on ciphertext attain the further outcomes of plaintext [6]. By using the presented model, the plaintext is 0 or else 1, they easily discover the plaintext and discard them. Mostly, the ultimate result is distorted by the malicious user and it is explained in the following:

Key generation: Assume $M = u \cdot v$. Then, u and v are large primes independent of one another. Thereby, the Legendre symbols y/u = y/v = −1 select a non-residue y. Therefore, the private and public keys are characterized as (M, y) and (u, v) also there y/M = +1 is the Jacobi symbol [15].

Encryption: The encrypted messages are regarded as d and non-zero random numbers namely $R \in Z_M^*$ is chosen. Therefore, the cipher-text a is characterized as follows:

$$a = R^2 \cdot y^d \bmod M \tag{7}$$

Decryption: The cipher text is a and if the a is quadratic residue mod M, then it was checked by prime factor (u, v). First, compute $a_v = a \bmod v$ and $a_u = a \bmod u$, o denote the quadratic residue mod M hold $a_u^{(u-1)/2} \equiv 1 \bmod u$ and $a_v^{(v-1)/2} \equiv 1 \bmod v$.

Monetary Cost
Now, the query plan Q with monetary cost can be formulated by $C(Q)$. It refers to the

reward paid for implementing crowdsourcing operator $(C(P_Q = \sum_{0 \in 0} C(o))$. From this, the cost for the execution of operator $o \in O$ is (0). Based on the crowdsourcing task calculating condition C^s with the unit, the cost is ψ_S. The high the unit cost C^s is $|C^s|$. When there were additional join conditions C^i in the operator, large unit cost ψ_i provides C Join operator

$$P_q^* = \arg_{P_q} \min C(P_q). \tag{8}$$

In Eq. (8), the query plan P_q^* can be defined as the query q that diminishes the cost.

Latency
The query assessment speed can be measured by latency. The optimization and latency prediction is nontrivial. The worker pool simultaneously completes the crowd task and alter the size of the pool. The public crowd framework comprises a limited amount of crowd workers. In real-time crowdsourcing, there exist many latency uncertainties.

$$P_q^* = \arg_{P_q} \min L(P_q). \tag{9}$$

In Eq. (9), the cost budget C with query q. It defines one with the minimum cost where there exist many plans with minimal delay.

6 Results and Discussion

In this experiment, two data sets were employed as simulation assessment and realworld crowdsourcing platform. (i) The presented study in domain sizes, changing number of condition were needed for evaluating its performances. Therefore, the bulk of attribute with synthetic dataset Auto1 can be produced. (ii) The 2014 car models having real dataset Auto2 were utilized. Table 1 demonstrates brief description on datasets.

Table 1. Dataset details

Relation	Dataset - Auto 1		Dataset - Auto 2	
	No. of attributes	No. of tuples	No. of attributes	No. of tuples
Vehicle	9	300	4	111
Image	11	3508	6	111
Review	10	2045	2	111

Table 2 and Fig. 6 provide a comparative cost examination of the EHOA-IQOCSS model with recent models on selection query evaluation [14]. The experimental values highlighted that the EHOA-IQOCSS model has accomplished optimized cost under all selection conditions. For instance, with 2 selection conditions, the EHOA-IQOCSS model has offered lower cost of 62.77 whereas the existing models such as parallel, sequential, CrowdOp, and MF-TSA models have obtained higher costs of 81.74, 80.76,

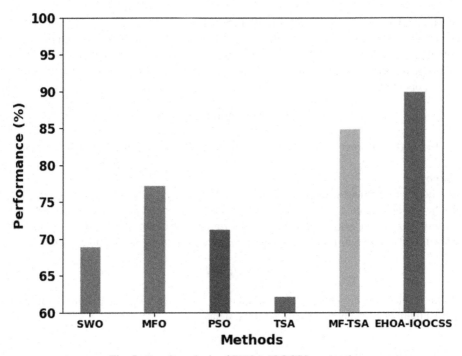

Fig. 5. Result analysis of EHOA-IQOCSS approach

77.36, and 75.90 respectively. Along with that, with 3 selection conditions, the EHOA-IQOCSS method has offered lower cost of 65.68 whereas the existing models such as parallel, sequential, CrowdOp, and MF-TSA models have acquired higher costs of 100.22, 86.60, 79.79, and 77.84 correspondingly.

Table 2. Cost analysis of EHOA-IQOCSS approach under selection conditions

Cost					
No. of selection conditions	Parallel	Sequential	CrowdOp	MF-TSA	EHOA-IQOCSS
2	81.74	80.76	77.36	75.90	62.77
3	100.22	86.60	79.79	77.84	65.68
4	119.68	96.81	91.95	74.44	64.71
5	140.11	99.73	87.57	72.49	56.93
6	158.59	109.46	95.84	72.49	62.77

In addition, with 4 selection conditions, the EHOA-IQOCSS model has granted lower cost of 64.71 whereas the existing models such as parallel, sequential, CrowdOp,

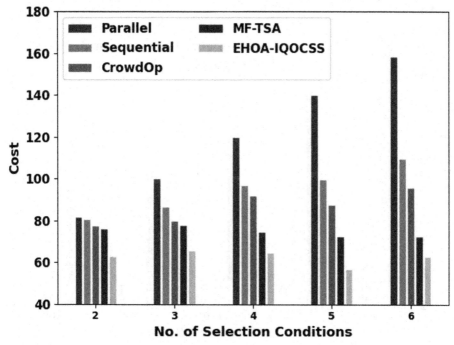

Fig. 6. Cost analysis

and MF-TSA models have obtained higher costs of 119.68, 96.81, 91.95, and 74.44 correspondingly. Then, with 5 selection conditions, the EHOA-IQOCSS model has offered lower cost of 56.93 whereas the existing models such as parallel, sequential, CrowdOp, and MF-TSA models have obtained higher costs of 140.11, 99.73, 87.57, and 72.49 correspondingly.

Table 3 and Fig. 7 offer a comparative latency analysis of the EHOA-IQOCSS model with recent models on Latency. The experimental values highlighted that the EHOA-IQOCSS method has accomplished best cost under all selection conditions. For example, with 80 User Required Budget, the EHOA-IQOCSS model has rendered lower cost of 2.36 whereas the existing models such as parallel, sequential, CrowdOp, and MF-TSA models have obtained higher cost of 9.20, 7.35, 4.96, and 2.84 respectively. Also, with 160 User Required Budget, the EHOA-IQOCSS model has offered lower cost of 1.11 whereas the existing models such as parallel, sequential, CrowdOp, and MF-TSA models have obtained higher costs of 4.72, 3.39, 1.83, and 1.70 respectively.

Table 4 and Fig. 8 provide a comparative Join query evaluation scrutiny of the EHOA-IQOCSS model with recent models on Latency. The experimental values highlighted that the EHOA-IQOCSS model has established best cost under all selection conditions. For example, with 430 User Required Budget selection conditions, the EHOA-IQOCSS model has offered lower cost of 0.29 whereas the existing models such as parallel, sequential, CrowdOp, and MF-TSA models have obtained higher costs of 4.70, 5.04, 0.80, and 0.43 respectively. Besides, with 530 User Required Budget selection conditions, the EHOA-IQOCSS model has offered lower cost of 0.36 whereas the existing models such

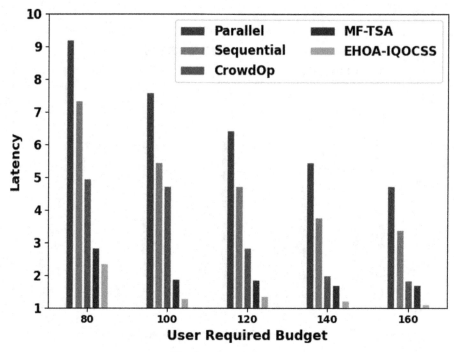

Fig. 7. Latency analysis

Table 3. Latency analysis of EHOA-IQOCSS approach under user required budgets

Latency

User required budget	Parallel	Sequential	CrowdOp	MF-TSA	EHOA-IQOCSS
80	9.20	7.35	4.96	2.84	2.36
100	7.58	5.44	4.72	1.88	1.30
120	6.44	4.72	2.84	1.85	1.35
140	5.44	3.76	1.99	1.70	1.22
160	4.72	3.39	1.83	1.70	1.11

as parallel, sequential, CrowdOp, and MF-TSA models have obtained higher costs of 2.46, 3.07, 0.89, and 0.50 correspondingly.

Then, with 730 User Required Budget conditions, the EHOA-IQOCSS model has offered lower cost of 1.70 whereas the existing models such as parallel, sequential, CrowdOp, and MF-TSA models have obtained higher costs of 2.17, 1.98, 2.04, and 1.97 correspondingly. From the detailed performance evaluation, the experimental outcomes inferred that the EHOA-IQOCSS model has accomplished enhanced performance over other models.

Table 4. Join query evaluation analysis of EHOA-IQOCSS approach under user required budgets

Latency

User required budget	Parallel	Sequential	CrowdOP	MF-TSA	EHOA-IQOCSS
430	4.70	5.04	0.80	0.43	0.29
480	3.68	4.05	0.75	0.60	0.46
530	2.46	3.07	0.89	0.50	0.36
580	2.72	3.05	1.02	0.24	0.16
630	2.86	3.02	3.94	0.72	0.56
680	2.66	3.02	3.05	2.97	2.59
730	2.17	1.98	2.04	1.97	1.70

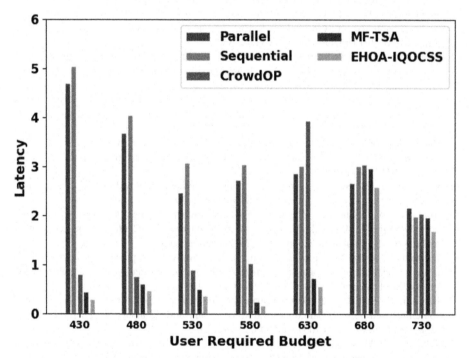

Fig. 8. Join query evaluation analysis of EHOA-IQOCSS

7 Conclusion

In this study, a new EHOA-IQOCSS algorithm has been projected for query optimization process. The presented EHOA-IQOCSS model mainly based on the enhanced version of HOA using chaotic concepts. The proposed model plans to accomplish a better tradeoff between latency and cost in the query optimization process along with security. Besides, homomorphic encryption technique is utilized for data encryption process. In addition, the EHOA-IQOCSS model optimizes the selection and joined queries with minimal latency and cost. The experimental validation of the EHOA-IQOCSS model is carried out under a series of simulations. The comparative analysis stated the betterment of EHOA-IQOCSS method than recent methods. In future, the hybridization of two metaheuristic algorithms can be developed to improve the performance of the EHOA-IQOCSS model.

References

1. Sharma, V., You, I., Jayakody, D.N.K., Atiquzzaman, M.: Cooperative trust relaying and privacy preservation via edge-crowdsourcing in social Internet of Things. Futur. Gener. Comput. Syst. **92**, 758–776 (2019)
2. Tsou, Y.T., Lin, B.C.: PPDCA: privacy-preserving crowdsourcing data collection and analysis with randomized response. IEEE Access **6**, 76970–76983 (2018)
3. Renukadevi, M., Mary Anita, E.A., Mohana Geetha, D.: An efficient fuzzy logic cluster formation protocol for data aggregation and data reporting in cluster-based mobile crowdsourcing. In: Shakya, S., Du, K.L., Haoxiang, W. (eds.) Proceedings of Second International Conference on Sustainable Expert Systems. LNNS, vol. 351, pp. 427–446. Springer, Singapore (2022). https://doi.org/10.1007/978-981-16-7657-4_35
4. Priya, J.S., Bhaskar, N., Prabakeran, S.: Fuzzy with black widow and spider monkey optimization for privacy-preserving-based crowdsourcing system. Soft Comput. **25**(7), 5831–5846 (2021). https://doi.org/10.1007/s00500-021-05657-w
5. Moayedikia, A., Yeoh, W., Ong, K.L., Boo, Y.L.: Improving accuracy and lowering cost in crowdsourcing through an unsupervised expertise estimation approach. Decis. Support Syst. **122**, 113065 (2019)
6. Renukadevi, M., Anita, E.M., Mohana Geetha, D.: An efficient privacy-preserving model based on OMFTSA for query optimization in crowdsourcing. Concurr. Comput. Pract. Exp. **33**(24), e6447 (2021)
7. Li, T., Luther, K., North, C.: Crowdia: solving mysteries with crowdsourced sensemaking. Proc. ACM Hum.-Comput. Interact. 2(CSCW), 1–29 (2018)
8. Ye, G., Zhao, Y., Chen, X., Zheng, K.: Task allocation with geographic partition in spatial crowdsourcing. In: Proceedings of the 30th ACM International Conference on Information and Knowledge Management, pp. 2404–2413, October 2021
9. Hashem, T., Hasan, R., Salim, F., Mahin, M.T.: Crowd-enabled processing of trustworthy, privacy-enhanced and personalised location based services with quality guarantee. Proc. ACM Interact. Mob. Wearable Ubiquitous Technol. 2(4), 167 (2018)
10. Bhaskar, N., Kumar, P.M.: Optimal processing of nearest-neighbor user queries in crowdsourcing based on the whale optimization algorithm. Soft. Comput. **24**(17), 13037–13050 (2020). https://doi.org/10.1007/s00500-020-04722-0
11. Tabassum, M.M., Hashem, T., Kabir, S.: A crowd enabled approach for processing nearest neighbor and range queries in incomplete databases with accuracy guarantee'. Perv. Mob. Comput. **39**, 249–266 (2017)
12. Moldovan, D.: Horse optimization algorithm: a novel bio-inspired algorithm for solving global optimization problems. In: Silhavy, R. (ed.) CSOC 2020. AISC, vol. 1225, pp. 195–209. Springer, Cham (2020). https://doi.org/10.1007/978-3-030-51971-1_16
13. Vinodha, D., Mary Anita, E.A., Mohana Geetha, D.: A novel multi functional multi parameter concealed cluster based data aggregation scheme for wireless sensor networks (NMFMP-CDA). Wirel. Netw. **27**(2), 1111–1128 (2020). https://doi.org/10.1007/s11276-020-02499-6
14. Vinodha, D., Mary Anita, E.A.: Secure data aggregation techniques for wireless sensor networks: a review. Arch. Comput. Methods Eng. **26**(4), 1007–1027 (2018). https://doi.org/10.1007/s11831-018-9267-2

15. Gong, Y., Guo, Y., Fang, Y.: A privacy-preserving task recommendation framework for mobile crowdsourcing. In: Proceedings of the 2014 IEEE Global Communications Conference, pp. 588–593 (2014)

Design of Energy Efficient IoT-Based Smart Street Light System

Pranav Chaudhary, Vishal Singh, Aayush Karjee, Gaurav Singal,
and Abhinav Tomar$^{(\boxtimes)}$

Netaji Subhas University of Technology, Delhi, India
abhinav.tomar@nsut.ac.in

Abstract. In today's world, as each aspect of our lives is becoming more and more enhanced, IoT plays a major role in all development areas. However, the same has not been implemented on a major scale for interior and exterior lighting systems. A plethora of research is being carried out and people are looking for a clean and better solution for the next generations. The street light system of India is still not automated and consumes huge amounts of energy. This paper introduces a prototype system which revolutionises the street lighting system in India. The prototype system uses two sensors (LDR and IR), LED lights and a microcontroller to have varying brightness levels (for different levels of natural brightness and presence of people on the streets). The microcontroller is also used to send sensor data to a web server over the internet, which explores its potential to be as a monitoring system. The system successfully reduces energy consumption massively with the implementation of LEDs and varying brightness. At the same time, it can also be used as a monitoring system which could help with various types of analysis. Further, we investigate a model which supports zero carbon footprint and complete sustainability.

Keywords: Internet of Things · Intelligent sensors · Smart cities · Lighting

1 Introduction

It is well known that technology is advancing day by day and thus it is a prior matter to develop an exclusive smart streetlight system with an aim to reduce energy consumption and increase road safety. This paper focuses on some of the most demanding problem domains in today's world: Economy, Energy & Environment. We have tried to create a solution that contributes to all these domains simultaneously. With depleting non-renewable resources, the focus has shifted to create solutions that employ renewable energy sources (such as solar panels). At the same time, we also need to employ technology that is cheap, reliable, and energy-efficient (such as LED lights). With these systems requiring heavy energy usage, the economy is heavily affected when such systems are evolved with the help of new technologies and automation. This is exactly where IoT plays a major role. IoT has been a boon to many smart applications which is witnessed by existing research [5, 6]. Thanks to the rapid growth in new domains like automation and

© The Author(s), under exclusive license to Springer Nature Switzerland AG 2023
I. Woungang et al. (Eds.): ANTIC 2022, CCIS 1797, pp. 250–262, 2023.
https://doi.org/10.1007/978-3-031-28180-8_17

embedded systems, Internet of Things has been an emerging technology and has helped a lot [7, 8]. The Internet of Things is a network of multiple connected smart devices which can communicate with each other and independently configure themselves using the network [9–11]. With the help of low-power consuming microcontrollers and sensors, we can automate systems while reducing our energy consumption.

We currently focus on reducing the immense amount of energy being wasted by the streetlights of India. As of 2016, global trends show that 18% to 38% of the total energy being generated in a country goes for powering streetlights, and India is no exception to this. This is a field which needs our immediate attention. A vast number of the street light systems in India are set up using CFL, high pressure sodium lamps or metal halide bulbs, which are inefficient and not the best solution that we could implement. Streetlights stay on well beyond sunrise and stay off well into the evening. This happens because the toggling of streetlights is currently manual, so human delay in toggling the street lights not only leads to a waste in energy, but also an untimely, unsafe and unreliable system for the general public.

By scrutinizing the past researches, it is found that the existing traditional street light system is facing various issues like information gap about the real time status of the street lights in an area, no proper system for monitoring and operating lights or a toggling schedule, no process to optimize the efficiency of street light system as per requirement and no management of independent unit of street light in terms of toggling, fault detection & replacement [1–5]. In view of these facts, the prime motivation behind the proposed work is twofold: The first is to reduce power consumption and energy expenditure. Majority of the resources that are used to generate electricity over the world are non-renewable. Streetlights are a major contributor in a nation's total energy expenditure, and our Smart Street Light System would make a significant impact in terms of energy efficiency. The second motivation, which is just as important as the first, is safety. Traditional street light systems, which are operated manually, may accidentally be switched off due to negligence or may not be switched on at the appropriate times. This would make commuting through the affected areas very dangerous. Smart Street Lights would be automatically operated, negating the "human error" factor, and making the streets safer.

Our IoT-based Smart Street Light System aims not only to significantly reduce the amount of energy consumed by the streetlights of India, but also aims to work in a sustainable manner. We have made the following contributions to the system:

- Researched about the effects of this automated system on energy consumption and have found that the energy consumption goes down by an average of 40% depending on the environment it's installed in and the components being used. The automation of toggling contributes little to this. However, the variation of the intensity of light depending on the environment helps us save a lot of energy. Again, this depends on the environment the system is being setup for.
- We have currently used a prototype to analyse the parameters involved in light sensitivity and to send sensor data to a web server. We have proposed two setups. One of which is powered through battery cells and the other powered through solar panels. The motive of proposing this is to show that even though at a minuscule level,

achieving zero carbon footprint is easily done. This can possibly be replicated at an industrial level with industrial equipment.

- We have built a simple web server for receiving the sensor data from the microcontroller. We plot these values on real time charts on a fixed frequency. This allows us to explore one of the many communication methods that could be used to communicate a plethora of information that can be collected using the street light system. Street lights are everywhere and are a natural candidate for the collection of environment data. For the purpose of our prototype, we have used a Wi-Fi - based communication method, which is simple and efficient for short distance communications.

- We have researched the integration of solar panels in order to reduce our carbon footprint to zero and implemented it on a separate system which uses the Arduino UNO board. This approach is also crucially beneficial in a country like India where power outages are common. By enabling the usage of solar panels, we can increase the reliability of the system as it would no longer be connected only to a central power grid. This is similar to how datacentres use two power sources, one being an Uninterruptible Power Supply (UPS). The street light system can hence be provided with a power supply which is not only cost-efficient and environment friendly, but also highly reliable.

This paper is organized as follows: Sect. 2 presents Literature Summary. Our approach is explained in Sect. 3. Thereafter, results are presented in Sect. 4 followed by observations. Finally, work is concluded in Sect. 5.

2 Literature Summary

This section has gone through relevant research papers to understand the problem better [1–8]. Here is a short summary of what we have gathered from the papers.

Street lighting systems are one of the few systems that are not yet automated in almost every country in the world. In India, it still is a manual system where lights are toggled at a fixed time. This is highly problematic as power consumption is very high in a country that still depends heavily on non-renewable resources of energy. The authorities that handle the street lighting systems in India are usually unreliable and inefficient as well, with lights staying ON even after dawn or staying OFF even after dusk which results in power wastage and traffic accidents, respectively. The current technology used is also not efficient. LEDs have taken over interior lighting but have not yet been implemented on the streets. The current system has an increased maintenance cost and power consumption.

The solution proposed is hence to automate the street lighting system and also make it efficient. The automation is based on two criteria, natural light detection and object detection. Various architectures have been explored where the streetlights are dependent on or independent of each other. Various sensors like LDR (Light Dependent Resistor), PIR and IR are used for the same [2]. Other components can include dimmers, communication modules, etc. The automated street lighting system uses LEDs which are more reliable and use less power for the same output. This decreases power consumption and maintenance cost. The system works in a simple way, the lights switch ON and

OFF based on the natural light detected and also have varying intensity based on object and light detection. This entire module is handled with the help of microcontrollers like ATmega [1] and AVR. In case the streetlights are communicating with each other, then various communication methods can be used like LoRaWAN, ZigBee, NB-IoT, etc. for wireless connection, or one could connect the multiple street lights using wired connection [2, 5].

Switching to LEDs, an automated system and varying intensity of light, all help towards an efficient, power-saving and reliable system. Various data from the object detection sensors can be used for the analysis of traffic. A centralised system can be used for collecting and analysing streetlight activity. This system evidently saves around 15–60% of energy and reduces the carbon footprint significantly [1, 3]. Maintenance costs are also low as the system is composed of highly reliable components. The system is also highly modifiable where light sensitivity thresholds and intensity can be modified depending on the environment for different settings (cities, societies, college campuses, etc.).

The system can be improved further by the implementation of solar panels. Solar energy can be used to charge batteries during the daytime and use the charged batteries to power the streetlights during night. This is a zero-carbon footprint approach to the problem and is highly sustainable. The streetlights can be further modified to be used for predicting the weather and monitoring the pollution content in the environment [4].

3 Proposed System

Figures 1, 2 and 3 highlight the components used in the designed smart street light system. During the proposed approach, we have explored two separate circuit setups. Both these circuit setups are prototype systems and do not scale anywhere near to what would be used on an industrial level which will be discussed in following sections.

3.1 ESP32 DevKitC Based Circuit

As the name suggests, in this circuit we have used the ESP32 DevKitC V4 development board. The board is manufactured by Espressif Systems. We used the development board as it provides support for hassle-free Wi-Fi connection and also a flash chip for storing our web server files using the SPIFFS. However, the board does not support solar powered inputs particularly well. As it is a low-energy consuming board, stepping down the voltage (coming from solar panels directly or from batteries) takes a significant part of the energy. This is highly inefficient and hence powering the development board via USB is the best way.

3.2 Arduino UNO Based Circuit

In this circuit, we used the Arduino UNO R3 microcontroller board. We chose the Arduino UNO R3 in this circuit as it can be powered easily using a Solar Panel (to charge the batteries) and batteries (to power the Arduino). However, we observed that the Wi-Fi module (ESP8266) does not work well with the Arduino board and is not reliable.

Sensors
In both circuit setups, we have used the same sensors, LDR and IR. The LDR sensor is used to measure the intensity of atmospheric brightness. The LDR sensor is connected to one of the GPIO pins of the ESP32 board, which converts it into digital values in the range of 0–4095 corresponding to 0–3.3V. Using these values, we have set thresholds for the automatic toggling of the LED light. The IR sensor is activated only when the light is switched ON and the atmospheric brightness is below a set threshold (dark times of the day/night). Initially, the LED has a minimal brightness or intensity. As soon as the IR sensor detects an object, the intensity of the LED light is increased and then decreased again once the object has moved out of the detection zone.

LED PWM Input
The LED is connected to a GPIO pin of the ESP32 board. In order to implement the varying brightness system, we use PWM input for the LED. In the ESP32 board, we use a PWM channel and set the frequency to 5000 Hz. We use an 8-bit resolution, which lets us set values in the range of 0–255 for the duty cycle. This can be changed to a higher or lower resolution. In order to set up the LED pin, we use two functions in the Arduino IDE:

```
ledcSetup(0,5000,8);
ledcAttachPin(LED,0);
```

In order to write analogue values to the LED, we use the following commands in the Arduino IDE:

```
ledcWrite(0,50); //Base brightness
ledcWrite(0,250);  //Max brightness
```

Communication – Wi-Fi
In the prototype system, we use the in-built Wi-Fi module of the ESP32 development board. This module supports the 2.4 GHz band and hence can offer three different standards, IEEE 802.11 b/g/n. The three standards differ with the data rates that they can offer. We have used Wi-Fi in this prototype system as it helps transfer huge amounts of data at high speeds within a short range. Other communication protocols may be considered for the same.

Using Wi-Fi, we connect to the internet. This helps us send sensor data in real time to our web server. We use the "WiFi.h" library to help us with the same in the Arduino IDE.

Web Server
In the prototype system, we have built a simple asynchronous web server. This is done as an asynchronous web server can handle multiple connections at the same time. It can also communicate with other connections while sending the response to a particular connection in the background. We achieve this with the help of the "ESPAsyncWebServer" library in the Arduino IDE. Apart from this, we have built an HTML file for handling the requests and also the look of our web page. After receiving the readings from the microcontroller, we plot them on our web page using the Highcharts library. The plot created gives us a time stamp and real-time trend of the sensor readings.

SPI Flash File Storage (SPIFFS) System
To store the HTML file on our ESP32 board, we use its flash memory and use the SPIFFS system. We use the "SPIFFS.h" in the Arduino IDE in order to load the files. The sketch data is uploaded to the board beforehand through the IDE.

4 Experimental Setup and Results

This Section explains the circuits used to setup experimental environments followed by results.

ESP32 DevKitC V4
The ESP32 DevKitC V4 is a ESP32 based board developed by Espressif. It's a low entry and developmental board that's part of the ESP32 Series. Most of the I/O pins are broken out to the pin headers on both sides for easy interfacing. Developers can connect these pins to peripherals as needed. Standard headers also make development easy and convenient when using a breadboard.

Some of the key components of this board are:

- the USB-to-UART bridge which allows for transfer with rates up to 3 Mbps.
- Micro USB Port which is the USB interface. It functions as the power supply for the board and is the communication interface between itself and the computer.
- I/O Connectors, which have multiple functions such as PWM, ACD, DAC, I2C, I2S, SPI, etc.

The power for the board can be supplied either through the Micro USB port, 5V/GND or the 3v3/GND pins. Note that the power can be supplied through either one of these connections, using multiple connections to power the board may damage the board.

Arduino UNO R3
The Arduino UNO R3 is a board based off of the ATmega328P. It has 14 pins in total out of which 6 can be used for PWM outputs and 6 for analogue inputs. It consists of

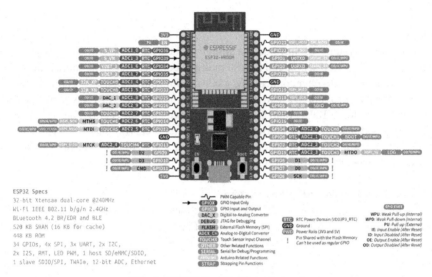

Fig. 1. ESP32 DevKitC based circuit

a 16 MHz ceramic resonator, a USB Port which serves both as a power supply and as a communication interface between itself and the computer. It further has a VIN pin to connect to an alternate power source such as a battery. It must be noted that even though the Arduino gives an output of 5 V, the power supply must be greater than 5 V. The power supply must be minimum of 8 V and a maximum of 15 V to avoid the risk of damage to the board and to successfully power the circuit.

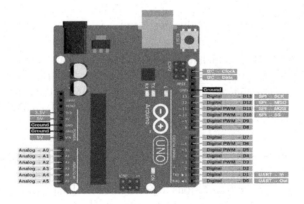

Fig. 2. Arduino UNO R3

One of the benefits of using this board is that the ATmega328P chip is easily replaceable as it isn't soldered to the board. The EEPROM has 1 Kb of memory that is not erased even when the board powers down. The 14 pins can very well be used for digital input as well.

LDR Sensor

The LDR is a light dependent resistor, i.e., its resistance varies with the intensity of light that falls on it. Also known as photoresistors, they're made of high resistance semiconductor material.

Fig. 3. LDR sensor

We use the LDR in the current experiment to detect the amount of natural light in the surroundings since its analogue output changes depending on the intensity of light. Using this value, we set a threshold in our system that determines whether the streetlights have to be turned ON or OFF. Receiving a higher value of the LDR, we determine that the amount of light in the surroundings do not warrant the use of streetlights, and the lights are hence turned OFF. If we were to receive a value lower than a certain threshold, the lights would be turned ON at low intensity.

IR Sensor

The IR sensor emits infrared rays with the purpose of sensing its surroundings. It is used for measuring heat and detecting the motion of objects. The IR sensor we use in our circuit has three pins, the VCC, GND and OUT (Fig. 4).

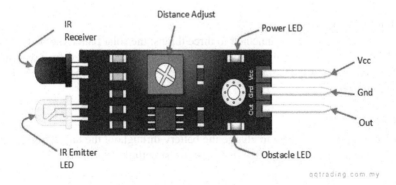

Fig. 4. IR sensor

The VCC pin is used for receiving power to power the sensor and the GND pin is used for grounding the sensor. The OUT pin gives us a digital output which we can use to detect whether there is some motion in our surroundings. Our streetlight system at night is turned ON at some base brightness (currently experimented at 20%). In the event that some motion is detected using the IR Sensor, we increase the brightness of the streetlight (to 100%).

Solar Module
The solar module used in this paper consists of 3 components, namely:

- Li-Ion battery

We use a Li-Ion battery of around 8V to power our microcontroller board. We can use either one Li-Ion battery of between 8−12 V or solder multiple lower voltage batteries to achieve the desired voltage. It must be noted that the batteries being used must be rechargeable, else they will not be able to be recharged by the solar panel (Fig. 5).

Fig. 5. Li-ion battery

- Li-Ion battery Charging Chip
     The charging chip is connected to three things: the solar panel, the battery and to the board. The power from the solar panel during the day is used for powering the battery and the power from the charged battery is used during the night to work the streetlights (Fig. 6).

- Solar Panel
     The solar panel is used to charge the battery throughout the day using the Li-Ion battery charging chip, since there is no use for streetlights during the day.

     As mentioned before, we have explored two different circuits:
     Arduino UNO R3 Circuit
     As shown in the circuit diagram below, our board is connected to 3 components; the LDR sensor, the IR sensor and the LED Light which we control. The outputs are taken

Fig. 6. Li-Ion battery charging chip

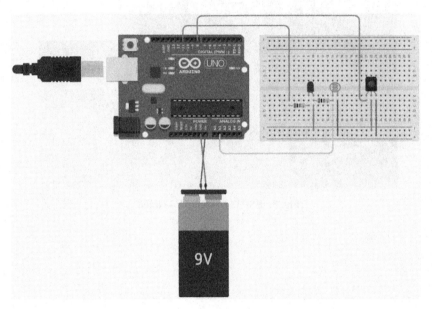

Fig. 7. Arduino UNO R3 circuit

from LDR and the IR sensor directly into the board, where we determine whether or not the LED has to be turned ON or OFF (Fig. 7).

The board is also connected to an external power supply through the VIN and GND pins of the Arduino. A power supply of greater than 7V but lower than 15V has to be used in order to make sure that there is no damage to the board. The connections are as follows:

- Pin 11 of the board to LED Light
- Pin A1 of the board to LDR to receive analogue output
- Pin 8 of the board to the OUT pin of the IR sensor
- The GND and VCC pins connected to the sensors necessary

The LDR is the main determiner of whether or not the street lights need to be toggled. Only when the street lights are turned on are the inputs from the IR sensor used to determine the brightness of the lights.

ESP32 DevKitC V4 Circuit

The same sensors are used with the ESP32 DevKitC V4 board. The board here is connected to the PC through the USB port and receives power from it. The circuit works as described previously (Fig. 8).

Fig. 8. ESP32 DevKitC V4 circuit

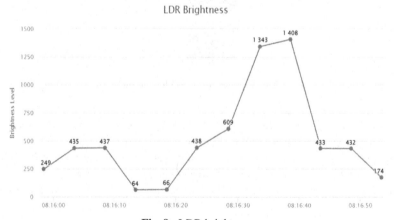

Fig. 9. LDR brightness

Results and Observations:

On implementing the circuit, we have gained a few insights. Environment affects our circuit greatly. On an average, the daylight readings were noted to be at a digital value of 330–400. Whereas night-time always gave a digital value of 0. The varying brightness system was implemented successfully with the LED glowing at two different brightness levels (100% and 20%) depending on whether motion was detected or not. The sensor readings were uploaded to the web server every five seconds. The plot created is shown in Fig. 9.

Observations

The first parameter on the basis of which we judge our model's performance is energy efficiency. In India, street lighting, electricity and maintenance costs can consume 5 to 10% of municipal budgets in large cities and up to 20% in smaller cities. Hence, it is essential to have a model of street lighting where the energy consumption is significantly reduced, while also requiring less maintenance than traditional streetlights.

The second parameter that our model is judged upon is pedestrian and passenger safety. Perceived personal safety can be defined as a person's immediate sense of security, and an absence of anxiety of becoming victimised, while travelling through a particular environment [12]. Street lighting is usually the most important physical feature of an environment when it comes to determining its perceived safety. Not only perceived safety, but the actual importance of visibility when the natural environment is poorly lit cannot be understated. Improving street lighting is also an effective means in combating crime. As far as vehicle safety is concerned, visibility is the single most important factor when it comes to determining how safe a street is.

5 Concluding Remarks

The benefit of proposed model lies in the fact that it is easy to implement and flexible as it can be deployed as soon as required. The energy savings are also evident from the results section. The LED lights and other components used, significantly reduce maintenance costs and increase the quality of the street lighting service and the system itself solves the problems that arise with manual operation of the existing street lighting system. Dimming the streetlights when the streets are empty will save a significant amount of energy. For the future, we see the potential for implementing a Solar Module for the ESP32 DevKitC based circuit. Even though the board's recommended power source is the micro-USB port input, it can also be powered using batteries or solar panels. Connecting to the grid and using solar panels at the same time might help in reducing the carbon footprint. Aside from this, the solar panels would also provide reliability. Solar panels can also be used for just generating energy and not powering the circuit. In the long run, the panel would produce more energy than the circuit would expend as the circuit would use minimal electricity.

References

1. Jagadeesh, Y.M., Akilesh, S., Karthik, S.: Intelligent street lights. Procedia Technol. **21**, 547–551 (2015)
2. Badgaiyan, C., Sehgal, P.: Smart street lighting system. Int. J. Sci. Res. **4**(7), 271–274 (2015)

3. Gupta, A., Gupta, S.: Design of automatic intensity varying smart street lighting system. In: IOP Conference Series: Materials Science and Engineering, vol. 225, no. 1, p. 012126. IOP Publishing (2017)
4. Dizon, E., Pranggono, B.: Smart streetlights in smart city: a case study of Sheffield. J. Ambient. Intell. Humaniz. Comput. **13**(4), 2045–2060 (2021). https://doi.org/10.1007/s12652-021-029 70-y
5. Khan, R.S., MR, P.: Intelligent Street Lighting System for Smart City (2021)
6. Thomas, A., Singal, G., Kushwaha, R.: Smart traffic control system using vanet a survey report. In: Vehicular Cloud Computing for Traffic Management and Systems, IGI Global (2018). https://doi.org/10.4018/978-1-5225-3981-0
7. Sharma, M., et al.: Intervenor: intelligent border surveillance using sensors and drones. In: 6th International Conference for Convergence in Technology (I2CT). IEEE 02–04 April, 2021, Pune, India (2021)
8. Jethani, S.: Surveillance system for monitoring social distance. In: 10th International Advanced Computing Conference (IACC), Communications in Computer and Information Science, vol. 1367. Springer, Singapore (2020)
9. Jain, S.S., Singal, G., Garg, D., Gupta, S.K.: SecureDorm: sensor-based girls hostel surveillance system. In: Somani, A.K., Shekhawat, R.S., Mundra, A., Srivastava, S., Verma, V.K. (eds.) Smart Systems and IoT: Innovations in Computing. SIST, vol. 141, pp. 327–337. Springer, Singapore (2020). https://doi.org/10.1007/978-981-13-8406-6_32
10. Pareek, B., Gupta, P., Singal, G., Kushwaha, R.: Person identification using autonomous drone through resource constraint devices. In: Sixth International Conference on Internet of Things: Systems, Management and Security (IOTSMS), pp. 124–129. IEEE (2019)
11. Fahrnberger, G., Gopinathan, S., Parida, L. (eds.): ICDCIT 2019. LNCS, vol. 11319. Springer, Cham (2019). https://doi.org/10.1007/978-3-030-05366-6
12. Blöbaum, A., Hunecke, M.: Perceived danger in urban public space: the impacts of physical features and personal factors. Environ. Behav. **37**(4), 465–486 (2005)
13. Kumavat, R., et al.: Intelligent street light system. Int. J. Res. Publ. Rev. **3**(11) (2022)
14. Deshpande, P., Jagtap, S.: IoT based energy management system. In: International Conference on Recent Trends in Engineering Science, Technology and Management (2022)
15. Verma, S., et al.: Smart street light based on IR sensor. Int. J. Eng. Sci. Comput. (IJESC) **10**(5) (2020)

An Optimized Low-Cost 4 × 4 Multiplier Circuit Design Using Reversible Logic Gates

Sriparna Bhattacharya[1], Soham Bhattacharya[2(✉)], Asima Adak[1], and Anindya Sen[1]

[1] Department of Electronics and Communication Engineering, Heritage Institute of Technology, Calcutta, India
[2] Department of Electrical and Computer Engineering, Rowan University, New Jersey, USA
bhatta22@students.rowan.edu

Abstract. Reversible logic gates, which are proven to provide zero power dissipation under ideal conditions, are in high demand for future computing technologies. Using reversible logic gates, this study provides an improved design for a low-cost 4 × 4 multiplier circuit module. The module can implement 8 × 8, 16 × 16 and up higher order multiplier circuits. In terms of gate counts, garbage outputs, constant inputs, and quantum cost, the suggested multiplier circuit using minimum number of half adders and full adders excels existing designs. Moreover, this concept can be used to implement different complex systems in the field of nanotechnology. The RTL design of the suggested multiplier circuit is then shown, followed by a simulation waveform that illustrates how the design works. The Xilinx ISE 14.7 software tool is also used to evaluate experimental results based on the on-chip power, delay, and other relevant parameters.

Keywords: Logic circuits · Reversible logic · Quantum cost · Garbage outputs · Multiplier

1 Introduction

Multiplication is the fundamental operation in mostly used digital signal processing. Multiplication time is still the dominating factor in determining the instruction cycle times of a DSP chip. However multipliers occupy large areas, have long latency, and consume considerable power. Hence, low power multiplier design has become a priority in the area of low power VLSI design. This work presents an efficient and modular 4 × 4 multiplier using reversible logic. The proposed multiplier circuit outperforms existing designs in terms of various parameters of reversible logic. Furthermore, this concept can be applied to the implementation of various complex systems in the field of nanotechnology.

In recent years, reversible logic has acquired a lot of attention because of its ability to reduce power consumption, which is a key criterion in low-power VLSI design. Prof R. Landauer in the year 1961 first demonstrated that KTln2 joules of energy are dissipated due to each bit of loss of information [1]. This loss of energy is associated with logical irreversibility where the input cannot be mapped back from output. Logical irreversibility

© The Author(s), under exclusive license to Springer Nature Switzerland AG 2023
I. Woungang et al. (Eds.): ANTIC 2022, CCIS 1797, pp. 263–281, 2023.
https://doi.org/10.1007/978-3-031-28180-8_18

in turn implies physical irreversibility and is associated with heat dissipative effects which affects performance in case of high speed computational work. Considering the new age computers and devices this concept of irreversibility gives rise to limited use of resources as only a fraction of transistors can be made to operate at a time to avoid thermal emergencies bringing in the concept of what is called dark silicon [2].

C. H. Bennett [3] through his pioneer work first paved the path of reversible logic which shows the feasibility of the existence of thermodynamically reversible computers dissipating much less than KT of energy at every step of computation. Reversible logic gates not only have the benefit of less heat dissipation but also have the advantage of no loss of information. Backward computing is possible with reversible logic gates where any previous stage can be recovered from the present stage. Toffoli in 1980 [4] stated that a sequential PC is feasible with zero internal power dissipation using reversible logic gates.

Several works have been done so far on combinational circuits using reversible logic gates. Reversible logic has significant application in low power CMOS, quantum computing, nanotechnology, and optical computing and efficient multipliers are required in each of these fields of applications. Any arithmetic and logic unit requires a multiplier as one of its basic components. Multiplier has huge applications starting from the field of microprocessor, communication, DSP, embedded system and many more. Three fourths of the instruction set in the microprocessor performs binary addition and multiplication [5]. The role of execution time of a multiplier is of major importance in any of the Digital Signal Processing Systems. Moreover power consumption should also be minimized leading to a low power computing system. All these criteria can be made feasible if multipliers are designed using reversible logic gates.

2 Materials and Methods

2.1 Reversible Logic

Reversible computing is a computing model in which the computational process is reversible at some point. That means it can store data for as long as it takes to be used when needed, along with time. A reversible logic gate is an n-input n-output device with no scope of direct fan-out. In order to have fanout in reversible circuits additional gates are to be used. Designing a circuit with a minimum number of gates is also another major characteristic of any computing system consisting of reversible logic gates. There are many parameters which determine the complexity and performance of reversible circuit design [4, 6, 7]. These are as follows:

i)   **The number of Reversible gates (N):** This refers to the number of reversible gates used in a circuit.
ii) **Constant inputs (CI):** This refers to the number of inputs which should be maintained constant at either logic 0 or 1 in order to synthesize the proposed logical function.
iii) **Garbage outputs (GO):** This refers to the number of unused outputs used in the reversible gates. Although this is an unnecessary output parameter but is not avoidable in order to achieve reversibility.

iv) The following formula is used to determine the relation between number of garbage outputs and constant inputs:

v) Input + Constant input = output + garbage output.

vi) **Quantum cost (QC):** This refers to the number of primitive reversible logic gates (1 × 1 and 2 × 2) that are required to realize the circuit.

Some properties of quantum cost are:

a.   **V*V = NOT**
b.   **V*V + = V + *V = 1**
c.   **V + *V + = NOT**

vii) **Gate levels (GL):** This refers to the number of levels which are essential to realize the logic circuit.

viii) **Hardware Complexity:** It refers to the number of AND, OR and XOR logic operations performed in the circuit.

2.2   Different Types of Reversible Gates

- *NOT Gate:* The simplest reversible logic gate is 1 × 1 NOT Gate, with input 'A' and output, 'P = **NOT A**'. The quantum cost of NOT is zero (Fig. 1).

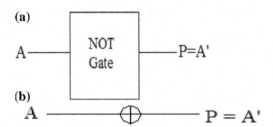

Fig. 1. A. Symbol of NOT gate. B. Quantum representation of NOT gate.

We can calculate the **FORWARD COMPUTATION** as
P = A', if A = 0, then P = A'; else P = A.
As well as, the **REVERSE COMPUTATION** as
A' = P, if P = 0, then A = P'; else A = P.

- *Feynman Gate:* It is a 2 × 2 reversible logic gate. It has two inputs, 'A' & 'B' and two outputs, 'P = **A**' &.'Q = **A xor B**'. The quantum cost of the Feynman gate is 1 [8] (Fig. 2).

FORWARD COMPUTATION will be:
P = A, If A = 0, then Q = B; else Q = B'.

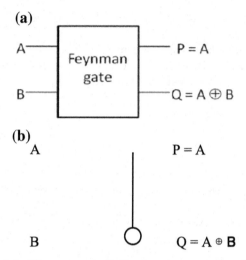

Fig. 2. A. Symbol of Feynman gate. B. Quantum representation of Feynman gate.

REVERSE COMPUTATION:
A = P; If P = 0 then B = Q; else B = Q'.

- ***Peres gate:*** It is a 3 × 3 reversible gate. Inputs are 'A', 'B' & 'C' and outputs are 'P = A', 'Q = A xor B' & 'R = A.B xor C'. The quantum cost of Peres gate is 4 [9].

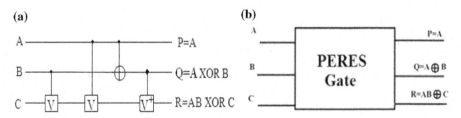

Fig. 3. A. Symbol of peres gate. B. Quantum representation of peres gate.

FORWARD COMPUTATION:
P = A, If A = 0, then Q = B and R = C; else Q = B' and R = B xor C.

REVERSE COMPUTATION:
A = P; If P = 0 then B = Q and C = R; else B = Q' and C = Q xor R.

- ***Toffoli gate:*** It is a 3 × 3 reversible gate. Inputs are 'A', 'B' & 'C' and outputs are 'P = A', 'Q = B', 'R = A.B ⊕ C'. The quantum cost of the Toffoli Gate is 5 [10] (Fig. 4).

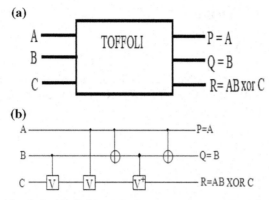

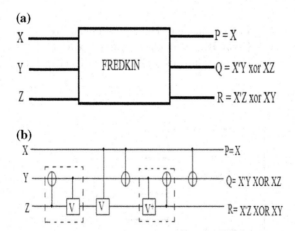

Fig. 4. A. Symbol of Toffoli gate. B. Quantum representation of Toffoli gate.

FORWARD COMPUTATION:
P = A; Q = B; If A AND B = 0, then R = C; else R = C'.

REVERSE COMPUTATION:
A = P; B = Q; If P AND Q = 0 then C = R; else C = R'.

- *Fredkin gate:* It is a 3 × 3 reversible gate. Inputs are 'X', 'Y' & 'Z' and outputs are 'P = **X**', 'Q = **X'Y xor X.Z**', 'R = **X'Z xor XY**'. The quantum cost of the Fredkin Gate is 5 [11] (Fig. 5).

Fig. 5. A. Symbol of Fredkin gate. B: Quantum representation of Fredkin gate.

FORWARD COMPUTATION:
P = X, If X = 0 then Q = Y and
R = Z, else Q = Z and R = Y.

REVERSE COMPUTATION:
X = P, If X = 0 then Y = Q and
Z = R; else Z = Q and Y = R.

- **HNG gate:** It is a 4 × 4 reversible gate. The inputs are 'A', 'B', 'C' & 'D' and outputs are 'P = A', 'Q = B', 'R = A xor B xor C', & 'S = (A xor B). C xor A.B xor D'. The quantum cost of this gate is 6 [13].

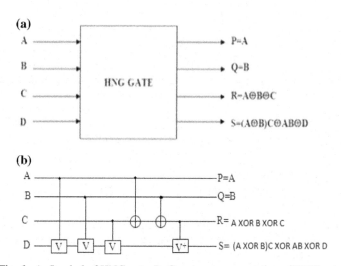

Fig. 6. A. Symbol of HNG gate. B: Quantum representation of HNG gate.

- **TSG gate:** It is a 4 × 4 reversible gate. The inputs are 'A', 'B', 'C' & 'D' and outputs are 'P = A', 'Q = A'C xor B'', 'R = (A'.C' xor B') xor D', & 'S = (A'C' xor B). D xor (A.B xor C)'. The quantum cost of this gate is 17 [15] (Fig. 7).

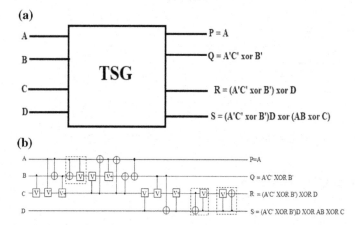

Fig. 7. A. Symbol of TSG gate. B. Quantum representation of TSG gate.

3   4-Bit Multiplier Circuit

A binary multiplier is an electrical circuit that multiplies two binary integers in digital electronics, such as a computer. Binary multiplication is significantly easier than decimal multiplication because there is no multiplication table to remember: just shifts and adds. This method is mathematically valid, and it has the advantage of allowing a compact CPU to do multiplication using its arithmetic logic unit's shift and add features rather than a specialized circuit. However, because there are so many intermediate additions, the procedure is sluggish. These additions take a long time to complete [12] (Fig. 8).

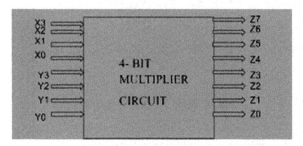

Fig. 8. Basic operational block diagram of a 4 × 4 multiplier circuit.

3.1   Partial Product Generation and Summation Network:

To accomplish 4 × 4 multiplications, it uses 16 partial product bits from the X and Y inputs. The suggested multiplier is designed in two steps using parallel multipliers.

Step I: Product Product generation.
Step II: Multi-Operand Addition.

The product of each bit of multiplicand to multiplier is generated in partial product generation. Carry save adder is used for 4 bit addition in multi-operand addition, and afterwards carry propagation adder is employed.

For example,

Suppose **X3X2X1X0** and **Y3Y2Y1Y0** are two binary numbers. So, the partial product table will be like:

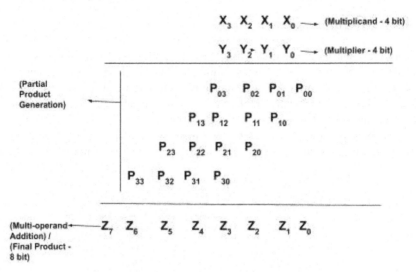

Fig. 9. Basic 4 × 4 multiplication.

From Fig. 9, the multi-operand addition will be:

$$Z_0 = X_0 Y_0 = P_{00}$$
$$Z_1 = X_0 Y_1 + X_1 Y_0 = P_{01} + P_{10}$$
$$Z_2 = X_0 Y_2 + X_1 Y_1 + X_2 Y_0 = P_{02} + P_{11} + P_{20}$$
$$Z_3 = X_0 Y_3 + X_1 Y_2 + X_2 Y_1 + X_3 Y_0 = P_{30} + P_{21} + P_{12} + P_{03}$$
$$Z_4 = X_1 Y_3 + X_2 Y_2 + X_3 Y_1 = P_{31} + P_{22} + P_{13}$$
$$Z_5 = X_2 Y_3 + X_3 Y_2 = P_{32} + P_{23}$$
$$Z_6 = X_3 Y_3 + CARRY = P_{33} + CARRY$$
$$Z_7 = CARRY$$

In Partial Product Generation, a total of 16 products will be generated. It is denoted as: $P_{ij} = X_i * Y_j$, where X_i is the ith bit of the multiplicand and Y_j is the jth bit of the multiplier.

3.2   Operation of a 4-bit Multiplier Circuit:

Three 4 bit adders were utilized in the circuit configuration seen in Fig. 10. Two four-bit inputs, comprising multiplicands (X0, X1, X2, and X3) and multipliers, have been taken (Y0, Y1, Y2, Y3). The bits of the multiplier will determine how much of the partial product is produced. The initial AND operation of X0Y0, which is also P00, will directly produce the multi-operand summation Z0. The first 4-bit adder will be used to create the multi-operand summation Z1, and the other outputs will be passed on to the following 4-bit adders as inputs. Z2 will be produced by the 4-bit adder's second operation. Last but not least, the most recent 4-bit adder operation, which will add up the partial products, Z3, Z4, Z5, Z6 and Z7 will be generated.

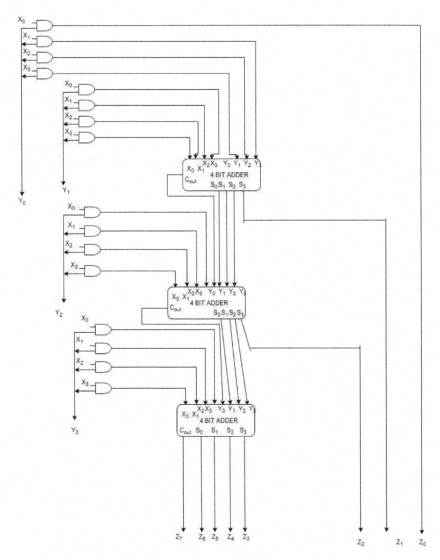

Fig. 10. Basic 4 × 4 multiplier operation.

4 Reversible Multiplier

The 4 × 4 reversible multiplier circuits have two main parts:

a) Partial Product Generation, and
b) Summation Network.

4.1 Partial Product Generation

For implementing the Partial product generation, it was previously stated that any of the four reversible gates like Feynman, Fredkin, Peres and Toffoli gates are required. In order to make the generation more equivalent in order to the minimum number of gates, minimum quantum cost, minimum number of constant inputs and minimum number of garbage outputs, we will choose **PERES GATE**, as it has covered all the previous possible criterions.

In Fig. 10, the partial product generation has been considered using **sixteen** PERES gates, which is the **minimum number of gates** to be used to implement the partial product generation of a 4×4 Multiplier circuit.

Constant inputs from the circuit are **16**. **Garbage outputs** of the circuit are **20**. As the quantum cost of each Peres gate is 4 and 16 Peres gates have been used in the circuit, hence, the total **Quantum Cost** of the circuit is **64**.

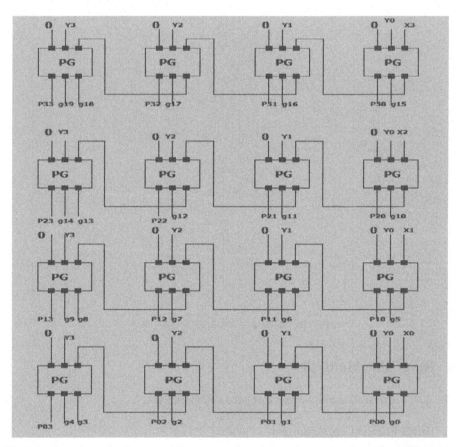

Fig. 11. The schematic diagram of the proposed partial product generation using LTSpice III simulator.

A comparative analysis of the partial product generation circuit is given below in Table 1, based on the different parameters of the properties of the reversible logic gates, with several references.

Table 1. Comparative analysis of the partial product generation of 4 × 4 multiplier circuit using reversible logic gates.

Partial product generation	Number of gates used	Constant inputs	Quantum cost	Garbage outputs
[9]	16	16	64	32
[10]	28	40	88	32
[11]	16	16	64	32
[13]	20	28	92	20
Proposed	**16**	**16**	**64**	**20**

4.2   Summation Network

In multi-operand addition, sixteen partial products are used as inputs, and an eight-bit answer is generated as the multiplier's answer. A ripple carry adder has been used in Fig. 12. A ripple carry adder is a logical circuit in which each carry bit gets rippled to the next stage. HNG gate is used as a reversible full adder and Peres gate is used as a half adder in the proposed four operand adder depicted in the figure. The summation network requires eight full adders and two half adders in order to achieve the required outputs. HNG gates singly perform the full adder operation and Peres gates singly operate the half adder. The schematic diagram of the proposed 4 × 4 multiplier circuit is represented in Fig. 12.

The schematic diagram of the proposed 4 × 4 multiplier circuit is represented in Fig. 12.

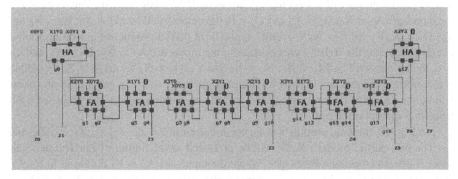

Fig. 12. The schematic diagram of the proposed 4 × 4 reversible multiplier circuit.

A comparative experimental study of the 4×4 Multiplier circuit using Reversible logic gates is given in Table 2, which states that this circuit can be better than the other previous methodologies.

Table 2. Comparative experimental analysis of the 4×4 multiplier circuit using reversible logic gates.

4×4 Reversible multiplier circuit	Number of gates used	Constant inputs	Garbage outputs	Quantum cost
[13]	28	28	52	–
[14]	40	52	52	152
[15]	52	52	52	184
[16]	32	40	40	140
[17]	28	32	56	–
[18]	40	31	56	–
[19]	29	34	58	–
Proposed	**26**	**26**	**38**	**120**

5   Analysis of the Proposed Work

For the partial product generation of the proposed reversible multiplier in Fig. 11, for the first Peres gate, where the inputs $A_0 = X_0$, $B_0 = Y_O$ and $C_0 = 0$, the outputs which will be produced are $M_0 = X_0$, $N_0 = X_0$ xor Y_0, $O_0 = X_0 Y_0$ xor $0 = X_0 Y_0$ (from the gate logic equation in Fig. 3.A), which is the first partial product of a 4-bit multiplier circuit (P_{00}). The output $M_0 = X_0$ will be carried forward to the next input of the Peres gate operation, whereas N_0 is treated as a garbage output. Similarly, from Fig. 3.A, for the second Peres gate operation, the inputs are $A_1 = X_0$, $B_1 = Y_1$ and $C_1 = 0$, the outputs will be $M_1 = X_0$, $N_1 = X_0$ xor Y_1, $O_1 = X_0 Y_1$ xor $0 = X_0 Y_1$, which is the second partial product of a 4-bit multiplier circuit (P_{01}). For the third Peres operation, the inputs are $A_2 = X_0$, $B_2 = Y_2$ and $C_2 = 0$, the outputs will be $M_2 = X_0$, $N_2 = X_0$ xor Y_2, $O_2 = X_0 Y_2$ xor $0 = X_0 Y_2$, which is the third partial product of a 4-bit multiplier circuit (P_{02}). For the fourth Peres operation, the inputs are $A_3 = X_0$, $B_3 = Y_3$ and $C_3 = 0$, the outputs will be $M_3 = X_0$, $N_3 = X_0$ xor Y_3, $O_3 = X_0 Y_3$ xor $0 = X_0 Y_3$, which is the third partial product of a 4-bit multiplier circuit (P_{03}). The generation processes will be the same for the remaining phases of the partial products of the proposed 4-bit reversible multiplier circuit.

For Fig. 12, the final outputs will be generated from Z_0, Z_1, Z_2, Z_3, Z_4, Z_5, Z_6, and Z_7. The first partial product $X_0 Y_0$ will be produced as the output of Z_0. The first half adder is generated using a Peres gate, where the inputs are $A_0 = X_1 Y_0$, $B_0 = X_1 Y_0$, $C_0 = 0$ and the outputs are $M_0 = X_1 Y_0 =$ first garbage output (g_0), $N_0 = X_1 Y_0 + X_1 Y_0 = P_{10} + P_{01} = Z_1$, using the logic equation of Fig. 3.A. O_0 will be carried forward to the next full adder. Z_2 will be generated from the second full adder operation by HNG gate, where the inputs will be $A_2 = X_2Y_0 + X_0Y_2$, $B_2 = X_1Y_1$, $C_2 = 0$, $D_1 =$ carry from R_1 (Carry of the first full adder) and the outputs will be $M_2 = g_3$, $N_2 = g_4$, $O_2 = X_2Y_0 + X_0Y_2 + X_1Y_1 = P_{20} + P_{02} + P_{11} = Z_2$, using the logic equation of Fig. 6.A. R_2 will be carried forward to the next full adder. Following the same procedure, $Z_3 = X_0Y_3 + X_1Y_2 + X_2Y_1 + X_3Y_0 = P_{30} + P_{21} + P_{12} + P_{03}$ will be generated from the fifth full adder circuit; $Z_4 = X_1Y_3 + X_2Y_2 + X_3Y_1 = P_{31} + P_{22} + P_{13}$ will be generated from the seventh full adder circuit, $Z_5 = X_2Y_3 + X_3Y_2 = P_{32} + P_{23}$ will be produced from the eighth full adder circuit, Z_6 will be produced from the second half adder circuit using Peres gate, where the outputs will be $M_9 = g_{17}$ (eighteenth garbage output of the circuit), $N_9 = X_3Y_3 + $ carry $= Z_6 + $ carry; $O_9 = $ carry forwarded from the whole circuit $= Z_7 = $ final summation output of the proposed 4-bit multiplier circuit.

[Here, $A_{0,1,2....9}$, $B_{0,1,2....9}$, $C_{0,1,2....9}$, $D_{0,1,2....9}$======> *Denoted as* 'inputs of the specific reversible gates';
$M_{0,1,2....9}$, $N_{0,1,2....9}$, $O_{0,1,2....9}$, $R_{0,1,2....9}$======>*Denoted as* 'outputs of the specific reversible gates'.]

In Table 3, the final outputs are presented from the mode of operations along with the specific inputs.

Table 3. Final output generation of the proposed reversible 4 × 4 multiplier circuit.

Phases	Inputs	Mode of operations	Final Outputs Generation
1	X0Y0	–	$Z_0 = X_0Y_0$
2	X1Y0	**1st Half adder circuit**	$Z_1 = X_0Y_1 + X_1Y_0$
	X0Y1	**(Peres gate)**	
3	X2Y0	**1st Full adder circuit**	–
	X0Y2	**(HNG gate)**	
	0		
	Carry of half adder		
4	$X_2Y_0 + X_0Y_2$	**2nd Full adder circuit**	$Z_2 = X_0Y_2 + X_1Y_1 +$
	X1Y1	**(HNG gate)**	X_2Y_0
	0		
	Carry of 1st Full adder		
5	X3Y0	**3rd Full adder circuit**	–
	X0Y3	**(HNG gate)**	
	0		
	Carry of 2nd Full Adder		

(continued)

Table 3. (*continued*)

Phases	Inputs	Mode of operations	Final Outputs Generation
6	$X_3Y_0 + X_0Y_3$	**4th Full adder circuit (HNG gate)**	–
7	$X_3Y_0 + X_0Y_3 + X_2Y_1$	**5th Full adder circuit (HNG gate)**	$Z_3 = X_0Y_3 + X_1Y_2 + X_2Y_1 + X_3Y_0$
	$X1Y2$		
	0		
	Carry of 4th Full adder		
8	X_1Y_3	**6th Full adder circuit (HNG gate)**	–
	X_3Y_1		
	0		
9	$X_1Y_3 + X_3Y_1$	**7th Full adder circuit (HNG gate)**	$Z_4 = X_1Y_3 + X_2Y_2 + X_3Y_1$
	X_2Y_2		
	0		
	Carry of 6th Full adder		
10	$X3Y2$	**8th Full adder circuit(HNG gate)**	$Z_5 = X_2Y_3 + X_3Y_2$
	$X2Y3$		
	0		
	Carry of 7th Full adder		
11	X_3Y_3	**2nd Half adder circuit (Peres gate)**	$Z_6 = P_{33} + CARRY$
	0		$Z_7 = CARRY$

6   Experimental Results

6.1   Register Transfer Logic Design

The RTL design has been implemented for our proposed 4×4 Reversible multiplier circuit is shown in Fig. 13. The behavioral and test-bench codes for the proposed circuit have been written in VHDL hardware descriptive language using the Xilinx ISE 14.7 Software tool.

6.2   Simulating Waveforms

With the help of the Xilinx ISE 14.7 ISim simulator, the simulation waveform has been generated for our proposed 4×4 reversible multiplier circuit in Fig. 14.

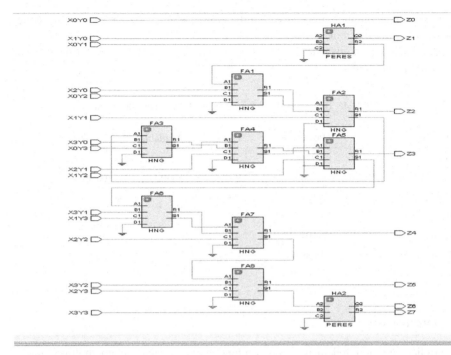

Fig. 13. The schematic RTL design of the proposed 4 × 4 reversible Multiplier circuit.

Fig. 14. Simulation waveform generated for our proposed 4 × 4 reversible multiplier circuit.

6.3 Power Analysis and Other Experimental Results

The total on-chip power generated after implementation for our proposed circuit is 3.689 W. Other simulation results which are derived from the circuit analysis are of delay of 8.051 ns, and the number of slice look-up tables is 7 with utilization of 1%. The total number of occupied slices is 4 with a utilization of 1% as well as the total number of bonded Input output buffers 24 with utilization of 8%. All these results are generated using the Xilinx ISE tool.

A table has been given according to the results generated of the synthesized circuit using the Xilinx tool.

Table 4. Total On-Chip power details of the proposed circuit.

On-Chip	Power (W)	Used	Available	Utilization(%)
Slice logic	0.034	10	–	–
LUT as logic	0.034	7	63400	0.01
Signals	0.109	26	–	–
I/O	3.438	24	210	11.43
Static power	0.107	–	–	–
Total on-Chip power	**3.689 W**	–	–	–

7   Discussion

Multipliers are in high demand in any arithmetic circuit. Hence many multipliers have been designed so far using reversible logic to optimize both the characteristics as well as the results. In 2006, Himanshu Thapliyal et.al proposed a 4 × 4 reversible multiplier using TSG gate and Fredkin gates [19]. The proposed 4 × 4 bit multiplier is designed with only 29 reversible gates compared to the existing counterpart which has 40 reversible gates [18]. In 2008, a novel reversible 4 × 4 multiplier was designed using HNG which could have been generalized for N × N multiplication [9]. Masoumeh Shams et. al designed a novel 4 × 4 bit reversible multiplier circuit with MKG gates having lesser number of garbage inputs compared to existing counterparts [17]. A novel low-cost quantum realization of reversible multiplier was proposed in 2009 by M.S. Islam et.al. in 2009 [15]. An improved design of a multiplier using reversible logic gates was proposed in 2010.This is again a 4 × 4 multiplier designed using DPG and BVF gate [14]. In 2012, H R Bhagyalakshmi et.al designed a 4-bit multiplier using a new 5 × 5 reversible logic gate called BVPPG gate. Toffoli gates were also used to construct the designed multiplier[20].A new architecture was proposed for multiplication using some reversible logic BVF gate and Peres Gate in 2012 [21]. Another reversible multiplier circuit was proposed using HNG gate which can multiply two 4-bits binary numbers and can be generalized for N × N bit multiplication in 2015 [22]. In [23], the design and comparison of a component scalable reversible logic multiplier has been presented. The authors have used Xilinx Vivado for the verification and simulation and the suggested design offered a 12.5% lower quantum cost and a 27% lower gate count. A new 3 × 3 SSG-I reversible gate has been introduced in [24] and it offered solution of 38.77% improvement while being very cost-effective. Consequently, it becomes more appropriate for nano-scale applications. In [25], the authors implemented an 8 8 Baugh-Wooley Wallace tree multiplier. There were two uses for the proposed multiplier:

Convolution Neural Networks and one-level decomposition of images using a rationalized db6 wavelet filter bank are two examples of image processing (CNN). In [26], the authors states that the reversible logic is used to demonstrate performance of various designs used in a MAC unit. Based on the number of Toffoli gates, the proposed designs [27] were compared to the other designs. Based on the comparison, it was possible to conclude that the design uses up to 72% fewer Toffoli gates and up to 1% fewer Toffoli gates than the designs available in the literature. In [28], the authors included viper, shift register, and multiplier liberation. The reversible entryway is bidirectional and uses little power. The strategy and results are completed in Xilinx programming, and the resistor transfer level (RTL) and waveform are checked. A binary multiplier was implemented using the Karatsuba and Urdhva-Tiryagbhyam algorithms community. The algorithms were written in Verilog (HDL) and are intended for use with the Xilinx ISE simulator for the FPGA Spartan-3E board. This reduced the FFT architecture and computing resources required for design [29]. The authors [30] proposed a system that uses Vedic multipliers and reversible gates to perform multiplications with high throughput and low power. The designed system was optimized by combining reversible logic's low power strategy with the high speed calculation of the Urdhava Tiryakbhyam Vedic multiplier.

Comparing the above references, in [18, 19], the authors used Fredkin gates for partial product generation. In [13], the authors used Peres gates in order to achieve the same. Our proposed design also uses Peres gates, but the difference is that the first outputs of the three blocks of each column can be carried forward to the next blocks as the first input, so that our garbage outputs can be gained as less numbers, which is one of the major constraints in designing a reversible logic circuits. Other than this property, other possibilities are equal as the other methodologies.

In the case of the 4 × 4 multiplier circuit in Table 2, our proposed methodology is better in terms of the number of gates used. Our proposed reversible multiplier circuit requires 26 gates whereas some of the references require 28, 29, 32, 40, 52 etc. numbers of gates.

Our proposed circuit requires 26 constant inputs and 38 garbage outputs respectively, which are quite less compared to the other designs given in Table 2. For the quantum cost calculation, 16 Peres gates have been used for the partial product generation, which concludes to 64 [16 * 4 (each Peres gate has a quantum cost of 4)] as a quantum cost computation. In case of the 4 × 4 reversible multiplier circuit, 8 HNG gates have been used as Full adders which concludes to 8*6 = 48, and 2 Peres gates have been used as Half adders, which results to 2* 4 = 8. These sum up to (64 + 48 + 8) = 120. This states that the proposed design is better than the other designs towards lessening the quantum cost of the circuit.

Based on the results of the investigation, in our opinion, the proposed design is superior to the other current designs because the total circuit cost is significantly lower than the other designs.

8 Conclusion

Using HNG gates and Peres gates, we presented a novel 4 × 4 bit reversible multiplier circuit in this study. In terms of number of gates, garbage outputs, constant inputs, and quantum cost, Table 2 shows that the proposed reversible multiplier circuit outperforms existing solutions. Table 3 shows the final output generation of the proposed 4X4 reversible multiplier circuit. Our proposed reversible multiplier circuit can be used for designing various complex systems in nanotechnology. Table 4 shows all the necessary performance analysis of the proposed circuit such as power analysis, delay, slice LUTs and their utilization.

Acknowledgment. We would like to express our profound gratitude to the Department of Electrical and Computer Engineering at Rowan University in the United States, as well as the Department of Electronics and Communication Engineering at Heritage Institute of Technology in India, for their ongoing assistance with this research.

References

1. Landauer, R.: Irreversibility and heat generation in the computing process. IBM J. Res. Dev. **5**(3), pp. 183–191 (1961)
2. Wikipedia Details about Dennard Scaling & Dark Silicon
3. Charles, H.B.: Logical reversibility of computation. IBM J. Res. Dev. **17**(6), 525−532 (1973)
4. Toffoli, T.: Reversible Computing. In: de Bakker, J., van Leeuwen, J. (eds.) ICALP 1980. LNCS, vol. 85, pp. 632–644. Springer, Heidelberg (1980). https://doi.org/10.1007/3-540-10003-2_104
5. Kumar, N., Bansal, M., Kumar, N.: VLSI architecture of pipelined booth wallace MAC unit. Int. J. Comput. Appl. (0975–8887) (2012)
6. Fredkin, E., Toffoli, T.: Conservative logic. Int. J. Theor. Phys. **21**, 219–253 (1982)
7. Bhattacharya, S., Sen, A.: A Review on reversible computing and its applications on combinational circuits. Int. J. Emerg. Trends Eng. Res. **9**(6), 806–814 (2021)
8. Das, J.C., De, D.: Feynman gate based design of n-bit reversible inverter and its implementation on quantum-dot cellular automata. Nano Commun. Netw. **24**, 100298 (2020). ISSN 1878–7789
9. Reshi, J.I., Tariq Banday, M.: Realization of peres gate as universal structure using quantum dot cellular automata. J. Nanosci. Technol. **2**(2), 115–118 (2016)
10. James, R.K., Jacob, K.P., Sasi, S., Ao, S.I., Rieger, B., Chen, S.S.: Reversible binary coded decimal adders using toffoli gates. Proc. Adv. Comput. Algor. Data Anal. LNEE. **28**(15), 117-31 (2008)
11. Patel, R.B., Ho, J., Ferreyrol, F., Ralph, T.C., Pryde, G.J.: A quantum Fredkin gate. Sci. Adv. **252**(3), e1501531 (2016)
12. Wikipedia Details about Binary Multiplier
13. Haghparast, M., Jassbi, S., Navi, K., Hashemipour, O.: Design of a novel multiplier circuit using HNG gate in nanotechnology. World Appl. Sci. J. **3**(6), 974–978 (2008)
14. Bhagyalakshmi, H.R., Venkatesha, M.K.: An improved design of a multiplier using reversible logic gates. Int. J. Engg. Sci. Tech **2**(8), 3838–3845 (2010)
15. Islam, M.S., et al.: Low cost quantum realization of reversible multiplier circuit. Inf. Technol. J. **8**, 208 (2009)
16. Rangaraju, H.G., et al.: Design and optimization of reversible multiplier circuit. Int. J. Comput. Appl. **52**(10), 44–50 (2012)
17. Shams, M., Navi, K., Haghparast, M.: Novel reversible multiplier circuit in nanotechnology. World Appl. Sci. J. **3**(5), 806−810 (2008)

18. Thaplyal, H., Srinivas, M.B., Arabnia, H.R.: A reversible version of 4x 4 bit array multiplier with minimum gates and garbage outputs. In: The 2005 International Conference on Embedded System and Applications (ESA 2005), Las Vegas, USA, vol. 18, pp. 106–114 (2005)
19. Thaplyal, H., Srinivas, M.B.: Novel reversible multiplier architecture using reversible TSG gate. In: IEEE International Conference on Computer Systems and Applications, pp. 100–103 (2006)
20. Bhagyalakshmi, H.R., Venkatesha, M.K.: Optimized multiplier using reversible multi-control input toffoli gates. Int. J. VLSI Des. Commun. Syst. 3(6), 27 (2012)
21. Mujumder, K., Pandit, M.K., Jana, A.K.: Design of a novel economic multiplier in VLSI using reversible logic gates. Int. J. Engineering and Adv. Tech. 2(2), 317–321 (2012)
22. Kumar, M.V., Babu, K.P., Basha, S.A., Devanna, H., Sudhakar, K.: Design of low power adder and multiplier using reversible logic gates. Int. J. Innov. Sci. Eng. Tech. 2(9) (2015)
23. AJ, K.R., Sakkara, S., Komal, M.: A novel, scalable n* n reversible logic multiplier design. In: 2022 3rd International Conference on Intelligent Engineering and Management (ICIEM), pp. 249-255. IEEE (2022). https://doi.org/10.1109/ICIEM54221.2022.9853070
24. Bhat, S.M., Kakkar, V.: Design and modeling of an ultra-efficient 3 x 3 SSG-1 reversible gate for nanoscale applications. In: 2021 International Conference on Emerging Smart Computing and Informatics (ESCI), pp. 720-723 (2021).https://doi.org/10.1109/ESCI50559.2021.9397042
25. Raveendran, S., Edavoor, P.J., Kumar, Y.B.N., Vasantha, M.H.: Inexact signed wallace tree multiplier design using reversible logic. IEEE Access 9, 108119–108130 (2021). https://doi.org/10.1109/ACCESS.2021.3100892
26. Pandimeena, R., Annapoorani, A., Kaviya, T.D., Rajalakshimi, A., Dhanagopal, R.: Design and comparison of power, area and delay of 32-bit reversible MAC unit. In: 2020 6th International Conference on Advanced Computing and Communication Systems (ICACCS), pp. 1412–1416 (2020). https://doi.org/10.1109/ICACCS48705.2020.9074179
27. Autade, P.P., Turkane, S.M., Deshpande, A.A.:Design of multipliers using reversible logic and toffoli gates. In: 2022 International Conference on Emerging Smart Computing and Informatics (ESCI), pp. 1-4 (2022). https://doi.org/10.1109/ESCI53509.2022.9758329
28. Dubey, A., Singh, S.: Area-time efficient of 2-D DWT using modified DA technique and reversible gate. In: 2022 IEEE 3rd Global Conference for Advancement in Technology (GCAT), pp. 1–5 (2022). https://doi.org/10.1109/GCAT55367.2022.9972239
29. Sultana, S.F., Patil, B.: Area efficient VLSI architecture for reversible radix_2 FFT algorithm. In: 2021 International Conference on Emerging Smart Computing and Informatics (ESCI), pp. 136-141 (2021)https://doi.org/10.1109/ESCI50559.2021.9396952
30. Eshack, A., Krishnakumar, S.: Speed and power efficient reversible logic based vedic multiplier. In: 2019 International Conference on Recent Advances in Energy-efficient Computing and Communication (ICRAECC), pp. 1-5 (2019).https://doi.org/10.1109/ICRAECC43874.2019.8995165

An Improved Resource Allocation Process Using Modified Max-Min Algorithm for Dynamic Cloud

J. Praveenchandar[(✉)] [iD]

Department of CSE, Saveetha School of Engineering, Saveetha Institute of Medical and Technical Sciences, Chennai 602105, India
praveenjpc@gmail.com

Abstract. Cloud computing is an emerging resource sharing platform, which provides the resources on-demand. It follows the pay-per-use pattern. The Cloud Service provider offers a variety of services such as Platform, Infrastructure, and software. They should assure that each user receives a high-quality service. But cloud usage has increased drastically day by day. To keep the SLA (Service Level Agreement) in a cloud system, heavy load should be distributed across the system. Here, we propose a novel technique of effective load balancing for resource scheduling technique that boosts profitability and stability. Max-Min algorithm is fine-tuned based on Profit and priority of the tasks named as Modified Max-Min algorithm. It is designed and adopted in cloud environment. Simulation result are observed, that shows the given approach improves the stability of load balancing and assures maximum profit by optimizing the response time and waiting time of the cloud users. This increases the cloud's overall efficiency which results more profitability.

Keywords: Resource allocation · Improving stability · Balancing dynamic work-load

1 Introduction

Distributed cloud platform implements the resource sharing and data sharing. It is one of the examples of distributed computing. In this environment all physical resources are virtualized. It enables the platform for remote resource access and resource sharing. All remote resources could be accessed with the help of software called as Hypervisor. It is a layer, creates the virtualized resources. So, this is called everything as a service. It provides the scalable resources to the customers. The cloud resource providers can exchange, sell, buy and trade the resources to their customers. Sometimes the resources are heterogeneous in nature. The cloud has two parts, cloud platform and networking. Based on the network, the services provided by the cloud may be varied. So all virtualized resources are represented as virtual clusters. It is a collection of physical machines connected by a network such as LAN (Local Area Network). All installed VM's (Virtual Machine) in distributed physical machines, builds the cluster. In a virtual cluster all

© The Author(s), under exclusive license to Springer Nature Switzerland AG 2023
I. Woungang et al. (Eds.): ANTIC 2022, CCIS 1797, pp. 282–294, 2023.
https://doi.org/10.1007/978-3-031-28180-8_19

VM's are connected each other logically through the virtual networks. Clusters are implemented in data centers. In recent years' data centers have grown a lot in all IT (Information Technology) sectors and other related fields. Even Amazon, Google, Yahoo are pouring their resources into constructing the new datacenters. Billions of dollars are invested on datacenters and automation of all operations. To ensure QoS (Quality of Service), the datacenter allocates the resources dynamically to all cloud users.

Now a day's virtualization technology moves towards increasing the number of clients and reducing the downtime. In various physical machines, multiple and heterogeneous workloads are running at various times. The workload can be categorized as two types. First one is non interactive workloads and another one is chatty workloads. Video streaming is an implementation of chatty workload. It will burst at some time. And non-interactive workloads don't need any people's efforts to show progress, after they submitted. Resource management complexity is increased by using the VM's. So an efficient resources utilization becoming one of the challenge. Because the server utilization must enhance the hardware utilization, maintenance cost and power consumption of the cloud operations. In most of the data centers, servers are underutilized. So lots of power, maintenance cost and physical infrastructure are wasted. To improve the low utility ratio of resources, a number of physical machines can be reduced or an efficient load balancing technique must be implemented. Though there are many load balancing techniques available, still there is some lack of stability in balancing the loads in heterogeneous environment. And bidding value coded by the customers is considered as secondary factor. That will improve the business. At the same time the service level agreement must also be satisfied with each customer. Virtualization based clustering is the most powerful technology of efficient resource management in cloud environment. Here the challenge is to increase the resources without affecting the QoS in datacenters. Then the datacenter automation is another major emerging scenario nowadays. Architectural support, analytical model, resource scheduling is some of the important constrains of it. Fine grained efficient scheduler is one of the important factors to achieve this task. Scheduling must be done effectively and rescheduling also must be implemented. It acts as an interface between the resources and gateway. It manages the available resources in the cloud environments. Overloading must be prevented in this dynamic environment to ensure the QoS. To manage workloads, we analyze two solutions. (i) Increasing the capacity of PM's. But already some of the PM's (Physical Machine) are underutilized. So that It is not an effective solution. (ii) Adopting the dynamic and efficient load balancing technique with the network. That will help to change unevenness in loads running on each physical machine.

The objective of the work is to balance the workload in the dynamic cloud using the Modified Max-Min algorithm, In this the existing algorithm is taken and modified with respect to the problem constrains. This new algorithm will improve the profit for CSP (Cloud Service Provider). This research paper organizes as bellow, Sect. 2 analyzed all similar works, Sect. 3 explains the derived algorithm, Sect. 4 analyzed the Experimentation and results. In this section the experimentation is done with the help of the cloud load balancing simulation software Cloud Analyst with Cloudsim and the results are observed and analyzed. Then the comparative analysis is also represented as graphs. Sect. 5 discussed about the conclusion and future work.

2 Related Work

In this section, Different load balancing strategies for cloud environment are examined.

Jin et al. [1] discussed a new compatible auction technique based on an incentive approach. Mainly this is applicable for mobile services. Lin et al. [2] analyzed more practical multiservice model, which is dynamic in nature. In this approach, a multimedia task is handled by server clusters, and for different types of multimedia requests different types of multimedia resources are allocated at different time. Wang et al. [3] have taken Heterogeneous virtual machines for consideration. A multi-tenant approach is proposed which is stochastic in nature and gives the model for an effective services of customer requests. Balakrishna et al. [4] discussed a new load balancing technique. In this, the network workload is equally distributed among all available nodes. This approach is mainly implemented for IOT (Internet of Things) nodes. For cloud integrated network infrastructure this load balancing algorithm is designed. Shahapure, N.H et al. [5] designed and implemented a new load balancing technique which is more secure and sustainable. In this work Edge data centers are taken for consideration in Fog computing. Sharma, S.C.M. et al. [6] discussed an advanced load balancing technique. When the fog or cloud is not available in the working environment, a new solution is proposed. Network of queues are used to model the sensor networks. Then linear programming technique is adopted for scheduling. Kaur, A., Kaur, B et al. [7] discussed another cost based optimization model for cloud environment. This gives an effective and flexible solution to allocate the resources available with cloud environment with respect to cost. Mao et al. [8] implemented with fair and efficient resource allocation. In this method, a load balancing avoids bottlenecks and minimizes uneven VM utilization. This approach is especially developed for cloud computing. A traditional Max-Min algorithm is analyzed for an effective load balancing in elastic cloud environment. Kim et al. [9] described two models. First is a model of real time services for real time request and the second one is VM provisioning of datacenters. And several power minimization schemes are also addressed. In [10] mapping process for each request to island of resources is also discussed by implementing heuristic approach. Xiao et al. [11] proposed an another effective approach for load balancing. This presents a virtualization technology that will allocate the datacenter resources to the user requests effectively and dynamically. Unevenness in the utilization of server is calculated. This is named as "skewness". By combining variety of workloads, we could minimize the "Skewness", it improves overall server utilization. Such a way the dynamic workload is balanced in cloud environment.

In [12], when a system gets heavy workloads, this approach is adapted to improve the performance of resource allocation. Application performance is reduced when the burstyness arises in user demand. The traditional load balances ignores the bursty arrivals. By balancing the bursty workloads across all computing nodes, overall system performance is improved. Tomita et al. [13] discussed another resource allocation with an effective congestion control. Congestion occurs when several types of resources, including as bandwidth, computing power, and storage, are taken from a common pool and allocated to a request.

Rani, Set al [14] proposed a new method by implementing DSC (Dominant sequence clustering) to schedule the task and WLC (Weighted least connection) algorithm to balance the load. Yeh. [15] discussed the cross-Identity Provider (IdP) architecture for resource scheduling to improve the performance. Chitra Devi et al. [16] have given the improved load balancing algorithm by fine-tuning the round-robin algorithm which gives improved results. Kaur, R. et al. [17] have analyzed a Resource allocation approach for the effective load balancing process both are dynamic Fog environments. In [18], a new model for mobile cloud platforms is discussed. Benet et al. [19] have given a protocol that is based on load balancing and policy-based routing for some specific datacenters. In [20] Rawat, P.S et al. discussed an improved approach to allocate the resource and Live migration is discussed. It identifies the cold spot and hot spot and manages them dynamically. Lee et al. [21] have given a advanced design for effective storage in cloud that is an enhanced proxy encryption mechanism that is searchable. Yakubu, I.Z et al. [22] analyzed a resource allocation approach for some specific type of heterogeneous cloud platform that is energy efficient.

3 Proposed Methodology

In this algorithm, a novel technique for balancing the workload is proposed during the resource scheduling process in cloud environments. In addition to the existing load balancing constrains, profit is also taken for consideration. The existing load balancing algorithm (Max-Min) is upgraded with respect to taken scenario. Bid amount of each resource is also included as one among the factor for task scheduling process. In this load balancing approach two different improved data structures are designed to keep track of the dynamic data's.(i) Resource Status Table (RST) and (ii) Task Status Table (TST). Figure 1 illustrate the system architecture.

Both associates with the Task scheduling and load balancing Algorithm respectively. Here, queuing model helps has been attached to the system to increase the processing speed, optimized results are obtained. Next modules describe, how the loads are balanced using proposed algorithm, and how it improves the profit and overall efficiency of the resource allocation process.

RST and TST are adopted with the system and updated per every unit time. RST consists of all the information about the resources such as Number of PM's, total number of Virtual Machines available, Idle Virtual Machines and length of every running Virtual Machines etc. TST consists of all information about the status of all tasks running on each virtual machine. In this scenario, for RST, input is supplied from TST. Task status is categorized as four types and based on that, RST is updated. And for TST, input is supplied from the physical infrastructure. Algorithm 3 and algorithm 4 are designed for dynamic updating of both TST and RST. Modified Max Min algorithm 1 is designed and adopted to implement load balancing.

Newly arrived tasks $Y(p)$ is acquired and bring to task scheduling module for every unit time. All $Y(p)$ are scheduled and put in to the dynamic priority queue. Here the buffer contains infinite size; 'n' number of tasks could be accommodated. All resultant array of identified tasks Dp are waiting for an idle agent. An agent may be in two states. Idle or engaged. Check for a status, if it is idle assign, otherwise next agent will be checked. This is continued for all $D(p)$. Agents do the mapping process of $D(p)$ with identified resources $Z(p)$. Since it is a dynamic process, it is being executed for every unit time. Based on these process TST and RST are updated periodically. During this

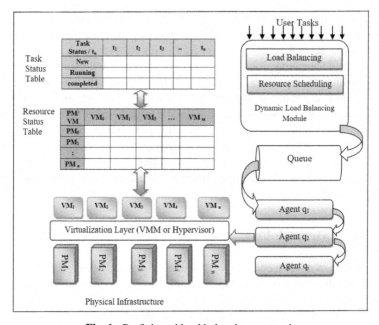

Fig. 1. Profit based load balancing approach

process, all the running tasks are being monitored and status of each assigned tasks with allocated resource are updated with both Tables. The proposed load balancing approach is described in following section, let us consider the requests from the clients taken as set R and tasks set T. S is a set of sizes of arrived tasks and I is Inter arrival time of all arrived tasks. Here E is a set of execution time of all tasks. Once the user request is received, the task scheduler makes each request in terms of tasks and each will have different sizes.

3.1 Proposed Load Balancing Approach

Max-min load balancing approach is a traditional algorithms used for cloud environments. It assigns all user requests to various computing resources. All resources are distributed by virtualization technology using the software hypervisor. Assigning virtualized versatile resources to all requests are NP Hard in nature. Though there are so many scheduling algorithms are available such as SJF, FCFS, Round Robin and priority scheduling, In addition to the resource allocation, various criteria's like resource utilization, user bandwidth and throughput are also must be considered. Max-min algorithm is one of the simplest and popular cloud scheduling algorithms. In this scenario, all the large tasks are allocated to faster resources and small tasks are allocated to slower resources with respect to its completion time. So waiting time of all smaller requests are minimized, by assigning those tasks to faster executing resources Static algorithms like opportunistic and Round Robin approaches schedules randomly. But the dynamic load balancing deals with the real time workloads and task executions. Though there are many dynamic load balancing approaches are available, still there exists some inefficiency in stability during load balancing due to versatility of loads. This approach is purely business oriented, to increase the profit to the Service Providers. At the same time, the challenge arises on Quality of Services (QoS). In addition to the profit; Service Level Agreements (SLA) must be maintained effectively with all received requests. That is also ensured in the proposed algorithm and it is modified from the existing load balancing algorithm.

3.2 Improved Load Balancing Algorithm (M-Max-Min)

Load balancing in distributed networks with versatile workload becomes one of the toughest tasks. Because the cloud usage is increased drastically day by day [2]. Workload should not be a factor to affect the QoS. Meanwhile SLA must be maintained effectively. Even if there are numerous load balancing techniques available, such as policy-based load balancing, multiservice load balancing, WLAN (Wireless Local Area Network) load balancing, and so on, there is still some variance in stability. And the profit in not taken for consideration in all these approaches.

Algorithm 1
Proposed M-Max-Min Load Balancing Algorithm
1) **Input:** Length if VM's Z(q), Y(p) and B(p)
2) **Output:** Balanced Workloads based on M-Max-Min
3) Sort all VM based on Z(q)
4) Sort reversely all Y(p) based on S(p) save as U(p)
5) Consider B(p) for all U(p)
6) Find mean of B(p)
7) x= $\lceil 0 + p \rceil$ / 2
8) do for all U(p) then
9) if B[*U[i]] > Bmean then
10) D[j] ← B[*U[i]]
11) Increment j & i values
12) else
13) D[x+1] ← B[*U[i]]
14) Increment x & i values
15) Assign all D [0...p] to Z [0...p]

Here we propose a new method to maximize the profit and stability, and provides an effective load balancing based on bid amount coded by the customer. In the sense, Customers that are willing to pay a higher price for a particular resource (Special customers) will receive faster service over others. So the traditional Max-Min approach for balancing load is slightly improved with respect to the above said scenario. As per the traditional approach VM's are allocated based on two factors (i) workload size (ii) completion time of VM [4]. When 'p' number of tasks arrived newly (Y), it is sorted based on sizes. Execution time of each Y is calculated. Expected finishing time of each task in all available Virtual Machines, based on the VM length is calculated. Request with largest running time is taken and mapped to faster VM, so that the maximum load is balanced and finished by minimum time. Algorithm 1 explains the proposed approach.

In this approach, in addition to existing factors, bidding amount given by every user is also considered. Let B is a set of bidding value coded by the customer. And U (p) is a set of reversely sorted order of all Y (p) based on S (p). Length of all VM's Z(p) are calculated based on the remaining capacity and sorted from faster to slower. New arrival tasks Y(p) are sorted reversely from bigger to smaller based on S(p) and taken it as U(p). Mean value of all B (p) is calculated (B mean). Using Divide and Conquer method, resultant array D(p) is divided by two equal half's. First one is the customer's tasks, those who coded higher bids M(0...p/2) and second half is remaining tasks M((p/2) + 1...p). This is categorized based on B_{mean}.if bidding value of U(i) is greater than B_{mean} (here 'i' is the random variable), first half of the resultant array D(p) is filled,or else second half is filled. Before that median 'x' of D(p) is calculated. In both cases, successive pointers are incremented. After D(p) got filled for all p', all D(p) will be allocated to Z(p). After adopting this algorithm, some of the performance metrics are observed and analyzed. Here we are adopting M/M/n queuing model and n servers are operated independently each other. The average waiting time (Q_{wait})of the newly arrived tasks can be calculated Eq. (1) as

$$Q_{wait} = \frac{\frac{\rho^m}{m!} \frac{1}{1-b}}{\sum_{i=0}^{m-1} \frac{\rho^i}{i!} + \frac{\rho^m}{m!} \frac{1}{1-b}} = \frac{\frac{\rho^m}{m!} \frac{1}{m-\rho}}{\sum_{i=0}^{m-1} \frac{\rho^i}{i!} + \frac{\rho^m}{m!} \frac{1}{m-e}} \tag{1}$$

3.3 Task Status Table (TST)

Task Status table (TST) is table which keeps track of data of all received and allocated tasks. Status of those tasks is updated for each unit time, since it is a dynamic process [7]. Once a request is represented as task, it entered into this Task Status Table along with the information such as inter arrival time, size of the task Sj, and status of the task. Then task status is updated periodically based on the data obtain from Resource Status Table (RST) [8]. This TST updating scenario is described in Algorithm 2 given as follows.

Algorithm 2
Algorithm (Task Status Table)
1) **Input:** Meta data of newly arrived tasks
2) **Output:** Final Tasks schedule.
3) Get all newly arrived tasks
4) Get the available resources from RST.
5) If Task ==New, then
6) Call Resource Allocation
7) If Task == Completed, then
8) Remove the task from TST
9) If Task == Running, then
10) Update TST and RST
11) End

TST is also updated dynamically for each unit time. Meanwhile Algorithm-1 is associated with Algorithm-2 and Algorithm-3. Two sets of tasks are taken for consideration (i) Tasks currently running all VM's and (ii) newly arrived tasks (Yp). Four categories of status are assigned to each task given in Table 1.

Depending on the current state of each task Tj, TST is updated. The running time of every task is measured. Resource Allocation and remove are the two functions for resource mapping to newly arriving tasks and removing the completed tasks from resource tag respectively. RST supplies the status of each task in VM which is described in next module. Based on TST & RST, load balancing process is initiated based on algorithm 1. Finally, we obtain the mean response time Eq. (2) as follows,

$$\overline{T} = \int_0^\infty tR(t)dt = \frac{1}{\mu} + \frac{1}{m\mu} \frac{(\lambda/\mu)^m}{m!} Q_0 \frac{1}{(1-g)^2} = \frac{1}{\mu} + W \quad (2)$$

3.4   Resource Status Table

Resource Status Table (RST) is a table which contains both information about resources and tasks. This RST updating scenario is described detailed in Algorithm 3. In Algorithm 3, Available Physical Machines and Virtual Machines are represented in table which contains tasks assigned to each VM and, the condition of each task is dynamically changed based on task completion time.

Algorithm 3
Algorithm Resource Status Table
1)   Input: Physical Infrastructure data in real time.
2)   Output: Final Resource availability
3)   Get the status of each VM in every PM
4)   If VM == Idle, then
5)   Update to agent and wait for allocation.
6)   If VM == Busy, then
7)   Mark as Engaged & measure the length
8)   Update the RST in every unit time.
9)   **End**

Task currently running in each VM, Execution time of each task, VM life cycle and last updated time are also updated simultaneously in RST. It assigns the status for each tasks based on its completion time and supplies the status information of each task to TST for each unit time. Available Physical Machines and Virtual Machines, busy VM's, Number of Idle VM's, length of every VM's are kept in RST [9]. Then the distribution of response time of a task could be calculated in Eq. (3) as

$$= \mu d^{-\mu t}(1 + \frac{(\frac{\lambda}{\mu})^m Q_0 1 - (m - \lambda/\mu)d^{-\mu\left(m-\frac{\lambda}{\mu}\right)t}}{m!(1-g)m - 1 - \lambda/\mu}) \quad (3)$$

All data are updated periodically with respect to task status. Simulation outcomes of this approach is analyzed in Experimentation section.

4 Experimentation

In experimentation part, we analyze the efficiency metrics of this approach after it adopts to the cloud system.

The experimentation is done using simulation tool cloudsim 3.0.3 and cloud Analyst then the results is observed. Modified Max-Min load balancing algorithm is written using Java programming as described, for cloudsim and configured with cloud analyst simulator then simulation gets initiated from the obtained results, some of the performance metrics are taken for consideration and analyzed. Comparative analysis is done with state of art Load balancing methods. First approach is Round Robin (RR) and next one is throttled load balancing approaches. The comparative analysis has demonstrated that the proposed approach provides the optimized results in terms of efficiency, task running time, and minimized waiting time. Table 1 and Fig. 2 represent the specification of simulation.

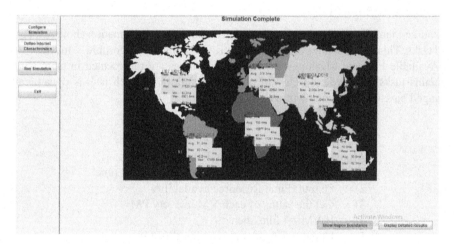

Fig. 2. Simulation environment

4.1 Task Movement Analysis

In the task movement from one VM to another VM determine the response time of the running tasks. Most of the load balancers achieve the minimum migration of tasks, because while identifying the most appropriate VM for a particular task which is being in queue for busy VM, It follows the static algorithm [17]. So the load balancers are unable to think of some advanced optimization to complete the job with minimum time.

Tasks running with heavy loaded VM's must be shifted to underutilize VM's with respect to given constrain. Figure 3 represents that the task movement analysis of this algorithm compared to other existing methods. Though, the task migration ratio gets minimum variant with other approaches, different set of tasks are identified for migration. Using formula (4) is calculated.

$$T_{Movement} = 1000 * \left(T_{Incoming} - T_{Outgoing}\right)/T_{Running} \qquad (4)$$

Table 1. Simulation specifications

Cloud	Configuration	Specification
Virtual machine	Host machines	12
Remote cloudlet	No of scientific workflows	200 to 500
	Task size (kb)	1900 to 3800
Physical machines	Memory	800
	Bandwidth	40,00,00
	Storage	1TB
	MIPS/PE	850

Here

$T_{Movement}$- *Tasks movement*

$T_{incoming}$- *Total arrived tasks for a VM*

$T_{outgoing}$- *Total completed tasks by a VM*

$T_{running}$- *Total running tasks in a VM*

If a task is migrated from one VM to another, most of the load balancers are failed to continue from its current state. Instead, it terminates the execution and restarts again. It results waste of time and resource.

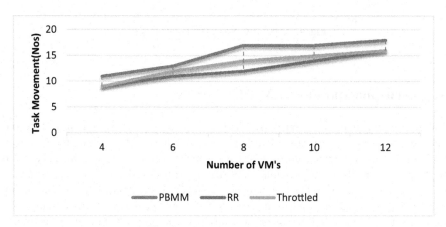

Fig. 3. Task movement analysis

4.2 Successful Task Completion Analysis

In a cloud system study, the number of effectively finished tasks is critical. Because specified tasks are transferred from one Virtual machine to another while usage virtual machines. Some tasks will be interrupted and others will be restarted during this process.

This has an impact on the task's current execution time. It will reduce the overall system's performance.

Furthermore, it is vital to ensure that all completed duties are completed. Our proposed approach ensures task completion by monitoring them from start to finish as they are moved. Figure 4 depicts the successful task execution analysis. The results show that the proposed methodology has the maximum task throughput when compared to alternative approaches.

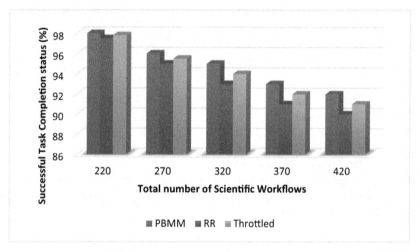

Fig. 4. Successful task completion analysis

5 Conclusion and Future Work

The recommended algorithm increases the load balancing process's stability. "Unevenness" of the workloads running in various VM's is balanced by shifting the workload from overburdened to under-utilized virtual machines. The work load is balanced based on the availability of virtual machines and size of the user tasks. Users who are having small sized tasks are given priority in resource allocation and balancing. By minimizing the response time, waiting time of those users, they could get faster services. It improves the user satisfaction, which leads for more business and profit. At the same time others task's execution flow is also ensured. When compared to previous load balancing methods, the suggested method yields better outcomes in terms of response time and waiting time. To improve the throughput of this load balancing process, Task live migration is considered and analyzed with various aspects as a future work.

References

1. Jin, A.L., Song, W., Zhuang, W.: Auction-based resource allocation for sharing cloudlets in mobile cloud computing. IEEE Trans. Emerg. Top. Comput. **6**(1), 45–57 (2018)

2. Lin, C.C., Chin, H.H., Deng, D.J.: Dynamic multiservice load balancing in cloud-based multimedia system. IEEE Syst. J. **8**(1), 225–234 (2014)
3. Wang, Z., Hayat, M.M., Ghani, N., Shaban, K.B.: Optimizing cloud-service performance: efficient resource provisioning via optimal workload allocation. IEEE Trans. Parallel Distrib. Syst. **28**(6), 1689–1702 (2017)
4. Balakrishna, G., Moparthi, N.R.: ESBL: design and implement a cloud integrated framework for IoT load balancing. In: Int. J. Comput. Commun. Control (IJCCC) **14**(4), 459–474 (2019)
5. Shahapure, N.H., Jayarekha, P.: Virtual machine migration based load balancing for resource management and scalability in cloud environment. Int. J. Inf. Technol. **12**(4), 1331–1342 (2018). https://doi.org/10.1007/s41870-018-0216-y
6. Sharma, S.C.M., Rath, A.K., Parida, B.R.: Efficient load balancing techniques for multi-datacenter cloud milieu. Int. J. Inf. Technol. **14**(2), 979–989 (2020). https://doi.org/10.1007/s41870-020-00529-2
7. Kaur, A., Kaur, B., Singh, D.: Meta-heuristic based framework for workflow load balancing in cloud environment. Int. J. Inf. Technol. **11**(1), 119–125 (2018). https://doi.org/10.1007/s41870-018-0231-z
8. Mao, Y., Chen, Xi., Li, X.: Max–min task scheduling algorithm for load balance in cloud computing. In: Patnaik, S., Li, X. (eds.) Proceedings of International Conference on Computer Science and Information Technology. AISC, vol. 255, pp. 457–465. Springer, New Delhi (2014). https://doi.org/10.1007/978-81-322-1759-6_53
9. Kim, K.H., Beloglazov, A., Buyya, R.: Power-aware provisioning of cloud resources for real-time services. In: MGC '09 Proceedings of the 7th International Workshop on Middleware for Grids, Clouds and e-Science, Urbana Champaign, Illinois – November 30 – December 01, pp. 1–6 (2009)
10. Papagianni, C., Leivadeas, A., Papavassiliou, S., Maglaris, V., Cervello´-Pastor, C., Monje, A.: On the optimal allocation of virtual resources in cloud computing networks. IEEE Trans. Comput. **62**(6), 1060–1071 (2013)
11. Xiao, Z., Song, W., Chen, Q.: Dynamic resource allocation using virtual machines for cloud computing environment. IEEE Trans. Parallel Distrib. Syst. **24**(6), 1107–1117 (2013)
12. Tai, J., Zhang, J., Li, J., Meleis, W., Mi, N.: ArA: Adaptive resource allocation for cloud computing environments under bursty workloads. In: 30th IEEE International Performance Computing and Communications Conference, pp. 1–8 (2011)
13. Tomita, T., Kuribayashi, S.: Congestion control method with fair resource allocation for cloud computing environments. In: Proceedings of 2011 IEEE Pacific Rim Conference on Communications, Computers and Signal Processing, pp. 1–6, 23–26 Aug 2011, Victoria, BC, Canada (2011)
14. Rani, S., Suri, P.K.: An efficient and scalable hybrid task scheduling approach for cloud environment. Int. J. Inf. Technol. **12**(4), 1451–1457 (2018). https://doi.org/10.1007/s41870-018-0175-3
15. Yeh, K.H.: An efficient resource allocation framework for cloud federation. Inf. Technol. Control, **44**(1), 64–76 (2015)
16. Chitra Devi, D., Rhymend Uthariaraj, V.: Load balancing in cloud computing environment using improved weighted round robin algorithm for nonpreemptive de-pendent tasks hindawi publishing corporation. Sci. World J. 3896065 (2016)
17. Kaur, R., Laxmi, V.B.: Performance evaluation of task scheduling algorithms in virtual cloud environment to minimize makespan. Int. J. Inf. Tecnol. 1–5 (2021). https://doi.org/10.1007/s41870-021-00753-4
18. Li, C., Li, L.: An efficient scheduling strategy in mobile cloud: model and algorithm. Inf. Technol. Control **44**(1), 7–19 (2015)

19. Benet, C.H., Noghani, K.A., Kassler, A., Dobrijevic, O., Jestin, P.: Policy-based routing and load balancing for EVPN-based data center interconnections. In: 2017 IEEE Conference on Network Function Virtualization and Software Defined Networks (NFV-SDN), pp. 1–7. Berlin, Germany (2017)
20. Rawat, P.S., Dimri, P., Saroha, G.P.: Virtual machine allocation to the task using an optimization method in cloud computing environment. Int. J. Inf. Technol. 12(2), 485–493 (2018). https://doi.org/10.1007/s41870-018-0242-9
21. Lee, C.C., Li, C.T., Chen, C.L., Chiu, S.T.: A searchable hierarchical conditional proxy re-encryption scheme for cloud storage service. Inf. Technol. Control 45(3), 289–299 (2016)
22. Yakubu, I.Z., Aliyu, M., Musa, Z.A., Matinja, Z.I., Adamu, I.M.: Enhancing cloud performance using task scheduling strategy based on resource ranking and resource partitioning. Int. J. Inf. Technol. 13(2), 759–766 (2021). https://doi.org/10.1007/s41870-020-00594-7

A Load Threshold Allocation Approach: Tackling Blackouts Through Brownout

Anshul Agarwal[✉][iD]

Department of Computer Science and Engineering, Visvesvaraya National Institute
of Technology (VNIT) Nagpur, Nagpur, India
anshulagarwal@cse.vnit.ac.in

Abstract. A significant gap exists between the supply and demand of
electricity as a result of the increasing energy needs of residential buildings and the absence of the required infrastructure and technology. To
address this issue, power utility companies typically employ a simple
strategy known as a blackout, in which the power supply to different
regions is interrupted at different times. However, this method increases
the inconvenience for users. In this paper, a more pragmatic approach is
proposed in which a power threshold limit is imposed on households during times of peak electricity demand. This paper presents a novel framework that is developed using different algorithms designed to allocate
load thresholds to households in an equitable manner. The algorithms
are evaluated on a real-world dataset, and the results demonstrate the
effectiveness of the developed technique in the implementation of the
brownout scheme in practise.

Keywords: Blackout · Brownout · Demand side management · Peak
power demand · Smart grid · Smart meter

1 Introduction

Globally, the residential sector has seen a sharp rise in energy consumption as
a result of population growth and different technological advancements. The
majority of countries, however, do not have the infrastructure needed to satisfy
these growing demands, and as a result, the gap between the demand for and
supply of power in these countries is growing over time.

Worldwide, the residential sector accounts for the largest share of a nation's
overall power consumption [5,9,15]. As a result, the majority of research focuses
on reducing home occupiers' peak power use and energy demand.

When power utility companies are unable to deliver the required amount of
electricity to houses, they implement rolling blackouts. It indicates that the utilities disconnect the energy supply to various regions of the distribution territory
for distinct periods of time. This helps utilities manage the lower demand for
power. Even while blackouts are simple to arrange, they result in greater user
discomfort and frustration. In addition, if the circuit breakers are not engaged

I. Woungang et al. (Eds.): ANTIC 2022, CCIS 1797, pp. 295–307, 2023.
https://doi.org/10.1007/978-3-031-28180-8_20

on time, a massive blackout may occur. Another method utilised by utilities is demand side management. Demand Side Management (DSM) is gaining popularity for managing the demand and consumption of consumers. It applies to Smart Grids that employ Information and Communication Technologies (ICT) to monitor the state of the grid and the behaviour of consumers. Albadi & El-Saadany [4] and Strbac [14] have discussed different DSM techniques. The primary focus in it has been on the architecture and development of the solution for only two layers. Energy management at building level is also an important problem and relevant issues need to be tackled [2, 16]. Shafie-Khah et al. [12] have proposed a novel decentralised DR model that relies on bi-directional communications. Peak power demand can also be reduced by asking the customers to shift their appliances in a systematic manner. Various approaches have been proposed [1, 3, 8, 10, 11, 13] to flatten the peak power consumption demand. But these techniques require the consumers and providers to participate actively (with increased inconvenience), which can be difficult in the real world scenarios.

To address these blackout-related concerns, a more intelligent method known as brownout may be used. In contrast to blackouts, it permits a dip in voltage, which reduces the demand on the grid and allows households to use part of their appliances. However, the implementation of this brownout plan necessitates investment and upgrade of the electric network, resulting in an increase in capital expenditures. It may also cause equipment failure [7, 17]. This research proposes a more realistic way to addressing this issue by building a unique framework. It involves assigning load thresholds to the distribution region (containing of families) during periods when the utility provider cannot meet the energy demands of the households. It guarantees that a) load thresholds are assigned to families in an equitable way and b) a minimal violation of this threshold should be observed across all households.

2   Methodology

Whenever there is a deficit of power supply relative to demand in a certain time slot, utilities establish a maximum power limit (called a load threshold) that can be consumed without penalty during this time slot. If the region's electricity usage exceeds this limit, the utility will levy a penalty. In this work, the utility's load threshold for a distribution zone in time slot t is indicated by E_t. The proposed algorithms then distribute the local load threshold to individual homes. It is indicated by the notation $e_{t,h}$ for household h in time slot t. Table 1 provides specifics on the various notations utilised in this article.

The utility assigns a predetermined load threshold to the distribution zone for a certain time slot. Before the commencement of the time slot, it is required to select the load threshold that will be assigned to each home. This assures that the threshold does not change within the allowed time period. Average percentage violation (AV) is the measure used to determine the violation of the imposed threshold limit that happened due to the consumption behaviour of these households. It is defined as the average percentage of power that exceeds

Table 1. Description of symbols

Symbol	Description
E_t	Load threshold allocated by the utility to the distribution region for time slot t
$\{H\}$	Set of households present in the distribution region
t	Time slot
$|S|$	Slot size
$p_{t,h}$	Power consumption of household h in time slot t
$p'_{i,h}$	Power consumption of household h at time instance x
p_h^{max}	Maximum power that may be consumed by household h
$algo$	Load threshold allocation algorithm
$e_t^{algo}[h]$	Local load threshold allocated to household h by algorithm $algo$ in time slot t
rr^{turn}	Household id that is selected for maximum load threshold allocation while implementation of round robin based threshold allocation
$vcnt_h$	Number of violations incurred by household h

the assigned load threshold. It is utilised to compare the threshold allocation performance of each algorithm in relation to the violation of these households. The details of different algorithms used are discussed as follows.

2.1 Equitable Distribution

This technique guarantees that each household within a distribution zone is assigned the same load threshold. The information is delivered using Algorithm 1.

Algorithm 1. Equitable Distribution

---
1 **foreach** $h \in \{H\}$ **do**
2 $\quad \lfloor\ e_t^{eq}[h] \leftarrow \frac{E_t}{|H|}$
3 **return** d_t^{equal}

This algorithm is the most straightforward to implement of all algorithms. It is effective when families have comparable energy consumption requirements over a specified time period. In scenarios where some households have high power demands and others have lower power demands, this algorithm will result in a high of the region, as households with high power demands will have more violations and households with lower demands will waste a (considerable) portion of their thresholds. Consequently, this method is not adaptable to the fluctuating (electricity consumption) requirements of homes.

2.2 Distribution by Proportion

This method assigns the load threshold proportionally, based on the ratio of each family's electricity consumption to the total household demand. This is specified by Algorithm 2.

Algorithm 2. Distribution by Proportion

---

1 **foreach** $h \in \{H\}$ **do**

2 $\qquad e_t^{prop}[h] \leftarrow \left(\dfrac{p_{t,h}}{\sum_{h' \in \{H\}} p_{t,h'}} \right) \times E_t$;

3 **return** e_t^{pr}

Unlike the equal allocation of load threshold, this method takes into account the differing energy consumption needs of families. Nonetheless, it has the following flaws: a) it does not reward homes with lower energy needs, and b) it unfairly assigns high load thresholds to homes with high energy needs (owing to excessive power waste).

Algorithm 3. Distribution by usage

---

1 **foreach** $h \in \{H\}$ **do**

2 $\qquad val_h \leftarrow 1 - \left(\dfrac{p_{t-1,h}}{\sum_{i=1}^{|S|} \max(p|p_{h,j} \forall j = 1 \ldots |S|)} \right)$;

3 $val^{sum} \leftarrow \displaystyle\sum_{h \in \{H\}} val_h$

4 **foreach** $h \in \{H\}$ **do**

5 $\qquad e_t^{power}[h] \leftarrow \left(\dfrac{val_h}{val^{sum}} \right) \times E_t$;

6 **return** e_t^{power}

2.3 Distribution by Usage

The primary heuristic used by Algorithm 3 to assign load thresholds is the ratio of a household's power consumption in the preceding time slot to the maximum power it could have consumed. This facilitates equitable distribution among households. On the basis of this ratio, households are ranked, and those with lower values are assigned higher load thresholds. Therefore, this algorithm incentivizes households whose power consumption behaviour is more prudent and frugal - a feature absent from proportional distribution. This results in fewer violations of household-specific thresholds.

2.4   Round Robin Based Distribution

This distribution algorithm distributes threshold load levels in a round-robin fashion. Each time slot (usually of one hour) is selected as the time epoch. Initially, the household with minimum house id is selected. In the next slot, house with next minimal power demand and one that has not been selected in the previous $|H|$ slots is selected for threshold allocation. This method is executed for each time slot that is available. Unlike previous algorithms, it provides each home with at least one opportunity per $|H|$ time slots to satisfy the maximum power demand. Nevertheless, this strategy has the following drawbacks:

- AV of households allotted the remaining threshold will be extremely high because the remaining threshold is typically quite low.
- A household selected in a time slot that is allowed to meet its maximum power demand may waste the allotted threshold because it may not consume its maximum power at this time.
- If there are a large number of homes, it will take longer for a family to satisfy its total electricity demand.

2.5   Novel Distribution Algorithm

One of the discussed algorithms may have a low AV value in a particular time slot, but none of them guarantees minimal AV in all time slots. Before the start of each time slot, it simulates these algorithms and calculates their AV value (using the function get_AV); it then selects the allocation algorithm with the smallest AV value. This results in a load threshold allocation with minimal AV across all time slots. Set $algorithms$ is initialised with the list of threshold allocation algorithms. Algorithm 4 outputs algorithm $algo$ with minimum AV value, load threshold allocated by the optimal algorithm and mean of the AV value of the optimal algorithm.

The main benefit of this algorithm is that it guarantees a minimum amount of AV in each time slot. In addition, it is more comprehensive in terms of load threshold allocation fairness because it takes into account different algorithms in different time slots; thus, a household whose threshold is not allocated fairly due to a particular algorithm will be allocated fairly by another algorithm. Therefore, it prevents households from going without load threshold allocation.

```
 1 function get_ AV(t)
 2 foreach algo ∈ {algorithms} do
 3 │   foreach h ∈ {H} do
 4 │   │   v₁ʰ ← 0
 5 │   │   foreach i ∈ {t} do
 6 │   │   │   if l'ᵢ,ₕ > dₜᵃˡᵍᵒ[h] then
 7 │   │   │   └   v₁ʰ ← v₁ʰ + l'ᵢ,ₕ
 8 │   │   valₕ ← v₁ʰ / Σᵢ∈{t} l'ᵢ,ₕ
 9 │   └   AVₜᵃˡᵍᵒ[h] ← valₕ × 100.0
10 return AV
11 end function
```

The code lines 4, 6, 7, 8, 9 in proper math:

- Line 4: $v_1^h \leftarrow 0$
- Line 6: $\text{if } l'_{i,h} > d_t^{algo}[h] \text{ then}$
- Line 7: $v_1^h \leftarrow v_1^h + l'_{i,h}$
- Line 8: $val_h \leftarrow \dfrac{v_1^h}{\sum_{i \in \{t\}} l'_{i,h}}$
- Line 9: $AV_t^{algo}[h] \leftarrow val_h \times 100.0$

Algorithm 4. Optimal Threshold Allocation

```
 1 optimalₜᵃˡᵍᵒ ← φ
 2 ∀h ∈ {H} : optimalₜᵈ[h] ← 0
 3 meanₜᴬⱽ ← 0
 4 AV = get_ AV(t)
 5 foreach algo ∈ {algorithms} do
 6 └   meanₜᵃˡᵍᵒ ← mean (AVₜ,ₕᵃˡᵍᵒ | h ∈ {H})
 7 optimalₜᵃˡᵍᵒ ← argminₐₗₒ (meanₜᵃˡᵍᵒ | algo ∈ {algorithms})
 8 foreach h ∈ {H} do
 9 └   optimalₜᵈ[h] ← dₜᵒᵖᵗⁱᵐᵃˡₜᵃˡᵍᵒ[h]
10 meanₜᴬⱽ ← min (meanₜᵃˡᵍᵒ | algo ∈ {algorithms})
```

3 Results and Evaluation

This section describes and compares the outcomes of applying the algorithms developed in this paper to an actual dataset.

3.1 Description of Dataset and Metric of Evaluation

Smart* Dataset [6] is the dataset used to evaluate the developed algorithms. It contains minute-by-minute electricity consumption data for over 400 anonymous households. To understand the efficacy of the developed algorithms, a ten-household distribution region is considered. In the case study examined in this paper, a total of twenty-four one-hour time slots are examined. As shown in Fig. 1, the load threshold allocated by the utility to the distribution region is simulated as 70 to 80% (uniform random sampling) of the total aggregate power of the distribution region in the given time slot. Figure 2 minute depicts the minute-by-minute consumption of electricity by each of the households on the first day of December. The results obtained after applying the developed algorithms to the households are evaluated as follows.

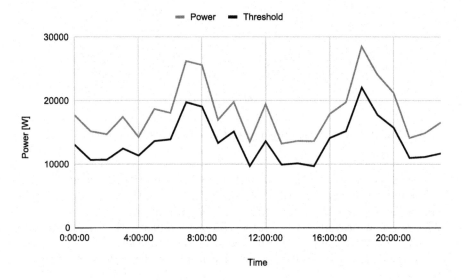

Fig. 1. Total power and threshold power allocated by the utility

Performance of Algorithms in the Distribution Region. AV is used to compare the performance of developed algorithms. A household-wide algorithm with a lower AV value is preferred over one with a higher AV value. Figure 3 depicts a summary of algorithms when applied to all of the region's households. It demonstrates that AV for the optimal algorithm is the lowest across all time slots. This is the objective of the utilities. From this graph, it is possible to conclude:

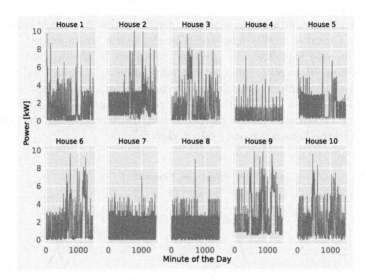

Fig. 2. Power consumption of all the households for a given day

- In the majority of time slots, the difference between the AV values of round robin and usage based distribution is minimal. Thus, the novel algorithm can choose between these two algorithms in the majority of time slots.
- The novel algorithm never chooses proportion-based threshold allocation because its AV value is never the lowest in any time slot.
- In all the time slots, the Proportion algorithm has the highest AV value.

In Table 2, the various algorithms selected by the novel algorithm in each time slot are described in detail. The novel algorithm allocates load thresholds based on the power usage ratio 37.5% of the time. Equal threshold allocation is chosen 25.00% of the time. Round robin distribution is also chosen 37.5% of the time. Therefore, the round robin and usage based distribution algorithms are superior to equitable distribution methods. The proportion allocation algorithm is never chosen by the optimal algorithm; therefore, allocation based on their relative power consumption does not significantly reduce the AV value. In comparison to other heuristics for threshold allocation, it can be concluded that allocation based on the power usage ratio of each household and round robin distribution has the greatest effect on the AV value of the region. Consequently, to minimise the AV value across all households, the novel method allocates threshold primarily based on the power usage ratio of the households, as the usage algorithm has dominated threshold allocation in the majority of time slots.

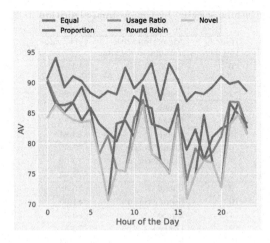

Fig. 3. Mean AV values of algorithms

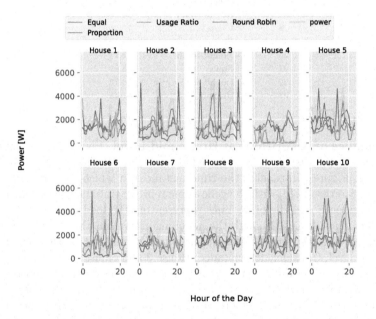

Hour of the Day

Fig. 4. Thresholds distribution to different houses by the developed algorithms (thick yellow line denotes the power consumption) (Color figure online)

Table 2. Algorithms selected by the optimal algorithm in each time slot

Hour of the day	Algorithm with minimal AV value	AV value
0	Equal	84.19
1	Round robin	86.35
2	Usage	84.86
3	Usage	83.92
4	Usage	83.49
5	Usage	83.81
6	Round robin	77.96
7	Round robin	70.62
8	Usage	75.65
9	Usage	75.38
10	Round robin	81.00
11	Equal	86.35
12	Usage	78.31
13	Equal	77.03
14	Equal	75.03
15	Equal	84.16
16	Round robin	70.92
17	Round robin	74.90
18	Usage	77.20
19	Round robin	76.79
20	Round robin	72.71
21	Equal	83.09
22	Round robin	84.73
23	Usage	81.48

Performance of Algorithms at Household Level. Figure 3 represents mean AV values of the distribution approaches across all the households in different time slots. Figure 4 illustrates the time instances in which each household violated the load threshold, with the yellow line representing the power consumption of each residence and the other lines representing the load thresholds allocated by various algorithms. Although the novel algorithm has the lowest AV in each time slot for the respective distribution region, it may not be the lowest at the household level. Consider, for instance, House 3 and House 6. It can be deduced that the novel algorithm never generates minimum AV for each house. In contrast, if we consider House 5, the novel algorithm is not preferred for the first twelve hours due to its high AV; however, it is preferred afterward due to its low AV. Figure 3 demonstrates that, when the mean textitAV of all households for a given time slot is considered, the optimal algorithm achieves the lowest value in each time slot.

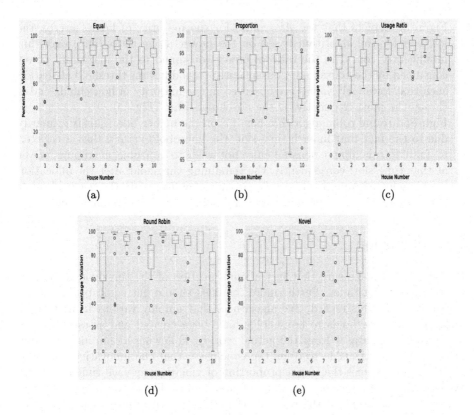

Fig. 5. Box plots denoting of distribution algorithm AV values

Overall Behaviour of the Algorithms. Figure 5 depicts a box plot for each algorithm applied to all households. It indicates the difference in AV values. The following are the conclusions drawn from this chart:

- From Fig. 2, it can be seen that House 2 consumes significantly less energy during all time periods compared to the other houses. As shown in Fig. 5, the AV values of this residence for equal and usage algorithms are low. This is due to the fact that these algorithms incentivize this low consumption behaviour, whereas round robin and proportional allocation do not.
- The Equal algorithm reveals that the majority of houses have high AV values (Fig. 5a). This is due to the fact that it does not account for the energy needs of households. Houses 2, 3, 9, and 10 have a lower AV value because they have a lower power consumption profile. The majority of the allocated threshold for these residences is lost due to their low consumption. As a result, other homes have high AV values. Figure 5b depicts that the proportion allocation algorithm has a high violation rate for all houses. Therefore, it is never chosen by the optimal algorithm for threshold allocation to regional households.

- Figure 5c depicts that the AV values for the majority of homes are on the low end for the algorithm based on the power usage ratio. This algorithm intelligently considers the ratio of power consumed to the maximum power consumed by the household. Consequently, it modifies the threshold allocation such that lower AV values are observed in the majority of households and is chosen the most frequently by the novel algorithm (Fig. 5e).
- Figure 5d round robin algorithm has AV on the higher side. This is primarily due to the fact that in each time slot, the household *rrturn* that is selected to fulfil its maximum demand may not wish to consume maximum power at that time slot; consequently, the remaining threshold after the allocation to this selected household is typically quite low to satisfy the needs of other households. This results in elevated AV values for the remaining homes.

4   Conclusion

It is crucial to make sure that just a small portion of the threshold for homes is breached at all times. Furthermore, families should get equitable threshold distribution. In this regard, five algorithms that employ various heuristics for assigning fair thresholds to households have been created and assessed in this study (using a dataset from the actual world). Following a thorough analysis of the data, it is feasible to draw the conclusion that the innovative optimum algorithm guarantees the lowest proportion of violations in each time slot while averting threshold allocation famine for households. The outcomes support the use of this technique for the realistic and effective deployment of brownout in the peak power demand management of the electric grid.

References

1. Agarwal, A.: A novel approach to save energy by detecting faulty HVACs. J. Inst. Eng. (India) Ser. B **103**(2), 305–311 (2021). https://doi.org/10.1007/s40031-021-00666-7
2. Agarwal, A., Ramamritham, K.: A novel approach for deploying minimum sensors in smart buildings. ACM Trans. Cyber-Phys. Syst. **6**(1), 1–29 (2021). https://doi.org/10.1145/3477929
3. Akasiadis, C., Chalkiadakis, G.: Cooperative electricity consumption shifting. Sustain. Energy Grids Netw. **9**, 38–58 (2017). https://doi.org/10.1016/j.segan.2016.12.002, http://www.sciencedirect.com/science/article/pii/S2352467716301850
4. Albadi, M.H., El-Saadany, E.F.: Demand response in electricity markets: an overview. In: 2007 IEEE Power Engineering Society General Meeting, pp. 1–5 (2007). https://doi.org/10.1109/PES.2007.385728
5. Amatya, V.B., Chandrashekar, M., Robinson, J.B.: Residential sector energy-supply-demand analysis: a modelling approach for developing countries and fuelwood-supply sustainability in Nepal. Energy **18**(4), 341–354 (1993). https://doi.org/10.1016/0360-5442(93)90069-P, http://www.sciencedirect.com/science/article/pii/036054429390069P

6. Barker, S., Mishra, A., Irwin, D., Cecchet, E., Shenoy, P.: Smart*: an open data set and tools for enabling research in sustainable homes. In: Proceedings of the ACM SustKDD, 12 August 2012. Association for Computing Machinery, New York, NY, USA (2012)

7. Blume, S., Sons, J.W.: Electric Power System Basics: For the Nonelectrical Professional. IEEE Press Series on Power Engineering. Wiley-Interscience (2016). https://books.google.co.in/books?id=lxFrnQAACAAJ

8. Ebrahimi, J., Abedini, M., Rezaei, M.M.: Optimal scheduling of distributed generations in microgrids for reducing system peak load based on load shifting. Sustain. Energy Grids Netw. 23, 100368 (2020). https://doi.org/10.1016/j.segan.2020.100368, http://www.sciencedirect.com/science/article/pii/S235246772030299X

9. Eia.gov: EIA - Electricity Data (2018). https://www.eia.gov/electricity/monthly/epm_table_grapher.php?t=epmt_5_01

10. Irwin, D., Iyengar, S., Lee, S., Mishra, A., Shenoy, P., Xu, Y.: Enabling distributed energy storage by incentivizing small load shifts. ACM Trans. Cyber-Phys. Syst. 1(2), 1–30 (2017). https://doi.org/10.1145/3015663

11. Kumar, G.K., Maniadarsh, S., Thungeshwaran, R., Ashwin, M., Jayabarathi, R.: Remotely controllable consumer perspective demand response using genetic algorithm. In: 2020 Fourth International Conference on I-SMAC (IoT in Social, Mobile, Analytics and Cloud) (I-SMAC), pp. 904–908 (2020). https://doi.org/10.1109/I-SMAC49090.2020.9243490

12. Shafie-Khah, M., Talari, S., Wang, F., Catalão, J.P.S.: Decentralised demand response market model based on reinforcement learning. IET Smart Grid 3(5), 713–721 (2020). https://doi.org/10.1049/iet-stg.2019.0129

13. Stamatescu, G., Stamatescu, I., Arghira, N., Fagarasan, I.: Data-driven modelling of smart building ventilation subsystem. J. Sens. 2019, 1–14 (2019). https://doi.org/10.1155/2019/3572019

14. Strbac, G.: Demand side management: benefits and challenges. Energy Policy 36(12), 4419–4426 (2008). https://doi.org/10.1016/j.enpol.2008.09.030, http://www.sciencedirect.com/science/article/pii/S0301421508004606

15. Subbiah, R., Pal, A., Nordberg, E., Marathe, A., Marathe, M.: Energy demand model for residential sector: a first principles approach. IEEE Trans. Sustain. Energy 8, 1215–1224 (2017)

16. Tanted, S., Agarwal, A., Mitra, S., Bahuman, C., Ramamritham, K.: Database and caching support for adaptive visualization of large sensor data. In: Proceedings of the 7th ACM IKDD CoDS and 25th COMAD. Association for Computing Machinery, New York, NY, USA (2020)

17. Wyatt, A.: Electric Power: Challenges and Choices. The Book Press Limited, Toronto (1986)

Predictive Analysis of Ambient Environment for Urban N Cultivation Using IOT Based Hydroponic System

Yokesh Babu Sundaresan[1](✉), S. A. Hariprasad[1], K. Nikhil[1], Ezhilmaran Devarasan[2], and M. Anbarasi[1]

[1] School of Computer Science and Engineering, Vellore Institute Technology, Vellore, India
`{yokeshbabu.s,manbarasi}@vit.ac.in`, `{sa.hariprasad2018, kavuru.nikhil2018}@vitstudent.ac.in`
[2] School of Advanced Sciences, Vellore Institute Technology, Vellore, India

Abstract. In a rapidly developing country like India, which has the world's highest growing GDP Urbanization is being seen in every nook and corner of the country. The difference between the population density of the cities and rural areas are very high. The population of the cities are growing exponentially every year, because of which the agricultural farms in and around the cities are being converted into residential skyscrapers. The need and demand for crops and food is growing up but the area to grow is going down. Due to this alarming scenario, hydropic agriculture has risen in popularity and practice. It is a form of agriculture in which the plants are grown with restricted water supply. In this work, we are growing coriander plants in a controlled environment with constant monitoring, the controlled environment being restricted water supply I,e Hydroponic farming. Various parameters like Soil pH (percentage hydrogen), Moisture levels etc. are recorded on a daily basis and made into a data set. This data set, then with the help of Supervised Machine Learning algorithms we are going to Co-Relate the data collected via IOT (Internet of Things) by the help of Regression Models, find the trends within the taken parameters and give an idea as to which conditions give a better yield. The main objective of our work is to find and show the correlation between various parameters taken into account while growing a crop through hydroponic agriculture and predict the range of parameters which result in the best growth of the crops.

Keywords: Supervised Machine Learning Algorithm · Regression models · Controlled environment · Hydroponic

1 Introduction

In a rapidly developing country like India, which has the world's highest growing GDP (Gross Domestic Product) Urbanization is being seen in every nook and corner of the country. The difference between the population density of the cities and rural areas are very high. The population of the cities are growing exponentially every year, because of

I. Woungang et al. (Eds.): ANTIC 2022, CCIS 1797, pp. 308–330, 2023.
https://doi.org/10.1007/978-3-031-28180-8_21

which the agricultural farms in and around the cities are being converted into residential skyscrapers. The need and demand for crops and food is growing up but the area to grow is going down. Due to this alarming scenario, hydroponic agriculture has risen in popularity and practice. It is a form of agriculture in which the plants are grown with restricted water supply (Table 1).

Table. 1. Population density of Indian metropolitan cities

No.	City	Population (in lakhs)	Area (sq km)	Density (pph (person per hectare))	Core area density (pph)	Core area (in sq.km)
1	Mumbai	124.87	437	286	460	67.7
2	Kolkata	44.96	205	219	219	205
3	Chennai	67.27	426	157	270	176
4	Bengaluru	84.25	712	118	214	216
5	Delhi	164.19	1397	118	391	22.74
6	Hyderabad	67.31	650	104	232	172.6

Agriculture is India's principal employment and the backbone of the Indian economy. Agriculture, in addition to supplying food, gives job possibilities to rural people on a big scale in impoverished and emerging countries. It is the process of producing food, fiber and many other desired products by the cultivation and raising of domestic animals. Agriculture is a primary source of income for more than 58% of India's population.

As the population of the city grows significantly the need to feed the city heavily lays on the need of agricultural land. As most of the agriculture lands are dried up due to lack of water the need for starvation increases. Hence cities have to start cultivating crops and the need for automated farming in cities becomes crucial.

Climate changes will have a significant impact on agriculture by increasing water demand and limiting crop productivity in areas where irrigation is most needed. Some of the strategies established to create better crops that may not use water effectively include irrigation systems, rain fed agriculture, and groundwater irrigation. A smart system is intended to use water effectively. In the system farmers need not make the water flow into fields manually, but the system automatically does that efficiently (Fig. 1).

People's traditional practices of water conservation may result in massive water waste. As a result, the notion of robotized farming with a combination of IoT (Internet Of Things) has emerged. Technological developments began to significantly boost manufacturing efficiency, resulting in a dependable system. The understanding of soil qualities causes the water supply to be driven in an intelligent manner. Agriculture practiced wisely aids in the acquisition of understanding about soil and temperature conditions. Developing smart agriculture employing IoT-based devices not only boosts output but also reduces water waste.

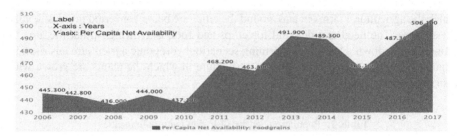

Fig. 1. Per capita net availability: food grains: pulses

2 Background

Hydroponic farming is heavily dependent upon water retention. The limited amount of water available will be retained with the help of a special soil mixture provided whose key role is to maintain the water level without losing the soil moisture.

A lot of work has already been done on the aspect of hydroponic farming. We have gone through various papers and found the following drawbacks and concepts.

Feature Selection has not yet been used in the creation of the machine learning model in this study. As a result, the outcome was less than satisfactory. The lettuce was standing straight one day and swaying to the side the next due to the blowing wind. Other errors were influenced by the amount of sunlight and temperature on that particular day. A lot of sunlight causes the plant to wither and unfold. When measured on a day with less sunlight and temperature, the width is smaller than when measured on a day with more sunlight and temperature [4]. Finally, these flaws caused the model to fail to produce a good learning result.

This work focuses on a model which maintains soil moisture level which is optimum for the crop growth. This level of soil moisture will be maintained constantly for the next 24 h with no impact and consideration of the weather condition. This work also talks about a smart irrigation system which helps in apt water management and provides ideal crop suggestions based on historic soil data.

This work also provides the type and quantity of various minerals needed [9]. This work does not talk about the plant diseases, this can further be extended so as to detect diseases and automated dispersal of pesticides and insecticides.

This work emphasizes the importance of IoT based technologies in agriculture. This paper works on the use of Low-Power Wide-Area Network (LPWAN) to reduce the power consumption and increase the wireless range by eliminating the unnecessary dependency of third party and backhaul networks. It also describes the comparisons between Coverage Range, Quality of Service, Battery Life, Latency, Scalability, Payload Length and Development model between LPWAN technologies. The only major drawback of the paper is the maintenance the LPWAN requires to keep it running as the technology used won't have the ideal conditions to run in an agricultural setup even though the battery life and power consumption are ideal [7].

Multi-Level IOT framework, which uses Application Layer, Internet Layer, Sensor and Actuator Framework along with Distribution middleware and follows MQTT (MQ Telemetry Transport) protocol. In the output, the End User Experiences VPS (Virtual

Private Server) interaction in one aspect and in the other aspect, it uses VPS and Local Server Interaction. This work falls back in implementing limiting factors such as nitrate, nitrate and ammonia via the electronic sensors. Automated data collection can be implemented into this work so that the system can function with better efficiency and maybe it could send alerts to the sender if there is any change or drastic changes in the parameters [1].

The paper focuses on five main concepts, namely Hydroponics, Need for Automation Control, Climate Statistics, Data Analytics and Cloud, Proposed System. The sensors record analog Data through a Hydroponic system with the help of MCP3008 chip ADC (Analog to Digital Converter). This work acts as an eye mainly to farmers but this technology can sometimes act more of a ban than a boon for the farmers. This work is done solely on the famer end so, it can be implemented in other factors as well [2].

3   System Architecture

3.1   Hydroponic Farming

In the present fast pace world, the form of hydroponic farming is taking over. The ongoing research paved new ways and paths for a better and substantial way of farming. Noticing the ways and researching the present trends, mainly followed in metropolitan cities and technologically advanced countries makes lives a lot easier in terms of hydroponic farming.

The work done by us addresses the key issues of automation and IoT integration into the way of sustainable farming in constraints such as limited water supply and space.

3.2   Necessity for Automation

The work being done needs constant monitoring as various sensors are used in a confined and controlled environment. As pre-processing homo sapiens, we tend to make unavoidable errors in our work. To avoid such mistakes that in other ways cannot be avoided, automation is the way. With the help of Arduino, ESp 8266 and aurd SpreadSheet the reading from the sensors are directly stored into the spreadsheet with almost no error. The readings are recorded once every 10 min which without automation requires an immense amount of manpower which may lead to loss or errors in recorded results.

3.3   Climate Maintained

Farming mainly depends on ambient climatic conditions but the city environment is not suitable for the growth of crops in the traditional way.

For our work as we targeted the metropolitan cities we made sure that the temperature range varied from 28 °C to 36 °C. In hydroponic farming, the crops are not exposed to sunlight throughout. Rather than exposing them to sunlight throughout, we made sure that adequate sunlight was available which in the day reaches approximately 240 cd and in the night for the integrity of the results, we made sure no light from any source was available which resulted in 0 cd.

Speaking about the soil moisture, for better understanding of the impact of moisture retention of the soil we grew the crops in early summer because of which there is humidity in the air than normal. The humidity varied from 40% to 80% which is the normal range in a coastal city (Table 2, Table 3, Table 4 and Table 5).

Table 2. Range of parameters full phase of crop growth

Parameter	Max	Min
PH	8.37	4.23
Luminous intensity	228	0
Humidity	76.2	50.3
Temperature	34.6	25.5
Soil moisture	687	676
Water level	252	161

Table 3. Range of parameters initial phase of crop growth

Parameter	MAX	MIN
PH	27.13	6.68
Luminous intensity	226	0
Humidity	82.5	47.8
Temperature	38.6	25.7
Soil moisture	687	579
Water level	731	153

Table 4. Range of parameters growing phase of crop growth

Parameter	Max	Min
PH	12.59	0
Luminous intensity	220	0
Humidity	72.7	43.6
Temperature	36.3	27.7
Soil moisture	685	676
Water level	661	272

Table 5. Range of parameters harvesting phase of crop growth

Parameter	Max	Min
PH	27.13	0
Luminous intensity	228	0
Humidity	82.5	43.6
Temperature	38.6	25.5
Soil moisture	693	676
Water level	731	153

3.4 Data Analysis

All the information collected from the sensors is stored in the personal systems directly rather than cloud as cloud is heavily dependent upon an uninterrupted internet connection which sometimes may not be possible. The data collected is stored and processed with the help of python to create results which help in better understanding of the data.

3.5 Proposed System

An innovative form of hydroponic farming is used. A coco pit is used as an soil replacement as the water retention capacity is much higher in this compared to general soil. The coco pit is connected to a water supply which is regulated. Six different sensors are connected to the system. The sensors being, pH sensor which monitors the pH of the water in the coco pit. The water in coco peat pH initially at the time of laying it down was 6.5. The second sensor used is Luminous Intensity Sensor. This sensor monitors the amount of luminescence around the setup. The third sensor is a Humidity sensor, this sensor monitors the humidity in the surroundings of the setup. Next sensor used was a temperature sensor, this sensor monitors the temperature of the surroundings. The fifth sensor used was soil moisture sensor, this sensor measured the amount of moisture in coco pit throughout the experiment. The final sensor used is a water level sensor, this sensor measures the amount of water provided to the system daily. The seeds used were coriander seeds as they take less time to grow which afforded us a chance to cross verify the results by repeating the experiment.

4 Experimental Process

According to the proposed system, the experiment is designed in such a way that it is a prototypical implementation. The design procedures are explained with a block Diagram.

4.1   Block Diagram

In the following proposed system, the analogue and digital sensors collect information from the hydroponic setup. With the help of Arduino Mega 2560 data is sent to the spreadsheet in a very smooth and effective manner. The data is collected and saved in a database using a wifi module. The block figure is represented for the proposed system (Fig. 2).

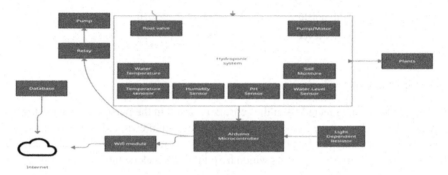

Fig. 2. Block diagram of proposed hydroponic system.

Major Steps explained in the proposed system are mentioned as flow charts.

4.2   Circuit Diagram and Components

The proposed circuit is created in such a way that the cost of components is economical and also the quality of the components is not compromised and also the performance of the components are very good.

The Major components involved in proposed system are:

- Arduino Mega 2560
- DHT-22 Sensor (Digital Temperature and Humidity Sensor)
- Water Level Sensor
- Soil Moisture Sensor
- PH Sensor
- Luminous Intensity Sensor
- WIFI (Wireless Fidelity) module (ESP 8266)
- Breadboard
- Jumper wires
- Pump
- Water Tube
- 5V motor
- 5V power supply

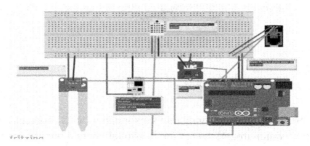

Fig. 3. Circuit diagram of proposed hydroponic system

The main component of the automated system is Arduino Uno Mega 2560 which is a very stable model which provides proper power supply and also helps in uploading large bundles of code (Fig. 3).

Fig. 4. Economic PH sensor with luminous intensity sensor.

PH Sensor - In both soil and hydroponics gardening, optimal pH levels are crucial for healthy plants and excellent harvests. Maintaining those ideal values necessitates frequent, reliable pH testing, especially in soilless growth systems. A plant's nutrient uptake is maximized at ideal pH values. The vigor and productivity of a plant are increased as a result of these nutrients. Luminous Intensity Sensor helps to capture the amount of sunlight hitting the product (Fig. 4).

Fig. 5. DHT-22 humidity and temperature sensor

DHT22 Temperature/Humidity Sensor - The DHT22 is a Temperature and Humidity sensor with digital interface temperature. The sensor is made in such a way that it can get propper calibrated value of humidity and temperature (Fig. 5).

Fig. 6. Image of soil moisture sensor

Soil Moisture Sensor - This soil moisture sensor can be used to detect soil moisture or evaluate if there is water around the sensor. It also tells you if the plants in the mesh pot need to be watered (Fig. 6).

Fig. 7. Image of water level sensor

Water-Level Sensor - A water-level sensor is a device that detects the level of water in a container. Maintaining the water level allows the roots to absorb the proper amount of water and prevents the plant from being spoilt (Fig. 7).

5   Dataset Analysis

5.1   Variation of PH with Respect to Time

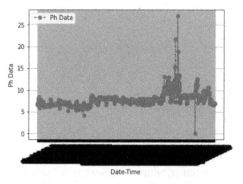

Fig. 8. Time series analysis of PH

Figure 8 shows the pH values of the water through the experiment. The minimum value recorded is 5.5 on the ph scale and this was recorded during the Initial phase of the experiment. The maximum recorded is 13 and it was recorded during the growth phase due to the addition of mineral water to the water supply, it became more basic. After the growth phase we supplied general water again, so, the pH dropped gradually making it more neutral.

5.2 Variation of Sunlight with Respect to Time

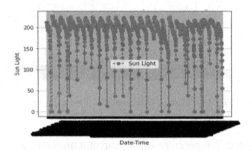

Fig. 9. Time series analysis of luminous intensity/sunlight for plant

Figure 9 depicts the Luminous intensity on candle scale over the whole duration of the experiment. The least recorded is Zero as during the night, it is made sure that the experimental setup is not exposed to any form of light energy. The highest value recorded is around 250 candela during the day.

5.3 Variation of Humidity with Respect to Time

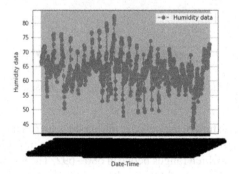

Fig. 10. Time series analysis of humidity

Figure 10 shows the humidity in the surroundings of the setup. As the experiment setup was in a coastal city, the humidity is relatively high but is under the normal humidity levels for the city. The lowest recorded is 45% and the highest is around 80%. To make sure that the humidity level doesn't go overboard, we conducted the experiment during early summer.

5.4   Variation of Temperature with Respect to Time

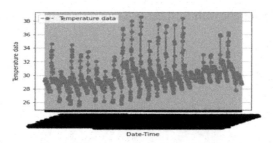

Fig. 11. Time series analysis of temperature

Figure 11 represents the Temperature of the surroundings throughout the experiment. The temperature kept on rising during the experiment gradually. The lowest recorded temperature was 26°C and highest was 36°C. The lowest average temperature was during the initial phase and the highest average was during the harvesting phase.

5.5   Variation of Soil Moisture with Respect to Time

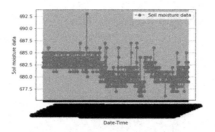

Fig. 12. Time series analysis of soil moisture

Figure 12 shows the moisture in the coco pit during the experiment timeline. During the initial phase the moisture level was between 682–686. The moisture level was highest during the growth phase which ranges between 680–692. The moisture level during the harvest phase is lowest in terms of average, its range varies from 676–680.

5.6 Variation of Water Level with Respect to Time

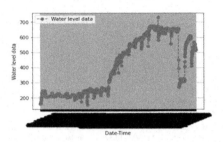

Fig. 13. Time series analysis of water level

Figure 13 depicts the water level in the experiment. The water level gradually increases till the growth phase and decreases there on. The water level during the initial phase was between 160 and 240 ml, during the growth phase it was between 200 ml and 650 ml. During the harvest phase, the water level required is low, it ranges from 200−500 ml.

6 Result and Discussion

The main objective of the result is to correlate the various parameters of the experiments with the help of four evaluation parameters, namely.

- Mean Absolute Error (MAE)
- Root Mean Square Error (MASE)
- Root Mean Square Log Error (RMSE)
- R Squared(R2)

The lower the value of MAE, the more the parameters are correlated. The R2 specifies the error in the calculations I,e the lesser the value of R2, the better the correlation is.

6.1 Predictive Analysis of Parameters Using Linear Regression

Table 6. Linear regression between parameters for initial phase of coriander plant growth

Parameter vs Parameter	PH	Sunlight	Humidity	Temperature	Soilmoisture	Water level
PH	Perfect linear correlation	MAE = 26.54 MASE = 1702.59 RMSE = 41.26 R2 = −0.00288	MAE = 3.13 MASE = 17.055 RMSE = 4.1298 R2 = 0.03718	MAE = 0.9522 MASE = 2.0584 RMSE = 1.43474 R2 = −0.003785	MAE = 0.9161 MASE = 1.1950 RMSE = 1.0931 R2 = −0.011836	MAE = 11.9423. MASE = 233.031 RMSE = 15.265 R2 = −0.0039

(*continued*)

Table 6. (*continued*)

Parameter vs Parameter	PH	Sunlight	Humidity	Temperature	Soilmoisture	Water level
Sunlight	MAE = 0.3905 MASE = 0.2885 RMSE = 0.5371 R2 = −0.00707	Perfect linear correlation	MAE = 2.9133 MASE = 16.551 RMSE = 4.0683 R2 = 0.0650	MAE = 0.7492 MASE = 1.268 RMSE = 1.126 R2 = 0.145	MAE = 0.902 MASE = 1.160 RMSE = 1.077 R2 = −0.0417	MAE = 1.0388 MASE = 1.521 RMSE = 1.233 R2 = 0.078
Humidity	MAE = 0.3817 MASE = 0.253 RMSE = 0.503 R2 = −0.0074	MAE = 21.29 MASE = 1630.14 RMSE = 40.375 R2 = 0.157	Perfect linear correlation	MAE = 0.831 MASE = 1.205 RMSE = 1.097 R2 = 0.517	MAE = 0.875 MASE = 1.06 RMSE = 1.033 R2 = −0.0056	MAE = 9.843 MASE = 174.68 RMSE = 13.21 R2 = 0.0941
Temperature	MAE = 0.409 MASE = 0.316 RMSE = 0.562 R2 = 0.0032	MAE = 22.06 MASE = 1529.58 RMSE = 39.109 R2 = 0.216	MAE = 2.64 MASE = 10.3 RMSE = 3.214 R2 = 0.505	Perfect linear correlation	MAE = 0.9160 MASE = 1.190 RMSE = 1.090 R2 = −0.012	MAE = 9.714 MASE = 168.86 RMSE = 12.99 R2 = 0.087
Soilmoisture	MAE = 0.389 MASE = 0.278 RMSE = 0.527 R2 = −0.0094	MAE = 24.12 MASE = 1462.23 RMSE = 38.23 R2 = 0.0032	MAE = 0.933 MASE = 2.1119 RMSE = 1.453 R2 = −0.0231	MAE = 2.890 MASE = 15.77 RMSE = 3.97 R2 = −0.018	Perfect linear correlation	MAE = 11.212 MASE = 229.93 RMSE = 15.16 R2 = −0.0049
Water level	MAE = 0.339 MASE = 0.232 RMSE = 0.4819 R2 = 0.0221	MAE = 22.450 MASE = 1350.67 RMSE = 36.75 R2 = 0.190	MAE = 3.35 MASE = 2.043 RMSE = 1.4296 R2 = 0.0010	MAE = 3.356 MASE = 18.41 RMSE = 4.29 R2 = 0.039	MAE = 0.797 MASE = 1.540 RMSE = 1.240 R2 = 0.0032	Perfect linear correlation

From Table 6, it can be inferred that water level and pH are the most correlated parameters in the initial phase of the experiment as MAE = 0.339. This means, with a given Water Level, we can predict the value of pH required for a good yield. The parameters that cannot be correlated are pH and Sunlight as the MAE = 26.54, this means that the value of Luminous intensity cannot be predicted with the pH level.

Table 7. Linear regression between parameters for growing phase of coriander plant growth

Parameter vs Parameter	PH	Sunlight	Humidity	Temperature	Soilmoisture	Water level
PH	Perfect linear correlation	MAE = 21.157 MASE = 1228.42 RMSE = 35.04 R2 = −0.0048	MAE = 3.400 MASE = 21.329 RMSE = 4.618 R2 = −0.0108	MAE = 1.155 MASE = 3.1804 RMSE = 1.783 R2 = −0.0061	MAE = 1.6315 MASE = 3.9975 RMSE = 1.999 R2 = 0.0096	MAE = 136.46. MASE = 23789.17 RMSE = 154.2 R2 = 0.1199
Sunlight	MAE = 0.944 MASE = 2.5054 RMSE = 1.582 R2 = 0.0000523	Perfect linear correlation	MAE = 3.309 MASE = 20.457 RMSE = 4.522 R2 = 0.194	MAE = 1.010 MASE = 2.544 RMSE = 1.595 R2 = 0.1704	MAE = 1.556 MASE = 3.836 RMSE = 1.958 R2 = 0.0247	MAE = 1.562 MASE = 3.678 RMSE = 1.917 R2 = 0.033
Humidity	MAE = 0.9677 MASE = 2.328 RMSE = 1.525 R2 = 0.00814	MAE = 19.44 MASE = 1072.59 RMSE = 32.750 R2 = 0.1304	Perfect linear correlation	MAE = 0.943 MASE = 1.686 RMSE = 1.298 R2 = 0.5603	MAE = 1.6009 MASE = 3.845 RMSE = 1.96 R2 = 0.00245	MAE = 134.715 MASE = 24155.87 RMSE = 155.42 R2 = 0.1037
Temperature	MAE = 0.8932 MASE = 1.6079 RMSE = 1.268 R2 = −0.0076	MAE = 18.107 MASE = 888.58 RMSE = 29.80 R2 = 0.165	MAE = 2.487 MASE = 10.05 RMSE = 3.171 R2 = 0.563	Perfect linear correlation	MAE = 1.780 MASE = 4.511 RMSE = 2.123 R2 = −0.0042	MAE = 142.16 MASE = 25289.25 RMSE = 159.02 R2 = 0.0057

(*continued*)

Table 7. (*continued*)

Parameter vs Parameter	PH	Sunlight	Humidity	Temperature	Soilmoisture	Water level
Soilmoisture	MAE = 0.959 MASE = 2.385 RMSE = 1.544 R2 = 0.01081	MAE = 19.289 MASE = 834.443 RMSE = 28.88 R2 = 0.0037	MAE = 1.0317 MASE = 2.1168 RMSE = 1.454 R2 = −0.0373	MAE = 3.3324 MASE = 21.27 RMSE = 4.612 R2 = −0.00273	Perfect linear correlation	MAE = 130.00 MASE = 23137.316 RMSE = 152.109 R2 = 0.0110
Water level	MAE = 0.886 MASE = 2.728 RMSE = 1.65 R2 = 0.1177	MAE = 20.0011 MASE = 1183.82 RMSE = 34.406 R2 = 0.0038	MAE = 1.563 MASE = 3.701 RMSE = 1.923 R2 = 0.0199	MAE = 3.494 MASE = 20.4542 RMSE = 4.5226 R2 = 0.073	MAE = 1.173 MASE = 2.624 RMSE = 1.62 R2 = 0.0017	Perfect linear correlation

From Table 7, it can be inferred that temperature and pH are the most correlated parameters in the growth phase of the experiment as MAE = 0.8932. This means, with a given temperature, we can predict the value of pH required for a good yield. The parameters that cannot be correlated are temperature and water level as the MAE = 142.16, this means that the value of Water level cannot be predicted with a given temperature.

Table 8. Linear regression between parameters for harvesting phase of coriander plant growth

Parameter vs Parameter	PH	Sunlight	Humidity	Temperature	Soilmoisture	Water level
PH	Perfect linear correlation	MAE = 22.685 MASE = 1027.818 RMSE = 32.059 R2 = −0.020	MAE = 4.589 MASE = 33.367 RMSE = 5.77 R2 = −0.154	MAE = 0.906 MASE = 1.836 RMSE = 1.35 R2 = 0.0653	MAE = 1.1328 MASE = 1.821 RMSE = 1.349 R2 = 0.032	MAE = 100.54. MASE = 15723.309 RMSE = 125.392 R2 = −0.05177
Sunlight	MAE = 0.9731 MASE = 1.421 RMSE = 1.192 R2 = −0.0967	Perfect linear correlation	MAE = 3.446 MASE = 20.575 RMSE = 4.535 R2 = 0.1587	MAE = 0.7630 MASE = 1.6451 RMSE = 1.282 R2 = 0.2184	MAE = 0.945 MASE = 1.470 RMSE = 1.212 R2 = −0.0047	MAE = 1.0651 MASE = 1.972 RMSE = 1.404 R2 = 0.00676
Humidity	MAE = 0.8707 MASE = 1.2903 RMSE = 1.1359 R2 = 0.153	MAE = 19.1465 MASE = 1114.27 RMSE = 33.38 R2 = 0.205	Perfect linear correlation	MAE = 0.725 MASE = 1.277 RMSE = 1.130 R2 = 0.290	MAE = 1.008 MASE = 1.796 RMSE = 1.340 R2 = 0.01474	MAE = 108.25 MASE = 14820.36 RMSE = 121.738 R2 = 0.207
Temperature	MAE = 0.9607 MASE = 1.441 RMSE = 1.2004 R2 = 0.075	MAE = 20.242 MASE = 1750.404 RMSE = 41.837 R2 = 0.2634	MAE = 3.8819 MASE = 25.495 RMSE = 5.049 R2 = 0.3559	Perfect linear correlation	MAE = 1.130 MASE = 2.060 RMSE = 1.435 R2 = 0.00103	MAE = 111.24 MASE = 16898.54 RMSE = 129.99 R2 = 0.026065
Soilmoisture	MAE = 0.9433 MASE = 2.2974 RMSE = 1.515 R2 = = −0.0189	MAE = 23.149 MASE = 1434.32 RMSE = 37.87 R2 = −0.00766	MAE = 1.0291 MASE = 1.813 RMSE = 1.346 R2 = −0.1067	MAE = 4.599 MASE = 33.304 RMSE = 5.770 R2 = −0.0732	Perfect linear correlation	MAE = 105.00 MASE = 16357.032 RMSE = 127.894 R2 = −0.004
Water level	MAE = 0.9163 MASE = 1.311 RMSE = 1.145 R2 = 0.0459	MAE = 28.312 MASE = 2365.95 RMSE = 48.641 R2 = 0.000481	MAE = 1.055 MASE = 1.63225 RMSE = 1.2775 R2 = 0.0771	MAE = 4.03624 MASE = 25.24 RMSE = 5.024 R2 = 0.16178	MAE = 0.9096 MASE = 1.342 RMSE = 1.158 R2 = 0.0436	Perfect linear correlation

From Table 8, it can be inferred that humidity and temperature are the most correlated parameters in the harvesting phase of the experiment as MAE = 0.723. This means, with a given humidity level, we can predict the temperature required for a good yield. The parameters that cannot be correlated are temperature and water level as the MAE = 111.24, this means that the value of Water level cannot be predicted with a given temperature.

Table 9. Linear regression between parameters for full phase of coriander plant growth

Parameter vs Parameter	PH	Sunlight	Humidity	Temperature	Soilmoisture	Water level
PH	Perfect linear correlation	MAE = 23.313 MASE = 1591.03 RMSE = 39.88 R2 = 0.00118	MAE = 3.9601 MASE = 27.939 RMSE = 5.285 R2 = 0.00598	MAE = 1.210 MASE = 3.0650 RMSE = 1.750 R2 = 0.0599	MAE = 1.8210 MASE = 4.899 RMSE = 2.213 R2 = 0.0378	MAE = 137.684 MASE = 22732.459 RMSE = 150.772 R2 = 0.2893
Sunlight	MAE = 1.0360 MASE = 2.128 RMSE = 1.459 R2 = −0.000246	Perfect linear correlation	MAE = 3.419 MASE = 21.26 RMSE = 4.61 R2 = 0.157	MAE = 1.147 MASE = 2.604 RMSE = 1.613 R2 = 0.185	MAE = 1.921 MASE = 5.188 RMSE = 2.277 R2 = −0.0118	MAE = 1.8404 MASE = 2.155 RMSE = 2.155 R2 = −0.0026
Humidity	MAE = 0.9411 MASE = 1.633 RMSE = 1.278 R2 = 0.0245	MAE = 20.003 MASE = 1241.13 RMSE = 35.22 R2 = 0.1857	Perfect linear correlation	MAE = 0.929 MASE = 1.478 RMSE = 1.216 R2 = 0.375	MAE = 1.811 MASE = 4.672 RMSE = 2.161 R2 = 0.023	MAE = 165.664 MASE = 31591.99 RMSE = 31591.99 R2 = 0.02649
Temperature	MAE = 0.9259 MASE = 2.554 RMSE = 1.598 R2 = 0.0676	MAE = 20.468 MASE = 1358.52 RMSE = 36.85 R2 = 0.176	MAE = 3.1046 MASE = 16.046 RMSE = 4.005 R2 = 0.4775	Perfect linear correlation	MAE = 1.658 MASE = 4.024 RMSE = 2.006 R2 = 0.0590	MAE = 166.6700 MASE = 31745.512 RMSE = 178.172 R2 = 0.0422
Soilmoisture	MAE = 0.936 MASE = 1.618 RMSE = 1.27 R2 = 0.113	MAE = 22.930 MASE = 1473.35 RMSE = 38.23 R2 = −0.0140	MAE = 1.185 MASE = 3.058 RMSE = 1.748 R2 = 0.0505	MAE = 3.6435 MASE = 24.41 RMSE = 4.94 R2 = 0.0159	Perfect linear correlation	MAE = 125.65 MASE = 22858.07 RMSE = 151.18 R2 = 0.288
Water level	MAE = 0.850 MASE = 1.518 RMSE = 1.23 R2 = 0.2719	MAE = 23.489 MASE = 1536.91 RMSE = 39.20 R2 = 0.0056	MAE = 3.864 MASE = 28.33 RMSE = 5.322 R2 = 0.0316	MAE = 1.185 MASE = 2.916 RMSE = 1.707 R2 = 0.0823	MAE = 1.451 MASE = 3.329 RMSE = 1.824 R2 = 0.3089	Perfect linear correlation

From Table 9, it can be inferred that water level and pH are the most correlated parameters in the full phase analysis of the experiment as MAE = 0.850. This means, with a given water level, we can predict the pH required for a good yield. The parameters that cannot be correlated are temperature and water level as the MAE = 166.67, this means that the value of Water level cannot be predicted with a given temperature.

6.2   Predictive Analysis of Parameters Using Support Vector Regression

Table 10. Support vector regression between parameters for initial phase of coriander plant growth

Parameter vs Parameter	PH	Sunlight	Humidity	Temperature	Soilmoisture	Water level
PH	Perfect linear correlation	MAE = 22.102 MASE = 2351.64 RMSE = 48.493 R2 = −0.0852	MAE = 2.9432 MASE = 15.363 RMSE = 3.919 R2 = 0.2227	MAE = 0.82803 MASE = 1.598 RMSE = 1.2642 R2 = 0.0446	MAE = 0.8812 MASE = 1.423 RMSE = 1.193 R2 = −0.174	MAE = 10.6116 MASE = 218.732 RMSE = 14.789 R2 = −0.0377
Sunlight	MAE = 0.3460 MASE = 0.227 RMSE = 0.4766 R2 = −0.0458	Perfect linear correlation	MAE = 2.836 MASE = 13.770 RMSE = 3.710 R2 = 0.264	MAE = 0.518 MASE = 0.871 RMSE = 0.933 R2 = 0.450	MAE = 0.8686 MASE = 1.362 RMSE = 1.167 R2 = −0.120	MAE = 0.989 MASE = 1.627 RMSE = 1.275 R2 = −0.225
Humidity	MAE = 0.310 MASE = 0.174 RMSE = 0.417 R2 = 0.275	MAE = 17.27 MASE = 1259.407 RMSE = 35.48 R2 = 0.0078	Perfect linear correlation	MAE = 0.683 MASE = 0.825 RMSE = 0.908 R2 = 0.3423	MAE = 0.833 MASE = 1.378 RMSE = 1.174 R2 = −0.057	MAE = 9.329 MASE = 169.081 RMSE = 13.0031 R2 = 0.0302
Temperature	MAE = 0.396 MASE = 0.317 RMSE = 0.563 R2 = 0.00755	MAE = 13.68 MASE = 1172.59 RMSE = 34.24 R2 = 0.2142	MAE = 2.742 MASE = 11.737 RMSE = 3.425 R2 = 0.466	Perfect linear correlation	MAE = 0.842 MASE = 1.325 RMSE = 1.151 R2 = −0.1810	MAE = 7.9547 MASE = 137.199 RMSE = 11.713 R2 = 0.25006
Soilmoisture	MAE = 0.348 MASE = 0.199 RMSE = 0.4461 R2 = = −0.0110	MAE = 20.962 MASE = 2052.051 RMSE = 45.299 R2 = −0.0695	MAE = 3.7415 MASE = 23.297 RMSE = 4.8267 R2 = −0.0293	MAE = 0.896 MASE = 1.852 RMSE = 1.3611 R2 = −0.1329	Perfect linear correlation	MAE = 8.9695 MASE = 161.8012 RMSE = 12.7201 R2 = −0.00836
Water level	MAE = 0.359 MASE = 0.2667 RMSE = 0.5165 R2 = −0.0788	MAE = 23.2524 MASE = 2417.059 RMSE = 49.1636 R2 = 0.0059	MAE = 2.9750 MASE = 16.440 RMSE = 4.05465 R2 = 0.02438	MAE = 1.00006 MASE = 2.70294 RMSE = 1.6440 R2 = 0.1164	MAE = 0.7492 MASE = 1.0809 RMSE = 1.0396 R2 = −0.1662	Perfect linear correlation

From Table 10, it can be inferred that humidity and pH are the most correlated parameters in the initial phase of the experiment as MAE = 0.310. This means, with a given humidity level, we can predict the pH required for a good yield. The parameters that cannot be correlated are water level and sunlight as the MAE = 23.025, this means that the value of Water level cannot be predicted with a given luminous intensity.

Table 11. Support vector regression between parameters for growing phase of coriander plant growth

Parameter vs Parameter	PH	Sunlight	Humidity	Temperature	Soilmoisture	Water level
PH	Perfect linear correlation	MAE = 17.013 MASE = 1014.28 RMSE = 31.84 R2 = −0.0743	MAE = 3.8003 MASE = 25.36 RMSE = 5.0361 R2 = 0.0470	MAE = 0.995 MASE = 2.330 RMSE = 1.526 R2 = 0.1112	MAE = 1.638 MASE = 4.429 RMSE = 2.104 R2 = 0.0109	MAE = 120.94 MASE = 24176.55 RMSE = 155.48 R2 = 0.026

(continued)

Table 11. (*continued*)

Parameter vs Parameter	PH	Sunlight	Humidity	Temperature	Soilmoisture	Water level
Sunlight	MAE = 1.005 MASE = 4.719 RMSE = 2.172 R2 = −0.0719	Perfect linear correlation	MAE = 3.602 MASE = 23.974 RMSE = 4.896 R2 = 0.1506	MAE = 0.802 MASE = 1.444 RMSE = 1.2019 R2 = 0.430	MAE = 1.6199 MASE = 4.0536 RMSE = 2.013 R2 = 0.0220	MAE = 139.698 MASE = 29287.10 RMSE = 171.134 R2 = −0.1414
Humidity	MAE = 0.822 MASE = 1.879 RMSE = 1.370 R2 = −0.0892	MAE = 17.210 MASE = 1090.04 RMSE = 33.015 R2 = 0.0421	Perfect linear correlation	MAE = 0.745 MASE = 0.958 RMSE = 0.979 R2 = 0.7400	MAE = 1.749 MASE = 4.602 RMSE = 2.1453 R2 = 0.0295	MAE = 134.739 MASE = 24557.9 5 RMSE = 156.709 R2 = −0.0675
Temperature	MAE = 0.839 MASE = 1.934 RMSE = 1.391 R2 = −0.0447	MAE = 18.473 MASE = 1451.83 RMSE = 38.102 R2 = 0.1318	MAE = 2.618 MASE = 11.78 RMSE = 3.43 R2 = 0.572	Perfect linear correlation	MAE = 1.564 MASE = 3.69 RMSE = 1.922 R2 = 0.0255	MAE = 139.68 MASE = 26889.48 RMSE = 163.980 R2 = −0.00359
Soilmoisture	MAE = 0.886 MASE = 2.831 RMSE = 1.682 R2 = −0.037	MAE = 18.183 MASE = 1149.82 RMSE = 33.909 R2 = −0.0549	MAE = 4.1329 MASE = 30.32 RMSE = 5.5065 R2 = 0.0070	MAE = 1.1566 MASE = 3.419 RMSE = 1.84 R2 = −0.0083	Perfect linear correlation	MAE = 136.775 MASE = 24782.89 RMSE = 157.42 R2 = 0.0698
Water level	MAE = 0.5868 MASE = 1.542 RMSE = 1.241 R2 = 0.3133	MAE = 17.654 MASE = 1008.07 RMSE = 31.750 R2 = −0.04008	MAE = 3.581 MASE = 24.307 RMSE = 4.930 R2 = 0.1196	MAE = 1.176 MASE = 3.361 RMSE = 1.83 R2 = 0.0380	MAE = 1.2847 MASE = 2.611 RMSE = 1.616 R2 = 0.368	Perfect linear correlation

From Table 11, it can be inferred that water level and pH are the most correlated parameters in the growth phase of the experiment as MAE = 0.586. This means, with a given water level, we can predict the pH required for a good yield. The parameters that cannot be correlated are temperature and water level as the MAE = 139.68, this means that the value of Water level cannot be predicted with a given temperature.

Table 12. Support vector regression between parameters for harvesting phase of coriander plant growth

Parameter vs Parameter	PH	Sunlight	Humidity	Temperature	Soilmoisture	Water level
PH	Perfect linear correlation	MAE = 14.519 MASE = 1121.40 RMSE = 33.487 R2 = −0.055	MAE = 3.750 MASE = 23.179 RMSE = 4.814 R2 = 0.2572	MAE = 0.8486 MASE = 1.7209 RMSE = 1.311 R2 = 0.0536	MAE = 1.2121 MASE = 2.518 RMSE = 1.586 R2 = 0.0438	MAE = 109.77 MASE = 21901.17 RMSE = 147.99 R2 = −0.1792
Sunlight	MAE = 0.975 MASE = 1.782 RMSE = 1.334 R2 = 0.0502	Perfect linear correlation	MAE = 3.642 MASE = 23.84 RMSE = 4.883 R2 = 0.2922	MAE = 0.5587 MASE = 0.9602 RMSE = 0.979 R2 = 0.537	MAE = 1.033 MASE = 1.731 RMSE = 1.315 R2 = −0.109	MAE = 110.02 MASE = 21459.37 RMSE = 146.49 R2 = 0.334
Humidity	MAE = 0.733 MASE = 1.0997 RMSE = 1.0487 R2 = 0.1170	MAE = 15.693 MASE = 1416.608 RMSE = 37.637 R2 = 0.1004	Perfect linear correlation	MAE = 0.6907 MASE = 1.549 RMSE = 1.244 R2 = 0.144	MAE = 1.197 MASE = 2.227 RMSE = 1.492 R2 = −0.087	MAE = 112.208 MASE = 21545.41 RMSE = 146.783 R2 = −0.1230

(*continued*)

Table 12. (*continued*)

Parameter vs Parameter	PH	Sunlight	Humidity	Temperature	Soilmoisture	Water level
Temperature	MAE = 0.848 MASE = 1.307 RMSE = 1.143 R2 = −0.0404	MAE = 7.830 MASE = 209.74 RMSE = 14.482 R2 = 0.491	MAE = 2.654 MASE = 13.02 RMSE = 3.609 R2 = 0.3560	Perfect linear correlation	MAE = 0.9160 MASE = 1.190 RMSE = 1.090 R2 = −0.012	MAE = 103.405 MASE = 18617.395 RMSE = 136.445 R2 = −0.0513
Soilmoisture	MAE = 0.908 MASE = 1.576 RMSE = 1.255 R2 = 0.0711	MAE = 14.502 MASE = 1074.906 RMSE = 32.785 R2 = −0.0437	MAE = 4.892 MASE = 38.307 RMSE = 6.189 R2 = 0.0917	MAE = 1.027 MASE = 2.190 RMSE = 1.480 R2 = −0.0648	Perfect linear correlation	MAE = 117.428 MASE = 22258.28 RMSE = 149.192 R2 = 0.1749
Water level	MAE = 0.868 MASE = 2.479 RMSE = 1.574 R2 = 0.069	MAE = 13.670 MASE = 525.301 RMSE = 22.919 R2 = −0.1050	MAE = 3.9546 MASE = 25.571 RMSE = 5.056 R2 = 0.3047	MAE = 0.785 MASE = 1.084 RMSE = 1.041 R2 = −0.011	MAE = 0.9191 MASE = 1.329 RMSE = 1.152 R2 = 0.298	Perfect linear correlation

From Table 12, it can be inferred that sunlight and temperature are the most correlated parameters in the harvesting phase of the experiment as MAE = 0.558. This means, with a given luminous intensity, we can predict the temperature required for a good yield. The parameters that cannot be correlated are soil moisture and water level as the MAE = 117.428, this means that the value of Water level cannot be predicted with a soil moisture.

Table 13. Support vector regression between parameters for full phase of coriander plant growth

Parameter vs Parameter	PH	Sunlight	Humidity	Temperature	Soilmoisture	Water level
PH	Perfect linear correlation	MAE = 18.38 MASE = 1347.984 RMSE = 36.71 R2 = −0.0432	MAE = 3.538 MASE = 22.984 RMSE = 4.7942 R2 = 0.0380	MAE = 1.002 MASE = 2.368 RMSE = 1.539 R2 = 0.189	MAE = 1.506 MASE = 3.971 RMSE = 1.992 R2 = 0.1733	MAE = 127.77. MASE = 22839.3 RMSE = 151.12 R2 = 0.288
Sunlight	MAE = 0.9430 MASE = 2.927 RMSE = 1.711 R2 = −0.00975	Perfect linear correlation	MAE = 3.621 MASE = 23.651 RMSE = 4.8632 R2 = 0.21463	MAE = 1.111 MASE = 2.539 RMSE = 1.593 R2 = 0.3130	MAE = 1.9406 MASE = 5.305 RMSE = 2.3033 R2 = −0.0322	MAE = 162.013 MASE = 31499.0 RMSE = 177.479 R2 = 0.0218
Humidity	MAE = 0.9039 MASE = 1.6860 RMSE = 1.298 R2 = −0.0062	MAE = 18.2066 MASE = 1258.105 RMSE = 35.469 R2 = 0.0738	Perfect linear correlation	MAE = 0.974 MASE = 1.814 RMSE = 1.3470 R2 = 0.486	MAE = 1.715 MASE = 4.422 RMSE = 2.102 R2 = 0.0019	MAE = 161.61 MASE = 30181.06 RMSE = 173.72 R2 = 0.057
Temperature	MAE = 0.898 MASE = 2.785 RMSE = 1.668 R2 = 0.0656	MAE = 18.518 MASE = 1583.68 RMSE = 39.109 R2 = 0.115	MAE = 2.86 MASE = 13.61 RMSE = 3.689 R2 = 0.4670	Perfect linear correlation	MAE = 1.609 MASE = 4.139 RMSE = 2.034 R2 = 0.0995	MAE = 136.567 MASE = 26169.03 RMSE = 161.76 R2 = 0.148
Soilmoisture	MAE = 0.8068 MASE = 1.744 RMSE = 1.320 R2 = 0.0942	MAE = 20.280 MASE = 1555.81 RMSE = 39.443 R2 = −0.055	MAE = 3.8521 MASE = 27.5794 RMSE = 5.251 R2 = 0.0213	MAE = 1.179 MASE = 3.128 RMSE = 1.768 R2 = 0.0436	Perfect linear correlation	MAE = 110.411 MASE = 21951.64 RMSE = 148.160 R2 = 0.312
Water level	MAE = 0.682 MASE = 1.331 RMSE = 1.153 R2 = 0.388	MAE = 19.253 MASE = 1462.55 RMSE = 38.243 R2 = −0.0474	MAE = 3.608 MASE = 25.069 RMSE = 5.0069 R2 = −0.00369	MAE = 1.0911 MASE = 2.591 RMSE = 1.609 R2 = 0.1359	MAE = 1.237 MASE = 2.696 RMSE = 1.642 R2 = 0.4985	Perfect linear correlation

From Table 13, it can be inferred that water level and pH are the most correlated parameters in the full phase analysis of the experiment as MAE = 0.682. This means, with a given water level, we can predict the pH required for a good yield. The parameters that cannot be correlated are sunlight and water level as the MAE = 162.013, this means that the value of Water level cannot be predicted with a given luminous intensity.

6.3 Predictive Analysis of Parameters Using Decision Tree Regression

Table 14. Decision tree regression between parameters for initial phase of coriander plant growth

Parameter vs Parameter	PH	Sunlight	Humidity	Temperature	Soilmoisture	Water level
PH	Perfect linear correlation	MAE = 25.117 MASE = 1570.68 RMSE = 39.631 R2 = −0.0493	MAE = 3.4989 MASE = 21.020 RMSE = 4.584 R2 = 0.262	MAE = 1.085 MASE = 2.704 RMSE = 1.644 R2 = −0.415	MAE = 0.952 MASE = 1.3727 RMSE = 1.171 R2 =−0.1289	MAE = 11.330 MASE = 266.11 RMSE = 16.312 R2 = −0.303
Sunlight	MAE = 0.4213 MASE = 0.329 RMSE = 0.573 R2 = −0.227	Perfect linear correlation	MAE = 3.117 MASE = 16.69 RMSE = 4.085 R2 = 0.216	MAE = 0.637 MASE = 1.028 RMSE = 1.014 R2 = 0.5450	MAE = 1.126 MASE = 2.266 RMSE = 1.505 R2 = −0.0655	MAE = 0.996 MASE = 1.558 RMSE = 1.248 R2 = −0.3035
Humidity	MAE = 0.408 MASE = 0.292 RMSE = 0.541 R2 = −0.365	MAE = 36.44 MASE = 4653.88 RMSE = 68.219 R2 = −0.3042	Perfect linear correlation	MAE = 0.9103 MASE = 1.477 RMSE = 1.215 R2 = 0.174.	MAE = 1.0399 MASE = 2.304 RMSE = 1.517 R2 =−0.2165	MAE = 11.833 MASE = 332.31 RMSE = 18.22 R2 = −1.0522
Temperature	MAE = 0.389 MASE = 0.280 RMSE = 0.529 R2 = −0.0033	MAE = 23.802 MASE = 2150.406 RMSE = 46.37 R2 = 0.322	MAE = 2.903 MASE = 11.880 RMSE = 3.446 R2 = 0.410	Perfect linear correlation	MAE = 1.1320 MASE = 1.858 RMSE = 1.363 R2 = −0.433	MAE = 8.271 MASE = 122.69 RMSE = 11.07 R2 = 0.303
Soilmoisture	MAE = 0.406 MASE = 0.294 RMSE = 0.542 R2 = = −0.0160	MAE = 28.44 MASE = 2407.91 RMSE = 49.070 R2 = −0.0055	MAE = 3.018 MASE = 16.75 RMSE = 4.093 R2 = −0.020	MAE = 0.7735 MASE = 1.104 RMSE = 1.050 R2 = −0.0059	Perfect linear correlation	MAE = 11.341 MASE = 217.46 RMSE = 14.74 R2 = −0.205
Water level	MAE = 0.334 MASE = 0.218 RMSE = 0.4672 R2 = −0.129	MAE = 21.03 MASE = 1526.93 RMSE = 39.075 R2 = 0.2402	MAE = 3.323 MASE = 18.834 RMSE = 4.339 R2 = 0.05843	MAE = 0.919 MASE = 2.70294 RMSE = 1.5006 R2 = 0.0072	MAE = 1.0835 MASE = 1.879 RMSE = 1.3707 R2 = −0.5531	Perfect linear correlation

From Table 14, it can be inferred that water level and pH are the most correlated parameters in the initial phase of the experiment as MAE = 0.334. This means, with a given water level, we can predict the pH required for a good yield. The parameters that cannot be correlated are water level and humidity as the MAE = 11.833, this means that the value of Water level cannot be predicted with a given humidity.

Table 15. Decision tree regression between parameters for growing phase of coriander plant growth

Parameter vs Parameter	PH	Sunlight	Humidity	Temperature	Soilmoisture	Water level
PH	Perfect linear correlation	MAE = 23.487 MASE = 1556.330 RMSE = 39.450 R2 = −0.133	MAE = 4.4440 MASE = 33.518 RMSE = 5.789 R2 = −0.066	MAE = 1.067 MASE = 2.294 RMSE = 1.514 R2 = 0.0555	MAE = 1.662 MASE = 4.845 RMSE = 2.201 R2 = 0.0173	MAE = 86.23 MASE = 14214.92 RMSE = 119.22 R2 = 0.422
Sunlight	MAE = 1.210 MASE = 5.287 RMSE = 2.299 R2 = −0.220	Perfect linear correlation	MAE = 3.764 MASE = 24.775 RMSE = 4.977 R2 = 0.1022	MAE = 0.902 MASE = 2.036 RMSE = 2.036 R2 = 0.3970	MAE = 1.852 MASE = 5.100 RMSE = 2.258 R2 = −0.126	MAE = 140.63 MASE = 28070.58 RMSE = 167.54 R2 = −0.131
Humidity	MAE = 1.085 MASE = 2.475 RMSE = 1.57 R2 = −0.264	MAE = 19.74 MASE = 1059.71 RMSE = 32.55 R2 = −0.2786	Perfect linear correlation	MAE = 0.9107 MASE = 1.569 RMSE = 1.252 R2 = 0.438	MAE = 1.816 MASE = 5.153 RMSE = 2.270 R2 = −0.4041	MAE = 142.944 MASE = 32162.22 RMSE = 179.338 R2 = −0.161
Temperature	MAE = 0.947 MASE = 1.723 RMSE = 1.312 R2 = −0.142	MAE = 15.279 MASE = 11.047 RMSE = 28.127 R2 = 0.2953	MAE = 2.512 MASE = 11.047 RMSE = 3.323 R2 = 0.475	Perfect linear correlation	MAE = 1.775 MASE = 4.988 RMSE = 2.233 R2 = −0.105	MAE = 134.80 MASE = 25756.83 RMSE = 160.48 R2 = −0.010
Soilmoisture	MAE = 1.0263 MASE = 4.360 RMSE = 2.088 R2 = −0.0082	MAE = 21.63 MASE = 1319.71 RMSE = 36.32 R2 = −0.0284	MAE = 3.285 MASE = 19.059 RMSE = 4.365 R2 = −0.0023	MAE = 1.063 MASE = 2.231 RMSE = 1.493 R2 = 0.0132	Perfect linear correlation	MAE = 121.68 MASE = 22438.58 RMSE = 149.79 R2 = 0.1508
Water level	MAE = 0.698 MASE = 1.371 RMSE = 1.171 R2 = 0.0499	MAE = 22.549 MASE = 1676.62 RMSE = 40.94 R2 = −0.261	MAE = 3.063 MASE = 20.044 RMSE = 4.477 R2 = 0.2023	MAE = 1.067 MASE = 3.0071 RMSE = 1.734 R2 = 0.09765	MAE = 1.528 MASE = 3.8184 RMSE = 1.9540 R2 = 0.0723	Perfect linear correlation

From Table 15, it can be inferred that water level and pH are the most correlated parameters in the growth phase of the experiment as MAE = 0.698. This means, with a given water level, we can predict the pH required for a good yield. The parameters that cannot be correlated are water level and humidity as the MAE = 142.944, this means that the value of Water level cannot be predicted with a given humidity.

Table 16. Decision tree regression between parameters for harvesting phase of coriander plant growth

Parameter vs Parameter	PH	Sunlight	Humidity	Temperature	Soilmoisture	Water level
PH	Perfect linear correlation	MAE = 22.732 MASE = 2045.76 RMSE = 45.230 R2 = −0.0708	MAE = 4.569 MASE = 45.141 RMSE = 6.718 R2 = −0.4399	MAE = 0.882 MASE = 2.502 RMSE = 1.581 R2 = −0.225	MAE = 1.471 MASE = 4.134 RMSE = 2.0333 R2 = −0.8793	MAE = 83.55 MASE = 18340.29 RMSE = 135.42 R2 = −0.069
Sunlight	MAE = 1.146 MASE = 2.743 RMSE = 1.656 R2 = −0.0261	Perfect linear correlation	MAE = 3.395 MASE = 21.554 RMSE = 4.642 R2 = 0.414	MAE = 0.6377 MASE = 1.308 RMSE = 1.143 R2 = 0.498	MAE = 1.5740 MASE = 1.307 RMSE = 1.959 R2 = −0.453	MAE = 129.51 MASE = 25884.24 RMSE = 160.885 R2 = 0.4367

(*continued*)

Table 16. (*continued*)

Parameter vs Parameter	PH	Sunlight	Humidity	Temperature	Soilmoisture	Water level
Humidity	MAE = 1.062 MASE = 2.186 RMSE = 1.478 R2 = −0.724	MAE = 15.92 MASE = 505.16 RMSE = 22.47 R2 = 0.59	Perfect linear correlation	MAE = 0.841 MASE = 2.206 RMSE = 1.485 R2 = −0.262	MAE = 1.522 MASE = 3.722 RMSE = 1.929 R2 = −0.926	MAE = 87.022 MASE = 15484.1 RMSE = 124.43 R2 = 0.135
Temperature	MAE = 0.723 MASE = 0.985 RMSE = 0.992 R2 = 0.4802	MAE = 7.183 MASE = 198.86 RMSE = 14.102 R2 = 0.787	MAE = 3.359 MASE = 23.251 RMSE = 4.822 R2 = 0.342	Perfect linear correlation	MAE = 1.123 MASE = 1.954 RMSE = 1.397 R2 = −0.4325	MAE = 93.27 MASE = 15132.8 RMSE = 123.01 R2 = −0.0493
Soilmoisture	MAE = 1.046 MASE = 1.781 RMSE = 1.33 R2 = = −0.018	MAE = 28.62 MASE = 2623.48 RMSE = 51.220 R2 = −0.0750	MAE = 4.297 MASE = 29.772 RMSE = 5.456 R2 = −0.190	MAE = 1.060 MASE = 1.905 RMSE = 1.380 R2 = −0.3879	Perfect linear correlation	MAE = 117.64 MASE = 22102.11 RMSE = 148.66 R2 = −0.1676
Water level	MAE = 0.7400 MASE = 1.444 RMSE = 1.201 R2 = 0.158	MAE = 22.803 MASE = 1843.464 RMSE = 42.935 R2 = −0.616	MAE = 4.103 MASE = 32.056 RMSE = 5.661 R2 = 0.0454	MAE = 1.00740 MASE = 2.8656 RMSE = 1.6928 R2 = −0.9196	MAE = 1.197 MASE = 2.6819 RMSE = 1.6376 R2 = −0.33059	Perfect linear correlation

From Table 16, it can be inferred that sunlight and temperature are the most correlated parameters in the harvesting phase of the experiment as MAE = 0.6377. This means, with a given temperature, we can predict the luminous intensity required for a good yield. The parameters that cannot be correlated are water level and sunlight as the MAE = 129.51, this means that the value of Water level cannot be predicted with a given sunlight.

Table 17. Decision tree regression between parameters for full phase of coriander plant growth

Parameter vs Parameter	PH	Sunlight	Humidity	Temperature	Soilmoisture	Water level
PH	Perfect linear correlation	MAE = 23.667 MASE = 26.197 RMSE = 39.67 R2 = −0.0871	MAE = 3.77 MASE = 3.1117 RMSE = 5.118 R2 = 0.0070	MAE = 1.162 MASE = 1.764 RMSE = 1.764 R2 = 0.0277	MAE = 1.375 MASE = 3.4744 RMSE = 1.863 R2 = 0.2968	MAE = 70.152 MASE = 13362.83 RMSE = 115.597 R2 = 0.589
Sunlight	MAE = 1.0190 MASE = 2.469 RMSE = 1.571 R2 = −0.1476	Perfect linear correlation	MAE = 3.674 MASE = 22.97 RMSE = 4.7930 R2 = 0.171	MAE = 1.0661 MASE = 2.232 RMSE = 1.494 R2 = 0.2434	MAE = 1.857 MASE = 5.101 RMSE = 2.258 R2 = −0.155	MAE = 163.11 MASE = 34396.27 RMSE = 185.46 R2 = −0.0659
Humidity	MAE = 1.032 MASE = 1.956 RMSE = 1.398 R2 = −0.219	MAE = 22.217 MASE = 1540.602 RMSE = 39.250 R2 = 0.1037	Perfect linear correlation	MAE = 0.961 MASE = 1.620 RMSE = 1.272 R2 = 0.3378	MAE = 1.906 MASE = 5.624 RMSE = 2.371 R2 = −0.1596	MAE = 162.59 MASE = 36533.3 RMSE = 191.13 R2 = −0.152
Temperature	MAE = 0.911 MASE = 1.703 RMSE = 1.305 R2 = 0.11710	MAE = 17.664 MASE = 1005.81 RMSE = 31.714 R2 = 0.0440	MAE = 3.0675 MASE = 16.238 RMSE = 4.0296 R2 = 0.3001	Perfect linear correlation	MAE = 1.650 MASE = 4.224 RMSE = 2.055 R2 = 0.0587	MAE = 147.269 MASE = 29019.5 RMSE = 170.351 R2 = 0.1299

(*continued*)

Table 17. (*continued*)

Parameter vs Parameter	PH	Sunlight	Humidity	Temperature	Soilmoisture	Water level
Soilmoisture	MAE = 0.9751 MASE = 2.7447 RMSE = 1.656 R2 = 0.0873	MAE = 20.854 MASE = 1216.04 RMSE = 34.87 R2 = 0.00587	MAE = 3.995 MASE = 28.318 RMSE = 5.321 R2 = −0.0553	MAE = 1.0834 MASE = 2.619 RMSE = 1.618 R2 = 0.109	Perfect linear correlation	MAE = 112.74 MASE = 20885.92 RMSE = 144.519 R2 = 0.3583
Water level	MAE = 0.706 MASE = 1.328 RMSE = 1.152 R2 = 0.210	MAE = 23.019 MASE = 1913.38 RMSE = 43.74 R2 = 0.0553	MAE = 3.665 MASE = 25.972 RMSE = 5.096 R2 = 0.0735	MAE = 1.1366 MASE = 3.302 RMSE = 1.8172 R2 = −0.2404	MAE = 1.253 MASE = 2.836 RMSE = 1.684 R2 = 0.4258	Perfect linear correlation

From Table 17, it can be inferred that water level and pH are the most correlated parameters in the full phase analysis of the experiment as MAE = 0.706. This means, with a given water level, we can predict the pH required for a good yield. The parameters that cannot be correlated are water level and sunlight as the MAE = 163.11, this means that the value of Water level cannot be predicted with a given luminous intensity.

7   Conclusion and Future Works

In conclusion, our whole work can be split into two main parts. The first one being the growth of plants and creation of data sets, in this we have grown the crops and taken the data with the help of sensors. In this aspect, there is minimal automation. The dataset is then created by taking the data and cleaning it to make sure that the anomalies are removed. With the help of this data set, we then move onto the second phase of the work. The second phase of this work is processing of the data set created and correlating the data to establish the best scenario for plant growth and good yield. With the help of Linear Regression, Support vector regression and Decision Tree Regression, we have established the parameters which are best correlated. For the work that can be done to further the progress done by us is to fully automate the system. With the correlation achieved by us, the parameters can be used to know the ambient conditions required when a certain parameter is fixed and cannot be altered in any way possible especially in the city environment in countries like India.

References

1. Nichani, A., Saha, S., Upadhyay, T., Ramya, A., Tolia, M.: Data acquisition and actuation for aquaponics using IoT. In: 2018 3rd IEEE International Conference on Recent Trends in Electronics, Information & Communication Technology (RTEICT), pp. 46–51 (2018). https://doi.org/10.1109/RTEICT42901.2018.9012260
2. Srinidhi, H.K., Shreenidhi, H.S., Vishnu, G.S.: Smart hydroponics system integrating with IoT and machine learning algorithm. In: 2020 International Conference on Recent Trends on Electronics, Information, Communication & Technology (RTEICT), pp. 261–264 (2020). https://doi.org/10.1109/RTEICT49044.2020.9315549

3. Srivani, P., Devi, Y.C., Manjula, S.H.: A controlled environment agriculture with hydroponics: variants, parameters, methodologies and challenges for smart farming. In: 2019 Fifteenth International Conference on Information Processing (ICINPRO), pp. 1–8 (2019). https://doi.org/10.1109/ICInPro47689.2019.9092043

4. Joshitha, C., Kanakaraja, P., Kumar, K.S., Akanksha, P., Satish, G.: An eye on hydroponics: the IoT initiative. In: 2021 7th International Conference on Electrical Energy Systems (ICEES), pp. 553–557 (2021). https://doi.org/10.1109/ICEES51510.2021.9383694

5. Gertphol, S., Chulaka, P., Changmai, T.: Predictive models for lettuce quality from Internet of Things-based hydroponic farm. In: 2018 22nd International Computer Science and Engineering Conference (ICSEC), pp. 1–5 (2018). https://doi.org/10.1109/ICSEC.2018.8712676

6. Jaisankar, S., Nalini, P., Rubigha, K.K.: A study on IoT based low-cost smart kit for coconut farm management. In: 2020 Fourth International Conference on I-SMAC (IoT in Social, Mobile, Analytics and Cloud) (I-SMAC), pp. 161–165 (2020). https://doi.org/10.1109/I-SMAC49090.2020.9243486

7. Farooq, M.S., Riaz, S., Abid, A., Abid, K., Naeem, M.A.: A survey on the role of IoT in agriculture for the implementation of smart farming. IEEE Access 7, 156237–156271 (2019). https://doi.org/10.1109/ACCESS.2019.2949703

8. Islam, N., Ray, B., Pasandideh, F.: IoT based smart farming: are the LPWAN technologies suitable for remote communication?. In: 2020 IEEE International Conference on Smart Internet of Things (SmartIoT), pp. 270–276 (2020).https://doi.org/10.1109/SmartIoT49966.2020.00048

9. Chaikhamwang, S., Janthajirakowit, C., Fongmanee, S.: IoT for smart farm: a case study of the fertilizer mixer prototype. In: 2021 Joint International Conference on Digital Arts, Media and Technology with ECTI Northern Section Conference on Electrical, Electronics, Computer and Telecommunication Engineering, pp. 136–139 (2021). https://doi.org/10.1109/ECTIDAMTNCON51128.2021.9425708

10. Syed, F.K., Paul, A., Kumar, A., Cherukuri, J.: Low-cost IoT+ML design for smart farming with multiple applications. In: 2019 10th International Conference on Computing, Communication and Networking Technologies (ICCCNT), pp. 1–5 (2019). https://doi.org/10.1109/ICCCNT45670.20

Blockchain-Aided Keyword Search over Encrypted Data in Cloud

Uma Sankararao Varri[✉]

GITAM Institute of Technology, GITAM Deemed to be University,
Visakhapatnam, Andhra Pradesh, India
uvarri@gitam.edu

Abstract. Attribute-based keyword search (ABKS) achieved significant attention for data privacy and fine-grained access control of outsourced cloud data. However, most of the existing ABKS schemes are designed based on a semi-honest and curious cloud storage system in which the search fairness between two parties becomes questionable. Hence, it is vital to building a protocol that provides mutual trust between the cloud and its users. This paper proposes a blockchain-aided keyword search over encrypted data, which achieves search fairness between the cloud and its users using Ethereum blockchain and smart contracts. Additionally, the system accomplishes fine-grained access control, limiting access to the data to only those who have been given permission. Besides, the scheme allows multi keyword search by the users. The security analysis shows that our scheme is indistinguishable against chosen-plaintext attack and other malicious attacks. The performance analysis shows that the scheme is efficient.

Keywords: Searchable encryption · Blockchain · Smart contract · Access control

1 Introduction

Information technology is escalating with every piece of data outsourced into the cloud. Even though the cloud provides many benefits, most organizations still hesitate to outsource their data to the cloud. This is because of sensitive data, including account information, credit information, debit information, transaction information, and contracts. Alongside, providing the rights to only authorized users to access the outsourced data is a challenging problem. Hence, protecting the privacy of the outsourced data and providing access control is essential. Traditional encryption achieves data privacy, but it is computationally inefficient when searching encrypted outsourced data.

Searchable encryption (SE) is one of the solutions to search over ciphertext without decrypting it. In past decade, several SE schemes were proposed based on traditional searchable symmetric encryption (SSE) [1,2] and searchable public-key encryption (SPE) [3,4]. Although SSE and SPE schemes achieve

© The Author(s), under exclusive license to Springer Nature Switzerland AG 2023
I. Woungang et al. (Eds.): ANTIC 2022, CCIS 1797, pp. 331–348, 2023.
https://doi.org/10.1007/978-3-031-28180-8_22

data privacy, they don't provide fine-grained access control (FGAC). Notably, in real-world applications, every file may have access privileges. For example, in the banking industry, some files are accessible by the manager and the deputy manager, and some are accessible by the manager and employees.

Attribute-based keyword search (ABKS) [5] achieves searching on ciphertext along with FGAC. The users whose attributes match the policy embedded with the file can access the file. In ABKS, the policy is created with all possible attributes of the system users. ABKS are divided into two types, based on where this policy is embedded: ciphertext-policy ABKS (CP-ABKS) and key-policy ABKS (KP-ABKS). In KP-ABKS, the policy is embedded in the user's secret key, and in CP-ABKS, the policy is embedded in the ciphertext.

CP-ABKS is widely studied because the control over access policy is with the data owner, whereas in KP-ABKS, this control is given to the third-party authority. There are various authors proposed CP-ABKS [5–19] schemes with different functionalities. However, the existing CP-ABKS schemes lack search fairness: The cloud may not be honest in searching and may return incorrect results by sending the previously searched results and claiming that the search is genuine. On the other hand, the user may be malicious or dishonest with the search results. In both scenarios, either participant is not fair to the system. Therefore, the system should establish search fairness to justify both parties.

Blockchain technology is a promising solution with built-in features like verifiability, unforgeability, anonymity, and tamper-free. There are few Blockchain-based searchable encryption (BBSE) [20–22] schemes that have been proposed to achieve search fairness. Nevertheless, it is an open research topic to improve efficiency and security. Hence, designing a blockchain-aided ABKS scheme with efficient algorithmic construction is essential.

1.1   Major Contributions

This paper presents a scheme named "Blockchain-aided attribute-based keyword search over encrypted data in the cloud". The following are the major contributions:

- **Fairness:** Our scheme uses the Ethereum blockchain and smart contracts (SM) to accomplish fairness between the cloud and its users. SM rewards the cloud after verifying the results returned by the cloud. Maintaining third-party authority is also a solution for verifying the search results. However, there is more probability for the third-party authority to be malicious. Hence, we replaced the third-party authority with blockchain technology to verify the results fairly.
- **Authorized multi-keyword search:** Our scheme enables multi-keyword search. It returns the most relevant search results with multiple search keywords compared to a single keyword search. Moreover, our scheme allows only authorized users to decrypt the encrypted files by providing FGAC. Here, FGAC states that the users whose attributes are satisfied with the predefined policy can only access the data in plaintext form.

- **Security:** Our scheme is indistinguishable against chosen-plaintext attack (IND-CPA) under Decisional Bilinear Diffie-Hellman (DBDH) Assumption. Further, we show that our scheme is secure by considering different security measures such as fairness and soundness.
- **Performance:** We experimented with all the algorithms designed for the proposed scheme and showed that our scheme is efficient. Further, we simulate and study the performances of different smart contracts used in our scheme.

1.2 Paper Organization

The remaining sections are organized as follows: This article's related work is presented in Sect. 2. Preliminaries are provided in Sect. 3. The system model is explained in Sect. 4. Section 5 explains the detailed scheme construction. Section 6 presents the security analysis. Section 7 presents the performance analysis. We concluded our scheme in Sect. 8.

2   Related Work

Searchable Encryption: SE was first introduced by Song et al. [1] to achieve searching on encrypted data without decryption. It allows only a single_keyword_search on the outsourced ciphertext index. After years, Cao et al. [23] presented a scheme to support multi-keyword search by using inner-product-similarity to find the similarity between the number of query keywords and the encrypted index. Further, different authors put forward the schemes based on SSE [2] and SPE [3,4]. However, these schemes do not provide FGAC.

Attribute-Based Keyword Search: ABKS allows searching on ciphertext along with FGAC. The data owner defines the policy containing user attributes. Hence, the users whose attributes match the policy can access the data. Wang et al. [5] proposed a scheme based on CP-ABKS, in which the data owner creates the policy. Then, Sun et al. [6] proposed a scheme that supports file-level authentication in a multi-user, multi-owner setting. The scheme also achieves verifiability along with conjunctive keyword search. Multiple approaches for assisting hidden policy-based search were put out by Chaudhari and Das [7,8]. [7] maintains receiver anonymity and data privacy when a user searches with keywords.

A multi-keyword searchable CP-ABKS technique was proposed by Sun et al. [9] to ensure the veracity of search results. The system protects against targeted plaintext and keyword assaults. Li et al. [10] suggested an effective method for building an index, and multi-keyword search is accomplished via secure inner product computing. A multi-keyword searchable CP-ABKS technique was given by Miao et al. [11], and user revocation was also achieved. Later, a CP-ABKS strategy for lightweight devices was presented by [12,18]. To lessen the impact on devices with resource constraints, the schemes have adopted fog architecture. Then, concerned about the significant computation burdens imposed on end users by ABKS methods on devices with limited resources, Zhang et al. [13] developed a lightweight technique. Since the earlier systems only used a single keyword, Zhang et al. [14] determined that they have computational and bandwidth issues. Then an ABKS system with multiple keywords allowing search result verifiability was proposed. Zhou et al. [15] presented a CP-ABKS scheme supporting multi-keyword search. Later, numerous other schemes based on ABKS were presented [16,17,19] by including various capabilities. These solutions, however, do not support search fairness between the user and the cloud.

Blockchain-Based Searchable Encryption: In recent times, verifying the search results' correctness and integrity got significant attention in searchable encryption since the results are received from a semi-trusted cloud. Hu et al. [20] constructed a privacy-preserving decentralized search scheme to achieve assured search results and not worry about potential attacks. The scheme stores the encrypted index in the smart contract such that the index is immutable. Then, Li et al. [21] integrated SSE and blockchain technologies to ensure fair payment between the user and the cloud. In their scheme, the blockchain sits between both parties and ensures fair payment by verifying that both users and the cloud are not malicious. Later, Chen et al. [22] proposed a scheme using a blockchain-based health-record sharing scheme on decentralized storage. The index for accessing the health record is created based on complex Boolean expressions. However, these schemes [20–22] do not support multi-keyword search and FGAC. We present a blockchain-aided ABKS scheme to achieve multi-keyword search, data privacy, keyword privacy, FGAC, and search fairness.

Notations: Table 1 shows the main notations/symbols used in this article.

3   Preliminaries

3.1   Bilinear Map

"Let G_1 and G_2 are multiplicative groups, Consider the prime p and generator g. The bilinear map $e : G_1 \times G_1 \to G_2$ must satisfy the following conditions: 1) $e(g^a, g^b) = e(g, g)^{ab}$, 2) $e(g, g) \neq 1$, and 3) It should be efficiently computable."

3.2   Access Policy

Definition 2: "The participants $\{P_1, P_2, \ldots, P_n\}$, a monotone collection $A \subseteq 2^{\{P_1, P_2, \ldots, P_n\}}$, $\forall B, C$ if $B \in A$ and $B \subseteq C$ then $C \in A$. Access structure A contains the subsets of the set $\{P_1, P_2, \ldots, P_n\}$. The collection in A contains a set of authorized participants and the rest are unauthorized."

3.3   Linear Secret Sharing Scheme (LSSS)

LSSS [24] Π with participants $\{P_1, P_2, \ldots, P_n\}$ is linear if it satisfies:

1) "The shares of each entity forms a vector over Z_p,
2) There exist a matrix M of size $l \times n$ and mapping $\rho(i)$ from $\{1, \ldots, l\}$ to P for LSSS Π. Select $v = \{s, v_2, \ldots v_n\} \in Z_p$ random where s is shared as secret. Then $M.v$ is the vector with l shares of the secret s according to Π. The share $\chi_i = M_i.v$ related to the party $\rho(i)$.

Let Π be an LSSS for a policy $\mathbb{A}$. Let authorized set $S \in \mathbb{A}$ and $I \subset \{1, 2, \ldots, l\}$ then $I = \{i : \psi(i) \in S\}$. If χ_i is a valid share of secret s based on Π then there exists a constant set $\{\omega_i \in Z_p\}_{i \in I}$ in which $\sum_{i \in I} \omega_i \chi_i = s$ and no such constant exists in the case of an unauthorized set."

Table 1. Symbols

Symbol	Meaning
$\mathbb{A}$	A matrix of size $l \times n$
ρ	A mapping function from each row of a matrix $\mathbb{A}$
U_{attr}	User attribute set
$\cup$	Universal attribute set
n	Number of universal attributes
H_1	Hash function
e	Bilinear pairing
rl	Revocation list
U_{id}	Users' Ethereum public key
kw	Keyword set
I	Index

3.4 Blockchain and Smart Contracts

Blockchain is a shared and distributed ledger that stores all the transactions orderly and permanently. A unique ID identifies each transaction in the blockchain. An efficient hash algorithm can compute this unique ID. The typical form of the blockchain is shown in Fig. 1. Each block is divided into header, Merkle hash root, and transactions. The header contains the version information, timestamp, nonce, and the previous block's hash. Merkle hash root contains the root of the Merkle tree. The transaction part contains all the transaction information in the present block. The hash algorithm guarantees the immutability of the transactions in each block and ensures that blocks in the blockchain cannot tamper by attackers.

Ethereum, Ether, and Gas: Ethereum is a decentralized blockchain that allows the writing of smart contracts. Bitcoin uses predefined operations, whereas Ethereum allows users to write and execute complex operations. Along with cryptocurrency, Ethereum has many decentralized blockchain applications. Ethereum allows users to execute their smart contracts. Two types of accounts on the Ethereum platform: contract accounts and externally owned accounts (EOA). External users' private keys are managed by

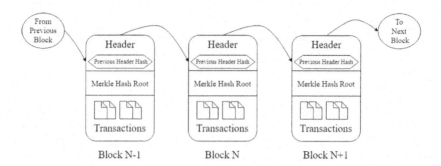

Fig. 1. Blockchain structure

EOA. Both these accounts are a 20-byte hexadecimal string, for example. 0x67b46A60cb74B3914d9Ed349722e47027aAE6c73. In Ethereum, Ether is used as a currency/token, and Ethereum Virtual Machine (EVM) is used to implement smart contracts. Every operation in Ethereum consumes a unit of gas. Gas can be used as a unit to pay the transaction fee.

Proof of Work (PoW): The process followed by the PoW is called mining; the nodes in this process are known as miners. In PoW, all miners race to solve complex mathematical problems. The miner who solved the problem first can mine the next block and gets the amount of Ether associated with that block as a reward. Ethereum takes up to 20 s to mine a block, whereas it takes 10 min for a Bitcoin block at the time of writing this paper.

Smart Contract: N. Szabo [25] proposed the first smart contract. The smart contract is a digitized version of a legal contract that can be written using a programming language and run on a computer. It builds trust between two parties without involving the third party in the communication. Once EVM converts the contract into byte code, the Application Binary Interface (ABI) and the contract address will be saved. The smart contract can communicate to other contracts only through the contract address. We have used smart contracts to verify the results returned by the cloud which achieves search fairness.

4   System Model

This section discusses the block diagram, the workflow, and the algorithm description of our scheme.

As shown in Fig. 2, the system model consists of four participants: Data Owner (DO), Data User (DU), Cloud Server (CS), and Blockchain and Smart Contracts. The role of each participant is described in detail as follows:

DO: generates the system parameters and outsources the encrypted files and index to the cloud.

DU: DU has to register with the DO to interact with the system. DU can submit the search query with interesting keywords to receive the results from the cloud.

Cloud Server

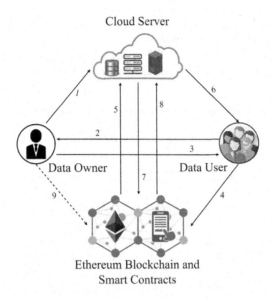

Data Owner

Data User

Ethereum Blockchain and
Smart Contracts

Fig. 2. Architecture of our proposed model

Once DU receives the search results, can decrypt them using a secret key if DU is authorized.

CS: searches the trapdoor on encrypted index. After a successful search, CS has to send the proof to the smart contract to receive the reward for the search operation. CS also sends the ciphertext results to the DU.

Blockchain and Smart Contracts: receives the search query from the user and validates the user. The smart contract outsources the search query to CS if the user is authorized. The smart contract is also responsible for validating the proof sent by the CS, and if the proof is valid, it sends the search fee to the CS.

The workflow of our proposed framework, shown in Fig. 2, is described as follows: Initially, DO creates the master secret key (MSK) and public parameters (PP), 1) then DO obtains the keywords from the file collection and creates an inverted index. Later, DO outsources the ciphertext related to the file collection, the encrypted index, and the proof containing file information to the CS, 2) DU sends the request to the DO for registering into the system, 3) DO generate a secret key and communicates it to the DU, 4) DU submits the search query to the smart contract. Later, the smart contract verifies whether the DU is valid and has enough search fee or not, 5) if so, the smart contract sends the search query along with user identity to the CS, 6) CS performs the search operation and returns the ciphertext results to DU, 7) CS also returns the file identifiers and the proof related to the search operation to the smart contract, 8) smart contract regenerates the proof with the file identifiers and the verification key. If the proof generated by the smart contract and the proof sent by the CS are equal, the smart contract sends the fee to the CS; meanwhile, DU can decrypt the results received by the CS by using his secret key. DU can only receive the actual plaintext if DU is authorized.

Note: If the proof generated by the smart contract and the proof sent by the CS are not equal, the smart contract does not send the fee to the CS.

4.1   Algorithm, Functional and Variable Description

This section discusses different algorithms, functions, and variables used in this paper.

Setup: Algorithm start by DO. It inputs the security parameter λ and outputs PP and MSK.

Key Generation: Algorithm start by DO. By taking inputs are MSK and user attributes, it produces the secret key.

File Encryption: Algorithm start by DO. This algorithm takes the file F, and file decryption key K as an input and outputs the file's ciphertext form.

Key Encryption: Algorithm start by DO. It takes the file decryption key K, access policy Π as an input, and produces the key ciphertext as an output.

Build Index: Algorithm start by DO. It takes the keywords and produces the encrypted index as output.

Trapdoor Generation: Algorithm start by DU. It inputs the secret key and user keywords and outputs the trapdoor.

Search: Algorithm start by CS. It inputs the trapdoor and encrypted index and produces the search results.

Decryption: Algorithm start by DU. By using a secret key, DU initially decrypts the file decryption key. If the attributes of DU match the access policy presented in the file decryption key, DU can get the file decryption key. Later, DU decrypts the file.

Deposit(): Function executed by DU. DU must deposit the amount to pay the search service cost.

\$msg.value: It represents the number of *wei* involved in the transaction, where *wei* is the smallest denomination of Ether.

\$cost: It involves the fixed number of *wei* that must be paid by the user per transaction.

msg.sender: It refers to an address of an EOA or a smart contract. *msg.sender* has the user's address if the user invokes the smart contract. *msg.sender* has the owner's address if another smart contract invokes the smart contract.

tx.origin: It is used to retrieve the address of the initial call. For example, if a user invokes a smart contract and the smart contract calls another, then *tx.origin* holds the entire chain along with the initial call address.

5   Scheme Construction

This section presents the construction of our proposed scheme algorithms in detail.

Setup: DO select two cyclic groups $\mathbb{G}, \mathbb{G}_T$ and $e : \mathbb{G} \times \mathbb{G} \rightarrow \mathbb{G}_T$ as a pairing function. The generator g is chosen from the group $\mathbb{G}$, p is a prime. Then, choose two random keys $p_1, p_2 \in [0,1]^\lambda$, where λ is a security parameter. Selects SHA-256 hash function $H_1 : \{0,1\}^* \in \mathcal{Z}_p^*$. DO selects the universal attribute set $\cup = \{\cup_1, \cup_2, \ldots, \cup_n\}$, where n is number of universal attributes. Later, for each $x \in \cup$ selects $p_x \in \mathcal{Z}_p^*$ and computes $Attr_x = g^{p_x}$. Then selects random $\alpha, \beta \in \mathcal{Z}_p^*$. Finally, publishes PP and MSK as follows,

$$PP = \{\mathbb{G}, \mathbb{G}_T, e, g, p, g^\alpha, e(g,g)^\beta, \{Attr_x\}_{x \in \cup}\}, MSK = \{\alpha, \beta, p_1, p_2\}$$

Key Generation: DO assigns relevant attributes U_{attr} to the user and choose $t \in \mathcal{Z}_p^*$ to calculate $S = g^\beta g^{\alpha t}, S_1 = g^t$ and $S_x = H(x)^{t/p_x}$ for all $x \in U_{attr}$. The following is the user's secret key:

$$SK = \{S, S_1, \{S_x\}_{x \in U_{attr}}\}$$

Encryption:
This process is divided into three parts: file encryption, key encryption, and index encryption.

File Encryption: DO selects a random symmetric key K from key space for a file F_i and computes the file ciphertext $CT(F_i) = Enc_K(F_i)$.

Key Encryption: The access policy $\Pi = (\mathbb{A}, \rho)$ where $\mathbb{A}$ is matrix with size $\ell \times n$ and ρ is a mapping function from matrix row to attributes. Then DO selects $(r_2, \ldots, r_n) \in \mathcal{Z}_p^*$ randomly. The secret $s \in \mathcal{Z}_p^*$ is chosen randomly to complete the vector $\overrightarrow{r} = (s, r_2, \ldots, r_n)$. The secrets for each share $1 \leq i \leq \ell$ is calculated as $\chi_i = \mathbb{A}_i . \overrightarrow{r}$ where $\mathbb{A}_i$ is the share of ith-row of a matrix. Finally, the ciphertext is calculated as follows,

$$C_1 = K.e(g,g)^{\beta s}, C_2 = g^s, \{C_{3,i} = g^{(\chi_i \alpha)} H(\rho(i))^{v_i}, C_{4,i} = g^{p_{\rho(i)} v_i}\}_{i \in [1...\ell], v_i \in \mathcal{Z}_p^*}$$
$$CT_K = \{C_1, C_2, C_{3,i}, C_{4,i}\}_{i \in [1...\ell]}$$

Build Index: The encrypted index looks like a dictionary structure as $\mathcal{D} =<$ $key, value >$, where the key part contains the encrypted keyword set and $value$ part contains the address of the files collection for that set of keywords along with proof of the data for multi-keyword search. Finally, the structure of $\mathcal{D}$ is as $<key, [value, proof]>$. Then, DO calculate $p_1(kw)$ for each keyword set of the inverted index and stores in key part of $\mathcal{D}$, then computes $\mathcal{D}[p_1(kw)].value = address(F(kw)) \oplus (p_1(kw)\|0)$, $\mathcal{D}[p_1(kw)].proof = p_2(p_1(kw)\|F_1(kw)\| \ldots \|F_k(kw))$, where $F_k(kw)$ is the $top - k$ file identifiers of the keyword kw. Later, the file identifiers in $F_k(kw))$ are encrypted as $EF(kw) = F_1(kw) \oplus (p_1(kw)\|1), \ldots, F_k(kw) \oplus (p_1(kw)\|1)$. Finally, DO outsources the encrypted index $I = \{\mathcal{D}, EF(kw)\}$ to the cloud.

The verification key p_2 is only with the DO and uses this key in the payment contract as a private argument.

Trapdoor Generation: DU creates a search query with multiple keywords by using the search key p_1 and the keywords kw of his interest. DU generates the search query as $TD = p_1(kw), (p_1(kw)||0), (p_1(kw)||1)$. Before submitting the search query, DU invokes the data user contract Contract 1 to deposit the search fee. Later, DU invokes the payment contract Contract 2 to submit the search query.

Contract 1. Data User Contract

    Contract DUC {
1: address DU;
2: address PC;
3: **Event GenToken (bytes32 token, address DUC)**
4: **function** DEPOSIT($msg.value)
5:     **if** ($msg.value! = 0$) **then**
6:         address[msg.sender].balance += $msg.value
7:     **end if**
8: **end function**

Search: Once the payment contract receives the search query, it checks whether or not the user is authorized. DO maintains a list rl which contains all the users who are not authorized to the system. For every submitted query, the payment contract checks this list rl first. If the user is authorized, the search query is transferred to the CS for a search operation. CS uses $p_1(kw)$ and searches in the dictionary with $\mathcal{D}[p_1(kw)]$ ad gets $\mathcal{D}[p_1(kw)].value$ and $\mathcal{D}[p_1(kw)].proof$. Then, CS receives the address of the file identifiers by performing $\mathcal{D}[p_1(kw)].value \oplus (p_1(kw)||0)$ and receives file identifiers by computing $EF_i(kw) = F_i(kw)) \oplus (p_1(kw)||1)$, for all $i \in k$.

Verify: Once the file identifiers $F_k(kw)$ and the proof $\mathcal{D}[p_1(kw)].proof$ are received from the CS, payment contract performs verification by computing the $proof'$ as, $proof' = p_2(p_1(kw)||F_1(kw)||\dots, ||F_k(kw))$. If the proof returned by the CS and the proof computed by the smart contract are same, then the payment contract transfers the search fee to the cloud. This payment contract Contract 2 is used as the main contract of our scheme where the role of this contract is to validate the user, check the correctness of the search results, and achieve a fair payment process.

Decryption: DU receive CT_K and $CT(F_i)$ from the cloud. Then, the key K can be retrieved by computing the following:

$$K = \frac{C_1 \cdot \prod_{i \in I} e(C_{3,i}, S_1)^{\omega_i}}{e(S, C_2) \cdot \prod_{i \in I} e(C_{4,i}, S_{\rho_i})^{\omega_i}}$$

Contract 2. Payment Contract

```
Contract PC {
1:  Struct dataUser {
2:  bytes32 token;
3:  unit256 balance;
4:  address DUC;
5:  }
6:  address payable CS;
7:  mapping(address => dataUser) private addrDU;
8:  bytes32 private p₂;
9:  uint256 private fee;
10: Event getToken (bytes32 token, address DUC)
11: function VALIDATETOKEN(bytes32 token, address DUC)
12:     var = VerifyUser(DUC)
13:     if (var = = FALSE) then
14:         assert addrDU[$msg.sender].balance >= fee
15:         addrDU[$msg.sender].token = token
16:         addrDU[$msg.sender].DUC = DUC
17:         emit getToken(token, $msg.sender)
18:     else
19:         User is not valid
20:     end if
21: end function
22: function VERIFYUSER(address DUC)
23:     Invoke rl
24:     if DUC isExist in rl then
25:         return TRUE
26:     else
27:         return FALSE
28:     end if
29: end function
30: function VERIFYRESULTS(UserAddr, fileids, proof)
31:     proof' = p₂(token||fileid₁|| ... ||fileidₖ)
32:     if proof = = proof' then
33:         CS.transfer = fee
34:         addrDU[UserAddr].balance -= fee
35:     end if
36: end function
37: }
```

Since the key K is composed of attributes, the user with a valid attribute set can get the key K. The decryption occurs only when the user attributes satisfy the access policy. If it happens, for each $I = [i : \rho(i) \in U_{attr}]$ there will be a constant $\omega_i \in \mathcal{Z}_p^*$ such that $\sum_{i \in I} \chi_i \omega_i = s$. Once DU receives the valid key, compute $F_i = DEC_K(CT(F_i))$ to receive the plaintext form of the file.

Decryption Correctness:

$$K = \frac{C_1 \cdot \prod_{i \in I} e(C_{3,i}, S_1)^{\omega_i}}{e(S, C_2) \cdot \prod_{i \in I} e(C_{4,i}, S_{\rho_i})^{\omega_i}} = \frac{K.e(g,g)^{\beta s} \cdot \prod_{i \in I} e((g^{(\chi_i \alpha)} H(\rho(i))^{v_i}), g^t)^{\omega_i}}{e(g^\beta g^{\alpha t}, g^s) \cdot \prod_{i \in I} e(g^{P_{\rho(i)} v_i}, H(\rho(i))^{t/P_{\rho(i)}})^{\omega_i}}$$

$$= \frac{K.e(g,g)^{\beta s} \cdot \prod_{i \in I} e(g^{\chi_i \alpha}, g^t)^{\omega_i} e(H(\rho(i))^{v_i}, g^t)^{\omega_i}}{e(g^\beta g^{\alpha t}, g^s) \cdot \prod_{i \in I} e(g^{v_i}, H(\rho(i))^t)^{\omega_i \cdot P_{\rho(i)}/P_{\rho(i)}}}$$

$$= \frac{K.e(g,g)^{\beta s} \cdot \prod_{i \in I} e(g,g)^{\chi_i \alpha t \omega_i} e(H(\rho(i)), g)^{v_i t \omega_i}}{e(g^\beta g^{\alpha t}, g^s) \cdot \prod_{i \in I} e(g, H(\rho(i)))^{v_i t \omega_i}}$$

$$= \frac{K.e(g,g)^{\beta s}.e(g,g)^{\alpha t \sum_{i \in I} \chi_i \omega_i}}{e(g,g)^{\beta s}.e(g,g)^{\alpha t s}} = \frac{K.e(g,g)^{\alpha t \sum_{i \in I} \chi_i \omega_i}}{e(g,g)^{\alpha t s}} = K$$

6   Security Analysis

This section shows how our scheme achieved security in terms fairness, data privacy, and soundness. We also show that our scheme is IND-CPA under the DBDH assumption.

6.1   Fairness

Our scheme's fairness of search results is achieved by using the Ethereum blockchain. In Ethereum, the consensus nodes execute all the transactions to attach a new block to the existing blockchain and get a reward for their work. In effect, all the users who use the blockchain services have to pay the gas price ($cost) fixed for each transaction. Further, the consensus nodes will identify the malicious transactions, and the dishonest user will not get any benefit in return. This property is not included in previous centralized cloud storage systems since users have to pay for search services before initiating the search. After the user gets the incorrect results, there is nothing to do with the already paid amount, i.e., the amount will not be refunded by the cloud. However, the user will be charged only when receiving valid search results in our scheme.

6.2   Data Privacy

Each file is encrypted with a different symmetric key K in our scheme before outsourcing to the cloud. This achieves file privacy. The access policy further encrypts the key K. The actual key K can only be obtained by users whose attributes satisfy the policy, as a result.

6.3   Soundness

The strong security of Ethereum guarantees the soundness of our proposed system. Since we adopt the PoW mechanism, where each miner solves the computationally complex mathematical problem, no adversary can tamper with any

Table 2. Theoretical comparison between our scheme and other recent schemes

Scheme Name	Setup	key_Gen	Encryption	Index_Gen	Trapdoor	Search	Decryption
Nui et al. [26]	$3E$	$(3+3S_a)E$	$(3+N_u)E+P$	$(2+N_k+2N_u)E$	$(1+N_{tk})E$	$(2+N_k+N_u)P$	$3P$
Miao et al. [27]	$(3+N_u)E+P$	$(10+4S_a)E$	$(1+3N_u)E+P$	$(2+N_u)E+P$	$4E$	$2P$	$3P+E$
Our scheme	$(1+N_u)E+P$	$(4+S_a)E$	$(2+N_u)E+P$	–	–	–	$3P$

P : Pairing Operation, E : Exponential Operation, N_u : Universal attributes
S_a : User attributes, N_k : Keywords, N_{tk} : Query keywords

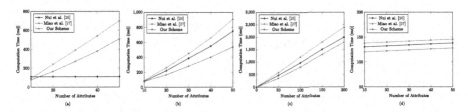

Fig. 3. Computation cost: (a) Setup **(b)** Key Generation **(c)** Encryption **(d)** Decryption

smart contract transaction. The adversary must hold more than 50% of the Ethereum network's computation power to tamper with any transaction. Hence, no individual can change the smart contract logic or any running transactions. The characteristics of consensus nodes in the blockchain ensure that the user gets correct and relevant results without verifying further.

6.4 Formal Proof

Theorem 1. *Our scheme is IND-CPA under DBDH assumption.*

IND-CPA Security Game:
Setup: Challenger $\mathcal{B}$ initializes the setup algorithm and generates PP and MSK. $\mathcal{B}$ holds the MSK and issues PP to $\mathcal{A}$.
Phase 1: $\mathcal{A}$ issues the secret key request. $\mathcal{B}$ runs the Key generation algorithm and issues the content requested by $\mathcal{A}$.
Challenge: $\mathcal{A}$ chooses two equal length messages m_0, m_1 and submits to $\mathcal{B}$. $\mathcal{B}$ picks a random bit $r \in [0, 1]$ and if $r = 0$, $\mathcal{B}$ outputs the original index otherwise outputs a random index.
Phase 2: Same as Phase 1 but the messages m_0, m_1 should not be same.
Guess: The adversary $\mathcal{A}$ has to guess $r' = [0, 1]$ of r. To win the game $\mathcal{A}$ has an advantage $\frac{\epsilon}{2}$.

Proof: If $\mathcal{A}$ wins the game then $\mathcal{B}$ can decode the DBDH problem.
Setup: $\mathcal{B}$ selects $\alpha, \beta \in \mathcal{Z}_p^*$ randomly and generates PP $= \{g^\alpha, e(g,g)^\beta, g\}$ and MSK $= \{\alpha, \beta\}$.
Phase 1: $\mathcal{A}$ generates secret key query to $\mathcal{B}$. Then $\mathcal{B}$ responds to $\mathcal{A}$ with secret key oracle as follows:

- **Secret Key:** $\mathcal{B}$ computes $S = g^\beta g^{\alpha t}, S_1 = g^t, S_x = H(x)^{t/p_x}$ and send it to $\mathcal{A}$.

Challenge: $\mathcal{A}$ generates two same length messages m_0, m_1 and submits to $\mathcal{B}$, where m_0, m_1 are previously not been asked by $\mathcal{A}$. Then, $\mathcal{B}$ coins a random bit $r \in [0,1]$. If $r = 0$, $\mathcal{B}$ outputs $C_1 = m_r.e(g,g)^{\beta s}, C_2 = g^s, \{C_{3,i} = g^{(\chi_i \alpha)} H(\rho(i))^{v_i}, C_{4,i} = g^{p_{\rho(i)} v_i}\}_{i \in [1...\ell], v_i \in \mathcal{Z}_p^*}$. Otherwise, $\mathcal{B}$ outputs a random message from ciphertext space.

Phase 2: Same as Phase 1 except m_0, m_1 are not asked in Phase 1.

Guess: $\mathcal{A}$ has to output the guess r' of r. If the ciphertext is a true oracle, then the probability that $\mathcal{A}$ outputs r' of r is $\frac{1}{2} + \epsilon$. If the ciphertext is random oracle then the probability that $\mathcal{A}$ outputs r' of r is $\frac{1}{2}$. The advantage for $\mathcal{A}$ to solve the game is, $\left[\frac{1}{2}\left(\frac{1}{2} + \epsilon\right) + \frac{1}{2}\left(\frac{1}{2}\right) - \frac{1}{2}\right] = \frac{\epsilon}{2}$.

Finally, we say that the DBDH problem is hard, so $\frac{\epsilon}{2}$ is negligible. To be specific, the advantage for $\mathcal{A}$ to break the scheme is negligible. Therefore, the challenger $\mathcal{B}$ has a negligible advantage in breaking the DBDH problem.

7   Performance Analysis

This section analyzes our scheme's performance related to the smart contract design and ABKS algorithms.

7.1   Performance of ABKS Algorithms

The theoretical comparison of our scheme with [26,27] schemes is presented in Table 2. From Table 2, the comparison is based on the number of pairing P and exponential operations E involved in constructing the schemes. We ignored the time taken to perform hashing and multiplication operations since these two operations involve negligible overhead compared to pairing and exponential operations. It is further observed from Table 2 that there are no exponential and pairing operations involved in our scheme for Index build, Trapdoor, and Search algorithms that made our scheme unique.

We simulated the ABKS algorithms (Setup, Key Generation, Encryption, and Decryption) on a Laptop running Windows with 2.50 GHz Intel(R) Core(TM)i5 7200U processor, 500 GB hard drive, and 8 GB RAM. Further, we implemented using Python 2.7 programming language in PyCharm IDE having Charm Crypto 0.42 library. The implementations are based on a 160-bit elliptic curve with a 512-bit finite field. We have used the Enrol Email Dataset [28] to implement our ABKS algorithms as shown in Fig. 3. The documents and keywords are randomly extracted from the dataset and conducted experiments 20 times. Figure 3 shows the computation cost for all the ABKS algorithms of our scheme compared with [26,27] schemes. It is observed from Fig. 3a that the computation cost for the setup algorithm increases linearly with the number of attributes in our scheme and [27]. Because these schemes calculate a component related to attributes. For example, $Attr_x = g^{p_x}$ for each attribute x in the universal attribute set $\cup$. Whereas [26] has no component related to attributes. Figure 3b shows that the computation cost for generating the user secret key grows with the increase in the number of attributes. Since attribute-related component $Attr_x$ for each attribute presented in the system is already calculated in the setup phase, it minimizes the exponential operations in the key generation phase. Whereas schemes [26,27] involve more exponential operations. Figure 3c indicates the computation cost for the encryption algorithm, and our scheme's computation cost is less compared to [26,27] schemes because it involves less number of complex operations. Figure 3d represents the computation cost of the decryption algorithm. The decryption cost is hardly constant since every time the user performs decryption, the same number of operations are involved.

7.2   Performance of Smart Contract

In our scheme, the smart contracts are designed using the Solidity programming language. The simulations of smart contracts are done using Ethereum Virtual Machine (EVM). Further, We ran and tested the smart contracts in the Ethereum network locally using a simulated network called *Ganache* [29] (Formerly known as *TestRPC*).

The execution of the smart contracts involves cryptocurrency, i.e., for each smart contract execution, the service receiver has to pay cryptocurrency. The

Table 3. Smart contract cost for different functions

Function	Gas consumed	ETH (10^{-3})	USD
Deployment of Payment contract	285962	0.571924	0.2745
Deployment of Data user contract	239748	0.479496	0.2301
Execution of ValidateToken function	56017	0.112034	0.0537
Execution of Verify user function	35745	0.07149	0.0343
Execution of Verify results function	25745	0.05149	0.0247
Execution of Deposit function	20112	0.040224	0.0193

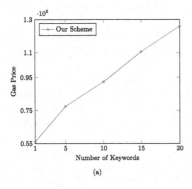
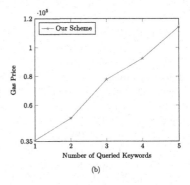

Fig. 4. Gas Prices: (a) Amount of gas required to execute validate token function **(b)** Amount of gas required to execute verify user function.

amount of gas, ether (ETH), and USD consumed by executing different contracts and functions are presented in Table 3. At the time of implementing the scheme, cost for 1 ETH = 480 USD and the gas price is 1 gas = $2 \times 10^9 wei$, wei = $10^{-18}ether$. Hence, 1 gas = $2 \times 10^{-9}ether$. As shown in Table 3, deployment of payment and data user consumes 0.2745 USD and 0.2301 USD, respectively. These expenditures for the deployment of contracts occur only once, whereas the expenditure for other functions in Table 3 occurs for every event generated by the data owner or data user. The DO executes the ValidateToken function to check whether the incoming search query is valid or not. Figure 4a exhibits the gas price required to perform the validate token function with a different number of tokens. Alongside, the gas price required for executing the verify user function varies concerning the number of users, as shown in Fig. 4b. Later, for each successful search, the user has to pay a fixed amount, which goes to the data owner, who has to pay for the blockchain usage.

8   Conclusion

This paper proposed a blockchain-based keyword search over encrypted data with fine-grained access control in the cloud. The scheme used the Ethereum blockchain and smart contracts to achieve fairness between the cloud and its users. The system also enables users to do multi-keyword searches by including multiple keywords in their search query. The scheme also achieved an efficient user revocation by maintaining a revocation list in smart contracts. The security analysis showed that the scheme is secure against IND-CPA and achieved security requirements like data privacy, fairness, and soundness. Our scheme's theoretical and experimental analysis showed that the scheme is efficient.

References

1. Song, D.X., Wagner, D., Perrig, A.: Practical techniques for searches on encrypted data. In: Proceeding 2000 IEEE Symposium on Security and Privacy. S&P 2000, pp. 44–55. IEEE (2000)
2. Minxin, D., Wang, Q., He, M., Weng, J.: Privacy-preserving indexing and query processing for secure dynamic cloud storage. IEEE Trans. Inf. Forensics Secur. 13(9), 2320–2332 (2018)
3. Miao, Y., Ma, J., Jiang, Q., Li, X., Sangaiah, A.K.: Verifiable keyword search over encrypted cloud data in smart city. Comput. Electr. Eng. 65, 90–101 (2018)
4. Farràs, O., Ribes-González, J.: Provably secure public-key encryption with conjunctive and subset keyword search. Int. J. Inf. Secur. 18(5), 533–548 (2019). https://doi.org/10.1007/s10207-018-00426-7
5. Wang, C., Li, W., Li, Y., Xu, X.: A ciphertext-policy attribute-based encryption scheme supporting keyword search function. In: Wang, G., Ray, I., Feng, D., Rajarajan, M. (eds.) CSS 2013. LNCS, vol. 8300, pp. 377–386. Springer, Cham (2013). https://doi.org/10.1007/978-3-319-03584-0_28

6. Sun, W., Yu, S., Lou, W., Hou, Y.T., Li, H.: Protecting your right: attribute-based keyword search with fine-grained owner-enforced search authorization in the cloud. In: IEEE INFOCOM 2014-IEEE Conference on Computer Communications, pp. 226–234. IEEE (2014)
7. Chaudhari, P., Das, M.L.: Keysea: keyword-based search with receiver anonymity in attribute-based searchable encryption. IEEE Trans. Serv. Comput. (2020)
8. Payal Chaudhari and Manik Lal Das: Privacy preserving searchable encryption with fine-grained access control. IEEE Trans. Cloud Comput. 9(2), 753–762 (2019)
9. Sun, J., Ren, L., Wang, S., Yao, X.: Multi-keyword searchable and data verifiable attribute-based encryption scheme for cloud storage. IEEE Access 7, 66655–66667 (2019)
10. Li, H., Yang, Y., Dai, Y., Yu, S., Xiang, Y.: Achieving secure and efficient dynamic searchable symmetric encryption over medical cloud data. IEEE Trans. Cloud Comput. (2020)
11. Miao, Y., Ma, J., Liu, X., Li, X., Jiang, Q., Zhang, J.: Attribute-based keyword search over hierarchical data in cloud computing. IEEE Trans. Serv. Comput. 13(6), 985–998 (2020)
12. Miao, Y., Ma, J., Liu, X., Weng, J., Li, H., Li, H.: Lightweight fine-grained search over encrypted data in fog computing. IEEE Trans. Serv. Comput. 12(5), 772–785 (2018)
13. Zhang, K., Long, J., Wang, X., Dai, H.-N., Liang, K., Imran, M.: Lightweight searchable encryption protocol for industrial internet of things. IEEE Trans. Industr. Inform. 17(6), 4248–4259 (2021)
14. Zhang, Y., Zhu, T., Guo, R., Xu, S., Cui, H., Cao, J.: Multi-keyword searchable and verifiable attribute-based encryption over cloud data. IEEE Trans. Cloud Comput. (2021)
15. Zhou, Y., Nan, J., Wang, L.: Fine-grained attribute-based multikeyword search for shared multiowner in internet of things. Secur. Commun. Netw. 2021 (2021)
16. Varri, U.S., Pasupuleti, S.K., Kadambari, K.V.: Key-escrow free attribute-based multi-keyword search with dynamic policy update in cloud computing. In: 2020 20th IEEE/ACM International Symposium on Cluster, Cloud and Internet Computing (CCGRID), pp. 450–458. IEEE (2020)
17. He, K., Guo, J., Weng, J., Weng, J., Liu, J.K., Yi, X.: Attribute-based hybrid Boolean keyword search over outsourced encrypted data. IEEE Trans. Depend. Secure Comput. 17(06), 1207–1217 (2020)
18. Varri, U.S., Kasani, S., Pasupuleti, S.K., Kadambari, K.V.: Felt-ABKS: fog-enabled lightweight traceable attribute-based keyword search over encrypted data. IEEE Internet Things J. (2021)
19. Varri, U.S., Pasupuleti, S.K., Kadambari, K.V.: CP-ABSEL: ciphertext-policy attribute-based searchable encryption from lattice in cloud storage. Peer-to-Peer Network. Appl. 14(3), 1290–1302 (2021)
20. Hu, S., Cai, C., Wang, Q., Wang, C., Luo, X., Ren, K.: Searching an encrypted cloud meets blockchain: a decentralized, reliable and fair realization. In: IEEE INFOCOM 2018-IEEE Conference on Computer Communications, pp. 792–800. IEEE (2018)
21. Li, H., Tian, H., Zhang, F., He, J.: Blockchain-based searchable symmetric encryption scheme. Comput. Electr. Eng. 73, 32–45 (2019)
22. Chen, L., Lee, W.-K., Chang, C.-C., Choo, K.-K.R., Zhang, N.: Blockchain based searchable encryption for electronic health record sharing. Future Gener. Comput. Syst. 95, 420–429 (2019)

23. Cao, N., Wang, C., Li, M., Ren, K., Lou, W.: Privacy-preserving multi-keyword ranked search over encrypted cloud data. IEEE Trans. Parallel Distrib. Syst. **25**(1), 222–233 (2013)
24. Beimel, A., et al.: Secure schemes for secret sharing and key distribution. Faculty of Computer Science, Technion-Israel Institute of Technology (1996)
25. Szabo, N.: Formalizing and securing relationships on public networks. First Monday (1997)
26. Niu, S., Lixia, C., Jinfeng, W., Fei, Y.: Electronic health record sharing scheme with searchable attribute-based encryption on blockchain. IEEE Access **8**, 7195–7204 (2019)
27. Miao, Y., Deng, R.H., Liu, X., Choo, K.-K.R., Wu, H., Li, H.: Multi-authority attribute-based keyword search over encrypted cloud data. IEEE Trans. Depend. Secure Comput. **18**(4), 1667–1680 (2021)
28. Enron Email Dataset (2015). https://www.cs.cmu.edu/./enron/. Accessed 16 August 2021
29. Ganache: Ethereum ganache overview. https://www.trufflesuite.com/ganache/

Impact of Selfish Nodes
on the Performance of AODV and DSR
Routing Protocols

Priyanka Pandey[(✉)] and Raghuraj Singh

Harcourt Butler Technical University, Kanpur, India
priyankapandey07@gmail.com

Abstract. Mobile Ad Hoc Network (MANET) is a set of mobile nodes that are moving continuously within their terrain. Such kind of networks performs its operation without any infrastructure. In order to route the packets from source to destination several routing protocols have been designed. Among them, AODV (Ad Hoc On Demand Distance Vector Routing) and DSR (Dynamic Source Routing) are most widely used in MANET environment. To perform routing operation efficiently, intermediate nodes should cooperate in forwarding data and control packets. However, selfish nodes or misbehaving nodes do not cooperate and may lead to overall degradation of routing performance. In this work, a simulation has been conducted to analyse the performance of AODV and DSR routing protocols in presence of selfish nodes.

Keywords: MANET · Selfish nodes · Routing protocols · AODV · DSR

1 Introduction

In recent years, due to extensive utilization of mobile devices like laptop, PDAs and mobile phones etc. Mobile Ad Hoc Network (MANET) [1,2] has become an important area of research. It is a transient network established dynamically by a set of arbitrarily moving nodes. In this kind of networks, no dedicated router is required instead each node acts as a router or packet forwarder. Communication between sender and receiver is generally carried out in multi-hop fashion.

Routing protocols are essential for such environment to discover routes for forwarding of data packets. These protocols are designed to establish routes between nodes regardless of frequent topological changes. Depending on the network conditions, they are widely categorized as reactive and proactive approaches.

In proactive scheme, nodes periodically broadcast control packets to maintain routing information. Whenever, a source node has to transfer data packets, it checks in its routing table and immediately initiates data transmission process. However, in this strategy control overhead is higher and condition becomes worst with highly dynamic and dense environment.

© The Author(s), under exclusive license to Springer Nature Switzerland AG 2023
I. Woungang et al. (Eds.): ANTIC 2022, CCIS 1797, pp. 349–361, 2023.
https://doi.org/10.1007/978-3-031-28180-8_23

On the other hand, reactive approach performs better in dynamic environment. Route between any pair of nodes is constructed only when required. Consequently, it has less control packet overhead as compared to proactive approach. Some of the popular reactive approaches in this category are AODV [3], DSR [4] and TORA [5]. AODV and DSR routing protocols are also known as on demand routing approaches. In AODV, routing information automatically gets deleted from the routing table when route is not utilized for the longer period of time. On the other hand, route information in DSR is stored in the cache and for deletion of stale route special mechanism is needed. During broadcasting it appends the source address to the route request packet. However, these protocols are designed by assuming that all nodes perform well. This assumption causes the network more vulnerable to security threats. Misbehaving node could be malicious or selfish. The malicious node pretends itself as cooperating node but drops data packets instead of forwarding them. These nodes may also flood the network with control packets which further causes congestion. On the other hand selfish node do not cooperate in data forwarding or routing process to preserve its battery power. In this work, selfish nodes have been launched over AODV and DSR routing protocols. Further, the performance of both protocols has been evaluated to study the effects of selfish nodes.

The rest of the paper is organized as mentioned: Sect. 2 discusses the related work. Section 3 consists of a brief description of the misbehaving nodes. In Sect. 4, simulation environment and results have been discussed and the last section concluded the overall work.

2   Related Work

Routing protocol plays a vital role in governing overall routing operation. It should be designed in such a manner so that sender and receiver can communicate efficiently. Many protocols such as AODV, DSR, TORA exist that meet this requirement. However, these protocols do not consider existence of any malicious node. Consequently, during routing, if such kind of node enters into the network, it may lead to overall routing performance degradation. This section discusses about the previous conducted simulation analysis on different routing protocols to study the impact of misbehaving nodes.

Azfar S. et al. [6] categorized and explained possible misbehaviours of nodes. Further, simulation was conducted to analyze the performance of AODV routing protocol with misbehavior and selfish nodes under different mobility and traffic conditions. After that, a detection technique was proposed to identify node responsible for misrouting packets.

Mishra D, et al. [7] analysed the effects of malicious node i.e. blackhole node under AODV and DSR. From simulation results, it was observed that AODV protocol performs better as compared to DSR routing in terms of performance on total data loss.

In [8], impact of selfish nodes under different DTN routing protocols was studied and analyzed. From simulation results it was concluded that in the presence of selfish nodes, performance of protocols i.e. Prophet, Epidemic and SawBinary have shown better results. However, performance of all DTN protocols decrease with increase in number of selfish nodes.

Hollick M. et al. [9] presented an analytical model which covers different types of misbehaving nodes. The AODV routing protocol was considered to estimate impact of these nodes on routing performance. Results reveal that selfish nodes and blackhole nodes have great impact on performance of AODV routing.

In [10], performance of AODV, DSR and DSDV has been compared under various network conditions i.e. while streaming MPEG4 traffic, realistic environment, under security attacks and routing misbehavior. As per simulation results throughput of both AODV and DSR is better as compared to DSDV. Further, delay of DSR is higher among considered protocols and control overhead performance of DSDV is considerably better.

Suman A. et al. [11] studied the performance of ZRP, DSR and STAR routing protocols in presence of some misbehaving nodes. The performance of the protocols was evaluated by varying node speed. As per simulation results, it was concluded that DSR routing protocol performs better as compared to others.

Gorine D. et al. [12] analysed the performance of AODV and DSR in presence of malicious and selfish nodes. As per results, DSR routing protocol was more affected in presence of selfish nodes.

Shan A. et al. [13] analysed performance of AODV in terms of packet delivery ratio and end to end delay. From simulation results, it can be concluded that PDR performance was more affected in presence of selfish nodes as compared to end to end delay performance.

The paper proposed in [14] examined the performance of AODV and DSDV in presence of selfish nodes attack. Results reveal that AODV protocol was more resistant to selfish node attack in terms of throughput and delay as compared to DSDV.

The proposed approaches have been summarized as shown below in Table 1.

Table 1. Summary of related works

Reference	Protocol name	Remarks
[6]	AODV	Analaysed and proposed selfish node detection technique
[7]	AODV, DSR	AODV performs better
[8]	Delay Tolerant Routing Protocol	With increase in number of selfish nodes performance of all DTN protocols degraded
[9]	AODV	Selfish nodes have great impact on AODV performance
[10]	AODV, DSR and DSDV	Delay of DSR is higher and control overhead of DSDV is considerably better
[11]	ZRP, DSR and STAR	DSR outperforms than others
[12]	AODV and DSR	DSR protocol was more affected
[13]	AODV	Huge reduction in packet delivery ratio performance as compared to delay
[14]	AODV and DSDV	Performance of AODV in terms of delay and throughput was better as compared to DSDV

From the literature survey, it can be seen that various protocols have been analyzed in presence of misbehaving nodes. However, performance analysis of AODV and DSR in presence of selfish nodes by taking into account important performance parameters with considered network conditions has not been evaluated. In most of the papers, only packet delivery ratio has been considered as a major performance parameters ignoring other metrics such as delay, throughput and normalized routing load which are also important. Therefore, in this paper, we have analyzed these performance parameters by inserting selfish nodes in AODV and DSR routing protocols.

3   Misbehaving Nodes

Misbehaving nodes do not co-operate in routing process and may lead to overall degradation of the network performance. Such nodes could be malicious or selfish. Description about these categories of nodes has been given in the following sub-sections.

3.1   Malicious Nodes

Malicious nodes intentionally disrupt the routing operations to severely affect the routing performance. Some of the popular attacks under this category have been described below:

Blackhole Attack. In this kind of attack [15], whenever a malicious node receives RREQ message, it immediately sends reply with false RREP packets towards the source node containing highest sequence number and less hop count. After that a source node initiates a data transmission process. Now when a malicious node receives data packets, it drops them. Therefore, this kind of attacks severely affect packet delivery ratio performance.

Grayhole Attack. It is similar to blackhole attack, however, this type of attacks does not drop all the packets instead the node sometime act as malicious node and sometime as legitimate node.

Flooding Attack. In this attack [16], a malicious node transmits multiple duplicate fake packets for the purpose of consuming more bandwidth and making the goal node unreachable.

Rushing Attack. Rushing attack mainly harms the on demand routing protocols and uses duplicate suppression during operations [17]. In this attack, a malicious node rushes the network with RREQ message to become a part of a route.

3.2   Selfish Nodes

Selfish nodes do not intentionally harm the system instead they don't co-operate in routing process in order to preserve battery power or other limitations. According to [18] selfish nodes can be of two types. The first category of selfish node can participate in route establishment process but does not forward data packets. Second category of node does not even co-operate during route discovery operation.

4 Simulation Environment and Performance Metrics

In this work, a simulation has been conducted to analyse the effects of selfish nodes which participate in route discovery process but do not forward data packets over AODV and DSR routing protocols by varying maximum node speed and simulation time.

4.1 Simulation Parameters

Simulation has been conducted using NS 2.35 [19] simulator. Total 55 nodes have been deployed in 1000×1000 region. The work considers Constant Bit Rate (CBR) traffic type and Random Waypoint Point mobility model has been chosen for node mobility pattern. To analyse the effects of selfish nodes, total six selfish nodes have been injected in AODV and DSR routing protocols. Other important simulation parameters are given in Table 2.

4.2 Performance Metrics

Following metrics have been considered for performance evaluation for routing protocols.

Table 2. Main simulation parameters

Simulator	NS 2.35
Simulation area	$1000\,m \times 1000\,m$
Propagation model	Two ray ground
MAC type	IEEE802.11
Antenna	Omni antenna
Mobility model	RWP
Simulation time	100, 200, 300, 400, 500 s
Number of Nodes	55
Max node speed	5, 10, 15, 20, 25 m/s
Pause time	6.0 s
Protocols	AODV, DSR

Packet Delivery Ratio (PDR): It is a proportion of number of packets received to the number of packets actually sent.

Throughput: It is a rate at which information is sent via link.

End to End Delay: Delay is the total time taken by the packet to arrive at the destination from the packet generating node.

Normalized Routing Load (NRL): It is an amount of control packets needed to transmit single data packet.

5   Result Analysis

After simulation, performance of considered routing protocols in presence of selfish nodes have been analyzed in terms of packet delivery ratio, throughput, normalized routing load and delay. Results obtained after simulation are represented through graphs.

5.1   Effects of Varying Simulation Time

Performance of considered routing protocols in presence of six selfish nodes have been evaluated by varying simulation time 100, 200, 300, 400 and 500 s and maximum node speed is fixed to 20 m/s. Results obtained after simulation in this network condition have been represented through Fig. 1, Fig. 2, Fig. 3, Fig. 4 and Table 3.

Table 3. Performance on varying time

Simulation time (sec.)	AODV				DSR			
	PDR	Throughput	NRL	Delay	PDR	Throughput	NRL	Delay
100	65.05	97.43	3.02	.09	59.96	86.55	1.03	.15
200	60.60	134.26	3.6	.17	56.59	116.51	.86	.29
300	60.83	147.37	3.3	.17	51.29	119.71	1.87	1.26
400	56.05	143.63	4.05	.19	47.94	118.36	1.73	1.15
500	57.76	152.82	4.11	.23	42.38	108.18	4.3	2.8

Figure 1 shows packet delivery ratio performance of both AODV and DSR by injecting selfish nodes. From simulation, it can be observed that on varying simulation time PDR of AODV is 16% better than DSR. This is because, information about routes in the routing tables of AODV protocol automatically gets deleted after expiration time. Due to which any selfish node stored as a part of a route also gets removed from the stored path.

As shown in Fig. 2, throughput of AODV is 22% better as compared to DSR while varying simulation time as 100, 200, 300, 400 and 500 s.

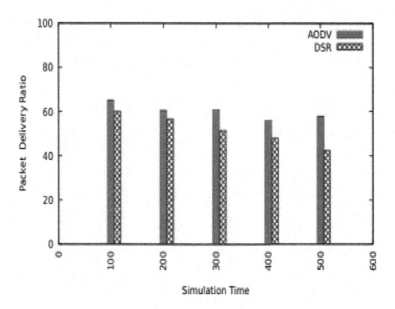

Fig. 1. Packet delivery ratio vs simulation time (sec.)

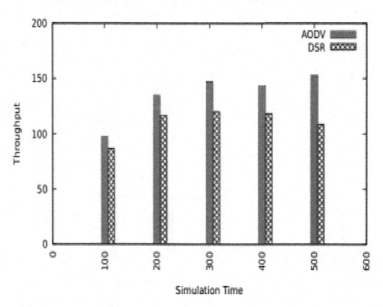

Fig. 2. Throughput (kbps) vs simulation time (sec.)

Normalized routing load performance has been represented in Fig. 3. From where, it is observed that number of control packets required to transmit single data packet in DSR is 45% less than AODV.

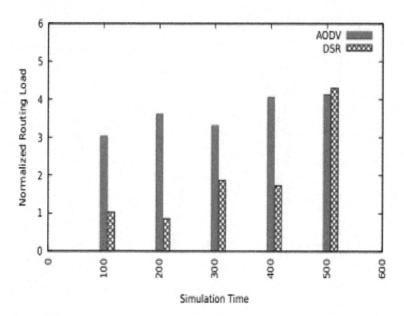

Fig. 3. Normalized routing load vs simulation time (sec.)

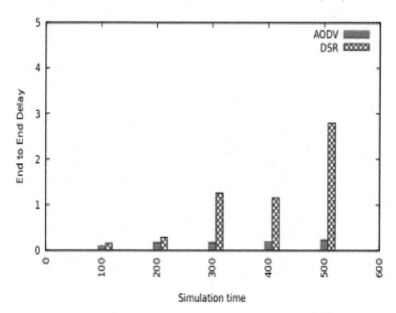

Fig. 4. End to end delay (sec.) vs simulation time (sec.)

Figure 4 shows end to end delay performance of AODV and DSR routing protocols in presence of selfish nodes. Results reveal that delay of AODV is 84% less than that of DSR.

5.2   Effects of Varying Maximum Node Speed

Simulation study has also been conducted by varying node speed as 5, 10, 15, 20 and 25 m/s. In this case simulation time has been fixed to 200 s. Results obtained are represented through Table 4 and From Fig. 5, Fig. 6, Fig. 7 and Fig. 8.

Table 4. Performance by varying max node speed

Speed (m/s)	AODV				DSR			
	PDR	Throughput	NRL	Delay	PDR	Throughput	NRL	Delay
5	59.16	126.54	2.6	.12	63.92	131.89	.73	.72
10	61.35	130.77	3.06	.15	58.77	121.22	.71	.30
15	64.78	138.53	3.28	.16	57.63	119.03	.96	.67
20	61.85	132.43	3.88	.18	49.78	102.79	2.67	1.39
25	61.82	132.31	3.76	.18	47.67	98.39	3.188	1.3

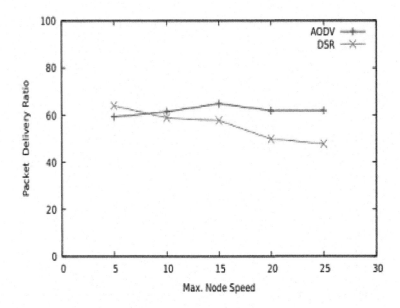

Fig. 5. Packet delivery ratio vs max node speed (m/s)

Packet delivery ratio on varying node speed is represented in Fig. 5 which shows that as the node speed increases, the PDR of DSR decreases. As per results, PDR of AODV is 11% better that DSR.

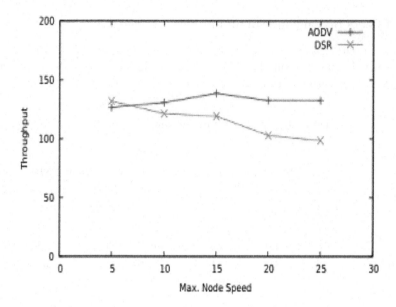

Fig. 6. Throughput (kbps) vs max node speed (m/s)

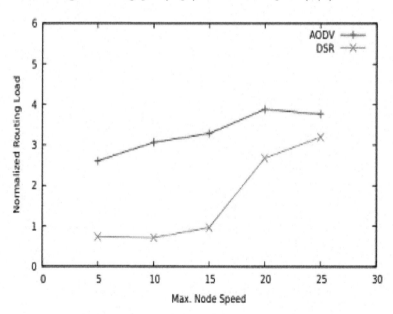

Fig. 7. Normalized routing load vs max node speed (m/s)

Throughput on varying the node speed has been shown in Fig. 6. Results prove that the AODV achieves 15% higher throughput as compared to DSR in presence of selfish node.

Figure 7 depicts normalized routing load of both AODV and DSR on injecting six selfish nodes. Result shows that DSR has 50% less normalized routing load as compared to AODV.

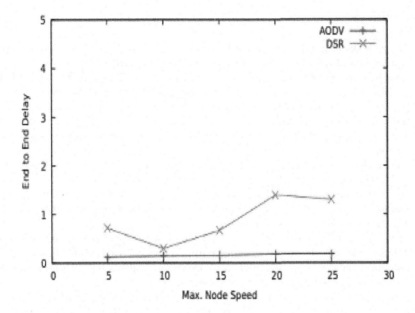

Fig. 8. End to end delay (sec.) vs max node speed (m/s)

Figure 8 represents end to end delay on varying node speed. In case of AODV, delay is almost constant. On the other hand, delay of DSR increases with increase in the node speed. Overall delay of AODV routing protocols is 82% less than DSR.

6   Conclusion

This paper presented an analysis of most popular on demand MANET routing protocols i.e. AODV and DSR in presence of selfish nodes. Selfish nodes do not intentionally harm the system rather due to some constraints such as for battery power preservation, they do not co-operate fully in route discovery and data forwarding operation. We have considered first category of selfish node which does not forward data packets to the next hop. Simulation has been conducted over network simulator NS 2.35 and results have been further analysed to study the effect of selfish nodes over the considered routing protocols. From the results, it is concluded that on varying node speed as well as simulation time, packet delivery ratio, throughput and delay performance of AODV is better than DSR. However, DSR requires less number of control packets in transmitting single data packet.

In future, it is planned to propose an effective scheme which would prevent the system from selfish nodes by applying cryptographic algorithms.

References

1. Bang, A.O., Ramteke, P.L.: MANET: history, challenges and applications. Int. J. Appl. Innov. Eng. Manag. (IJAIEM) **2**(9), 249–251 (2013)
2. Roy, R.R.: Handbook of Mobile Ad Hoc Networks for Mobility Models, vol. 170. Springer, New York (2011). https://doi.org/10.1007/978-1-4419-6050-4
3. Perkins, C., Belding-Royer, E., Das, S.:RFC3561: ad hoc on-demand distance vector (AODV) routing (2003)
4. Johnson, D.B., Maltz, D.A., Broch, J.: DSR: the dynamic source routing protocol for multi-hop wireless ad hoc networks. Ad Hoc Network. **5**(1), 139–172 (2001)
5. Gupta, A.K., Sadawarti, H., Verma, A.K.: Performance analysis of AODV, DSR & TORA routing protocols. Int. J. Eng. Technol. **2**(2), 226 (2010)
6. Azfar, S., Nadeem, A., Ahsan, K., Sarim, M.: Impact analysis and a detection method for misbehaving nodes in Mobile ad-hoc networks. J. Basic Appl. Sci. Res. 4(8), 15–28 (2014)
7. Mishra, D., Jain, Y.K., Agrawal, S.: Behavior analysis of malicious node in the different routing algorithms in mobile ad hoc network (MANET). In: 2009 International Conference on Advances in Computing, Control, and Telecommunication Technologies, pp. 621–623. IEEE, December 2009
8. Samyal, V.K., Sharma, Y.K.: Analysis of selfish node behavior in delay tolerant networks routing protocols. Proc. Int. J. Innov. Res. Sci. Eng. **3**(1), 377–384 (2017)
9. Hollick, M., Schmitt, J., Seipl, C., Steinmetz, R.: On the effect of node misbehavior in ad hoc networks. In: 2004 IEEE International Conference on Communications (IEEE Cat. No. 04CH37577), vol. 6, pp. 3759–3763. IEEE, June 2004
10. Tomar, G.S., Sharma, T., Bhattacharyya, D., Kim, T.H.: Performance comparison of AODV, DSR and DSDV under various network conditions: a survey. In: 2011 International Conference on Ubiquitous Computing and Multimedia Applications, pp. 3–7. IEEE, April 2011
11. Suman, A., Nagar, A.K., Jain, S., Saurav, P.: Simulation analysis of STAR, p. 15. DSR and ZRP in presence of misbehaving nodes in MANET. Proc. Manuscript received November 2009
12. Gorine, D., Saleh, R.:Performance analysis of routing protocols in MANET under malicious attacks. Int. J. Netw. Secur. Appl. (IJNSA) **11** (2019)
13. Shan, A., Xiumei, F A N., Zhang, X.: Quantitative study on impact of node selfishness on performance of MANETs. In: 2020 IEEE International Conference on Smart Internet of Things (SmartIoT). IEEE (2020)
14. Abdelhaq, M., et al.: The impact of selfishness attack on mobile ad hoc network. Int. J. Commun. Netw. Inf. Secur. **12**(1), 42–46 (2020)
15. Verma, M., Barwar, N.C.: A comparative analysis of DSR and AODV protocols under Blackhole and Grayhole attacks in MANET. Int. J. Comput. Sci. Inf. Technol. **5**(6), 7228–7231 (2014)

16. Gurung, S., Chauhan, S.: A novel approach for mitigating route request flooding attack in MANET. Wirel. Netw. **24**(8), 2899–2914 (2018)
17. Moudni, H., Er-Rouidi, M., Mouncif, H., El Hadadi, B.: Attacks against AODV routing protocol in mobile ad-hoc networks. In: 2016 13th International Conference on Computer Graphics, Imaging and Visualization (CGIV), pp. 385–389. IEEE, March 2016
18. Babakhouya, A., Challal, Y., Bouabdallah, A.: A simulation analysis of routing misbehaviour in mobile ad hoc networks. In: 2008 The Second International Conference on Next Generation Mobile Applications, Services, and Technologies, pp. 592–597 (2008). https://doi.org/10.1109/NGMAST.2008.56
19. Issariyakul, T., Hossain, E.: Introduction to network simulator 2 (NS2). In: Issariyakul, T., Hossain, E. (eds.) Introduction to Network Simulator NS2, pp. 1–18. Springer, Boston (2009). https://doi.org/10.1007/978-0-387-71760-9_2

A Deadlock-Free and Adaptive Prime Perspective Turn Model for 3D-Mesh Based Network-on-Chips

Pradeep Kumar Sharma[1]([✉]), Pinaki Mitra[1], and Santosh Biswas[1,2]

[1] Indian Institute of Technology (IIT) Guwahati, Assam, India
cspradeepindia@gmail.com, pinaki@iitg.ac.in
[2] Indian Institute of Technology (IIT), Bhilai, India
santosh@iitbhilai.ac.in

Abstract. With the tremendous demands for core-based digital systems, routing algorithms play a key role in improving metrics like performance parameters (delay, throughput) and cost effectiveness of network-on-chips (NoCs). A 3D-mesh-based NoC essentially stacks many layers of 2D-meshes integration to achieve greater performance, a high integration density, shorter interconnects, and lower power consumption. We propose a 3D-mesh routing model that is adaptive, deadlock-free, and that forbids certain turns depending on the prime number of stacks up layer as well as vertical and horizontal directions without virtual channels. The proposed routing model extends the two dimension repeating turn model (RTM-2D) into 3D-mesh by applying certain additional rules based on prime perspective, and it balances the degree of adaptiveness accordingly as prime perspective plane. According to the simulation results, our routing method outperforms in terms of performance metrics to the six typical routing systems in the uniform, transpose, and hotspot cases.

Keywords: Network-on-Chip (NoC) · PTM · Turn model · Mesh topology · Deadlock-freedom

1 Introduction

The adjacent processing cores communicate with one another through a number of topological routers in a network-on-chip (NoC), which is an organised system of point-to-point connections. The structure of network communication is depicted in Fig. 1 from [2,18] as follows: (a) traditional bus-based network communication among cores of SoCs where only one core can communicate at a time in the network system, (b) point-to-point interconnection links where each core dedicated to each other via a link, and (c) router-based network communication called NoC where each router either pass the communication to a local core or it passes to the next destined address. NoC overcomes the limitations of standard System-on-Chips (SoCs) bus-based communication architectural system by providing a scalable, reuseable, and parallel communication platform for large applications.

© The Author(s), under exclusive license to Springer Nature Switzerland AG 2023
I. Woungang et al. (Eds.): ANTIC 2022, CCIS 1797, pp. 362–375, 2023.
https://doi.org/10.1007/978-3-031-28180-8_24

High-performance real-time and application processors, a dedicated graphics core, and programmable logic are all combined into one unit to produce an MPSoC (MultiProcessor System on Chip), which delivers a high-performance processing system [10,14]. Efficient task mapping [18,22] and routing model [4,16,21,23] can help greatly to reduce the overall communication energy and communication overheads.

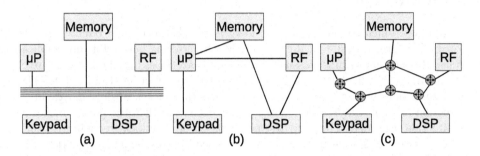

Fig. 1. Network communication structures (a) traditional bus, (b) dedicated point-to-point interconnection, and (c) router-based interconnection

To construct a deadlock-free routing algorithm, there are 12 possible ways to prohibit two combinations of turns in a 2×2 mesh topology as shown in Fig. 2. Consequently, for a 10×10 2D-mesh topology, it has $(12)^{81}$ possible routing ways because it contains total $(10-1) \times (10-1) = 81$ 2×2 subnetworks. To design a deadlock-free and highly adaptive high performance routing algorithm from such a hugh search space is an NP-hard problem.

The 2D-mesh-based NoC is the most commonly accepted topology. However, in order to achieve higher performance, recent trends suggest that a network's routing algorithm is slightly moving to 3D-mesh on integration of stacks over 2D-meshes. The routing method can be implemented in two different ways: table-based (look-up table) and logic-based (combination circuit). In terms of area, power, latency, and throughput; Dimension order Routing (DoR) [8], turn model routing [12], Odd-even turn model [6], balanced-plane odd-even turn model [7], repetitive turn model (RTM-2D) [21], RTM-3D [4] are the most basic examples of logic-based routing algorithms. Table-based approach maintains a look-up table at each switch/router to store routing paths for its every destination pairs. It is implemented to any topology but has poor scalability. SR [17], PM [20], LBDR [11] are examples of table-based routing algorithms.

Since RTM-3D [4] (3D extension of RTM-2D) outperforms over BOE, OE-3D, NF-3D turn models in 3D-mesh network. So, the fundamental objective is to define a new deadlock-free and adaptive routing algorithm that outperforms RTM-3D and the earlier turn models for 3D-mesh networks.

Following is the arrangement of the remaining sections. We provide a brief summary of the associated work for the forbidden turn model in Sect. 2. Prohibited turn model (PTM-3D) routing and an illustrated example are found in Sect. 3. The comparative simulation results of six fundamental routing methods are shown in Sect. 4. Finally, Sect. 5 concludes the paper work.

2 Related Work

A topology which has low diameter, low average distance, high bandwidth and low node-degree, doesn't mean that it always performs better for any applications. Routing algorithms classified into several categories based on the nature of application problems [1,2]. The most famous Dimension order Routing (DoR) [8] is a fully deterministic XY routing in which the packet always moves in x-direction first until x-direction vanishes if needed, and then the packet moves in y-direction if needed. The very first paper based on deadlock-free adaptive turn model routing in 2D-mesh architecture proposed by Glass *et al.* in 1992 [12]. The *XY, West-first, North-last, and Negative-first* routing algorithms are deadlock-free and not using any virtual channel or buffer. A new partially adaptive routing technique based on Odd-Even columns turned in a 2D-mesh was proposed by chiu *et al.* in 2000 [6]. It slightly solves the adaptiveness problem of turn model routing and it also works without using virtual channels and buffers in the router design architecture. By proposing two additional modified odd-even rules, Dahir *et al.* developed a balanced degree of adaptiveness odd-even routing for 3D-mesh network in 2012 [7]. PAAD (partially adaptive and deterministic routing) is a switch based routing: *deterministic* when there is no congestion and *partially adaptive* when there is congestion in 2D-mesh bassed network [15]. The RTM-2D [21] repetitive prohibited turns are based on *column%3* instead of odd-even so that the maximum column repetitive distance increases and the routing pressure [19] decreases. The deadlock-free routing models, prime turn model and

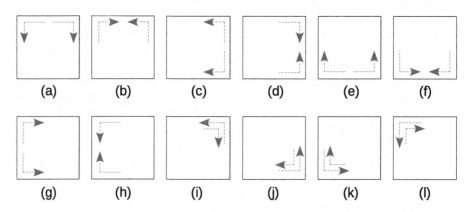

(a)   (b)   (c)   (d)   (e)   (f)

(g)   (h)   (i)   (j)   (k)   (l)

Fig. 2. The deadlock-free routing algorithms for 2D-mesh (2×2) topology

last first turn model [16], and column/row-partitioning routing model [3] implemented on 2D-mesh topology and their performances are slightly better than odd-even routing turn model. In 3D mesh based NOCs, FT-DyXYZ, an adaptive fault tolerance routing that employs proximity congestion information to balance traffic, may tolerate permanently damaged links which do not require routing tables, or global information about pathways and defects [13]. RTM-3D [4] is basically an extension of repetitive turn model by deploying two addition rules for inter-layer prohibited turn. It shows the performance result over basic turn model routing and odd-even for 3D-mesh network. Adaptive thermal-aware routing (ATAR) [9] is thermal-aware prohibited turn based deadlock-free routing which can also alleviate the peak temperature.

Therefore, we got the motivation as well as set the objective to design a new routing algorithm called, prime perspective turn model (PTM) which has the longest MRD distance, low routing pressure, and better performance metrics (average packet delay (cycles), throughput (flits/cycle/node) to others routing algorithms, RTM-3D and MRD-3D, OE-3D and others 3D routing algorithms.

3   Proposed Model

For a 3D-mesh based network topology, a particular node is identified by a three-element-vector (x_c, y_c, z_c), where x_c denotes coordinate along x-axis, y_c denotes coordinate along y-axis, and z_c denotes coordinate along z-axis. Each node can be labeled(l) by the following formula: $l = x_c + y_c * N + z_c * N * N$. Assume that N is the size of each dimension. Each node (x_c, y_c, z_c), therefore meets the condition that $0 < x_c, y_c, z_c < N$. Each node in the same plane has the same value of z_c.

Definition 1. *A prime number (or prime) is a natural number that is divisible exactly only by one (1) and the number itself.*

From the above definition, isPrime(z_c) is a function which returns *true* if z_c is prime, otherwise returns *false*.

Definition 2. *Routing, $\langle S, D \rangle$ is the higher-level decision-making process that determines the path for traffic within a network, between networks, or across multiple networks from the source node (S) to the destination node (D) through intermediary network nodes (routers/switches/gateways).*

3.1   PTM-3D

PTM-3D (Prime perspective Turn Model for 3D-Mesh), which restricts turns based on prime position of coordinate axes, is the proposed deadlock-free routing algorithm for 3D-mesh based NoCs. PTM-3D is a combination of RTM-3D (which is an extension of RTM-2D), OE-3D, MRD-3D and BOE-3D. A message/packet forwards possibly in six available directions: **Up** ($z_e > 0$), **Down** ($z_e < 0$), **North** ($y_e > 0$), **South** ($y_e < 0$), **East** ($x_e > 0$), and **West**

$(x_e < 0)$. When a new message is injected into 3D-mesh network then the proposed PTM-3D routing is following turn rules to avoid deadlock in layer to layer communication,

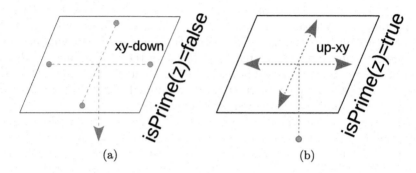

Fig. 3. Prohibited turn: (a) xy-down turn, (b) up-xy turn

– **Rule 1**: A message is not allowed to take a turn at any node (x_c, y_c, z_c) in xy-down direction, if the current layer z_c is not a prime, i.e., $isPrime(z_c) = false$ as shown in Fig. 3(a)
– **Rule 2**: A message is not allowed to take a turn at any node (x_c, y_c, z_c) in Up-xy direction, if the layer z_c is a prime, i.e., $isPrime(z_c) = true$ as shown in Fig. 3(b).

To avoid the deadlock, the injected message follows Rules 1 and 2 in inter-layers communication. For example, the injected message is prohibited from *xy-plane-to-down* direction at $z_c = 1, 4, 5, 6$ by Rule 1, and it is prohibited *Up-to-xy-plane* at $z_c = 2, 3, 5$ by Rule 2 as shown in Fig. 3.

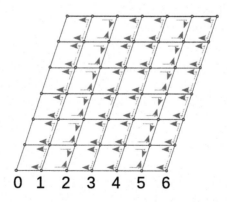

0 1 2 3 4 5 6

Fig. 4. Prohibited turn: column (x-axis) perspective turn

- **Rule 3**: Any message is not allowed to take a turn at any node (x_c, y_c, z_c) in North-West (NW) and South-West (SW) turns, if the column x_c is not a prime number, i.e., $isPrime(x_c) = false$ as shown in Fig. 4.
- **Rule 4**: Any message is not allowed to take a turn at any node (x_c, y_c, z_c) East-North (EN) and East-South (ES) turns, if the coordinate x_c is a prime number, i.e., $isPrime(x_c) = true$ as shown in Fig. 4.

To avoid the deadlock in intra-layer (i.e., within a xy-plane), the injected message follows Rules 3 and 4. For example, the injected message is restricted North/South to West turn at non-prime column, $x_c = 1, 4, 5, 6$ according to Rule 3, and Rule 4 forbids East to North/South turn at prime column, $x_c = 2, 3, 5$ as shown in Fig. 4.

The Algorithm 1, PTM-3D divides the routing problem based on plane-wise prohibited turn model along z-direction perspective. Let us assume that current node(x_c, y_c, z_c), source node(x_s, y_s, z_s), destination node(x_d, y_d, z_d) are the coordinate points of 3D-mesh having three coordinate axes (x-direction, y-direction, and z-direction).

The Algorithm 1 divides basically into three cases ($z_e = 0$, $z_e > 0$, $z_e < 0$) based on offset(z) along z-axis ($z_e = z_d - z_c$). For the first case ($z_e = 0$), it calls algorithm PTM-2D as shown in Fig. 4. In the second case ($z_e > 0$),

---

ALGORITHM 1: PTM-3D

Input : current node(x_c, y_c, z_c), source node(x_s, y_s, z_s), destination node(x_d, y_d, z_d)

Output: $Avail\_Direction\_Set$

1: $Avail\_Direction\_Set = \phi$;
2: $x_e = x_d - x_c$;
3: $y_e = y_d - y_c$;
4: $z_e = z_d - z_c$;
5: **if** $z_e = 0$ **then**
6:    call PTM-2D;
7: **else if** $z_e > 0$ **then**
8:    **if** $x_e = 0$ *and* $y_e = 0$ **then**
9:       Add **Up** $(z_c + 1)$ to $Avail\_Direction\_Set$;
10:   **else**
11:      **if** $isPrime(z_c) = false$ or $z_c = z_s$ **then**
12:         call PTM-2D;
13:      **if** $z_c = 1$ *and* $z_d = 3$ **then**
14:         **return** $(Avail\_Direction\_Set)$;
15:      **if** $z_e > 1$ *or* $isPrime(z_d) = false$ **then**
16:         Add **Up** $(z_c + 1)$ to $Avail\_Direction\_Set$;
17: **else**
18:    Add **Down** $(z_c - 1)$ to $Avail\_Direction\_Set$;
19:    **if** $isPrime(z_c) = true$ *and* $(x_e \neq 0$ *or* $y_e \neq 0)$ **then**
20:       call PTM-2D;
21: **return** $(Avail\_Direction\_Set)$;

---

if both offsets along x_e and y_e becomes zero then the packet adds route Up $(z_c + 1)$ direction in available direction set; if the current plane is non-prime $(isPrime(z_c)=$false) or the current plane is source plane, then it calls PTM-2D, and if a situation becomes $z_c = 1$ and $z_d = 3$ then the packet routes to a low congested immediate neighbor from the avail directions set; otherwise the packet also adds Up direction in available direction set if the current offset $z_e > 1$ or $isPrime(z_d) = false$. For the last case $(z_e < 0)$, the available direction set adds Down $(z_c - 1)$ direction and it also calls PTM-2D, if the current plane is prime whereas $(x_e \neq 0$ or $y_e \neq 0)$. Therefore, The current message firstly analyzes all possible available paths/routes using PTM-3D routing algorithm and forwards to one of direction in *Avail_Direction_Set* where network traffic is low and update the current position.

Based on the above cases, Algorithm 2 called by Algorithm 1. Initially Avail_Direction_Set is empty(ϕ), and both x_e and y_e are the offset between current position and destination node along x-direction and y-direction respectively. If both offsets are zero, that means, the current packet reached to the destination node, hence the packet goes to the local core and return from it. But, for $x_e = 0$, the available direction set contains either North $(y_c + 1)$ or South $(y_c - 1)$ direction, depend on its case, $y_e > 0$ or not. For $x_e > 0$, if offset $y_e = 0$ then it adds East$(x_c + 1)$ in available direction set otherwise, for the case isPrime$(x_c) =$ false or $x_c = x_s$, the available direction set contains either North $(y_c + 1)$ or South $(y_c - 1)$ direction depend on its case, $y_e > 0$ or not, and if a situation $x_c = 1$ and $x_d = 3$ occured then the packet moves to one of the direction from available direction set, that means $y_c \to y_d$. The East $(x_c + 1)$ direction is available, either the current packet is far at least two hops distance $(x_e > 1)$ or the destination node is not at prime position along x-direction (isPrime(x_d) = false). For the third case, $x_e < 0$, the available direction set contains West as well as North/South direction depends on, $y_e > 0$ becomes true or false. At the end of the algorithm, it returns all available directions set, and among all, any one can took as current path.

The repetitive (prohibited turn) distance for RTM-3D is three(3) but, the repetitive distance for PTM-3D is not repetitive (not constant) under any size of network. Since, higher the maximum column repetitive distance (MRD) has lower the routing pressure observed in [21]. So, we can say that the repetitive distance for PTM-3D is the size of network (e.g., Δz) and it has low routing pressure.

ALGORITHM 2: PTM-2D

Input : current node(x_c, y_c), source node(x_s, y_s), destination node(x_d, y_d)
Output: *Avail_Direction_Set*
1: *Avail_Direction_Set* = ϕ;
2: $x_e = x_d - x_c$;
3: $y_e = y_d - y_c$;
4: **if** $x_e = 0$ *and* $y_e = 0$ **then**
5:    Packet goes to local core and **exit**;
6: **if** $x_e = 0$ **then**
7:    **if** $y_e > 0$ **then**
8:       Add **North** ($y_c + 1$) to *Avail_Direction_Set*;
9:    **else**
10:      Add **South** ($y_c - 1$) to *Avail_Direction_Set*;
11: **else**
12:    **if** $x_e > 0$ **then**
13:      **if** $y_e = 0$ **then**
14:        Add **East** ($x_c + 1$) to *Avail_Direction_Set*;
15:      **else**
16:        **if** $isPrime(x_c) = false$ *or* $x_c = x_s$ **then**
17:          **if** $y_e > 0$ **then**
18:            Add **North** ($y_c + 1$) to *Avail_Direction_Set*;
19:          **else**
20:            Add **South** ($y_c - 1$) to *Avail_Direction_Set*;
21:          **if** $x_c = 1$ *and* $x_d = 3$ **then**
22:            **return** (*Avail_Direction_Set*);
23:          **if** $x_e > 1$ *or* $isPrime(x_d) = false$ **then**
24:            Add **East** ($x_c + 1$) to *Avail_Direction_Set*;
25:    **else**
26:      Add **West** to *Avail_Direction_Set*;
27:      **if** $isPrime(x_c) = true$ **then**
28:        **if** $y_e > 0$ **then**
29:          Add **North** ($y_c + 1$) to *Avail_Direction_Set*;
30:        **else**
31:          Add **South** ($y_c - 1$) to *Avail_Direction_Set*;
32: **return** (*Avail_Direction_Set*);

3.2 Illustrative Example

A 3D-mesh ($7 \times 7 \times 7$) topology where each joint (black dot) of mesh topology depicted as router (6 ports) and it is dedicated to a local core, is shown in Fig. 5. Both Rules 1 and 2 are applicable if the packets are communicating from layer to layer (inter-plane) whereas both Rules 3 and 4 are applicable if packet moves in the same plane (intra-plane) where x-coordinate decides prohibited turn model for xy-plane.

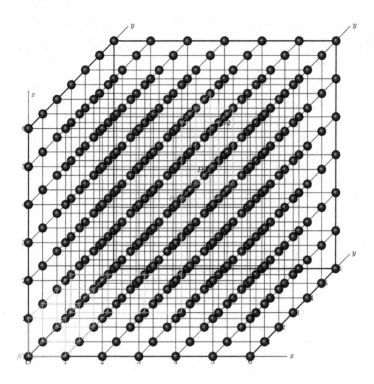

Fig. 5. $7 \times 7 \times 7$ 3D-mesh architecture.

In Fig. 5, two source-destination pairs, $\langle S1, D1 \rangle$ and $\langle S2, D2 \rangle$, are marked with red and blue, respectively, to illustrate the PTM-3D routing algorithm in 3D mesh ($7 \times 7 \times 7$) topology. The first pair (red), $\langle S1, D1 \rangle$ routes a message from S1(0,0,0) to D1(3,3,3), whereas the second pair (blue), $\langle S2, D2 \rangle$, routes a message from S2(4,3,5) to D2(3,5,3) and the the available direction set for each message/packet is taken as empty, i.e., $Avail\_Direction\_Set = \phi$.

For the first pair (red) $\langle S1(0,0,0), D1(3,3,3) \rangle$, initially, the offsets are $x_e = y_e = z_e = 3$ along x-axis, y-axis, and z-axis respectively. First, the source node S1(0,0,0) can add a route (1,0,0) or (0,1,0) to available direction set by calling PTM-2D since ($z_c = z_s$), or it can add a route to the immediate upper plane arriving at (0,0,1), so the Available_Direction_Set is {(1,0,0), (0,1,0), (0,0,1)}. The current packet is arriving at any of the available directions, thus let's assume that (0,0,1). The message at (0,0,1) cannot be routed to (0,0,2) since Rule 2 is violated, and hence the message at (0,0,1) routes either at (1,0,1) or (0,1,1) in its plane($z_c = 1$), and let's assume that the packet is receiving at (1,0,1). The message at (1,0,1) cannot be routed to (1,0,2) because a situation, $z_c = 1$ and $z_d = 3$ occured, or to (2,0,1) because again a situation, $x_c = 1$ and $x_d = 3$ occured. Therefore, the message at (1,0,1) reached to (1,1,1), and similarly, from (1,1,1) to (1,2,1), from (1,2,1) to (1,3,1). For the message at $y_e = 0$ and $z_c = 1$, only East direction is available. When the message where $x_e = 0$ and $y_e = 0$, it routes to Up direction only and reached to the destination D1(3,3,3). Therefore, for the first pair(red) $\langle S1, D1 \rangle$, the message at source S1(0,0,0) can travel via 28 alternative paths to reach the destination D1(3,3,3) using the PTM-3D routing algorithm. One of the routing path is as: $\langle S1(0,0,0) \rightarrow (0,0,1) \rightarrow (1,0,1) \rightarrow (1,1,1) \rightarrow (1,2,1) \rightarrow (1,3,1) \rightarrow (2,3,1) \rightarrow (3,3,1) \rightarrow (3,3,2) \rightarrow D1(3,3,3) \rangle$. Likewise, another routing path is as: $\langle S1(0,0,0) \rightarrow (0,1,0) \rightarrow (0,2,0) \rightarrow (0,3,0) \rightarrow (1,3,0) \rightarrow (2,3,0) \rightarrow (3,3,0) \rightarrow (3,3,1) \rightarrow (3,3,2) \rightarrow D1(3,3,3) \rangle$.

For the second pair (blue) $\langle S2(4,3,5), D2(3,5,3) \rangle$, the packet at source (S2) can find one of the routing path as: $\langle S2(4,3,5) \rightarrow (4,3,4) \rightarrow (4,3,3) \rightarrow (4,4,3) \rightarrow (3,4,3) \rightarrow D2(3,5,3) \rangle$; likewise, another path is as: $\langle S2(4,3,5) \rightarrow (4,3,4) \rightarrow (4,3,3) \rightarrow (3,3,3) \rightarrow (3,4,3) \rightarrow D2(3,5,3) \rangle$. Therefore, for the second pair(red) $\langle S2, D2 \rangle$, has 08 alternative paths to reach destination D2(3,5,3).

3.3 Deadlock-Freedom Proof

To ensure deadlock-freeness in intra-layer (PTM-2D), the algorithm must obey 12 possible ways of prohibited turns in each 2×2 submesh network as shown in Fig. 2, e.g., Rules 3 and 4. In PTM-3D, Rules 1 and 2 are implemented to make sure that no cycle exists between any two layers, which is one of necessary condition for inter-layer deadlock-freeness.

4 Experimental Results

In this section, we compare the performance metrics (delay, throughput) of the proposed model, *prime number based turn model routing for 3D-mesh topology (PTM-3D) to maximum column repetitive distance based 3D routing (MRD-3D routing)* [4], *repetitive turn model for 3D routing (RTM-3D)* [4], *balanced odd-even turn model for 3D routing (BOE-3D)* [7], *odd-even turn model for 3D routing(OE-3D)* [6,7] *and negative-first turn model for 3D routing (NF-3D)* [12]. These all are simulated on network simulator, Noxim [5] using virtual cut-through technique for $5 \times 5 \times 5$ mesh as well as $5 \times 5 \times 7$ mesh up to 12000 cycles. PTM-3D model is illustrated in detail on $7 \times 7 \times 7$ 3D-mesh to show two complex cases separately so that all four rules can be practicednbut it efficiently works also in $5 \times 5 \times 5$ 3D-mesh. Here, we have chosen $5 \times 5 \times 5$ 3D-mesh to show and compare performance parameters with different-different recent routing models in experimental results because most of the routing models (for example, RTM-3D, MRD-3D etc.).

Now, we calculate the performance parameter (delay, throughput) in respect of packet injection rate for each message. We also considered three different typical traffic patterns namely: uniform, transpose and hotspot traffic. In uniform traffic, the source node and the destination node are fully randomly distributed in the network topology. In transpose traffic, both source node (i, j, k) and destination node (j, k, i) should be the mirror image of each other along the principal diagonal axis. Now, in hotspot traffic, a particular node chosen as hotspot that receive 4 percent extra packets in addition to the uniform traffic.

372   P. K. Sharma et al.

PTM-3D routing model works under uniform, transpose, and hotspot cases and compared to RTM-3D Fig. 6 demonstrates the performance metrics(average packet latency and throughput) versus packet injection rate in uniform, transpose, and hotspot cases for $5 \times 5 \times 5$ 3D-meshes. In Fig. 6(a), PTM-3D got saturated (sat) when PIR is 0.36 in uniform traffic. Higher the saturation point offers less congestion over lower saturation point. Figure 6(b), the throughput of PTM-3D also performs better than the previous routing schemes under uniform traffic case. In most of the cases, PTM-3D performed better result than the previous turn models under the transpose traffic (Fig. 6(c) and (d)) as well

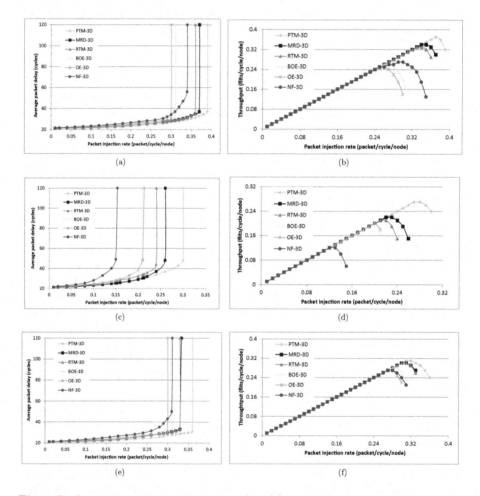

(a)   (b)

(c)   (d)

(e)   (f)

Fig. 6. Performance metrics in $5 \times 5 \times 5$ meshes. (a) Average packet delay versus Packet injection rate (PIR) under uniform traffic, (b) Throughput Vs PIR under uniform traffic, (c) Average packet delay Vs PIR under transpose traffic, (d) Throughput Vs PIR under transpose traffic, (e) Average packet delay Vs PIR in hotspot traffic, (f) Throughput Vs PIR in hotspot traffic.

as hotspot traffic (Fig. 6(e) and (f)) having two hotspot positions (**3, 1, 1**) and (**2, 3, 4**). PTM-3D also performed better results in case of cuboid 3D-meshes in uniform, transpose, and hotspot cases.

Tables 1 and 2 show more concrete view of average packet delay against PIR and throughput against PIR for the above six mentioned routing strategies under uniform, transpose, hotspot traffics. In most of the cases, they concludes that PTM-3D has reduced average packet delay and increased throughput than the other routing strategies.

Table 1. Average packet delay (cycles) against Packet injection rate (packet/cycle/ node) in uniform, transpose and hotspot traffics in $5 \times 5 \times 5$ meshes

PIR	Average packet delay (cycles)																	
	Uniform traffic						Transpose traffic						Hotspot traffic					
	PTM-3D	MRD-3D	RTM-3D	BOE-3D	OE-3D	NF-3D	PTM-3D	MRD-3D	RTM-3D	BOE-3D	OE-3D	NF-3D	PTM-3D	MRD-3D	RTM-3D	BOE-3D	OE-3D	NF-3D
0.04	21.17	21.2	21.2	21.4	21.42	22.05	21.5	21.5	21.9	22	22	22.8	21.17	21.2	21.2	21.4	21.42	21.8
0.08	21.36	21.5	21.5	22	22.04	22.8	22.55	22.5	23.3	23.5	23.5	25.2	21.36	21.5	21.5	22	22.04	22.8
0.12	21.59	22.35	22.35	22.9	22.96	23.75	24	23.85	25.5	26	25.5	33	21.59	22.35	22.35	22.9	22.96	24
0.16	22.2	23	23	23.8	23.88	25	26.25	25.75	28.5	30	29	sat	22.2	22.9	22.9	24.1	23.88	25.5
0.2	23.1	24.1	24.1	25	25.1	26.5	29.25	29	32.5	41	38.5	–	23.1	24.3	24.3	26	25.1	27.25
0.24	24.2	25.5	25.5	26.85	27	28.3	33.75	37	44	sat	sat	–	24.2	26.2	26.2	28.4	27	29.5
0.28	25.5	27.2	27.3	28.7	28.7	30.5	40	sat	sat	–	–	–	25.5	28.4	28.5	30.9	28.7	35
0.32	28.1	29.5	29.65	sat	sat	41.5	sat	–	–	–	–	–	28.1	31.35	31.6	sat	sat	sat
0.36	31.3	34.8	35	–	–	sat	–	–	–	–	–	–	30.8	sat	sat	–	–	–
0.4	sat	sat	sat	–	–	–	–	–	–	–	–	–	sat	–	–	–	–	–

Table 2. Throughput (flits/cycle/node) against Packet injection rate (packet/cycle/ node) in uniform, transpose and hotspot traffics in $5 \times 5 \times 5$ meshes

PIR	Throughput (flits/cycle/node)																	
	Uniform traffic						Transpose traffic						Hotspot traffic					
	PTM-3D	MRD-3D	RTM-3D	BOE-3D	OE-3D	NF-3D	PTM-3D	MRD-3D	RTM-3D	BOE-3D	OE-3D	NF-3D	PTM-3D	MRD-3D	RTM-3D	BOE-3D	OE-3D	NF-3D
0.04	0.04	0.04	0.04	0.04	0.04	0.04	0.04	0.04	0.04	0.04	0.04	0.04	0.04	0.04	0.04	0.04	0.04	0.04
0.08	0.08	0.08	0.08	0.08	0.08	0.08	0.08	0.08	0.08	0.08	0.08	0.08	0.08	0.08	0.08	0.08	0.08	0.08
0.12	0.12	0.12	0.12	0.12	0.12	0.12	0.12	0.12	0.12	0.12	0.12	0.12	0.12	0.12	0.12	0.12	0.12	0.12
0.16	0.16	0.16	0.16	0.16	0.16	0.16	0.16	0.16	0.16	0.16	0.16	0.16	0.16	0.16	0.16	0.16	0.16	0.16
0.20	0.20	0.20	0.20	0.20	0.20	0.20	0.20	0.20	0.20	0.20	0.20	–	0.20	0.20	0.20	0.20	0.20	0.20
0.24	0.24	0.24	0.24	0.24	0.24	0.24	0.24	0.24	0.21	0.15	sat	sat	0.24	0.24	0.24	0.24	0.24	0.24
0.28	0.28	0.28	0.28	0.25	0.22	0.26	0.27	sat	–	–	–	–	0.28	0.28	0.28	0.28	0.27	0.27
0.32	0.32	0.32	0.32	sat	sat	0.25	sat	–	–	–	–	–	0.31	0.29	0.29	sat	sat	sat
0.36	0.36	sat	sat	–	–	sat	–	–	–	–	–	–	0.24	sat	sat	–	–	–
0.4	sat	–	–	–	–	–	–	–	–	–	–	–	sat	–	–	–	–	–

Table 3 shows the PIR saturation point and % improvement of performance parameters (average packet delay, throughput) PTM-3D routing scheme to the rest mentioned routing schemes under uniform, transpose, and hotspot traffics. In this table, PIR saturation point = 0.36 and % improvement = 10.57 for the RTM-3D routing scheme under uniform traffic that means, when the PIR reaches to 0.36 under uniform traffic then RTM-3D routing scheme got fully saturated, did not receive any data more and at that point PTM-3D routing scheme improve the performance over RTM-3D routing scheme by 10.57%.

Table 3 concludes that PTM-3D routing schemes performs better than the previous routing schemes, but when the 3D-mesh size increase, its performance get more enhance.

Table 3. Saturation point and % improvement (delay, throughput) of PTM-3D to five different routing strategies under uniform, transpose, and hotspot traffic

Routing strategies	PTM-3D											
	Average packet delay (cycle)						Throughput (flits/cycle/node)					
	Uniform		Transpose		Hotspot		Uniform		Transpose		Hotspot	
	PIR saturation point	% improvement	PIR saturation point	% improvement	PIR saturation point	% improvement	PIR saturation point	% improvement	PIR saturation point	% improvement	PIR saturation point	% improvement
MRD-3D	0.37	11.35	0.26	23.4	0.33	13.1	0.36	09.0	0.26	42.3	0.33	11.1
RTM-3D	0.36	10.57	0.24	23.3	0.33	13.6	0.36	24.13	0.24	37.5	0.33	15.4
BOE-3D	0.31	12.7	0.21	40	0.31	17.3	0.31	66.7	0.21	23.5	0.31	34.8
OE-3D	0.31	11.1	0.21	38.6	0.3	09.3	0.3	87.7	0.21	14.3	0.3	26.6
NF-3D	0.34	47.5	0.15	47.8	0.31	46.9	0.35	2.5x	0.15	2.5x	0.31	47.6

5   Conclusions

In this paper, we briefly discussed various prohibited turn routing models to ensure adaptive deadlock-freeness for 2D/3D-mesh networks. The prohibited turn models are working even without virtual channels. A packet can route prime based prohibited turn model using proposed algorithm, PTM-3D (Prime perspective Turn Model for 3D-Mesh) which ensure deadlock-freedom adaptiveness, in 3D-mesh network. To measure the performance, we have shown the comparison based simulation results of the average packet delay (in cycles) as well as thorughput (flits/cycle/node) along packet injection rate (packet/cycle/node) among six different routing strategies, PTM-3D, MRD-3D, RTM-3D, BOE-3D, OE-3D, NF-3D under uniform, transpose and hotspot cases cases of $5 \times 5 \times 5$ 3D-meshes. After all, the results conclude that, PTM-3D is performed relatively better than other routing models in 3D-cube mesh or 3D-cuboid mesh in most of the cases (uniform, transpose, or hotspot).

PTM-3D has some limitations as: (a) PTM-3D works efficiently if mesh size is not beyond the $36 \times 36 \times 36$ 3D-mesh, (b) for smaller 3D-meshes (between $2 \times 2 \times 2$ to $4 \times 4 \times 4$), it gives similar results to RTM-3D, (c) PTM-3D do not have awareness of faults (switch/router) but in near future, we are considering fault-aware cases.

References

1. Abbas, A., et al.: A survey on energy-efficient methodologies and architectures of network-on-chip. Comput. Electr. Eng. **40**(8), 333–347 (2014)
2. Bjerregaard, T., Mahadevan, S.: A survey of research and practices of network-on-chip. ACM Comput. Surv. (CSUR) **38**(1), 1 (2006)
3. Cai, Y., Luo, W., Xiang, D.: The column-partition and row-partition turn model. In: 42nd Annual Computer Software and Applications Conference (COMPSAC), vol. 1, pp. 687–694. IEEE (2018)
4. Cai, Y., Xiang, D., Ji, X.: Deadlock-free adaptive routing based on the repetitive turn model for 3d network-on-chip. In: International Conference on Parallel & Distributed Processing with Applications, Ubiquitous Computing & Communications, Big Data & Cloud Computing, Social Computing & Networking, Sustainable Computing & Communications, pp. 722–728. IEEE (2018)
5. Catania, V., Mineo, A., Monteleone, S., Palesi, M., Patti, D.: Noxim: an open, extensible and cycle-accurate network on chip simulator. In: IEEE 26th International Conference on Application-specific Systems, Architectures and Processors (ASAP), pp. 162–163. IEEE (2015)

6. Chiu, G.M.: The odd-even turn model for adaptive routing. IEEE Trans. Parallel Distrib. Syst. **11**(7), 729–738 (2000)
7. Dahir, N., Al-Dujaily, R., Yakovlev, A., Missailidis, P., Mak, T.: Deadlock-free and plane-balanced adaptive routing for 3d networks-on-chip. In: Proceedings of the Fifth International Workshop on Network on Chip Architectures, pp. 31–36. ACM (2012)
8. Dally, W.J., Towles, B.P.: Principles and practices of interconnection networks. Elsevier (2004)
9. Dash, R., Majumdar, A., Pangracious, V., Turuk, A.K., Risco-Martin, J.L.: ATAR: an adaptive thermal-aware routing algorithm for 3-D network-on-chip systems. IEEE Trans. Components Packaging Manuf. Tech. **8**(12), 2122–2129 (2018)
10. Delgado, R., Park, J., Choi, B.W.: MPSoC: the low-cost approach to real-time hardware simulations for power and energy systems. IFAC-PapersOnLine **52**(4), 57–62 (2019)
11. Flich, J., Duato, J.: Logic-based distributed routing for NOCs. IEEE Comput. Archit. Lett. **7**(1), 13–16 (2008)
12. Glass, C.J., Ni, L.M.: The turn model for adaptive routing. ACM SIG. Comput. Archit. News **20**(2), 278–287 (1992)
13. Jouybari, H.N., Mohammadi, K.: A low overhead, fault tolerant and congestion aware routing algorithm for 3D mesh-based network-on-chips. Microprocess. Microsyst. **38**(8), 991–999 (2014)
14. Kumar, S., et al.: A network on chip architecture and design methodology. In: Proceedings IEEE Computer Society Annual Symposium on VLSI, pp. 105–112. IEEE (2002)
15. Manzoor, M., Mir, R.N., et al.: PAAD (Partially adaptive and Deterministic routing): a deadlock free congestion aware hybrid routing for 2D mesh network-on-chips. Microprocessors and Microsystems, p. 104551 (2022)
16. Manzoor, M., Mir, R.N., et al.: Prime turn model and first last turn model: an adaptive deadlock free routing for network-on-chips. Microprocess. Microsyst. **89**, 104454 (2022)
17. Mejia, A., Flich, J., Duato, J.: On the potentials of segment-based routing for NOCs. In: 2008 37th International Conference on Parallel Processing, pp. 594–603. IEEE (2008)
18. Sharma, P.K., Biswas, S., Mitra, P.: Energy efficient heuristic application mapping for 2-D mesh-based network-on-chip. Microprocess. Microsyst. **64**, 88–100 (2019)
19. Tang, M., Lin, X., Palesi, M.: Routing pressure: a channel-related and traffic-aware metric of routing algorithm. IEEE Trans. Parallel Distrib. Syst. **26**(3), 891–901 (2013)
20. Tang, M., Lin, X., Palesi, M.: An offline method for designing adaptive routing based on pressure model. IEEE Trans. Comput. Aided Des. Integr. Circuits Syst. **34**(2), 307–320 (2014)
21. Tang, M., Lin, X., Palesi, M.: The repetitive turn model for adaptive routing. IEEE Trans. on Computers **66**(1), 138–146 (2016)
22. Tosun, S., Ozturk, O., Ozkan, E., Ozen, M.: Application mapping algorithms for mesh-based network-on-chip architectures. J. Supercomput. **71**(3), 995–1017 (2015)
23. Wu, J.: A deterministic fault-tolerant and deadlock-free routing protocol in 2-D meshes based on odd-even turn model. In: Proceedings of the 16th International Conference on Supercomputing, pp. 67–76. ACM (2002)

Effect of Channel Slot Time on Performance of IEEE 802.15.6-Based Medical Body Area Network

Khushboo Dadhich[⊠] and Devika Kataria

JK Lakshmipat University, Jaipur, India
{khushboodadhich,devikakataria}@jklu.edu.in

Abstract. The IEEE 802.15.6 standard is an emerging technology that supports low data rate, short-range wireless communication. Medical Body Area Networks (MBAN) are a special type of wireless communication where multiple sensor nodes are deployed on the human body to measure vital parameters. The data is sent by the nodes to a coordinator, the latter aggregates the data and sends it to a central server using standard protocols. The coordinator allows the nodes to access the channel using different access modes-beacon mode with the super frame, non-beacon mode with super frame and non-beacon mode without super frame. The standard allows different user priorities to be assigned to the nodes. The nodes may access the channel using scheduling done by the coordinator (scheduled access) or may randomly access the channel using the CSMA/CA (for narrowband PHY) or Slotted Aloha for UltraWideBand (UWB PHY) protocols. In this work we have conducted an analytical study to understand the performance parameters of different user priority nodes using CSMA/CA protocol and operating in the Beacon access mode with super frame boundaries. Parameters like the probability of successful transmission (reliability) which in turn depend on the probability of packet drop due to channel access failure and the probability of failure due to insufficient time slot available have been studied. This study reveals that once a channel is assessed by a node, then the probability of sufficient time slot of 60% yields the best packet transmission probability. The successful delivery of the packet also depends on back off counter. Markov chain models for nodes with different priorities have been developed using backoff stage and backoff counter as parameters.

Keywords: Markov chain · MAC layer · Medical body area network · Time Slot · User Priority

1 Introduction

Remote health monitoring has become an emerging technology and many health parameters are measured using sensor nodes on human body. These sensor nodes send the measured data to coordinator using IEEE 802.15.6 standard. The nodes along with the coordinator form network which follow the standard and are known as Medical Body Area Networks (MBAN). The rules defined for the PHY and MAC layers of MBAN have

© The Author(s) 2023
I. Woungang et al. (Eds.): ANTIC 2022, CCIS 1797, pp. 376–385, 2023.
https://doi.org/10.1007/978-3-031-28180-8_25

non-optimized parameters and there is scope for improving the QoS by varying these parameters. The channel available time slot has a significant impact on the performance of the MBAN, specially with understanding that the standard keeps the Super-frame length fixed but allows slot lengths to be varied. Several research groups are working on optimizing the slots and achieving better traffic management.

A research group has recommended mini slots for emergency packet communication [1]. Each slot in the super-frame is split into two sections ordinary slots and mini slots. Mini slots are used to facilitate emergency packet transfer without the CSMA/CA access procedure. The MAC protocol controls vital traffic in the beacon-enabled super-frame using mini slots and regular traffic using a predefined slots allocation technique based on data rate. The high energy consumption of nodes with high data rates is a significant disadvantage of this technology. Another group of authors have developed two Time division multiple access-based scheduling techniques to increase reliability and energy efficiency, specifically adaptive scheduling, and dynamic scheduling techniques. The first technique dynamically assigns time slots to nodes by evaluating their network and storage health in both emergency and non-emergency situations. As opposed to the first method, the second grants time slots to nodes based on their queue length. Nonetheless, node prioritizing is not considered in these slot allocation algorithms [2]. Dynamic Slot Scheduling (DSS) technique for optimizing slot scheduling in the super-frame by utilizing a temporal autocorrelation model has been developed by researchers [3]. Actual on-body data is examined to ascertain the unpredictability of communication networks obtained from certain wireless transceivers. The disadvantage of this system is that each node has the same signal strength. In another work it has been suggested that a non-overlapping contention window-based dynamic slots allocation approach. This technique introduces two algorithms: the Non-Overlapping Backoff Algorithm (NOBA) and the Dynamic Slot Allocation (DSA) scheme. The NOBA removes backoff-induced inter-priority conflicts, whereas the DSA distributes dynamic slots to decrease waste caused by the fixed slot size of the super-frame structure. However, this system has not been evaluated in several healthcare event [4]. Author in [5] have suggested the 'varyschedslots' approach, which allows the number of slots assigned to a node to be varied depending upon the packet arrival rate from the node.

Various analytical models have been developed using Markov chain and analysis done for saturated and non-saturated regimes. Researchers [6, 7] have proposed models that use queueing sub model for buffers and have analyzed the mean waiting time and transmission success probability for all the eight user priorities. Performance enhancement have been recommended by a new model where collision avoidance between nodes assigned same user priority has been suggested by another group [8]. Monte Carlo simulations have been done so as to study the reliability and throughput for the different user priority for different payloads and the simulations have been compared with analytical model [9]. Backoff counter regulation has been done based on random parameter generator and a model for Back off counter has been developed to study the effect on reliability of data transmission [10].

From the state of art study, it may be summarized that some of the algorithms work by assuming that there are no default user priorities assigned to the nodes. The nodes are assigned priority dynamically, according to data rate or data buffer size. Super-frame utilization is kept flexible in some methods so that the various phase lengths are varied according to emergency or normal data [11]. In some cases back off counter values are varied, so that there is minimum collision and delay between the data transmitted by different nodes. In this work, we plan to explore the effect of channel slot length for preassigned priority nodes so as to study its effect on probability of data transmission and successful packet delivery.

Optimization of throughput, packet delivery, latency, energy consumption, lifetime, relay mechanism, and channel utilization are done using analytical models. Markov chain model have been used for developing relation between performance metrics. In this study we have identified the following objectives:

(a)   To develop an analytical model to study stationary state transitions and develop an understanding of how packets are transmitted and successfully delivered by a node under test.
(b)   Develop equations for state transition probabilities using the mathematical model
(c)   Studying the effect of variation in channel slot length on the probability of packet transmission and the probability of successful delivery.

The model has been implemented using MATLAB for nodes with different user priorities.

The paper has been organized as follows: Sect. 2 contains an overview of IEEE 802.15.6 standard where CSMA/CA used graphs in MAC layer have been discussed. Section 3 deals with the mathematical model and the expression for three probabilities used as performance metric. Results have been presented in Sect. 4 where the graphs have been plotted and analyzed. The outcomes of the study have been summarized in the conclusion.

2   Overview of IEEE 802.15.6 MAC Protocol

In the access phase Beacon mode with super frame, the different access periods for nodes are: Exclusive Access Periods (EAP1, EAP2), Random Access Periods (RAP1 and RAP2), Managed Access Periods (MAP1, MAP2) and optional Contention Access Period (CAP). To manage network congestion, eight user priorities (UP0–UP7) are assigned to nodes depending upon the data traffic as shown in Table 1. In the standard beacon mode with Superframe, the nodes contents for EAP or RAP and CAP using CSMA/CA or slotted aloha mechanism. While the EAP periods are reserved for emergency data, the RAP and CAP periods are available for all nodes. The CAP period is preceded by beacon B2 so as to synchronize with the node. MAP is used by coordinator to allocate resources using polling mechanisms.

In CSMA/CA protocol the data transmission process is controlled by two parameters: the back-off counter and Contention Window (CW). Table 1 shows that the CW is variable and depends on node's priority. The CW size is large for low priority nodes (UP 0) and smallest for the high priority nodes at UP7. The back-off counter plays a vital role in the case of MAC layer of MBAN as it is loaded with CW_{min} value which depends on priority of node as per Table 1. The goal of incorporating a backoff counter in the CSMA/CA

Table 1. Node priorities as per traffic classification and contention window bounds as per IEEE 802.15.6 standard

User priority	Traffic designation	Contention window minimum (CW_{min})	Contention window maximum (CW_{max})
UP0	Background	16	64
UP1	Best effort	16	32
UP2	Excellent effort	8	32
UP3	Video	8	16
UP4	Voice	4	16
UP5	Network control	4	8
UP6	High priority data	2	8
UP7	Emergency or medical implant data	1	4

method is to create different time delay between nodes contesting to transmit data so that the hub can regulate node collisions.

At the start of CSMA/CA procedure, the node loads its backoff counter to a random value between 1 to CWmin and remains in its idle state till the channel is busy. When the channel is found to be free, the node begins to decrease the back-off counter by 1. After every decrement of the back-off counter, the channel is sensed and if found busy or if the current slot time is insufficient for the transmission, the back-off counter is made to freeze. The node stays in that state till the channel is sensed-free and has sufficient time length available for the data packet. After the backoff counter becomes zero, the node starts transmitting data. If the data is transmitted successfully to the node, the transmission is continued till completion or till collision is sensed. However, if the transmission is a failure, then the back-off stage is increased by 1, and the process is repeated, till maximum back-off stages are reached. The back-off counter gets updated with CW depending on the number of failures, using the following algorithm as shown in Eq. 1.

$$CW = \begin{cases} CW_{min} & \text{successful transmission} \\ CW & \text{same as the previous value for odd number of failures} \\ 2 * CW_{min} & \text{for even number of failures} \end{cases} \quad (1)$$

3 Mathematical Model

Markov chain model has been developed for different user priorities, as an example, Markov model for UP6 is shown in Fig. 1. The Markov model shows three parameters: user priority (UP), backoff stage (s), and backoff counter (j). The user priorities in this model vary from 0 to 7, the backoff stage (s) runs from 1 to m, the value of m is calculated by the formula $2^m * CW_{min} = CW_{max}$ [12] these value of CW_{max} and CW_{min} have been taken from the Table 1 and the backoff counter (j) varies from 1 to CWmin [12] The probabilities of transition between different states of the model have been shown in Table 2.

Table 2. Probabilities definition for Markov model

Notation	Description
P_{busy}	Probability of channel is busy
P_{idle}	Probability for start carrier sensing by nodes
P_L	Probability for insufficient time slot length
P_s	Probability of successfully packet deliver
Pt	Probability of transmission
P_f	Probability of collision
P_{cf}	Probability of packet drop due to channel access failure
N	Number of sensor nodes in MBAN

In Fig. 1, the process begins with the idle state (0, 0, 0), which occurs when all nodes are in the queue or idle state. Probability 1-P_{idle} is computed when nodes are unable to get access and remain in the same condition. The P_{idle} defines the likelihood of node starting carrier sensing to see if the channel is free. After gaining access, the node updates all index values and begins decrementing the backoff counter number by one for very time slot. If the channel is not free, then the node continues in the same state with probability P_{busy}. If the channel is free then the node moves to the next stationary state with probability determined in terms of P_{busy} and P_L, as per Eqs. 6 and 8. The Eq. 6 shows that probability that the channel is free and Eq. 8 shows the probability of sufficient length time slot availability. This process is continued vertically down within a back off stage as shown by arrows in Fig. 1, till the stationary state where the back off counter decrements to zero. The node now attempts to transmit the data packet and if not successful then enters the next Back off stage, where again the back off counter is reloaded and the procedure is repeated until it does not exceed its maximum limit.

The stationary states of the Markov chain are represented by the equation

$$S_{s,j} = \lim_{t \to \infty} p((a(t) = s, \quad b(t) = j)) \tag{2}$$

where backoff stage s ∈ [1, m], backoff counter j ∈ [0, CW_{min}]

From Fig. 1, we arrive at the following transition probabilities between the various stationary states of the Markov chain which are also proposed in ref [9] for evaluating reliability or probability of successful packet transmission.

The probability that the node stays in the idle state is given by Eq. 3.

$$P(0, 0, 0|0, 0, 0) = 1 - P_{idle} \tag{3}$$

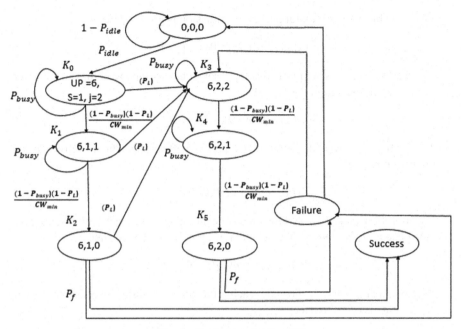

Fig. 1. Markov model for UP6

The probability that the node moves to the state where it loads the indices is determined by Eq. 4.

$$P(UP, m, CW_{min}|0, 0, 0) = P_{idle} \qquad (4)$$

The probability that the node senses that the channel is busy while decrementing its backoff counter is illustrated in Eq. 5.

$$P(UP, m, CW_{min}|UP, m, CW_{min}) = P_{busy} \qquad (5)$$

When the channel is free, the probability of moving the node to the next state is given by Eq. 6.

$$P(UP, m, CW_{min} - 1|UP, m, j) = \frac{(1 - P_{busy})}{CW_{min}} \qquad \text{for } j \in [1, CW_{min}] \qquad (6)$$

Equation 7 depicts the likelihood of a node going to the next backoff stage owing to a lack of time slots.

$$P(UP, s + 1, j|UP, s, j) = P_L \qquad \text{for } s \in [1, m] \qquad (7)$$

Equation 8 illustrates the likelihood of decreasing the backoff counter if the channel has an enough time slot.

$$P(UP, s, j - 1|UP, s, j) = 1 - P_L \qquad \text{for } j \in [1, CW_{min}], s \in [1, m] \qquad (8)$$

The probability of successful packet transmission is given by Eq. 9.

$$P(Success|UP, s, 0) = 1 - P_f \tag{9}$$

When a data packet is not reached at the receiver end owing to a collision, the failure probability is represented in the Eq. 10.

$$P(Failure|UP, s, 0) = P_f \tag{10}$$

The likelihood that a node will reach the last backoff stage and fail to deliver packets is provided in Eq. 11.

$$P(PacketDrop|UP, s, 0) = P_f \tag{11}$$

Equation 12 depicts the likelihood of a node moving into the packet drop state owing to inadequate time slot length on a node that is already in the final state.

$$P(PacketDrop|UP, s, j) = P_L \tag{12}$$

As shown in Eq. 13, once the node reaches the packet drop state, the chance of going to the idle state is equal to one.

$$P(0, 0, 0|PacketDrop) = 1 \tag{13}$$

Using these equations and the Markov chain model, the transition matrix for UP6 has been developed as shown in Fig. 2. The stages of Markov model shown in Fig. 1, for UP6 are used for developing this matrix.

$$
\begin{bmatrix}
P_{busy} & (1-P_{busy})(1-P_L)/CW_{min} & 0 & P_L & 0 & 0 \\
0 & P_L & (1-P_{busy})(1-P_L)/CW_{min} & P_L & 0 & 0 \\
0 & 0 & 0 & P_fP_L & 0 & 0 \\
0 & 0 & 0 & P_{busy} & (1-P_{busy})(1-P_L)/CW_{min} & 0 \\
0 & 0 & 0 & 0 & P_{busy} & (1-P_{busy})(1-P_L)/CW_{min} \\
0 & 0 & 0 & 0 & 0 & P_fP_L
\end{bmatrix}
$$

Fig. 2. Transition matrix for stationary states in Markov model for UP6

We investigate the impact of a channel time slot transmission probability P_t, and probability of successful packet delivery P_S.

The intermediate transmission Probability is defined as probability where the node is able to reach the zero value for backoff counter and start transmission in any backoff stage. From the Markov chain, P_t is calculated as follows

$$P_t = \sum_{j=1}^{CWmin} \sum_{s=1}^{m} \frac{(1 - P_{busy})}{CW_{min}} P_L^{s-1} (1 - P_L)^j \tag{14}$$

The probability of unsuccessful packet transmission P_f can be expressed in terms of transmission probability P_t

$$P_f = 1 - P_t^{N-1} \tag{15}$$

Reliability, also known as Probability of successful transmission Ps, is given by

$$P_S = 1 - P_{cf} \tag{16}$$

where P_{cf} is the probability of packet loss as a result of channel access failure. Channel access failure occurs when either the time slot length is insufficient or data transmission through other nodes collides. The Markov chain can now be used to calculate the probability of packet loss due to channel access failure.

$$P_{cf} = \sum_{j=1}^{CWmin} \sum_{s=1}^{m} P_L{}^{s-1}(1 - P_L)^j P_f P_L{}^m (1 - P_L)^{j-1} \tag{17}$$

4   Results Analysis

Using the transition matrix and Eqs. 14–17, the two probabilities reflecting the performance of network are calculated and plotted for varying probability of sufficient channel time slot $(1 - P_L)$ for UP 6, 4, 2, 0.

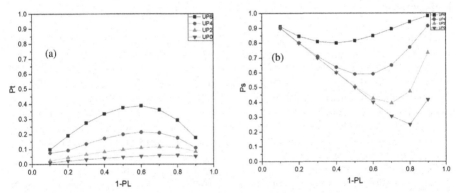

Fig. 3. Graphs for probability of transmission, probability of packet drops due to channel access failure, probability of successful packet delivery.

Figure 3(a) depicts the transmission probability of nodes for UP 6, 4, 2, 0. The graph shows that the P_t is higher for UP6 as compared to other nodes lower user priorities. The value of P_t increases as the probability of sufficient time slot increases and reaches a peak value when the probability of sufficient channel time slot is nearly 60%. As the probability of sufficient time slot increase, more nodes are now ready for transmission and as soon as their back off counters are zero, these nodes transmit data and collisions may occur. This reduces the transmission probability for node under test.

The graph in Fig. 3(b) depicts the likelihood of successful packet delivery for UP 6, 4, 2, 0. We notice that the UP6 has a higher probability of successful packet delivery than the other nodes of lesser priority. As previously stated, all nodes have different back counter values depending on their user priority; higher user priority nodes have a low value for the counter, whereas lower user priority nodes have a high value for the counter. Therefore, higher user priority nodes have a better chance of occupying a good fraction of channel time slot for data transmission, while lower priority nodes face the possibility of channel access failure. This increases the probability of successful packet delivery.

5 Conclusion

The study is a generalized approach for understanding the roles if back off counter and channel time slot in successful packet delivery when nodes with different user priority are ready for data transmission. It is seen that the higher user priority nodes have better probability of packet delivery as compared to lower user priority nodes when sufficient time slot of channel is available. The backoff counter also plays an important role in the transmission probability as nodes with higher user probability have a smaller contention window, which causes lower backoff counts as well as lower number of backoff stages. As a future scope of work, we plan to study the complete performance analysis including parameter- through-put by modifying the Markov chain to include retransmission.

References

1. Muthulakshmi, A., Shyamala, K.: Efficient patient care through wireless body area networks—enhanced technique for handling emergency situations with better quality of service. Wirel. Pers. Commun. **95**(4), 3755–3769 (2017). https://doi.org/10.1007/s11277-017-4024-7
2. Salayma, M., Al-Dubai, A., Romdhani, I., Nasser, Y.: Reliability and energy efficiency enhancement for emergency-aware wireless body area networks (WBANs). IEEE Trans. Green Commun. Netw. **2**(3), 804–816 (2018). https://doi.org/10.1109/TGCN.2018.2813060
3. Zhang, H., Safaei, F., Tran, L.C.: Channel autocorrelation-based dynamic slot scheduling for body area networks. EURASIP J. Wirel. Commun. Netw. **2018**(1), 1–17 (2018). https://doi.org/10.1186/s13638-018-1261-8
4. Saboor, A., et al.: Dynamic slot allocation using non-overlapping backoff algorithm in IEEE 802.15.6 WBAN. IEEE Sens. J. **20**(18), 10862–10875 (2020). https://doi.org/10.1109/JSEN.2020.2993795
5. Soni, G., Selvaradjou, K.: A dynamic allocation scheme of scheduled slots for real-time heterogenous traffic in IEEE 802.15.6 standard for scheduled access mechanism. J. Ambient Intell. Hum. Comput. (2021). https://doi.org/10.1007/s12652-021-03288-5
6. Rashwand, S., Misic, J.: Performance evaluation of IEEE 802.15.6 under non-saturation condition. In: 2011 IEEE Global Telecommunications Conference - GLOBECOM 2011, Houston, TX, USA, pp. 1–6, December 2011. https://doi.org/10.1109/GLOCOM.2011.6134262.
7. Rashwand, S., Misic, J., Khazaei, H.: Performance analysis of IEEE 802.15.6 under saturation condition and error-prone channel. In Wireless Communications and Networking Conference, Cancun, Mexico, March 2011, pp. 1167–1172 (IEEE). https://doi.org/10.1109/WCNC.2011.5779296
8. Adnan, M., Sallabi, F., Shuaib, K., Abdul-Hafez, M.: Performance enhancement of IEEE 802.15.6 using collision avoidance technique. J. Sens. Actuator Netw. **9**(3), 33 (2020). https://doi.org/10.3390/jsan9030033

9. Mukherjee, A., Bandyopadhyay, B., Das, D., Chatterjee, A., Ahmed, Sk.J., Naskar, M.: Markov chain based analysis of IEEE 802.15.6 MAC protocol in real life scenario. In: Proceedings of the 9th International Conference on Body Area Networks, London, Great Britain (2014). https://doi.org/10.4108/icst.bodynets.2014.257202

10. Das, K., Moulik, S.: PBCR: parameter-based backoff counter regulation in IEEE 802.15.6 CSMA/CA. In: 2021 International Conference on COMmunication Systems & NETworkS (COMSNETS), Bangalore, India, pp. 565–571, January 2021. https://doi.org/10.1109/COMSNETS51098.2021.9352747

11. Das, K., Moulik, S., Chang, C.-Y.: Priority-based dedicated slot allocation with dynamic superframe structure in IEEE 802.15.6-based wireless body area networks. IEEE Internet Things J. **9**(6), 4497–4506 (2022). https://doi.org/10.1109/JIOT.2021.3104800

12. Kumar, V., Gupta, B.: Performance analysis of IEEE 802.15.6 CSMA/CA protocol for WBAN medical scenario through DTMC model. J. Med. Syst. **40**(12), 276 (2016). https://doi.org/10.1007/s10916-016-0638-7

CoviBand - Wearable Social Distancing and Contact Tracing Device Using Signal Strength Indicator Metrics

Srishti Gohain, K. Santhi[✉], Ayush Pandya, Anbarasi Masilamani, and T. Chellatamilan

Vellore Institute of Technology, Vellore, India
santhikrishnan@vit.ac.in

Abstract. The Covid-19 pandemic has grown to be a highly hazardous threat to the survival of most of the human race. It has not only caused prolonged stay-at-home or lockdown policies in many countries but has also been eating away from the global economy. Staying at home for long durations has affected the lives of daily wage workers tremendously and has also had negative consequences on the mental health of many. This paper aims to reduce the risk of contracting the disease when people leave their homes for essential services and during the gradual lift of the lockdown restrictions. This is achieved through a wearable device (wristband) which constantly looks for other wristbands in the vicinity using a WiFi module. This WiFi module is inbuilt into a NodeMCU Amica board and the setup is used in addition to a buzzer which sounds an alarm when two wristbands are dangerously close. In addition to the warning feature using the buzzer, the device would also store the contact history and the duration of contact on a remote server which can then be used for contact tracing in case a person is found to test positive for Covid-19. The interface of the remote server would be such that it gives a detailed list of the other wristbands that came into contact with any particular wristband. This device would also have an edge over some of the contact tracing apps as many people fear that these apps are an invasion of privacy and drain their mobile batteries quickly.

Keywords: Acoustic buzzer · Covid-19 · IoT · NodeMCU Amica board · Wristband · WiFi

1 Introduction

The coronavirus pandemic is a global health crisis. Different countries are trying to control and slow down the transmission of the coronavirus by imposing lockdowns, banning travel and quarantining people so that they can have minimum physical interaction. One plausible method to reduce the spread of coronavirus is by practising social distancing. Keeping physical distance between yourself and others is referred to as social distancing. Specifically, it is staying at least 6 feet away from other people to avoid contracting coronavirus. However, social distancing is something that may be required to be followed even after the pandemic ends. But it can be difficult for humans to remember to maintain social distancing in public places and this may lead to violating social distancing

I. Woungang et al. (Eds.): ANTIC 2022, CCIS 1797, pp. 386–399, 2023.
https://doi.org/10.1007/978-3-031-28180-8_26

norms. Sometimes, people might think that it may be rude to ask others to move away. This paper proposes a solution to constantly remind people if they are violating social distancing norms. An inbuilt contact tracing mechanism is also present which records each violation of social distancing and transmits it to a remote server. The rest of the following paper is organized in the given manner: Sect. 2 provides a detailed study of related works. Section 3 elucidates the architecture which is proposed for overcoming the limitations found in Sect. 2 along with the algorithm implemented. Section 4 lists the components and the technologies used. Section 5 shows the results of the model and the inferences obtained from the proposed methodology. Section 6 includes the Conclusion and the Future scope of CoviBand is mentioned in Section 7.

2   Literature Survey

To deal with the effects of the COVID-19 pandemic, several technological strategies are emerging. Digital technologies, such as IoT, AI, blockchain, and 5G next-generation telecommunications networks, have been at the forefront of these developments.

[1] Greenlight (safe) can be used as a mobility pass [1]. The data recorded by each of the devices is available for access by the state, national data centres etc. [1] If a yellow/red person or gadget spends a lot of time with the green device, their light automatically turns yellow [1]. The device stores contact history only from the past 15 days and it cannot be removed once worn [1]. It contains three warning levels: safe, mildly suspect and highly suspect along with three coloured LEDs to indicate each level [1]. Three factors are recorded: device id, timestamp and duration [2]. The IOT-Q-Band supplies the real-time location of the subject to the authorities along with their health records [2]. The state of the band can also be viewed to check if the band has been tampered with [2]. It is designed to be use-and-throw to avoid infection from a used band [2]. The band depends on several smartphone features like GPS and the internet to save the band's battery [2]. Therefore, if the runaway quarantine subject does not have a smartphone with GPS/mobile data turned on, it cannot make use of the mobile application to transmit the geolocation and other required data to the cloud. Tripathy A.K., et al. (2020), have proposed a device that makes use of sensors to detect other such devices in the specified radius [3]. IoT Devices are helpful for healthcare workers to identify symptoms and provide better treatment rapidly [3]. Some of the advantages are mass screening, detection of crowds etc. [3]. In developing countries like India and many others the mobile penetration is around 40%, which means many people could still not be monitored.

[4] Digital technology, in the opinion of the WHO and CDC, can significantly enhance the public health response to the COVID-19 pandemic [4]. If implemented properly we can take the safety of patients and health workers both to a very efficient and much less risky model of operation [4]. This would ensure the safety of the health workers especially, those who are working tirelessly day and night for us [4]. But a major limitation is that due to the crushing of economies and the rise in cases exponentially the governments and corporations are not willing to invest in these technologies because they need to prioritize building the infrastructure for the patients who are currently infected with Covid-19 [4]. Any mechanism for dynamic patient monitoring, prevention of the spread of diseases and alarming the people or health workers on the expected spread rate will be of great help in controlling the spread to an extent if not for completely wiping

out the disease. Nandikattu R.R., et al. (2020), have suggested a gadget that uses a PIR sensor to detect infrared radiation from the human body to sound an alarm and send out a mobile alert [5]. An alert will be sent to the phone when someone enters the crucial range of six feet, indicating whether or not the individual in the area exhibits COVID symptoms, which aids in keeping social distance [5]. Accuracy depends on the cost of the sensor due to which the product is expensive [5]. Rashid M.T., et al. (2020), have put forward to track the COVID-19 outbreak and research the dynamics of the infectious disease's transmission, a novel concept for trustworthy social sensing-based information dissemination and risk warning systems called CovidSens has been developed [6]. It is a reliable and timely COVID-19 monitoring and alerting system for the mass population based on social sensing [6]. It is a dynamic and scalable AI-driven information retrieval and dispatching system [6]. Major challenges in this system include data collection, reliability, scalability, modality, presentation, and misinformation spread [6]. Singh V.K., et al. (2020), have elucidated a solution to control the spread of COVID-19 disease if the infected patients abscond from their quarantine facilities. To gather information for this research, a survey of recently suggested IoT devices that seek to help authorities and healthcare professionals during the pandemic was done. In three phases—"Early Diagnosis," "Quarantine Time," and "After Recovery"—they examined IoT-related technologies and their applications. They assessed how IoT-enabled/linked technology, such as wearables, drones, robots, IoT buttons, and smartphone applications, may be used to combat COVID-19 for each phase [7]. More patients can use IoT devices to engage in their treatment with peace of mind if IoT technology is implemented appropriately and securely. As a consequence, authorities and medical professionals can respond to pandemics more effectively. As a result, the effects of various illnesses, such as infections, hospitalizations, and death rates, can be greatly diminished [7].

The creation of an automated health monitoring system that responds or sounds an alert when a patient is in a critical state is required. To communicate with doctors and other concerned parties, messages are sent through email and Twitter when the data are evaluated by the Node MCU microcontroller. It also keeps track of and records the patient's prior diagnostic data on their health. The medical staff receives the patient's true condition through an online portal so that the right care may be given to cure the patient [8]. As the internet is a key communication route, the IoT-based system may provide real-time information on patient parameters [8]. Although artificial intelligence (AI) technologies are being employed for diagnosis, they are not as accurate as biological diagnosis. Telemedicine has undergone a paradigm change, and with more and more practical technologies emerging, AI has the potential to upend the healthcare sector. The standards established in several unique studies for the coronavirus pandemic can also be expanded to address any potential pandemics in the future. In the same way that artificial intelligence and machine learning have been highly effective at addressing the numerous issues that occur in healthcare systems, they have also been utilised to address the issues brought on by COVID-19 [9]. Hopefully, in the future, AI systems will be able to identify illnesses with a 100% accuracy rate [9]. Because it is dependable and simple to use, the gadget, which is essentially a "cap," may be worn by anybody, anywhere. The microcontroller is configured with a certain sensitivity level up to which the sensor detects infrared radiation, and the sensor detects infrared radiation that is either emitted or reflected from objects. In this manner, if somebody is close to the sensor, the alert will sound appropriate. Smart sensors are used by the apparatus. PIR sensors are used in the solution to detect human and animal bodies rather than random things [10]. By altering the PIR sensor's sensitivity, this gadget is capable of adapting to a variety of environments. The user can be informed if their temperature rises or falls from the usual, healthy body temperature by including a temperature sensor [10]. In the proposed face mask detection model named SSDMNV2, both the training and development of the image dataset, which was divided into categories of people having masks and people not having masks, have been done successfully [11]. The technique of OpenCV deep neural networks used in this model generated Fruitful results.

Classification of images was done accurately using the MobilenetV 2 image classifier, which is one of the uniqueness of the proposed approach [11]. In this paper, the authors have illustrated how an object can be remotely monitored using a NODEMCU ESP8266. They have used the Arduino IDE and communicated with an object via HTTP calls. It consists of four modules – A WiFi network, a Server, A client and a mobile access point [12]. This prototype is built using four NodeMCU modules (a static access point that supplies the WiFi network, a server, a client, and a mobile access point linked to the remote surveillance object), which are all created using the Arduino IDE and communicate with each other using the HTTP protocol [12]. In this paper, the author reviews the usage of NodeMCU in different IoT products. It gives a great insight into the versatility as well as the challenges one could face while working with NodeMCU. It elaborates on the self-contained Wi-Fi networking solution as well as the storage capabilities and the powerful onboarding processing [13]. Because NodeMCU is an open-source platform, anybody may edit, change, or develop it. The ESP8266 wifi-enabled chip is part of the NodeMCU Dev Kit/Board. Espressif Systems created the ESP8266, a low-cost Wi-Fi chip that uses the TCP/IP protocol [12]. More details can be found on ESP8266 Documentation. The IoT's potential integration into the system for epidemic prevention and control is discussed in this study. In particular, we present a possible fog-cloud combined IoT platform that can be used in systematic and intelligent COVID-19 prevention and control. This involves five interventions, including COVID-19 Symptom Diagnosis, Quarantine Monitoring, Contact Tracing & Social Distancing, COVID-19 Outbreak Forecasting, and SARS-CoV-2 Mutation Tracking [14]. The authors investigate and review the state-of-the-art literature on these five interventions to present the capabilities of IoT in countering the current COVID-19 pandemic or future infectious disease epidemics [14]. In this study, the role of IoT and AI in combating COVID-19 is studied, and the three key processes—network evaluation, implementation, and IoT industry review—are also covered. These steps include early detection, quarantine periods, and post-recovery activities. This study examines how IoT responds to the COVID-19 pandemic at a new level of healthcare [15]. In this research, the long short-term memory (LSTM) with recurrent neural network (RNN) is used for diagnosis purposes and in particular, its important architecture for the analysis of cough and breathing acoustic characteristics [15].

The present digital contact tracing based on these three elements is reviewed in this work. Researchers concentrate on smartphones and wearables, two private, close-to-the-user gadgets. Researchers talk about networking strategies, both centralized and decentralized, that are used to ease data flow. Last but not least, we look into the proximity sensing functionality offered by wearables and smartphones to determine the closeness between any two users and conduct tests comparing the performance of these two personal gadgets [16]. The purpose of this paper is to provide a thorough survey of user location-tracking, proximity detection, and digital contact tracing solutions in the literature from the last two decades, to analyze their benefits and shortcomings in terms of centralized and decentralized solutions, and to present the authors' ideas on potential future research directions in this timely research area [17]. Bluetooth is not needed for location-based trace methods. Instead, they detect the geolocations of app users using mobile phone network data, GPS, Wi-Fi signals, and other smartphone sensors, and they utilize location data to calculate proximity to infected people. Digital contact tracing alternatives include barcoding techniques. Users may register visited locations by scanning Quick Response (QR) codes, which are barcodes that can be seen in public places like bus doors and store entrances [18]. The key contribution is to explain why a contact-tracing method like this is likely to succeed in achieving the stated objective of restoring complete normality [19]. There is some opportunity for exceptions since they demonstrate using probabilistic models that universal acceptance is not required to accomplish the stated aim [20]. However, the adoption rate must be extremely high, for example, above 95% depending on the illness characteristics [21]. The number may be reduced to roughly 90% with increased attention in disease surveillance to identify mild instances early [22]. The findings suggest for public authorities at the state or federal levels spearhead the deployment effort to achieve the necessary adoption rate and a tracing coverage that is extensive enough to be useful for disease management [23]. To solve the majority of privacy issues with existing protocols, the protocol offers full-lifecycle data privacy protection on the devices as well as the back-end servers [24]. Researchers used Diffie-Hellman key exchange for participant secret sharing and Bloom filters to efficiently offer privacy-preserving storage. Researchers demonstrate how DIMY offers resistance to several well-known assaults while adding very little overhead. In comparison to other comparable cutting-edge apps, DIMY's storage footprint on client devices and back-end servers are substantially less [25].

3   Proposed Architecture

Since the viral disease, covid-19 has taken over the majority of the world, there have been many innovative solutions for social distancing and contact tracing. Some of them are apps which have induced the fear of data misuse and loss of privacy while others are devices which are either expensive or require to be paired with mobile phones for constant WiFi or bluetooth access. The aim of this paper is to create a low cost and privacy conscious device that can help in social distancing and contact tracing. This paper suggests a wristband using a NodeMCU Amica board, which is a microcontroller with a built-in WiFi module. Figure 1 shows the interconnections between the server, CBand and WiFi routers. The NodeMCU is used to create a soft access point using an SSID which is of the format 'CBand'+'<id>'. It constantly searches for other devices in the vicinity with SSID starting with 'CBand'. As soon as a CBand is detected, the wristband checks for the other CBand's Received Signal Strength Indicator (RSSI) and if it is higher than the given threshold, it indicates that the two wristbands are dangerously close by sounding an alarm. In addition to sounding an alarm, the wristband also maintains a persistent WiFi connection in station mode with a router. The id of the wristband that came into contact is then sent to a Flask server using this WiFi connection. The server then stores the contact information in the database, which can be retrieved using a web app for viewing and analyzing.

The **procedure** of detecting and storing contact history in the CBand is given below:

Step 1: Detect another CBand in the vicinity with RSSI > −40
Step 2: Send a POST request to the server with the contact information
Step 3: The server stores the contact information in the database
Step 4: Use the front end to view and analyze contact history of each band

The **Algorithm** performed by each CBand is given below (Fig. 2):

Workflow Diagram

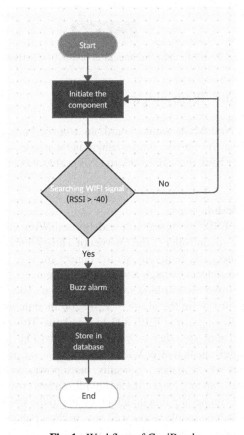

Fig. 1. Workflow of CoviBand

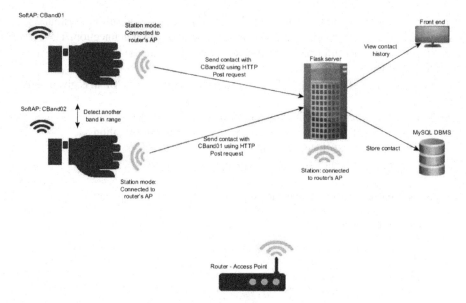

Fig. 2. Infographic architectural layout of CoviBand

4   Components and Technologies Used

The setup includes a NodeMCU Amica board, an acoustic buzzer and an LED which are connected using male to female jumper cables and a breadboard. The NodeMCU is powered using a power bank through its micro USB port as it is intended to be a mobile device.

NodeMCU Amica Module
The NodeMCU is an ESP8266 based is a widely used WiFi microchip incorporated with a light weight microcontroller in the Internet of Things domain. It has the capability to support the connectivity requirements to connect smart devices and also control and monitor data from sensors through a web server. Engineers are increasingly using this module as it is a low cost and ultra low power device. The Machine-To-Machine paradigm plays a major role in the usage of ESP8266 module as it allows devices to communicate with each other using IEEE 802.11 standards. This module also possesses a full TCP/IP stack. There are other embedded platforms like Raspberry Pi, ESP32, Intel Edison and BeagleBone that offer WiFi support. But these devices also have heavy computing capabilities which makes it consume more power and comparatively more expensive. The social distancing band aims at providing a low cost solution which would enable a majority of the general public to adopt it. Due to the stress on ultra low power consumption, the ESP8266 module works well only in short ranges. This drawback does not affect the performance of the social distancing band as it is required to be worn on the user's wrist at all times and it detects other bands only within a short range. So, the ESP8266 is the best choice for it.

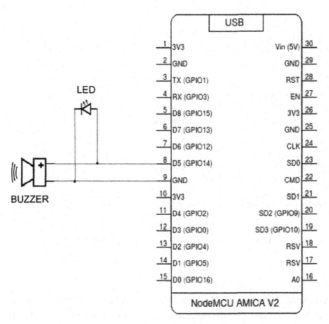

Fig. 3. NodeMCU AMICA V2 block diagram

Some of the relevant features of the ESP8266 WiFi module are:

- Supports IEEE 802.11 b/g/n, 2.4 GHz WiFi with support for WPA/WPA2, WiFi Direct
- Integrated full TCP/IP stack
- Integrated low power 32 bit microcontroller
- Integrated 10 bit analog to digital converter
- Smart Link function supports for both Android and iOS devices
- Supports Station mode, Soft Access Point mode, Station + Soft Access Point mode
- Wake up and transmit packets in less than 2 ms
- Standby mode power consumption is less than 1 mW.
- Deep sleep mode power is less than 10 μA and power down leakage current is less than 5 μA

Acoustic Buzzer

A 5 V passive acoustic buzzer whose anode is connected to D5 in the NodeMCU Amica the board and cathode are connected to GND. This acts as an indicator to alert the user if there is another person who is in close proximity. A more subtle indicator like a vibrator can be used in office spaces or other professional environments.

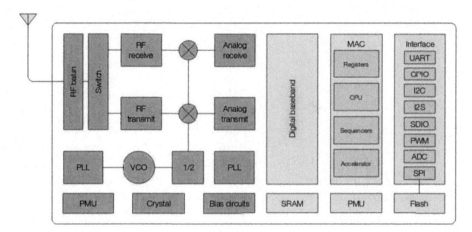

Fig. 4. Functional block diagram of ESP8266

LED
The LED is connected in parallel with the buzzer, thus eliminating the need for a resistor. The anode is connected to D5 and the cathode is connected to GND. This acts as a visual indicator to alert the user.

WiFi (IEEE 802.11)
IoT frequently uses Wi-Fi as a short-range communication medium. The word "Wi-Fi" is an acronym for Wireless Fidelity and refers to the IEEE 802.11 standard for wireless local area networks (WLANs). This serves as an alternative to wired connections, which are frequently made between gadgets in wireless mode. Connection on the physical layer and data link layer are both dependent on this.The ESP8266 module supports IEEE 802.11b, IEEE 802.11g and IEEE 802.11n standards. There are three wifi modes in an ESP8266 module namely station mode, soft access point mode and station+soft access point mode. Station mode refers to the state when the ESP8266 is connected to a WiFi network established by an access point. A device which provides access to a Wi-Fi network to other devices (stations) and connects them further to a wired network is called an access point (AP). ESP8266 can provide a similar functionality except it does not have the capability to connect to a wired network. A soft access point (soft-AP) is an AP which does not have an interface with a wired network. ESP8266 can operate in both soft-AP and Station mode so it can act as a node of a mesh network. The CBand operates in the third wifi mode which is station+SoftAP mode to create an access point other CBands can detect and use station mode to send contact information to a server.

HTTP
The Hypertext Transfer Protocol (HTTP) is a communication protocol that enables communication between clients and servers. Hypertext Transfer Protocol (HTTP) is the application layer protocol that forms the foundation of the World Wide Web (WWW). The protocol follows a request-response model where a client sends requests to a server using HTTP commands. Each HTTP request is independent of other requests. Some of

the HTTP methods are GET, POST, PUT, HEAD, DELETE, PATCH, OPTIONS among which the CBand makes use of the POST method to send contact information to the server. The POST method requests the server to process the data enclosed in the body of the HTTP request.

MySQL
MySQL is the RDBMS used to store contact history which is then retrieved for viewing and analyzing.

Flask
Flask is a web development framework based on python. It is used to create a server which stores and retrieves data from the DBMS and also projects a front-end for users and concerned authorities for contact tracing.

Fig. 5. CoviBand circuit layout

5 Results and Discussion

The setup consists of the NodeMCU, Buzzer and an LED which is shown in Fig. 3. The CBand successfully sent the contact information to the remote server which can be viewed by each user upon login. This is depicted in Fig. 4. A provision for concerned authorities (admins) to view contact history of all users is also incorporated. Other basic functionalities like filtering records for each day and generating a visual representation of the contact information is integrated as well. The graph generated for a user is shown in Fig. 5 (Figs. 6 and 7).

The issue at hand is how to stop the transmission of any airborne illness for which there is no vaccination, and social isolation is the most effective solution. Therefore, the question now is: How can we do it using technology? Since this issue involves the real world, hardware will be needed. We would employ software for the interface. Our research has revealed that prior initiatives to address the issue have fallen short for a variety of reasons. Devices have issues retaining data for more than 15 days or issues with exorbitant component costs, making them expensive. In contrast to currently

CoviBand Records

Date	User ID	Contact
08/26/2022, 12:27:50	01	3
08/26/2022, 12:27:53	01	3
08/26/2022, 12:27:55	01	3
08/26/2022, 12:27:57	01	3
08/26/2022, 12:27:59	01	3
08/26/2022, 12:28:02	01	3
08/26/2022, 12:28:04	01	3
08/26/2022, 12:28:06	01	3
08/26/2022, 12:28:08	01	3
08/26/2022, 12:28:11	01	3
08/26/2022, 12:28:13	01	3
08/26/2022, 12:28:15	01	3
08/26/2022, 12:28:17	01	3
08/26/2022, 12:28:20	01	3

Fig. 6. CoviBand records and contacts history

CoviBand Records

Date	User ID	Contact
08/26/2022, 12:27:50	01	3
08/26/2022, 12:27:53	01	3
08/26/2022, 12:27:55	01	3
08/26/2022, 12:27:57	01	3
08/26/2022, 12:27:58	01	3
08/26/2022, 12:28:02	01	3
08/26/2022, 12:28:04	01	3
08/26/2022, 12:28:06	01	3
08/26/2022, 12:28:08	01	3
08/26/2022, 12:28:11	01	3

Prediction Graph

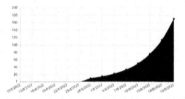

Fig. 7. CoviBand records and prediction graph

available software-based solutions, like the government-sponsored Aroyagya Setu app, which performs contact tracing with a similar function but makes use of the phone's GPS service, our solution makes use of wifi, which will enable it to do so with much greater accuracy and provide a much more accurate picture of the situation on the ground. Additionally, it addresses the issue of social distance on the ground by warning users if they approach one another too closely.

6   Conclusion

This paper is targeted towards the best possible support which each of us can give as civilians to curb the spread of Covid, that is social distancing. The paper is an amalgamation of common IOT components and database concepts to provide a real solution which could be applied to make a significant difference in dealing with the pandemic. As per the health experts the Corona Virus is here to stay for a while and we will have to deal with it in our everyday lives. Until the vaccine is approved and its manufacturing starts in a scale which is sufficient for a country of the size like India we will have to take precautions like social distancing, proper sanitation, avoiding crowds etc. IOT devices can be of huge help in monitoring and also providing the information which is needed in real time. Making use of devices like CBand to solve the pandemic, contributing more towards the development of devices using IOT techniques and equipping ourselves better for the next global crisis plays a vital role given the current state of health of an average human being. The proposed design is a response to the problem of having portable and affordable contact tracing equipment that can be readily used by the government for extensive use in containment zones, airports, train stations and other government run facilities. The problem that we are solving here is to curb the spread of any air borne disease for which the vaccine doesn't exist, and the best way to do that would be by social distancing. So now the question comes how can we achieve that using technology, as this problem is in the physical space hence hardware would be required. And for the interface we would use software. Our research has shown us that previous attempts at tackling the problem have failed because of a number of reasons. Devices had problems with storing data past 15 days or problems with high cost of components resulting in an expensive device. Compared to existing software based solutions for instance the government backed aroyagya setu app which has similar function that is contact tracing but it uses the GPS service of the phone, our solution uses wifi which will do it with much more accuracy and hence provides much more accurate situation on the ground. And also at the same time it solves the problem of social distancing on the ground, it alerts the users if they come dangerously close to one another.

7   Future Work

Future improvements to this work can be made by incorporating technologies like big data. The vast quantities of contact information transmitted to the server may be analyzed to instantly warn users of their level of risk. Artificial intelligence and machine learning can improve this. Another area for improvement could be the incorporation of an internal method for storing contact information in the event that WiFi access is lost. When a WiFi network is accessible, the saved data can subsequently be transferred to the distant server.

References

1. Tripathy, A.K., Mohapatra, A.G., Mohanty, S.P., Kougianos, E., Joshi, A.M., Das, G.: Easy-Band: a wearable for safety-aware mobility during pandemic outbreak. IEEE Consum. Electron. Mag. **9**(5), 57–61 (2020)

2. Singh, V., Chandna, H., Kumar, A., Kumar, S., Upadhyay, N., Utkarsh, K.: IoT-Q-Band: a low cost internet of things based wearable band to detect and track absconding COVID-19 quarantine subjects. EAI Endorsed Trans. Internet Things 6(21) (2020)

3. Soppin, S., Nagaraj, C.B., Iyer, M.: Tracking the crowd and Covid-19 patients for the prevention and spread of disease. Community Med. (2020)

4. Chamola, V., Hassija, V., Gupta, V., Guizani, M.: A comprehensive review of the COVID-19 pandemic and the role of IoT, drones, AI, blockchain, and 5G in managing its impact. IEEE Access 8, 90225–90265 (2020)

5. Nadikattu, R.R., Mohammad, S.M., Whig, P.: Novel economical social distancing smart device for Covid-19. Int. J. Electr. Eng. Technol. (IJEET) (2020)

6. Rashid, M.T., Wang, D.: CovidSens: a vision on reliable social sensing for COVID-19. Artif. Intell. Rev. 54(1), 1–25 (2020). https://doi.org/10.1007/s10462-020-09852-3

7. Nasajpour, M., Pouriyeh, S., Parizi, R.M., Dorodchi, M., Valero, M., Arabnia, H.R.: Internet of Things for current COVID-19 and future pandemics: an exploratory study. J. Healthc. Inform. Res. 4(4), 325–364 (2020)

8. Bhardwaj, V., Joshi, R., Gaur, A.M.: IoT-based smart health monitoring system for COVID-19. SN Comput. Sci. 3(2), 1–11 (2022)

9. Ghimire, A., Thapa, S., Jha, A.K., Kumar, A., Kumar, A., Adhikari, S.: AI and IoT solutions for tackling COVID-19 pandemic. In: 2020 4th International Conference on Electronics, Communication and Aerospace Technology (ICECA), pp. 1083–1092. IEEE, November 2020

10. Raghav, S., et al.: Suraksha: low cost device to maintain social distancing during COVID-19. In: 2020 4th International Conference on Electronics, Communication and Aerospace Technology (ICECA), pp. 1476–1480. IEEE, November 2020

11. Nagrath, P., Jain, R., Madan, A., Arora, R., Kataria, P., Hemanth, J.: SSDMNV2: a real time DNN-based face mask detection system using single shot multibox detector and MobileNetV2. Sustain. Cities Soc. 66, 102692 (2021)

12. Ouldzira, H., Mouhsen, A., Lagraini, H., Chhiba, M., Tabyaoui, A., Amrane, S.: Remote monitoring of an object using a wireless sensor network based on NODEMCU ESP8266. Indones. J. Electr. Eng. Comput. Sci. 16(3), 1154–1162 (2019)

13. Parihar, Y.S.: Internet of Things and NodeMCU. J. Emerg. Technol. Innov. Res. 6(6), 1085 (2019)

14. Dong, Y., Yao, Y.D.: IoT platform for COVID-19 prevention and control: a survey. IEEE Access 9, 49929–49941 (2021)

15. Kollu, P.K., et al.: Development of advanced artificial intelligence and IoT automation in the crisis of COVID-19 Detection. J. Healthc. Eng. (2022)

16. Ng, P.C., Spachos, P., Gregori, S., Plataniotis, K.N.: Personal devices for contact tracing: smartphones and wearables to fight COVID-19. IEEE Commun. Mag. 59(9), 24–29 (2021)

17. Shubina, V., Holcer, S., Gould, M., Lohan, E.S.: Survey of decentralized solutions with mobile devices for user location tracking, proximity detection, and contact tracing in the covid-19 era. Data 5(4), 87 (2020)

18. Kleinman, R.A., Merkel, C.: Digital contact tracing for COVID-19. CMAJ 192(24), E653–E656 (2020)

19. Xia, Y., Lee, G.: How to return to normalcy: fast and comprehensive contact tracing of COVID-19 through proximity sensing using mobile devices. arXiv preprint arXiv:2004.12576 (2020)

20. Anglemyer, A., et al.: Digital contact tracing technologies in epidemics: a rapid review. Cochrane Database Syst. Rev. (8) (2020)

21. Mokbel, M., Abbar, S., Stanojevic, R.: Contact tracing: beyond the apps. SIGSPATIAL Spec. 12(2), 15–24 (2020)

22. Mufti, T., Gupta, B., Sohail, S.S., Kumar, D.: Contact tracing: a cloud based architecture for Safe Covid-19 mapping. In: 2021 International Conference on Computational Performance Evaluation (ComPE), pp. 874–877. IEEE, December 2021
23. Ahmed, N., et al.: DIMY: enabling privacy-preserving contact tracing. J. Netw. Comput. Appl. **202**, 103356 (2022)
24. Bay, J., et al.: BlueTrace: a privacy-preserving protocol for community-driven contact tracing across borders. Government Technology Agency-Singapore, Technical report, 18 (2020)
25. Vangipuram, S.L., Mohanty, S.P., Kougianos, E.: CoviChain: a blockchain based framework for nonrepudiable contact tracing in healthcare cyber-physical systems during pandemic outbreaks. SN Comput. Sci. **2**(5), 1–16 (2021)

Average Time Based PRoPHET Routing Protocol for Opportunistic Networks

Mehul Kumar Gond[1], Mohini Singh[1], Anshul Verma[1](✉) (iD), and Pradeepika Verma[2]

[1] Department of Computer Science, Banaras Hindu University, Varanasi, India
anshulverma87@gmail.com
[2] Technology Innovation Hub, Indian Institute of Technology, Patna, Bihta, India

Abstract. An Opportunistic Network is an intermittently connected Mobile Ad-hoc Networks that exploits the communication opportunity between the nodes for data transmission whenever they are within the communication range of each other even for a short time. In contrast to the Mobile Ad-hoc Networks, Opportunistic Networks follow store-carry-forward approach for the data transmission. Routing in this type of network depends on many factors, like the direction of the node's movement, the supported interface bandwidth (Bluetooth, high-speed Internet, etc.), the node's speed, and the node's buffer size. In this research work, a context-aware routing protocol is proposed that uses the frequency of contacts among nodes as context information. The frequency of meetings between any two nodes is found to be a good heuristic to identify the message's best forwarder. The proposed routing protocol is simulated on opportunistic network environment (ONE) simulator and the results are compared with the most prominent routing protocols of context-oblivious and context-aware classes, and it was found that the proposed routing protocol performs better than other protocols in terms of delivery probability and buffer average time.

Keywords: Delay tolerant network · Opportunistic network · Mobile ad-hoc network · Time to live · Buffer size · PRoPHET · ONE simulator

1 Introduction

The development of an Opportunistic network (OppNet) begins from the development of its parent information centric network mobile ad-hoc network (ICN MANET) [1, 2]. The mobile ad-hoc network (MANET) and OppNet are both members of the Unstructured Mobile Network (UMN) class. An UMN has less or no pre-installed infrastructure [3]. UMNs can be further divided into two subgroups MANETs and delay tolerant networks (DTNs) [4]. In MANETs path from sender to receiver is assumed upon which data is to be transferred, while in OppNets and DTNs networks path from sender to receiver [5] may never exist due to the high mobility of the nodes.

In the Fig. 1, there are three separate networks connected to each other. Networks 1 and 2 are connected through a satellite link, while networks 2 and 3 are connected using a vehicular-based network. The networking link established using a satellite link is more likely to be predictable and can be scheduled accordingly, while the vehicle-based communication link can be intermittent due to the high mobility of the vehicle,

I. Woungang et al. (Eds.): ANTIC 2022, CCIS 1797, pp. 400–412, 2023.
https://doi.org/10.1007/978-3-031-28180-8_27

so the connection is very unpredictable and can be treated as opportunistic. Whenever vehicular nodes come into contact with each other, then ICN nodes are responsible for managing data transfer between disconnected clusters of the network. When nodes come into contact, they can send as well as receive bundles (arbitrary sized data units). These bundles have time to live (TTL) property which decides the expiration of packets. Sometimes when the node or link is not available at the moment, the relay node can wait for some time and has to store bundles or else send these bundles to its neighbouring node with better-probability, one that is more likely to reach the desired location.

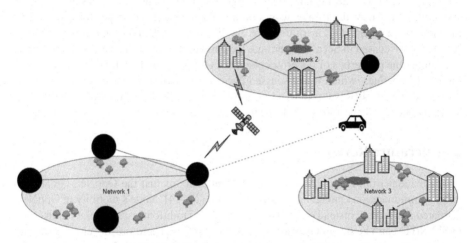

Fig. 1. Information centric network (ICN)

In MANET, the message is only sent once unless a packet is damaged or lost during transmission [6]. However, in DTNs, as the connections between the nodes are very unpredictable, and the future connections and disconnections are intermittent; the networks follow a safe approach of replicating several copies of packets in the network. Unlike MANETs which aim to offer a connected path for transmission in a dynamic network environment, an OppNet only seeks to provide the next best "storage node" that moves towards the destination node [7]. In MANETs, the nodes are connected as receiver during communication through some common network. This condition of the common internetwork is rarely possible in the case of dynamic-network environments like the OppNets environment. In such environments, some nodes may have high mobility (like cars, trams, and bikes), while some nodes may frequently connect and disconnect with the network, like pedestrians who may switch off their smart devices [8]. OppNets may have static nodes along with immense quantity of mobile nodes. The devices in OppNets interconnected each other via interfaces like Bluetooth, Wi-Fi, etc. OppNets initially start from a single seed node and expand during communication using neighbouring nodes, which helps in routing and forwarding [8].

OppNets are used in scenarios where there is no pre-installed infrastructure for communication, and it is not worth investing in [9]. OppNets have applications in domains where on-demand connections are required or where there is no pre-existing infrastructure for communication, for example, OppNets can be used to collect data on wildlife animals. Sensors are attached to the animals, and data can be downloaded at fixed collection points. OppNets also come as an alternative for communication in rural areas where there is no pre-existing infrastructure; one example of this is the Daknet project developed by MIT Media Lab researchers [10]. Daknet has been successfully tested and deployed in remote areas of both India and Cambodia. The objective of this paper is to observe different OppNet protocols to verify the properties of protocols and to make a new better routing protocol.

Section 1 of the paper is dedicated to a brief introduction of DTNs and OppNets. Different routing protocols [11] have been categories in the context-oblivious and context-aware classes, where the former works on a naive approach of simple forwarding and the latter were designed to learn to adapt the dynamics of the topology of the network, which was discussed in Sect. 2 (Literature Review) of this paper. The aim of the paper is to examine the properties of the protocols of the OppNets and how it behaves by changing the TTL values, which was discussed in Sect. 3. Analysis of the results obtained is discussed in Sect. 4 (Results and Discussion). At last in Sect. 5 (Conclusion and Future Works) conclusion and future works of the paper are discussed.

2   Literature Review

It was evident from reading through several publications that the OppNets' goal is to build communication among highly mobile nodes [12–14]. Node's mobility in OppNets is treated as a feature instead of a drawback [15–17]. Traditional routing algorithms used in MANETs can't be straight forward applied to OppNets. Therefore, developing routing protocols for OppNets is an important research direction [18, 19]. Several routing protocols have been developed in OppNet are classified into two classes: context-oblivious, and context-aware, on the basis of whether they use context information to take route decisions or not. Most prominent routing protocols of OppNets are discussed following.

First Contact: The simplest protocol of OppNets is the First Contact [20] in which the message is randomly forwarded by source or intermediary nodes to a node they encounter first. Therefore, regardless of whether a node is a good forwarder or not, any nodes that enter the communication range will be notified [4]. In this routing, each node randomly selects a contact to transmit a message. Because of this there is only one copy of each communication in the network. Once the message is delivered, the sending node removes the local copy of the message from its buffer. Thus, at a time only a single copy of the message is present in the network, which results in low congestion in the network. However, if the carrier node does not successfully transfer the message, then the message will be lost. First Contact also suffers from path loops. When there exists frequent contact between a same pair of nodes that stay in the connection for a long time, then the message is only revolving around this pair of nodes. First Contact has a poor delivery ratio and high message delivery delay as the next hop is chosen randomly and at a time only a single copy of the message is present in the network.

Direct Delivery: The source node holds the message until the destination node [1] comes with in its communication range. The intended message is transmitted directly to the recipient in a single hop, hence it is named "direct delivery". This message uses the least amount of bandwidth and network resources. However, it is also suffered by significant transmission delay. An indefinite transmission delay may also occur if the sender and destination nodes do not encounter. There is only one copy of the message in the network, if the source node fails to relay it, the message is lost. It has very less delivery rate and almost zero overhead.

Epidemic: The flooding method is used by the epidemic routing protocol to send messages. Every node keeps two buffers, the first one is used to store messages that the node generates itself, while the second one is used to store messages that the node receives from other nodes. There is a distinct ID assigned to each message in a summary vector, each node keeps track of the message IDs it has in its buffer and which message delivery is still pending. When two nodes meet, they compare their summary vectors and exchange the messages those are new to them [21]. By this process, the duplicate copies of the messages are flooded throughout the network like an epidemic. This routing technique has a high bandwidth and buffer capacity demand.

Spray and Wait: By reducing flooding [22], the Spray and Wait scheme [23] enhances the epidemic protocol. It includes two steps, the Spray stage and the Wait stage, as the name suggests. The flooding is limited to only L copies during the Spray phase by forwarding L copies of a message to L different nodes. If destination is not found among these L relay nodes, the relay node can only transfer the message to the destination node, hence will enter into wait stage if the destination node is not directly reachable. As a result, the Spray and Wait scheme has the advantages of the epidemic and direct delivery protocols. If L is too small, it behaves like direct delivery, and if L is too large, it behaves like an epidemic protocol.

Probabilistic Routing Protocol Using History of Encounters and Transitivity (PRoPHET): PRoPHET routing system is context-aware and leverages the abundance of meetings between two devices to determine the context [24]. Each node computes the probabilistic delivery matrix for each known destination prior to transmitting the message. The nodes' prior interactions are used to generate this delivery probability matrix. The nodes those are frequently encountering, have higher delivery predictability, and whenever two nodes meet, they exchange their delivery predictability matrix.

From the above discussion it is clear that each routing protocol has some advantages and disadvantages. Therefore, it is necessary to develop a new routing protocol for OppNets that perform better in terms of delivery probability and buffer average time that is the core of this research work.

3 Proposed AT-PRoPHET Routing Scheme

An opportunistic network environment with N wireless nodes that are presumably cooperative and have enough energy to participate in data transmission is taken into consideration. Each node does not behave maliciously and has sufficient buffer capacity to retain information. When designing routing protocols for OppNets, the context information of a node is taken into consideration that includes its current location, movement, direction, delivery probability, frequency of encounter, distance between source and destination, energy, and so on [27]. In our proposed protocol, interaction history of nodes is used to forecast the next best forwarding node to the destination. It is the extension of PRoPHET routing protocol [24], readers may refer to PRoPHET protocol for more details regarding calculation of frequency of encountering a node.

The AT-PRoPHET protocol is described in the algorithm 1 and 2. Algorithm 1 shows that source node has message m with it. It has two neighbouring nodes, both nodes calculate their respective frequencies with respect to the source node and return the sum of frequencies, in the later step each neighbour node calculate the average frequency of encounter with respect to the source node if their frequency is greater than 0. Let assume value of average frequency at source node 0.3 which has two neighbouring nodes A and B (Fig. 2). The value of average frequency for A and B are 0.2 and 0.4 respectively. Thus, according to the AT-PRoPHET, node B with value 0.4 is selected and other node with value 0.2 will be rejected because the node A has higher average frequency than node B. The selected node is inserted into the hash map table. Algorithm 2 shows the transfer process from source node to hash map node. For each node in the hash-map, transfer the message from the current node to the current node in the hash-map. Otherwise, if average frequency of the node is equal to 0, it will be rejected.

Algorithm 1: AT-PRoPHET

1. Begin

2.   For each message to do

3.   Calculate the frequency of node

4.   Return sum of node frequency

5.   End for

6.   For each message

7.   If node frequency $\neq 0$

8.   Calculate the average frequency of node

9.   Else

10.   reject

11.   End for

12.   For each message

13.   If neighbour average frequency > current average frequency

14.   Insert the node on the hash map

15.   End for

16. End

Algorithm 2: Hash map Transfer

1. Begin
2.   For each node in hash map
3.   Check the node in hash map
4.   Transfer the message from current node to hash map node
5.   End for
6. End

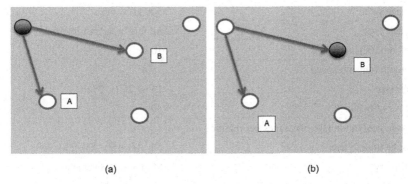

(a)   (b)

Fig. 2. Proposed algorithm (a) Initial phase (b) After transmit phase

4   Results and Discussion

4.1   ONE (Opportunistic Network Environment) Simulator

In scenarios like opportunistic and delay-tolerant networks, the ONE simulator is used for simulation and for visualising node mobility. It is a discrete event simulation engine based on agents. Several modules that perform the essential simulation tasks are updated by the engine at each stage of the simulation. The main duties of the ONE simulator include simulating node mobility, inter-node connections, routing, and message processing. Results are gathered and analysed using other tools for visualisation, reporting, and post-processing. Movement models are used to put node movement into practise. Either artificial models or actual movement traces are being used. The location, communication range, and bit-rate of the nodes determine their connectivity to one another. The communications always have a single source host and a single destination host inside the simulation environment, and they are unicast [28]. Report modules gather data from the simulation engine's events and provide output. The outputs produced might be aggregated statistics computed in the simulator or logs of events that are further processed by other post-processing tools.

4.2   Simulation Environment Setup

We use the ONE simulator for the simulation of the proposed protocol and for the comparison of results with Direct Delivery, Epidemic, PRoPHET, and Spray-And-Wait. Below is the simulation setup. The ONE simulator is supported by java, so we used Java 17.0.2. The simulation default settings file is shown in Table 1 and Table 2 with significant parameter values.

Table 1. Simulation setup

Parameter	Values
Simulation area size	(4500 × 3400) M
Message size	500 kb–1 mb
Interface type	Simple broadcast interface
Bluetooth transmit range	10 m
Bluetooth transmit speed	250k
Buffer size	15 m, 20 m, 25 m
Number of hosts	40
Message generation rate (messages per minute)	1
Message time to live	50, 100, 150, 200, 250, 300
Mobility type	Map route movement
Movement model	Shortest path based movement
Interval of update	0.1
Interface	High speed
High speed interface type	Simple broadcast interface
High speed Internet transmit speed	1000
High speed Internet transmit range	10 m

Table 2. Routing algorithms used for comparison

Routing algorithm	Parameter	Value
Epidemic	n/a	n/a
PRoPHET	Number of copies(L)	6
Direct delivery	n/a	n/a
AT-PRoPHET	Number of copies(L)	6

4.3   Results Discussion

The results of proposed routing protocol are compared with PRoPHET, Epidemic, Direct Delivery, and First Contact in terms of delivery probability and buffer average time at different scales of TTL and Buffer sizes. From the Fig. 3, Fig. 4 and Fig. 5, it was a clear depiction that the average buffer-time of all protocols increases with an increase in message TTL. It was found that the average buffer time was maximal in the case of direct delivery protocol and minimal in the case of AT-PRoPHET protocol and other routing protocols performance lies between Direct Delivery and AT-PRoPHET and, from the Fig. 6, Fig. 7 and Fig. 8, it was also clear that the delivery probability of protocols increases as the message TTL increases. It was found that delivery probability

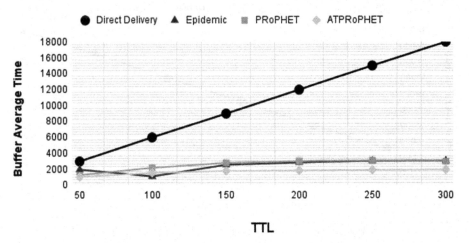

Fig. 3. TTL vs buffer average time (Buffer size = 15 m)

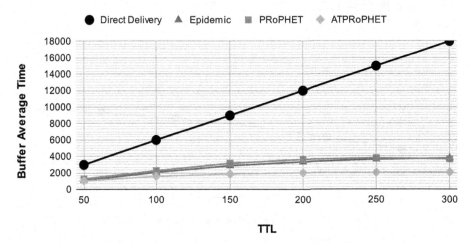

Fig. 4. TTL vs buffer average time (Buffer size = 20 m)

is minimal in the case of the Direct Delivery protocol and maximal in the case of AT-PRoPHET protocol and all other routing protocol's performance lies between the Direct Delivery protocol and the AT-PRoPHET protocol. According to the results it is found that the buffer-average time vs. TTL parameter of the proposed protocol for buffer size between 15 m to 25 m is 34.6% to 50.7% less than PRoPHET, 36% to 51.7% less than Epidemic, and 88.4% to 89% less than Direct delivery protocol, and also the delivery probability of the proposed protocol for buffer size between 15 m to 25 m is 37% to 48% greater than PRoPHET, 30.4% to 41.7% greater than Epidemic, and 53.6% to 56.4% greater than Direct delivery protocol. It is evident by the results that the proposed protocol performs better than other protocols.

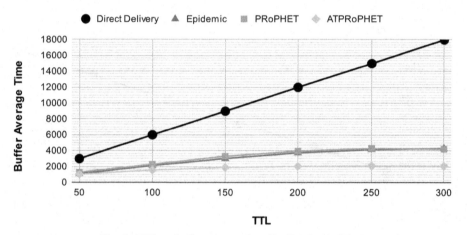

Fig. 5. TTL vs buffer average time (Buffer size = 25 m)

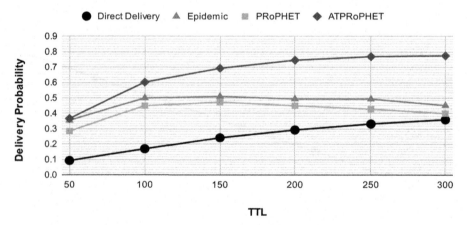

Fig. 6. TTL vs delivery probability (Buffer size = 15 m)

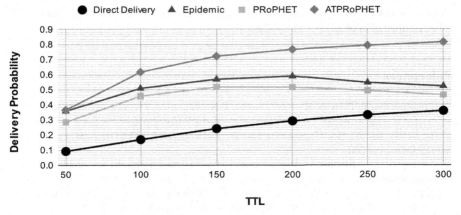

Fig. 7. TTL vs delivery probability (Buffer size = 20 m)

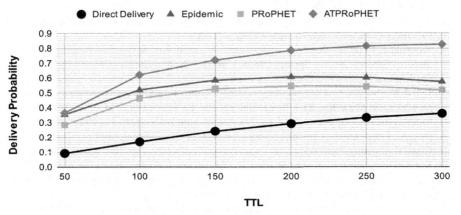

Fig. 8. TTL vs delivery probability (Buffer size = 25 m)

5   Conclusion and Future Work

Several routing protocols have been proposed for OppNets in literature [29–35]. This research work simulated and discussed the performance of the proposed routing protocol along with other routing protocols i.e., PRoPHET, Epidemic, Direct Delivery, and First Contact. The frequency of encounters of nodes is used as context information and from the results obtained, it is justified that the proposed routing algorithm performs better with high delivery probability and less buffer average time. A good performance is achieved, however some upgrades need to be done to make this protocol more suitable for real-world application, for example the overhead and the message dropped value of the protocol increases as the buffer size is increased.

Acknowledgment. This research work is part of the research work funded by "Seed Grant to Faculty Members under IoE Scheme (under Dev. Scheme No. 6031)" granted to Anshul Verma at

Banaras Hindu University, Varanasi, India, and is also supported by Technology Innovation Hub, Indian Institute of Technology Patna, India.

References

1. Spyropoulos, T., Psounis, K., Raghavendra, C.S.: Single-copy routing in intermittently connected mobile networks. In: 2004 First Annual IEEE Communications Society Conference on Sensor and Ad Hoc Communications and Networks, IEEE SECON 2004, pp. 235–244. IEEE October 2004
2. Spyropoulos, T., Psounis, K., Raghavendra, C.S.: Spray and focus: efficient mobility-assisted routing for heterogeneous and correlated mobility. In: Proceedings of the - Fifth Annual IEEE International Conference on Pervasive Computing and Communications Workshops (PerComW 2007), 79–85 (2007). https://doi.org/10.1109/PERCOMW.2007.108
3. Del Duca Almeida, V., Oliveira, A.B., MacEdo, D.F., Nogueira, J.M.S.: Performance evaluation of MANET and DTN routing protocols. In: IFIP Wireless Days (2012). https://doi.org/10.1109/WD.2012.6402866
4. Jones, E.P., Ward, P.A.: Routing strategies for delay-tolerant networks. Submitted to ACM Computer Communication Review (CCR), 1 (2006)
5. Woungang, I., Dhurandher, S.K., Anpalagan, A., Vasilakos, A.V. (eds.): Routing in Opportunistic Networks, p. 83. Springer, New York (2013). https://doi.org/10.1007/978-1-4614-3514-3
6. Jindal, A., Psounis, K.: Contention-aware analysis of routing schemes for mobile opportunistic networks. In: MobiOpp 2007 Proceedings of the 1st International MobiSys Workshop on Mobile opportunistic Networking, pp. 1–8 (2007). https://doi.org/10.1145/1247694.1247696
7. Dev, A.: Opportunistic network routing protocols. In: 2019 9th International Conference on Cloud Computing, Data Science & Engineering (Confluence), pp. 100–106 (2019)
8. Kumar Dhurandher, S., Kumar Sharma, D., Woungang, I.: Energy-based Performance Evaluation of Various Routing Protocols in Infrastructure-less Opportunistic Networks. http://www.scs.ryerson.ca/. Accessed 13 Oct 2022
9. Bjurefors, F.: Opportunistic networking congestion, transfer ordering and resilience (2014)
10. Jain, S., Fall, K., Patra, R.: Routing in a delay tolerant network. Comput. Commun. Rev. 34(4), 145–157 (2004). https://doi.org/10.1145/1030194.1015484
11. Ramesh, S., Ganesh Kumar, P.: Opportunistic Network Environment simulator Department of Communications and Networking Special assignment (2008). https://scialert.net/fulltext/?doi=jai.2013.123.133#ab
12. Kaur, N., Mathur, G.: Opportunistic networks: a review 18(2), 20–26 (2016). https://doi.org/10.9790/0661-1802032026
13. Sharma, D.K., Kukreja, D., Aggarwal, P., Kaur, M., Sachan, A.: Poisson's probability-based Q-routing techniques for message forwarding in opportunistic networks. Int. J. Commun. Syst. 31(11), 1–23 (2018). https://doi.org/10.1002/dac.3593
14. Boldrini, C., Conti, M., Passarella, A.: Autonomic behaviour of opportunistic network routing. Int. J. Auton. Adapt. Commun. Syst. 1(1), 122–147 (2008). https://doi.org/10.1504/IJAACS.2008.019203
15. Chen, L.J., Yu, C.H., Tseng, C.L., Chu, H.H., Chou, C.F.: A content-centric framework for effective data dissemination in opportunistic networks. IEEE J. Sel. Areas Commun. 26(5), 761–772 (2008). https://doi.org/10.1109/JSAC.2008.080603
16. Akestoridis, D.G., Papapetrou, E.: A framework for the evaluation of routing protocols in opportunistic networks. Comput. Commun. 145, 14–28 (2019). https://doi.org/10.1016/j.comcom.2019.06.003

17. Huang, C., Lan, K., Tsai, C., Architecture, A.: A survey of opportunistic networks, pp. 1672–1677 (2008). https://doi.org/10.1109/WAINA.2008.292
18. Fall, K.: A delay-tolerant network architecture for challenged internets. In: Proceedings of the 2003 Conference on Applications, Technologies, Architectures, and Protocols for Computer Communications - SIGCOMM 2003 (2003). https://doi.org/10.1145/863955
19. Pelusi, L., Passarella, A., Conti, M.: Opportunistic networking: data forwarding in disconnected mobile ad hoc networks. IEEE Commun. Mag. **44**(11), 134–141 (2006). https://doi.org/10.1109/MCOM.2006.248176
20. Jain, S., Fall, K., Patra, R.: Routing in a delay tolerant network. In: Proceedings of the 2004 Conference on Applications, Technologies, Architectures, and Protocols for Computer Communications, pp. 145–158, August 2004
21. Vahdat, A., Becker, D.: Epidemic routing for partially connected ad hoc networks. Technical report CS-2000-06, Computer Science Department. Duke University (2000)
22. De Rango, F., Amelio, S., Fazio, P.: Epidemic strategies in delay tolerant networks from an energetic point of view: main issues and performance evaluation. J. Netw. **10**(01) (2015). https://doi.org/10.4304/JNW.10.01.4-14
23. Spyropoulos, T., Psounis, K., Raghavendra, C.S.: Spray and wait: an efficient routing scheme for intermittently connected mobile networks. In: Proceedings of the ACM SIGCOMM 2005 Workshop on Delay-Tolerant Networking, WDTN 2005 (2005), pp. 252–259. https://doi.org/10.1145/1080139.1080143
24. Lindgren, A., Doria, A., Schelen, O.: Probabilistic routing in intermittently connected networks. ACM Mob. Comput. Commun. Rev. **7**, 19–20 (2003)
25. Burgess, J., Gallagher, B., Jensen, D., Levine, B.N.: MaxProp: routing for vehicle-based disruption-tolerant networks. In: Proceedings of the IEEE INFOCOM (2006). https://doi.org/10.1109/INFOCOM.2006.228
26. Wang, S.X.: The improved Dijkstra's shortest path algorithm and its application. Procedia Eng. **29**, 1186–1190 (2012). https://doi.org/10.1016/j.proeng.2012.01.110
27. Dhurandher, S.K., Borah, S., Woungang, I., Sharma, D.K., Arora, K., Agarwal, D.: EDR: an encounter and distance based routing protocol for opportunistic networks. In: Proceedings of the International Conference on Advanced Information Networking and Applications AINA, vol. 2016, pp. 297–302, May 2016. https://doi.org/10.1109/AINA.2016.15
28. Keranen, A.: Opportunistic network environment simulator. Special Assignment report, Helsinki University of Technology, Department of Communications and Networking (2008)
29. Verma, A., Verma, P., Dhurandher, S.K., Woungang, I. (eds.): Opportunistic Networks: Fundamentals, Applications and Emerging Trends. CRC Press, Taylor and Francis (2021). ISBN: 9780367677305
30. Verma, A., Srivastava, A.: Integrated routing protocol for opportunistic networks. Int. J. Adv. Comput. Sci. Appl. (IJACSA) **2**(3), 85–92 (2011). https://doi.org/10.14569/IJACSA.2011.020315
31. Singh, M., Verma, A., Verma, P.: Security in opportunistic networks. In: Opportunistic Networks: Fundamentals, Applications and Emerging Trends, Chapter 14, pp. 299–312. CRC Press (2021)
32. Verma, A., Singh, M., Pattanaik, K.K., Singh, B.K.: Future networks inspired by opportunistic network. In: Opportunistic Networks: Mobility Models, Protocols, Security & Privacy, Chapter 12, pp. 229–246. CRC Press, Taylor & Francis (2019). https://doi.org/10.1201/9780429453434
33. Verma, A., Pattanaik, K.K.: Routing protocols in opportunistic networks. In: Opportunistic Networking: Vehicular, D2D and Cognitive Radio Networks, Chapter 5, pp. 125–166. CRC Press, Taylor and Francis (2017). https://doi.org/10.1201/9781315200804

34. Verma, A., Pattanaik, K.K., Ingavale, A.: Context-based routing protocols for OppNets. In: Woungang, I., Dhurandher, S., Anpalagan, A., Vasilakos, A. (eds.) Routing in Opportunistic Networks, pp. 69–97. Springer, New York (2013). https://doi.org/10.1007/978-1-4614-351 4-3_3

35. Singh, M., Verma, A., Verma, P.: Empirical analysis of the performance of routing protocols in opportunistic networks. In: Research Advances in Network Technologies. CRC Press (2023, in Press). ISBN 9781032340487

Analysis and Implementation of Microservices Using Docker

Keshav Sharma[1], Anshul Verma[1]($\boxtimes$) (iD), and Pradeepika Verma[2]

[1] Department of Computer Science, Banaras Hindu University, Varanasi, India
anshulverma87@gmail.com
[2] Technology Innovation Hub, Indian Institute of Technology, Patna, India

Abstract. Implementation of micro-services is among the most challenging and important tasks in the field of Computer Science. For implementing the microservice architecture, Docker has been used in the current scenario. Creating a machine learning model that works on one computer is not really difficult. But creating a model that can scale and run on all types of servers around the world, it's more challenging. This work proposed a way to deploy a certain type of trained model in microservice architecture using Docker to use anywhere. For practical implementation, two models for machine learning has been used. One that addresses the handwritten digit recognition problem which has been an open problem in pattern classification since a long time, and another model resolves the issue of house pricing based on several attributes. The purpose of implementation of machine learning model in microservice architecture using Docker is to enable a method from which anyone can use a machine learning model without worrying for their machine configuration and dependencies of the machine learning model.

Keywords: Container · Docker · Cloud · Microservices · Machine learning model · Dependencies · Server

1 Introduction

The main idea of microservices is to implement an architecture in which different parts or component of a software design are created and deployed as separate isolated services. They get their name because each application function works as an independent service.

1.1 Background

This architecture allows each service to scale or update without disrupting other services in the application. Each is deployed separately and they communicate through well-defined network-based interfaces [1]. Due to their isolation and strict requirement to communicate over well-defined interfaces, microservices avoid the quick and dirty solutions often found in monoliths [4]. These microservice architecture results in a loss of cohesion and an increase in coupling, having two main causes of complexity. The microservices style is typically organized around business capabilities and priorities.

I. Woungang et al. (Eds.): ANTIC 2022, CCIS 1797, pp. 413–421, 2023.
https://doi.org/10.1007/978-3-031-28180-8_28

Unlike a traditional monolithic development approach, each team having a specific focus on user interfaces, databases, technology layers, or server-side logic where microservice architecture uses cross-functional teams [2].

After a model has been developed, it may work perfectly on one system or server, but not really on other systems, for example, when the model has been moved to the production stage or to another server, many challenges comes into the picture such as performance issues, app crashing, and not well optimized. Another challenging situation is that machine learning model can certainly be written using a single programming language like python, but the application will certainly need to interact with other applications written in other programming languages for data ingestion, data preparation, front-end, etc. Docker allows to manage all these interactions in better way because micro-services can be written in a different language that allows for scalability and easy addition or removal of independent services. Thus, Docker brings reproducibility, portability, ease of deployment, granular updates, lightness and simplicity.

1.2 Objective

The purpose of implementation of machine learning model in microservice architecture in docker is to enable a method from which anyone can use a machine learning model without worrying about their machine configuration and dependencies for a certain machine learning model. The deployed machine learning model can be accessed through the exposed APIs or the UI provided by another microservice which internally connect the APIs of the Machine learning models. One Model resolves the problem of handwritten digit recognition has long been an open problem in the field of pattern classification [6]. Another model resolves the issue of house pricing based on several attributes [7].

For implementing the microservice architecture Docker has been used. Docker is an open-source containerization platform that enables developers to package applications into containers that standardized executable components combining application source code with the operating system (OS) libraries and dependencies required to run that code in any environment [17]. Docker enables developers to use the docker container which consists the environment and dependencies for a certain type of machine learning model without worrying about the environmental setup of the system it consists, just need docker installed on their system. The major objectives of this work are described below:

- Build a customized docker image with all the dependencies of our ML model.
- Creation of API which is customizable according to the model.
- Build a microservice architecture which is independent of system configuration.
- Enable usage of a trained ML model without installing a single dependency.
- Make deployment and configuration of whole microservice architecture easier.

2 Literature Review

The development of microservices using docker is implemented in some of the papers in the past also. Some of the papers have discussed below.

2.1 Microservices Using Docker

A study on the microservices using Docker was conducted in [8]. The study concluded that while Docker alone itself is not a silver bullet that can solve every problem of building a microservices architecture, together with surrounding tools, it is very helpful in improving efficiency, automation, and other necessary fundamentals to achieve the most important principles of building a microservices architecture. The study also discussed about how Docker can be useful to successfully apply the beneficial architectural style with a well working case study.

A study on Distributed microservices systems using docker demonstrates the shortcomings of traditional monolithic architectures by enabling the independence of development, deployment, updating, and scaling of components, but designing such systems is not without Challenges [21]. The authors described the design and structure of Serfnode (an extensible solution to the service discovery problem for microservices running in Docker containers that aims to be as simple to use as possible). It doesn't change the original containers and no special infrastructure is needed to start. Thus, all we need is Docker and the Serfnode image. The new images form a decentralized cluster of Serfnodes, where they advertise and provide search service. In the near future, the authors have plan to increase code coverage for Serfnode, including functional and performance tests. They also have a higher-level API planned for common tasks.

2.2 Machine Learning on Docker

As Docker becomes the most popular containerization platform, accurate modeling of application performance in docker containers is very important both for users and cloud service providers [20]. In this article, the performance of the application in docker containers has been modeled using three machine learning techniques. First, the impact of key containers resource allocation parameters that affect the performance of containerized applications is identified [18]. Then, modeling techniques over CPU, memory and I/O parameters to characterize the performance of applications running in containers is presented [13]. Experimental results shows that the proposed models can achieve a prediction error as low as 2.27%, with an average of 10.13% for most applications. In addition, the prediction accuracy of SVM and ANN models are significantly better than LR based approaches, with improvements of 48.13% and 29.30%, respectively [9].

3 Methodology

When a model is ready, scientists worry about the model not reproducing real-life results or when the work is shared with teammates. Sometimes, it does not happen because of the model, but because of the need to reproduce the whole stack. Docker makes it easy to reproduce the workspace used to train and run a machine learning model anywhere. Docker allows to package code and dependencies into containers that can be moved to different servers even if they are on different hardware or operating system. A training model can be developed on a local computer and can be easily transferred to external clusters with additional resources such as GPUs, additional storage, and powerful CPUs.

It is easy to deploy and make a model available to the world by wrapping it in an API in a container and deploying the container using technology like OpenShift, a Kubernetes distribution. Simplicity is also a good argument in favour of the containerizing machine learning applications, as containers can be created automatically with templates and have access to open-source registry containing existing containers added by users. Docker allows developers to track different versions of a container image, check who built a version with what, and roll back to previous versions. Another argument is that the machine learning application can continue to run even if one of its services is updated, patched, or down. For example, if there is need to update an output message that is part of the entire solution, there is no need to update the entire application and to interfere with other services.

3.1 Architecture

To build a microservice architecture for each application, a separate container has been deployed for machine learning model and to reduce the coupling further UI is deployed on a different docker container as a different microservice. Here, since in docker, the storage used is ephemeral i.e., last for a short span of time because it belongs to a container and will lose their existence with the termination of the container. Since storage should not to be ephemeral, a persistence storage for container provided by base operating system is used. In proposed architecture (illustrated in Fig. 1), the machine learning model is deployed independently and communicate through well-defined network-based interfaces. Because of their isolation and strict requirement to communicate through well-defined interfaces results in increase of cohesion and decrease in coupling [11].

This - architecture proposes a way to implement microservices on a single machine using docker. Two containers working as a microservice consist of the trained machine learning model and one container consist of the UI server for the client. Since all three servers resides on a single network, distinguishing base on networking IP is not possible so far. Thus, going one step deeper for the Transport layer and distinguishing based on the port number is efficient way. In this architecture, the concept of **PATing** is used i.e. all three containers can be accessed through same IP but from different port number hence, each microservice have their own socket for access [3, 12].

The web server simply consists of simple html files having options of choosing a model, giving necessary files or attributes through a form and having a submit button to call our API of ML model.

The servers for ML model having trained machine learning model and an exposed API to access the model. The exposed API is accessed through the CGI, which is also responsible for storing the request from the client. Then, the API will get the request attributes and will perform some tasks based on the request and return the response.

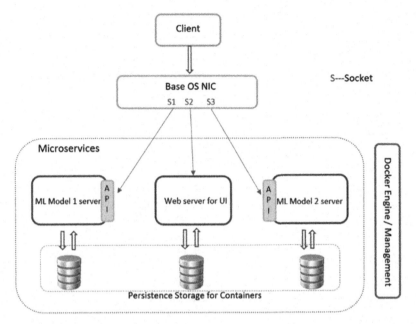

Fig. 1. Proposed microservice architecture

Further, since the containers of docker are just an instance of an image so they have ephemeral storage, the data logs and other information will be deleted when the container will shut down [14]. Thus, for the persistence storage the architecture will use the base OS storage mounted on the containers. For that a Docker storage has been created and mounted it while launching a container [10].

3.2 Approach

To build the proposed architecture, a way to implement microservices on a single machine using Docker is illustrated here.

The given block diagram (Fig. 2) explains the work flow to build the architecture. Initially, we have trained the model and saved it in a Joblib file [5]. Thereafter, we have created a Docker image from a Docker file that resolves all the dependencies of the models [15]. Building a docker image with all the requirements need iteratively building and checking the further dependencies [16]. Next step incudes launching a docker container from the build image and setup code in that container, committing the container to an image and pushing it to the repository. This step is also iterative since after implementation, testing of the code has been carried out and further improvement has been done in the next iteration. After committing a satisfactory image for model, we create persistence volumes for all the containers and launch the containers to deploy our architecture.

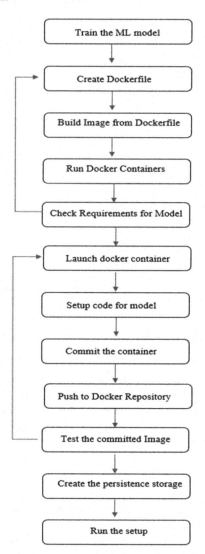

Fig. 2. Approach followed for the architecture

4 Results and Discussion

4.1 Evaluation of the Trained Models

Let's evaluate the trained ML models model used in the architecture with the help of cross validation score method provided by sklearn toolkit.

The cross-validation technique, used for evaluating the models (shown in the Table 1), requires scoring techniques and cross validation to evaluate the model. For Handwritten digit recognition, the Sorting techniques accuracy has been used and for house price prediction neg. Mean squared error has been used here.

Table 1. Evaluation of the trained model

Model	Scoring technique	CV (Cross validation)	Scores	
Handwritten digit recognition	Accuracy	3	Mean	0.9285
			Standard deviation	0.0043
Handwritten digit recognition	Accuracy	5	Mean	0.92834
			Standard deviation	0.00426
House price prediction	Neg mean squared error	3	Mean	3.7035
			Standard deviation	0.2813
House price prediction	Neg mean squared error	5	Mean	3.3385
			Standard deviation	0.4364

4.2 Analysis of Results

The objective to build the microservice architecture for each application, in this case, for machine learning model a separate container has been deployed and to reduce the coupling further, UI has been deployed on a different docker container as a different microservice. Since the storage is not to be ephemeral, so we use a persistence storage for container provided by base operating system. In the proposed architecture, our machine learning model is deployed independently and communicated through well-defined network-based interfaces.

The designed architecture proposes a way to implement microservices on a single machine using docker. In the two containers working as a microservice, one consists of the trained machine learning model and another consists of the UI server for the client.

The micro servers for ML model consist of trained machine learning model and an exposed API to access the model. The exposed API is accessed through the CGI, which is also responsible for storing the request from the client. Then, the API will get the request attributes and will perform some tasks based on the request and return the response.

5 Conclusion and Future Works

The previously developed Machine learning model, generally have lots of dependencies issues and very difficult to use by other users. Also, if someone is training a model and other want to utilize it, they face multiple issues including dependencies issue, difficult in accessing the model and more. Thus, it has needed a solution to enable using a trained model by another user get easier. The developed and deployed model on docker is independent of its dependency of operating system, libraries and their versions because all these dependencies are packed into a container and the only dependency, we have, is the docker installed on any operating system. The trained model is pushed to a centralized repository, i.e., hub.docker.com which can be pulled by any user irrespective of their system configuration and the dependencies of the model. The model can also be accessed by a user-interface through the exposed API in the docker image itself and can be used by the common non-technical users also. The model can also be used directly by exposed API directly.

The developed architecture is a model that can be used to deploy application in microservice architecture without worrying about the dependencies. To further increase the performance on this task, several approaches can be used further in the future, such as changing the architecture of the docker, further code can be optimized which is used to access the data.

Docker supports Container reuse means existing containers can be used as base images essentially as templates for building new containers [19]. The architecture is built only for experimental purpose, to use it for the business purpose, multiple instances of an identical server should be launched to deal with large amount of hits. Since docker support container reuse, the resource utilization for multiple instances will very low. The experiments performed in this report is a roadmap. As discussed earlier, docker provides isolation, so deploying an application in microservice architecture using docker will give isolation in minimum footprint.

Acknowledgment. This research work is part of the research work funded by "Seed Grant to Faculty Members under IoE Scheme (under Dev. Scheme No. 6031)" granted to Anshul Verma at Banaras Hindu University, Varanasi, India, and is also supported by Technology Innovation Hub, Indian Institute of Technology Patna, India.

References

1. Salah, T., Zemerly, M.J., Yeun, C.Y., Al-Qutayri, M., Al-Hammadi, Y.: The evolution of distributed systems towards microservices architecture. In: 2016 11th International Conference for Internet Technology and Secured Transactions (ICITST), pp. 318–325. IEEE, December 2016
2. Dragoni, N., et al.: Microservices: yesterday, today, and tomorrow. Present Ulterior Softw. Eng., 195–216 (2017)
3. Bansal, A., Goel, P.: Simulation and analysis of network address translation (NAT) & port address translation (PAT) techniques. Int. J. Eng. Res. Appl. 7(7 Part 2), 50–56 (2017)
4. Ponce, F., Márquez, G., Astudillo, H.: Migrating from monolithic architecture to microservices: a rapid review. In: 2019 38th International Conference of the Chilean Computer Science Society (SCCC), pp. 1–7. IEEE, 4 November 2019
5. Sahu, V.L., Kubde, B.: Offline handwritten character recognition techniques using neural network: a review. Int. J. Sci. Res. (IJSR) 2(1), 87–94 (2013)
6. Gu, Y., Wells, L.J.: Offline Handwritten Digits Recognition Using Machine learning (2018)
7. Bae, J.K.: Using machine learning algorithms for housing price prediction: the case of Fairfax County, virginia housing data 42(6), 2928–2934 (2015)
8. Jaramillo, D., Nguyen, D.V., Smart, R.: Leveraging microservices architecture by using Docker technology. In: SoutheastCon 2016, pp. 1–5. IEEE, March 2016
9. Gorgevik, D., Cakmakov, D.: Handwritten digit recognition by combining SVM classifiers. In: EUROCON 2005-The International Conference on "Computer as a Tool", vol. 2, pp. 1393–1396. IEEE, November 2005
10. Zhao, N., et al.: Large-scale analysis of docker images and performance implications for container storage systems. IEEE Trans. Parallel Distrib. Syst. 32(4), 918–930 (2020)

11. Dua, R., Raja, A.R., Kakadia, D.: Virtualization vs containerization to support paas. In: 2014 IEEE International Conference on Cloud Engineering, pp. 610–614. IEEE, March 2014
12. Cisco: Port Address Translation, Cisco. https://www.cisco.com/assets/sol/sb/RV320_Emulat ors/RV320_Emulator_v1-1-0-09/help/Setup13.html. Accessed 02 July 2022
13. Ye, K., Kou, Y., Lu, C., Wang, Y., Xu, C.Z.: Modeling application performance in Docker containers using machine learning techniques. In: 2018 IEEE 24th International Conference on Parallel and Distributed Systems (ICPADS), pp. 1–6. IEEE, December 2018
14. n2ws.com: Ephemeral Storage Mirror on an EBS Volume, 26 May 2022. https://n2ws.com/ blog/how-to-guides/ephemeral-storage-on-ebs-volume. Accessed 02 July 2022
15. Zhang, Y., Yin, G., Wang, T., Yu, Y., Wang, H.: An insight into the impact of dockerfile evolutionary trajectories on quality and latency. In: 2018 IEEE 42nd Annual Computer Software and Applications Conference (COMPSAC), vol. 1, pp. 138–143. IEEE, July 2018
16. Skourtis, D., Rupprecht, L., Tarasov, V., Megiddo, N.: Carving perfect layers out of docker images. In: 11th USENIX Workshop on Hot Topics in Cloud Computing (HotCloud 19) (2019)
17. I. C. Education: Docker, IBM, 23 June 2021. https://www.ibm.com/cloud/learn/docker. Accessed 02 July 2022
18. Shirinbab, S., Lundberg, L., Casalicchio, E.: Performance evaluation of container and virtual machine running cassandra workload. In: 2017 3rd International Conference of Cloud Computing Technologies and Applications (CloudTech), pp. 1–8. IEEE, October 2017
19. Rufino, J., Alam, M., Ferreira, J., Rehman, A., Tsang, K.F.: Orchestration of containerized microservices for IIoT using Docker. In: 2017 IEEE International Conference on Industrial Technology (ICIT), pp. 1532–1536. IEEE, March 2017
20. Singh, S.: How to build application inside and outside Docker. Dockerfile structure and commands. Medium, 8 October 2018. Accessed 02 July 2022
21. Stubbs, J., Moreira, W., Dooley, R.: Distributed systems of microservices using docker and serfnode. In: 2015 7th International Workshop on Science Gateways, pp. 34–39. IEEE, June 2015

Automated Energy Modeling Framework for Microcontroller-Based Edge Computing Nodes

Emanuel Oscar Lange[1], Jiby Mariya Jose[2], Shajulin Benedict[2(✉)], and Michael Gerndt[1]

[1] TUM School of Computation, Information and Technology, Technical University of Munich, 85748 Garching, Germany
ge35xor@tum.de, gerndt@in.tum.de
[2] Department of Computer Science and Engineering, Indian Institute of Information Technology Kottayam, Valavoor P.O., Kottayam 686635, Kerala, India
{jiby.phd2102,shajulin}@iiitkottayam.ac.in
http://www.sbenedictglobal.com

Abstract. When IoT-enabled applications utilized edge nodes rather than cloud servers, they aimed to apply diligent energy-efficient mechanisms on edge devices. Accordingly, frameworks and approaches that monitor/model microcontrollers, including Espressif-Processor-based (ESP) edge nodes, have drawn mainstream attention among researchers working in the edge intelligence domain. The traditional approaches to measuring the energy consumption of edge nodes are either not online or prone to complex solutions. This article attempts to develop an Automated Energy Modeling Framework (AEM) for microcontroller-based edge nodes of IoT-enabled applications. The proposed approach baselines the energy consumption values; models energy consumption values of components using a random forest (RF) algorithm; and, automatically suggests the energy consumption of edge nodes in real-time – i.e., during the execution of IoT-enabled applications on edge nodes. Experiments were carried out to validate two applications' automated energy modeling approach using Espressif's ESP devices. The proposed mechanism would benefit energy-conscious IoT-enabled application developers who focus on minimizing the energy consumption of embedded-based edge nodes such as ESPs.

Keywords: Automation · Energy modeling · Energy consumption · Framework · IoT

1 Introduction

Applying edge intelligence, an emerging area of research in the IoT domain, has become central to the minds of researchers and practitioners due to the latency

I. Woungang et al. (Eds.): ANTIC 2022, CCIS 1797, pp. 422–437, 2023.
https://doi.org/10.1007/978-3-031-28180-8_29

and privacy issues of traditional pure cloud-based learning mechanisms. Various domains, including smart finance, smart healthcare, smart transportation, and smart industry, have preferred edge computing with tiny battery-operated devices, mostly embedded-based devices, to process their learning tasks nearer to sensor nodes.

Although edge intelligence paves a way for enabling the full potential of businesses shortly, designing energy-efficient edge-enabled applications is considered a primordial challenge to developers. This is because of the following key points:

1. non-availability of a holistic energy measurement framework for microcontroller-based edge computing devices [7]. In fact, energy consumption of edge nodes need to be evaluated without much overheads so that the scarce resources are efficiently handled;
2. a few available solutions are either expensive or complex in nature; and,
3. the most utilized methods are offline monitoring methods – i.e., the energy consumption of applications are assessed only after the execution of them.

This article proposes an Automated Energy Modeling (AEM) framework for embedded-based edge devices of an IoT-enabled application. The proposed approach attempts to baseline the potential energy consumption of instructions when executed on edge devices, more specifically Expressif Processors (ESP); develops energy models using Random Forest (RF) algorithm; and, suggests the energy consumption of edge nodes based on embedded systems in runtime. In this way, applications that are prone to energy inefficiencies could be stopped before draining the associated batteries of devices, if any.

Experiments were carried out at our research laboratory to baseline the energy consumption of ESP's components such as CPU, memory, and WIFI/Bluetooth. Next, the energy consumption of applications is modeled using random forests (RF) algorithm based on the previously created baseline results. Next, utilizing our proposed AEM framework, we demonstrated the online approach of displaying the energy consumption of IoT-enabled applications.

The major contributions of the article are listed as follows: i) we developed an automated energy modeling framework for embedded-enabled edge nodes of IoT applications; ii) we revealed the baseline creation approach for performing energy measurements on these embedded devices; iii) we modeled the energy consumption values using RF to automatically suggest the energy consumption of applications in real-time; and, iv) we demonstrated the proposed AEM framework using two applications namely Google Cloud's firebase-application and computer vision-based application.

The rest of the paper is written as follows: Sect. 2 describes the state-of-the-art work in the field of energy efficiency in edge-enabled applications; Sect. 3 expresses the inner working details of the proposed automated energy modeling framework; Sect. 4 explains about the modeling approaches implemented in the framework; Sect. 5 demonstrates the experiments held to validate the importance of the proposed mechanism; and, Sect. 6 concludes our work with a few outlooks for researchers who intends to extend our research work.

2   Related Work

Edge-enabled applications have increased in recent years in various domains such as, agriculture [13], healthcare [14], finance, industry, and so forth, owing to the potential business possibilities and latency/privacy/cost improvements. Most of the machine learning tasks are offloaded to embedded-based edge devices [15] to complement the learning processes.

The notable challenges of edge-based IoT-enabled applications, including energy inefficiency, have been attempted by a few researchers in the recent past. For instance, authors of Huned et al. [16] studied the procedure to offload tasks considering the energy efficiency during the edge-cloud orchestration; authors of [17] developed a few resource allocation strategies based on energy efficiency in edge environments; and, so forth.

A few researchers have attempted to study the performance/energy efficiency aspects of microcontrollers which are often low-cost devices. These research works have been oriented in two major subdivisions: i) Instruction-Level analysis – here, analysis was carried out based on instructions when executed on microcontrollers. For instance, authors of [1] investigated the impact of instructions and formulated a base cost when executed on microcontrollers; ii) Functional-Level analysis – in this case, the characteristics of components were studied and mapped onto the observed energy consumption values. For instance, in [2], authors have characterized the power consumption of different components of a system in the form of algorithmic and architectural parameters.

Establishing models after the execution of applications on embedded systems has been accomplished in the recent past. Notably, authors of [3] modeled the processing unit based on three parameters namely, degree of parallelism, number of instructions, and the input data. Similarly, authors of [5] revealed the methodology to apply state machines for modeling the effects of WiFi and Bluetooth components of embedded systems. Apart from modeling the energy consumption of individual components, a few authors have developed simulations which pinpoints the energy consumption values with respect to task scheduling [9], scalability, and so forth [10–12].

In general, modeling is a good approach for embedded-based edge nodes due to the limited utility of potential batteries or energy sources. However, most of the existing solutions are not online – i.e., the existing methods require the completion of applications in order to assess the energy consumption values. Also, very few frameworks exist in the market that investigates the energy consumption of applications in a holistic manner. Recently, WattEdge was developed by [8]. But, this framework focuses on only powerful edge nodes such as Raspberry pi, JetsonNano, and so forth. In fact, measuring and modeling tiny devices such as microcontroller-based ESP32 is a challenging effort due to skilled external measurements.

This article attempted to design an automated energy modeling framework that created a baseline and modeled the energy consumption values of the individual components of low-power microcontroller-based edge nodes such as ESP-32, RaspberryPi-Pico, Arduinos, and so forth, in real-time.

3   Automated Energy Modeling Framework (AEM)

An automatic approach to analyzing the energy consumption of IoT-enabled applications is a needy process, especially in battery-operated tiny low-cost microcontroller-based edge nodes. This section describes the proposed AEM framework that automatically provides the energy consumption values of applications. Additionally, the key functionalities of these components are explained in detail.

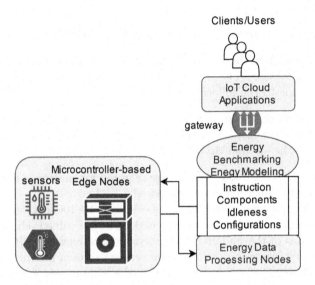

Fig. 1. AEM framework

3.1   AEM Framework Components

The proposed AEM framework focuses on measuring and modeling energy consumption of low-power embedded-based edge devices (see Fig. 1). It assesses the energy consumption values using current sensors and configurations. The major components and their functionalities are listed below:

1. User Applications – IoT-enabled applications are often connected with cloud environments such as Amazon Web Services or Google Compute Cloud. The service instances utilize sensor networks or their establishments through IoT gateways.
2. Energy Modeling – The energy modeling framework works in two phases. The first phase is organized in an offline mode – i.e., the energy measurements of potential configurations, instructions, communication aspects, and so forth, are captured and modeled. This phase is required only once to collect typical energy consumption values of a target microcontroller-based edge node so that a baseline energy measurement is calculated.

Later, in the second phase, the created model is applied to predict the energy consumption of microcontrollers in online mode. Prediction models such as RF, Support Vectors, Linear Regression, and so forth. This work is restricted to low-power microcontroller edge nodes such as ESP-based boards.
3. Edge Nodes and Sensors – These are end devices of any IoT-enabled application. The edge nodes are either battery-operated or power-sourced machines. In this study, we focus on battery-operated microcontroller nodes. Typically, these nodes have a tiny version of operating systems such as FreeRTOS.

3.2   Energy Measurements – Methodology in First Phase of AEM

In general, measuring the energy consumption of microcontroller-based edge nodes is a tedious task. The major factors that impact the direct energy measurements are due to the following reasons [7]:

1. non-availability of low-impact hardware counters on embedded devices,
2. a minimal number of parallel threads to capture energy measurements, and
3. potential overheads that drain associated batteries of these edge nodes.

Obviously, external measurements are required for capturing the energy consumption values of microcontroller-based edge nodes.

In AEM, the power supply voltage of 5 V with 10–100 mA current is offered to the target microcontroller-based edge node. The 5 V value is chosen because of the specifications of the underlying microcontrollers such as ESPs. To calculate the energy values, we monitor the current sensor values of microcontroller-based edge nodes. However, there is a possibility of a wide range of shifts in the current sensor values of target devices – i.e., between sleep states and computation states. Therefore, a shunt resistor is utilized to avoid inaccuracies or the possible brownout conditions of microcontrollers.

In our framework, the current I values are captured using INA219 sensors. These sensors support range switching while minimizing the sampling error. In AEM, sampling of current measurements is carried out every 532 µs before they are averaged to calculate the average power value. This value was chosen considering the resolution of the current sensor utilized in the framework. Next, based on the start and stop timestamps, the energy consumption values are calculated. All these energy consumption values are stored in energy data processing nodes of AEM (see Fig. 1).

4   Baseline Data Creation and Modeling

To model the energy consumption of IoT-enabled applications on microcontroller-enabled edge nodes, initially, we need to collect the current I values of these nodes. Next, the energy consumption values are calculated. Based on the energy measurements, we could baseline the energy consumption values of the target microcontrollers considering different configurational settings.

4.1   Configurations – Baseline

In AEM, current I values need to be collected from microcontroller-based edge nodes using four different configurational settings. These settings are enabled based on diligently designed code functions that are written in C++. The different configurational settings of AEM are explained below:

1. *Idle Condition* – In this stage, the edge computing devices are powered ON without issuing any specific tasks or instructions on it. The measured current sensor values of these target devices are processed in the energy data processing nodes and stored in a CSV file format for further modeling processes.
2. *Instruction-level* – In this stage, machine code instructions that target the *ALU* operations or *Loading* operations are executed over a long period. The current I values due to these instructions executed on edge nodes are recorded as similar to the previous step in CSV files.
3. *Component-level* – To collect the baseline energy consumption values of edge nodes, functions are developed in C++ such that they are either computational, memory, or I/O intensive tasks. In ESP microcontrollers, there is a feature to collect the CPU utilization and background processes of nodes – i.e., uxTaskGetSystemState().
4. *Parallelism Condition* – In this stage, task scheduling features [6] are utilized in source codes such that certain tasks are executed on multiple available cores of edge computing devices. In this way, parallel threads and cores are utilized in embedded devices.
   Calculating the energy consumption values of I/O is particularly a critical task. For instance, to measure the energy consumption of Bluetooth devices of ESPs, we need to enable the Generic Attribute Profile (GATT) feature in ESP devices.
   The GATT feature of ESP-32 [4] entails three different states – i) Firstly, the GATT server advertises its services to potential clients; ii) Secondly, the GATT server executes background event-triggered processes analogous to the WiFi module [5], which can be put to the standard CPU measurements; and, iii) Lastly, the GATT server hosts attributes that can be read or written to external storage units.
   Measuring current I due to Bluetooth devices is performed based on state machines in AEM. Figure 2 depicts the state machines that switch between different modes of operations. To get more accurate measurements, AEM executes tasks over a period in different modes of BLE.

4.2   RF Modeling

Once after the receipt of sufficient measurements using various configurational settings, models are developed in AEM. In general, models are real-world representations of a situation in a mathematical form. In AEM, RF models are utilized to represent the energy consumption of IoT-enabled applications that utilize edge-enabled nodes.

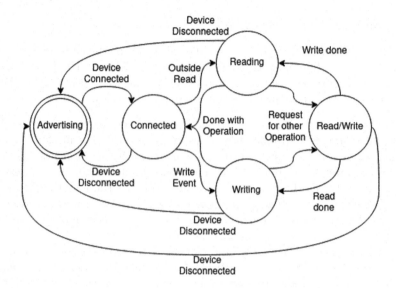

Fig. 2. State machine BLE

The random forests (RF) algorithm is an ensemble-based learning algorithm. It creates trees based on variances found in the data during the training processes. In AEM, decision trees are created based on the energy consumption values observed from baseline datasets. Among the statistical data, a few portions are utilized as training datasets and the other portion as testing datasets. While training, RF classifiers are utilized to split trees as shown in Algorithm 1.

Algorithm 1. Random Forest Algorithm of AEM Framework

Require: Training Process
Ensure: Baseline Data
    for B **do**ags == 1 . . . B
        Generate bootstrap sample N
        Create a Root tree R
        Select m variables $\in$ p *variables*
        iteration = 1 . . . m
        Randomly samples the baseline energy consumption data.
        Elect the best variable on split process
    end for
    Store Model
    Proceed with Prediction

---

5   Experimental Results

Initially, this section explains the setup utilized to measure/model the energy consumption values of embedded microcontroller-based edge nodes. Next, the current sensor values for different states such as idleness, basic instructions, parallelism stages, and WiFi/Bluetooth communications are explained. Finally, the effect of the RF algorithm when compared to the traditional equation-based polynomial fitting approach is discussed.

5.1   Experimental Setup

Throughout the experiments, we have measured the ESP-32 WROOM microcontroller board as a target device for collecting baseline data. In fact, any other microcontroller-based edge devices could be studied in the same fashion. The experimental layout utilized for measuring current I from the target device ESP-32 is shown in Fig. 3.

The current sensor relays the measurements through an Scl/Sda protocol to data processing nodes – i.e., collecting sensor data and storing them for further modeling is carried out in processing nodes. In our experiments, we utilized Raspberry Pi 4. Also, throughout the experiments, the voltage of the measurement system was kept static at 4.96 V. 4.96 V was chosen as the operating voltage value of raspberry pi is between 4.75 to 5.25 V.

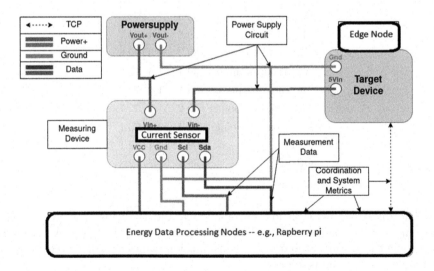

Fig. 3. Measuring circuit

5.2   Current I – Baseline Data Preparation

To create baseline data for edge nodes, we collected current sensor values from ESP-32 boards under different configurational settings of ESP-32. Table 1 lists the current values measured using the AEM framework. These measurements are carried out based on specifically written programs that included 100 instructions of similar types such as *add*, *sub*, *mul*, or *div* operations. To enable different modes of operations such as light sleep and deep sleep, the clocked gates are turned off based on the configurational specifications of ESP32.

Table 1. Current measured in AEM framework to create baseline data

Conditions	Frequencies		
	80	160	240
Current measured in μm			
Idle state	32.3	37.9	48.7
Sleep modes			
Light sleep	12.2	12.2	12.1
Deep sleep	10.8	10.8	10.8
Instructions			
NOOP	37.5	48.6	67.6
Add (integer)	39.2	51.8	72.6
Sub (integer)	39.3	52.2	73.6
Mul (integer)	39.8	53.4	75.7
Div (integer)	39	50.3	72.6
Add (floating point)	39.1	51.5	72.2
Sub (floating point)	39.1	51.4	72.1
Mul (floating point)	39.2	51.7	72.7
Div (floating point)	39.4	52.1	73.1
AND	39	51.4	72.1
OR	39.2	51.7	72.8

The difference between idle current value and the value due to executing certain instructions is considered as base cost of an instruction. Accordingly, component-level current and power consumption values are calculated based on polynomial equation as follows:

$$I_{CPU} = I_{Base} + aF^2 + bF \tag{1}$$

$$P_{CPU} = P_{CPU} * V \tag{2}$$

Typically, the energy consumption value is derived based on the time evaluated for CPU cycles and power consumption values that depend on idle and running states as shown below:

$$E_{CPU} = (t_{running} * P_{running}) + ((1 - t_{running}) * P_{idle}) \quad (3)$$

We observed the current I values increasing while applying parallelism. Figure 6 demonstrates the increasing current sensor value with higher number of cores in ESP32. Also, it could be observed that the current values increased with increasing frequencies of microcontrollers. In this demonstration, we utilized linked-list application written specifically to choose multiple cores of ESP-32.

The type of instruction has a small impact on the power consumption of a program. However, due to varying cycle lengths, the energy consumption of a program is influenced by the type of instruction. The time of an instruction t_{instr} is dependent on the frequency of the CPU and the amount of cycles needed for execution (C_{instr}). Therefore the frequency of the CPU has a minimizing effect on the power consumption as it reduces execution time:

$$t_{instr} = C_{instr} * 1/F \quad (4)$$

The energy consumption of a single instruction is currently defined as:

$$E_{instr} = t_{instr} * P_{CPU} \quad (5)$$

And, it can be rewritten as:

$$E_{instr} = (C_{instr} * 1/F) * P_{CPU} \quad (6)$$

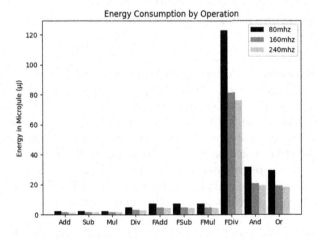

Fig. 4. Energy consumption operations

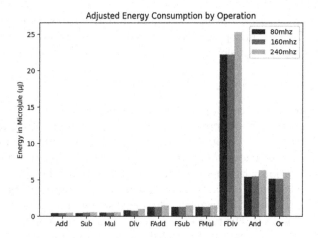

Fig. 5. Adjusted energy consumption operations

In Fig. 4, the Eq. 6 was used to draw the energy consumption of each operation. Even though *Frequency* has a negative effect on average current, it has a positive effect on time to execute. So, the larger the cycle length, the better the improvements from a higher frequency. Although this is not totally accurate, this model assumes that the energy consumed is reduced to zero after the instruction finishes. After an application finishes, there is still some energy consumed for idle mode. Thus, the cost of instruction should be compared to the cost of running idle, which is done in Fig. 5. The Figure shows the additional cost that occurs when running the instruction compared to the idle state.

Combining the Eqs. 6 and idle CPU power, the energy consumption of an embedded system can be modeled entirely by frequency, cycle length, and parallelism degree as seen in Eq. 7.

$$E_{instr} = (C_{instr} * 1/F)/\beta * P_{CPU} \tag{7}$$

Figure 7 shows the impact of different speedups and frequencies on the power consumption of applications. Generally, higher frequency and higher speedup reduce the run time such that energy consumption decreases. To show this effect, a logarithmic scale is applied to the heatmap. Although especially the effect of higher frequency diminishes as the cost of average power consumption grows, the positive effect is a constant division. At a certain point around 300 MHz, the effects of Frequency reverse and actually result in higher energy consumption with the assumption being that frequencies above 240 MHz behave the same. This breaking point is dependent on the number of cycles and the degree of parallelism.

ESP-32 offers WiFi and BLE capabilities. These programs have increased complexity to the before-mentioned tests as they require background event processes and external conditions from other devices. For this reason, a cycle-specific approach is not recommended. Instead, there is an application implemented for

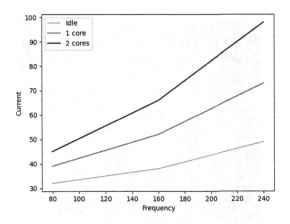

Fig. 6. Increasing current with increasing number of cores

Table 2. Current for bluetooth and wifi

Current I values for WiFi/BLE	
Operation	Current
WiFi connecting	44.65
WiFi connected	44.33
WiFi linkedlist	55.0
BLE advertising	54.22
BLE connected	47.65
BLE reading	50.71
BLE writing	62.54
BLE read/write	54.31

each component that covers all the standard necessities for communicating with other devices. The purpose is to compare their average power consumption to the previous tests that could be used to add to the existing knowledge. Additionally, the frequency is capped at the standard 160 MHz, so they will only be measured for that frequency. The current measurements observed in our experiments are given in Table 2.

5.3   Energy Modeling – RF

The previous experiments were held in an offline approach. This step is required only once for a micro-controller-based edge node. However, after the collection of a large number of experimental results, we could train the baseline data to create models. In the AEM framework, we applied the RF model to train the data. Additionally, we compared the previous method of examining the energy consumption of applications with RF models.

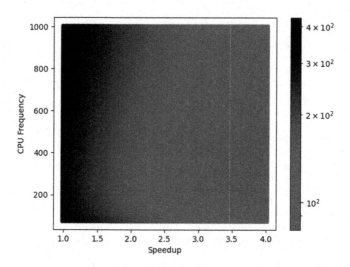

Fig. 7. Logarithmic heat map frequency and speedup

The equation-based evaluation of edge nodes shows the average energy consumption to CPU frequency and power consumption. Luckily, the additional internal measurements and the real-time streaming has little impact on energy consumption. As shown in Table 1, arithmetic operations consume 73–75 mA for a Frequency of 240 MHz combined with an average current of 4.9, which results in average energy consumption of roughly 357.7–367.5 mJ. The average power consumption for the real-time measurements is about 350 mJ.

The Random Forrest (RF) was tested with different available variables such as CPU utilization, task run time length, CPU frequency, and the type of test run (which component is stress tested). Originally, some electrical measurement data was considered but that would require a measuring setup to predict consumption. That defeats the purpose as it is possible to just measure consumption.

During the testing stages, 500000 measurement points were looked at, and the final model used 180000 of the most recent measurements with the newest framework version. The RF was tested on different Forest sizes. But, after a size of 500 trees, the used error function (squared error) did not reduce significantly anymore. For each split, only one parameter is considered, the minimum sample split size was 2 and the minimum sample size for a split node was 1.

The root node and the two underlying nodes only differentiate between Frequency and Utilization, and the average error at these nodes is already down to 70 mJ. While some differentiation between work nodes is made, the utilization is further divided into underlying nodes.

The error between the traditional equation-based approach and the Random Forrest are minimal. For four independent runs of the online framework running a 30-minute setup (70000 sample size), the relative error was between 2.5 and 3% of the overall consumption. This error is mostly due to the high restart frequency, where the energy consumption is hard to predict as seen by the high number of spikes in the power, current, voltage, and shunt windows. These spikes combined with the fact that there is no cycle accurate estimation but rather a trend analysis the r-squared value of the random forest is at 0.6. Therefore it is more important to look at the long-term error rate instead of the r-squared value as a high variance is expected.

To validate the AEM framework and test its efficacy, two applications were deployed. The two applications were chosen based on the previously modeled parameters and their relevance in edge computing. The first application tests the validity of the model based on sending frequent HTTP requests. ESP-32 is often used to relay heat and humidity information to a real-time database. The sample application uses the google cloud real-time database from Firebase. Random heat and humidity values are generated, and a heat index is calculated from a polynomial expression. These values are sent to the database via HTTP. The second example is computation and memory heavy. In this application, the ESP-32 reads data from a camera and prepossesses information for later computation in computer vision applications.

In the sample application, a random image is created. This image is then converted to grayscale. Afterward, the values are normalized in values between 0 and 1. Lastly, the image is cropped and resized to the original size. These are some common operations one would expect in image pre-processes. The average power consumption for these tests (250, 330–350) is slightly higher than the averages of all applications combined (240, 345) but tracks closely to the linked list (260 mA, 350 mA) example. These applications have a higher diversity of instructions and higher access to memory or the WiFi component as a reason for higher current consumption.

This also explains the error difference of 2.4% for the Random Forrest in comparison to the 3% for the equation-based approach, which does not take the type of application into consideration. The polynomial approach could easily be extended with an if-then condition that takes the type of application into consideration, like the Random Forrest. The difference in power consumption is minimal, and the other factors are much more relevant. Also, CPU utilization reduces the impact of applications by the percentage of run time. The new applications track very close to the discussed model with an expected error rate of 2–3%. The fact that the frequency of a processor is one of the biggest impacts on energy consumption is not a new concept, the concept of dynamic voltage and frequency scaling is well-researched and implemented into many microprocessors.

6   Conclusion

Energy efficiency is considered one crucial aspect in several IoT-enabled applications, including healthcare. However, capturing the energy consumption of applications from embedded system-based microcontrollers is prone to several challenges. This article proposed an automated energy modeling framework that collected current values of individual operations and modeled them using the RF algorithm. The framework was experimented with using real-world applications such as computer vision problems to manifest the importance of the framework. In the future, the framework will be validated on various other edge nodes considering the external triggers or interrupts.

References

1. Tiwari, V., Malik, S., Wolfe, A.: Power analysis of embedded software: a first step towards software power minimization. IEEE Trans. VLSI Syst. (1994). Department of Electrical Engineering, Princeton University Princeton
2. Laurent, J., Nathalie, J., Senn, E., Martin, E.: Functional level power analysis: an efficient approach for modeling the power consumption of complex processors. In: IEEE Xplore, Design, Automation and Test in Europe Conference and Exhibition, France (2004)
3. Schneider, M., Blume, H., Noll, T.G.: Power estimation on functional level for programmable processors. Adv. Radio Sci. (2004). Aachen, Germany
4. Espressif Systems: ESP32-WROOM-32 Datasheet, Version 3.3, www.espressif.com, Time of access: 29.08.2022 16:00 (2022). www.espressif.com/sites/default/files/documentation/esp32-wroom-32_datasheet_en.pdf
5. Akintadeorcid, O.O., Yesufu, T.K., Kehinde, L.O.: Development of power consumption models for ESP8266-enabled low-cost IoT monitoring nodes. Adv. Internet Things **9**(1) (2019). Department of Electronic and Electrical Engineering; Obafemi Awolowo University, Ile-Ife; Nigeria
6. Gomez, A., et al.: Reducing energy consumption in microcontroller-based platforms with low design margin co-processors. In: IEEE Design, Automation and Test in Europe Conference and Exhibition (2015)
7. Chen, G., Song, C., Yanglin, Z., Yang, Y.: A survey of energy consumption measurement in embedded systems. IEEE Access (2021)
8. Sadegh, A.M., Adel, T., Raj, G., Muhammad, C.: WattEdge: a holistic approach for empirical energy measurements in edge computing, service-oriented computing, November 2021
9. Tariq, U.U., Ali, H., Liu, L., Hardy, J., Kazim, M., Ahmed, W.: Energy-aware scheduling of streaming applications on edge-devices in IoT-based healthcare. IEEE Trans. Green Commun. Network. (2021)
10. Irfan, M., Masud, S., Pasha, M.A.: Development of a high level power estimation framework for multicore processors. In: IEEE Advanced Information Management, Communicates, Electronic and Automation Control Conference, May 2018
11. Jin, Z., Zhang, C., Jin, Y., Zhang, L., Su, J.: A resource allocation scheme for joint optimizing energy consumption and delay in collaborative edge computing-based industrial IoT. IEEE Trans. Industr. Inform. **18**, 6236–6243 (2022)
12. Premsankar, G., Ghaddar, B.: Energy-efficient service placement for latency-sensitive applications in edge computing. IEEE Internet Things J. **18**, 17926–17937 (2022)
13. Yin, Y., et al.: Development and application of subsoiling monitoring system based on edge computing using IoT architecture. Comput. Electron. Agric. **198**, 106976 (2022). https://doi.org/10.1016/j.compag.2022.106976
14. Benedict, S.: IoT-enabled remote monitoring techniques for healthcare applications - an overview. Informatica (Slovenia) **46**(2), 131–149 (2022). https://doi.org/10.31449/inf.v46i2.3912

15. Liu, J., Zibo, W., Liu, J., Xiaoguang, T.: Distributed location-aware task offloading in multi-UAVs enabled edge computing. IEEE Access **10**, 72416–72428 (2022). https://doi.org/10.1109/ACCESS.2022.3189682
16. Materwala, H., Ismail, L., Shubair, R.M., Buyya, R.: Energy-SLA-aware genetic algorithm for edge-cloud integrated computation offloading in vehicular networks, **135**, 205–222 (2022). https://doi.org/10.1016/j.future.2022.04.009
17. Gao, Y., Li, Z.: Energy and delay-aware task offloading and resource allocation in mobile edge computing. In: 2022 IEEE 25th International Conference on Computer Supported Cooperative Work in Design (CSCWD), pp. 1335–1340 (2022). https://doi.org/10.1109/CSCWD54268.2022.9776276

An Intelligent Safety Stock Computing Agent for Safety Inventory Maintenance in the Supply Chain Environment

Satyananda Swain[✉] and Manas Ranjan Patra

Department of Computer Science, Berhampur University, Berhampur, Odisha, India
sswaincse1985@gmail.com, mrpatra.cs@buodisha.edu.in

Abstract. In most businesses, products or services need to be delivered on time to the customer on demand. Failure to do so can result in customer dissatisfaction and consequently damage business. Therefore, many business units, especially manufacturing industries being guided by the safety stock policy maintain tactical buffer inventories to optimize service to the customers. Safety stock consists of an extra inventory held to deal with both demand and supply uncertainties to prevent stockout. In this paper, we adopt software agent technology for safety stock calculation and management. An intelligent safety stock computing Agent (ISSC-Agent) is deployed to optimize replenishment planning and maintain inventory as per the actual demands of the customers by avoiding backorders and improper demand forecasting.

Keywords: Safety stock · Safety stock management · Software agent · Supply chain management · Uncertainties

1 Introduction

The supply chain is an exclusive network that integrates different commercial processes. The supply chain life cycle includes procurement, manufacture, distribution, and retail operation with customer service. A strategic business strategy is the core of any supply chain management (SCM) system. Inventory supervision is a tricky aspect of SCM which relies on expert decisions to handle the problem of stockouts. It is a real challenge to determine the operational inventory levels. On one hand, maintaining higher inventory levels can be non-profitable, but on the other hand low inventory levels can lead to stock-out issues. The buffering technique, called Safety stock can be a possible solution to such problems. The calculation of safety stock using the mathematical formula and evaluating its performance is the main idea of this research study. The second objective is to automate the process of safety stock calculation with the help of a software agent. Safety stock consists of an extra inventory held to deal with both demand and supply uncertainties to prevent stockout situations. An intelligent safety stock computing Agent (ISSC-Agent) is deployed to optimize replenishment planning and maintain inventory as per the actual demands of the customers.

© The Author(s), under exclusive license to Springer Nature Switzerland AG 2023
I. Woungang et al. (Eds.): ANTIC 2022, CCIS 1797, pp. 438–451, 2023.
https://doi.org/10.1007/978-3-031-28180-8_30

1.1 Background

Safety Stock
Safety stock is an additional amount of a product that is warehoused in the storeroom. It serves as preventive coverage against fluctuations in demand. Safety stock eliminates the hassle of running out of stock. If a firm holds sufficient safety stock, then the firm doesn't rely on suppliers to deliver quickly or turn away customers because of depleted inventory levels. There are several mathematical stochastic methods or formulas for calculating safety stock. The standard formula for calculating safety stock consists to multiply the safety factor by the deviation of the demand during the replenishment time, that is, determining the safety stock as the function of service level.

Safety Stock Management
Caridi and Cigolini [1] defined safety stock management as " the managing issue deals with finding the appropriate time for safety stock replenishments and with setting the appropriate delivery dates for replenishment". Two fundamental aspects of safety stock management are when to order and how to order. The amount of safety inventory necessary to satisfy a given level of demand can be determined with the help of statistical techniques. It is important that supply chain managers at the time of calculating safety inventory, consider the joint impact of demand and the replenishment cycle variability. For the calculation of safety inventory, the supply chain manager must refer to the recent sales volume chart and the replenishment cycle chart, with the help of the data from these charts, it's easy for the managers to determine safety inventory using the formula:

$$\sigma_C = \sqrt{\overline{R}(\sigma_s^2) + \overline{S}(\sigma_R)^2} \tag{1}$$

Here,

σ_C = Safety Stock Requirements
σ_s = Standard Deviation of the daily sales.
σ_R = Standard Deviation of the replenishment cycle.
$\overline{R}$ = Average Replenishment Cycle.
$\overline{S}$ = Average Daily Sales.

Software-Agent
A software agent is an autonomous entity equipped with a knowledge base and driven by self-developed or induced objectives [2]. It is a computational paradigm characterized by responsiveness, autonomy, and goal-driven ability which can provide a good solution for distributed control and monitoring. It is situated in an environment and is capable of autonomous behavior to meet its design objectives.

1.2 Motivation

Recently, Researchers have begun to explore the area of safety stock management, as there are a lot of levers and dials available in the realm of safety stock. Appropriate management will help the organization to reduce idle inventory, smooth lead times, and reduce or eliminate the line-down situation. Safety stock calculation is a hectic task with different formulated approaches. Choosing a particular approach to safety stock calculation and using it appropriately for demand forecasting drags many researchers' attention. That motivates us to develop a software agent-oriented schema where an intelligent agent can evaluate and provide safety stock estimated results to avoid business loss.

1.3 Objective of the Work

This research study intended to address the following questions:

- How a software agent can be adopted for the calculation of safety stock in a supply chain environment?
- How an intelligent agent be used to safeguard the effective implementation of safety stock management strategies?
- How an intelligent computing agent be employed to guarantee operation automation in safety stock calculation and management in SCs?
- How agents can be effectively used for Demand and Supply Control in the SCM scheme?

2 Literature Review

Kumar, Kunal, Aouam, and Tarik. Discuss the process of integrating strategic safety stock placement and tactical lot sizing while considering the production cycle time of each stage in a network of production facilities. They demonstrate a dynamic programming paradigm to solve the integrated problem and show a simulation study that specifies there is a reduction in PCT variability due to this integration [3].

Trapero J. R, Cardós M, and Kourentzes N. display a combination of empirical methods that minimizes tick loss to show that combining quantile forecasts yield safety stocks with a lower cost. They consider real data experiments for different lead times to illustrate a simulation model that can enhance safety stock [4].

Lee C-J, Rim S-C. proposed a consistent safety stock calculation formula for demand-driven materials requirement planning(DDMRP) replenishment approach by considering average inventory and stockout rates to improve the performance while inventory management [5].

Bahroun, Z. and Belgacem, N. produced an experimental analysis for determining dynamic safety stock levels in cyclic production schedules to adapt cyclic production with a proper demonstration of the limitation of legacy approaches considered in traditional patterns. Their dynamic approach modeled a production sequence that is repetitive in nature with consideration of manufacturing orders for a particular case with a uniform probability distribution for all demands [6].

Sellitto M. A. proposed a quantitative modeling approach for calculating the lead time, inventory and safety stock in job shop manufacturing. In his studies, they describe the importance of stochastic variables like safety stock for optimizing inventory management activity in a complete industrial application scenario [7].

Brunaud B, Laínez-Aguirre JM, Pinto JM, and Grossmann IE proposed a concept to optimize inventory policies based on supply chain planning models. Their work revolves around demand uncertainty problems, and they formulated four prospects about safety stock as a proportion to throughput, risk pooling effect, explicit risk pooling, and service time guarantee [8].

Schuster Puga M, Minner S, and Tancrez J-S. improved supply chain design by integrating facility location strategy with safety stock placement and delivery decisions in an interdependent environment. They developed a non-linear model as a conic quadratic mixed integer program that can be extended to include demand correlation and stochastic lead times [9].

Woerner Stefan, Laumanns Marco, and Wagner Stephan M. studied assembly systems and explain the fundamental idea of joint optimization of capacity and safety stock allocation. Their main strategy is to minimize inventory holding costs with satisfying service and budget constraints [10].

Lu Hui, Wang Hongwei, Xie Yong, and Li Heng. Developed an inventory balance equation based on the linear order release rule and modified base stock definition in construction material management. A numerical analysis is conducted to investigate the performance of the safety stock approach and days of supply rules [11].

Prak Dennis, Teunter Ruud, and Syntetos Aris presented an approach that represents corrected lead time demand variance expressions and reorders levels for inventory systems with a constant lead time where fluctuation of demand plays a vital role [12].

3   Methodology

3.1   Proposed Framework

The safety stock calculation framework consists of many distinct phases. The basic idea proposed, is to develop a specific business-oriented safety inventory management milieu using agent technology [13]. The distributed operation includes an intelligent agent named ISSC-Agent that controls and monitors the safety stock calculation operation.

The proposed work advocates a technical approach for handling and monitoring multiple operations of safety stock maintenance without much human intervention. This approach consists of the ISSC-Agent, with the basic function of calculating the safety stock from the predefined formula. The ISSC-Agent tracks all aspects of the safety inventory management operation in the supply chain. An Agent-oriented approach for safety stock computation has been developed comprising different operational steps as depicted in Fig. 1.

The action of the agent is triggered by state transitions. The typical operational states along with their descriptions are presented in Table 1.

3.2   Operational Procedure of the Framework

Step-1: Start. At first, the safety stock calculation operation is initiated by the ISSC-Agent. The entire operation is controlled and monitored by ISSC-Agent. The ISSC-Agent

Fig. 1. Proposed agent-oriented safety stock computation workflow diagram

initiates the operation by implementing the *Safety_Stock_Manage_Op ()* function with the operation status initiated to the "*CREATED*" state.

Step-2: In this step, the ISSC-Agent checks the status to be matched to the "*CREATED*" status. The ISSC-Agent calls the function *SL_INPUT_REQ ()* to store the daily sales details with their respective frequencies. The function *S_INPUT_REQ( )* is called by the ISSC-Agent to perform the input operation followed by a status updated to "*SL_INPUTTED*" mode.

Step-3: Then, the ISSC-Agent performs the calculation of the Daily sales average by calling the function *DAILY_SALE_AVG_CALCULATION()*. This step also includes the calculation of the frequency total by the function *SL_FREQ_TOTAL ()*. Thereafter, the status update is done by the ISSC-Agent to "*SALES_AVG_CALCULATED*".

Table 1. The different states and their description for ISSC-Agent

State name	Description
CREATED	Indicates that the ISSC-Agent initiates the calculation of safety stock for inventory maintenance
SL_INPUTTED	Indicates that the ISSC-Agent loads the sales information and their frequencies as preliminary inputs
SALES_AVG_CALCULATED	Indicates that the ISSC-Agent calculated the sales average and frequency total for the given input values
SL_DEVIATED	Indicates that the ISSC-Agent finds out the sales deviation and squared the deviation from the preliminary input values
SD_DAILY_SALES	Indicates that ISSC-Agent calculates the standard deviation from sales deviations
REPLENISHED	Indicates that ISSC-Agent loads the sales lead information and their frequencies as inputs
LEAD_DATA_AVAILABLE	Indicates that the ISSC-Agent calculated the sales lead average and frequency total for the given input values
SD_REPL_CYCLE	Indicates that the ISSC-Agent calculates the Replenishment cycle standard deviation from sales lead deviations
SAFETY_STOCK_CALC	Indicates that the ISSC-Agent calculated the safety stock using the given formula
FINISHED	Indicates that the ISSC-Agent finished the operation after calculating the safety stock

Step-4: In this step, after the ISSC-Agent checks the status information as "*SALES_AVG_CALCULATED*", the agent performs the calculation of sales deviations followed by Sales deviations squared by calling the function *SALES_DEVIATION_CALCULATION ()* and *SALES_DEVIATION_SQUARED ()* respectively with updating the operation status to "*SL_DEVIATED*" state.

Step-5: One of the major work in the calculation of safety stock for inventory management is, to find out the Standard deviation of daily sales, and the formula to calculate the standard deviation is as follows:

$$\sigma_s = \sqrt{\frac{\sum fd^2}{n-1}} \tag{2}$$

Here,

σ_s = Standard Deviation of the daily sales.
f = Frequency of the event.
d = Deviation of event from the mean.
n = Total No. of observation.

The standard deviation of the daily sales can be low or high about the mean value. A low standard deviation defines high reliability due to the reason of close relation to the average and a higher value of standard deviation describes low reliability with high variation in sales related to the calculated average. The ISSC-Agent calls the function *SD_DAILY_SALES()* and uses the given formula to calculate the standard deviation followed by status updating to "*SD_DAILY_SALES*".

Step-6: In this section, the agent performs input of sales leads time with frequencies for replenishment cycles. Lead time refers to the time it takes to order and restock inventory. The function called by the ISSC-Agent is *S_LEAD_TIME_INPUT_REQ ()* for providing input values of sales lead time and their respective frequencies.

Step-7: The ISSC-Agent then performs a calculation of the lead average for replenishment cycles with frequency total by using the functions *LEAD_AVG_CALCULATION()* and *LEAD_FREQ_TOTAL ()*. In this step, the status is updated to "*REPLENISHED*" mode by the ISSC-Agent.

Step-8: The ISSC-Agent performs a Calculation of Sales lead deviations and Sales lead deviations squared using functions *LEAD_DEVIATION_CALCULATION()* and *DEVIATION_SQUARED()* respectively. The operation status is then updated to "*LEAD_DATA_AVAILABLE*"

Step-9: The ISSC-Agent then finds out the Standard deviation of the replenishment cycle using the following formula:

$$\sigma_R = \sqrt{\frac{\sum fd^2}{n-1}} \tag{3}$$

Here,

σ_R = Standard Deviation of the replenishment cycle.
f = Frequency of the event.
d = Deviation of event from the mean.
n = Total No. of observation.

This standard deviation measures the average amount of variability in the data set. It defines the average time required to restock after considering the variability of the actual time to receive orders. Finally, the operation status is updated to "*SD_REPL_CYCLE*" by the ISSC-Agent.

Step-10: In the function *SEFTY_STOCK_CALCULATOR()*, the final calculation of safety stock is done using the formula

$$\sigma_C = \sqrt{\overline{R}(\sigma_s^2) + \overline{S}(\sigma_R)^2} \tag{4}$$

Here,

σ_C = *Safety STock Requirements*
σ_s = Standard Deviation of the daily sales.
σ_R = Standard Deviation of the replenishment cycle.
$\overline{R}$ = Average Replenishment Cycle.
$\overline{S}$ = *Average Daily Sales*

The given formula determines average customer demand to maintain inventory at a safe state based on the reorder time frame from the sales volume average. The operation status is next updated to *"SAFETY_STOCK_CALC"*.

Step-11: At last, the ISSC-Agent prints the computed result, and using which, we can perform demand forecasting. The final verdict of operational status is "FINISHED" to specify operation completion.

Step 12: Stop.

3.3 Proposed Algorithm

The algorithms for key operations of the safety stock computation process are presented below:

Pre-conditions

1) Daily Sales Details and Lead Time Details must be available before the firm.
2) Status: "CREATED" by ISSC-Agent.

Safety_Stock_Manage_Op ()
This algorithm computes and manages the entire safety stock computation operation by ISSC-Agent.

1: Start.

2: if Status== "CREATED":

3:         Print "Input Operation Request Initiation"

4:         SL= SL_INPUT_REQ ()

5:         UPDATE_STATUS("SL_INPUTTED")

6: Else if Status== "SL_INPUTTED":

7:         Print " Sales Average and Total Frequency Calculation Initiation".

8:         $\bar{S}$ = DAILY_SALE_AVG_CALCULATION (SL)

9:         SL_N = SL_FREQ_TOTAL (SL)

10:        UPDATE_STATUS ("SALES_AVG_CALCULATED")

11: Else if Status == "SALES_AVG_CALCULATED":

12:        Print "Deviation Calculation and Squared operation Initiation"

13:        SL_DEV = SALES_DEVIATION_CALCULATION (SL, $\bar{S}$)

14:        SL_DEV_SQ = SALES_DEVIATION_SQUARED (SL_DEV)

15:        UPDATE_STATUS ("SL_DEVIATED")

16: Else if Status== "SL_DEVIATED":

17:        Print "Standard Deviation of Daily Sales Calculation"

18:        σ_s = SD_DAILY_SALES (SL, SL_N, SL_DEV_SQ)

19:        UPDATE_STATUS ("SD_VALUED")

20: Else if Status== " SD_VALUED":

21:         Print "SD Value Calculation Initiation for Replenishment Cycles"

22:        LD= S_LEAD_TIME_INPUT_REQ ()

22:        $\bar{R}$= LEAD_AVG_CALCULATION (LD)

23:        LD_N= LEAD_FREQ_TOTAL(LD)

24:        UPDATE_STATUS ("REPLENISHED")

25: Else if Status== "REPLENISHED ":

26:         Print "Deviation Calculation Operation Initiation for Replenishment"

27:                LD_DEV = LEAD_DEVIATION_CALCULATION (LD, $\bar{R}$)

28:        LD_DEV_SQ = LEAD_DEVIATION_SQUARED(LD_DEV)

29:        UPDATE_STATUS ("LEAD_DATA_AVAILABLE ")

30: Else if Status== " LEAD_DATA_AVAILABLE":

31:        Print "Standard Deviation of Replenishment Cycle"

32:        σ_R= SD_REPL_CYCLE (LD, LD_N, LD_DEV_SQ)

33:        UPDATE_STATUS("SD_REPL_VALUED")

34: Else:

35:   Print "Safety Stock Calculation"

36: σ_C= SEFTY_STOCK_CALCULATOR (σ_s, $\bar{S}$, σ_R, $\bar{R}$)

37:   Print "Safety Stock Computed Value=", σ_C

38:   UPDATE_STATUS ("SAFETY_STOCK_CALC")   [End of if of step-2]

39: if Status== "SAFETY_STOCK_CALC "

40:   print "Safety Stock Computation Finished"

41:   UPDATE_STATUS ("FINISHED").

42: Stop.

3.4   Experimental Setup and Simulation Data Scenario

As an experimental setup, the AgentPy simulation platform uses Python language for the development of the agent and its associated goal-oriented functions. In this paper, we ponder a watch trader with daily sales data and replenishment cycle data as depicted in Table 2 and Table 3 respectively. The specified scenario is provided as input to the *Safety_Stock_Manage()* operation by the ISSC-Agent to compute safety stock value for the watch trader. The agent proceeds as per the agreed algorithm and after completion of its execution, it produces the safety stock result. In the next section, we produce the implementation outcome and analyze the simulation result in detail.

Table 2. Daily sales data and their frequencies for safety stock computation

Sl. no	Daily sales	Frequency
1	60	1
2	70	2
3	80	3
4	90	4
5	100	5
6	110	4
7	120	3
8	130	2
9	140	1
	$\bar{S} = 100$	N = 25

Table 3. Lead time data and their frequencies for safety stock computation

Sl. no	Lead time in days	Frequency
1	7	1
2	8	2
3	9	3
4	10	4
5	11	3
6	12	2
7	13	1
$\overline{R} = 100$		N = 16

4   Result and Discussion

4.1   Simulation Results for Safety Stock Computation by ISSC-Agent

The following result establishes the output of the whole safety stock computation by ISSC-Agent for the given watch trader scenario.

OUTPUT:
Current Status of Safety Stock Computation Operation ['**CREATED**']
1. INPUT OPERATION REQUEST INITIATION:
INPUT OF DAILY SALES AND THEIR FREQUENCIES
[[60 70 80 90 100 110 120 130 140]
 [1 2 3 4 5 4 3 2 1]]
Current Status of Safety Stock Computation Operation ['**SL_INPUTTED**']
Completed: 1 step
This step provides a demonstration of initiating an input operation that offers the daily sales details with their frequencies respectively.
2. CALCULATE THE DAILY SALES AVERAGE
CALCULATION OF DAILY SALES AVERAGE
100.0
TOTAL FREQUENCY(SL_N)
25
Current Status of Safety Stock Computation Operation
['**SALES_AVG_CALCULATED**']
Completed: 2 steps
In this step, the sales average value gets calculated by adding all sales values divided by the number of observed sale values.
3. DEVIATION CALCULATION
DEVIATION CALCULATED
[-40.0, -30.0, -20.0, -10.0, 0.0, 10.0, 20.0, 30.0, 40.0]
DEVIATION SQUARED
[1600.0, 900.0, 400.0, 100.0, 0.0, 100.0, 400.0, 900.0, 1600.0]

Current Status of Safety Stock Computation Operation ['SL_DEVIATED']
Completed: 3 steps
This step specifies the calculation of sales deviation followed by the computation of deviation squared values.
4. STANDARD DEVIATION OF DAILY SALES
[1600.0, 1800.0, 1200.0, 400.0, 0.0, 400.0, 1200.0, 1800.0, 1600.0]
10000.0
20
Current Status of Safety Stock Computation Operation ['SD_VALUED']
Completed: 4 steps
In this step, the standard deviation of daily sales gets calculated by the software agent.
5. SD VALUE CALCULATION FOR REPLENISHMENT CYCLES
LEAD TIME
[[7 8 9 10 11 12 13]
 [1 2 3 4 3 2 1]]
LEAD AVG
10.0
TOTAL FREQUENCY(LD_N)
16
Current Status of Safety Stock Computation Operation ['REPLENISHED']
Completed: 5 steps
This step offers to provide lead time and the frequencies needed to calculate the standard deviation value for the replenishment cycles
6. DEVIATION CALCULATION FOR REPLENISHMENT
DEVIATION CALCULATED1
[-3.0, -2.0, -1.0, 0.0, 1.0, 2.0, 3.0]
DEVIATION SQUARED1
[9.0, 4.0, 1.0, 0.0, 1.0, 4.0, 9.0]
Current Status of Safety Stock Computation Operation
['LEAD_DATA_AVAILABLE']
Completed: 6 steps
This step calculates the standard deviation and squares the calculated standard deviation for the inputted lead data values.
7. STANDARD DEVIATION OF REPLENISHMENT CYCLE
SD_REPL_CYCLE
[9.0, 8.0, 3.0, 0.0, 3.0, 8.0, 9.0]
40.0
1.632993161855452
Current Status of Safety Stock Computation Operation ['SD_REPL_VALUED']
Completed: 7 steps
This step executes the operation of standard deviation calculation for the replenishment cycle.
8. SAFETY STOCK CALCULATION
SAFETY STOCK CALCULATOR
SAFETY STOCK COMPUTED VALUE=175.1190071541826
SAFETY STOCK COMPUTATION FINISHED
Current Status of Safety Stock Computation Operation ['FINISHED']
Completed: 8 steps
Run time: 0:00:00.007980
Simulation finished. In this last step, the final calculated values of safety stock get displayed as a result and the operational status is updated to finished signifying operation closure.

Degree of Safety Attained

From the above result, we can settle that in a situation in which the daily sales diverge from 60 to 140 watches and the replenishment cycle fluctuates from 7 to 13 days, the watch trader would necessitate a safety stock of 175 watches to offer *84%* of all conceivable occurrences.

4.2 Limitations of the Proposed Framework

1. The ISSC-Agent plays a central role in the operation of the proposed framework, its failure can adversely affect the working of the management procedure.
2. Choice of safety stock computation formula is a scary task. Different formulae as per different scenarios are available. So, wisely select the formula.
3. Integration of the given agent-oriented framework with the legacy inventory management system is a real challenge.

5 Future Work

In future, we will investigate in detail the role-played by the cycle service level or the fill rate in a supply chain, how it can lead to product availability and the overall profitability of the business firm. In addition to that, we try to find the solution to a few large orders or frequent small orders for a given usage because a few big orders involve low acquisition and high holding costs whereas many small orders result in low holding and high acquisition costs. Calculation of economic order quantity (EOQ) using an intelligent software agent is the final goal to be achieved in near future.

6 Conclusion

The safety stock problem in the context of SCM has been an active research topic. In this paper, we demonstrate an agent-based safety stock computation strategy using a software agent. The proposed model provides a buffering policy through an intelligent computing agent for solving the inventory management problems linked to safety stock management. We make use of an intelligent agent for the effective implementation of safety stock management plans and to ensure the execution of future stock-related transactions as per demand forecasting.

References

1. Caridi, M., Cigolini, R.: Improving materials management effectiveness: a step towards the agile enterprise. Int. J. Phys. Distrib. Logist. Manag. 32(7), 556–576 (2002)
2. Buterin, V.: A next-generation smart contract and decentralized application platform. White paper (2014). https://github.com/ethereum/wiki/wiki/White-Paper
3. Kumar, K., Aouam, T.: Integrated lot sizing and safety stock placement in a network of production facilities. Int. J. Prod. Econ. 195, 74–95 (2018)
4. Trapero, J.R., Cardós, M., Kourentzes, N.: Empirical safety stock estimation based on kernel and GARCH models. Omega 84, 199–211 (2019)

5. Lee, C.-J., Rim, S.-C.: A mathematical safety stock model for DDMRP inventory replenishment. Math. Probl. Eng. **2019**, 10 (2019). https://doi.org/10.1155/2019/6496309. Article ID 6496309
6. Bahroun, Z., Belgacem, N.: Determination of dynamic safety stocks for cyclic production schedules. Oper. Manag. Res. **12**(1–2), 62–93 (2019). https://doi.org/10.1007/s12063-019-00140-0
7. Sellitto, M.A.: Lead-time, inventory, and safety stock calculation in job-shop manufacturing. Acta Polytech. **58**(6), 395–401 (2018)
8. Brunaud, B., Laínez-Aguirre, J.M., Pinto, J.M., Grossmann, I.E.: Inventory policies and safety stock optimization for supply chain planning. AIChE J. **65**(1), 99–112 (2019)
9. Puga, M.S., Minner, S., Tancrez, J.-S.: Two-stage supply chain design with safety stock placement decisions. Int. J. Prod. Econ. **209**, 183–193 (2019)
10. Woerner, S., Laumanns, M., Wagner, S.M.: Joint optimisation of capacity and safety stock allocation. Int. J. Prod. Res. **56**(13), 4612–4628 (2018)
11. Lu, H., Wang, H., Xie, Y., Li, H.: Construction material safety-stock determination under nonstationary stochastic demand and random supply yield. IEEE Trans. Eng. Manag. **63**(2), 201–212 (2016)
12. Prak, D., Teunter, R., Syntetos, A.: On the calculation of safety stocks when demand is forecasted. Eur. J. Oper. Res. **256**(2), 454–461 (2017)
13. Swain, S., Patra, M.R.: A distributed agent-oriented framework for blockchain-enabled supply chain management. In: 2022 IEEE International Conference on Blockchain and Distributed Systems Security (ICBDS), pp. 1–7 (2022). https://doi.org/10.1109/ICBDS53701.2022.9936015

Designing a Secure E Voting System Using Blockchain with Efficient Smart Contract and Consensus Mechanism

Durgesh Kumar$^{(\boxtimes)}$ and Rajendra Kumar Dwivedi

Department of Information Technology and Computer Application, Madan Mohan Malaviya University of Technology Gorakhpur, Gorakhpur, India
ydurgesh120@gmail.com

Abstract. These days, most people are not satisfied with the final result of the voting system. This is because the current system for voting is centralized and fully controlled by the election commission. So, there is a chance that the central body can be compromised or hacked and the final result can be tampered. In this direction, a decentralized, Blockchain and Internet of Things (IoT) based methodology for voting system is devised and presented in this paper. The efficient smart contracts and consensus mechanism are applied in the proposed system to enhance the security. Blockchain is totally transparent, secured and immutable technique because it uses concept like encryption, decryption, hash function, consensus and Merkle tree etc. which make Blockchain Technology an appropriate platform for storing and sharing the data in a secured and anonymous manner. IoT makes use of biometric sensors using which people can cast their votes in not only physical mode but also in digital mode. As a response, a message is received to the owner for casting his vote to ensure the authentication. In this way, we can make the present voting system more secure and trust-worthy using the properties of both Blockchain and IoT, and therefore, we can give more value to the election process in the democratic countries. The proposed method ensures security as well as reduces the computational time as compared to the existing approaches.

Keywords: Inter Planetary File System (IPFS) · Cloud storage · Security · Blockchain · Consensus · Smart contract · Merkle tree · Hash · Nonce · IoT

1 Introduction

These days, Blockchain has been used in several applications viz., healthcare information system, smart agriculture system, and smart city to enhance the security [1–6]. It is also widely used in the areas of vehicular area networks, social networks, and e voting systems to provide the secure and efficient models [7–11]. Currently, we are using two ways for voting system in the Indian constituency system. The paper ballot system is the first, and the electronic voting machine is the second (EVM). The ballot paper system is not a secure voting system because anyone can change their ballot papers. In this case, we are not able to perform a fair election. Apart from the ballot paper the second method

© The Author(s), under exclusive license to Springer Nature Switzerland AG 2023
I. Woungang et al. (Eds.): ANTIC 2022, CCIS 1797, pp. 452–469, 2023.
https://doi.org/10.1007/978-3-031-28180-8_31

is using EVM (electronic voting machine) which is a digital form of voting this method is also not secure because people may think that EVM can be hacked and vote can be tampered. So, we will put in place a digital voting system that is entirely based on blockchain technology.

1.1 Blockchain for Security

It is a decentralized distributed ledger system in which transactions are stored in blocks and the blocks are connected together with the help of hashes. In a blockchain network, all blocks have the same authority to check and verify the transaction details across the whole network. Blockchain use in public key cryptography to encrypt and decrypt the transaction over the peer-to-peer network. The blocks in the blockchain have several fields: Merkle root, the previous block hash, time stamp, and the actual transaction. The structure of blocks is divided into two parts: headers and bodies. The headers consist of the hash of the previous block, time stamp, nonce, and Merkle tree. The body consists of all transactional data. The block header 80-byte field contains that metadata – the data about the blocks.

- **Time Stamp.** It's the digitally recorded moment of time when the block has been mined. It is used to validate the transactions.
- **Previous Block Hash.** It is a 32-byte field that carries a 256-bit hash of the preceding block that was generated using the SHA-256 cryptographic hashing algorithm. This aids in building a block chain that is linear.
- **Nonce.** Its root number is contained in the 4-byte-long field. These are the only elements in a block of transactions that can be changed. Miners in PoW change their announcements until they locate the correct block hash.
- **Merkle Root.** A 32-bytes field containing a 256-bit root hash. It is built hierarchically by merging the hashes of each transaction into a block.
- **Transactional Data.** The list of all transactions in the block is contained in a variable-size field. Just so you know, there are roughly 2000 transactions in each bitcoin block. Each block is roughly 1 MB in size. Blockchains have different limits on block size and the quantity of transactions. A decision is made based on communication overhead and network congestion.

1.2 Motivation

Use of blockchain technology can make the process of elections very easy and convenient [12–16]. In the present situation, voters leave their homes and go to the election center to cast their votes, which is not very voter-friendly [16–20]. Therefore, we are to implement our work so that users do not need to go to election center for casting their vote and they can cast their vote from home by just using a simple web application or mobile application.

1.3 Contribution

This paper contributes to improve the election process in the democratic countries by proposing a blockchain based methodology for the security enhancement in the voting system. This technique ensures the trust among various political parties and the people as well as prevents the debate over vote tampering. Apart from this, it will also make the election process much easier for the voters and will maintain the security, privacy, transparency, and anonymity of the users.

1.4 Organization

Rest of the paper is organized as follows. Section 2 presents background. Section 3 presents the literature review of the related work. The electronic voting system is illustrated in Sect. 4. Section 5 describes the current electronic voting system technology. The experimental results are reported in Sect. 6.

2 Background

The blockchain-based system has the potential to give residents a safe environment, foster trust, and help them get through any uncertain circumstances. Blockchain technology could be crucial for protecting voter registration. As a blockchain by its very nature produces an audit trail of modifications, including information on whose account made the change and when, citizens and authorized government employees might update voter rolls more securely. Independent watchdogs might keep an eye out for purges or other questionable activity by tracking the alterations being made to voter data on a blockchain in real-time. Additionally, it offers accurate vote tallies and complete transparency during an election.

In the early stages of its growth, voters had always struggled with trust concerns in relation to their ballots. After they voted in person or by mail, they either believed their ballot was being changed, rejected, or replaced. The danger of votes being altered after they are cast and before they are tallied can be decreased by using electronic voting methods supported by the security features of blockchain. In such a system, voters cast their ballots using electronic voting equipment in the polling places, which then stores the data onto a blockchain and gives a voter a printed receipt of their vote for auditing purposes. Then, voters may confirm that their vote was accurately recorded on the ballot. In this manner, the blockchain technology will assist in providing accurate election results and vote counting that is free from human mistake. For those who were worried about the security of their data, this decentralized system is irreversible; no one can transfer votes or encourage vote-buying because of the way the programme works. Additionally, blockchain internet voting by its very nature creates an audit trail of changes, which includes details on which account made the change and when. Independent watchdogs might keep an eye out for purges or other questionable activity by tracking the alterations being made to voter data on a blockchain in real-time.

A touch screen attached to a computer makes up a conventional DRE. On the touch screen, ballots are shown for the voters to choose from and cast their votes. The touch-screen display may be utilized to help voters in a number of ways, such as showing large fonts and strong contrast for individuals with poor vision, warning them when someone undervotes, and discouraging overvotes. A secure procedure known as a DRE immediately records the votes cast and preserves the information in memory. Votes are therefore composed, cast, and recorded using the same equipment. The voter is unaware of the third stage, which involves recording the cast ballot on a memory device. Testing the hardware and software of the machine before the election and having faith that the software being used during the election is the same as the software tested prior to the election are requirements for assurance that the vote is recorded as cast. Both of these are hotly debated topics. Voters form their ballots on a computer screen in other optical scanning methods. The computer prints an optical scanning ballot after a ballot is finished. The ballot is checked by the voter, who then places it into a different machine to be scanned and counted. These two procedures are regarded as electronic voting procedures.

For many years, research has focused on the use of computer tools and equipment for voting as well as the generation of accurate results that capture the views of the participating voters. Various tactics have been used to support the election process. Computerized voting systems initially allowed for paper ballot voting. At each polling location, the cards were afterwards scanned and totaled on a central server. Direct Recording Electronic (DRE) voting systems were eventually put into use, received great praise, and were adopted by the electorate despite objections from computer experts.

This method is particularly useful for those who do not have access to polling places or live in remote areas, as well as when overseas and military voters require blank absentee ballots in order to cast their ballots by the deadline on Election Day but cannot obtain them in time. It was formerly commonly accepted that the greatest solution to these issues would be to use the internet or other online voting platforms. Today, however, there are a lot fewer restrictions on overseas and military voters. By law, absentee votes must now be made accessible 45 days before election day. However, in certain states, cast ballots can still be counted if they are received after election day. Additionally, ballots must be made electronically accessible so that the majority of voters may obtain them. Blockchain technology is widely used around the world in a variety of economic areas, including cryptocurrencies, media, entertainment, and yes, even the voting process! Blockchain is a sort of shared database that varies from traditional databases in how it saves data. It functions as a digital ledger.

Blockchains store data in units called "blocks," which are subsequently connected by means of encryption. New blocks are created as new pieces of data are received. Data is chained together in chronological order once each block has been filled with information. This is accomplished by chaining each block onto the one before it. We can readily assess how effective blockchain would make the voting system after it is implemented by linking it to it. First off, the blockchain voting system fully reduces the possibility of hacking, altering, or tampering with the sensitive data by tracking the rising or falling vote total every second. Even abroad voters may be benefitted from this since they may quickly access the election procedure on their mobile devices via blockchain networks. Voters can easily cast a vote remotely using online voting with only one click on a mobile device.

3 Related Work

Bajpai et al. [21] proposed In this paper, the author focuses on providing the best digital voting system for voters and organizers in democratic countries. It has long been challenging to develop a safe electronic voting system that maintains current voting techniques, fairness and anonymity while offering the flexibility and transparency that come with electronic systems.

As a result, by incorporating the qualities of an ideal voting system into the digital realm, the effectiveness of the voting system is strengthened. As a result, election expenses and inspector labor have come down significantly. As described in this paper, we propose the architecture of a new electronic voting system using open-source blockchain technology. Blockchain is offering new potential to develop new categories of digital services. Blockchain technology has changed many aspects of our lives, including the ability to secure digital transactions made over the Internet, to validate their validity, to license them, and to offer the highest level of security and encryption. To store data, this system provides a distributed architecture that spreads the data between multiple servers. This technology not only protects voter identity outside of the voting process but also makes the voting process visible.

Mani et al. [22] explained in this paper, blockchain is a distributed system that validates security and dependability. A new era of a reliable and consensus-based system has begun as a result. Since blockchain places a strong emphasis on security, many other activities and processes are following its lead. The offered digital Ethereum network currently encourages almost all activities and operations to be carried out electronically. We have seen how the current COVID-19 pandemic situation has changed as a result of the election process. The suggested solution implements the college voting mechanism utilizing the Aadhaar API and the Ethereum network on a blockchain platform. E-voting will contribute to increased transparency and voter trust, which will help to eliminate fraud and corruption in the voting process. As a result of the usage of blockchain technology, this method will enable voters to cast their ballots from home with total security and dependability.

Keerthi et al. [23] The Writer's Discussion in this article contains numerous suggestions for an entirely online-based voting system. The majority of nations continue to use paper ballots for voting. Over the past ten years, electronic voting systems have grown widely, yet there are still a lot of problems. The main issues with electronic voting are safety, legality, reliability, openness, transparency, and usability. The choices are constrained for blockchain, though. With the use of blockchain technology, which also provides advantages like immutability and decentralization, it is possible to overcome all the problems outlined. The lack of testing and comparison, as well as the emphasis on a single theme, are the key problems with blockchain technology as it relates to electronic voting.

This study presents a general-purpose electronic voting system based on blockchain. The blockchain allows for the completion of all processes. Once voting has started, decentralization makes sure that the platform is totally independent and cannot affect the results of the vote. Voters' identities are protected thanks to homomorphic encryption. On three different blockchains, our solution was examined and compared. The results demonstrate that both public and private blockchains are accessible at very modest speeds. Due to the homomorphic encryption employed to safeguard voter data, we have created a novel method that completely decentralizes the management of the e-voting platform.

Patil et al. [24] The authors of this paper largely concentrate on the electronic voting mechanism. Digital technology has recently benefited the lives of many people. This is unlike the voting process, which mostly relies on conventional paper for implementation. The issues of security and transparency are threatened by the growing use of the conventional (offline) electoral process. General elections are still conducted using a centralized system, which is supervised by a single organization. Traditional electoral systems have problems with the ability of the entity to completely control the database and the system's tampering with the database of the crucial opportunity, among other things. Blockchain is one of the technological answers since it is based on a decentralized system in which various people own the complete database. The blockchain is employed by the bitcoin system, commonly referred to as the decentralized banking system. One of the primary methods for manipulating databases Blockchain technology can be used to spread datasets on the electronic voting system, thereby reducing this risk. This study looks at how vote results from each election site are recorded using blockchain algorithms. This thesis proposed a technology that relied on each node in the underlying blockchain taking a specific turn on the system, as opposed to Bitcoin's proof-of-work.

Rathee et al. [25] In this article, the author discusses blockchain and IoT-based voting systems. A smart city is an intelligent environment created by the coordinated and intelligent deployment of all available resources and cutting-edge technologies. When 5G technology and intelligent sensors (Internet-of-things (IoT) devices) operate together, users' needs are met more efficiently and with greater ease. E-voting, among other IoT use cases, is a significant application that advances IoT to the next stage in the development of smart city technology. In traditional applications, it's common to presumptively trust and cooperate with every single device. However, in reality, intrusions may cause disruptions in devices, causing them to act maliciously and degrade network functions. Because of this, there is a serious issue with the privacy and security problems in e-voting systems in particular, where hackers could commit a multitude of frauds to rig the election.

4   Proposed Model

The suggested design will be based on a smart contract made with Ethereum software to construct an electronic voting application where the user will establish an account and appropriate account verification is completed via voter identification and other biometric techniques. Each action taken with this account is a vote that has to be verified by a miner. The miner will assign the vote to a vote pool for that constituency based on the voter's identity and take into account the voter's permanent address. The opportunity to register to vote will be available for a brief period of time. Each registered vote will be processed using biometric techniques, and the miner will confirm the validity of each vote. The miner will cancel the request when the constituency's election date has passed and any additional votes have been registered. The request will also be cancelled by the miner if the user's biometric authentication fails. Voting in more than one constituency will not be permitted by the same account holder.

As a result, in order to save time and minimize security risks, IoT devices needed to be protected by projecting an effective and trustworthy framework. By implementing a biometric login system that will verify that only one individual is linked with each vote, it will be possible to combat the common scenario where document forgeries allow a single person to cast several ballots. The electronic voting system and this biometric system can both be implemented in the same application. We would need separate ledgers for voter preferences and biometric data, and each miner would have to verify the data before confirming a voting transaction. In this instance, the accounts would be created using your physical data rather than documents or emails. The ledgers would also need to be updated daily with information on the number of deaths and people reaching 18 (the legal voting age in India), and they would need to be in sync with the census. The actual data entered can be checked using police records, public records, and, in situations of suspicion, in person at a procedure that the government has allowed. For a huge portion of the Indian populace who are not particularly familiar with the technical complexities of technology, such as the password reset and document update possibilities, it is also a simpler way.

4.1 Blockchain Based Voter Authentication

These factors may cause people to forgo the entire voting process, which would be detrimental rather than beneficial. A one-touch option that takes them to the parties of their choice and another single-touch option that allows them to cast their ballots while remaining in the comfort of their homes sounds like a much more practical solution. The procedure flowchart for blockchain electronic voting is shown in Fig. 1.

Before ensuring a secure E-voting process utilizing blockchain technology, it is crucial to verify each person's credentials, including name, age, date of birth, and address, using an identification card, such as a passport, voter identity card, ration card, etc. No two people could engage in the voting process twice or cast two votes since each individual has a unique Passport. This approach may also be used to catch bogus users who have stolen someone else's Passport or those who are voting in someone else's name after they have passed away. Voting is permitted if the voter's status is null. You will receive a notification stating that "you have already cast your vote." The proposed framework's pseudo code is also presented by Algorithm 1.

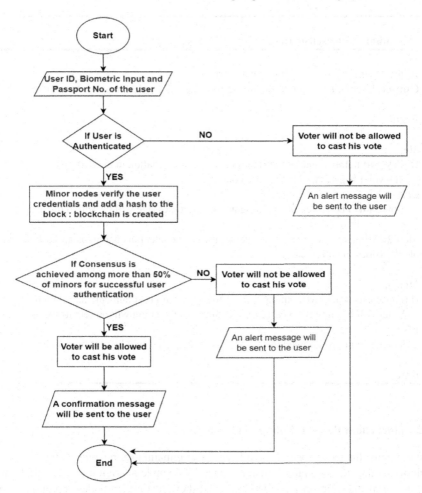

Fig. 1. Proposed methodology for blockchain based voter authentication

---

Algorithm 1: Blockchain Based Voter Authentication

Input: User ID, Biometric Input, Passport No
Output: User authentication for casting the vote and an alert message to the user

Begin:

Step 1:
If (Passport number and biometric input = voter information in the database) then
   The voter is permitted to cast the vote
Else
   Voter's will be barred from voting and an alert message will be sent to the user

Step 2: Miners m_1, m_2, m_3,.... m_n verify the user credentials and adds an hash to the block : Blockchain is created

Step 3:
If (consensus is achieved among minors for successful user authentication) then
   Voter will be allowed to cast his vote and a confirmation will be sent to the user
Else
   Voter will not be allowed to cast his vote and an alert will be sent to the user

End

4.2 Blockchain Based E Voting to Cast a Vote

Additionally, thanks to a Blockchain feature, the remaining admin authorities would be able to quickly identify any intrusions made by a single alteration or other malicious action during the voting process. The flowchart shown in Fig. 2 provides a comprehensive overview of the whole blockchain-enabled electronic voting process, with step-by-step instructions for each stage as follows:

- A smart phone E-voting application would be highly beneficial for minimizing the time and effort while waiting in line, which would increase the country's voting rate.
- Every individual who is qualified to vote may successfully log in after installing the E-voting programme by entering their passport number or password. Every individual is identified or confirmed using this eye scan or finger print identity in a biometric password system that ensures security and guards against fake identities.
- A person is only allowed to proceed with the process if their passport number and associated password credentials match information that has already been saved in the database; otherwise, they are not authorized to take part in any E-voting procedures.
- The peer and miner nodes that make up the blockchain network are in charge of voting for or confirming the network's participating nodes.

- If miners have successfully validated a person's identification information, including their date of birth, Passport number, residence, and voting status, they are then permitted to cast ballots.
- Else
- The voter will be identified as a false user.
- Additionally, the voting record is compared with a database to avoid single people from repeating their vote.

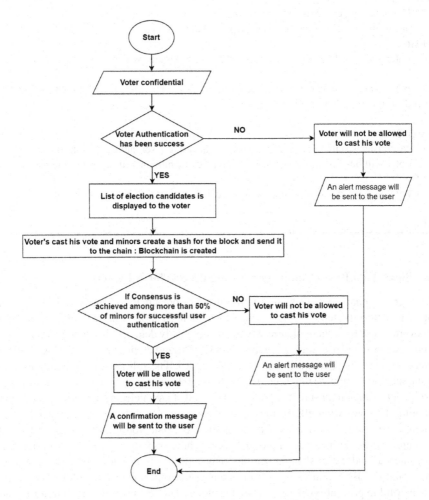

Fig. 2. Proposed methodology for blockchain based E voting to cast a vote

The entire process of casting a vote in a blockchain-based electronic voting system is shown by the algorithm in the second phase of the voting system using discus in the form of an Algorithm 2.

Algorithm 2: Blockchain Based E Voting to Cast a Vote

Input: Voter Credentials
Output: Casting of vote and an alert message to the voter

Begin:

Step 1:
If (Voter authentication is successful) then
    List of the Election Candidates is displayed to the voter
Else
    Voter's will be barred from voting and an alert message will be sent to the user

Step 2: Voter casts his vote and Miners m_1, m_2, m_3,.... m_n create hash for the block and sends to the chain : Blockchain is created

Step 3:
If (consensus is achieved among minors for successful user authentication) then
    Voter will be allowed to cast his vote and a confirmation will be sent to the user
Else
    Voter will not be allowed to cast his vote and an alert will be sent to the user

End

4.3 Blockchain Based Complete E Voting Process for All Voters

Consider a scenario where some of the invaders breach IoT devices and attempt to vote under false pretenses. Then, when voter identification is done using a biometric password, these fraudulent identity voters may be easily detected. If attackers manage to bypass the initial phase, they will undoubtedly be found at the subsequent stage, where voters are once more identified using miner nodes. The full person's identification is maintained on a database that is connected through Blockchain, and miner nodes further verify each person to ensure a valid vote. The next stage in electronic voting is to begin counting the votes when the voting procedure is completed. Blockchain technology is crucial at the stage where it truly protects the electronic voting process against fraud or tampering throughout the counting phase. There may be a strong possibility that both internal and external organizations may modify the provided record during the vote counting. By retaining user transparency, the blockchain technology would be very helpful in preventing these security problems. The remaining polling authority can promptly identify or discover any modification or alteration of a single vote or record and take the appropriate measures for that station. The blockchain technology offers a high degree of security in the E-voting process, whereas smart based E-voting apps are regarded to be smart devices where users are identified or authorized to complete their votes using the application. Let's suppose a situation as shown in Fig. 3 in order to comprehend the advantages of blockchain throughout the voting or counting procedure.

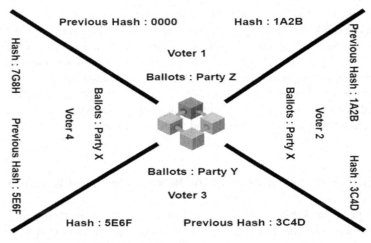

Fig. 3. Blockchain based complete E voting process for all voters

---

Algorithm 3: Blockchain Based Complete E Voting Process for All Voters

---

Input: Voters' data
Output: Blockchain of voters' data

Begin:

If (Voter casting is successful) then
    Miners m_1, m_2, m_3,.... m_n create hash for the block and records in the chain
    //Blockchain is created for the successful votes

Else
    It is also recorded in the chain of blocks
    //Blockchain is created for the unsuccessful casting

End

The blockchain hashes are highly useful when someone wants to identify or spot any changes in the current blocks. A single modification to any recorded data, such as vote totals or individual identities within the block, will, according to a blockchain feature, affect the current hash. Each block includes the hash of the previous and current blocks, creating a chain of blocks and guaranteeing the security of the blockchain. Let's have a look at where a 3-block chain sequence is worn to get a better understanding of it in the context of E-voting. Each block in Fig. 3 denotes a cast vote or the total number of votes cast by voters. Voter data, the current hash, and the hash of the following block are the three components of each block. Numerous authorities are assigned to record or preserve each vote's tally using Blockchain. Let's assume that a hacker tries to alter the data of the second block from the outside or from the inside. In such a case, any modification to the counting might have an impact on all blocks that come after the data or vote information has been uploaded. This results in an irrational update of the hash of the present block as well as of blocks 3 and all succeeding blocks because they no longer have a valid hash of the prior block. Therefore, changing a single chunk will render all the following blocks unusable. This paper's focus is on analyzing the legitimacy of IoT devices where hackers attempt to exploit them in order to cast fraudulent votes. The suggested framework is examined in relation to a number of networking aspects, including the likelihood that it is accurate, the potency of an attack, and the requests that hacked IoT devices in the network may perform.

5 Experimental Environment for Blockchain Based E Voting

In this paper, using Ethereum-based blockchain technology to implement the e-voting system to perform online mode voting for all users who are connected to the entire network for maintaining transparency, immutability, and enhancing all security-related issues in this system. In the beginning, a new user must register before their information is stored in the database. If the user is already registered, the system will request their credentials for verification. The procedure will end if the OTP is invalid; otherwise, if the verification is successful, the system will request the user's fingerprint. The system will halt if the fingerprints don't match. The system will examine the gas value when the fingerprint has been successfully verified. Each voter may only have one vote, and the system will halt if the admin cannot allocate a gas value to each voter. Blockchain employs the digital signature (SHA256) technique to maintain and verify the integrity of the data and to encrypt it. This depends on the availability of gas. When a voter casts a ballot, the information from that ballot is uploaded to an IPFS server, which then creates a hash for that vote that Ethereum will keep up to date. The database will be updated with the vote's status at its conclusion. Permissioned Blockchain is used for designing the proposed model.

5.1 Solidity

The Ethereum Network team created Solidity, an object-oriented programming language, for the purpose of building and developing smart contracts on blockchain systems. It is applied to the development of smart contracts, which apply business logic and produce a series of transaction records within the blockchain framework. It serves as a tool for writing machine-level code and compiling it for use with the Ethereum Virtual Machine (EVM). It is quite similar to C and C++ and is rather easy to learn and comprehend. A "main" in C is comparable to a "contract" in Solidity, for instance.

5.2 Metamask

In this paper explore the scattered web of the present in your browser with Metamask. Additionally, it enables you to run Ethereum on your browser without having to run a full Ethereum node. It contains a secure identification block that gives users an interface to maintain their identities across many websites and sign blockchain transactions.

5.3 NodeJS

NodeJS is an open-source, cross-platform environment for creating networking and server-side applications. Applications created using NodeJS can be used on Linux, OS X, and Microsoft Windows and are written in JavaScript. Additionally, it offers a variety of JavaScript modules, greatly facilitating the creation of web applications using NodeJS.

5.4 ReactJS

A JavaScript package called ReactJS is used to create a variety of reusable UI components. It produces user interface (UI) elements that can display dynamic data. React is frequently used as the V in MVC. React provides a more straight forward programming model and higher speed. Node may be used to build React on the server, while React Native can be used to build native apps. One-way reactive data flow, which React implements, is less boilerplate and simpler to understand than conventional data binding.

5.5 IPFS

In a distributed file system, data is stored and shared via the Inter Planetary File System (IPFS), a protocol and peer-to-peer network. By using of IPFS in e-voting system to storing ledger of all valid and invalid voter access in the online system and in all nodes transparently. Here's the working process of IPFS in its first stage. Examine what transpires when you add a file to IPFS. A cryptographic hash, or digital fingerprint, is created for our file and every block included inside it. By keeping just the material that interests each network node and a small amount of indexing data that identifies which node is holding what, IPFS eliminates duplications throughout the network. When looking for a file to read or download, one can also ask the network to locate the nodes that contain the data hidden by the hash of the file. But you don't need to memorize the hash since the decentralized naming system known as IPFS allows you to search for any file using its human-readable name.

6 Results and Discussion

As a result, time consumption during transaction processing on the blockchain network is reduced. If user requests are increasing, then computational time will also increase, as seen in Fig. 4. User demand is decreasing, so computation time also decreases. Power consumption is also increasing in blockchain transactions.

When the number of voters in the system grows, so does the authentication time increase because there are many processes for very detailed information available in the system, like passport number, biometric details, etc. During the voting process, the system verifies all of the voter's information. In this case, the authentication process takes more time for a complete transaction on the blockchain network, as seen in Fig. 5.

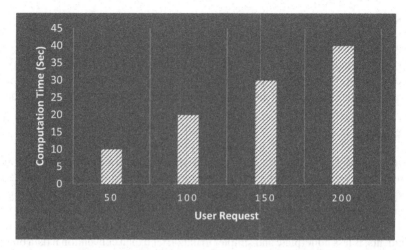

Fig. 4. Number of user requests vs computational time

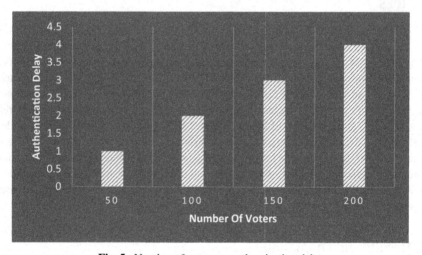

Fig. 5. Number of voters vs authentication delay

In the blockchain network, miners verify the accuracy of voters by performing transactions by the valid voters in the system. As the number of miners on the blockchain network increases, accuracy also increases, as seen in Fig. 6. During executing the transaction number of users, the accuracy is also perfect.

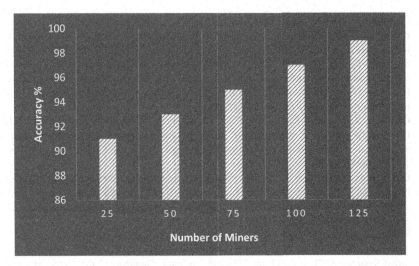

Fig. 6. Number of miners vs accuracy

7   Conclusion and Future Directions

A hybrid system that allows for scenarios where whitelisted access is necessary but all transactions are visible to the public is a permissioned, public, shared blockchain. Transparency will be provided, which is essential in democracies. However, there are solutions for some of the additional issues that e-voting may bring, such as preserving privacy, particularly in the case of public permission-less blockchains. Another issue is how quickly the transactions can be validated. Therefore, while many problems are claimed to be solved by blockchain technology, one area where it may ultimately make sense is electronic voting systems.

In future, the work can be emphasized on consensus protocols and smart contracts to enhance the security and improve the computational time. The work can also be extended to provide some possible solutions for the areas where remote voting is not possible.

References

1. Shrivastava, A.L., Dwivedi, R.K.: Designing a secure vehicular Internet of Things (IoT) using blockchain: a review. In: 1st IEEE International Conference on Advances in Computing and Future Communication Technologies (ICACFCT 2021), Meerut, India, 16–17 December 2021. MIET (2021)
2. Shrivastava, A.L., Dwivedi, R.K.: A secure design of the smart vehicular IoT system using blockchain technology. In: 9th IEEE International Conference on Computing for Sustainable Global Development (16th INDIACom 2022), New Delhi, India, to be held on 23–25 March 2022. Bharati Vidyapeeth (2022). https://doi.org/10.23919/INDIACom54597.2022.9763216
3. Chauhan, N., Dwivedi, R.K.: A secure design of the healthcare IoT system using blockchain technology. In: 9th IEEE International Conference on Computing for Sustainable Global Development (16th INDIACom 2022), New Delhi, India, to be held on 23–25 March 2022. Bharati Vidyapeeth (2022). https://doi.org/10.23919/INDIACom54597.2022.9763187

4. Chauhan, N., Dwivedi, R.K.: Designing a secure smart healthcare system with blockchain: a review. In: 1st IEEE International Conference on Informatics (ICI 2022), Noida, India, to be held on 14–16 April 2022. JIIT (2022). https://doi.org/10.1109/ICI53355.2022.9786895
5. Shrivastava, A.L., Dwivedi, R.K.: Designing a secure vehicular Internet of Things (IoT) using blockchain. In: Suma, V., Baig, Z., Kolandapalayam Shanmugam, S., Lorenz, P. (eds.) Inventive Systems and Control. LNNS, vol. 436, pp. 669–679. Springer, Singapore (2022). https://doi.org/10.1007/978-981-19-1012-8_46
6. Chauhan, N., Dwivedi, R.K.: Designing a secure smart healthcare system with blockchain. In: Suma, V., Baig, Z., Kolandapalayam Shanmugam, S., Lorenz, P. (eds.) Inventive Systems and Control. LNNS, vol. 436, pp. 443–456. Springer, Singapore (2022). https://doi.org/10.1007/978-981-19-1012-8_30
7. Chauhan, N., Dwivedi, R.K.: A survey on designing a secure smart healthcare system with blockchain. In: Shakya, S., Ntalianis, K., Kamel, K.A. (eds.) Mobile Computing and Sustainable Informatics. LNDECT, vol. 126, pp. 391–403. Springer, Singapore (2022). https://doi.org/10.1007/978-981-19-2069-1_27
8. Kumari, T., Kumar, R., Dwivedi, R.K.: Design of a secure and smart healthcare IoT with blockchain: a review. In: Choudrie, J., Mahalle, P., Perumal, T., Joshi, A. (eds.) IOT with Smart Systems. SIST, vol. 312, pp. 229–238. Springer, Singapore (2023). https://doi.org/10.1007/978-981-19-3575-6_25
9. Yadav, A.K., Singh, K.: Comparative analysis of consensus algorithms and issues in integration of blockchain with IoT. In: Tiwari, S., Trivedi, M.C., Mishra, K.K., Misra, A.K., Kumar, K.K., Suryani, E. (eds.) Smart Innovations in Communication and Computational Sciences. AISC, vol. 1168, pp. 25–46. Springer, Singapore (2021). https://doi.org/10.1007/978-981-15-5345-5_3
10. Yadav, A.K., Singh, K.: Comparative analysis of consensus algorithms of blockchain technology. In: Hu, Y.-C., Tiwari, S., Trivedi, M.C., Mishra, K.K. (eds.) Ambient Communications and Computer Systems. AISC, vol. 1097, pp. 205–218. Springer, Singapore (2020). https://doi.org/10.1007/978-981-15-1518-7_17
11. Yu, B., et al.: Platform-independent secure blockchain-based voting system. In: Chen, L., Manulis, M., Schneider, S. (eds.) ISC 2018. LNCS, vol. 11060, pp. 369–386. Springer, Cham (2018). https://doi.org/10.1007/978-3-319-99136-8_20
12. Hsiao, J.-H., Tso, R., Chen, C.-M., Wu, M.-E.: Decentralized E-voting systems based on the blockchain technology. In: Park, J.J., Loia, V., Yi, G., Sung, Y. (eds.) CUTE/CSA -2017. LNEE, vol. 474, pp. 305–309. Springer, Singapore (2018). https://doi.org/10.1007/978-981-10-7605-3_50
13. Li, C., Xiao, J., Dai, X., Jin, H.: AMVchain: authority management mechanism on blockchain-based voting systems. Peer-to-Peer Netw. Appl. **14**(5), 2801–2812 (2021). https://doi.org/10.1007/s12083-021-01100-x
14. Xiao, S., Wang, X.A., Wang, W., Wang, H.: Survey on blockchain-based electronic voting. In: Barolli, L., Nishino, H., Miwa, H. (eds.) INCoS 2019. AISC, vol. 1035, pp. 559–567. Springer, Cham (2020). https://doi.org/10.1007/978-3-030-29035-1_54
15. Pawlak, M., Guziur, J., Poniszewska-Marańda, A.: Voting process with blockchain technology: auditable blockchain voting system. In: Xhafa, F., Barolli, L., Greguš, M. (eds.) INCoS 2018. LNDECT, vol. 23, pp. 233–244. Springer, Cham (2019). https://doi.org/10.1007/978-3-319-98557-2_21
16. Abayomi-Zannu, T.P., Odun-Ayo, I., Tatama, B.F., Misra, S.: Implementing a mobile voting system utilizing blockchain technology and two-factor authentication in Nigeria. In: Singh, P.K., Pawłowski, W., Tanwar, S., Kumar, N., Rodrigues, J.J.P.C., Obaidat, M.S. (eds.) Proceedings of First International Conference on Computing, Communications, and Cyber-Security (IC4S 2019). LNNS, vol. 121, pp. 857–872. Springer, Singapore (2020). https://doi.org/10.1007/978-981-15-3369-3_63

17. Chaieb, M., Yousfi, S., Lafourcade, P., Robbana, R.: Verify-your-vote: a verifiable blockchain-based online voting protocol. In: Themistocleous, M., Rupino da Cunha, P. (eds.) EMCIS 2018. LNBIP, vol. 341, pp. 16–30. Springer, Cham (2019). https://doi.org/10.1007/978-3-030-11395-7_2

18. Yang, X., Yi, X., Nepal, S., Han, F.: Decentralized voting: a self-tallying voting system using a smart contract on the ethereum blockchain. In: Hacid, H., Cellary, W., Wang, H., Paik, H.-Y., Zhou, R. (eds.) WISE 2018. LNCS, vol. 11233, pp. 18–35. Springer, Cham (2018). https://doi.org/10.1007/978-3-030-02922-7_2

19. Braghin, C., Cimato, S., Cominesi, S.R., Damiani, E., Mauri, L.: Towards blockchain-based E-voting systems. In: Abramowicz, W., Corchuelo, R. (eds.) BIS 2019. LNBIP, vol. 373, pp. 274–286. Springer, Cham (2019). https://doi.org/10.1007/978-3-030-36691-9_24

20. Cucurull, J., Rodríguez-Pérez, A., Finogina, T., Puiggalí, J.: Blockchain-based internet voting: systems' compliance with international standards. In: Abramowicz, W., Paschke, A. (eds.) BIS 2018. LNBIP, vol. 339, pp. 300–312. Springer, Cham (2019). https://doi.org/10.1007/978-3-030-04849-5_27

21. Bajpai, M., Haider, A., Mishra, A., Perwej, Y., Rastogi, N.: A novel vote counting system based on secure blockchain. Int. J. Sci. Res. Sci. Eng. Technol. 69–79 (2022). https://doi.org/10.32628/ijsrset22948

22. Mani, A., Patil, S., Sheth, S., Kondaka, L.S.: College election system using blockchain. In: ITM Web Conferences, vol. 44, p. 03005 (2022). https://doi.org/10.1051/itmconf/20224403005

23. Keerthi, K., Venkatesh, N., Lakshmi, G.D., Chand, N.S., Haritha, D.: E-voting system using blockchain technology. J. Crit. Rev. 9(4), 243–254 (2022). https://doi.org/10.31838/jcr.09.04.31

24. Patil, B., Naringrekar, D., Mahapatro, P.: EasyChair preprint voting system based on blockchain technology. Voting System Based on Blockchain Technology (2022)

25. Rathee, G., Iqbal, R., Waqar, O., Bashir, A.K.: On the design and implementation of a blockchain enabled E-voting application within IoT-oriented smart cities. IEEE Access 9, 34165–34176 (2021). https://doi.org/10.1109/ACCESS.2021.3061411

Systemic Review of AI Reshaped Blockchain Applications

Mohammad Shamsuddoha[1] ⓘ, Mohammad A. Kashem[2] ⓘ, and Saroj Koul[3(✉)] ⓘ

[1] Western Illinois University, Macomb, Illinos, USA
m-shamsuddoha@wiu.edu
[2] Feni University, Feni, Chittagong, Bangladesh
kashem@feniuniversity.ac.bd
[3] OP Jindal Global University, Sonipat, Haryana, India
skoul@jgu.edu.in

Abstract. The perceived benefits of integrating Blockchain Technology (BT) and Artificial Intelligence (AI) have profound importance from qualitative and quantitative perspectives to real-world applications. However, the academic literature connecting the two is largely absent. This study reviews the adoption of Blockchain applications in diversified sectors that contribute to its reshaping through AI and are not limited to digital currency, trade connection, or information processing. A term-searching mechanism addresses the research question through a formalized plan for reviewing field-wise blockchain papers. The keywords *Blockchain, blockchain-based applications, and artificial intelligence* assess the secondary literature published until the first quarter of 2021. Twenty-one use cases where BT proved its permanence theoretically or empirically about AI are identified based on equality and feasibility.

Moreover, the potential of BT goes beyond the hindrances of techno-socio-economic space concerns, thus contributing to research and business innovation. This study can be considered one of the first academic articles connecting BT and its application spread over IT and related industrial environments/sectors/ fields for improving the movement of AI. In addition to trust and awareness, integrating AI and Blockchain will lead to a future beyond the reactive machine's limitation.

Keywords: Blockchain · Blockchain technology · Artificial intelligence · AI · Systemic review · Blockchain applications

1 Introduction

Artificial intelligence (AI) has a broad appeal in real-time data handling, and improved responses increase consumer expectations [1] in the modern world. But, surprisingly, AI today limits its full utilization and potential due to the complexity and incapability of its understanding [2]. Besides, Blockchain, a continuous ledger technology, is augmented substantially with fast changes that avoid disruptive surprises or missed opportunities [3]. However, science and industry improvements and computer technology revolutions ensure equal opportunity for all. But, the roles of AI in ensuring sustainable development

© The Author(s), under exclusive license to Springer Nature Switzerland AG 2023
I. Woungang et al. (Eds.): ANTIC 2022, CCIS 1797, pp. 470–494, 2023.
https://doi.org/10.1007/978-3-031-28180-8_32

goals (SDGs) play a sophisticated landmark in digital transformation [4] from a techno-centric viewpoint.

Also, AI, the trust machine-driven business model, creates values to maintain and address technical and moral standards and innovation design [5]. In this regard, the term 'double-edged sword' behaviour is used for AI to avoid human errors and associated risks. Still, it is 'purposefully misused', for instance, in gathering personal and behavioural data for data mining [6]. But on the other hand, BT promises efficiency (disinter-mediation and ease of operations), control and security (superior protection and reducing risks through cryptocurrency) [7]. So, the common issues that arose under the cognizance of AI are supposed to be reduced by shifting towards Blockchain in the sense that Blockchain involves transparency (accessibility and visibility), immutability (restriction in changing recorded data) [8] and confidence (shared reading at the same time). For instance, using BT's standard mechanisms, transparency issues in AI can be resolved because there are fewer chances to corrupt the data or information in the Blockchain (a decentralized and distributed ledger mechanism) [9]. However, blockchain-induced modelling and verification of data ensure electronic documents and data integrity reliably [10]. Similarly, the limitation of AI reasoning in internal processes, especially for deep learning, transforms a trustworthy blockchain [11]. Such complicated issues arise due to a sense of ethics or security [12].

Blockchain Technology (BT) generally is grounded on distributed consensus, network protocols, smart contracts, privacy, security through peer-to-peer communication [13], and control and security [7, 14]. Furthermore, the significant improvement of BT has added a crucial contribution in the management domain as substantiated by maturing research agenda [15], such as in carbon tax policy [16] and ledger-commitment latency [17]. Even so, [18] prioritized the perceived benefits of BT towards real-world applications irrespective of basic research, especially in qualitative and quantitative perspectives [19]. As a result, adopting BT factually rather than maintaining sustainability [20].

As an emerging technology, Blockchain enraptures its feasibility of being versatile irrespective of confining cryptocurrency. Nevertheless, the sorted-out applicability of Blockchain is gradually shifting in practice with regulation. For example, [21] investigated the ambiguities of Blockchain by justifying individual characteristics in contrast to the success of Blockchain, visualizing different dimensions, e.g., hyper ledger fabric on permissioned Blockchain [22]. Similarly, [23] reviewed the impact of smart contracts on the blockchain process for setting automated business logic, but a great deal of uncertainty surrounds its real potential. In addition, a few research papers on smart contracts termed BT's substantial progress as security, integrity and anonymity [24], with a debate over legal implications and regulatory uncertainties [25]. Both technologies are not alternatives to one another but complementary for the betterment of collaborative performance and collective intelligence. Hence, the integration between AI and Blockchain accelerates the self-execution mechanism of AI in all aspects of trustworthy real-time assessment and forecasting.

This study thus literally justifies the roles and gradual development that occurred in multidimensional sectors such as finance, banking, supply chain, insurance, and business process, subject to the advancement of both AI and BT. This paper is organized as follows: Sect. 2 discusses the research questions and methodology with an article selection flowchart. Section 3 describes the common features of BT and differentiating role of both AI and BT, Sect. 4 presents the applications of both AI and BT based on the systematic literature review, and Sect. 5 relates the inter-dependencies of both AI and BT. Lastly, in Sect. 6, the conclusion and future research are presented.

2 Methodology and the Research Question

With the guided format from [26], the process set up is into sequential steps such as identifying the required type of research, selecting suitable studies assessing quality and synthesizing data, tabulating, and reviewing the recent contribution of blockchain application with its fundamental characteristics.

2.1 Term Selection, Systematic Searching, and Snowball Effect

The authors used major databases, including Google Scholar, Mendeley and JSTOR, as the search platform because of the diverse nature of acceptance and their profuseness in incorporating academic journal articles, especially from scholarly societies and commercial publishers. However, the authors utilized the advanced searching options by using exact phrases and keywords in the title or the entire article to fine-tune the best articles on each referred sector. In addition, the study reviewed several blockchain-based applications and secondary literature to set the research goals [27]. In the blockchain literature review, the study used the following keywords: "{'AI', 'blockchain'; 'AI applications' and blockchain-based applications; 'blockchain and AI finance'; 'blockchain and AI stock market'; 'blockchain and AI central bank'; 'blockchain and AI real estate'; 'blockchain and AI power system'; 'blockchain and AI healthcare'; 'blockchain and AI tourism'; 'blockchain and AI social engagement'; 'blockchain and AI marketplace'; 'blockchain and AI mathematics'; 'blockchain and AI transport and logistics management'; 'blockchain and AI entertainment'; 'blockchain and AI e-government; 'blockchain and AI charity; 'blockchain and AI technology'; 'blockchain and AI retailing'; 'blockchain and AI shipping'; 'blockchain and AI money transfer'; 'blockchain and AI business process management'; 'blockchain and AI insurance'; "and 'blockchain and AI education'}" to assess the literature available until the second quarter of 2021.

Research Question: How did the correlative movement of BT and AI accelerate the world standards throughout the decade on diversified sectors?

To address the research question, we used a term-searching mechanism. Of the listed articles, the first 400 hits were selected. Then, based on their relevance to the study, followed by a further search, guidelines were prepared [28] for significant understanding (Fig. 1). Thus, potentiality and relevancy were prioritized in searching and selecting the articles.

Due to the bounding of time and relevancy of the selected blockchain applications, the primary questions worked as the critical stimulus for selecting research articles. Earlier, [21] included the grey literature's priority and pure research bases. In contrast, this limit-redundancy mechanism accumulated many substantial applications of blockchain adoption applications instead of adding more references to similar articles [29].

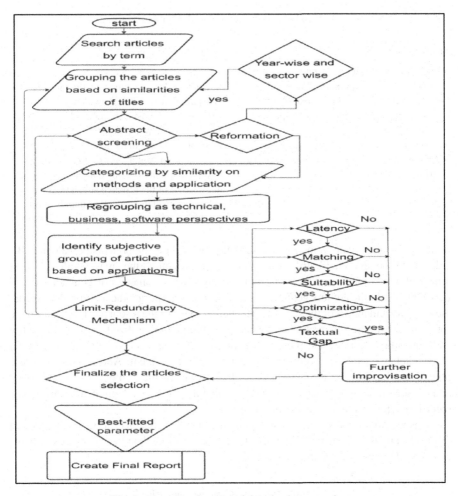

Fig. 1. Flowchart for the article selection procedure

2.2   Inclusion and Exclusion Criteria

Various studies on Blockchain as an emerging technology create ambiguity in selecting and reviewing field-wise AI and Blockchain papers. That is why, depending on the screening structure by scrutinizing abstracts and keywords and their relevancy, a splitting application-wise-paper selection was the basis of inclusion and exclusion parameters, as in Table 1.

The selected study should be in AI, Blockchain or blockchain-based applications. Literature that combined more than one sector for selected applications or solely blog-based details was excluded except for rich materials. Peer-reviewed publications were preferred. Another criterion that had given preference for selecting papers is the relevancy of answering the research question. As a result, the authors were able to fix the sector-wise application of Blockchain into 21 distinct sectors from an initial categorization

Table 1. Inclusion and exclusion area

Inclusion Criteria	Exclusion Criteria
• Peer-reviewed research papers, conference papers/ proceedings, books/book chapters • Limit-Redundancy Mechanism: Avoid articles having similarities with applications of Blockchain • New judgment for field-related applications • Prioritize the selection of empirical research articles	• Technical papers • Articles addressing technical judgement of BT, pure software-based application irrespective of business applications • Only literary works or articles having a low level of relevance to the topic matter, with "little to no potential" for future extensions • Appealing but not related to the selected application of the research subject matter • Articles in a language other than English

of about 40 areas. Due to the related attributes in the key components prevalent to BT [21, 23, 24, 26–28, 37, 43, 46], these 21 sectors represent all the areas. While selecting articles for citation, the authors did not set any prior parameters of equivalence and feasibility. Still, the authors genuinely endeavour to incorporate the ideologies covering the viability and merits of the sectors and whether to fit for the resources, time, and scope for solid substructure reassessment. Therefore, the authors utilized the term "equality and feasibility" to represent prevalent featured sectors associated with the entire field of Blockchain, which is supposed to be genuinely equivalent. And in meeting these objectives, that was not to incorporate all the advancements of blockchain technology in each sector but to justify the universal applicability of Blockchain in all transactions, record-keeping or common daily affairs.

This methodological approach using inclusion and exclusion criteria was performed (Table 2), and the sector-wise features of BT (Table 3) based on the 43 selected articles considered were reviewed and analyzed in Sect. 3.

Table 2. Methodological approach

Term selection and Systematic searching	Searched based on the keywords (Sect. 2.1) resulted in **402** articles
Inclusion and exclusion criteria	Depending on the mapping through inclusion and exclusion criteria, this number filtered to **194** articles
Abstract and sector-wise screening	By prioritizing relevancy through scrutinizing abstracts and keywords, then splitting up into application-wise-paper-selection, this selection was limited to **109** articles
Currency and best-fitted parameter	Justifying sectoral feasibility and accommodating the latest contribution until 2021, the final selected list was **46** articles

Table 3. Common features of BT in the 21 selected areas (All author's view; Source [21, 23, 24, 26–28, 37, 43, 46]

1) Finance	8) Technology	15) Shipping
• Trusted sources • International money transfer • Hassle-free borrowing and lending • Efficient foreign exchange	• Complete automation and user-centric paradigm • Decentralized internet • Cloud/storage sharing/renting • Smart contacts by machine to commands	• Reduce paperwork • Transparent and secure global trading
2) Central Banking	9) Tourism	16) Business Process Management
• Increased high uptime • Digital currency • Resiliency and transparency • Crack-down money laundering	• Efficient customer identification, reward and loyalty system • Baggage tracking and management • Secure and traceable payment Immediate booking through tracking	• Accurate charging of consultancy/fees for expert • Patent protection • Smart legal contracts
3) Insurance	10) Social Engagement	17) Retailing
• Eliminate fraud • Secured medical record data	• Share-and-collect points • Manage user reputation and create a new community	• Trade loyalty rewards • Gift cards • Real-time tracking or source of origin
4) Money Transfer	11) Media & Entertainment	18) Power System
• Transfer savings • Digital-will option	• Pay-per-use facility • Authenticity • Micropayment • Rights protection • Proof-of-ownership	• Monitor power usage • Saving cost
5) Stock Market	12) Charity	19) Healthcare
• Share issue, secure trading and settlement • Independent trading • Price stabilization and reduction of volatility authentic prediction	• Pay digital content creators • Highly visible and transparent donation • Real-time data updates and rapid delivery of emergency aid	• Accurate health records • Tracing genuine medicine

(continued)

Table 3. (*continued*)

6) Marketplace/Mobile Commerce	13) Education	20) E-Government
• Low-fee Ad • Secured product-related digital data • Targeted audience • Zero platform fees • Distributed identity platform	• Digital certification • Genuine talents engagement for recruitment open innovation platform	• Fast borrowing and lending • Tracking property • Exclusive digital platform
7) Mathematics	14) Logistics & Supply Chain	21) Real Estate
• Solve complex mathematical problems relating to prime numbers • Massive technical support to discover and prove • Digital signature algorithm and data integrity	• Secure identity and remove heavy resilience on intermediary • Operational and financial transparency • Dispute resolution • Fool-proof track and tracing • Real-time hitch riding • Origin tracking and cost reduction on each transaction • Peer-to-peer ridesharing	• Smart city with smart devices • Sensor-embedded physical objects • Untampered voting

3   Differentiating Roles of AI and BT

AI can utilize Blockchain to authenticate information (trusted and transparent), whereas BT maximizes the involvement of large data with the emergence of AI. Furthermore, Blockchain ensures a decentralized recording mechanism whilst the true emphasis - *intelligent growth* (prompt response) runs over AI. So, both technology interchangeably materializes the benefits of each other. In addition, the integration based on the algorithm ensures actionable insights and improved decision-making validity. In this section, the authors discuss the common technological advancement in selected sectors through AI and BT (Table 4). By differentiating the role of these sectors (a contribution of this paper), the authors initially emphasize how Blockchain would effectively be a decentralized and immutable system for storing encrypted data. At the same time, AI enables analyses of accumulated data for better decision-making. In some respects, our focus was on the augmentation of Blockchain over the privacy issues of AI, in reverse governance and personalization of AI over the scalability issues of Blockchain.

Briefly, AI crunches massive volumes of data. But, at the same time, BT allows users to protect their data while allowing agents to create and transfer data of commercial importance on a tighter budget.

Table 4. Differentiating roles of AI and BT in the 21 selected areas

Sl	Sectors	Artificial Intelligence	Blockchain Technology
1	Finance	Technologically sophisticated forecasting cash flow events, changing credit scores, and detecting fraud	Tracking and recording digital transactions by reducing transaction costs and friction
2	Central Banking	Managing record-level, high-speed data and getting useful insights with digital payments, AI bots, and biometric fraud detection systems	Simplify complicated procedures and improve internal processes instead of siloed systems
3	Insurance	Managing claims, customer service, underwriting, marketing and fraud detection	Automate claims operation, Streamline payments between parties - claims and administrative expenses
4	Money Transfer	By acquiring and analyzing data, offering unique insights, a sales funnel, and suggestions to grow the connection and drive sales and IT supports	Facilitating digital P2P transfers or the absence of the intermediary as a natural stimulus
5	Stock Market	Introducing Robo-advisers to look into millions of data points and execute transactions at the best price	Stocks may be purchased and sold using blockchain technology with real-time and fluctuating prices and entire peer-to-peer exchanges
6	Marketplace/ M-commerce	Anticipating buying trends- what customers buy and when they buy	Maintaining all previous transactions in a digital ledger in 'Blocks,' with unique cryptography value and logical matching
7	Mathematics	Contributing toward basic mathematical computation tools like linear algebra	Setting the proven logic of math-based models to establish an ecosystem that works for all users (Bitcoin)
8	Technology	Advancing the capacity of a computer or a robot to control activities normally require human intelligence and judgment	Decreasing expenses, and avoiding regulatory barriers, and bureaucratic procedures to become a more transparent, democratic, decentralized, efficient, and safe technological movement

(*continued*)

Table 4. (*continued*)

Sl	Sectors	Artificial Intelligence	Blockchain Technology
9	Real Estate	Algorithmic calculations of millions of papers in a matter of seconds for examining property valuations, debt levels, house upgrades, and even some personal information about a homeowner	Transmit the purchase price for transactions utilizing existing cryptocurrencies and initial coin offerings (ICOs) (tokenization)
10	Tourism	Providing online support to clients, answering inquiries, and offering useful information to customers even when a customer support representative is unavailable	Facilitating crypto transactions in place of services, building effective loyalty programs that reward their customers, and even betokening real assets (resort and spaces) in the form of Non-fungible Tokens (NFTs)
11	Social Engagement	Promoting businesses and getting closer to audiences by knowing about their preferences, setting up targeted advertisements, and developing content	Transparent data sharing, community participation and disseminating royalty payment options in streaming services, movies, and music
12	Media and Entertainment	Automate sound production methods, split screenplays, produce shortlists, construct timetables, story-boarding, and guide movie resources, and automatically sync the group's captured video and amusement	Tracing the lifespan of any item, reducing intellectual property infringement, protecting digital content, and making true digital collectables more accessible
13	Charity	Evaluating large data sets and detecting patterns to choose when and where to disperse resources to serve consumers	Digital fundraising to receive money securely, transparently, and internationally without paying currency conversion costs (Crypto Giving Tuesday)
14	Education	Providing students with better and quicker learning materials and alerting professors about issues	Authorizing academic identities owning personal information, and the veracity of the qualifications
15	Shipping	Reducing cost, appropriate forecasting, lessening risks and quicker delivery	Shipment tracking with increased efficiency and secure necessary documentation

(*continued*)

Table 4. (*continued*)

Sl	Sectors	Artificial Intelligence	Blockchain Technology
16	Logistics & Supply Chain	Improving supply chain and transportation processes by decreasing costs, reducing risk, enhancing forecasts, and delivering faster delivery via more optimal routes	Tracking shipments in real-time, minimizing risk (/expenses) by automatically (and securely) issuing and monitoring the appropriate shipping, insurance and financing documents
17	Business Process Management	Digital transformation in operations, automating redundant tasks, predictive analysis, and improved customer experiences	Improving efficiency by building trust and reducing friction through access (for permissioned users)
18	Retailing	Improved consumer experiences, forecasting, and inventory management and yielded additional business insights through the cloud system	Tracing the product fault, if any, based on tracking the entire product history and identifying the tainted suppliers, manufacturer and batches to correct supply chain concerns
19	Power System	Encompassing expert systems, artificial neural networks, fuzzy diagnostic theory, and genetic algorithms for bunches of benefits	Recording and facilitating transactions between energy providers and consumers on a peer-to-peer basis through automated intelligent contracts
20	Healthcare	Using machine-learning algorithms, or AI, replicating human cognition in analyzing, displaying, and interpreting complicated inpatient and outpatient data	Transforming healthcare through improved security, transparency, and accessibility of records
21	E-Government	Connecting with the government and accessing government services, for example, chat-bots, to respond to inquiries	Maintaining public ledger for asset transactions such as land, property, and cars and tracking registry and property ownership

Source: [21, 23, 24, 26–28, 37, 43, 46]

4 AI and Blockchain-Based Applications and Research

BT has proved supportive with authentic footprints in every sphere of business and industry with trust, whereas AI keeps paces adding new footsteps. Typical applications surrounding us are finance, power, healthcare, real estate, tourism, social engagement, and the marketplace. Similarly, this technology deals with mathematics, transport, entertainment, e-government, charity, technology, retailing, business process management, and education, each described below in Tables 5–9.

4.1 Applications of BT and AI in Finance, Central Banking, Insurance, Money Transfer, and Stock Market

BT has played a promising role in providing the best possible services to clients and adapting full financial and banking services [30]. Although BT empowers decentralized financial services for innovators and entrepreneurs, issues still exist within cryptocurrency [31]. The significant services embedded under the Blockchain in insurance processes are client registration, policy issuance, handling claims, and detecting suspicious transaction patterns [32]. Like other sectors, BT has created a great hope to eliminate risk against fraudulent practices in electronic fund transfers [30]. In addition, the private Ethereum Blockchain diversifies stock trading logic by smart contract [33]. Table 5 exhibits research in domain-specific areas 1–5 of Table 3.

In the same way, while AI does accurate forecasting [34] by using machine learning, for instance, IBM's Watson, in today's world, especially for financial matters, the reluctance to get the advantages of AI leads to risks in competition, organization performance, and market capitalization [35]. However, Turchin [36] argued that the chances of proving the existence of AI are not far away with proper changes, though pessimists doubted it [37]. Also, digital transformation for value co-creation enhances the domination of finance and banking activities [38] and public distribution to a greater extent by maximizing trust [39].

Table 5. Finance, stock market, central banking, insurance and money-transfer

Areas of research	AI/BT	Authors	Theme of research	Contribution/Innovation
Finance	BT	[31]	Decentralized financing for entrepreneurship and innovation	Bitcoin, Libra, Bitcoin Lightning Network
	AI	[38]	Value co-creation for consumer comfort by AI and mobile banking service platforms	Introducing a digital self-service transaction technology-oriented mechanism and transformation
Stock market	BT	[33]	Trading and deployment of decentralized stock exchange platforms	Private Ethereum, smart contract
	AI	[25]	Portfolio optimization, AI-based stock market forecasting and monetary estimation and investigation,	Critical mechanical improvement and recognizable proof of times of expanded revenue for ventures

(continued)

Table 5. (*continued*)

Areas of research	AI/BT	Authors	Theme of research	Contribution/Innovation
Central banking	BT	[42]	Systematic Mapping Study for Blockchain adoption	Digital Currency, Regulatory Compliance, and Payment Clearing and Settlement Systems
	AI	[34]	Instability, intricacy and ambiguity in banking transactions	An open and collaborative movement against decreasing cost and adding ways to differentiation
Insurance	BT	[41]	STEEP (social, technological, environmental, economic and political /legal) framework for strategic decision making	FinTech and InsurTech
	AI	[40]	The effects of computerized reasoning on the protection area on insurability criteria	Measurement of the insurability of risks for an exact expectation of misfortune probabilities and risks
Money transfer	BT	[30]	Money transfer system, robust banking practices	Secured money transfer flow and documentation through smart contracts
	AI	[35]	The transformative business trend in core processes, business models and operations	Mechanics of AI acceptance in financial Transactions and its effect on capitalization

On the other hand, the motto of stock trading lies in the right prediction of stocks from historical time series data, which is much easier due to the advent of AI, for example, economic sentiment analysis [25]. This task involves the optimization of the portfolio—some development as seen in diversified methodologies, including multi-objective models and heuristic methods. For insurance concerns, the shifting of loss from reimbursement to calculation and ways to avert the loss allows the acceptability of AI to a great extent [40]. This shifting also works for risk transformation through new products of insurance and coverage. However, the insurance company faces challenges in the applicability and accuracy of multidimensional product diversity.

4.2 Applications of BT and AI in Marketplace/M-Commerce, Mathematics, Technology and Real Estate

A blockchain is a trust machine [43] in consensus and cryptography [44]. Likewise, an algorithmic movement of AI for mathematics and science has overcome the common issues and difficulties of learning and analyzing data through data mining [45]. Also, for mobile commerce (m-commerce), MobiChain ensured secure transactions in the mining process following Android Core Module [46].

Due to technological innovation developments, for the digitized organization, capabilities create synergy for the innovation process to solve associated constraints [47]. Henceforth, the common limitations of this advancement are the inability to recognize information demands and cope with complexity. Moreover, this transformation also keeps changes in attitude and purchase [48], especially in marketing and 'human-machine interaction'. However, the future marketplace for value-generating products and services is reshaping under ethical considerations and socially responsible actions [49].

Blockchain movements elevate operational capabilities by digitizing logistics financing in e-commerce logistics real estate [50]. In addition, real estate advancement was reshaped by using data-driven techniques for data validation and a complete end-to-end market mechanism [51]. This advancement in real estate for automation poised a dramatic engagement of autonomous machines, computer-aided design in dealing, planning, construction [52–54] and data compliance, e.g., RegTech, PropTech, ConTech and PlanTech (Ibid). On the other hand, an initiative of Blockchain, viz., "*proptech*" [55], is quite effective for smart real estate management through a design-and-interaction mechanism [56]. Nevertheless, digital real estate platforms are justified under the social context for document dispossession [57] and accumulation strategies [58]. Table 6 catalogues the major domain-specific research in 6, 7, 8 & 21 of Table 3.

Table 6. Marketplace/mobile commerce, mathematics, technology & real estate

Areas of research	AI/BT	Author	Theme of research	Contribution/Innovation
Marketplace	BT	[59]	Decentralized autonomous organizations	Public Blockchain, smart contract, IoT
	AI	[49]	A multi-layered ethical analysis of opportunities prevailing in the marketplace	Changes in preferences and perceptions of consumers' evaluation toward products and services and CSR
Mobile commerce	BT	[46]	Android application, mobile security	Bitcoin, cloud computing, and IoT
	AI	[48]	AI-powered digital assistantship	Identifying the factors and developing a model for upgrading buying intentions and attitudes of consumers based on perceived intelligence

(*continued*)

Table 6. (*continued*)

Areas of research	AI/BT	Author	Theme of research	Contribution/Innovation
Mathematics	BT	[60]	Mathematics, cryptography, cryptocurrency and Blockchain	Data integrity, cryptography and encryption algorithm,
	AI	[45]	Data mining in mathematics and science education	Learning frameworks for Text mining techniques to foster supporting instructors' guidance and learning
Technology	BT	[43]	Technology adoption, diffusion of innovation	Disruptive technology
	AI	[47]	Consistency in the innovation process for transformation and digital association of innovation	AI's information processing capabilities by understanding the readiness level of AI in a digitized organization
Real estate	BT	[51]	Visionary procedure for completely advanced digital and automated real estate marketplace	Distributed Ledger Technology, Smart contract
	AI	[57]	Digitization of residential real estate and critics of housing scholars	Platforms' convenience and focus on the contemporary political economy of housing

4.3 Applications of BT and AI in Tourism, Social Engagement, Media & Entertainment, Charity and Education

Different ways and formats of data origins, either form of data sources, even welcome and unwelcome, containing expressions of online client engagement, are combined and analyzed by AI-enabled systems and how to increase the involvement in online social engagement [61]. Still, this diversity is prevalent in online learning or learning-records-storage facilities by maintaining accountability and transparency [39]. Furthermore, the emotional behaviours' contextual meaning is tricky; AI gives this platform a shape of sentiment detection and analysis [62] for handling idioms, emotional expressions, and humour.

Also, in education, Blockchain-based distributed systems are used for academic reputation and record keeping. As a result, the instructional design of traditional modes of education can be replicated, such as MOOC predictive modelling and AIEd application [63]. In addition, the advancement of AI flourishes due to an enormous level of continuity in services that is usually impossible for a human being in the global landscape, especially in labour services and changes in the experiences of tourists [64]; for example, Mioji

Travel [65]. Table 7 lists domain-specific research in the areas mentioned in 9, 10, 11, 12 & 13 of Table 3.

Table 7. Tourism, social engagement, media & entertainment, charity, and education

Areas of research	AI/BT	Authors	Theme of research	Contribution/Innovation
Tourism	BT	[66]	Applicability and Adoption of BT	Cryptocurrencies, internal smart contracts viz., BedSwap, LockTrip, Winding Tree
	AI	[67]	Justified opportunities in advanced Tourism sectors	Destination government, the travel industry ventures and traveller experiences
Social engagement	BT	[68]	Social media analytics	A smart contract, data authenticity and security, transparency
	AI	[61]	Online customer engagement behaviours	Estimation of customer-related information processing
Media and entertainment	BT	[69]	Rights and royalty management, reputation management	Distributed ledger, smart contract
	AI	[62]	Deep emotions modelling and analysis on the social web	Principles of self-structuring modelling for unstructured and un-labelled social media data
Charity	BT	[39]	Decentralized Donation tracking system to record the transactions	Ethereum, smart contracts
	AI	[70]	Moral competence, ethics and the attributes of moral agency	Computing the morality and social impacts
Education	BT	[71]	Transparency in the assessments and personalization of the curriculum	Distributed ledger, smart contracts, and Hyperledger
	AI	[72]	Characterization into learner, collaborator and leader paradigms	Empowerment of learner agency and personalization

4.4 Application of BT and AI in Logistics & Supply Chain, Shipping, Business Process Management, and Retailing

The Internet of Things (IoT) has a long historical contribution to transport and logistics management through Radio-Frequency Identification (RFID) technology, the cloud ecosystem and Namecoin are used for progressiveness in managing document workflow and financial processes [73]. However, scalability and robustness are approved duly in business process decentralization. For instance, business processes digital software revolution turned the reliable source, process, and quality of entire business artefacts into physical consequences [74].

On the other hand, Blockchain-induced Business Process Management and Runtime Verification of accounting, compensation and documentation could be the possible solution against business process orchestration [42]. Besides, due to the introduction of internet technology or big data, an e-commerce platform or Blockchain-based AI has enhanced the research on shipping and consumer online shopping to generate more revenue [75]. Again inventory network digitalization improves proficiency in the global supply chain, and compliance issues create disruptions in the coordination and commercializing of a new product [76]. However, the movement of AI goes beyond the limitations of automated transport cost and payment handling and manages delivery with the standard [77].

With micro-cloud computing, robotics, Augmented Reality, 5G, Virtual Reality, and Mixed Reality, significant retail changes give integrated and active involvement in retailing [78]. However, feasibility issues and personal data use made technology adaptation questionable [78]. Similarly, information plays a key role in shipping, irrespective of traditional maritime operations and transportation involving autonomous stakeholders [79]. AI, the digital future [35], advances the accuracy, speed and inputs for process control [80], for example, in the hybrid intelligent system. This technology encompasses different applications. However, transitioning operations is one of the keys to the widespread use of AI [80]. Table 8 lists the major domain-specific research at 14, 15, 16 & 17 under Table 3.

Table 8. Logistics & supply chain, shipping, business process management, and retailing

Areas of research	AI/BT	Authors	Theme of research	Contribution/Innovation
Logistics	BT	[81]	Technology, trade, traceability/transparency	Distributed ledger technologies, IoT
	AI	[77]	Approaches to smart logistics frameworks	Smart logistics technologies and applications

(continued)

Table 8. (*continued*)

Areas of research	AI/BT	Authors	Theme of research	Contribution/Innovation
Supply chain	BT	[76]	Difficulties related to global supply chain and pertinent abilities and possibilities of Blockchain	Smart contract
	AI	[80]	Potentiality of AI techniques for practical judgement of SCM	Inclusion and exclusion criteria aggregation in SCM, along with logistics, marketing and production
Shipping	BT	[73]	Document management, financial processes and device connectivity	Maritime port environment, port community system, IoT
	AI	[80]	Self-Organizing ecosystem for shipping	The global shipping industry's complexity and autonomous stakeholders' operations and maintenance among different cultural participants in a competitive market
Business process management	BT	[82]	Inter-organizational business processes and their lifecycle	Mutual trust, cryptocurrency transactions, proof of existence, authenticity. Smart contract
	AI	[83]	Analyzing, implementing, executing, and monitoring business processes to stimulate transformative thinking and prospects	Transformative trends, Social Computing, Big Data Analytics, Smart Devices, and Real-Time Computing
Retailing	BT	[75]	E-commerce platforms, Contingent free shipping, and discount coupons to improve the performance and consumers' purchase decisions	Internet technology, IoT
	AI	[78]	Changes in retailing for technological advancement	Technology-based retail drivers, technology adoption for shoppers, retailers, employees, and suppliers

4.5   Application of BT and AI in Power Systems, Healthcare and E-Government

The innovative blockchain-based e-participation model simplifies all spheres of public affairs to create smart citizens and public transparency [84]. This diversity also prevails in government mechanisms, land registration and rightful ownership [85]. In addition, the government allows and seeks to update the role of AI in identifying suspicious fund transfers [34].

Similarly, for dropping maintenance and operational costs in the power sector, appropriate AI operation techniques include controlling voltage, fault diagnosis, proper estimation, and real-time predictions [86]. A large-scale adaptation of AI has surrounded healthcare for real-time information of the patients in recent years with value co-creation, but for the generalization of ideas in all aspects of existing systems [87]. The domain-specific research areas under 18, 19 & 20 (Table 3) are in Table 9.

Table 9. Power systems, healthcare, and E-government

Areas of research	AI/BT	Authors	Theme of research	Contribution/Innovation
Power system	BT	[88]	Energy trading and marketing	Bitcoin, cryptocurrency
	AI	[86]	Conditions of operating and identifying power system intelligence different from the traditional system	Enhancing the productivity of the power system and load frequency control of equipment and devices
Healthcare	BT	[10]	Privacy and security for patient data	Composer, Docker Container, Hyperledger Fabric & Caliper
	AI	[87]	Co-creating values in B2B industrial healthcare markets by perceptive and responsive mechanisms	Context-specific solutions and network boundaries of healthcare mechanism
E-government	BT	[85]	Developing new concepts for e-government against the challenges of Blockchain	Cryptographically secured distributed ledger
	AI	[89]	Services of central government departments, local governments and public institutions	Quality and privacy of e-government services

From the above section, while AI works to ease mechanisms and process large data sets, BT allows and securely generates records and information.

5 Reshaping of Blockchain and the Diversified Fields with the Advent of AI

The best goal from the advent of AI depends largely on the comprehensive understanding of AI strategy and policy for international competitiveness [90]. Transformational capabilities of AI beyond the acceptances of supply chain management differentiate traditional digitalization [91]. Besides, empowerment is facilitated through AI, like in education, retailing and transportation [92]. However, the business value and practical implications show the greater contribution of AI to knowledge-building experience [93]. So, the diversity belonging to AI considers multistep reasoning and innovative artefacts.

On the other hand, automation's feasibility and attractiveness increased extensively in society depending on sophisticated computation [94]. The acceleration of AI also covered value chain, blockchain integration and organizational strategy development [28]. From the similar representation related to Blockchain, the coverage segregated to blockchain-based data management for decentralized intelligence, increasing transparency, data marketplace and smart contract [95]. Consequently, AI contributed decipherably to Blockchain irrespective of AI-related business reigns.

The understanding of AI (behaviour) for secure and efficient optimization of Blockchain, but for generalization, their integration is yet not reflected in the literature [96, 97]. More specifically, the common roles of AI are contented with mitigating risks, information fusion, optimization and mining [96]. Again, the interdependency between Blockchain and AI enlarged data protection and privacy at a low cost [98], empowering AI on smart BT to share information reliably between participants. Reasonably, the AI-based strong fairness is triggered through automated and compensated mechanisms [95]. In addition, the integration also reduces uncertainty in decentralization by automated execution of smart contracts and secure data sharing [99]. The computation complexity has been limited in a distributed fashion by an efficient mechanism of edge intelligence in permissioned Blockchain [100]. So, the enhancement of the feasibility of the integration enlightens the structure and common characteristics of Blockchain, for example, decentralization, smart contract, and data management.

Though few issues, one of the fundamental improvements has itemized in distributed and knowledge learning models like 'Federated Learning' opted for data privacy in blockchain intelligence [101]. Furthermore, the major development of AI dramatized the Blockchain in reinforcement learning, decision-making, and effective reasoning [102]. For instance, PayPal works faster than on Blockchain, but Blockchain has become competitive in scalable issues using the Directed Acyclic Graph (DAG). In addition, AI also empowered BT to simplify decisions and optimize higher performance than human operations [96]. Moreover, the AI algorithm enhanced the query performance of Blockchain [103]. In reverse, cyber security issues of IT accused of AI were dismantled and found irrelevant in a few cases. Hence, the potentiality of AI is workable to reshape Blockchain and contributes to related fields to a greater extent.

By contrast, how AI surmounts the issues of BT, and the dependency of both technologies has a history of inter-dependency between them. On the present technical surface, their integration enhances data aegis by retaining individual privacy and granting people control over their data. Subject to novel possibilities, BT and AI integration can improve data protection by maintaining individual privacy and giving people control over their data [23]. Additionally, AI-powered systems swiftly detect and respond to online threats, for instance, by accurately detecting proof of stake systems in real-time [61]. AI maintains globally distributed, scalable, and affordable computing capacity to accommodate enormous volumes of data, once more adopting a cloud technology approach. On the other side, by adding digital signatures at the end of the Blockchain and reducing the time between blocks, throughput can be significantly boosted, and latency can be substantially decreased while maintaining decentralization [66].

6 Conclusions

AI-based BT has been accelerating the database structure and recording unanimously by connecting everything from day-to-day affairs. While this achievement has fluctuated due to many issues and its varied existence in the industry, it must be tackled to better smooth, secure and risk-free transactions. This paper's advantages and challenges must be unconditionally fragmented to update current AI and Blockchain-based applications and their key features. This study considers literature review-based 'quality evaluations' in a widespread phenomenon concerning the limitations of Blockchain [21, 23, 24, 43, 46]. This study established blockchain problems and obstacles to illustrate the standard features and applications. Besides, potential researchers may consider an in-depth analysis of each sector to include a new approach to finding suitable solutions. Moreover, this study's multifaceted philosophies will give investors, practitioners, and academics considerable learning. In this regard, the comprehensive analysis of these variables' direct and indirect effects will boost the Blockchain and AI without any potential bias.

6.1 Future Trends of Blockchain Research and AI

Future research contributions go with smart-contract, cryptocurrency, permissioned and public Blockchain, distributed ledger, and disruptive technology depending on the research area and themes. These are differential contributions related to domains based on suitable technology fit within the sector. Still, for future fellow researchers, the challenges and future trends are diverted to BT adoption. The systematic procedures and legislation are still under the development process for a few of the sectors. While this article depicted a flavour of Blockchain-based applications and technological advancements, it is still a long way to go.

References

1. Shabbir, J., Anwer, T.: Artificial intelligence and its role in near future (2018). arXiv preprint arXiv:1804.01396
2. Vinuesa, R., et al.: The role of artificial intelligence in achieving the sustainable development goals. Nat. Commun. **11**(1), 1–10 (2020)
3. Atlam, H.F., Alenezi, A., Alassafi, M.O., Wills, G.: Blockchain with internet of things: benefits, challenges, and future directions. Int. J. Intell. Syst. Appl. **10**(6), 40–48 (2018)
4. Nerini, F.F., et al.: Connecting climate action with other sustainable development goals. Nature Sustainabil. **2**(8), 674–680 (2019)

5. Sena, V., Nocker, M.: AI and business models: the good, the bad and the ugly. Found. Trends® Technol. Inf. Oper. Manag. **14**(4), 324–397 (2021)
6. Gupta, S., et al.: Assessing whether artificial intelligence is an enabler or an inhibitor of sustainability at the indicator level. Transp. Eng. **4**, 100064 (2021)
7. Di Silvestre, M.L., et al.: Blockchain for power systems: current trends and future applications. Renew. Sustain. Energy Rev. **119**, 109585 (2020)
8. Risius, M., Spohrer, K.: A blockchain research framework. Bus. Inf. Syst. Eng. **59**(6), 385–409 (2017)
9. Greenblatt, D.J., et al.: Gender differences in pharmacokinetics and pharmacodynamics of zolpidem following sublingual administration. J. Clin. Pharmacol. **54**(3), 282–290 (2014)
10. Tanwar, S., Parekh, K., Evans, R.: Blockchain-based electronic healthcare record system for healthcare 4.0 applications. J. Inf. Secur. Appl. **50**, 102407 (2020)
11. Nassar, M., Salah, K., Rehman, M.H., Svetinovic, D.: Blockchain for explainable and trust-worthy artificial intelligence. Wiley Interdisc. Rev.: Data Min. Knowl. Disc. **10**(1), e1340 (2020)
12. Frank, M.R., Wang, D., Cebrian, M., Rahwan, I.: The evolution of citation graphs in artificial intelligence research. Nature Mach. Intell. **1**(2), 79–85 (2019)
13. Nakamoto, S.: Bitcoin: A Peer-to-Peer Electronic Cash System (2008). https://bitcoin.org/bitcoin.pdf
14. Underwood, S.: Blockchain beyond bitcoin. Commun. ACM **59**(11), 15–17 (2016)
15. Tandon, A., Kaur, P., Mäntymäki, M., Dhir, A.: Blockchain applications in management: a bibliometric analysis and literature review. Technol. Forecast. Soc. Chang. **166**, 120649 (2021)
16. Jiang, S., et al.: Policy assessments for the carbon emission flow and sustainability of Bitcoin blockchain operation in China. Nat. Commun. **12**(1), 1–10 (2021)
17. Lee, S., Kim, M., Lee, J., Hsu, R.H., Quek, T.Q.: Is blockchain suitable for data freshness? an age-of-information perspective. IEEE Netw. **35**(2), 96–103 (2021)
18. Wang, Y., Chen, C.H., Zghari-Sales, A.: Designing a blockchain-enabled supply chain. Int. J. Prod. Res. **59**(5), 1450–1475 (2021)
19. Garg, P., Gupta, B., Chauhan, A.K., Sivarajah, U., Gupta, S., Modgil, S.: Measuring the perceived benefits of implementing blockchain technology in the banking sector. Technol. Forecast. Soc. Chang. **163**, 120407 (2021)
20. Saurabh, S., Dey, K.: Blockchain technology adoption, architecture, and sustainable agri-food supply chains. J. Clean. Prod. **284**, 124731 (2021)
21. Casino, F., Dasaklis, T.K., Patsakis, C.: A systematic literature review of blockchain-based applications: current status, classification and open issues. Telemat. Inf. **36**, 55–81 (2019)
22. Novotny, P., et al.: Permissioned blockchain technologies for academic publishing. Inf. Serv. Use **38**(3), 159–171 (2018)
23. Ante, L., Steinmetz, F., Fiedler, I.: Blockchain and energy: a bibliometric analysis and review. Renew. Sustain. Energy Rev. **137**, 110597 (2021)
24. Lone, A.H., Naaz, R.: Applicability of blockchain smart contracts in securing internet and IoT: a systematic literature review. Comput. Sci. Rev. **39**, 100360 (2021)
25. Ferreira Santana, F., Mira da Silva, M. and Galvão da Cunha, F., 2021. Blockchain for Real Estate: A Systematic Literature Review
26. Briner, R.B., Denyer, D.: Systematic review and evidence synthesis as a practice and schol-arship tool. In: Handbook of Evidence-Based Management: Companies, Classrooms and Research, pp. 112–129 (2012)
27. Kitchenham, B., Charters, S.: Guidelines for performing systematic literature reviews in software engineering. Engineering **2**, 1051 (2007)

28. Borges, A.F., Laurindo, F.J., Spínola, M.M., Gonçalves, R.F., Mattos, C.A.: The strategic use of artificial intelligence in the digital era: systematic literature review and future research directions. Int. J. Inf. Manag. **57**, 102225 (2021)
29. Shamsuddoha, M., Kashem, M.A.: A revolutionary paradigm shift in supply chain management: the blockchain mechanism. Explor. Latest Trends Manag. Literat. **1**, 15–33 (2022)
30. Deer, M.S., Al-Mejibli, I., Yassin, A.T.: Money Transfer System Using BT: A Case Study of Banks in Iraq (2020). http://www.xajzkjdx.cn/gallery/313-mar2020.pdf. Accessed 29 May 2022
31. Chen, Y., Bellavitis, C.: Blockchain disruption and decentralized finance: the rise of decentralized business models. J. Bus. Ventur. Insights **13**, e00151 (2020)
32. Raikwar, M., Mazumdar, S., Ruj, S., Gupta, S.S., Chattopadhyay, A., Lam, K.Y.: A blockchain framework for insurance processes. In: 2018 9th IFIP International Conference on New Technologies, Mobility and Security (NTMS), pp. 1–4. IEEE (2018)
33. Al-Shaibani, H., Lasla, N., Abdallah, M.: Consortium blockchain-based decentralized stock exchange platform. IEEE Access **8**, 123711–123725 (2020)
34. Ashta, A., Herrmann, H.: Artificial intelligence and fintech: an overview of opportunities and risks for banking, investments, and microfinance. Strateg. Chang. **30**(3), 211–222 (2021)
35. Kumari, J.P.: Instrument development of microfinance on poverty reduction: pilot study in Sri Lankan microfinance sector (2021)
36. Turchin, A.: Assessing the future plausibility of catastrophically dangerous AI. Futures **107**, 45–58 (2019)
37. Makridakis, S.: The forthcoming Artificial Intelligence (AI) revolution: its impact on society and firms. Futures **90**, 46–60 (2017)
38. Payne, E.H.M., Peltier, J., Barger, V.A.: Enhancing the value co-creation process: artificial intelligence and mobile banking service platforms. J. Res. Interact. Mark. (2021)
39. Singh, A., Rajak, R., Mistry, H., Raut, P.: Aid, charity and donation tracking system using Blockchain. In: 2020 4th International Conference on Trends in Electronics and Informatics (ICOEI), vol. 48184, pp. 457–462. IEEE (2020)
40. Eling, M., Nuessle, D., Staubli, J.: The impact of artificial intelligence along the insurance value chain and on the insurability of risks. The Geneva Papers on Risk and Insurance-Issues and Practice, pp. 1–37 (2021)
41. Grima, S., Spiteri, J., Romānova, I.: A STEEP framework analysis of the key factors impacting the use of blockchain technology in the insurance industry. Geneva Papers Risk Insur.-Issues Pract. **45**(3), 398–425 (2020)
42. Dashkevich, N., Counsell, S., Destefanis, G.: Blockchain application for central banks: a systematic mapping study. IEEE Access **8**, 139918–139952 (2020)
43. Frizzo-Barker, J., Chow-White, P.A., Adams, P.R., Mentanko, J., Ha, D., Green, S.: Blockchain as a disruptive technology for business: a systematic review. Int. J. Inf. Manag. **51**, 102029 (2020)
44. Riasanow, T., Jäntgen, L., Hermes, S., Böhm, M., Krcmar, H.: Core, intertwined, and ecosystem-specific clusters in platform ecosystems: analyzing similarities in the digital transformation of the automotive, Blockchain, financial, insurance and IIoT industry. Electron. Mark. **31**(1), 89–104 (2021)
45. Shin, D., Shim, J.: A systematic review on data mining for mathematics and science education. Int. J. Sci. Math. Educ. **19**(4), 639–659 (2020). https://doi.org/10.1007/s10763-020-10085-7
46. Suankaewmanee, K., Hoang, D.T., Niyato, D., Sawadsitang, S., Wang, P., Han, Z.: Performance analysis and application of mobile Blockchain. In: 2018 International Conference on Computing, Networking and Communications (ICNC), pp. 642–646. IEEE (2018)

47. Haefner, N., Wincent, J., Parida, V., Gassmann, O.: Artificial intelligence and innovation management: a review, framework, and research agenda. Technol. Forecast. Soc. Chang. **162**, 120392 (2021)
48. Balakrishnan, J., Dwivedi, Y.K.: Conversational commerce: entering the next stage of AI-powered digital assistants. Ann. Oper. Res., 1–35 (2021)
49. Du, S., Xie, C.: Paradoxes of artificial intelligence in consumer markets: ethical challenges and opportunities. J. Bus. Res. **129**, 961–974 (2021)
50. Harish, A.R., Liu, X.L., Zhong, R.Y., Huang, G.Q.: Log-flock: a blockchain-enabled platform for digital asset valuation and risk assessment in E-commerce logistics financing. Comput. Ind. Eng. **151**, 107001 (2021)
51. Treleaven, P., Barnett, J., Knight, A., Serrano, W.: Real estate data marketplace. AI Ethics **1**(4), 445–462 (2021). https://doi.org/10.1007/s43681-021-00053-4
52. Sun, J., Yan, J., Zhang, K.Z.K.: Blockchain-based sharing services: What blockchain technology can contribute to smart cities. Finan. Innov. **2**(1), 1–9 (2016). https://doi.org/10.1186/s40854-016-0040-y
53. Koeleman, J., Ribeirinho, M.J., Rockhill, D., Sjödin, E., Strube, G.: Decoding digital transformation in construction| McKinsey. McKinsey Co. (2019)
54. Perera, S., Nanayakkara, S., Rodrigo, M.N.N., Senaratne, S., Weinand, R.: Blockchain technology: is it hype or real in the construction industry. J. Ind. Inf. Integr. **17**, 100125 (2020)
55. Nasarre-Aznar, S.: Collaborative housing and Blockchain **66**(2), 59–82 (2018)
56. Ullah, F., Al-Turjman, F.: A conceptual framework for blockchain smart contract adoption to manage real estate deals in smart cities. Neural Comput. Appl., 1–22 (2021)
57. Fields, D., Rogers, D.: Towards a critical housing studies research agenda on platform real estate. Hous. Theory Soc. **38**(1), 72–94 (2021)
58. Aalbers, M.B., Christophers, B.: Centring Housing in political economy. Hous. Theory Soc. **31**(4), 373–394 (2014)
59. Pace, A.: Mathematics, Cryptography, Blockchains, and Cryptocurrencies: Myths and Realities (2019). https://indico.cern.ch/event/848910/. Accessed 28 May 2022
60. Schär, F., Schuler, K., Wagner, T.: Blockchain vending machine: a smart contract-based peer-to-peer marketplace for physical goods2020
61. Perez-Vega, R., Kaartemo, V., Lages, C.R., Razavi, N.B., Männistö, J.: Reshaping the contexts of online customer engagement behavior via artificial intelligence: a conceptual framework. J. Bus. Res. **129**, 902–910 (2021)
62. Adhikari, B.: Use of screen media and mental health: effects on adolescents and pre-adolescents. J. Nepal Med. Assoc. **59**(241), 962–964 (2021)
63. Hwang, G.J., Xie, H., Wah, B.W., Gašević, D.: Vision, challenges, roles and research issues of Artificial Intelligence in Education (2020)
64. Sasaki, A., et al.: A study on the development of tourist support system using ICT and psychological effects. Appl. Sci. **10**(24), 8930 (2020)
65. Kaplan, A., Haenlein, M.: Rulers of the world, unite! the challenges and opportunities of artificial intelligence. Bus. Horiz. **63**(1), 37–50 (2020)
66. Valeri, M., Baggio, R.: A critical reflection on the adoption of Blockchain in tourism. Inf. Technol. Tour. **23**(2), 121–132 (2021)
67. Tuo, Y., Ning, L., Zhu, A.: How artificial intelligence will change the future of tourism industry: the practice in China. In: Wörndl, W., Koo, C., Stienmetz, J.L. (eds.) Information and Communication Technologies in Tourism 2021, pp. 83–94. Springer, Cham (2021). https://doi.org/10.1007/978-3-030-65785-7_7
68. Choi, T.M., Guo, S., Luo, S.: When Blockchain meets social-media: will the result benefit social media analytics for supply chain operations management? Transp. Res. Part E: Logist. Transp. Rev. **135**, 101860 (2020)

69. Bilow, S.C.: Introduction: blockchain in media and entertainment. SMPTE Motion Imag. J. **129**(1), 20–21 (2020)
70. Crook, N., Nugent, S., Rolf, M., Baimel, A., Raper, R.: Computing morality: synthetic ethical decision making and behaviour, pp. 79–82 (2021)
71. Lam, T.Y., Dongol, B.: A blockchain-enabled e-learning platform. In: Interactive Learning Environments, pp. 1–23 (2020)
72. Ouyang, F., Jiao, P.: Artificial intelligence in education: the three paradigms. Comput. Educ.: Artif. Intell. **2**, 100020 (2021)
73. Tsiulin, S., Reinau, K.H., Hilmola, O.P., Goryaev, N., Karam, A.: Blockchain-based applications in shipping and port management: a literature review towards defining key conceptual frameworks. Rev. Int. Bus. Strat. **30**, 201–224 (2020)
74. Meroni, G., Baresi, L., Montali, M., Plebani, P.: Multi-party business process compliance monitoring through IoT-enabled artifacts. Inf. Syst. **73**, 61–78 (2018)
75. Li, C., Chu, M., Zhou, C., Xie, W.: A 2020 perspective on "'Is it always advantageous to add on item recommendation service with a contingent free shipping policy in platform retailing?'" Electron. Commer. Res. Appl. **40**, 100960 (2020)
76. Chang, S.E., Chen, Y.C., Lu, M.F.: Supply chain re-engineering using blockchain technology: a case of smart contract-based tracking process. Technol. Forecast. Soc. Chang. **144**, 1–11 (2019)
77. Issaoui, Y., Khiat, A., Bahnasse, A., Ouajji, H.: Toward smart logistics: engineering insights and emerging trends. Arch. Comput. Methods Eng. **28**(4), 3183–3210 (2021)
78. Shankar, V., et al.: How technology is changing retail. J. Retail. **97**(1), 13–27 (2021)
79. Watson, R.T., Lind, M., Delmeire, N., Liesa, F.: Shipping: a self-organising ecosystem. In: Lind, M., Michaelides, M., Ward, R., Watson, R.T. (eds.) Maritime informatics. PI, pp. 13–32. Springer, Cham (2021). https://doi.org/10.1007/978-3-030-50892-0_2
80. Toorajipour, R., Sohrabpour, V., Nazarpour, A., Oghazi, P., Fischl, M.: Artificial intelligence in supply chain management: a systematic literature review. J. Bus. Res. **122**, 502–517 (2021)
81. Pournader, M., Shi, Y., Seuring, S., Koh, S.L.: Blockchain applications in supply chains, transport and logistics: a systematic review of the literature. Int. J. Prod. Res. **58**(7), 2063–2081 (2020)
82. Mendling, J., et al.: Blockchains for business process management-challenges and opportunities. ACM Trans. Manag. Inf. Syst. (TMIS) **9**(1), 1–16 (2018)
83. Beverungen, D., et al.: Seven paradoxes of business process management in a hyperconnected world. Bus. Inf. Syst. Eng. **63**(2), 145–156 (2021)
84. Benítez-Martínez, F.L., Hurtado-Torres, M.V., Romero-Frías, E.: A neural blockchain for a tokenizable e-Participation model. Neurocomputing **423**, 703–712 (2021)
85. Khayyat, M., Alhemdi, F., Alnunu, R.: The challenges and benefits of blockchain in E-government. IJCSNS **20**(4), 15 (2020)
86. Yousuf, H., Zainal, A.Y., Alshurideh, M., Salloum, S.A.: Artificial intelligence models in power system analysis. In: Hassanien, A.E., Bhatnagar, R., Darwish, A. (eds.) Artificial Intelligence for Sustainable Development: Theory, Practice and Future Applications. SCI, vol. 912, pp. 231–242. Springer, Cham (2021). https://doi.org/10.1007/978-3-030-51920-9_12
87. Leone, D., Schiavone, F., Appio, F.P., Chiao, B.: How does artificial intelligence enable and enhance value co-creation in industrial markets? an exploratory case study in the healthcare ecosystem. J. Bus. Res. **129**, 849–859 (2021)
88. Rouzbahani, H.M., Karimipour, H., Dehghantanha, A., Parizi, R.M.: Blockchain applications in power systems: a bibliometric analysis (2020)
89. Cho, S., Mossberger, K., Swindell, D., Selby, J.D.: Experimenting with public engagement platforms in local government. Urban Aff. Rev. **57**(3), 763–793 (2021)

90. Roberts, H., Cowls, J., Morley, J., Taddeo, M., Wang, V., Floridi, L.: The Chinese approach to artificial intelligence: an analysis of policy, ethics, and regulation. AI & Soc. **36**(1), 59–77 (2020). https://doi.org/10.1007/s00146-020-00992-2

91. Dubey, R., Bryde, D.J., Foropon, C., Tiwari, M., Dwivedi, Y., Schiffling, S.: An investigation of information alignment and collaboration as complements to supply chain agility in humanitarian supply chain. Int. J. Prod. Res. **59**(5), 1586–1605 (2021)

92. Sun, W., Bocchini, P., Davison, B.D.: Resilience metrics and measurement methods for transportation infrastructure: state of the art. Sustain. Resil. Infrastruct. **5**(3), 168–199 (2020)

93. Collins, C., Dennehy, D., Conboy, K., Mikalef, P.: Artificial intelligence in information systems research: a systematic literature review and research agenda. Int. J. Inf. Manag. **60**, 102383 (2021)

94. Sipior, J.C.: Considerations for development and use of AI in response to COVID-19. Int. J. Inf. Manage. **55**, 102170 (2020)

95. Singh, H.J., Hafid, A.S.: Prediction of transaction confirmation time in Ethereum blockchain using machine learning. In: Prieto, J., Das, A.K., Ferretti, S., Pinto, A., Corchado, J.M. (eds.) BLOCKCHAIN 2019. AISC, vol. 1010, pp. 126–133. Springer, Cham (2019). https://doi.org/10.1007/978-3-030-23813-1_16

96. Zhang, J., Yalcin, M.G., Hales, D.N.: Elements of paradoxes in supply chain management literature: a systematic literature review. Int. J. Prod. Econ. **232**, 107928 (2021)

97. Pan, Y., Zhang, L.: Roles of artificial intelligence in construction engineering and management: a critical review and future trends. Autom. Constr. **122**, 103517 (2021)

98. Prada-Delgado, M.Á., Baturone, I., Dittmann, G., Jelitto, J., Kind, A.: PUF-derived IoT identities in a zero-knowledge protocol for Blockchain. Internet of Things **9**, 100057 (2020)

99. Liu, Y., Li, Y., Lin, S.W., Yan, Q.: ModCon: a model-based testing platform for smart contracts. In: Proceedings of the 28th ACM Joint Meeting on European Software Engineering Conference and Symposium on the Foundations of Software Engineering, pp. 1601–1605 (2020)

100. Lin, C., He, D., Huang, X., Khan, M.K., Choo, K.K.R.: DCAP: A secure and efficient decentralized conditional anonymous payment system based on Blockchain. IEEE Trans. Inf. Forensics Secur. **15**, 2440–2452 (2020)

101. Yang, K., Jiang, T., Shi, Y., Ding, Z.: Federated learning via over-the-air computation. IEEE Trans. Wirel. Commun. **19**(3), 2022–2035 (2020)

102. Zheng, Q., et al.: Artificial intelligence performance in detecting tumour metastasis from medical radiology imaging: a systematic review and meta-analysis. EClinicalMedicine **31**, 100669 (2021)

103. Gawas, M., Patil, H., Govekar, S.S.: An integrative approach for secure data sharing in vehicular edge computing using Blockchain. Peer-to-Peer Netw. Appl. **14**(5), 2840–2857 (2021). https://doi.org/10.1007/s12083-021-01107-4

Distributed Secure Data Aggregation for Smart Grid Using Partial Homomorphic Encryption

Aniket Agrawal[1], Kamalakanta Sethi[2(✉)], Kasturi Routray[1], and Padmalochan Bera[1]

[1] Indian Institute of Technology, Bhubaneswar, India
{aa22,s21ee09001,plb}@iitbbs.ac.in
[2] Indian Institute of Information Technology, Sri City, India
kamalakanta.s@iiits.in

Abstract. Today, smart grid advanced metering infrastructure (AMI) is a critical cyber-physical system where energy providers generate and distribute energy to different clients depending on their changing demands. Suppliers collect and aggregate energy usage data online for billing, control and statistical analysis. However, performing such operations over an insecure channel exposes the AMI network to various cyberattacks. In this paper, we propose fault-tolerant privacy-enhanced data aggregation scheme for computing total energy consumption at different levels in the smart grid AMI network. First, a trusted authority (TA) initiates the operation by constructing a client-server tree and assigning pseudonyms to the existing members. Here, the client refers to the data generator who introduce random noise into their power consumption readings. Then, they use Paillier homomorphic encryption to facilitate the additive computability and secrecy of their reading data. They sign their ciphertexts to enable its integrity verification. The successfully verified ciphers are progressively aggregated by their parent servers. Finally, the root server delegates the final aggregate decryption to TA. The distributed architecture of our scheme supports pseudonymized data processing from multiple participants. We present the experimental results and security proofs to demonstrate the usability of our scheme.

Keywords: Smart grid · Paillier homomorphic encryption · Fault tolerance · Pseudonymization · Random noise

1 Introduction

Smart grid advanced metering infrastructure (AMI) employs networking and communication technologies that integrate digital smart metres for scalable, demand-driven and intelligent delivery power to the consumers. It allows service providers to collect the energy usage data for control, understanding consumption pattern and investigating malicious activities. As a result, these data-driven

I. Woungang et al. (Eds.): ANTIC 2022, CCIS 1797, pp. 495–510, 2023.
https://doi.org/10.1007/978-3-031-28180-8_33

insights are one of the principal benefits provided by the smart grid and a major concern in terms of client privacy breaches [1]. Furthermore, adversaries may launch or introduce various forms of cyberattacks such as false data injection (FDI), where they manipulate large volumes of power statistics in their favour [2]. This may potentially cause significant damage to the AMI network to the extent of power outages. Therefore, there is a need for privacy enhanced data aggregation (PEDA) technologies to control various cyberattacks such as FDI, replay [3], impersonation, and so on [4]. The majority of the PEDA schemes exploited the additive homomorphic nature of Paillier [5] and modified Elgamal encryption [6], with a few requiring one extra multiplication employing Boneh-Goh-Nissim (BGN) cryptosystem [7]. [8] proposed a differential privacy based approach for preserving privacy on an individual basis. A few schemes introduced random noise in accordance with a distribution [9], while others performed anonymization [10]. In addition to secrecy, PEDA demands optimization via parallel and efficient cryptographic procedures. A few works applied mathematical techniques such as the Chinese remainder theorem (CRT) [11] and map-reduce framework (MRF) in order to scale a large encryption/decryption problem in terms of its smaller tasks that could be synchronised.

Data aggregation can be performed in a decentralized manner to achieve higher efficiency. The AMI network can be modelled as a graph where data is propagated and aggregated by various nodes in a graph. In general, such graphs reduce to the minimum spanning tree (MST) considering equal weights at different edges involved. Here, it is necessary to reduce the number of iterations of ciphertext propagation and the maximum aggregation cost per node. This requires keeping the height and width of the MST within a bound. However, finding an MST under both constraints is an NP-Complete problem. Therefore, a simple heuristic algorithm was proposed in [12] for efficient re-balancing of the tree. Additionally, fault diagnostics should be emphasized so that the system continues to function even when the intermediate aggregator (IA) or root is out of operation. Also, the ciphertext aggregation and vertical propagation technique must not be impeded by cyberattacks such as distributed denial of service (DDoS) and node overloading. A few schemes [8,12–14] achieved fault tolerance keeping a few or no constraints on the number of malfunctioning metres. The metres may go offline for a short period of time to save energy or become dysfunctional. Binary search based approach was used for abnormal node detection in [12]. In [14], MST fault tolerance is achieved by transmission of a parent request (PR) to the collector on failure in receiving keep-alive messages and broadcast of parent-child association updates to the nodes requesting adjustments. However, none of the existing works use efficient homomorphic encryption with distributed implementation for secure data aggregation in smart grid. Moreover, a majority of them do not consider heterogeneous security violations. In this paper, we present a distributed secure data aggregation scheme for smart grid.

1.1   Contributing Features of Our Proposed PEDA System

The design goal of our proposed scheme is to architect a robust and practical PEDA cryptosystem with the following features:

1) **Decentralized operation:** We construct a data aggregation tree (AT) in a top-down manner. Here, the server spawns a new member thread when a registered client node connects to it. This joining happens on the fly without disturbing the parameters of the system clients. The overall distributed aggregation is multi-threaded, where the leaf and intermediate aggregator (IA) nodes at the lowest level commence their operations in parallel. Moreover, achieving a balanced computational load is essential and requires a constraint relation between the height and maximum degree of a node while keeping an overall number of AT nodes constant. The basis of our mathematical formulation is to minimize the total number of levels or iterations at the expense of a minor increase in total average aggregation cost per node.

2) **Robust security:** We ensure pseudonymity and resilience towards FDI and replay attacks. To achieve individual privacy, clients inject noise following a normal distribution. Also, TA issues a pseudonym or artificial identity (PID) to the client. It establishes a mapping between PID and real ID (RID) for every client. Client j sends data using PID_j while keeping RID_j secrecy against its IA server. For source authentication, IA and TA together are involved in white-box traceability of malicious child nodes.

3) **Fault tolerance:** Our scheme identifies malfunctioning nodes in a decentralized model. We rely on the grandparent node to detect the parent node failure in data aggregation of its child nodes following a timeout. The temporary halt renders this protocol slightly time intensive. However, it does not necessitate regular monitoring and update transmission.

4) **Efficient cryptographic operations:** Our scheme uses additional methods to enhance the efficiency of the following:

    4.1) *Encryption:* The clients leverage the self-blinding property of the Paillier scheme, which requires them to perform costly cipher generation only once. Specifically, they can generate their new ciphers through a simple refresh mechanism.

    4.2) *Outsourced Decryption:* The root node responsible for calculating the total revenue delegates the decryption process to TA having sufficient computational resources. Furthermore, CRT quickens the Paillier decryption by a factor of three.

1.2   Paper Outline

We provide mathematical concepts applied in Sect. 2. In Sect. 3, we present our proposed system design and examine its security and performance in Sects. 4 and 5, respectively. Lastly, we conclude in Sect. 6.

2   Mathematical Background

2.1   Chinese Remainder Theorem (CRT)

It is a number theory theorem which is widely used while dealing with large integers [15]. Given pairwise co-prime positive integers $n_1, n_2, \ldots, n_k$ and arbitrary integers $a_1, a_2, \ldots, a_k$, the system of simultaneous congruences $x \equiv a_1 (\bmod\ n_1), x \equiv a_2 (\bmod\ n_2) \ldots, x \equiv a_k (\bmod\ n_k)$ has a unique solution modulo $n_1.n_2 \ldots n_k$. Hence, it allows replacement with several similar computations on small divisors.

2.2   Paillier Homomorphic Cryptosystem (PHC)

This non-deterministic partial homomorphic cryptosystem [16] involves the first three steps, which are as follows:

1) **Key Generation:** Firstly, two random, large and independent prime numbers p and q are chosen such that $gcd(pq, (p-1)(q-1)) = 1$. Then, $N = p.q$ and Carmichael's function $\lambda(N) = lcm(p - 1, q - 1)$ are computed (Carmichael's theorem: $a^{\lambda(N)} = 1\ mod\ N$ for co-prime integers a and n). A random integer $g \in Z_{N^2}^*$ is selected and $\mu = (L_N(g^\lambda mod\ N^2))^{-1} mod\ N$ is calculated using $L_N(x) = (x - 1)/N$.
   The public key (N, g) and private key (λ, μ) are obtained.
2) **Encryption:** For the given message $m \in Z_N^*$, $r \in Z_{N^2}^*$ is randomly chosen, and encryption is done to get the resultant ciphertext is $E(m) = c = g^m * r^n mod\ n^2$.
3) **Decryption without CRT:** The ciphertext $c \in Z_{N^2}^*$ can be decrypted to get the plaintext m using the private key (λ, μ) as: $m = (L(g^\lambda mod\ N^2)).\mu\ mod\ N$. The random constant can be computed as $r = (c * g^{-m}\ mod\ n)^{n^{-1} mod\ \lambda}\ mod\ n$.
4) **CRT assistance:** The cryptosystem is sped up using CRT (Sect. 7 of [16], [11]) as follows:
   4.1) **Extra pre-calculations for CRT:** Integer N^2 can be factored as $p^2.q^2$ to create two sub-problems for applying CRT. For this, $p' = p^{-1} mod\ q$, $\mu = (L_N(g^\lambda mod\ N^2))^{-1} mod\ N$ $c_p = (L_p(g^{p-1} mod\ p^2))^{-1} mod\ p$ and $c_q = (L_q(g^{q-1} mod\ q^2))^{-1} mod\ p$ are pre-computed.
   4.2) **Decryption using CRT:** Compute $m_p = c^{p-1} mod\ p^2$, $m_q = c^{q-1} mod\ q^2$, $m' = p' * (m_q - m_p)\ mod\ q$ and the plaintext $m = m_p + m'$.
5) **Homomorphic properties:** The encryption and decryption algorithms of the PHC have the following notable properties:
   5.1) **Plaintexts addition:** It allows multiplication of the ciphers to get the decrypted result as the addition of underlying messages i.e., $\forall m_1, m_2 \in M, E(m_1 + m_2) \leftarrow E(m_1) \cdot E(m_2)$.
   5.2) **Plaintext-Cipher multiplication:** A cipher corresponding to m_1 raised to the power of a plaintext m_2 will decrypt to the product of the two plaintexts, $D(E(m_2, r_1)^{m_1} mod\ n^2) = m_1 m_2 mod\ n$.
   5.3) **Self-blinding Feature:** It is easy to generate another cipher decrypting to same message m_1, $D(E(m_1, r_1) * r_2^n mod\ n^2) = D(E(m_1, r_1 * r_2))$.

3   Our Proposed Scheme Methodology

The sequence diagram of our proposed PEDA scheme is shown in Fig. 1. The operation begins with the creation of an aggregation tree (AT) by TA using top-down approach. TA assigns 256-bit pseudonyms or false identities to the new joinees of the created client-server tree after their registration. Threads are spawned for the leaf level clients who encrypt and sign their data. They pass it to their dedicated server parent IA node in parallel for aggregation and integrity verification using signature. The node for which signature verification fails is directed to send the data again by IA. IA reports the node involved in any malicious activity to TA, which then traces and revokes the real identity of the node. The bottom-up aggregation is carried out in a distributed manner until the energy sum cipher reaches the root node. If a node in the live system fails in between, the redundant links of AT allow the children of the failed node to re-route their data. The root node delegates the costly decryption process by outsourcing it to TA assumed to have decent computing power. TA sends the partially decrypted revenue cipher back to the root for final decryption requiring only one operation. The overall procedure is described in Fig. 2. The detailed algorithms are presented in the following subsections:

1) Aggregation tree (AT) and pseudonym creation: It describes how a new node j joins AT of current height h. E and V are the current set of edges and vertices in AT. The trusted authority (TA) having an identity as ID_{TA} provides a pseudonym (PID_j) to the new joinee j taking its real identity (RID_j) as input. All IDs are of size $M = 256$ bits.

1.1) **Dynamic Client Membership:** For controlling AT structure, constraints are placed on the root (R) and other non-leaf intermediate aggregator (IA) nodes under specific conditions. For instance, a bound is imposed on the number of immediate children $|C_x| \leq k * (h + 1)$. Here, $k = 2.5$ for root node $(x = R)$ and $k = 1.33$ and 1.66 (faulty node case) for IA node $(x = IA)$. Here, we assume that IA has weaker computation capability as compared to the R node. The overall procedure is shown in Fig. 3 where the number j on the node represents the order of its joining. Different notations used in the procedure are shown in Table 1 where Lv means level and $G_C = P_{P_C} = P_{U_C}$ is also the parent of P_C and U_C.

1.2) **Pseudonym generate:** TA uses SHA-256 function H and computes $PID_j = (H(ID_{TA}) \oplus RID_j) * ID_{TA} \, mod \, M$ and $Parent(j) = P_j$ stores the registered PID_j. It ensures that client j with (PID_j, RID_j) cannot find ID_{TA} easily.

2) Fault Tolerance: A fault-tolerant tree data structure AT' is created through the addition of redundant links between the two consecutive levels of AT. This is shown in Fig. 3. It is assumed that not more than one in the triplet (G_C, P_C, U_C) concerning C_P are non-functional, simultaneously.

2.1) **Re-construction:** Links are established between level 0 root node R' and C_R. The same is done between $\{C_P\}_{P \neq R}$ at level x and their $|C_P|$ uncle nodes U_{C_P} at level $x - 1$ $(x > 1)$.

2.2) **Diagnosis:** If the root $P_C = R$ node fails or is offline, its sibling uncle nodes $U_C = R'$ adopt the concerned orphans $O = \{1, 2, 3, 4, 5\}$ via their respec-

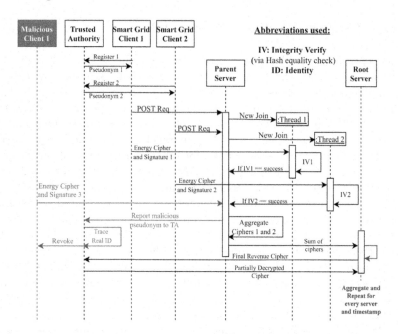

Fig. 1. Our proposed PEDA sequence diagram

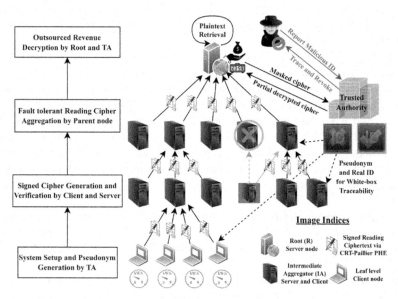

Fig. 2. Our proposed PEDA system design

tive $PIDs$. If the same happens to any IA node $P_C = 3$, $G_C = R$ senses that it is not getting any aggregate data from its child node after a timeout. Hence, it requests the concerned uncle nodes $U_C = \{1, 2, 4, 5\}$ to aggregate the data of

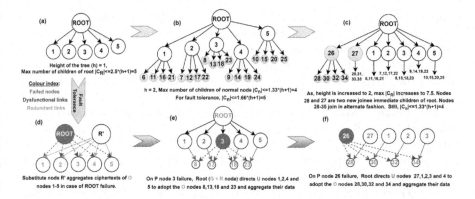

Fig. 3. Aggregation tree creation (a, b, c) and handling faulty node scenarios (d, e, f)

Table 1. Notation table for AT nodes

AT node	Notation	Details/Remarks
Root	R	Aggregate collector node of AT
Child	C_P	Sends its data to P for aggregation
Parent	P_C	$Lv(P_C) = Lv(C_P) - 1$, $(P_C, C_P) \in E$
Uncle	U_C	$Lv(U_C) = Lv(P_C)$, $(P_C, U_C) \notin E$
Grandparent	G_C	$Lv(G_C) = Lv(P_C) - 1$, $(G_C, P_C) \in E$
Orphan	O	It's parent P_O is offline temporarily

the orphans $O = \{8, 13, 18, 23\}$, taking into account their corresponding $PIDs$, respectively.

2.3) **Restoration:** AT retains its original state prior to the node failure and continues to function normally when the faulty node resurrects and resumes transmitting its data later.

3) Ciphertext and Signature generation: TA chooses two 512-bit prime numbers p and q. It calculates its Paillier public key $(N = p*q, g)$ where $g \in Z^*_{N^2}$ and private key (λ, μ). Power consumption data m_{ij} of node j at the 32-bit timestamp TS_j is encrypted to create the ciphertext c_{ij} and signature s_{ij}.

3.1) **Encrypt:** At the location of j, the noise following normal distribution $n_{ij} \sim N(0, \sigma_x^2)$ is added to the electricity consumption data $m_{ij} \in Z^*_N$. A random integer $r_{ij} \in Z^*_N$ is chosen to encrypt the noisy electricity consumption data $m'_{ij} = m_{ij} + n_{ij}$ at the timestamp TS_i to generate the 2048-bit ciphertext: $c_{ij} = g^{m'_{ij}} \cdot (r_{ij})^N \bmod N^2$.

3.2) **Sign:** Node j generates the 256-bit signature $s_{ij} = H(c_{ij}||TS_i||PID_j)$ and sends (c_{ij}, s_{ij}) to its parent P_j.

3.3) **Refresh:** Using same r_{ij} again at $TS_{i'}$ leaks information about the differential $c_{i'j}/c_{ij} = g^{m_{i'j}-m_{ij}}$. So, from the next timestamp $TS_{i'=i+1}$ onwards for a message $m_{i'j}$, j can use an 8-bit self-blinding integer $z_{i'j}$ and pre-computed ciphertext of zero $E(0) = (r_{ij})^N \bmod N^2$ to obfuscate $c_{i'j}$ as $c_{i'j} = g^{m_{i'j}} * E(0)^{z_{i'j}} \bmod N^2$ to combat the cryptanalysis. Here, $c_{i'j}$ is also a legal Paillier ciphertext with random integer $r_{i'j} = r_{ij}^{z_{i'j}}$.

4) Signed Cipher Processing: After receiving (c_{ij}, s_{ij}), $P_j = Parent(j)$ ensures the integrity of c_{ij} by the aid of s_{ij}. Successful verification is followed by aggregation.

4.1) *Verification:* Decentralized database independently managed by P_j contains IDs for all the registered $C_{P_j} = \{x_j\} \forall j \in [|C_{P_j}|]$ nodes. For the entries having a valid PID, P_j checks whether $H(c_{ij}||TS_i||PID_j) = s_{ij}$. Aggregation is performed if equality is satisfied for all the legitimate C_{P_j} nodes. If not, node j is directed to send its data again.

4.2) *Trace:* This procedure is called if the data is sent from the very same pseudonym PID_j more than once. TA traces and revokes the real identity RID_j corresponding to the leaked pseudonym PID_j of the malicious node i as $RID_j = (PID_j * ID_{TA}^{-1}) \oplus H(ID_{TA}) \bmod M$.

4.3) *Summation:* After P_i gets the correct data, it aggregates the data of itself and its $|C_{P_i}|$ immediate child nodes as:

$$C_{P_i} = c_{P_i} \prod_{j=1}^{|C_{P_i}|} c_{x_j} = c_{P_i} \cdot \prod_{j=1}^{|C_{P_i}|} g^{m'_{x_j}} \cdot (\prod_{j=1}^{|C_{P_i}|} r_{x_j})^N \bmod N^2$$

$$= g^{\sum_{j=1}^{|C_{P_i}|} m'_{x_j} + m'_{P_i}} \cdot (r_{P_i} * \prod_{j=1}^{|C_{P_i}|} r_{x_j})^N \bmod N^2$$

Note: It hashes it using step 2 of algorithm 3 and sends it to its parent P_{P_i}. The procedure is repeated until the aggregate ciphertext reaches level 1 nodes of AT having parent as R.

5) Final Computation: R node follows the previous step to get the level 1 aggregate cipher CP_0 at timestamp TS_0. It repeats this procedure for other timestamps for total aggregation and relies on TA for outsourced decryption.

5.1) *Masked Aggregation:* R gathers the ciphers for t timestamps each having 7-bit electricity cost $\{p_i\}_{i \in [t]}$ associated with it. It computes the aggregate encrypted revenue R_{AT} as, $R'_{AT} = \prod_{i=0}^{t-1} CP_i^{p_i}$. It chooses a random $w \in Z_N^*$ and uses it as an exponent to mask R'_{AT} as $Z_{AT} = R_{AT}'^w = \prod_{i=0}^{t-1} CP_i^{p_i * w}$. It outsources Z_{AT} to TA.

5.2) *Verifiable Decryption:* TA uses its private key (λ, μ) to obtain the partially decrypted revenue cipher $Z'_{AT} = Dec(Z_{AT}) = w * \prod_{i=0}^{t-1} (p_i * \sum_{j=1}^{|V|-1} m'_{i,j})$ (₹) which it sends back to R. Its correctness can be verified through an efficient procedure described in Sect. 5.2 of [18].

5.3) *Revenue Retrieval:* R fully decrypts Z'_{AT} using w to get the noisy summed revenue plaintext $Dec(Z_{AT})/w$ which differs from the accurate total RV_{AT} (₹) by temporal price weighted quotient $= (\prod_{i=0}^{t-1} (p_i * \sum_{j=1}^{|V|-1} n_{i,j}))/RV_{AT} \approx 0\%$.

4   Security Analysis

Security assumption: Semi-trusted IA nodes do not aggregate the data of illegal pseudonym holders and are expected to report it to the TA. They do not conspire with their child nodes C_{IA} to report fraudulent verification status. Also, they are assumed not to leak $PIDs$ of their children $PID_{C_{IA}}$ or adopted orphans (faulty node case).

1) **Eavesdropping Prevention:** The semantically secure Paillier ciphertext c_{ij} is indistinguishable under chosen plaintext attack (IND-CPA). It ensures the confidentiality of the plaintext $m'_{ij} = m_{ij} + n_{ij}$ against the channel eavesdropper as per Decisional Diffie-Hellman (DDH) assumption (Theorem 1 of [16]). Also, the refreshed ciphertext $c_{i'j}$ corresponding to the message $m_{i'j}$ uses secretive $z_{i'j}$ at time $TS_{i'>i}$. Even though R outsources decryption to TA, it maintains confidentiality against TA because of its retrieval key w unknown to TA. Also, there is no need for TA to reveal the private key to R.

2) **Robustness and Data Integrity:** Each node i hashes c_{ij} with TS_i. Any online data modification or injection of false data by the adversary can be efficiently detected by the IA nodes through a hash equality check. This ensures the integrity and authenticity of the power data m'_{ij} generated at fresh timestamps to prevent FDI and replay attacks.

3) **Non-repudiation and White-box Traceability:** Node i cannot deny the ownership of ciphertext c_{ij} as the signature s_{ij} carries PID_j not known to anyone except P_i and TA. So, it rules out any impersonation by the siblings of i as they are assumed to be oblivious of PID_j. Also, TA can authenticate the real source identifier (RID_j), assuring ciphertext non-repudiation and traceability.

4) **DoS and Sybil attack:** If a node i intends to overload the network by sending data via illegal re-use of the very same PID_j or creation of multiple fake $PIDs$, its semi-trusted parent node P_i discovers it through a small database storing valid child $PIDs$. After receiving the reports from P_i, TA invalidates the ID via a RID trace.

5) **Individual Privacy and Pseudonymity:** The linkage between the data m'_{ij} and the real sender identity (RID_j) is broken, and m'_{ij} is associated with PID_j. The PID_j cannot be easily determined given signature-cipher pair (s_{ij}, c_{ij}) at a given timestamp TS_i. Only a valid decryption key λ known to R can recover the aggregate of the power consumption ciphers. If it colludes with any IA node to decrypt individual ciphertext $c_{C_{IA}}$, it will get a noisy and pseudonymized message $m'_{C_{IA}}$, ensuring data privacy. The differential attack launched by taking the difference of aggregate ciphers from two servers is also countered.

6) **Decentralized Fault Tolerance:** The situation involving a faulty node is tackled via a mechanism securely. This is under the assumptions pertaining to the siblings of the failed node which appends the PID entry of the affected orphan to their database.

5   Performance Analysis

5.1   Simulation Tool, Platform and Device

The proposed PEDA employs a discrete-event network simulator NS-3.35 and python API of mosaik 3.0.0, a co-simulation framework for the smart grid. The network simulation is visualized through NetAnim which is an offline animator based on the multi-platform Qt4 GUI toolkit. We used Google Colab Notebook (MxNet) to simulate parallel cipher aggregation in the distributed architecture via encryption on the client GPUs followed by aggregation on the server CPU. For supporting fast multiple-precision arithmetic, gmpy2 module is used. The experiments are run on Ubuntu 20:04:2 LTS WSL system having an Intel Core(TM) i3-5005U CPU @ 2.00 GHz x64-based processor, 4.00 GB RAM.

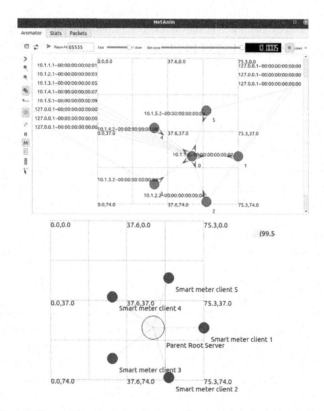

Fig. 4. Star AMI network topology visualization and simulation

In our scheme, star topology is the best way to visualize the network creation as shown in Fig. 4. For this, an XML trace file is generated using NetAnim and NS-3.35. Here, a new smart meter client node intends to join its corresponding parent server with specific IP and MAC addresses. The parallel communication

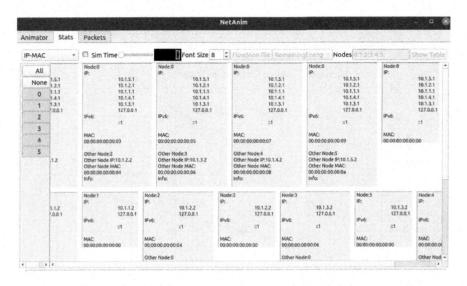

Fig. 5. Simulation results: packet routing statistics

between the five client and the root server node of AT is simulated and the statistics are shown in Fig. 5.

5.2   Theoretical Implementation Analysis

The maximum number of meter clients $f(h)$ in a complete AT of height h is computed as:

$$f(h) = Max(|V|_{actual} - 1) = \lfloor r_R \rfloor + \lfloor r_R \rfloor . \lfloor r_{IA} \rfloor + \lfloor r_R \rfloor . \lfloor r_{IA} \rfloor^2$$

$$+ \lfloor r_R \rfloor . \lfloor r_{IA} \rfloor^{h-1} = \lfloor r_R \rfloor . (1 + \lfloor r_{IA} \rfloor + \lfloor r_{IA} \rfloor^2 + \ldots + \lfloor r_{IA} \rfloor^{h-1})$$

$$= \lfloor r_R \rfloor . \frac{\lfloor r_{IA} \rfloor^h - 1}{\lfloor r_{IA} \rfloor - 1} = \lfloor 2.5.(h+1) \rfloor . \frac{\lfloor 1.33.(h+1) \rfloor^h - 1}{\lfloor 1.33.(h+1) \rfloor - 1}$$

With the help of above mentioned formula, the physical parameters of AT are computed and shown graphically on logarithmic scale in Fig. 6. It is trivial that a node cannot join in segments and must do so in its entirety. This condition can be ignored in order to weakly approximate the relation between $|V|_{max}$ and h.

$$g(h) = Max(|V|_{Approx} - 1) = r_R + r_R.r_{IA} + \ldots + r_R.r_{IA}{}^{h-1}$$

$$= 2.5.(h+1) + 2.5 * 1.33.(h+1)^2 + \ldots + 2.5 * 1.33^{h-1}.(h+1)^h$$

$$= 2.5.(h+1). \frac{1.33^h.(h+1)^h - 1}{1.33.(h+1) - 1} \approx \frac{2.5.(h+1)^{h+1}.1.33^h}{10^c.(1.33.h + 0.33)}$$

$$\approx \frac{\frac{5}{2}.(h+1)^{h+1}.(\frac{4}{3})^h}{10^c.(\frac{4}{3}.h + \frac{1}{3})} \approx \frac{5.2^{2h-1}.((h+1))^{h+1}}{10^c.(3)^{h-1}.(4.h + 1)} (c > 1)$$

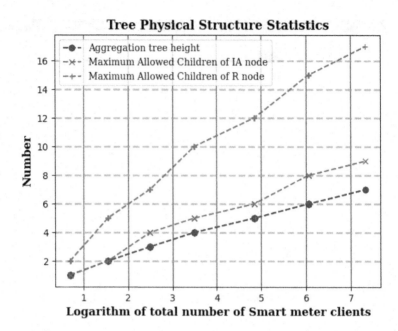

Fig. 6. Physical parameters

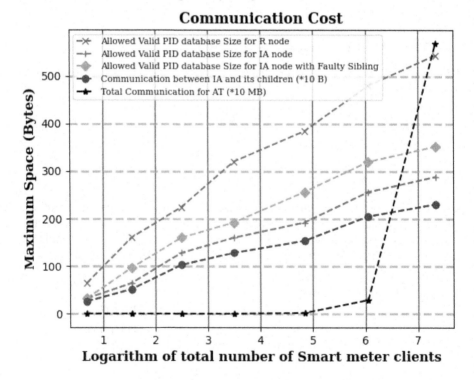

Fig. 7. Maximum computation time

Computation Cost

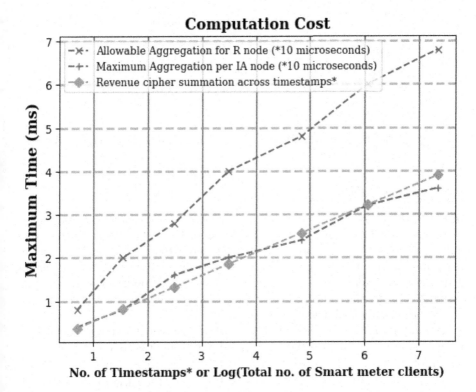

Fig. 8. Maximum communication space

In AT, the total transmitted data size for all the AT nodes $(|V|)$ is $Q(|V|) = (|V| - 1) * (|c_{ij}| + |H(c_{ij}||TS_i)|) = (|V| - 1) * (2048 + 256)$ bits $= 2304.(|V| - 1)$ bits or $Q_{max}(h) = 2304.f(h)$ bits. Also, each IA node contains mini PID data storage of size $256 * |C_{IA}| \leq 256 * \lfloor 4/3 * (h + 1) \rfloor$ bits. This is shown through a semi-log line graph in Fig. 7.

5.3   Practical Implementation Analysis

In Fig. 8, another semi-log line graph exhibits the time complexity for various algorithms assuming all the functional nodes of AT. The task of performing overall aggregation for AT with a total time complexity $\approx 0.3 * (|V| - 2)\,\mu s$ is distributed parallelly among R and IA nodes in proportion to $|C_R|$ and $|C_{IA}|$, respectively. R sums the revenue ciphers for T timestamps in $\approx T/2\,ms$. The generator $g = N + 1$ is utilised for quick encryption [18]. We have conducted 40 trials and shown the average results graphically in Fig. 8 and Table 2.

We can observe that all the plots except the total AT communication overhead are almost linear w.r.t the total number of AT clients varying exponentially. This explains the scalability of our distributed setup as the parametric values

Table 2. Algorithm timing analysis

Algorithm	Time (ms)	Optimization	Time (ms)
Encrypt (PHC)	1.9171	Cipher-refresh	0.0373
Decrypt (PHC)	1.9433	Decrypt (CRT+PHC)	0.6252

remain considerably low even for 10^7 clients. For example, the height of AT is 7 for $|V| \approx 2.22 * 10^7$ clients.

5.4   Noise Statistics

In Fig. 9, the normal noise produces a thick peak in the centre, enabling noise to be greater while being within a given range. In the proposed scheme, the individual noise (Wh) is allowed to lie in the range $[-100, 100]$ with a high chance assuming maximum reading of 1 kWh at an individual level for a timestamp. The aggregating servers IA and R obtain a noisy data from the clients who are assumed to inject the values following the normal distribution with mean as zero and a specific standard deviation σ_n.

Assuming around one lakh clients, the variance can be computed for the total absolute noise in the concerned timestamp to be less than one crore with 99% probability, i.e., $Pr(-10^7 \leq \sum_{i=1}^{|V|-1} n_{ij} \leq 10^7) = 0.99$. For $|V| \approx 100001$, $\mu + 2.577 * \sigma_n * \sqrt{|V| - 1} = 2.577 * \sigma_n * \sqrt{10^5} = 10^7$, the variance is calculated as $\sigma_n^2 = (10^7/2.577)^2/10^5 = 150581341.857 \, \text{Wh}^2 = 150.581 \, \text{kWh}^2$. The shaded region of Fig. 9 highlights the range of chosen noise values n with their probability $p(n)$. As the total number of AT nodes $|V|$ increases and tends to ∞, it is

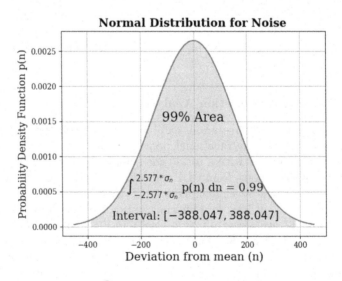

Fig. 9. Normal distribution

expected that the total noise quotient $(\prod_{i=0}^{t-1}(p_i*\sum_{j=1}^{|V|-1}n_{i,j}))/RV_{AT}$ approaches 0%.

The above-mentioned security and performance analysis results justify the usability, scalability and effectiveness of our proposed secure data aggregation scheme in large scale smart grid AMI system.

6 Conclusion

The proposed distributed PEDA cryptosystem uses additive homomorphic Paillier cryptosystem accelerated through obfuscation, CRT and outsourced decryption. This ensures confidentiality during the data aggregation process. It supports the dynamic joining of nodes using an effective tree based construction that adheres to physical constraints for load balancing. Client data privacy is enabled via the provision of pseudonyms and infusion of random normal noise. In addition, our scheme achieves ciphertext integrity, and resilience against major cyberattacks ensured through timestamp, traceability and hash signature. Lastly, the inclusion of a few inter-level redundant links as well as a suitable protocol together facilitate fault-tolerant energy data aggregation hierarchically.

Acknowledgments. This research is funded by a project under CPRI (Central Power Research Institute), Bangalore, India.

References

1. Prasad, V.K., Bhavsar, M., Tanwar, S.: Influence of monitoring: fog and edge computing. Scal. Comput. Pract. Exp. **20**(2), 365–376 (2019)
2. Guo, Y., Ten, C.-W., Jirutitijaroen, P.: Online data validation for distribution operations against cybertampering. IEEE Trans. Power Syst. **29**(2), 550–560 (2014)
3. Fan, H., Liu, Y., Zeng, Z.: Decentralized privacy-preserving data aggregation scheme for smart grid based on blockchain. Sensors (Basel) **20**(18), 5282 (2020)
4. Zhang, Y., Chen, X., Li, J., Wong, D.S., Li, H., You, I.: Ensuring attribute privacy protection and fast decryption for outsourced data security in mobile cloud computing. Inf. Sci. **379**, 42–61 (2017)
5. Saleem, A., et al.: FESDA: fog-enabled secure data aggregation in smart grid IoT network. IEEE Internet Things J. **7**(7), 6132–6142 (2020)
6. Cui, J., Shao, L., Zhong, H., et al.: Data aggregation with end-to-end confidentiality and integrity for large-scale wireless sensor networks. Peer-to-Peer Netw. Appl. **11**, 1022–1037 (2018)
7. Khan, H., Khan, A., Jabeen, F., Rahman, A.: Privacy preserving data aggregation with fault tolerance in fog-enabled smart grids. Sustain. Cities Soc. **64**, 102522 (2021)
8. Bao, H., Lu, R.: DDPFT: secure data aggregation scheme with differential privacy and fault tolerance. In: IEEE International Conference on Communications (ICC), pp. 7240–7245 (2015)
9. Chen, Y., Martínez, J.-F., Castillejo, P., López, L.: A privacy-preserving noise addition data aggregation scheme for smart grid. Energies **11**, 2972 (2018)

10. Ming, Y., Li, Y., Zhao, Y., Yang, P.: Efficient privacy-preserving data aggregation scheme with fault tolerance in smart grid. Secur. Commun. Netw. **2022**, 18 p. (2022), Article ID 5895176

11. Yao, L., Shuai, X.: Accelerate the Paillier cryptosystem in CryptDB by Chinese remainder theorem. In: 20th International Conference on Advanced Communication Technology (ICACT), pp. 74–77 (2018)

12. Li, F., Luo, B., Liu, P.: Secure information aggregation for smart grids using homomorphic encryption. In: Smart Grid Communications (SmartGridComm), pp. 327–332. IEEE (2010)

13. Grining, K., Klonowski, M., Syga, P.: On practical privacy-preserving fault-tolerant data aggregation. Int. J. Inf. Secur. 1–20 (2018)

14. Li, D., Aung, Z., Williams, J.R., Sanchez, A.: Efficient authentication scheme for data aggregation in smart grid with fault tolerance and fault diagnosis. In: IEEE PES Innovative Smart Grid Technologies (ISGT), pp. 1–8 (2012)

15. The Wikipedia website. https://en.wikipedia.org/wiki/Chinese_remainder_theorem

16. Paillier, P.: Public-key cryptosystems based on composite degree residuosity classes. In: International Conference on the Theory and Applications of Cryptographic Techniques, pp. 223–238 (1999)

17. Katz, J., Menezes, A.J., Van Oorschot, P.C., Vanstone, S.A.: Handbook of Applied Cryptography. CRC Press, Boca Raton (1996)

18. Damgård, I., Jurik, M., Nielsen, J.: A generalization of Paillier's public-key system with applications to electronic voting. Int. J. Inf. Secur. **9**, 371–385 (2010)

Author Index

Printed in the United States
by Baker & Taylor Publisher Services